W9-BFI-986

THE ORIGINS of
EVERYDAY THINGS

THE ORIGINS *of* E

EVERYDAY THINGS

Reader's Digest

PUBLISHED BY THE READER'S DIGEST ASSOCIATION LIMITED

LONDON • NEW YORK • SYDNEY • CAPE TOWN • MONTREAL

CONTRIBUTORS

THE ORIGINS OF EVERYDAY THINGS was edited and designed by :
The Reader's Digest Association Limited, London

Copyright ©1999 The Reader's Digest Association Limited
Copyright ©1999 The Reader's Digest Association, Inc.
Copyright ©1999 The Reader's Digest Association (Canada) Ltd.
Copyright ©1999 The Reader's Digest Association Far East Ltd.
Phillippine Copyright 1999 The Reader's Digest Far East Ltd.
Library of Congress Cataloging-in-Publication Data has been applied for.

All rights reserved. No part of this book may be reproduced, stored in a retrieval system, or transmitted in any form or by any means, electronic, electrostatic, magnetic tape, mechanical, photocopying, recording or otherwise, without permission in writing from the publishers.

® Reader's Digest, The Digest and the Pegasus logo are registered trademarks of The Reader's Digest Association, Inc, of Pleasantville, New York, USA.

Library of Congress Cataloging in Publication Data
The origins of everyday things / [editor, Ruth Binney].
        p.   cm.
    Includes index.
    ISBN 0-7621-0141-5
        1. Material culture—History. 2. Manners and customs—history.
    I. Binney, Ruth.   II. Reader's Digest Association.
    GN406.075 1999
    306'.09—dc21   98-46262

EDITOR Ruth Binney

SENIOR ART EDITOR Neal Martin

ASSISTANT EDITORS Kim Davies, Caroline Johnson, Peter Lawson, Marion Moisy

DESIGNERS Keith Miller, Rachael Stone

STAFF WRITER Rachel Warren Chadd

EDITORIAL ASSISTANT Rachel Robson

SENIOR RESEARCHER Fiona Plowman
RESEARCHERS Gisèle Edwards, Jane Egginton

PICTURE RESEARCHERS Wendy Brown, Carina Dvorak, Jane Lambert

PROOFREADERS Roy Butcher, Barry Gage

WRITERS Hannah Andrassy, Geraldine Carter, Stephen Escritt, Paul Evans, Irving Finkel, Colin Ford, Anne Gatti, Nigel Hawkes, Betty Kirkpatrick, Jon Kirkwood, Helen McCurdy, George Monger, Ruth Richardson, Henrietta Wilkinson, Andrew Williamson

SPECIAL ACKNOWLEDGMENT The Keeper and staff of The Museum of Welsh Life, St Fagans, Cardiff, Wales

CONSULTANTS Dorothy Bosomworth, Archivist, Cartier Ltd, London ; Christopher Breward, Tutor in the History of Design, Royal College of Art, London ; John Burnett, Curator of the History of Sport, National Museums of Scotland, Edinburgh ; Jennifer Chandler and George Monger, The Folklore Society, London ; Stephen Escritt, Research Consultant, Carlton Hobbs ; Irving Finkel, Assistant Keeper,

FOREWORD

Ingenuity defines humanity. Our ancestors, who walked the planet 2 million years ago, used this unique attribute to shape, change and control their surroundings, first by making simple tools, then by using them to make other implements. So the foundations of our everyday world were laid, and were built on in successive centuries as people settled down and learned how to organise their lives.

The Origins of Everyday Things tells the fascinating, entertaining and

Department of Western Asiatic Antiquities, British Museum, London; Colin Ford, Director, National Museums and Galleries of Wales; David Gordon, Secretary, The Royal Academy, London; Nigel Hawkes, Science Editor, *The Times*; James Harpur, Writer on Religions; John Kahn, Writer and Editor, WordCraft Ltd; Professor Malcolm McLeod, Director, Hunterian Museum and Art Gallery, Glasgow; Oded Schwartz, Food Writer; Kit Wedd, Writer and Editor; Professor Philip Whitfield, Division of Life Sciences, King's College, London

PHOTOGRAPHERS Jon Bouchier, John Chase, Vernon Morgan

ARTISTS Ian Atkinson, Peter Barrett, Richard Bonson, Sarah Fox-Davies, Lorraine Harrison, David Noonan, Graham White

EDITORIAL DIRECTOR Cortina Butler

ART DIRECTOR Nick Clark

EXECUTIVE EDITOR Julian Browne

MANAGING EDITOR Paul Middleton

EDITORIAL GROUP HEADS Ruth Binney, Noel Buchanan

STYLE EDITOR Ron Pankhurst

PICTURE RESEARCH EDITOR Martin Smith

often extraordinary stories behind the objects all around us. Yet it is much more than a book of inventions, for it looks at such central aspects of existence as our languages, societies, customs and traditions. In each of the thousand and more themes included here, the light of past achievements illuminates our present existence.

And what achievements they are— and how diverse—ranging from the button and buttonhole, invented more than 3000 years apart, to the silicon chips that control modern computers, and from the first stone cooking pots, put over fires more than 15 000 years ago, to the ancient art of acupuncture, which is still used to treat illness.

As the strands of history weave through the book clear patterns emerge, making it possible to discern the surges of inventiveness inspired by the rise of empires, the influences of religion, the legacies of the great explorers and the effects of increasing prosperity brought about by the Industrial Revolution.

We may marvel at the inventions of our technological age, but many advances we regard as modern are really centuries old. Equally, our traditional festivals and celebrations such as Christmas are adaptations of ancient rites and rituals.

Whether they are clearly documented in the historical record or disputed even by experts, the origins described here share a common characteristic. They all reveal the indomitable ingenuity of the human mind, which for countless generations has made progress possible.

CONTENTS

HOW IT ALL BEGAN
10

10	*In the Beginning*
12	*The Toolmakers*
14	*The Great Civilisations*

HOUSE AND HOME
16

18	*Every Room in the House*
20	*Elements of Construction*
22	*Furniture*
24	*Furnishings*
26	*Lighting*
28	*In the Kitchen*
30	*Heating and Cooking*
32	*The Bedroom*
34	*The Bathroom*
36	*Washday*
38	*Cleaning Chores*
40	*Safety and Security*
42	*Favourite Pets*
44	*Handy Housewares*
46	*Gadgets for the Home*
48	*The Indoor Garden*
50	*Earthly Paradise*
52	*Garden Flowers*
54	*Garden Tools*

MANNERS AND CUSTOMS
56

58	*Etiquette*
60	*Mealtimes*
62	*Dining Out*
64	*Courtship*
66	*Tying the Knot*
68	*Bringing up Baby*
70	*Spring and Summer*
72	*Autumn and Winter*
74	*Christmas Cheer*
76	*Superstitions, Signs and Omens*
78	*Foretelling the Future*
80	*Last Rites*

FOOD AND DRINK
82

84 *Farming and Wheat*

86 *Staple Sustenance*

88 *Meat and Poultry*

90 *Vegetables*

92 *Familiar Fruit*

94 *Harvesting the Water*

96 *Dairy Produce*

98 *Sweets and Treats*

100 *Herbs and Spices*

102 *Preserving*

104 *Pulses, Nuts and Oils*

106 *New and Synthetic Foods*

108 *Hot Drinks*

110 *Soft Drinks*

112 *Beer and Brewing*

114 *A World of Wine*

116 *Strong Liquor*

FASHION AND BEAUTY
118

120 *Essential Fabrics*

122 *Fine Fabrics*

124 *Making and Mending*

126 *The Dress and the Shirt*

128 *A Suit of Clothes*

130 *Coats, Gloves and Scarves*

132 *Dressing Up,*
Dressing Down

134 *Next to the Skin*

136 *Head to Toe*

138 *Everyday Accessories*

140 *Improving on Nature*

DESIGN FOR LIVING
142

144 *Essential Technology*

146 *Using Nature's Materials*

148 *Making Things from Metal*

150 *The Earth's Treasure*

152 *Generating Power*

154 *Practical Chemicals*

156 *Miracle Materials*

158 *Instruments*

160 *Clocks and Watches*

162 *The Computer Revolution*

164 *Civil Engineering*

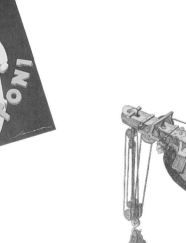

MOVING ABOUT
166

168 On Two Wheels

170 Carrying Passengers

172 The Car is Born

174 The Open Road

176 Railways

178 On the Water

180 First Flight

182 Air Travel for All

184 Finding the Way

LIVING TOGETHER
186

188 Settlements

190 Government and the People

192 The World of Work

194 The Marketplace

196 The World of Finance

198 Crime and Punishment

200 Health and Safety

202 Religious Beliefs

204 Teaching and Learning

206 Measuring the World

208 Water and Waste

THE WRITTEN AND SPOKEN WORD
210

212 The Making of Language

214 Characters and Alphabets

216 Signs and Symbols

218 Flags, Signs and Trademarks

220 The Language of Numbers

222 Pen and Paper

224 Print Spreads the Word

226 The Book

228 Newspapers and Magazines

230 Sending Messages

232 Long-distance Information

LEISURE AND SPORT
234

236 *Making Music*
238 *In Harmony*
240 *Dance Steps*
242 *On the Stage*
244 *Opera, Puppets and Magic*
246 *Photography*
248 *Moving Pictures*
250 *Sound Recording*
252 *Television and Video*
254 *High Days and Holidays*
256 *Holidays Abroad*
258 *Instant Riches*
260 *Marvels and Wonders*
262 *Ancient Games*
264 *Playing Fields*
266 *Bat and Ball*
268 *On Horseback*
270 *Popular Sports*
272 *Board Games*
274 *Cards and Puzzles*
276 *Children's Toys*
278 *Games and Pastimes*

SICKNESS AND HEALTH
280

282 *Infectious Diseases*
284 *Body and Mind*
286 *Guardians of Health*
288 *Making a Diagnosis*
290 *New Parts for Old*
292 *Surgical Skills*
294 *Nature's Medicine Chest*
296 *Alternative Treatments*
298 *Family Matters*
300 *Eyes and Ears*
302 *In the Dentist's Chair*

WORDS AND PHRASES
304

312 *Index*
320 *Acknowledgments*

IN THE BEGINNING

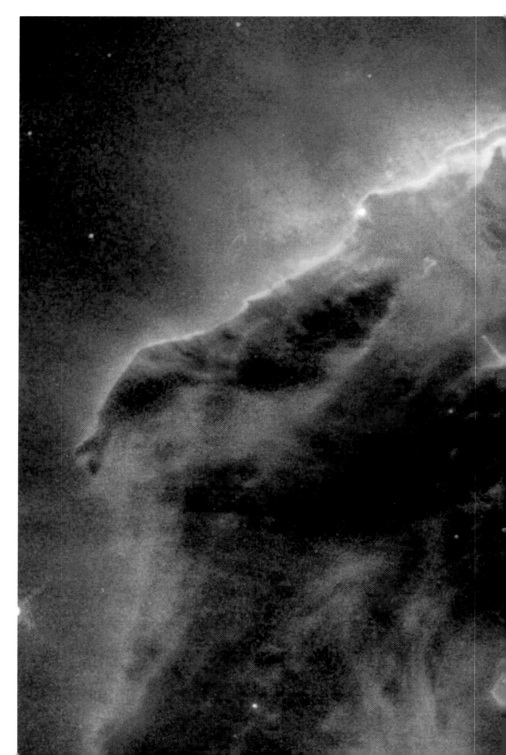

spinning disc of gas and dust around it condensed to form the planets about 4.5 billion years ago: these became rocky and solid close to the Sun, gaseous bodies made largely of hydrogen farther out. All the planets orbit the Sun in the same plane, evidence that they formed from a flat disc of dust.

Initially the Earth was molten. The oldest rocks began to soldify about

WE live in a Universe far removed from its violent beginnings. Time, space and matter all began about 12 to 15 billion years ago in an explosive event called the Big Bang. Cosmologists believe this because the Universe is still expanding: run time backwards, reversing this expansion, and both logic and the theory of relativity suggest that at the beginning all matter was concentrated into a single point of infinite density. To the question 'What happened before the Big Bang?' the answer is simple. Time, like matter, began at the Big Bang, so there was no 'before'.

The ultimate shape of the Universe was determined almost immediately. For a brief instant, expansion accelerated and the size of the Universe increased a trillion trillion times in a fraction of a second. It then settled down to a more modest enlargement. After a few minutes, the nuclei of simple atoms began to form, but it was another half a million years before the temperature fell to about 3000°C (5500°F) and atoms formed. There were three kinds: hydrogen, helium and tiny quantities of lithium.

Gravity began to draw these atoms together to form stars. Inside these stars hydrogen and helium burned in thermonuclear reactions that created heavier elements. As the stars grew old and eventually exploded, they spread into interstellar space the elements from which our world is made. These first stars were the factories in which the elements were forged.

Our own Sun, a fairly typical star, was formed about 5 billion years ago from a cloud of dust and gas. The spinning cloud turned from a ball into a flattish disc with a bulge at the centre. In the bulge hydrogen nuclei fused to make helium, creating the Sun. The

4 billion years ago, but the inner core remained fluid, driving volcanic activity. The gravity of the Earth was strong enough to prevent the gases released by volcanoes from escaping, and it was far enough from the Sun to allow water to exist in liquid form.

The oceans provided the cradle from which life emerged. Nobody knows exactly how this happened, but early in the Earth's history molecules with the ability to copy themselves appeared in the rich soup of chemicals in the oceans. By about 3.5 billion years ago, perhaps earlier, simple organisms that we would recognise as being alive existed in seawater. These were single-celled creatures, bacteria and algae, and they began to transform the planet.

At this time the Earth's atmosphere was dominated by carbon dioxide and nitrogen, although it contained some hydrogen, methane and ammonia. The first bacteria lived on these, but at some time around 3 billion years ago blue-green algae appeared in the sea. Using sunlight, carbon dioxide and water, they produced oxygen by the process of photosynthesis. Slowly they transformed the atmosphere, increasing the amounts of oxygen to 23 per cent and making possible the emergence of more complex life forms.

The next major step was the appearance, about 1.5 billion years ago, of protists, single-celled organisms like bacteria but larger and more complex. These were eukaryotes, the first organisms able to build complex structures with the huge variety of shape, structure and function that we see today. The first large organisms were sponges, which appeared about 570 million years ago, followed by jellyfish and marine worms. Fish with backbones were living by 450 million years ago, at about the same time as the first plants started growing on land.

The first animals to colonise land were millipedes, about 390 million years ago ; insects and amphibians appeared 60 million years later. Reptiles walked the planet around 290 million years ago, and dominated it as dinosaurs between 250 and 65 million years ago. Alongside them, from about 230 million years ago, were the mammals, to begin with a fairly insignificant group comparable with today's lemurs, shrews or squirrels.

When the dinosaurs disappeared in a global catastrophe possibly caused by the impact of a comet from outer space that caused huge climatic change, the mammals survived, rapidly increasing in numbers and diversity. Among their eventual descendants were many apes : the ancestors of humankind.

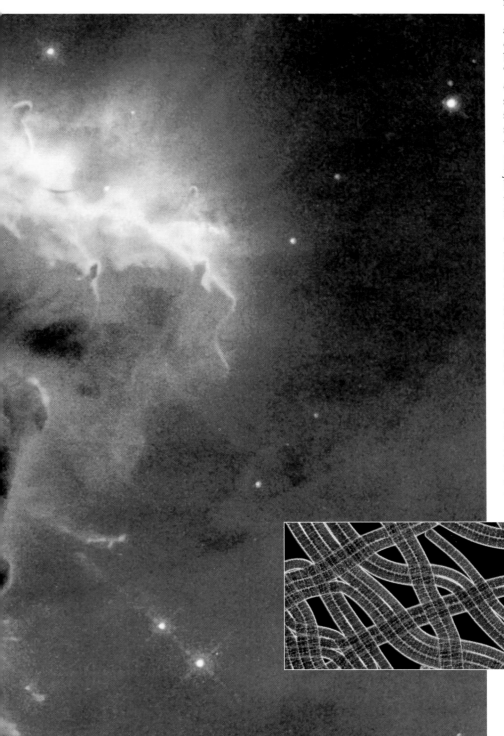

STAR BIRTH *In the Eagle Nebula, 7000 light years from Earth, stars similar to our Sun—on which human origins ultimately depend—condense from 'fingers' of gas and dust. Primitive blue-green algae (inset) have lived on our planet for at least 3 billion years.*

THE TOOLMAKERS

Fossils discovered in Ethiopia during 1993-4 have provided the clearest idea yet of what the first 'proto-humans' looked like. About 4.5 million years ago *Ardipithecus ramidus* was an ape that had some human features: small eye teeth and a narrow base to the skull. It also walked upright, had a small brain and lived in the forests, feeding mainly on fruit.

The course of evolution that led from *Ardipithecus* to *Homo sapiens*, our own species, is complex and far from clear. But some 3.5 million years ago an ape emerged which stood upright at about 1.2 m (4 ft) high, with short legs and long arms. Named after the region of Ethiopia where its fossil remains have been found, *Australopithecus afarensis* seems to have become extinct about 3 million years ago, around the time a related species, *Australopithecus africanus*, appeared in southern Africa.

The oldest creature to be given the name *Homo* exists as fossils about 2.5 million years old. Discovered in Tanzania in 1964, its most distinctive characteristic is its larger brain. It was given the name *Homo habilis* (Handy Man) because it seems to have been the first to use tools.

By 2 million years ago *Homo habilis* had been joined by a related species, *Homo erectus*, the first true human. A species had emerged that could control its own environment—the hallmark of humanity. Its members could hunt, make tools and use fire. The size of their brains was about three-quarters that of the modern human, but twice

as big as a chimpanzee's. And, unlike their predecessors in the human lineage, they colonised the world.

Exactly when this colonisation began is still disputed. Until recently the date was set at about 1 million years ago, but fossils of *Homo erectus* found in Java and dated to 1.6 million years ago suggest an earlier departure from Africa. By expanding its range by a few miles each year, the species as a whole spread far and wide. Certainly *Homo erectus* survived as a species until 100 000 years ago.

By then, *Homo erectus* had given rise to successors who could do all the same things, but better. From about 500 000 years ago there were creatures with brains bigger than those of *Homo erectus*. These archaic *Homo sapiens* include Boxgrove Man, who lived in what is now West Sussex. As time passed, their brains increased in size to reach roughly those of modern human beings. Yet they probably had no language, and the style of stone tools they used did not alter for hundreds of thousands of years.

Homo erectus had two descendants at least: modern man, *Homo sapiens*, who appeared about 120 000 years ago in Africa, and Neanderthal man, who existed at the same time and in some of the same places. We know nothing about the relations between them, but *Homo sapiens* ultimately proved more adaptable. Neanderthals appear to have become extinct about 35 000 years ago, and their remains suggest that, despite having brains as large as ours, they left no art and may have lacked language.

Homo sapiens was different. Paintings discovered in caves in both southern

ALL-PURPOSE IMPLEMENT *Homo erectus fashioned this stone axe, which was discovered in deposits dating from 700 000 years ago in Olduvai Gorge, Tanzania. Axes, which replaced pebble choppers, were used for skinning animals and scraping their hides, for cutting flesh and wood, and for digging.*

CUTTING EDGE *Around 2500 BC miners at Grimes Graves near Thetford in Norfolk transformed deer antlers into pickaxes. They sank 9 m (30 ft) shafts into the chalk to reach seams of flint, which they chipped out with picks. Animal shoulder blades were also fashioned into shovels.*

France and Spain attest to a cultural transition that began some 40 000 years ago. Stone tools became more sophisticated, and there is evidence of rope, bone spear points and fish-hooks. *Homo sapiens* also took to the sea, colonising Australia around 50 000 years ago. This cultural transition seems to have happened at about the same time in many places. But if modern humans had the brain power to develop so spectacularly, why did it take so many tens of thousands of years after their exodus from Africa for this change to occur?

The so-called 'Out of Africa' school of thought believes that *Homo erectus* and later *Homo sapiens* emerged first in Africa, and that each in succession spread through the world. However, not all anthropologists accept that *Homo sapiens* colonised the world after evolving in Africa.

The 'multiregional evolution model', however, accepts the first migration, but believes that all later changes took place everywhere, not just in Africa. According to this theory, *Homo sapiens* must have evolved independently in many parts of the world at about the same time.

Fossil and genetic evidence both argue against the multiregional model. In Israel, for example, fossils of modern humans have been found that are older than neighbouring Neanderthal fossils by 40 000 years. The genetic similarity of humans around the world—racial differences are superficial—argues for a common origin, giving the Out of Africa hypothesis the edge.

Early humans were hunter-gatherers who migrated according to the seasons and ate a diet of fruit, nuts, game and seafood. They also used food plants such as cereals where they could find them growing wild. By about 20 000 years ago people had knives that could be used for harvesting wild grain, together with mortars for grinding cereals. Between 12 000 and 9000 years ago agriculture began, apparently independently, in Africa, Asia and South and Central America.

EARLY BRITONS

The first humans in Britain for whom there is evidence were archaic *Homo sapiens* of 500 000 years ago. Britain was then linked to the rest of Europe by land and there were long periods when the land was covered with ice. Only in the interglacial eras— most importantly around 250 000 BC—did the population increase. In 10 000 BC, when the ice retreated for the last time, permanent settlement began at last.

At Star Carr in North Yorkshire, archaeologists have discovered traces of people who lived there in 7500 BC. They inhabited skin tents on a birch platform by a lake, made flint blades for spears and arrows, and kept dogs—the first domesticated animals in Britain.

By 6000 BC, when the marshy land bridge between Dover and Calais had been swept away by rising sea levels, Britain was an island. For the next 7000 years its history was shaped by a succession of invaders. Farming was brought around 3500 BC by people from France, while metalworking was introduced by the Beaker People, the builders of Stonehenge, skilled sailors who originated in Spain. The Celts brought ironwork around 600 BC. Then followed the Romans, who conquered Britain in AD 43.

Warfare, conquest and trade helped to spread techniques. The invention of paper and printing—both in China— transformed learning and the speed with which new ideas were spread. By 1500, 50 years after the printing press was established in Germany by Johann Gutenberg, about 40 000 separate works had been published. With this came the intellectual transformation

ART OF THE ICE AGE *The thrill of the chase is captured in a Spanish cave painting of a stag hunt that possibly dates to around 12 000 years ago. The artist would have applied the colour to the rock using simple brush-like tools.*

that led, in 1750, to the Industrial Revolution, the most profound change in the life of humankind since the spread of agriculture.

What distinguished the Industrial Revolution was the substitution of machinery for the work of the individual. Capitalism, money, trade and the concentration of people in cities already existed, but machinery empowered mass production. And that in turn altered the way people worked, creating the factory and requiring new prime movers such as the steam engine to power it.

THE GREAT CIVILISATIONS

The greater part of human history is unrecorded, save in the artefacts left behind by early humans. The oldest surviving ones come from the Palaeolithic era—or Old Stone Age—which began about 2.5 million years ago. The word 'Palaeolithic' was coined in 1836 by Christian Thomsen, a Danish archaeologist, to describe the only tools found from these times: flakes of stone sharpened to an edge. It is a misnomer, because the people of the Old Stone Age also used wood and leather, but little has survived.

The retreat of the ice from much of northern and western Europe, Siberia and North America at the end of the last glaciation, some 12000 years ago, led to the beginning of farming and the Neolithic era, or New Stone Age. This was a time of rapid advance. With the advent of agriculture and the domestication of animals the first permanent settlements were established. Pottery, spinning, weaving and the smelting of metals followed.

The Bronze Age began in China and the Middle East more than 5000 years ago—in Britain about 1900 BC—with the smelting of copper and then bronze, which is an alloy of copper and tin. It was during the Bronze Age that the first great civilisations emerged, in China, Mesopotamia, Sumer, Crete and Mycenae. The search for fresh sources of ore led to the process of exploration, colonisation and trade, which spread ideas across Europe. Iron was made into weapons in Anatolia by 2000 BC. By 1200 BC the secret of reheating iron and hammering it to produce a more hard-wearing edge had spread throughout the Near East.

When the Iron Age began in Europe around 700 BC—100 years later in China—city-based civilisations were already long established in the Middle East. The first was the Sumerian culture, which developed in the

BEE OF GOLD *The Minoans of Crete, who around 2000 BC developed the first European civilisation, created this fine brooch in about 1600 BC.*

4th millennium BC along the flood plains of the Tigris and Euphrates rivers, in what is now Iraq. The Sumerians had begun to keep records on clay tablets by about 3500 BC, a principle that was soon followed by the Egyptians. Egypt was founded about 3100 BC, and the Great Pyramid at Giza built between 2589 and 2566 BC. It was a theocratic state ruled by a divine king, but most of the people were peasant farmers. They depended on the seasonal flooding of the Nile and, subsequently, irrigation using pumps to ensure the productivity of the land. In Egypt, China and, later, Mexico the control of water created the need for firm administration—leading, in each case, to despotism.

Technically, Egyptian civilisation remained simple. It was the Greeks who invented science, while the Romans exploited technology, both creating cultures whose inheritance has proved more permanent than that of the Egyptians. The Greeks were great astronomers, began the science of medicine, and established the basis of philosophy. The Romans were empire-builders who, by the time of Christ's birth, controlled the entire Mediterranean and most of western Europe. Rome gave us law, our form of writing, many of our cities, and the Roman Catholic Church.

After economic and political crises in the 3rd century AD the Roman Empire split into Rome in the west, and Byzantium (Constantinople) in the east. The empire in the west declined, and by the end of the 5th century had given way to a series of kingdoms established by rulers of Germanic origin. The population of the city of Rome fell from 1 million in AD 400 to 100000 by 800. In the east, however, the Roman tradition survived.

From the 7th century Islam kept the spirit of inquiry alive, making many discoveries in astronomy, mathematics

and technology. It was in 1095 that Pope Urban II urged Christian men to wrest the holy places of Christianity from Muslim control. The first Crusade began two centuries of war between Christians and Muslims, but contact with Muslim culture brought back to Europe such novelties as paper, Arabic numerals and the windmill. These, together with the flowering of knowledge during the Renaissance, provided a springboard for the next 300 years of civilisation.

DISCOVERING THE PAST

Different methods are needed to trace the history of humanity and the things people have made. Archaeology is vital for earlier, unrecorded periods, and can fill in details of more recent times. The principle upon which it is based is that the deeper things are buried, the older they must be. Coins and fragments of pottery, whose style changed over time, can often help to date a particular archaeological level. Objects made of wood can be dated by tree rings, each reflecting a year's growth, which can be matched against a master chronology.

The discovery of radioactive isotopes has provided a new and independent form of dating. Elements

such as uranium, argon, potassium and carbon occur in more than one form, called isotopes. Over time one of these isotopes may decay, altering to form another isotope of the same element, or even another element. Dates can be calculated by observing how far this process has gone. Radiocarbon dating, used for any material from something that was once alive—wood, leather, bones, shells, charcoal—depends on the decay of carbon-14, an isotope formed in the upper atmosphere and incorporated into all living things. A carbon date proved that the Turin Shroud, believed to have wrapped the body of Jesus, was in fact medieval.

The discovery of the genetic material DNA has provided another technique for tracing human history. DNA survives in trace amounts in ancient bones—it has been extracted from a Stone Age skeleton found in Somerset—and also alters at a known rate as genetic mutations occur. This enables scientists to compare ancient populations with modern ones, and, by measuring the amount of change, make estimates of the time at which a common ancestor lived. The technique is proving a powerful tool in tracing human migrations.

UNEARTHING THE PAST *In AD 79 the small town of Herculaneum near Naples, Italy, was suddenly buried under lava from the volcano Vesuvius. After the site was discovered in 1709, excavations uncovered well-preserved mosaics, toys, pottery, graffiti, even medical kits, all giving a vivid picture of Roman life.*

THE TWO-MILLION-YEAR RIBBON OF PROGRESS

The ribbon shows many of the major ages, civilisations and periods that have marked the development of human society since *Homo erectus*, the first true human, appeared during the Palaeolithic era more than 2 million years ago. What also becomes clear is how rapidly progress was made after the advent of agriculture 12000 to 10000 years ago and, soon after, the beginning of metal smelting.

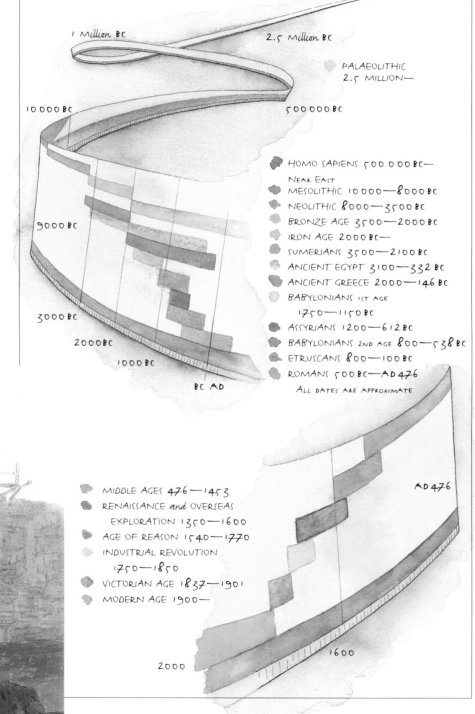

1 Million BC 2.5 Million BC

PALAEOLITHIC 2.5 MILLION—

10000 BC 500000 BC

HOMO SAPIENS 500000 BC—
NEAR EAST
MESOLITHIC 10000—8000 BC
NEOLITHIC 8000—3500 BC
BRONZE AGE 3500—2000 BC
IRON AGE 2000 BC—
SUMERIANS 3500—2100 BC
ANCIENT EGYPT 3100—332 BC
ANCIENT GREECE 2000—146 BC
BABYLONIANS 1ST AGE 1750—1150 BC
ASSYRIANS 1200—612 BC
BABYLONIANS 2ND AGE 800—538 BC
ETRUSCANS 800—100 BC
ROMANS 500 BC—AD 476
ALL DATES ARE APPROXIMATE

9000 BC

3000 BC
2000 BC
1000 BC
BC AD

AD 476

MIDDLE AGES 476—1453
RENAISSANCE and OVERSEAS
   EXPLORATION 1350—1600
AGE OF REASON 1540—1770
INDUSTRIAL REVOLUTION
   1750—1850
VICTORIAN AGE 1837—1901
MODERN AGE 1900—

2000 1600

HOUSE AND HOME

Sheltered from the storm, or shielded from a scorching sun, we are at home. Protected from the outside world, we share the same priorities of warmth, shelter and privacy as our early ancestors. Where there were no caves, humans first built homes with the materials around them—animal bones and hides, mud, turf, reeds, wood and stone. After 10000 BC in the Far East and central Europe, hunter-gatherer peoples made tent-like constructions of branches set in the ground with animal skins strung over them, sometimes weighted down or reinforced with mammoth bones. In southern Mesopotamia, farmers and fishermen built reed dwellings, while in the eastern Mediterranean people erected circular huts of twig, daub and stone.

From about 10000 years ago, with the beginnings of farming, communities began to settle across the Middle East and central Asia. Here people lived closely together for both security and companionship, often within a group of interconnecting homes enclosed by a defensive wall or barrier. At Jericho, north of the Dead Sea, the earliest city wall of the 8th millennium BC was some 6m (20ft) high, with a moat 9m (30ft) wide cut from solid rock.

At the same time at Çatal Hüyük, near Konya in present-day Turkey, small, rectangular mud-brick houses already had well-defined storerooms and living rooms with hearths, benches, ovens, and raised platforms for sleeping. The houses were grouped together and were accessed from the

adjoining flat roofs of other dwellings by ladders. The roofs also served as communal space.

In such secure settings, homemaking skills were born. Primitive brooms and feather dusters were probably fashioned for regular household chores. As cooking developed beyond roasting on an open fire, fireproof utensils were made for baking food in clay ovens. Plates and pots from the eastern Mediterranean and Mesopotamia, regions which had reached similar levels of civilisation between 8000 and 5000 BC, were decorated with geometric or, occasionally, animal designs.

Throughout the world, geography, climate, wars, technology and social class created myriad styles of home-building. The multi-tiered Chinese houses that first appeared around 255 BC, or the Neolithic turf houses built across the Northern Hemisphere from Holland to Iceland, owe little to Mesopotamia. The earliest British dwellings, built around 3000 BC to 1850 BC, were temporary, circular constructions of wood and thatch.

The oldest known British Neolithic settlement, Skara Brae in the Orkneys dating from around 1800 BC, was made entirely of stone, the only local building material. Because it is costly to transport, stone has nearly always been used near its source. Its colours, ranging from the warm, honeyed tones of Cotswold cottages to the harsh greys of Scottish crofts, endow homes with their regional traits.

Despite the technological advances of the 19th and 20th centuries, which have transformed our homes, many houses retain historic features such as the remnants of the medieval hall and still reflect ancient practices. We encircle and defend our homes with stone walls or wooden fences that echo Celtic palisades from 1000 BC. Within their boundaries we tame nature by planting flowers for pleasure and cultivating the plants our ancestors grew to feed themselves and to cure their ills.

EVERY ROOM IN THE HOUSE

'Mid pleasures and palaces though we may roam,
Be it ever so humble, there's no place like home...'

FROM THE POPULAR SONG 'HOME, SWEET HOME', JOHN HOWARD PAYNE, 1823

WORKING MAN'S CASTLE *By the 17th century a new home built in local stone by a successful Oxfordshire yeoman, or independent freeholding farmer, integrated home comforts established in medieval castles and manor houses. Visitors entered a panelled passage leading from the front door to the back. Business was conducted in the hall (or dining room) to the right of the passage; friends might proceed to the neighbouring parlour where the family could enjoy some privacy away from the bustle of servants and farm workers. Leaded glass windows and numerous fireplaces ensured light and warmth throughout.*

TIME FOR BED *A curving flight of steps, contained and supported by the central chimney stack, led from the dining room to interconnecting family bedchambers. In the loft above, reached by ladder-like steps, servants slept on simple pallet beds.*

COOK'S DOMAIN *A second chimney stack at the end of the house allowed food to be prepared and cooked in a separate kitchen. In humbler homes, cooking took place at the family hearth.*

ROOF RAISING *Huge curved beams were the defining element of the Anglo-Saxon cruck house, whose roof extended to the ground. By the Middle Ages, tie beams projecting beyond the crucks allowed for vertical side-walls, creating more headroom.*

When the Romans invaded Britain in AD 43, they found scattered settlements of people living in wattle-and-daub or stone dwellings, with thatch or turf roofs. Inside, families and cattle often shared a single, windowless, all-purpose living room.

Roman rulers constructed a series of luxurious country villas and walled cities of sophisticated two-storey brick houses. But after the departure of the Romans in the early 5th century, their materials were pillaged and their consummate building skills were unmatched for hundreds of years.

The emergent Anglo-Saxon civilisation created the first villages and built fine stone churches. Villagers still lived in primitive huts; their lords or thanes in long barn-like halls divided into bays for the family, servants, labourers and livestock.

Multistorey buildings reappeared when Norman barons built imposing stone fortresses at the end of the 11th century. Storage rooms took up the ground floor, quarters for garrison and servants the first. Above them, reflecting the communal lifestyle of early medieval times, was a great hall with steps to private family bedrooms. Rudimentary lavatories were set into the walls of the keep. For most people, indoor toilets would not arrive until after the First World War.

The high cost of transporting stone to the towns meant that timber, wattle and daub were the main building materials. After a severe fire in London in 1189, Richard I offered incentives to build in stone. A budding merchant class constructed town houses, but the city was still mostly timber-built at the time of the Fire of London in 1666.

In the countryside, knights lived in fortified manor houses. Early buildings consisted simply of ground-floor storage with a hall or single main room above. By the end of the peaceful 13th century the need for fortifications had faded and the main hall of a manor house was often built on the ground floor with adjoining storerooms.

As life became more secure, the lords began to seek more privacy for their families and guests. Ground-floor storerooms were expanded to support an extra room or solar adjoining the main hall. In time, this was known as the parlour, from the French *parler* ('to speak'), or as the drawing room to which people 'withdrew'. Soon this single room was extended into a wing tacked on to the 'upper' end of the hall, behind the head of the table, to create private family chambers complete with fireplaces.

Just as the hall reached its zenith of splendour in the 15th century, with carved beams and rafters and a large gallery, so its decline began. Its stately height was divided to provide bedchambers or servants' quarters, and less imposing, half-timbered manor houses began to be built. Brick, little used in Britain since Roman times, was reintroduced as a prestige building material during the 16th century.

Although Tudor homes and their rooms bore some resemblance to those of today, they were

LIVING ON ONE LEVEL

City crowding led the Romans to build the first blocks of flats from around AD 64. For similar reasons, flats reappeared in Paris in the 18th century built for middle-class and aristocratic tenants. In London, the Albany building in Piccadilly was converted to apartments in 1803 by the architect Henry Holland.

In 19th-century India, space was not a problem for the British elite, who transformed traditional Bengali huts into much grander single-storey homes—hence the term 'bungalow'.

BUNGALOW IN BRITISH INDIA, ABOUT 1880

usually places where people both lived and worked. A town merchant or craftsman would run his business in a shop or workshop on the ground floor below the living quarters; a farming villager might still share his house with his beasts. Home and the workplace gradually began to separate from the 17th century, when rooms such as the parlour and the dining room began to assume their modern functions.

The final knell for the great hall was sounded in 1650-2, when Roger Pratt, consulting with his fellow architect Inigo Jones, designed one of the early symmetrical houses, Coleshill in Berkshire, destroyed by fire in 1952. It reflected Italian and French themes with a hall reduced to a central vestibule dividing the building in half, and a double staircase with a flight rising up each side. By the late 1600s, town houses were being built with a hallway rather than a communal hall.

TEST OF TIME *The small hallways in modern homes, giving access to individual rooms, are remnants of the great hall of medieval castles and fortified houses. In the 13th century, all family life and household affairs took place there.*

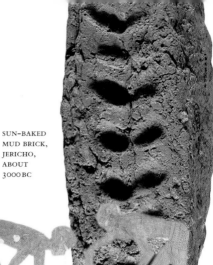

SUN-BAKED MUD BRICK, JERICHO, ABOUT 3000 BC

SHAPING MUD BRICKS IN MOULDS, EGYPT, ABOUT 1500 BC

THE BUILDING BLOCKS
Bricks and stone, mortar and concrete

Around 8000 BC the people of Jericho discovered that when fashioned into blocks, wet mud would, if it contained sufficient clay, harden in the sun. The resulting bricks were their building materials. Some 5000 years later the Mesopotamians baked bricks in kilns to make them stronger and more water-resistant. In Britain they were introduced by the Romans. It was common practice to use old Roman bricks—the earliest evidence of new ones dates to the late 1100s. Brick-making machines were developed in Britain from 1825.

Even before brick-making began, stones would have been gathered and piled on each other to form walls, but hunks of stone were first cut mechanically in ancient Egypt around 2500 BC. In the ancient world clay and bitumen were the most common bonding substances. A mortar containing the mineral gypsum was developed by the Egyptians. At Pompeii more than 2000 years later the Romans were building with a mortar of lime, water and sand.

By mixing mortar with pieces of stone and brick, the Romans created a type of concrete. The town walls of Cosa in central Italy, built in 273 BC, are an early example of a Roman concrete construction. From the 1st century AD they made concrete with volcanic sand. In Britain concrete fell out of use after the Romans left until the 18th century.

SNUG AND SECURE
Windows and doors

The word 'window' derives from the Old Norse *vindauga*, which expressively combines *vindr*, 'wind', and *auga*, 'eye'. For early housebuilders everywhere, climate and vulnerability to attack were the factors critical to window size. In many homes the doorway was the only source of daylight. Some 2000 years ago, wealthy Romans were the first to enjoy clear glass windowpanes, produced by casting thin glass blocks and then grinding and polishing them. During the 1st century AD glazed sun porches were a feature of the most luxurious country villas.

Until the 15th century a variation of the Roman method was the only way to make clear windowpanes, which remained expensive and were therefore used only in grand houses and ecclesiastical buildings. For ordinary medieval British homes, waxed parchment or oiled linen stretched over the windows excluded draughts but admitted some light.

At night, wooden shutters kept out the cold and wind and also gave some security. For the better-off, hinged casements came into use in the 15th century. In these, strips of lead held small panes made of droplets of molten glass poured into moulds.

The art of glass-making was revived in pre-Renaissance Italy via Byzantium. Craftsmen began to spin glass into large discs that were then cut to the required shapes. The first record of this type of glass being used in Britain is for the sash windows installed in the architect Inigo Jones's Banqueting House in London in 1685. In this early type of sash window only the lower frame could be moved. The double hung sash, which opened top and bottom, was in widespread use by the 1750s.

Throughout Mesopotamia and the ancient world the entrance to a home was closed with hides, cloth or a wickerwork of woven twigs, but doors of this kind were also prevalent. Most Roman homes had wooden doors, while the castles and manor houses of Norman Britain were generally sealed with solid oak doors reinforced with metal strips. But until the 16th century most British homes had doors made from planks butted together with internal rails and, occasionally, a crosspiece. Stone farmhouses and cottages often had the half-doors now seen mostly in stables. These allowed in daylight while keeping out the animals.

CLEAR AS DAY *Light is filtered through the elaborate leaded window of a 17th-century Dutch home. Soon new glass-making methods allowed for larger, cheaper panes.*

UP ON THE ROOF
Thatch, tiles and ceilings

Turfs, moss and thatch made of straw, leaves, branches or reeds, tied together in sheaves or bundles, were probably the first roofing materials employed to weatherproof Neolithic homes from around 10000 BC. In Britain, thatch became the favourite roofing material everywhere, although as a protection against house fires it was banned in London in 1212 in favour of stone tiles. Tiles of fired clay became economically viable in the 17th century.

Discoveries on the Greek island of Melos suggest that clay roof tiles date from earlier than 1400 BC. Their use became widespread in Asia and Europe, although wooden tiles were preferred in northern Europe and Russia. The

WOOD
SHINGLE
ROOF

OUTLET FOR SMOKE
FROM CENTRAL
HEARTH FIRE (BELOW)

WOODEN
FLOORBOARDS
ATTACHED TO
TIMBER FRAME

TIMBER FRAME FILLED
WITH WATTLE (TWIGS
WOVEN AROUND POLES)

BEATEN
EARTH
FLOOR

WOOD
PLANK DOOR

UNGLAZED WINDOW,
SEALED WITH WOODEN
INDOOR SHUTTERS

MUD AND HORSEHAIR
DAUB, COVERED WITH
WHITEWASH

FILLING THE GAPS *Workmen put the finishing touches to a late medieval home typical of south-eastern England, where wood from the vast forests was the most common building material. Although vulnerable to fire, timber-framed houses were easy to erect and the wattle-and-daub walls could be filled and repaired at little cost.*

Romans introduced stone tiles, usually made of easily workable sandstone and limestone. In Britain the high cost of transport meant that, until the 1700s, the use of slate was confined to houses near quarries.

During the Middle Ages the rafters supporting the roofs of better-quality houses were exposed within; rougher timbers were covered by packing the space between the joists with straw and clay and then plastering over. In two-storey buildings ceilings were often just the structural beams and floorboards of the storey above. In late medieval times 'ceiling', which probably stems from the Latin *caelum*, 'sky' or 'heaven', and *caelare*, 'to engrave', was also used of wooden wall panelling. Decorative plaster ceilings were seen in the 1400s and were common by the 18th century.

AS GOOD AS NEW *A thatcher freshens up a roof. As long as they are properly maintained, roofs of this type, which possess excellent insulating qualities, can last 70 years.*

UP AND DOWN
Stairways and floors

In the first two-storey homes, built in the Middle East from 8000 BC, storeys were linked internally with simple ladders. Staircases were developed in Egypt in the 2nd millennium BC. Most medieval British homes were single-storey, but tower houses had circular stone staircases built into the walls.

The Normans fitted staircases in their castles and fortified mansions. Steep, single-flight staircases appeared in humbler homes in the 1400s; the dog-legged design, with steps built against two perpendicular walls or a chimney stack, followed in the 1500s. By the 17th century some grander houses featured open-well staircases.

Ceramic floor tiles were known in ancient Egypt, but it was in Islamic countries that their use became widespread in the early 1100s. They arrived in Britain via Moorish Spain, appearing on the ground floors of wealthy homes in the 13th century. Stone slabs and floors of beaten earth covered in rushes remained common in ordinary houses for the next 400 years. Wooden flooring for ground-floor rooms was introduced in middle-class homes in the 1700s.

MARVELLOUS MOSAICS

In the 5th century BC artistic Greek builders designed the earliest known decorative mosaic floors, consisting of uncut pebbles pressed into a surface coated with mortar. Colour was first provided by painting the pebbles. The tessera technique, whereby stone is cut into tiny geometric shapes that fit in a grid, dates from the late 4th century BC. Glass, first used in about the 3rd century BC, was less suitable than stone for floors.

ROMAN MOSAIC, 1ST CENTURY AD

SITTING IN STYLE
Chairs, stools and sofas

REGENCY MAHOGANY
SOFA ON SABRE LEGS,
ABOUT 1820

From ancient times chairs have been used as symbols of authority, to elevate the mighty above lesser mortals. Some of the first known chairs were created by the Egyptians around 2650 BC for ceremonial occasions. Pharaohs and queens were enthroned in ebony armchairs that were richly inlaid with gold and precious stones. Medieval lords in England presided over meals from a raised chair at the head of the table while their servants sat in descending order of rank on benches. The word 'chairman', used to denote the leader of an organisation, reflects the traditional link between the chair and status.

The basic form of the common seat has changed little over the centuries. The Egyptian chair was similar to those used today, with a high upright back and four straight legs (often shaped like those of a lion or a bull). By 1350 BC the Egyptians had made simple square-seated household stools and more decorative royal ones, as well as wooden stools, which could be folded up, for domestic and military use. These had X-shaped frames topped with leather or fabric seats, and looked much like those used by campers today.

ROMAN BASKET CHAIR,
ABOUT 3RD CENTURY BC

The Greeks of around 500 BC were using stylish klismos chairs, with their simple curved legs balancing concave backs. The Romans knew of them, but developed other types of chair: one 3rd-century marble relief shows a woman in a wickerwork basket chair that would not look out of place in a modern bedroom. Likewise the 17th-century day bed of the Restoration period and the elegant chaise longue of the 18th century recall the couch beds used by the ancient Egyptians, Etruscans and Romans.

Even after the fall of the Roman Empire these furniture forms never quite disappeared in the West. They re-emerged strongly from the end of the Middle Ages when the craftsmen

GREEK–STYLE
KLISMOS CHAIR,
ABOUT 1815

CLASSICAL EASE *Influenced by painted decorations that showed the ancient Greeks at leisure, designers in Regency Britain (1811-20) turned such pieces of furniture as the klismos chair and sofa into high points of fashion.*

and artists of the Renaissance revived the classical models.

Sitting in comfort was a luxury only for the rich who had the time to enjoy it. The settle, a high-backed wooden seat with arms designed for two or more people, originated in Europe in the 10th century. This developed into the padded settee in the 17th century, when upholstered seating became common. The sofa, larger than the settee and made for reclining, became popular in the 19th century. Its name is derived from the Arabic *suffah*, 'cushion'.

In the early 19th century steel coil springs, patented by Georg Junigl in Vienna in 1822, were fixed within the upholstery to provide softer, bouncier seating. The idea of the three-piece suite, comprising two armchairs and a settee, did not catch on until the 1930s when it became stylish, practical furniture for suburban living rooms.

STORAGE SPACE
Chests and cupboards

For storing bed linen, the Egyptians crafted the earliest known chests from wood or woven reeds in about 3000 BC, while the Minoans of Crete used terracotta for their versions. Wall paintings in Pompeii show that the Greeks used cupboards, and a fine Roman example, complete with shelves and hinged folding doors, is illustrated in a fresco at Herculaneum, near Naples, created in the 1st century AD.

In Britain the skills for constructing such furniture seem to have been lost after the departure of the Romans, but from the 8th century simple caskets and boxes were made to hold jewels and relics. Later, in the early Middle Ages, larger 'trunks' or travelling chests were hollowed from tree trunks and fitted with lids for storing.

By the 12th century boards were joined to make basic chests or 'hutches' for storing valuables or clothes. As the

JACOBEAN OAK
CUPBOARD,
ABOUT 1620

CRAFTED IN OAK *Renaissance cabinet-makers in northern Europe carved architectural designs of columns, friezes and cornices on oak cupboards.*

PANELLED OAK
CHEST, ABOUT 1660

GATE-LEG TABLE,
ABOUT 1680

VERSATILE TABLE *The gate-leg table, designed by craftsmen of the Jacobean period (1603-25), occupied little space when not in use. This made it ideal for the modest dining rooms of middle-class homes.*

art of carpentry developed, chests were stacked and enclosed in a frame. A 'cup-borde with drawing boxes' recorded in a 1596 English inventory was undoubtedly an early chest of drawers.

Not until the 17th century did the term cupboard come to mean a piece of furniture used for general storage. The word had first been used in medieval Britain to denote a flat board used for storing cups and plates. Recesses or free-standing pieces of furniture, with doors, were known as ambries and used for storing food. Medieval Europeans also had armoires, decorated storage units that sometimes incorporated compartments, drawers or, in the case of a Spanish armoire made in 1441, arms for hanging clothes.

CHIPS OFF THE BLOCK

• The art of veneering furniture with sheets of decorative wood was practised by the ancient Egyptians.
• Cofferers, who originally made chests (coffers), and later chairs and desks, were Britain's most important craftsmen in the Middle Ages. When their supremacy was challenged by the import of 'Flaunders chests' from France, the cofferers appealed to Richard III, who imposed a ban on the trade in 1483.
• Self-assembly furniture was tried out in the USA during the 1850s but only became successful in the 1960s when Mullard Furniture Industries, or MFI, was founded in Britain.

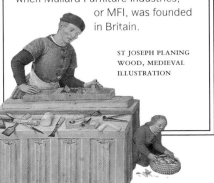

ST JOSEPH PLANING
WOOD, MEDIEVAL
ILLUSTRATION

A PLACE AT TABLE
Board and trestle

Used, it seems, for bearing sacrificial offerings the first tables had X-shaped frames and probably looked like over-sized stools. The Egyptians built the earliest recorded tables of the ancient world, around 2500 BC, using wood or alabaster. In Mesopotamia tables were made of various metals, while the Greeks used marble.

The Romans produced elaborate small tables, with decoratively inlaid surfaces of cedar, other exotic woods and precious metals, and bronze legs shaped to resemble those of animals. Both Greeks and Romans used their tables for dining and gambling. Large formal tables possibly did not exist in pre-Christian times. Furniture in general was scarce except in the homes of the very rich, and most of it was either built into the basic structure of a house or designed to be easily portable.

The huge dining table around which sat the medieval English lord and his retainers was of trestle construction. Huge oak or elm boards were laid on central supports and fixed in place with pegs until after the meal. Then the table would be dismantled, and the space cleared. The word 'board' meant a table, and this is the sense retained in such phrases as 'board and lodging' and 'board of directors'.

Tables that had fixed legs joined by stabilising stretchers or tie beams appeared in the 15th century. Over the next 100 years they incorporated such modifications as the three-leafed draw top in which two panels could be pulled out on runners to extend the table. From the mid 16th century various smaller occasional tables were crafted, including the card table with a baize-covered hinged top allowing it to be folded away.

Buffets, or tiers of shelves, were used from the mid 15th century to display precious silverware at formal dinners, and later to show food—hence the term 'buffet meal'. They were the ancestors of sideboards, developed in the late 18th century. By the Victorian era the sideboard was heavily decorated and incorporated side cupboards, drawers and shelves, and occasionally a mirror.

23

DECORATED WALLS
Interior style

KNOTTED IN SILK *The oldest carpets may have come from Turkmenistan in central Asia, but the finest were Persian. During the 16th century, book illuminations were translated into silk carpet designs such as this rich example made by hand in 1540.*

When, more than 30000 years ago, the cave painters of the Ardèche in south-east France used combinations of charcoal and earth pigments to make images of big cats, rhinoceroses and bears, they may have been trying to bring good luck in the hunt. But they also became some of the first known interior decorators. By 3000 BC the Egyptians, Sumerians and Assyrians were routinely painting the plaster-covered walls of their homes and palaces using natural pigments from plants and animals.

Magnificent tapestries from Assyria and Babylonia were described by early travellers, but the oldest surviving example is Egyptian. Dating to 1480 BC, and discovered in the tomb of the pharaoh Thutmose IV, it bears cartouches with hieroglyphs describing his life. Hanging painted canvas or other cloths on walls as a cheap alternative to tapestries was common practice in Egypt at this time, as it became much later in Britain between the 15th and 17th centuries AD.

In the 15th century, wood panelling, originally a Roman technique, was reintroduced into England by Flemish craftsmen. Because it withstood the smoke from fires better than cloth hangings, and also offered some protection against damp weather, it became popular in the great houses of the Elizabethan period. The first wallpapers were decoration for these wood panels: small squares of paper with images

SQUARE BY SQUARE
Hanging wallpaper in the 18th century was a labour-intensive affair (top). Small sheets had to be individually pasted and positioned. A sample book of 1821 from Connecticut, USA, was block printed on hand-painted backgrounds.

printed by wood blocks were stuck onto the panels, then coloured by hand.

The earliest example of wallpaper in Britain was found in 1911 on beams in the Master's Lodge of Christ's College, Cambridge. A pattern of pomegranates was revealed, along with the signature of the woodblock maker Hugo Goes of York on a proclamation issued on the accession of Henry VIII in 1509.

Around 1600 shavings of wool (later silk) were blown onto paper covered with adhesive, thus producing flock wallpaper. The technique was already used on cloth. Wallpaper became a less expensive alternative to tapestries and leather wall hangings from the 1680s. Individual sheets were joined together in groups of 12 or more to form a roll, enabling both more complex designs and faster printing. In France a machine for printing wallpaper was invented in 1785. By 1806 rolls of paper were in production in Britain.

COMFORT UNDERFOOT
Carpets and rugs

For comfort, furs and animal skins were thrown down on the earth and stone floors of the first homes. But the oldest complete carpet, found in the Pazyryk valley in central Asia, was made of camel hair and knotted wool. Found in a royal tomb in the Altai Mountains of southern Siberia, it dates from the 5th century BC. However, fragments from Persia (now Iran) and central Asia suggest that the knotted-pile technique was probably developed even earlier by

SHOW HOUSE *Renowned as a collector, Nicolaas Rockox, Burgomaster of Antwerp, displayed numerous treasures in his home, painted here in 1635 showing classical busts, paintings and fine rugs hung on the walls. Table-carpets were common by this time— when used at mealtimes they were protected by a linen cloth—but window curtains, although available, had not replaced shutters.*

nomadic shepherds, who used their versatile carpets on the ground, as coverings for walls and doorways, and as blankets. Nevertheless, well into the 19th century loose or plaited rushes were still strewn over the earthen or stone floors of poorer homes, as they had been since antiquity.

The fine handmade linen and wool rugs of Egypt and Syria were brought to Europe in the 12th century as booty from the Crusades. So precious were they that their wealthy owners displayed them on walls or laid them over beds, tables, seating or cupboards.

Royal charters were issued to the weavers of Axminster and Wilton in England in 1701. Aubusson and other smooth-surfaced carpets, which are woven in the same way as tapestries but with a bulkier weft, were the earliest carpets to be machine-made, at Kidderminster in 1735.

DESIGNED IN SETS *Modern interiors took shape when upholsterers offered such ready-made furnishings as these 1815 French patterns.*

CURTAINS AND SHUTTERS
Keeping out draughts

Cloth was such a prized commodity in medieval times that it was seldom used to cover window openings. Curtains were much more often used around beds, both to retain warmth and to provide privacy. Plain, heavy cloth, sometimes waxed and enclosed in frames known as fenestrals, might be put in windows to keep out draughts. But it was more common in houses between the 14th and 16th centuries—that is, before windows were glazed—to hang wooden shutters on the inside walls.

The earliest reference to window curtains appears in a 1509 inventory of the nobleman Edmund Dudley's house in Candelwykstrete, London. The inventory mentions 'courteyns of grene …hangyng in the Wynddowys', implying that the curtains were hung from a rod or securely fastened above the window. By the late 16th century the inventories of great houses such as Hardwick Hall in Derbyshire included window curtains suspended from a rod and pulled aside during the day. But curtains were unusual until the 1700s.

Early window blinds resembled medieval fenestrals, but were made with lighter cotton or silk, usually oiled and painted with decorative patterns. A cloth blind was patented by William Bayley in 1692 and from 1750 spring-loaded roller blinds, known as 'spring curtains', were available.

HOME EMBELLISHMENTS

• The carpet is named from the Latin *carpere*, 'to pluck' or 'to card' (comb out). It probably derives from the use of unravelled woollen thread for carpet-making.

• In 1769 the British designer Edward Beran enclosed wooden slats in a frame to adjust the amount of light let into a room. These became known as venetian blinds from their early use over Italianate windows.

• Until they were mass-produced from the late 18th century, ceramic ornaments were confined to opulent homes.

CERAMIC DUCKS, POPULAR BRITISH WALL DECORATIONS FROM THE 1930S

ROMAN BRONZE OIL LAMP,
1ST CENTURY AD

HOME LIGHTING
Lamps and candles

The first artificial light came from open fires, and the flares of burning fat dripping from cooking meat were probably the inspiration for the oil lamp. The earliest known lamps, fashioned by the Palaeolithic cave dwellers of western Europe around 40 000 BC, were hollowed out of stones and contained a wick of moss or other plant material soaked in animal fat. Ancient civilisations developed metal or pottery vessels to burn oil, but the Greeks of the 7th century BC introduced cup-shaped lamps with handles and nozzles or spouts for holding wicks.

Oil lamps changed little through Roman, medieval and Renaissance times. But in 1784 the Swiss chemist Aimé Argand designed a model with a tall glass chimney enclosing a large tubular wick. Draught allowed into the chimney fanned the flame, producing a much brighter light. Lamps burned olive oil, beeswax, fish and whale oil, or tallow, made from the fat of cattle, sheep or horses, until the 1860s when these fuels were superseded by paraffin.

Images of cone-shaped candles were painted on Egyptian tombs in around 3000 BC, and for millennia repeatedly dipping a wick, such as a length of rush or flax fibre, in animal or vegetable fat was the basic method of candlemaking. Beeswax candles, which produced a better quality of light and a sweet, not noxious odour, were too expensive for any but the wealthy.

The invention of moulds by the French nobleman Sieur le Brez around 1600 helped to make candles more plentiful, but poorer families still had to use rushes soaked in tallow. As late as the 18th century, the countryman Gilbert White recorded that 'the careful wife of an industrious Hampshire labourer obtains all her fat for nothing; for she saves the scummings of her bacon pot... A pound of common grease will dip a pound of rushes.'

SOCIAL REVOLUTION *In the Middle Ages a candle, placed in a draught-free spot, might burn for 4 hours—the average rushlight, 30 minutes. Gaslight transformed daily life, illuminating homes and streets, and extending working hours from the 19th century. Lamp chimneys helped to create brighter lights, but by the 1920s clean, consistent electricity was lighting up most of Britain.*

FRENCH OIL
LAMP, LATE
1800S

RUSHLIGHT
AND HOLDER,
EARLY 1700S

CANDLESTICK
INCORPORATING
BOX FOR TINDER,
STEEL AND FLINT,
MID 1800S

FRENCH OIL
LAMP, LATE
1800S

FRAGILE GLOW *Studious children of the 17th century, engulfed by shadowy gloom, strain their eyes in the dim candlelight. Even for people who could afford more candles, activity was severely curtailed at dusk.*

STATUS SYMBOL *The sparkle of light on cut glass first graced the rooms of European nobility in the late 17th century. The famed glass-makers of Venice and Bohemia set a trend for colour and ornament, but this 1770s chandelier reflects the English preference for clear drops and cascades.*

ELECTRIC
TABLE LAMP,
1902

EARLY LIGHT
BULB, 1910–30

ADVERTISEMENT
FOR GASLIGHTS
AND MANTLES,
1929

ALL LIT UP
From gas lamp to light bulb

The ancient Chinese discovered natural gas while mining for salt, and burned it to create light underground. But the gas lighting that was to take over from the candle and the oil lamp began in France during the 1790s. Gaslights were first installed on London's streets in 1807, and by the 1860s most of the homes and streets in Britain's towns and cities were lit by gas.

Early gas lamps burned dimly. Ceiling-mounted lamps with multiple flame fittings were designed to rival candle-burning chandeliers, previously a preserve of the Church and the wealthy, but these 'gasoliers' produced a tremendous heat.

Competition from the early electric lamps in the 1880s led the Austrian chemist Karl Auer to produce an incandescent gas mantle, made of cotton fabric impregnated with thorium and cerium salts, which gave a brighter, whiter light and used less gas. The cotton burned away leaving behind the metal oxides which were heated to glowing point by the burning gas but did not, themselves, ignite. Light was now so dazzling that it became necessary to shield the eyes from it, leading to the first lampshades.

The English chemist Humphry Davy demonstrated that electricity could be used to heat metal strips and make them glow in 1801, but electric lighting was not a possibility for householders until much later. In 1878 the English physicist Joseph Swan ran electricity through a carbon filament encased in a glass bulb from which the air had been evacuated, and produced an incandescent light that lasted for several hours. The following year the American inventor Thomas Edison created a light that burned for a couple of days. Honours for the first practical electric light went to Edison.

AT THE FLICK OF A SWITCH

• When electric lights were first installed in hotels and public places in the early 1900s, notices were needed to remind people not to light them with a match.

• Electric sockets incorporating switches to turn the current on and off were introduced by the English inventor David Salomons in 1888.

• 'If gas lamps are to be superseded, it must be by something that will bear harder knocks than a bulb of glass.' *Boy's Book of Science,* late 1800s.

CATCHING FIRE
The origins of the match

Rub two pieces of wood against each other until the friction creates enough smouldering dust to light dry tinder. Alternatively, strike a flint against steel or some other metal such as iron pyrites to create sparks. So might have read ancient instructions for starting a fire.

In Britain tinderboxes containing flint, steel and tinder of dry feathers or such plant material as moss were essential household items well before Roman times. The flint and steel 'strike-a-light' remained basically unchanged until the 19th century.

Matches of a sort had been known to the Romans, in the form of lengths of wood dipped into molten sulphur and ignited with the heat from smouldering tinder. But even after the Irish scientist Robert Boyle discovered in 1680 that phosphorus and sulphur burst into flame when rubbed together, self-igniting matches still took another 150 years to appear.

In 1805 the French scientist Jean Chancel discovered that slivers of wood tipped with potassium chlorate, sugar and gum ignited when dipped into sulphuric acid. A variety of safer matches was made in the following years, but the real precursor of the modern match was the 'friction light' devised by the English pharmacist John Walker in 1827. The head of this match ignited when rubbed against sandpaper.

VERITAS
MANTLES & BURNERS
BRITISH MADE

LUMME! IT MUST BE A VERITAS

S. JONES's
LUCIFER MATCHES,
That IGNITE BY THE FRICTION produced by drawing the Match briskly through a piece of SAND-PAPER, and an unrivalled never to linger by keeping.
Inventor of
THE PROMETHEANS, SELF-ACTING COFFEE POT,
Elixir, &c.
Light-House, 201, Strand, London.

EARLY FRICTION
MATCHES, 1827

MESOPOTAMIAN CLAY HUSKING TRAY, ABOUT 5000 BC

CHINESE CEREMONIAL BRONZE FOOD VESSEL, ABOUT 1200 BC

BATTERIE DE CUISINE *Nomadic hunter-gatherers, who needed to travel light, had no use for clay cookware. But as settled communities became reliant on cereal grasses they created a range of specialised utensils for removing the husks from wheat ears and for grinding and sifting grain.*

CLAY SIEVE, ISRAEL, 2ND MILLENNIUM BC

ROMAN SILVER SAUCEPAN, ABOUT 100 BC

THE PREHISTORIC COOK
Ancient utensils and techniques

Cooking probably began accidentally some 350 000 years ago, after a piece of raw flesh dropped into a fire. To avoid burnt and shrunken morsels, Neanderthal cooks buried portions of meat in the embers and baked tough vegetable roots on hot stones close to the flames. Carcasses were speared on pointed sticks, suspended between two forked branches and spit-roasted over the fire. Perhaps an early gourmet tried caking meat in mud or wrapping vegetables in leaves to help to retain their succulence.

Nature provided the first cooking pots. Where molluscs or large reptiles such as terrapins existed, their shells made handy heatproof containers. Stomachs and hides of animals were widely used as receptacles and hung over the fire; this method of cooking, used during the 5th century BC by the nomadic Indo-European Scythians, persisted in remote areas of Scotland until the 1700s.

Around 10 000 BC the first clay pots were hand-shaped in Japan; by 3 500 BC the Sumerians of Mesopotamia, who had fashioned cooking pots from stone a few thousand years earlier, were using turntables to throw pots and utensils such as colanders. Finer sieves for sifting flour in bread-making were made of interwoven reeds, rushes or papyrus.

Metal cooking pots were devised in China around 1000 BC, in the form of the iron wok. Metal pots were known to Britons around the same time. The Romans manufactured saucepans, skillets and frying pans in factories. Most of the cooking vessels now common in kitchens were used in Romano-British homes of the 1st and 2nd centuries AD. One notable exception is the kettle. The medieval 'kittle' was simply a large

STRONG AND SMOOTH

The invention of chemical and heat-resistant glass is credited to Otto Schott of Schott's Glass Works in Germany in 1884. But it was experiments in cooking with the glass by Mrs Jesse Littleton, wife of the chief physicist at the American Corning Glass Works, that led to that firm's development of Pyrex in 1915.

In 1954 the Frenchman Marc Grégoire used Teflon, a tough resin discovered 16 years earlier by the US company Du Pont, to lubricate fishing tackle. Inspired by Teflon's possibilities, Grégoire founded the Tefal company in 1955, making nonstick kitchenware.

STRAIGHT FROM THE OVEN TO THE TABLE

PYREX
OVEN - TABLE
GLASS WARE

1930S COOKWARE PROMOTION

pan with a lid, used for boiling water or food. Kettles with spouts appeared in the 1690s, but these were luxury items for those who could afford to drink tea. They were made in more affordable materials from the 1720s.

The bain-marie was devised in Egypt in the 1st century AD. Its invention is credited to an alchemist known as Mary the Jewess, who wrote under the name 'Miriam, sister of Moses'.

COPPER KETTLE, 19TH CENTURY

TAKING THE HEAT *Strong, conductive metal utensils were precious to the ancients and often kept for ceremonial occasions, but Roman factories made them commonplace. Spouted kettles date from the 17th century.*

KITCHEN SPACE
A room for cooking

In hot climates cooking long remained an outdoor activity, but as housing became more sophisticated food preparation changed its location. The Roman kitchen of the 6th century BC was set in the atrium, the open courtyard at the centre of the house, but by the 1st century AD small rooms containing raised hearth ovens had been tacked onto the back of the house.

In medieval castles and manor houses the kitchen was the centre for all

BAYEUX BARBECUE *The Norman feast of 1066 that followed victory at Hastings is recorded on the 11th-century tapestry. William the Conqueror's men are busy stewing, grilling and baking.*

activities requiring heat, including cooking, dyeing and basket-weaving. Early kitchens, modelled on monastery halls where mass catering programmes were carried out for the poor, had great open hearth fires and ceiling beams hung with bacon, salt beef and dried herbs. By the late 1600s, as smoke and cooking smells became offensive to polite society, the separate kitchen was an essential part of grander homes.

In the great town houses of the early 1800s, run by a battery of staff, kitchens were located in the basement and rarely visited by the mistress. The kitchen also comprised the cook's room and the pastry room, situated away from the range. A 'brewhouse' might form part of the scullery, so that the washtubs could be used for making beer.

Revolutions in kitchen design came with advances such as the gas cooker, first exhibited at the Great Exhibition of 1851, and the electric cooker, which was shown in Chicago in 1893. In 1869 Catherine Beecher, sister of the writer Harriet Beecher Stowe, had designed an integrated kitchen including a sink, drainer, worktops and cupboards.

The free-standing cabinet arrived in Britain in the 1920s. One early design by the Canadian Wilson Crowe consisted of storage space above and below a hinged enamelled work surface. Seeing the potential, the British furniture manufacturer Len Cooklin established Hygena Cabinets; by the late 1920s the company was producing cabinets equipped with a range of fittings such as a pull-out ironing board.

Prefabricated standardised kitchen units and worktops were commonplace in American homes by the late 1930s and reached Britain after the Second World War. By 1947 pottery sinks and wooden draining boards were being replaced with sink units pressed from a single sheet of metal and enclosed in a floor cupboard. Wipe-clean surfaces such as the heatproof plastic laminate Formica, developed in the USA in 1913, became standard.

Nostalgia precludes the loss of the distinctive kitchen dresser. The original early 17th-century dresser was no more than a board or table where food was prepared or 'dressed' prior to cooking. The single-unit dresser was created by uniting the worktop with the crockery shelves above it, while a cupboard to hold table linen was added underneath. The new dresser became more decorative in function and food preparation was transferred to tables elsewhere.

FOR PREPARING FOOD

- The Romans were evidently pastry eaters. They made bronze bun tins and also used pastry crimpers to decorate bread and pies.
- Britain's first pastry cutters were created in the 1500s for gingerbread figures. Pastry boards and rolling pins appeared in the 1600s.
- The earliest known recipes date from ancient Egypt, written on soft clay tablets that were then baked to preserve them. A papyrus from about 1200 BC lists more than 30 different sorts of bread and cakes.
- Before the 18th century, when it came to describe profitable, poor-quality fiction, 'pot-boiler' referred to big smooth stones heated in the fire and thrown into pots to cook food. This ancient method of transferring heat was used in remote parts of Scotland until the early 1900s.

It's easier than you think to have your 'FORMICA' dream kitchen!

THE SHRINKING KITCHEN
By the 19th century large, sprawling kitchens (left) were filled with a plethora of dishes, equipment and stand-alone furniture used by an army of servants. For the 1950s housewife, who had little or no domestic help, the ideal kitchen was uncluttered, with tools and implements stored away in prefabricated units. Sink, cooker, floor cupboards and wall cabinets were all placed within easy reach.

COOKING BREAD ON AN OPEN FIRE, EGYPT, 2500 BC

TAMING THE FLAME
Fire and fireplace

Greek mythology recounts that Prometheus stole fire from the gods to give to humankind—and was severely punished for his pains. History suggests, however, that fires were lit in caves occupied by Peking man some 350 000 years ago. Open fires that were contained by stones were the basic pattern for millennia and in the Britain of the 11th century such fires were still occupying the central position of a room.

Only in the 14th century, after chimneys became established, did the fire move permanently to the side of the room. By the 15th century the back wall of the fireplace was protected from the intense heat by a fireback of cast iron. Decorative carved chimney breasts made their debut in grand homes of the 1500s; the mantelpiece, introduced into Britain in Norman times, became fashionable in the late 17th century. Mass-produced cast-iron fireplaces were widely installed during the Victorian building boom.

When coal started to replace wood as the main domestic fuel in the early 18th century, fire grates were designed for burning the new fuel. The new grate incorporated fireback and irons or legs, creating a self-contained unit. From the mid 1700s built-in grates featured hobs, or flat tops on which pots and pans could be heated.

CONTROLLING THE HEAT *Fire tools evolved along with the fireplace. By the 15th century tongs and a fork to move logs and a long-handled shovel to scoop up ash were commonplace. The coal scuttle and the poker, used to break lumps of burning coal into smaller pieces, were introduced only in the 18th century after coal became the standard fuel.*

COOKING TEMPERATURE
Ovens and stoves

More than 25 000 years ago the peoples of the Ukraine circled their hearths with small cylindrical pits, lined them with embers or pebbles hot from the fire, and created the first 'ovens'. Later prehistoric peoples, such as the Neolithic Britons of 5000 BC, coated pits with flat, overlapping stones to cook food in water heated with stones from the fire. About 2000 BC the Egyptians devised the first clay ovens.

The Romans fried and grilled food on raised brick hearths. They introduced this technique into Britain, where similar hearths were still in use in the 1830s. The first ranges, produced in the 1780s, consisted of an open grate flanked by hobs, with an iron oven on one side. Ventilation adjustments to the grate helped to control temperature.

Ranges with insulated enclosed grates were introduced by American-born Benjamin Thompson, better known as Count Rumford. This highly inventive scientist, administrator, philanthropist and sometime spy devised his first closed range for the German army in 1798. Its sheet-metal oven was set into brickwork, wells were sunk into the hotplate to hold pots and pans, and beneath each hob was a small fire.

Despite Rumford's advances the enclosed ranges beloved of Victorian Britain were never fuel-efficient or easy to maintain. The survival of the solid-fuel range was ensured by the Swedish engineer and Nobel prize-winner for physics Gustav Dalen. Blinded in a laboratory accident and confined to his home, in 1924 Dalen created an efficient cooker with an insulated cast-iron firebox, connected to ovens and to hotplates insulated with hinged covers. Produced by the Swedish company Svenska Aktiebolaget Gasaccumulator, hence the acronym Aga, it arrived in Britain in 1929.

A DIRTY JOB *In large homes of the 1800s the laying of fires, their care and clearing up were all daily chores tackled by the servants. By the time its owners awoke, the house would be warm.*

COAL SCUTTLE AND SCOOP, LATE 1800S

PORTABLE GAS HEATER, 1860S

BELLOWS, EARLY 1900S

POKER, SHOVEL AND TONGS, MID 19TH CENTURY

INSTANT HEAT
From open fire to electric stove

The fire that warmed as well as cooked was the focal point of the family home until after the gas and electric revolutions were firmly established. Food was probably first cooked with gas at a natural gas spring near Wigan in Lancashire in the mid 17th century. In a letter to the physicist and chemist Robert Boyle in 1687, the Reverend John Clayton describes his experiments with a flame 'so fierce that several strangers have boiled eggs over it' and adds that 30 years earlier it had produced sufficient heat to boil a piece of beef.

This form of energy was destined to be harnessed for the first time in 1802 by the German-born Frederic Albert Winsor (who later brought gas street lighting to London) when he hosted dinner parties cooked by gas at his home

COOKING RANGE, 1929

in Braunschweig, Germany. Domestic gas fires appeared in the 1850s with the piping of gas into homes. But only when electric-lighting companies made a competitive thrust in the 1880s and 1890s did gas companies begin to improve gas and make it cheaper.

The first patent for an electric heating system was granted in 1887 in the USA to Dr W. Leigh Burton. In 1912 Charles Reginald Belling wrapped a filament around a fireproof clay frame to produce a radiant heater similar to those still used today.

In England St George Lane-Fox designed a means of passing electricity through an insulated wire placed around a cooking vessel. He then patented the first electric 'cooker' device, in 1879. The original electric oven, powered by a waterfall-driven generator, was installed in 1889 in the Hotel Bernina near St Moritz in Switzerland. During the 1890s cooking with electricity began to

be promoted but it did not become popular with home cooks until after the late 1930s, despite the eulogy from a Mrs Lancaster, writer on electricity, in 1914 : 'It is always willing to do its allotted task and do it perfectly *silently*, swiftly and without mess ; never wants a day off, never answers back…costs nothing when it is not actually doing useful work.'

Microwave energy was developed by the British physicists John Randall and Henry Albert Boot for radar installations during the Second World War. It was realised that food could be cooked with it after an exposed bag of maize turned into popcorn. The first microwave oven was patented in October 1945 by the US company Raytheon.

CONTROL FOR COMFORT
Central heating and air conditioning

In the 1st century BC the Roman fish and oyster farmer Caius Sergius Orata, aiming to keep his animals plumply content, raised their tanks on pillars so that hot air from a furnace could circulate beneath them and warm the water.

The Roman hypocaust, the first true central heating system, soon followed. Underground furnaces heated air, which was then directed along tiled flues and distributed under floors and through hollow walls. Until the collapse of the Roman Empire this system remained in common use throughout northern Europe. But the modern central heating revival dates to the early 1800s when many larger buildings, and institutions such as hospitals, were fitted with central boilers that sent steam through a network of pipes.

Fanning air over blocks of ice to cool a room, a task performed by slaves for an 8th-century caliph of Baghdad, was one of the methods employed in the ancient world to subdue heat. The first true air conditioner, featuring humidity control, powered ventilation as well as mechanical refrigeration, was patented in 1902 by the American inventor Willis Carrier. The addition of a dust filter in 1906 to improve the air in textile mills led to the term 'air conditioning'.

BELLING ELECTRIC HEATER, 1950S

GAS COOKER, ABOUT 1936

INSTANT RESPONSE *Housewives of the late 1800s, who eagerly purchased gas heaters and cookers, enthused over their new-found ability to control temperature at the turn of a knob. Electric models followed in the 1930s.*

MINIATURE 'BABY BELLING' ELECTRIC COOKER, 1950S

SLEEPING IN SAFETY
Beds above the ground

Huddled together for protection and warmth, prehistoric hunter-gatherers wrapped themselves in animal skins and slept in shallow pits lined with springy undergrowth. So that they could lie above ground—and slithering night-life—primitive people planted four forked branches in the ground, built a frame between them and wove thongs to support a 'mattress' of skins.

From this humble origin the bed became the status symbol of ancient civilisations, and up until the 17th century only the richest people owned one. The ancient Egyptian bed comprised a simple wooden frame and a sleeping surface of interlaced flaxen cords. The Greeks also made their bed frames from wood but wove together leather thongs to create flexible supports.

In medieval England the bed was large and ornate. Reflecting its evolution from the royal tents of military campaigns, it had panelling, curtains and overhead canopies to exclude draughts and drips. The mighty four-poster developed from this in the 16th century. Elizabeth I used her capacious version as a place from which to conduct state affairs and to meet ambassadors.

Metal bedsteads were made in the last days of the Roman Empire but did not re-emerge until the end of the 16th century in Sicily. At a time when many wooden beds were ridden with vermin, they were advertised in 18th-century France as 'bedbug-proof' ('*non sujets aux punaises*'). Iron bedsteads became standard in British hospitals, prisons and boarding schools from the 1840s.

The mattress had been developed by comfort-loving Romans. They used a cloth 'envelope' stuffed, according to the owner's economic means, with straw, reeds or herbs, wool, feathers or

EXUBERANT DESIGNS *By the 1880s iron and brass bedsteads were being produced in an array of extravagant styles for the bedrooms of Victorian homes.*

ETRUSCAN COUCH, CRAFTED IN TERRACOTTA ON A COFFIN LID, ABOUT 500 BC

swan's-down. In the 6th century BC rose petals were favoured by the sybarites in southern Italy, who were known for their pleasure seeking, which is why the good things of life may now comprise a 'bed of roses'.

The New Yorker James Liddy is sometimes said to have thought up the sprung bed in the mid 1850s when he fell against the seat of the wagon in which he was travelling and realised that a network of coiled springs would provide a more comfortable bed-base than the latticed ropes used. But in fact,

COIL SPRING MATTRESS, ADVERTISED IN 1930

Vi-Spring Mattress
"The Best for Rest"

LYING IN COMFORT *Ancient couch beds, and even the stuffed mattresses used by the Romans, afforded none of the luxury granted by the sprung mattress invented in the 19th century.*

DRESSING THE CURLS *A maid attends to her lady's needs in a Dutch bedchamber scene of about 1670. Purpose-made dressing tables originated at this time, but here the wash ewer, mirror and toiletries are simply set out on a covered table. The bed is curtained off for warmth and privacy.*

sprung mattresses had appeared in Britain soon after the spring was first patented in the 1820s.

The Egyptians used wooden or ivory headrests, which were made to suit the individual sleeper. But the Greeks reclined on more comfortable pillows filled with wool, feathers or plant fibres. Homer describes the 'choice fleeces', 'lovely purple blankets' and 'glossy bed-covers' of his hero Odysseus.

White linen bed sheets were used by the rich from the early 1300s, and pillowcases followed about a century later. In the late 1940s new fabrics and printing methods enabled coloured and patterned sheets to be mass-produced for the first time.

With the advent of the bed spring, feathers were used to stuff quilts rather than mattresses. The word 'eiderdown' reflects the popularity of eider ducks' plumage for this purpose. 'Duvet' is a translation of the French for 'down'.

WARM AND COSY
Clay hot-water bottles evolved in the 19th century from such bed warmers as hot coals wrapped in cloth and metal warming pans, first used in the 15th century. The rubberised hot-water bottle dates from the Victorian era.

CLAY HOT-WATER BOTTLE, ABOUT 1920S

ETRUSCAN BRONZE HAND MIRROR, 4TH CENTURY BC

ROMAN WOODEN COMB, ABOUT 2ND CENTURY AD

COMFORT AND STYLE
Furniture for the bedroom

An area containing a bed and bedside mat, a chest for valuables and a chamberpot formed the basic Roman 'bedroom'. In most of Europe the bedroom was part of everyday living quarters until the late Middle Ages, but in Britain rooms used primarily for resting were built in the Norman castles of the 11th century. Thus nobles retired to their chambers, while servants slept communally, among the smoke and smells of the great hall. First-floor bedrooms did not become common until homes were built with fireplaces and chimneys in the 16th century.

Within the medieval bedchamber, clothes were often folded over a *perche*, a horizontal pole fixed to the wall. The first 'wardrobe', mentioned in the 13th-century records of King John, was a combined storeroom, dressing room and lavatory adjoining the bedchamber.

The freestanding wardrobe evolved during the 17th century from the linen press, a tall double-doored cupboard enclosing large sliding trays for folded linen. By the mid 19th century the wardrobe was an enormous piece of furniture, and the typical cluttered bedroom of the Victorian age also included a washstand, ewer for water, basin and portable bathtub.

FOR PERSONAL CARE
Comb, brush and mirror

Some 10000 years ago Stone Age Scandinavians carved the first combs from bone, while the ancient Egyptians favoured ivory and wood for their double-sided designs. Teeth were cut individually until 1796, when William Bundy, a British textile-machine inventor, developed a device that consisted of several parallel saws. In 1862 the Birmingham chemist Alexander Parkes

IMAGE MAKERS *Accessories from thousands of years ago included finely cut combs and mirrors made from polished metals. The back of this early mirror (left) pictures a warrior being dressed for battle by his attendants.*

made the first plastic combs by mixing chloroform and castor oil to make a substance he named Parkesine. This formulation led to the development of celluloid, the material commonly used for combs today.

Compared with combs, brushes for untangling the hair are newcomers to the dressing table, dating back only to the late 18th century. Hogs' bristles from the Russian wild boar were favoured for hairbrushes until supplies dried up after the famine of 1920-1. The backs of the best early brushes were made from ivory, which was imported from Africa or India.

The first mirrors were made around 5000 BC in northern Italy and the Middle East by polishing the lustrous volcanic mineral obsidian. Until the Venetians of the Middle Ages perfected the process of silvering the back of a sheet of glass, reflecting surfaces were highly polished bronze, tin or silver.

AND SO TO BED

• Hammocks, the most portable of beds, were first woven in Central and South America from the bark of the *hamack* tree. Christopher Columbus saw them in Brazil during his voyage to the New World in 1492.
• Folding beds, also known as camp beds, were used in French military campaigns of the 15th century. They had elaborate canopies and curtains much like the fixed beds of the day. Napoleon Bonaparte died in a canopied metal camp bed in 1821.
• In 1832 the Scottish surgeon Neil Arnott devised water beds as a way of improving patients' comfort.
• The poor of the Middle Ages used dried pea pods as mattress fillings, from which the fairy tale 'The Princess and the Pea' may originate.

'THE PRINCESS AND THE PEA', EDWARDIAN ILLUSTRATION

WORKING UP A LATHER
Soap and its making

Ancient Babylonians of about 2800 BC washed their clothes with a form of soap made from wood ash and liquid animal fats. A Mesopotamian recipe from the 3rd millennium BC describes a liquid soap that was made from oil and potash. According to the ancient Roman writer Pliny the Elder, the Phoenicians of about 600 BC cleansed themselves with a soap of goat's tallow and wood ash.

The Romans anointed their skin with oils and hot water, then scraped themselves clean with a strigil. By the early centuries AD, however, they had

were mixed with wood ashes. Flowing down the mountain they formed a crude soap on the banks of the River Tiber. By the 13th century the Arabs were mixing olive oil with soda ash to make hard soap. Bars were exported from Damascus to Mediterranean cities before soap factories were set up in Castile, Marseilles, Genoa and Venice during the 15th century.

A British soap industry emerged in the late 1100s in Bristol, but a tax first levied on it in the 13th century made soap expensive. After it was abolished in 1853, a long and foul-smelling tradition of making soaps at home by boiling up ashes with the waste fats left over from cooking declined rapidly.

INSTRUCTIONS FOR MAKING CASTILE SOAP, 1667

RECIPE FOR CLEANLINESS
Factory-made soap bars were sold from the early 1900s. Until then, soap was so costly that householders made their own.

adopted a Gaulish soap based on the Phoenician recipe. Pliny called it *sapo*.

The ancient Hebrews discovered that boiling the roots of certain plants, of which there are many varieties, produced soapy water that removed dirt and dissolved grease. In Britain such species, particularly soapwort, *Saponaria officinalis*, were commonly used from the Middle Ages until the 1800s.

Hard soap was first mentioned at Mount Sapo in Rome, where melted animal fats from sacrificial rites

BOILING SOAP *A bucket of lye is carefully poured into hot olive oil to make soap at a factory in 18th-century Marseilles. Seen here is the surface of the boiler, which was 2.5m (8ft) deep. The liquid would be left to cool before being reboiled, then allowed to harden into blocks of pure white soap.*

KEEPING BUGS AT BAY *Lifebuoy soap, introduced by Lever Brothers in 1894, had disinfectant properties imparted by the carbolic acid it contained.*

CLEAN LIVING
Bathing through the ages

When Queen Victoria came to the throne in 1837 there was not a single bathroom in Buckingham Palace. Even in the 1930s some flats in Britain were being built without bathrooms. Yet in the ancient civilised world, cleansing the body with water was considered essential to a person's spiritual and physical well-being.

Around 2500 BC almost every house at Mohenjo-Daro, one of the great cities of the Indus Valley civilisation, had a bathroom. In these little brick structures bathers would douse themselves with water poured from a jug, which was carried away by chutes or pottery pipes in the floor and into the municipal drains.

Terracotta tubs for bathing were first used in Mesopotamia. Examples of these have been found in the palace at Mari on the River Euphrates in northern Iraq, built about 1700 BC, as well as in the Minoan palace of Knossos in

A WISE HABIT? *Taking a bath in the 15th century was a special occasion, afforded only by the wealthy. Servants had to heat and transport large volumes of water and then empty heavy wooden tubs. The medieval doctors of Salerno advised that 'Baths by art or nature warm, used or abused do men much good or harm', but by the time of the Reformation bathing was frowned upon.*

Crete from around the same period. Mohenjo-Daro also had a 'Great Bath' 12 m (39 ft) long, 7 m (23 ft) wide and almost 3 m (10 ft) deep, which appears to have been for communal use. Public bathing in large sunken pools was also favoured by the Egyptians, the Greeks, and especially the Romans, who brought an unrivalled sophistication to bathing and developed efficient plumbing and heating systems throughout their empire.

From the 11th century monasteries helped to spread an understanding of the virtues of washing. Monks observed religious rituals involving cleanliness, which were intended to keep them

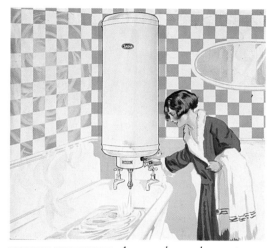

INSTANT HOT WATER *A 1930s showcard promotes an easy-to-use electric water heater. Geysers, gas-operated water heaters, were invented in 1868, but were not made safe from explosion until well into the 20th century. Electric immersion heaters installed in lagged water tanks had become popular by 1930.*

healthier than the general population. Advice came also from the *Salernitan Guide to Health*, produced before 1200 by the renowned medical school at Salerno, in southern Italy. As well as advocating daily washing and bathing every two or three weeks, it introduced the jug and basin, and the wooden bathtub, into the bedrooms of the wealthy. In 1351 Edward III installed the first recorded bathroom in Britain at the Palace of Westminster. It had fire-heated cisterns to provide hot water.

As bathing became accessible to the many, poorer people had the luxury of public baths as early as the 12th century. However, protests by the clergy about

hygiene and the immorality of mixed bathing brought about their closure. In the 17th century Samuel Pepys's wife was described as having some enthusiasm for public bathhouses, which were a popular meeting place for women. Published in 1640, the *Laws of Gallantry* recommended frequent washing, but despite this Louis XIV of France was said to take only one bath a year.

In the average home, wooden tubs, which tended to leak and also smelled unpleasant after use, only gave way to lighter metal baths towards the end of the 1700s. Although the Palace of Whitehall contained bathrooms with hot and cold running water in the 1670s, a room used exclusively for washing, complete with its own furnishings, developed once the technology was available from the 1820s. Victorian catalogues displayed elaborate examples of washbasins, towel rails, showers, toilets, bidets and cabinets with mirrors. Early Victorian showers were hand-pumped, but centuries earlier the ancient Greeks had used rooms with plumbed water that could be sprayed on bathers.

The idea of relaxing in a whirlpool originated in the United States from the Jacuzzi brothers, Italian emigrants who set up water jets to massage the arthritic joints of a member of their family. They perfected their eponymous whirlpool bath in the 1950s and launched it in 1968 in California.

A PRIVY PLACE
The toilet

The citizens of Mohenjo-Daro in the 4th and 3rd millennia BC had brick-built lavatories with wooden seats and chutes to a cesspit or street drain below. Around 2800 BC the inhabitants of Skara Brae in the Orkney Islands built simple recesses into the walls of their houses to make rudimentary toilets connected to drainage channels.

Brick lavatories dating from 2300 BC in Mesopotamia were equipped with a large water vessel to flush the toilet after use. The ancient Egyptians used

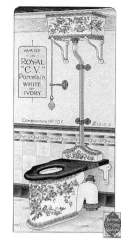

WASHDOWN TOILET BOWL AND CISTERN, 1902

CLOSET FANCY *Ornately decorated automatic flushing toilets with plumbed water were not in homes until the late 1800s. From 1880 perforated sheets of paper on a roll added the finishing touch.*

VICTORIAN TOILET PAPER HOLDER, 1880

toilet seats that were made from limestone and anatomically shaped. They were connected to a drainage system. Roman public baths afforded no privacy and had communal toilets set in a bench-like arrangement, where the waste dropped into a drain before being flushed away by running water. The wealthy had hand-flushed lavatories in their villas, with two seats set amicably side by side.

Waste disposal in early medieval Europe was generally as basic as emptying chamberpots into the central drainage channels of streets, although most castles had at least one 'garderobe'. In 1449 Thomas Brightfield of St Martin's Parish, London, developed a toilet flushed by water piped from a cistern, and in 1596 Elizabeth I's godson Sir John Harington published a design for a flushing 'water closet' with an overhead tank for his house near Bath. But neither had a public sewerage system equipped to deal with the waste.

In 1775 the English watchmaker Alexander Cummings patented a water closet with a valve, or 'stink-trap'— a pipe with an S-bend that trapped water and stopped noxious smells rising from the drain. Thomas Crapper, a London plumber, invented the valveless water cistern in 1884.

The Romans used a sponge attached to a stick. It was the Chinese who seem to have been the first to adopt paper. In AD 589 a court official wrote that he dare not use, for toilet purposes, documents with quotations or commentaries from revered Chinese literature.

DOING THE LAUNDRY
Keeping clothes clean

MACHINE AGE *Hastings women relax while staff at Britain's first automatic laundry in 1948 load the washes. Coin-operated machines were introduced the following year.*

ELBOW GREASE *In 1800 Welsh washerwomen risk the occupational hazard of chapped hands as they pound their clothes in the stream.*

Laundering the linen of the pharaohs during Egypt's 2nd dynasty (about 2830-2530 BC) was considered such an important task that it was supervised by court officials. Even then, the practice was already well established: cleaning clothes had been recorded on Egyptian tablets more than 1000 years earlier.

From ancient times clothes were washed by being pounded with the hands, or with rocks, in the shallows of a stream or lake. At English wellsides in the Middle Ages, linen was commonly beaten with a bat-shaped beetle or battledore. In isolated areas of Scotland as late as the 19th century, dirty clothes were still soaked in tubs and trampled clean with bare feet.

Commercial laundries were set up by the Romans, but after the collapse of their empire such businesses became a rarity in Britain. Washerwomen and laundresses were commonplace by the 17th century; in the early 1800s larger businesses were laundering for institutions such as workhouses. The first public laundry opened in Manchester in 1842, but such places were a last resort for the respectable. Only since the advent of the launderette in the late 1940s has it become acceptable to wash one's dirty linen in public. The first US 'Washateria' opened in 1934. Washing machines were charged by the hour.

CLEAN AND WHITE
The detergent story

Natron, a natural form of carbonate of soda, was probably the Egyptians' laundry aid. The Romans sprinkled fuller's earth, an absorbent clay, on their woollen garments before beating and washing them clean. This fulling, which also had a thickening effect, was traditionally carried out by men: a Company of Fullers was registered in the City of London in 1376, but meanwhile the toil of laundresses remained unsung.

Drying clothes in sunlight would have bleached them clean, but the Romans also exploited the bleaching properties of ammonia by soaking garments in a dilute solution of stale urine. In Britain, urine was used as a whitener well into the 19th century, as was dung, which has a similar effect, and lye, an alkali made from wood or plant ashes.

Until the end of the 18th century, soap was a luxury usually saved for personal hygiene. Clothes might be scrubbed with a harsh soap made from animal fat, but lye was extensively used for boiling laundry. Soda replaced lye from 1791, when sodium

sulphate was first produced on an industrial scale from salt by the French chemist Nicolas LeBlanc. The first soap powder, Babbitt's Best Soap, went on sale in New York in 1843. Persil, named from two of its vital ingredients, perborate and silicate, was introduced in Germany in 1907. Persil's secret was self-activation; it 'washed whiter', in the words of their 1930s advertising slogan, by slowly releasing oxygen.

Synthetic soapless detergents, whose molecules attach themselves selectively to dirt, were developed in Germany in the 1880s. Nekal, the first commercial detergent, was marketed there in 1917.

The Romans noticed that adding a faint blue dye to rinsing water masked the yellow tinge of much-laundered cotton and linen and gave the impression of snowy whiteness. The practice was introduced into Britain, along with starch, from Holland in the 1500s, when powdered crystals of cobalt blue or an extract of lapis lazuli were used. It became redundant in the mid 1940s after optical whiteners began to be incorporated into washing powders.

POWDER PACKETS *Industrial soap production in the early 1800s led to the packaging of soap powders for home use. From the 1930s synthetic detergents, popularised in the USA when fats needed for soap became scarce, helped to whiten the weekly wash.*

THE WASHING MACHINE
A force for freedom

In the notorious 'Monday wash' of the 19th century, which took at least two days to complete, water was lugged from pumps or wells, then heated in a copper, or boiler, over the fire. Clothes were churned around inside it with a multilegged dolly stick or 'peggy legs' before repeated hand rinsing.

Many attempts had been made to ease the arduous job of washing. Robert Hooke, who developed the modern microscope, described a system used at the home of Sir John Hoskins in 1677, in which a fine linen bag of laundry was immersed in water and attached to a rotating wheel. William Bailey's hand-cranked device of 1758 was reputed to do the work of three washerwomen.

Mechanical washers proliferated in the late 19th century. One typical early example, patented in 1858 by Hamilton Smith of Pennsylvania, consisted of a wooden drum in which a dolly was revolved by a hand crank. Although such machines made washing easier, tubs were still filled and emptied by hand. It took hot and cold water on tap, and electricity, to provide real freedom from such drudgery. In 1907 the first electric washing machine, the Thor, was designed in the USA by Alva J. Fisher.

ADVERTISEMENT FOR GERMAN ELECTRIC WASHING MACHINE, ABOUT 1925

HELP AT HAND *Mangles for wringing and pressing, ridged washboards for scrubbing wet fabrics, dollies for churning the wash and tongs for lifting laundry out of tubs of boiling water were familiar to Britain's housewives from the 1800s until the 1950s, when electric washing machines started to take the strain. Wooden clothespegs were hand carved long after the spring peg was invented in the USA in 1893.*

CLEAN BUT DRY

The Mycenaeans of 1600 BC drew out dirt from clothes by sprinkling earth on them then brushing it off. A French book of 1716 mentions the stain-removing properties of turpentine, but the dry-cleaning process was commercialised in the mid 1800s by the French dyer Jean Baptiste Jolly after his maid accidentally spilt turpentine on a piece of cloth.

WRING AND PRESS
Drying and ironing

From the earliest times, wet clothes were wrung by hand and spread in the sun to dry. Hand-operated mangles and wringers, recorded in Britain from the late 1690s, were standard in middle-class homes of the 19th century. From the 1860s, steam-powered dryers were used in public wash-houses. The first

electric tumble driers were installed in ships of the P&O Line in 1909, but it was the 1930s before domestic electric driers were successful. Until then only well-to-do homes had heated drying rooms and closets—forerunners of the airing cupboard.

The pleated clothes fashionable in Egypt from around 2000 BC were achieved by starching with gum. Until the 19th century many country folk would press their clothes with nothing more than a wooden roller. The Vikings who invaded Europe from the 9th century spread their clothes on whalebone plaques.

Heated irons were used in the Far East from the 8th century, when small pans were filled with hot coal or charcoal; similar box irons were in use in Europe in the 15th century. By the 1700s the flatiron had become a block of metal that was heated on the fire or stove. Gas irons were patented in the 19th century. Although it was developed in France, the earliest patent for an electric iron was taken out by the American Henry Seeley in 1882.

MANGLE, 1925-35

WOODEN DOLLY, 1920S

STARCH, 1940S

LAUNDRY TUB, 1920S

GLASS WASHBOARD, 1920-40

SMALL WASHTUB, 1920-40

GAS IRON, 1930-50

BOX IRON, ABOUT 1850

FLATIRON, ABOUT 1890

TONGS AND CLOTHESPEGS, 1930-50

A CLEAN SWEEP
Brooms and brushes

When people first kept house, 10000 and more years ago, dirt was swept up and out of huts with branches plucked from shrubs. So the brush was 'invented', and then improved by binding flexible sticks and twigs together around a wooden handle. In Europe, favourite plants for this purpose were broom, from which the brush took its name, heather, birch and the tufts of maize plants. The first American brush factory was founded in New York in 1859.

Brushes of bristles knotted together in bunches were made by the Romans, but not until the 15th century were hogs' bristles glued with pitch into blocks of wood and used for scrubbing, for brushing clothes, as well as for sweeping. In the USA the shape of

SWEEPING THE ALMSHOUSE FLOOR
WITH A TWIG BESOM, 1513

the broom was altered, and its efficiency tremendously increased, when in the late 18th century the members of the Shaker religious community, with elegant simplicity, converted its circular head into a flat wedge.

The feather duster, icon of house pride, may have an even more ancient origin than the besom, for brushes made of feathers were almost certainly used in around 25000 BC in the execution of cave paintings in northern Spain. In Britain, moss was another natural material employed for dusting, certainly until the 18th century.

GOBBLING UP THE GRIME
Vacuum cleaners and carpet sweepers

In 1901 the London engineer Hubert Cecil Booth placed a handkerchief on an upholstered seat and proceeded to suck air through it. By thus depositing grime on his handkerchief, he proved that suction could dislodge and trap dirt. Inspired by an unimpressive demonstration of a dust-blowing machine for cleaning railway carriages, Booth went on to build the first machine to combine a power-driven suction pump with dust-collecting. This cumbersome horse-drawn device, from which a long hose would be run into a building, was nicknamed the 'Puffing Billy'.

Smaller, bellows-operated vacuum cleaners evolved for domestic use, but were eclipsed by the 'electric suction sweeper' patented in the USA by James Murray Spangler, an asthmatic school caretaker, in 1907. Unable to capitalise on his invention, he sold it to a leather-goods maker, William Henry Hoover, whose original upright, bag-on-stick model of 1926 was marketed with the slogan 'It beats as it sweeps as it cleans'.

The vacuum cleaner's predecessor, the carpet sweeper, began in 1811 as a revolving brush in a box fixed to castors, patented in Britain by James Hume. The idea did not achieve commercial success until the American shop owner Melville Bissell patented a more efficient version in 1876.

DUST BUSTERS *The domestic vacuum cleaner revolutionised housework and made the carpet beater redundant, but ancient tools such as brooms, dusters and scrubbing brushes are still part of the cleaning arsenal.*

VACUUM CLEANER, 1930S

QUICK AND EASY *An advertisement from the 1930s shows how to make light, elegant work of sweeping up the crumbs.*

VACUUM CLEANER AND ATTACHMENTS, 1930S

DUSTPAN AND BRUSH, 1930S

BESOM, 18TH-CENTURY DESIGN

CARPET BEATER, 1940S

FEATHER DUSTER, 1930S

BLACKING BRUSHES, 1950S

A HELPING HAND *Rigorous standards of the 19th century were maintained by servants who worked for such low wages that even families of modest means could afford a domestic. As late as the 1930s, dust from coal fires was removed from rooms such as this every day.*

PURITY AND EFFICIENCY
The burgeoning of housework

Epitomised by the clarion call of the Methodist leader John Wesley, 'Cleanliness is, indeed, next to Godliness', a new ethos of purity flowered in the 18th century. Throughout the Industrial Revolution the prosperous middle classes created ever more housework by cluttering their homes with elaborate furnishings and ornaments and by heating their houses with dust-producing coal fires. However, homemade cleaning materials, such as bone ash and charcoal polish, dating from about the 17th century, remained in popular use.

Until the early 1900s the cleaning ritual began at dawn with raking out the kitchen range, then scrubbing it clean with a blacking solution and polishing it. Tea leaves or sand, scattered over stone and tile floors, helped to dampen down dust before sweeping, washing and scrubbing. Tea leaves or freshly pulled grass were also scattered on carpets before they were brushed clean; occasionally they were also taken outside to be beaten free of dust.

THE HYGIENIC HOME

• The Romans used weasels, not cats, to rid their homes of rodents. By the Middle Ages various kinds of mousetrap existed, including a metal contraption with a large spring and serrated jaws, illustrated in a German book of the 13th century.

• A paste of sand, grit and ashes was the usual 17th-century scourer. Victorian housewives used washing soda (sodium carbonate), but this was eclipsed by Brillo steel wool pads, first sold in the USA in 1913 with an accompanying bar of soap.

• Until the 1920s most people made their own cleaning products. From Roman times, furniture polish was made from beeswax mixed with juniper or cedar oil.

• Rubber gloves first protected hands from hot water in the early 1950s.

MOUSETRAP THAT CAPTURED THE CREATURE ALIVE, ABOUT 1850

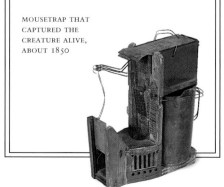

TACKLING THE DISHES
Washing-up and dishwashers

During the Middle Ages, when chunks of stale bread were used as 'plates', washing-up was non-existent. Even after wooden platters came into use they were generally simply wiped clean with bread or straw. It was the widespread introduction of china, following the expansion of the Staffordshire potteries at the end of the 18th century, that heralded the chore of washing-up.

The dishwasher was invented in 1885 by Eugène Daquin, a Frenchman. His machine used a revolving mechanism equipped with artificial hands that grabbed dishes and dunked them first in soapy water, then in a clear cold bath; rotating brushes scrubbed the dishes clean. A report on the machine in *Scientific American* assured readers that the dishwasher constituted 'no danger whatsoever to man or dish'.

In 1886 Josephine Cockran, an American housewife, patented a small domestic dishwasher. Inspired by the number of plates her servants broke, she designed an appliance in which a hand crank made the machine spray soapy water over the dishes. The first dishwasher to be electrically powered appeared in 1922.

MACHINE WASH *Dishwashers such as this 1929 German model were designed to reduce crockery breakages rather than time. They needed to be laboriously cranked by hand.*

TUMBLER OR
EGYPTIAN LOCK,
DEVISED IN THE
1ST MILLENNIUM BC

ARAB KEY CARRIER,
FIRST RECORDED
2ND MILLENNIUM BC

EGYPTIAN LOCK *In the original tumbler lock the bolt was held shut by pins that dropped from a box. To release the lock a long key was inserted into a slot in the bolt, levered to raise the pins and pulled back to draw the bolt. Such locks can still be found in rural parts of the Near and Middle East.*

UNDER LOCK AND KEY
Protected property

The need to keep thieves at bay is as old as the notion of property. Simple locks in which a wooden bolt was attached to a piece of rope, pulled into place through a hole in the door and secured with a complex knot, were known to the Chinese and the Egyptians as early as 2000 BC. The first tumbler lock, named after the falling pins that secured the bolt, was in use in Iraq during the 8th century BC. Its subsequent popularity in Egypt, where it was used for securing mummy cases, led to its name of Egyptian lock, and it spread through Greece to the rest of Europe.

In ancient Rome brides were ritually presented with the keys to their new households, and adulthood is often still marked with receiving 'the key of the door'. The symbolic power of the key can be traced to Greek mythology, in which it unlocked the door to Heaven and Hell. Its association with good luck, and the superstition that the key should be kept in a keyhole to prevent evil spirits from entering the home, originate from ancient Mediterranean culture.

By the Middle Ages elaborate locks were being made throughout Europe, but such locks were easily picked. The first major improvements in lock design came from Britain. In 1778 the locksmith Robert Barron patented the double-action tumbler lock, based on the principle by which

CODED OPENING *Key-operated padlocks were known to the Romans, but keyless combination locks were a later invention. The first models, using sequences of letters, not numbers, date from the early 17th century.*

TURN OF THE KEY
The patterned end of a Roman key matches the shape of the holes in the bolt. It would have been moved back and forth in the lock to open or secure the locked object.

ROMAN BRONZE LOCK
AND KEY (ABOVE),
ABOUT 2ND CENTURY AD

BRAMAH PADLOCK
AND CYLINDRICAL
KEY, 1801 (LEFT),
AND IN ITS
CHALLENGE BOARD
(RIGHT)

BRASS COMBINATION
LOCK, 18TH CENTURY

mortise locks operate. The tumblers were released by a first turn of the key, and the lock opened by a further turn. Some 40 years later the locksmith Jeremiah Chubb added a detector tumbler to jam the lock if anyone attempted to pick it. To prove the principle, in 1818 a Chubb lock was given to an imprisoned locksmith-turned-burglar with a promise of £100 and a pardon if he could pick it. After trying unsuccessfully for more than two months, the frustrated convict gave up.

Joseph Bramah was a cabinet-maker who became one of the most inventive engineers of his age. In 1784 he devised a lock operated by a complex cylindrical key containing slits and notches that lowered sprung segments in the lock.

The American locksmith Linus Yale made a lock based on the Egyptian principle of pin tumblers. Today's Yale lock was developed from this by Linus Yale Junior in 1856. Relatively difficult to pick, it has proved a lasting success.

PICKER'S DARE *Joseph Bramah was so sure of his lock that in the early 1800s he offered a reward to whoever could pick it. The challenge was finally met in 1851 by the American Alfred Charles Hobbs, who took 51 hours, spread over 16 days, to perform the feat.*

SAFES AND MONEY BOXES
Keeping assets hidden

In ancient times people concealed their valuables in caves or up trees, or simply buried them, but in Europe wooden chests were used to provide security for jewels and other precious objects from the 8th century AD. Strongboxes of wrought iron, strengthened with interlaced iron bands, were being made in large numbers in southern Germany by the late 16th century, in sizes ranging from a few centimetres to about 1.5 m (5 ft) long. Used throughout Europe, they became known in Britain in the mid 19th century as armada chests, in the mistaken belief that such chests had held the bullion that financed the Spanish Armada in 1588, or that they came from wrecked Spanish ships.

In the early 19th century various metal safes were patented, including several by Jeremiah Chubb. However, most of them were intended to be fireproof rather than burglarproof. The first patent for a fireproof safe was granted in 1834 to the Englishman William Marr. Safes continued to be simply variations on the theme of

the iron chest until the much publicised Cornhill robbery of 1865, after which they were more finely engineered.

The idea for a time lock, which opens only at a predetermined hour and runs by clockwork or electricity, was conceived in 1831 by the Scottish bank agent William Rutherford. These came into their own in the USA in the 1870s when burglars began torturing bankers to force them to hand over the strongroom keys or reveal the combination.

The penny-wise have long found ways to hide their savings. Hollowed flints filled with Roman coins from the 1st century AD have been unearthed in southern England. The first containers made specifically for keeping coins were used in ancient Egypt and Rome to store offerings to household gods.

Onion-shaped pottery money boxes with a slit for inserting coins were used by apprentices in medieval Britain to collect Christmas tips from their masters' customers. On Boxing Day the pots were broken to release their bounty. Animal figures date from the 17th century. The pig, which gave us the 'piggy bank', was one of the most popular figures, probably because of the importance of pigs in rural economies.

TREASURE TROVE *In the coffers used by the wealthy of the 17th and 18th centuries to secure their riches an elaborately engraved lock usually occupied the whole interior of the lid. The keyhole on the front of these early safes was usually a decoy, the real one being concealed beneath a panel on the lid. No such ingenuity went into the simple, but treasured, pottery money boxes of humble folk.*

GERMAN EARTHENWARE MONEY BOX, 16TH CENTURY

WROUGHT-IRON GERMAN ARMADA CHEST, ABOUT 1600

EARTHENWARE PIGGY BANK, 19TH CENTURY

BOLT FROM THE BLUE

Both the ancient Egyptians and the Minoans of Crete erected what seem to have been lightning rods on temples, although their exact function is unproven.

Lightning remained a puzzle until 1752, when the American statesman and inventor Benjamin Franklin proved that it was a form of electricity by flying a kite into a cloud during a storm and showing that a key attached to the kite had become electrified. His subsequent invention of the lightning conductor earned him the venom of the clergy, who accused him of interfering with the wrath of God.

SECURING THE GOODS
Rope, chains and barbed wire

Rope tied in a knot, the most basic way of securing things, began with vines used by Neolithic people for making things such as fishing nets. By 4000 BC tree bark fibre was being rolled to make yarn, but hemp, the most popular material for rope, was first used during the 2nd millennium BC by the Chinese. Weatherproof metal chains of connecting links, through which a padlock can be slipped if the links are large enough, were first fashioned in Egypt in the 3rd millennium BC to form handles on stone vessels.

Faced with a shortage of timber for fencing in their vast herds, US cattle ranchers adopted barbed wire in the 1870s as a cheap alternative for corralling their beasts. It helped to open up the West by providing settlers with affordable security. Blocks of barbed wood were strung along wires in the first design, patented by Lucien Smith in 1867. The following year M. Kelly improved on this with a twisted metal strand with protruding barbs. Modern barbed wire was made possible by the invention of a machine for mass-producing it, patented by Joseph Farwell Glidden in 1873.

LOGO FOR GLIDDEN BARBED WIRE, 1880

MAN'S BEST FRIEND
An ancient pedigree

From cosseted Pekingese to doleful bloodhounds, all our canine pets are descended from wolves. The ancestor of the wolf itself was a carnivorous tree-climbing mammal *Miacis*, which lived around 40 million years ago. Distinct canines first appeared 35 million years ago in North America.

Recent research by biologists in the United States suggests dogs have been domesticated for some 135 000 years—a process that started before modern humans began to leave Africa 100 000 years ago. But archaeological evidence of dogs goes back only to 12 000 BC, the date of a Palestinian grave. Buried dog remains have also been found in a Stone Age settlement in Yorkshire.

Domesticated dogs were trained to chase, bring down and retrieve prey, while their territorial instincts would have been used for guarding camps. In Mesopotamia, a greyhound-type dog was depicted chasing gazelle on a piece of pottery 8000 years old.

The Egyptians kept the first lap dogs, which they depicted sitting under the chairs of their owners. The Romans bred dogs for specific tasks, importing different types from all over the empire, and credited them with watchfulness, courage and loyalty. They were also the first to issue the warning 'Beware of the dog' (*cave canem* in Latin), which can be seen beneath a fierce-looking canine on a mosaic dating from the 1st century AD uncovered in Pompeii.

ROYAL FAVOURITES
Chinese emperors were often offered dogs as gifts. Around 3450 BC, Emperor Fo-Hi considered breeding tiny dogs to slip up his sleeves and keep his hands warm in winter, an idea put into practice by 15th-century Aztec priests with their chihuahuas in Central America.

Lap dogs were popular in China, where crossbreeding and strict diets to impair growth produced small dogs with bent legs and snub noses. Pekingese have existed for 2000 years. Originally they were the exclusive property of the Chinese imperial court.

Spaniels, whose name probably comes from the Old French *espaignol*

PAMPERED PETS *The luxury of owning a pet that could not earn its keep was beyond the means of most people during the Middle Ages. By the time this portrait was painted in 1759 dogs were popular among all classes, but noblewomen and wealthier citizens favoured small, lap-dog breeds.*

(Spanish dog), are first described in a French book on hunting from the 14th century. They became fashionable some 200 years later when Henry III of France surrounded himself with miniature spaniels. The King Charles spaniel is thought to have originated in either China or Japan, but earned its name in 17th-century England from Charles II's passion for his pet spaniels.

The first poodles were large gun dogs used by hunters to catch waterfowl—hence their German name, *Pudelhund*, meaning 'splashing dog'. French or German in origin, they were already known in the 13th century. Traditionally, the poodles' thick, curly coats were clipped to make them resemble lions. This also allowed them to swim more easily, while the bands of hair that were left around their legs and front quarters protected their joints and vital organs from the effects of the cold.

CAT COMPANIONS
Sacred, proud and beloved

Compared with their canine rivals, cats were late converts to domesticity. The earliest known remains of a tamed species, with teeth significantly different from those of Mediterranean wildcats, were uncovered in Khirokitia in Cyprus and date from around 6000 BC.

Cats were first depicted—hunting wildfowl, killing mice and playing under chairs—on tomb sketches and paintings in Egypt around 1500 BC. They were domesticated when it was noticed that they protected granaries from infestations of rats.

Egyptian cat owners would shave their eyebrows as a sign of mourning for their pet cat. They took the body to Bubastis, city of the elegant cat-headed goddess Bastet, also known as Bast or

FIDELITY SYMBOL *A tiny Chinese canine figurine, made in about AD 350, accompanied its owner to the grave. As in life, the dog rests in its bed.*

BEWARE OF THE DOG *In ancient times dogs such as the Assyrian mastiff were bred for their lion-hunting prowess. Dogs were also used in warfare to carry messages, attack the enemy and defend camps. Roman soldiers found that after defeating Celtic warriors it took another two days to overcome the dogs guarding their dead masters' supplies.*

ASSYRIAN RELIEF
OF HUNTER AND
MASTIFF, 600 BC

ADORED CAT *The tabby's distinctive marks were familiar to the ancient Egyptians, who developed the cult of the cat. The Romans, who kept cats from the 1st century AD, considered them the epitome of independence.*

PRIZED PETS

- In ancient Egypt, 'Mau' was an affectionate name given to cats. Dead cats were lovingly embalmed before being given ceremonial burials. In one grave, at a site of a temple to the cat-goddess Bastet, 300 000 mummified cats were discovered.
- The first widely reported dog show was held in 1859 at Newcastle upon Tyne. The world-renowned Cruft's, named after its founder, Charles Cruft, began in 1891.
- The earliest book to set guidelines for judging dogs was published in 1867 and listed 35 British breeds.
- Isaac Newton, the English physicist, is said to have invented the cat flap in the late 17th century.

Pasht, who was said to possess nine lives. She may also be the derivation of the affectionate term 'puss'.

Domestic Egyptian cats may have reached Europe on board ships plying the trade routes to Phoenicia (modern-day Syria and Lebanon). The association of cats and devil worship took hold in the 12th century. In the 13th century the Church launched a crusade against two French heretical sects who were said to have worshipped the devil in the form of a black cat, and the religious persecution of cats began.

Europe's cat population plummeted. When plague struck in the 14th century there were not enough cats to kill the rats that were the main carriers of the disease-spreading fleas. A quarter of Europe's human population perished.

Cats regained their domestic niche in the 17th century, when they were regularly portrayed in Dutch paintings. A century later they were beloved pets in many British households. Imported breeds were introduced from the 1880s, including the first Siamese cats ever to be exhibited, given to Owen Gould, a British consul general in Bangkok, by the king of Siam (now Thailand). Like Persians, Siamese cats are thought to be descended from an ancient species of Asian wildcat.

FUR AND FEATHERS
Other popular pets

Golden hamsters were first brought to Britain by James Henry Skene, a consul general at Aleppo in Syria, in 1880. Although these early arrivals and their offspring survived more than 30 years, all today's pet golden hamsters are believed to be the descendants of a litter captured in Syria in 1930 for use in scientific experiments and brought to London in 1931. A few were given to London Zoo in 1932 and from 1937 they were sold as pets to the public.

The guinea pig, a native of South America, was the first rodent to be domesticated, originally as a source of food for the Incas. It was introduced into Europe around 1580.

The ancient Egyptians delighted in the exotic bird life that surrounded them and depicted at least 70 different species in their art. The tuneful golden oriole, the lapwing, the hoopoe and the crane were among those birds that were kept in captivity.

The canary, named after its native Canary Islands, was domesticated in the 1500s. The budgerigar was brought to Britain from Australia in 1840 by the naturalist John Gould. Its name comes from the Aboriginal *budgeri*, 'good', and *gar*, 'cockatoo'. The affectionate term 'budgie' dates from the 1930s.

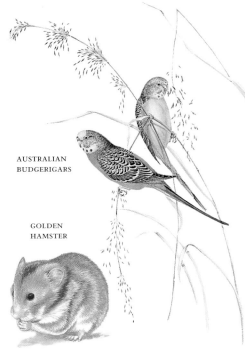

AUSTRALIAN
BUDGERIGARS

GOLDEN
HAMSTER

FAMILY FAVOURITES *Small pets such as budgerigars and hamsters became popular home companions in the 1950s. The breeding and showing of sweet-songed budgerigars began in earnest in the 1920s, while hamsters were exhibited for the first time in 1945.*

HIT ON THE HEAD *Nails in various stages of production lie on the workbench of a 15th-century nail-maker. Each rod had to be softened in the fire before being tapered in stages.*

CLEAN CUT
Scissors and shears

Among the handiest of all household objects, scissors first appeared in the Bronze Age. However, their origins go back more than a million years, when clubs made of antlers and hammers of stone were first employed as domestic tools, and when sharpened stones were mankind's only cutting implements.

Bronze, first made in Mesopotamia about 3500 BC, provided the material for better blades. The first scissors, in widespread use in Europe and Asia by 1000 BC, consisted of two blades connected at the handle end by a C-shaped spring. This design, which was used to cut everything from hair to animal hides, remained basically unchanged for millennia, and was being used for sheepshearing until recent times.

In the Middle Ages the nobility of Europe had made elaborately decorated gold or silver spring scissors inlaid with enamel, pearl and diamonds. Well into the 17th century humbler folk, and craftsmen such as tailors and seamstresses, used simpler versions made of either iron or brass.

Pivoted scissors, in which a screw or rivet axis connects two blades with handles looped at their ends to hold the fingers, were being made of bronze and iron 2000 years ago in Roman Europe and the Far East. More expensive to make than spring scissors, they did not become common for domestic use until the 16th century. Large-scale production began in 1761, when the Sheffield metalworker Robert Hinchcliffe began to make them from cast steel, which produced stronger blades.

Scissors inspire many superstitions, one of the most common being that accepting a pair as a gift from a friend risks severing the friendship. Traditionally a small coin is given in exchange.

PINNING THINGS DOWN
Nailing, screwing and bolting

The hammer, originally just a roughly shaped stone, has changed little since the Egyptians produced the first cast copper hammerhead around 3500 BC. Claw hammers, with a V-shaped opening opposite the head for extracting nails, appeared in Roman times.

Nails are equally ancient. The oldest known were found on a statue of a bull, consisting of copper sheets nailed to a wooden frame, made in Mesopotamia in about 3500 BC. But in the Middle Ages nails were still being made by craftsmen who hammered rods through a succession of holes of decreasing size, and flattened the end to make a head. Consequently they were expensive and used only to fix metal to wood. Most joiners and builders fastened timbers together with cheap wood joints and pegs. The first nail-making machines were developed by Ezekial Reed in the USA in 1786 and by Thomas Clifford in England in 1790.

Screw-type devices such as the water screw for raising water were known to the Egyptians. But the idea was applied to carpentry only in the 16th century, when it was realised that a nail with a twist in its stem stayed more securely in place. A slot was cut into the head to make it easier to fit and remove, and a 'turnscrew' designed. The first machine for cutting screws was patented by Job and William Wyatt in England in 1760.

Nuts and bolts appeared in about 1550, together with the spanners needed to tighten and undo the bolts. Like early screws, they were hand-made and of slightly different sizes. A screw-cutting lathe developed by Henry Maudslay in 1797 standardised production, making pieces interchangeable. Around 1700 the adjustable spanner appeared in France.

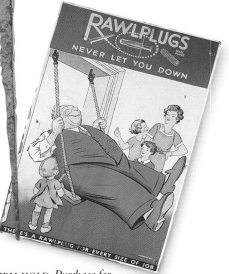

FIRM HOLD *Purchase for screws was provided by plugs of wood driven into chiselled holes until 1919, when the London building contractor John Rawlings devised an expandable fibre plug made of jute bonded with animal blood. The Rawlplug was an overnight success.*

CLEAR WINNER
The manufacturers of the first adhesive cellophane tape, devised in the 1920s for use in car spray painting workshops, soon realised it had much wider applications in the home.

FILM AND FOIL
Keeping it under wraps

Cellophane, a flexible, transparent film made from cellulose (a natural substance found in all plants), was invented by the Swiss chemist Jacques Brandenburger in 1908. It was originally used to wrap luxury items, but it was expensive and not moisture-proof. In 1927 chemists of the American company Du Pont patented a moisture-resistant cellophane that was widely used to encase packaged goods such as cigarettes. The earliest hygienic food wrap, made from rubber-based hydrochloride, was marketed in the USA as Pliofilm from 1934.

Adhesive cellophane film, or sticky tape, owes its invention to the 1920s American fashion for two-tone cars. To help painters to create sharp edges to the contrasting colour bands, in 1928 the Minnesota Mining & Manufacturing Company (3M) developed an adhesive tape that could be removed without taking paint away with it.

For reasons of economy, the original cellulose tape manufactured by 3M had adhesive only at the edges. It is claimed that one disappointed user suggested to the 3M salesman that he take 'this Scotch tape back to those bosses of yours and tell them to put adhesive coating all over it'. Deciding that meanness did not pay, the company began to coat the film fully, and both the tape and the name stuck. Sticky tape was marketed in Britain in 1934, followed by Sellotape in 1937.

An economical method of extracting aluminium from its ore was developed in 1886. The resulting material could easily be cold-rolled into strong, thin sheets that were greaseproof, odourless and tasteless, resistant to heat and corrosion, as well as impervious to gas. Marketed in the USA from 1947, rolled domestic aluminium foil did not arrive in British kitchens until 1962, under the trade name Bacofoil.

STICKING TOGETHER
Adhesives and glues

Excavations at Umm el Tlel in Syria have revealed that some 40000 years ago, early humans attached stone tools to wooden hafts with bitumen, a naturally occurring dark, sticky substance now used for surfacing roads and waterproofing roofs. For the ancient Sumerians of around 5000 BC, bitumen, oozing its way through cracks in the earth, was associated with the underworld and evil spirits, a belief that may be the origin of the Biblical Hell's 'lake of pitch'. The practical waterproofing qualities of bitumen were first exploited in about 2400 BC, when shipwrights in Babylon and Mesopotamia used it to caulk their ships.

The Egyptians manufactured glues by boiling animal skin, bone and sinew, and similar glues are still used by traditional carpenters. Other natural adhesives used since earliest times include beeswax, egg white, gum, resin and starch pastes. Synthetic glues, developed in the 20th century, are stronger and more versatile.

'Superglues', discovered accidentally by scientists of the American company Eastman Kodak in the 1950s and first sold in Britain in the mid 1970s, provide the tightest grip of all. Investigating the light-bending qualities of the substance ethyl cyanoacrylate, the scientists were surprised when the glass prisms of the refractometer stuck firmly together and could not be prised apart.

TIGHT COVER *Aluminium foil was introduced into British homes in 1929, when the first milk bottles with aluminium tops were delivered to doorsteps. But it took bluetits until the 1950s to learn how to pierce through these metal covers.*

INNOVATIONS ROUND-UP

- Rubber bands were first made by Perry and Co of London in 1845.
- Charles Gould invented the stapler in 1868 for use in bookbinding.
- A vacuum flask was demonstrated in 1892 by the Scottish physicist James Dewar. His mother-in-law remained sceptical of a flask that Dewar made for his son in 1902 and knitted a woollen cosy for it to make sure that its contents stayed warm.
- Vacuum flasks were first marketed in 1902 by the German Reinhold Burger, who held a competition to name the invention. The winning entry was Thermos, the Greek word for 'hot'.
- In 1900 the Norwegian Johann Vaaler patented the paperclip.
- The aerosol can was invented in 1926 by another Norwegian, Erik Rotheim, but the idea was not developed commercially until 1941, when Lyle Goodhue and William Sullivan took out a patent in the USA. They saw the spray can as the ideal container for insecticides.

AEROSOL INSECT KILLER, 1950s

GADGETS FOR THE HOME

'Every new invention that is practical and economical…will be brought to [your] notice…The time spent on housework can be enormously reduced in every home, without any loss to its comfort, and often with a great increase to its well-being…'

'THE REASON FOR GOOD HOUSEKEEPING', *Good Housekeeping* MAGAZINE, MARCH 1922

JOB IN HAND *Mechanical devices turned manually proliferated in the 19th century, mostly for use 'below stairs'. Typical was the knife cleaner, patented by the British manufacturer William Kent in 1851, made of leather leaves and abrasive powders such as emery to clean several knives at once. It was made redundant by stainless steel, but other gadgets, such as the coffee mill, remained little changed for 100 years.*

For nearly every domestic chore, and many tasks besides, a gadget has been invented. The process started early: as far back as the 1st century AD the Greek engineer Hero of Alexandria designed a tiny steam turbine for opening doors. In the 9th century the three Banu Musa brothers of Baghdad wrote *The Book of Ingenious Devices*, which included an oil lamp with an automatically rising wick. Roasting spits operated by the heat rising from a fire instead of by human spit-turners were known in the Middle Ages.

As the machine age took hold in the 19th century, so labour-saving machines multiplied. Among the more practical was the American Universal

KNIFE CLEANER, 1890–1910

FOOD MINCER, 1920S

SPICE OR COFFEE GRINDER, LATE 1700S

COFFEE MILL, MID 1800S

CAN OPENER, ABOUT 1895

CAN OPENER, 1990S (1930S DESIGN)

EGG WHISK, 1920–40

A WORLD OF DREAMS

A now forgotten device, patented in 1903, extinguished the flames under boiling milk thanks to levers operated by a float. The long list of gadgets that never made it ranges from an 'improved cup and saucer' (1902), featuring drainage channels in the saucer to keep the bottom of the cup dry after any spillage, via a bicycle-operated shower (1897) through to a ring door knocker (1905)—a brass ring worn on the finger for those who find knocking on doors tiring.

AUTOMATIC HAT TIPPER FOR TIRELESS GREETINGS, 1896

boot cleaner of 1882. Its hand-turned wheel had a row of bristles for brushing off dirt and another one for polishing.

Mechanical whisks, food mixers and mincers appeared in the 1850s. By the 1880s the classic mincer design had emerged from the London firm of Spong and Co. It had a hand-turned screw to drive the food through fixed blades, as well as attachments for slicing vegetables and meat. Smaller versions were sold for use at the dining table by those who had lost their teeth.

An earlier British invention was the coffee grinder, which came into use in the late 1600s. Until then spices and coffee had been ground using pestles and mortars. Small grinders for home use were first made in 1815 by the iron founder Archibald Kenrick. His much copied coffee mill consisted of a bowl at the top to hold the beans, a handle to turn the blades and a drawer into which the ground beans fell.

Canned food, produced from the early 1800s, demanded a means of getting at its contents. A can of veal

made of tin plate and taken on an Arctic expedition in 1824 bore the instructions: 'Cut round on the top with a chisel and hammer.' In the USA, pierce-and-prise can openers were introduced around 1858. Simple cutting wheels were used from 1870; only in 1931 did a design with pivoted handles and a turning key appear.

A pierce-and-prise can opener was one of the features of the pocket knife designed by Karl Elsener for the Swiss Army in 1891, in which a spring mechanism allowed many utensils to be folded next to the main blade. The Swiss Army knife, originally issued only to recruits, was so popular that by 1900 it became available to civilians.

In the late 19th century inventors rushed to make use of electricity. The first electric toaster, the Eclipse, was sold by the Crompton company, of Chelmsford in Essex, in 1893. Its

bare wires, glowing red hot as the current passed through them, toasted bread one side at a time. The pop-up toaster, using a clockwork timer to turn off the current and release a spring under the toast, was devised by Charles Strite, a mechanic from Stillwater, Minnesota, in 1927. The Proctor toaster of 1930 improved on this by using a thermostat to 'read' the surface temperature of the bread, a principle that is still employed in today's models.

The electric food mixer, introduced in the USA in 1910, was transformed by the British engineer Ken Wood, whose first Kenwood Chef was marketed in 1950. Cooks could now mix, shred, liquidise, mince, and even open cans, simply by fixing on one of a variety of tools.

Early electrical gadgets were not confined to kitchen use. In the late 1880s the French hairdresser Alexandre Godefroy produced a gas hair dryer, a bonnet fitted with a flexible tube that extended to a gas stove. By 1899 an electric hand-held dryer was available in Germany. The electric toothbrush, first patented in the USA in 1885, did not achieve commercial success until a practical design was made by the Squibb company of New York in 1961.

OUR FRIENDS ELECTRIC *It was electricity, first available in British homes in the early 1880s, that really made household gadgets desirable. Soon most mechanical devices invented by the Victorians had an electrical equivalent, including the coffee grinder (1937) and the can opener (1946).*

FOOD MIXER (KENWOOD CHEF), 1945

SMARTEN UP *John Corby of Windsor started his business in the 1930s with a simple 'valet stand' on which to hang a jacket. A pressing section for trousers was added in the 1950s.*

TOASTER, 1930S

ELECTRIC TOOTHBRUSH, ABOUT 1988

HAIR DRYER, 1920S

PENKNIFE, 1990S (1890S SWISS ARMY KNIFE DESIGN)

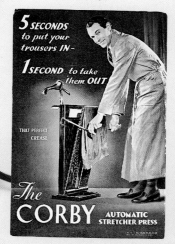

5 SECONDS to put your trousers IN –

1 SECOND to take them OUT

THAT PERFECT CREASE

The CORBY AUTOMATIC STRETCHER PRESS

THE JOY OF FLOWERS
Food for the soul

'If you have enough money for two loaves of bread, buy only one and spend the rest on flowers, because although bread feeds the body, flowers feed the soul.' So advised the Prophet Muhammad, and throughout history, flowers have been offered as gifts to the gods or variously endowed with divine significance.

The Aztecs of the 14th to the 16th centuries illustrated the desire to nurture plants with the legend of the lily of Mictlan, the lily of the valley. Wanting a flower for their heavenly gardens, the gods sent a bat to steal a tear from Xochiquetzel, the goddess of trees and flowers. The tear was then transformed into a lily that had the gift of eternal bloom, but it was both colourless and without fragrance.

So the gods sent the bat with the lily to Mictlan, the underworld, to be washed in the River of Death. There the lily received the gift of beauty but lost that of eternal bloom. Rejected by the gods since its beauty was doomed to fade, the lily finally took root on Earth, where for a brief season it has silver blooms and a wonderful fragrance. The lily is the property of Mictlan and its beauty is only on loan to the Earth.

In ancient Egypt, the water lily, also known as the sacred lotus, was cut to be

THE SACRED LOTUS *The water lily or lotus flower, which bloomed near the banks of great rivers, became a revered symbol in ancient civilisations. Tombs of kings and queens depicted such scenes as this Egyptian girl smelling a white lotus blossom.*

arranged in holy places. Vases dating from 2500 BC, found in the tombs of the necropolis Beni Hasan beside the River Nile, were put in place to hold the scented blue Nile lotus. The lotus also appears in early Indian Buddhist and Chinese Taoist scriptures and art.

Two thousand years ago, the fragrant sweet violet, which grew in the Mediterranean region, was linked to Aphrodite, the Greek goddess of love. It became one of Europe's favourite flowers, brought into homes for its scent and simple beauty.

A BLOOMING PASSION
Floral decorations and arrangements

The heroes of ancient Greece were wreathed with laurel, while a crown of periwinkle circled the head of a condemned man. Hibiscus flowers tied in the hair of Polynesian women, garlands in Renaissance portraits and Victorian corsages all reveal the long history of floral decorations as symbols of status and sexuality.

Displaying flowers in the home is as important now as it was in the 2nd century AD when cut flowers artfully arranged in a container were depicted in a mosaic for the emperor Hadrian's villa in Rome. Ikebana, the Japanese art of formal flower arrangement, began in the early 7th century and is based on Buddhist philosophy.

Flower arranging was not regarded as an art form in Europe until the 17th century, when exotic new flowers were imported from discovered lands. The lavish bouquets of baroque paintings gave way in the 18th century to a neo-Classical revival of Graeco-Roman floral tributes. In British homes, 'bough-pots' were used to arrange branches and flowers in the hearth during the summer months. The mass-production of goods made possible by the Industrial Revolution brought cheaper ceramic and glass containers, making flower arranging more popular.

Since ancient times flowers have been preserved. Tombs of Egyptian pharaohs from the 2nd millennium BC contained bunches of dried roses, preserved with salt. Sand was preferred in 14th-century India. Both methods became popular in Europe.

ART IN A VASE *The acceptance of flower arrangements as a form of interior design was reflected by the French artist Jean-Baptiste Chardin in this still life from the mid 18th century.*

KENTIA PALM, *Howea forsteriana*, LORD HOWE ISLAND

CAST-IRON PLANT, *Aspidistra elatior*, CHINA

AZALEA, *Rhododendron simsii*, ASIA

INDOOR EXOTICS
Popular house plants

The practice of house-plant cultivation began in earnest in Europe only after the late 1600s. In 1653 the agricultural authority Sir Hugh Plat published *The Garden of Eden*, a reissue of a 1608 title, *Floraes Paradise*. It was the first English guide to growing plants indoors; many of the tropical species covered were cultivated on a small scale. Soon after, the wealthy began to add greenhouses and conservatories to their homes.

Modest householders also looked for ways of using exotic plants to brighten

SWISS CHEESE PLANT, *Monstera deliciosa*, SOUTH AMERICA

the gloomy parlours typical of 18th and 19th-century homes. Plants that could withstand the fumes from gas lighting became popular, despite their lack of flowers. One example was the aspidistra, dubbed the cast-iron plant because of its durability and resistance to the smoke and dust from open fires. Its successful transition from Chinese forest undergrowth to Victorian parlour was possible because both its fleshy roots and its leathery leaves were naturally adapted to intermittent rainfall as well as to deep shade.

The Victorian fashion for palms was greatly encouraged by the opening of the Palm House in Kew Gardens near London in 1848. The exotic Canary Island date palm and fan palms became favourites and were considered sophisticated additions to any conservatory.

One of the most passionate of the Victorian house-plant crazes centred on ferns, the modern descendants of giant swamp forest inhabitants that thrived 350 million years ago in the Carboniferous Age. Because many ferns demand high levels of humidity, they were grown

PARLOUR PALM, *Chamaedorea elegans*, CENTRAL AMERICA

in Wardian cases, miniature table-top greenhouses named after their originator Nathaniel Ward, who invented the case in 1829. Of the ferns that survived the craze, the delicate ribbon brake and the tongue-like bird's-nest fern are still popular. Another favourite, the Swiss cheese plant, is an evergreen climber native to the moist tropical forests of Central and South America. It gained its name from the holes in its leaves.

As European empires expanded, plant hunters searching for plant seeds followed in the footsteps of diplomats, missionaries and travellers. North and South America were important areas of botanical exploration in the 1800s, and many species, including azaleas, *Begonia grandis* and lilies, were also brought from China. Orchids from tropical forests arrived in the West in Victorian times and their cultivation indoors quickly developed into 'orchidomania'.

GONE TO POT

• Succulents such as the American aloe or agave were introduced to British gardeners from the Americas in the early 18th century. Cacti were rarely gown outside botanical gardens until the 19th century.
• Plants were grown in terracotta pots and window boxes in the crowded urban communities of ancient Rome. Large, decorative plant pots, known as jardinières from the French *jardin*, 'garden', became popular in England in the 1800s.
• The popularity of flowers and cut flowers was revived in the late 1800s as electricity replaced gas lamps.

BIRD'S-NEST FERN, *Asplenium nidus*, TROPICAL ASIA

IN-HOUSE TRAINING *From the 1950s central heating and double glazing made European homes suitable habitats for a wide range of exotic plants, including the amaryllis, native to South America, azaleas from Asia and the African violet. These all added tropical splendour to living rooms and conservatories.*

AMARYLLIS *Hippeastrum* 'RED ANGEL', SOUTH AMERICA

AFRICAN VIOLET, *Saintpaulia*, AFRICA

49

EARTHLY PARADISE

*'And the Lord God planted a garden eastward, in Eden…
And out of the ground made the Lord God to grow every
tree that is pleasant to the sight, and good for food…'*

GENESIS, CH. 2, V. 8–9

The perfect garden, an enclosed space containing water, trees and flowers, is an ideal that has travelled from the origins of Western culture to towns, cities and suburbs around the world. Irrigation, and the protection of crops and other useful plants from the elements and from marauders, were the first motivations for gardening. But even plants grown for the table can be objects of delight, and the pleasures of the garden were quickly appreciated.

GARDEN SPLENDOUR

No records exist of gardens before the 2nd millennium BC, but Egyptian tomb paintings of about 1475 BC depict temple gardens, and the pharaohs brought plants from Africa, Europe and Asia for their gardens by the Nile. In about 1200 BC Rameses III made 'great vineyards; walks shaded by all kinds of sweet fruit trees, a sacred way splendid with flowers from all countries, with lotus and papyrus as numerous as the sand'.

Conquests and commerce carried the cultural development of the Egyptian garden to Persia, where emperors built intimate pleasure gardens full of shade and water, large enclosed game reserves and terraced parks planted with trees and shrubs. *Pairi-daeza*, the ancient Persian name for such gardens or parks, is the root of the word 'paradise'. The elaborate Hanging Gardens of Babylon, built in arid lands now in central Iraq by Nebuchadnezzar II during the 6th century BC, were one of the Seven Wonders of the World. The ancient Greek writer Diodorus recorded that 'the several parts of the structure rose from one another tier upon tier'.

Courtyard gardens of urban Greece were lined with colonnades, while at public sports grounds philosophers

RENAISSANCE SYMMETRY *In the garden of Ferdinando de Medici, and those of other Italian villa owners, broad, straight avenues and geometric designs imposed order over a natural landscape. 'Green' tunnels encircled orchard plantings to provide rainproof shelter. Both Italian and French styles of the 15th century were the inspiration for English formal gardens, such as Cardinal Wolsey's famed design at Hampton Court Palace.*

would stroll through groves of cypress and olive, fir and poplar. As the empire expanded, ideas from the East were employed to create luxurious orchards and vegetable gardens—and the 'smiling patch of never failing green' encountered by Odysseus on his visit to Alcinous, king of the Phaeacians.

The Romans adopted Hellenistic traditions but further adapted the garden paradise to the empire's diverse climatic conditions. In Italy's towns and cities villa courtyards were outdoor 'rooms', often with landscapes painted on the walls to create an illusion of space. Fruit trees, flowers and vegetables flourished in this sheltered environment. In the country the great villa gardens were parks planted with orchards and vineyards, and with decorative trees and shrubs. When the Romans reached Britain they brought with them lilies, as well as figs, mulberries and peaches.

A CULTIVATED TRADITION

Gardening in the Middle Ages became less flamboyant, but medieval monastic and castle gardens grew plants for their medicinal, cosmetic and culinary uses. The illuminated manuscripts and tapestries of that time also show plants

ORNAMENTAL FEATURES

• Garden gnomes first appeared in Britain in the mid 19th century, imported from Nuremberg by Sir Charles Isham of Lamport Hall, Northamptonshire. In Germany they had been used by miners as good-luck charms. Isham originally thought to use the figures to hold place names at the table, but later built a rockery for them with miniature plants and waterfalls.

• Grottoes were used in classical times to provide shelter from heat and glare. The Romans made them of tufa, a compressed volcanic ash that imparted a rustic look.

English cultivation, with meadow flowers outlawed as weeds. Garden neatness was seen as a virtue from the 18th century, when the lawn became a neutral green foil for flowering plants in borders. A passion developed for lawns manicured to appear, in the words of the 19th-century novelist Anthony Trollope, 'as much like velvet as grass has ever been made to look'.

ADDING WATER

In arid climates water, the life-giving source that made gardens possible, became central to their design. In the garden oases of ancient Egypt, Persia, the Mediterranean and northern India, irrigation technology progressed to produce fountains and waterfalls for geometric water gardens. During the 1st century BC the Roman architect Vitruvius described the Mediterranean water-garden tradition, which later provided the inspiration for Italian Renaissance architects. Their feats of engineering produced the Italianate water gardens renowned in Europe.

A new style emerged in Britain in the 1700s, led by the landscape designer Lancelot 'Capability' Brown, named from his habit of describing gardens as having 'capabilities of improvement'. As a result, formal water gardens were replaced with naturalistic lakes and pools.

clearly appreciated for their beauty. By the 16th century flowers had become cherished for their appearance and scent, and many of today's suburban garden features began to emerge.

Hedges of native British species such as hawthorn surrounded fields from Celtic, pre-Roman times, but the hedge became a major element of Tudor garden design when Henry VIII's cardinal Thomas

COOL DELIGHT *Friends meet among cypresses and canals of flowing water in a walled garden, one of 177 masterpieces built in the hills of Kashmir by the Mughal emperor Jahangir in the 17th century.*

Wolsey set out complex, rigid patterns using clipped box and yew. These evergreens soon became part of elaborate knot gardens and edged the borders of formal beds, known from the 1600s as parterres, from the French for 'on the ground'.

Ball games of all kinds were loved by the Tudor nobility, who needed flat areas of short grass for play, and the lawn evolved from the sports alleys and greens of 16th-century England. Many early lawns, made from meadow turf, were floral masterpieces of violets, daisies and speedwell. By the 1650s the bowling green had become distinctive to

THE GARDEN OF DELIGHTS
Flowers from around the world

The flowers of the ancient world were valued for their symbolism as well as their beauty. To the Greeks, the iris represented the goddess of the rainbow, messenger of the gods, and the narcissus was a youth turned into a flower for falling in love with his own reflection.

By the Middle Ages many garden plants were grown for their medicinal and culinary properties. Medieval gardens featured little but roses, lilies, pinks, cowslips, marigolds and violets, but by the end of the 16th century more than 200 kinds of plant were grown in England, including tulips, anemones, hyacinths and crocuses from the Middle East. In the following century lupins, phlox, goldenrod, Michaelmas daisies and Virginia creeper were all brought from North America. By the late 1830s the number of species grown in British gardens had risen to 18 000, with more plants emerging from both the Orient and the Americas.

The spread of printing and new written works from the late 15th century led to greater access to information about plants. Between the 16th and 19th centuries, the increasing availability of new species from around the world, the rise of nurseries and the publication of gardening books introduced flower cultivation to a wider public.

From Mexican gardens came the dahlia, introduced into Europe in the 1790s. In the early 1800s the Empress Josephine, wife of Napoleon I, developed dahlia hybrids and varieties. These later became part of her fantastic arrangements of exotics in the gardens of Malmaison, outside Paris.

Many of the flowers introduced into Europe were brought back by British 'plant explorers'. In the early 1600s, on expeditions financed by his employers, the Cecils, earls of Salisbury, John Tradescant Senior collected plants from across Europe and the Mediterranean region, including the gladiolus, rock roses and the lilac, which he named the Persian jasmine. John Tradescant Junior also brought back many new perennials and shrubs from his own journeys to North America.

Under the patronage of George III, Sir Joseph Banks, who had documented the flora of Australia on his travels with Captain James Cook, was made the first 'director' of Kew Gardens in 1771. Following this, and the foundation in 1804 of the future Royal Horticultural Society, many expeditions were initiated. The explorations of the Scottish botanist David Douglas in California in the mid 1820s led to the introduction of, among other species, the flowering currant, the California poppy and the monkey flower.

Rhododendrons and azaleas were the bounty of 19th-century botanical expeditions such as Sir Joseph Dalton Hooker's journeys to the Himalayas and Ernest Wilson's adventures in China. Wilson collected plants for the Veitch family, who ran one of the most influential nurseries of the 19th century and who made possible the introduction of countless plants. More than 400 of them were illustrated in William Curtis's *Botanical Magazine*. Founded in 1787, it was the first gardening magazine and is still published under the title *Curtis's Botanical Magazine*.

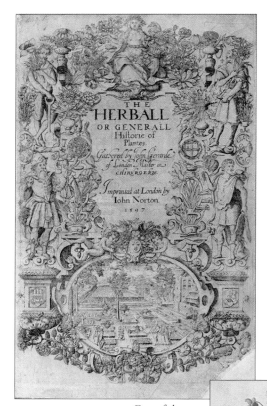

BOTANICAL BIBLE *One of the earliest, most influential works in English for gardeners was John Gerard's* Herball *of 1597, which listed plants for their ornamental and medicinal qualities.*

SPIDERWORT, *Tradescantia virginiana*, DRAWN IN 1629

JOHN TRADESCANT JUNIOR, 1608–62

GIFT FROM AFAR *In the early 1600s the nursery-owning Tradescants, father and son, received from the Americas the plant that now bears their name,* Tradescantia virginiana, *the spiderwort.*

IN A WORD *The violet (left) was named from the same Greek word as iodine, whose colour it shares. The Greek for 'rose tree' lent the rhododendron its descriptive name.*

Rosa Damascena Variegata.

GROWING FOR GOLD
Bulbs and their kin

Along with other flowering plants, bulbs, corms and tubers made their first appearance on Earth about 35 million years ago. Most are native to the Middle East and Mediterranean, and to places with similar climates, such as South Africa. Irises were grown in classical times, and lilies, irises and daffodils all adorned the Islamic gardens of the 7th century. Tulips, anemones and crown imperials were also nurtured in the gardens of the sultans.

In the 1550s Ghiselin de Busbecq, the Holy Roman Empire's ambassador to the sultan in Constantinople, was astounded to see narcissi, hyacinths and tulips growing in Turkish gardens. He sent bulbs to the imperial court in Vienna, where they were received by the botanist Carolus Clusius, who in 1594 took his tulip collection to the Low Countries.

Tulips first reached Holland during the 1570s. By the beginning of the 17th century 'tulipomania' had taken hold, and Dutch merchants were gambling large sums of money on single bulbs in the hopes of breeding flowers with streaked petals or 'breaks'.

In the early 1620s one bulb of the Semper Augustus tulip was sold for 20000 stuivers—this at a time when a skilled carpenter could earn an annual wage of just 8000 stuivers. Before the crash in 1637, another example of the same tulip was said to have sold for 260000 stuivers.

FLOWERS OF FORTUNE *In the 1920s, science revealed that the variegated tulip petals, which commanded such huge sums from 17th-century Dutch merchants, did not result from the skill of plant breeders but were caused by a virus transmitted by aphids. At the height of 'tulipomania', the price of a bulb could match that of a mansion in The Hague.*

FOSSILISED ROSE LEAVES, ABOUT 30 MILLION YEARS OLD

THE ROMANCE OF THE ROSE
Petals with divine beauty

The rose is red, it is said, because it blushed with pleasure when it was kissed by Eve in the Garden of Eden. In ancient Egyptian and Greek cultures the rose was linked to female deities : in Egypt to Isis, in Greece to Aphrodite. The Greeks also used rose petals to cure anyone bitten by a mad dog.

In Britain only a small selection of roses was grown before the reign of Elizabeth I. Nevertheless, one of the earliest uses of the rose as an English symbol occurred during the Wars of the Roses in the 15th century. The white rose of York was probably *Rosa alba*, a native of northern Europe that had been introduced by the Romans. The red rose of Lancaster was *Rosa gallica officinalis*, the old rose of Provins in central France. It was reputedly brought to Europe from the Middle East by Thibault IV, ruler of Navarre, during the Crusades. Later it became known as

FAVOURED BLOOM *The damask rose,* Rosa damascena versicolor, *striped red and white, became known as the Lancaster and York rose when Henry Tudor united the two houses in 1486. Fossilised stems with prickles and rose-like leaves date the popular rose to between 60 and 25 million years ago, but the first positively identified fossilised rose dates from 15 to 12 million years ago.*

the apothecary's rose because of its common use in ointments and potions.

From the 1500s rose breeding gained in popularity. The moss rose, *Rosa centifolia* 'Muscosa', a variant of the cabbage rose, appeared in a catalogue of 1727. Chinese roses were being grown in Kew Gardens by 1769. The first of the tea roses, *Rosa odorata*, also from China, was introduced by Sir Abraham Hume in 1810, but it was the plant collector John Parks who began to market them in the 1820s. Their scent was said to resemble that of fresh-packed tea.

SPADE WORK *The medieval gardener (above) dug the soil with a metal-rimmed wooden scoop. This tool was remarkably similar in design to the bronze spade fashioned in Ur in Mesopotamia around 1800 BC.*

Digging, weeding, watering, pruning and other gardening tasks have changed little through the ages. The plethora of hoes, spades, shovels, rakes, trowels, forks and shears listed in an inventory at Abingdon Abbey, Oxfordshire, in the 14th century still comprise the basic set of gardening tools.

Flint hoes with wooden handles were made in Mesopotamia around 4000 BC and both the ancient Egyptians and Romans used iron hoes. These were pulled towards the body—the technique still favoured by British gardeners today. Until the 19th century, short-handled hoes, which were used in a kneeling position, remained more common than long-handled designs.

Load-carrying shovels were made in the Stone Age from the shoulder blades of large food animals such as deer, and from these evolved the spade for digging. Early spades, probably devised by the Romans, were scoops fashioned from wood with an iron rim attached. Alternatively, a wooden handle was inserted into an iron cutting blade. The Romans also used the *trulla* or trowel.

Shears based on the same principle as Roman spring scissors were first used for sheepshearing, but shears for hedge trimming, lawn edging and pruning evolved from the 16th century with the introduction of pivoted scissors. Secateurs, with curved blades, had been developed in France by 1818 and proved useful for the new rose hybrids. These, unlike their shrubby predecessors, required careful pruning to ensure blooming in subsequent years. Named from the French for 'cutters', secateurs quickly became popular in Britain. In 1830 steel shears made by the Sheffield company Steers and Wilkinson were praised for their strength. 'By using both hands,' reported one tester, 'the most delicate person may cut through a branch of an inch in diameter.'

Lawns became the focus of suburban gardening in the early 19th century and in 1830 Edwin Budding found the way to make light of lawn care. Budding, a Gloucestershire textile engineer, had created a machine for shearing the nap from woollen cloth, but after representations by textile workers fearful of losing their jobs, he applied his machine to grass instead. Previously grass had been mown by hand with scythes or cutters pulled by donkeys. Ransomes,

ANCIENT AND MODERN *Gardeners in ancient Rome would have employed billhooks, trowels and rakes similar to those of today. The selection of tools widened greatly in the 19th century, when secateurs and lawn mowers were invented. Mechanisation brought sprinklers and hedge trimmers in the early 1900s, the date of the first hand forks.*

STEEL FORK, 19TH CENTURY

BOW RAKE, ABOUT 1890

LAWN MOWER FOR CUTTING NARROW BORDERS, ABOUT 1885

COPPER WATERING CAN, 18TH CENTURY

CERAMIC WATERING POT, 16TH-CENTURY DESIGN

A WATER SPRINKLER, USA, ABOUT 1900

STEEL SHEARS, 19TH CENTURY

FRENCH SECATEURS, 1890S

MECHANICAL HEDGE TRIMMER, ABOUT 1920

DAISY GRUBBER, ABOUT 1910

OUTDOOR DUTIES *Trees are planted, flowerbeds tidied and plants potted up by these early 17th-century workers. A carefully 'layed' hedge separates garden and farmland.*

lawn sprinkler was made practicable only through the invention of vulcanised rubber hosing in the 1860s. In 1871 the American J. Lessler of Buffalo, New York, patented the garden sprinkler.

Couch grass was deemed by the ancient Roman historian Pliny to be a 'problem plant'. Weeding was practised by the Elizabethans. By condemning 'darnel, hemlock and rank fumitory' as 'savagery', they broke with the prevailing belief that all plants have a purpose, whether medicinal, cosmetic or culinary. According to the 17th-century herbalist William Coles, weeds were useful to exercise 'the industry of man to weed them out. Had he nothing to struggle with, the fire of his spirit would be half extinguished.'

KEEPING PLANTS WARM
The greenhouse revolution

an agricultural machinery company, was manufacturing Budding's lawn mower by 1832. In 1902 Ransomes produced the first petrol-driven motor mower to be commercially successful.

Before specialised equipment was developed, gardeners used a wide range of devices for scooping and carrying water for their plants, including ladles and gourds. Early watering pots of the 1470s were made of clay. They had no spout but many small holes in the body that released fine streams of water.

Spouted pots were first depicted in the 1600s, with the term 'watering can'

appearing in 1692. *The Retir'd Gardener* of 1706 declared that 'Nothing is more useful in a garden than a watering-pot, so that a gardener cannot be without it. It imitates the rain falling from the Heavens.' However, copper watering cans with handles replaced clay pots from about 1700.

Garden hoses made from tubes of fabric originated in the 1400s, but the

When the Romans arrived in Britain they brought with them their own innovative garden technology. They grew plants such as cucumbers and melons in portable earth-filled baskets and created structures similar to greenhouses, glazed with thin, translucent sheets of the mineral mica.

After the demise of the empire, many Roman tools and techniques fell out of general use and were employed only in religious communities. But the passion for exploration and the study of nature in the 16th century heralded an explosion in kitchen-garden development. Frost-tender plants, including tomatoes and oranges, which required new growing methods, flooded in.

Glass had been used to protect plants from the 15th century. As it became more affordable from the 1550s specific structures were constructed to cover vegetables and fruit and to force early crops. Cloches were placed over young plants to protect them from the elements. Glass-covered hotbeds were trenches filled with animal dung covered with topsoil. As the manure in the bed decomposed, it released heat.

Lean-to greenhouses appeared in the walled kitchen gardens of the 18th century. These were heated by hotbeds enclosed in brick frames or by wood or coal-burning boilers connected by flues in the adjoining wall.

SOW AND GROW

- The 17th-century English diarist and writer John Evelyn is credited with the first use in print of the word 'greenhouse' for a device to protect evergreens over the winter.
- Local authorities began renting out allotments for growing vegetables and fruit in the 1800s, when the Industrial Revolution drew country folk into towns and cities. The first scheme was inaugurated at Brompton, Yorkshire, in 1805.
- The wheelbarrow was used in China in the 1st century AD for carrying goods and people, but until the Middle Ages European gardeners worked in pairs, shifting loads with boards resembling stretchers.

GLASS BELL JAR, ABOUT 1890

HAND FORK, ABOUT 1930

SWAN-NECKED ONION HOE, ABOUT 1910

TROWEL, ABOUT 1910

BILLHOOK, 1850s

MANNERS
AND
CUSTOMS

In the 2 million years that humans have lived together in communities, an intricate web of manners and customs, celebrations and beliefs has evolved. Learned from infancy, and handed down from generation to generation, these beliefs provide a structure for the individual lives whose great occasions—and final passing—are marked out by rites and rituals.

Our beliefs began to take shape among the tribes of hunter-gatherers. Unable to escape from or to control Nature's power, their existence was constantly threatened by wild beasts, floods, storms, famine, earthquakes and volcanic eruptions, freezing cold and searing heat. From their fears sprang religion and superstitions. They created deities of the Moon and the stars, thunder and lightning, and gradually developed rituals to appease the wrath of these spiritual rulers and to ward off danger.

As our ancestors tried to understand Nature they became aware of the cycle of the seasons. Applying this knowledge, the earliest farmers discovered the essentials of agriculture, including when and how to plant food crops. Spring was welcomed and celebrated as the time of rebirth, and thanks were given for autumn fruitfulness.

By the time of Christ a variety of annual festivals had developed in every civilisation. As well as marking the seasons these afforded a respite from working life and the chance for revelry. The early Christians incorporated many elements of heathen feasts into their commemorative calendar as a means of subduing paganism. The date for the Nativity, for instance, was calculated by adding nine months' 'gestation time' to the ancient spring festival on March 25, when creation and new growth were celebrated. Christmas consequently coincided neatly with the pagan festivities of the winter solstice, when fires were lit to encourage the Sun to return and ensure another year of fertility.

Christianity often exerted a sobering influence on celebrations. The lewd overtones of the Romans' spring Lupercalia, when men drew lots for women, was superseded by the more restrained St Valentine's Day celebrations. All Hallows (All Saints) on November 1 was instituted by the Church to replace the Celtic festivities of Samhain, and the spirits who roamed the Earth on Samhain Eve were retained in the celebrations of All Hallows Eve (Halloween).

All over the world, rules of manners and good behaviour were found to be essential to preserve the social order. Chivalry was a complex development of such a code of conduct, and in medieval times it proved its worth in taming the violence and lusts of knights. As etiquette has evolved—emanating largely from the upper classes and expressed in aspects of daily life from speech to clothes to table manners—it has also reflected fashion and marked out social distinctions.

But many of the traditions we customarily observe are far from ancient. The white wedding and Christmas trees and cards are largely Victorian inventions. Mass production and 20th-century commercialism have led to the observation of many new card occasions, from wedding anniversaries to Father's Day.

CODES OF POLITENESS
Common courtesy

With arms outstretched, displaying hands empty of weapons, early humans approached their neighbours to offer or ask for help. In these or similar gestures of peace and friendship the notion of etiquette was born. As civilised societies developed, so too did codes of conduct. Position and social identity played a significant role in matters of etiquette, a word derived from the French for 'label'. Social conventions often emanated from the royal courts, with monarchs devising courtesies applied selectively according to rank.

The earliest known documented etiquette advice was written in verse

KNIGHTLY BLESSINGS *Charlemagne, King of the Franks, is crowned Holy Roman Emperor by Pope Leo III in AD 800. Their alliance led to the integration of Christian codes of conduct into the rituals of chivalry.*

around 2000 BC. The *Instructions* of the Egyptian pharaoh Ptah-Hotep to his son included the advice:
'Be prudent whenever you open
    your mouth.
Your every utterance should be
    understanding.'
In ancient Greece it was also deemed important to teach children about the conventions of their society, or good

manners. Around 700 BC the poet Hesiod's advice to the young included such precepts as: 'At the abundant dinner of the gods, do not sever with bright steel the withered from the quick upon that which has five branches'. In other words, 'fingernails should not be cut at the table'.

The earliest reference in English literature to a strictly stratified society regulated by a code of conduct marking distinctions of class and rank appears in the 10th-century Anglo-Saxon epic poem *Beowulf*. It describes how Queen Wealtheow offers to drink to the king and then to his courtiers in a clearly defined order of precedence.

The tradition of etiquette in the West is intimately linked with the Church and early medieval chivalry. The *Pax Dei* (*Peace of God*) was a set of principles adopted during the 10th century for Christian warriors. It was instrumental in the evolution of the ideal of chivalry, which flourished between the 11th and the 13th centuries during the Crusades.

Throughout the Middle Ages rules that related to morals and manners were often communicated through popular songs and rhyming verses. Some examples appear in the English 15th-century *The Babees' Book*, for pages and maids-in-waiting. In one piece, entitled 'Urbanitatis' ('Of Politeness'), *The Babees' Book* instructs them:
'When you come before a
    lord
    In hall, in bower, or at board,
You must doff or cap or hood...'
Another line runs: 'Good manners always make good men.'

Historically, the covering of a person's head symbolises authority— the ultimate symbol being a crown. Removing the head covering, an act that at one time might have revealed the identity of the wearer, is a mark of social deference. Polite behaviour still demands that Christian men take off their hats while they are in church. This follows the teachings of St Paul, who, in his first letter to the Corinthians, declared that: 'Every-man praying or

prophesying...ought not to cover his head, for as much as he is the image and glory of God.' In contrast, his advice to women was to cover up their hair modestly, for: 'Judge in yourselves: is it comely that a woman pray unto God uncovered?'

GUIDING MANNERS
Establishing decorum

The Dutch scholar Desiderius Erasmus believed that most people not only aspired to gentility but also wanted to know the rules of behaviour. His short treatise *De civilitate morum puerilium* (*On the Civility of the Behaviour of Boys*), which was published in 1530, covered manners at school, in church, at mealtimes and even in bed. It also included

discreet guidelines on how to 'name some functions of the body that our sensibility no longer permits us to discuss in public'.

In France from the mid 17th to the early 18th century Louis XIV insisted that courtiers observe an elaborate timetable of civilities. Dandies such as Beau Nash and Beau Brummell set the rules of British etiquette during the 18th and early 19th centuries. Their whims swiftly became the fashion. The Prince Regent (later George IV) is said to have wept when his friend Brummell disapproved of the way his coat fitted.

In the United States, meanwhile, a new society was establishing itself. In the 18th century the statesman George Washington advised on good behaviour in his pamphlet *Rules of Conduct*. In the 19th century, letter writing and

MAKING PEACE *South African President F.W. de Klerk (left) and African National Congress leader Nelson Mandela clasp hands in a display of mutual trust in 1993.*

'How to Choose and Win Friends' were covered by 'Miss Manners', the journalist Judith Martin. America's most celebrated exponent of etiquette was Emily Post, whose 1922 book *Etiquette: the Blue Book of Social Usage* became an instant best seller.

The terms U (upper-class) and non-U (not upper-class), coined in 1954 by the British linguist Alan Ross, became widely known in 1956 through *Noblesse Oblige*, a collection of essays edited by the social commentator Nancy Mitford. Words such as 'pudding' were deemed to be 'U' while 'sweet' was 'non-U'.

BAD BEHAVIOUR

The V-sign, with the palm facing inwards, may have its origins in war. It is said that on the eve of the Battle of Agincourt in 1415 the French threatened to chop off the 'bow fingers' (first and second fingers) of every English archer. At dawn next day the victorious English extended the same two fingers in a mocking gesture. During the Second World War a V-sign, with the palm facing outwards, was used by Winston Churchill, the British Prime Minister, as a victory symbol.

A SKINHEAD GIVES THE V-SIGN ON BEING APPREHENDED BY A LONDON POLICE OFFICER.

AIRS AND GRACES
A Dutch gentleman doffs his hat and bows before a lady in a typically debonair display of 17th-century etiquette.

GREEK VASE, 5TH CENTURY BC

GREETINGS *Home from battle, a Greek soldier stretches out his hand in an open gesture of friendship.*

BONDING BEHAVIOUR
The handshake and the kiss

A hand signal can be seen before a face comes into focus—so we greet with a wave, then smile to demonstrate our welcome. To show that they came in unarmed friendship, the Romans greeted each other with outstretched arm and open palm. In the 20th century this salute took on a more sinister meaning when adopted by Nazis under the dictator Adolf Hitler.

In ancient civilisations, such as the Kingdom of Israel and the Roman Empire, the handshake signified the binding of a contract. In medieval times it marked a pledge of honour or allegiance; a subordinate would kneel while his superior initiated the handclasp. Shaking hands as a polite form of greeting across social classes, although considered too egalitarian to be acceptable in earlier ages, became acceptable in early 19th-century Europe.

If, as anthropologists argue, the loving kiss is related to sucking in babyhood, it is as old as the human race. The less intimate kiss on the cheek was used as a form of greeting or salutation among the ancient Greeks and Romans. The Hebrew Old Testament also records that 'Esau ran to meet him [his brother, Jacob] and fell on his neck, and kissed him'. Subsequently, kissing became a symbol of Christian brotherhood: 'Salute one another with a holy kiss,' St Paul urges in his Epistle to the Romans. Medieval lords would ceremonially kiss newly invested knights on the cheek. The knights, however, showed respectful submission or allegiance to their lord by kissing his hand.

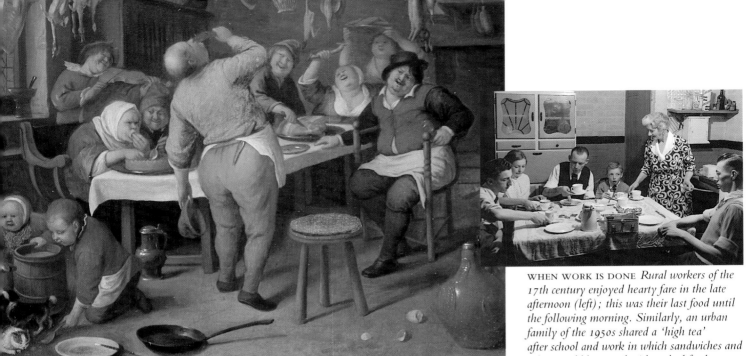

WHEN WORK IS DONE *Rural workers of the 17th century enjoyed hearty fare in the late afternoon (left); this was their last food until the following morning. Similarly, an urban family of the 1950s shared a 'high tea' after school and work in which sandwiches and cakes would be served with cooked food.*

FEASTING TOGETHER
Shared sustenance

When food was hard to come by, our earliest ancestors, the hunter-gatherers, had no regular breaks for eating. In fact, mealtimes are a mark of civilisation. They began to be adopted during the Neolithic Age, when humans started to control their food supply through agriculture and animal domestication, and settled down.

Mealtimes offer more than simple replenishment of the body's fuel, for they reflect the rituals, status, religion and etiquette of specific cultures. The roots of friendship lie in the sharing of food, and the word 'companion' stems directly from the Latin *com panis*, 'with bread'. Sharing food marked covenants, or promises, in both the Old and New Testaments. Today birth, marriage and death, as well as religious celebrations such as Passover and Christmas, are celebrated in meals.

In Western societies breakfast, lunch, tea and dinner form the standard daily pattern of meal-taking, although local variations abound. The timing of meals and their content are dictated by working hours and tradition, as well as by the availability of foodstuffs. In 13th-century Europe, for instance, the largely agricultural population ate two main meals each day. The first was dinner at about 9 or 10am, and then later there was supper at 5pm. Meals would consist typically of grain-based broth or cereal porridge. This was accompanied by onions and green vegetables such as cabbage, or bread. Except for the nobility and wealthy farmers, meat was rare. Only in the early 20th century in North America did 'dinner' become exclusive to the evening.

BREAKING THE FAST
Throughout the Middle Ages religious orders adhered to a daily two-meal regime, while the working classes would take short breaks for food during the day, the first of which would 'break the fast' of the previous night. By the 17th century, however, breakfast had become a substantial meal, consisting of cold meats, fish, cheese, bread, butter and wine or ale for the rich, and cereal pottages, or porridge, for the poor.

The traditional British breakfast dishes—thick, milky oat porridge or eggs and bacon—have rural roots, since both milk and eggs could be supplied fresh every morning after the farmer had attended to his cattle and poultry.

In the 18th century, when increased urbanisation meant that many working men ate chops and steaks at the newly established chophouses, rather than coming home from their jobs in the middle of the day, dinner was customarily at 5pm. The resultant gap between breakfast and dinner gradually led to the institution of a midday snack, which by the 19th century had stretched to become an extensive meal called luncheon, eventually shortened, both in duration and verbally, to 'lunch'.

As dinner became a later meal, eaten by the upper classes around 7.30 to 9pm, 'afternoon tea' evolved from a simple hot drink to a meal in its own right. At first, nursery teas were for children, who were sent to bed before dinner. In the mid 19th century taking tea became fashionable among middle-class and aristocratic women—who were possibly following the example of Anna, Duchess of Bedford—in an effort to legitimise the secret habit of snacking on cakes in their boudoirs.

Some families continue to dine early, and even today 'high tea' can be a substitute for, rather than an addition to, dinner. However, 'dinner' can also mean the midday meal.

MORNING GRAINS *Ready-to-eat breakfast cereals were mass-produced and marketed as 'health foods' in the late 19th century. Among the first to package porridge oats in Britain were Quaker (1877). In the USA Dr John Harvey Kellogg and his brother Will introduced cornflakes in 1898.*

EATING ETIQUETTE

Table manners are markers of society and culture. To eat with a knife and fork, first established as polite in the 17th century, is typically Western, while for many Muslims the convention is to use the right hand.

Pronouncements on etiquette have featured in almost every age. *The Babees' Book* of 15th-century manners for young people advised:

'When you are set before the
  meat,
Fair and honestly it eat.
First, look ye that your hands
  be clean…'

ANCIENT LUXURIES
Cutlery was once a prized possession. Spoons were shared among diners until the 16th century. This finely decorated early example of a more personal spoon could be folded and carried in a pocket. Before about 1600 the fork was used only for serving.

ANGLO-SAXON
FORK, ABOUT
AD 900

FLEMISH
FOLDING
SPOON, 1562

DISHES, PLATES AND CUTLERY
Varieties of tableware

Prehistoric diners ate off large leaves and flat pieces of wood, while for the Romans, pastry cases were served as both dish and food, rather like pizzas today. In medieval Europe, people ate off 'trenchers'—slices of stale bread which soaked up the juices and might later be fed to the dogs or given to the poor. A fresco dating from 1525 in the town of Mantua, Italy, depicts some of the earliest recorded flat metal plates, and by the end of the 17th century flat ceramic plates were common in France. In Britain the 'service' of matching plates, bowls and serving dishes became affordable only after Josiah Wedgwood developed mass-produced earthenware in the 18th century.

The first cutlery consisted of simple 'spoons' and scoops made of shells, hollowed-out pieces of wood and socket joint bones. When people first learnt to bake, clay spoons were among the earliest implements to be made. Egyptian spoons were bronze, and often had a pointed handle to extract the meat from snail shells. Wealthy Greek and Roman families used silver spoons. However, it was not until Georgian times that the knife, fork and

ON A PLATE *From the late 1700s, when sets decorated with designs such as this willow pattern were first mass-produced, ceramic plates replaced the metal ones of the 16th and 17th centuries. The pattern, although inspired by the East, was British in origin.*

SWANSEA PEARLWARE
PLATE, ABOUT 1800

spoon appeared together as eating implements on British tables.

Most cutlery now in everyday use was once a luxury available only to the wealthy. Even in Europe's aristocratic circles, diners shared drinking cups until the 16th century, and up until this time guests also brought their own knives to the table.

As late as 1662 in Britain the same applied to forks. Thomas Coryat, who described forks in his travel book *Coryat's Crudities*, probably introduced them in Britain, in the early 17th century. Before that time, diners speared meat with a knife-point or tore it with their fingers. Early table forks, like the serving forks of ancient Rome, had two prongs; in the 1800s three and four-pronged table forks were used.

The knife has a far longer history, founded on such cutting tools of prehistoric times as flints, the volcanic 'glass' obsidian, bones and shells. The art of slotting flints into wood and serrating the edges was refined by the Egyptians in the 4th millennium BC. By 1500 BC a variety of bronze cutting tools was being honed from Britain to China.

Rich Egyptian and Roman families owned ornamented table knives, and the Romans also devised knives that had steel blades. Until the 17th century the table knife generally had a pointed tip. The disgust of the French statesman Cardinal Richelieu at seeing his friends pick their teeth with their knife-tips is said to have prompted a change to broader blades with square, and later rounded, tips.

MEDIEVAL MANNERS *Before the 16th century knives were often the only cutlery. Even at the great feasts of the French Duc de Berry (above) neither forks nor spoons were used.*

EATING IN PUBLIC
Taverns, inns and restaurants

In the taverns of ancient Rome, slaves and other lowly members of society ate hunks of cheese washed down with cheap Cretan wine. Here, too, people exchanged the gossip of the day.

The taverns of early medieval Europe, which had evolved from the Roman *tabernae*, were also places frequented mainly by the poor and were devoted to the consumption of alcohol and simple foods. Such was their unsavoury reputation in Britain, however, that in the 8th century the Archbishop of York decreed that 'No

CULINARY PIONEER *The French chef Georges-Auguste Escoffier transformed restaurant cuisine. Simplifying food presentation, and organising teams of cooks to perform distinct tasks more efficiently, he set new standards across Europe and the USA.*

priest [should] go to eat or drink in a tavern'. Inns, where lodgings were provided for the increasing numbers of travelling merchants, were also popular in the Middle Ages. From the 16th century a set menu for dinner at a fixed price came to be called an 'ordinary' or *table d'hôte*, meaning 'host's fare'. The inns where it was available soon became known as 'ordinaries' too.

As food quality improved, these ancestors of today's restaurant became convivial meeting places for businessmen. According to Samuel Johnson, the 18th-century writer: '…there is nothing which has yet been contrived by man, by which so much happiness is produced as by a good tavern or inn.'

Until Johnson's time dining out had been predominantly for the poor, with

TASTE AND STYLE *From the 1880s, the Savoy Hotel in London (above) was one of several fine settings in which restaurants were established.*

BASIC SUSTENANCE *Taverns provided substantial meals at a cost that ordinary working people could afford. The Cock Tavern (left) in Fleet Street, London, was typically plain.*

the wealthy preferring to entertain in style in their own homes. The first restaurant to be described as such was opened in Paris in 1765 by a Monsieur Boulanger. Until then, only traders known as *traiteurs* were allowed to sell cooked meats, which people were not permitted to consume in public.

During the 19th century grand hotels, many of them incorporating excellent dining establishments and employing highly gifted chefs, grew to cater for the expanding middle classes. The renowned French chef Georges-Auguste Escoffier worked with the Swiss hotelier César Ritz at the Savoy in London and at the Hotel Ritz in Paris in the late 1800s. Escoffier did much to establish modern dining principles, shortening menus and speeding up service. He also courted his wealthy clientele, for instance by naming new dishes in their honour. Pêche Melba, a dessert of poached peach, ice cream and raspberry purée, was created for Dame Nellie Melba, the Australian soprano.

THE LANGUAGE OF FOOD
Words, phrases and conventions

MAJESTIC MENU *For the spectacular gala dinner arranged to celebrate the coronation of Edward VII in 1902, the management of the Carlton Hotel printed a special menu, surmounted by a royal crown. It stylishly set out each of the nine courses to be served.*

Like the restaurant itself, much of the modern language of dining comes from France, including the words '*chef*', '*maître d'hôtel*', a head steward or head waiter, and '*entrée*'—which in French means an 'entry', or starter, but which in the 1900s came to mean a main course in English. *Hors-d'oeuvres* are dishes placed 'outside the work': originally these appetisers were grouped around, or outside, the culinary centrepieces laid out for a banquet.

The French word '*menu*', from the Latin for 'small', acquired its sense of 'detailed' and then 'list' during the 19th century, appearing in the *menu de repas*, the 'meal list'. To 'wait', which came to be used for serving food at the table, emerged in the 1500s from the Germanic word *wahtan*, meaning 'to watch'. And *à la carte* dining—the 'card' being the menu—was introduced as an alternative to fixed *table d'hôte* meals after 1765, when Boulanger's restaurant was opened.

Since many of the staff in early restaurants had previously worked in the households of the nobility, their servants' outfits were smartly adapted to become the familiar black-and-white uniform of the waiter. The tradition of giving a gratuity to a waiter originated in 16th-century Europe from the popular practice of making small payments to boys for running errands. During the late 19th century European workers took the custom with them when they emigrated to the United States.

The term 'tip' probably came from coffee-houses in the City of London, where merchants gathered to conduct business in the 17th and 18th centuries. Messages for swift delivery were placed in a box with a small coin as payment, the lid of the box bearing the letters TIP—To Insure Promptitude.

FAST FOOD
Snacks and speedy meals

Nearly 4000 years ago, hungry residents of Ur in Mesopotamia could buy fried fish, roast meat and onions from the city's street vendors. Cookshops of the 6th century BC consisted of open-fronted booths that sold ready-cooked meat, and were Ur's 'takeaways'.

More recently, Vienna sausages and frankfurters were first sold as popular fast food in the USA from the early 19th century. The 'hot dog' gained its name in 1906 when the American cartoonist Tad Dorgan drew a dachshund (the 'sausage dog') in an elongated bun.

The fast-food boom that followed the Second World War was epitomised by the McDonald's chain. Richard and Maurice, the McDonald brothers, established a small drive-in

EASY DINERS

• In a French dictionary of 1692 *Pique nique*, meaning 'peck at a trifle', described an indoor meal to which every diner brought food. Only in the 1860s did an English picnic become a relaxed outdoor meal.
• Potato crisps were first made by a New York chef in 1853 after a customer complained that his fried potatoes were too thick.
• Only men were allowed to eat at the first self-service restaurant, the Exchange Buffet in New York, opened in 1885. Customers ate standing up.

restaurant in Pasadena, California, in 1937 selling hot dogs. By the 1940s hamburgers had begun to replace hot dogs, but not until 1948, at their San Bernardino outlet, did the McDonalds standardise low-cost food served at speed in clean surroundings.

But it was Ray Kroc, who was a salesman for electric milk shake mixers, who turned McDonald's into an internationally recognised brand name. In 1954 Kroc delivered an order to the kitchens of the San Bernardino branch. He was so impressed that he bought the rights to franchise the McDonald concept. In 1955 the first of the new restaurants opened, in Des Plaines, Illinois; Britain's first dates to 1974, in London.

CHAIN REACTION *The American motorist of 1955 could call for a meal at a McDonald's drive-in. At that time a hamburger cost 15 cents and french fries 10 cents, with a milk shake for 20 cents.*

VALENTINE'S DAY
Anniversary of love

Spring has long been considered the season of love. In ancient Rome revellers at the festival of Lupercalia on February 15 celebrated fertility and purification rites with bawdy bands of near-naked youths running around the streets and striking women with strips of goatskin.

Around the 4th century the Church initiated the festival of St Valentine's Day on February 14 to replace such pagan excesses. It appears that neither of two possible Valentines, both 3rd-century Christian martyrs, had any connection with romantic love. The hint of impending springtime, when animals usually mate, simply served to confirm the natural link with

ALLEGORY OF LOVE *Medieval suitors at court followed elaborate rituals in wooing the objects of their desire. Their garden of love recalled the Biblical Garden of Eden.*

Lupercalia. From the 13th century a set of customs developed around the festival. Women who were not partnered could be won in the Valentine lottery, a Lupercalian throwback which survived until the 19th century. Luck, accident and anonymity characterised the spirit of the festival. These resulted in the traditional belief that the first person seen on February 14 would be one's love for the rest of the year, and the unsigned card of today.

Red roses were first given as a St Valentine's Day gift in 18th-century France, in imitation of Louis XVI's love

tokens to his queen, Marie Antoinette, although these flowers of Aphrodite, the Greek goddess of love, had symbolised heavenly perfection and earthly passion since ancient times.

Credit for sending the first valentine often goes to Charles, duc d'Orléans, who conveyed to his wife 'poetical or amorous addresses', which he called *valentiens*, while he was imprisoned in the Tower of London after the Battle of Agincourt in 1415. However, the modern valentine, the earliest form of greetings card, evolved during the 16th century. Early valentines were handmade and decorated with knots, hearts, doves and cupids. In composing their messages, lovers could turn for inspiration to *Valentine Writers*, a handbook of standard rhymes and greetings referred to in 1723. The first printed valentine dates from the mid 18th century.

Subsequently, the practice of sending valentines grew more popular, and by the 19th century postmen were claiming a special

A RED ROSE, SYMBOL AND GIFT OF LOVE

meal allowance for the extra load of mail. Around this time a variety of decorative styles emerged, including mechanical valentines with figures that rolled their eyes and put out their tongues, and cards adorned with cupids that hovered or rowed boats when the cards were opened.

BECOMING ENGAGED
Pledges of betrothal

Betrothal was once much more than a verbal promise. In Roman times bridegrooms of the upper classes had to provide security for the completion of the bargain, while the early Church required a contract of betrothal to be sworn in front of witnesses. If either party died during the engagement, the survivor inherited a share of the other's estate.

The rules were often much more relaxed among poorer

VICTORIAN ST VALENTINE'S DAY CARD

POSTED PASSION *Handmade valentines were common during the 18th century. The 'puzzle card' (above) reads:*
'My dear the heart which you behold/Will break when you the same unfold/Even so my heart with love sick pain/Sure wounded is and breaks in twaine.'
By the Victorian period manufactured cards without a message—including some pop-ups—were hugely popular.

people, particularly in rural areas, and trial marriages were common. The Roman law of *usus*, or 'prescription', specified that if a woman lived with a man for a year without being absent for three nights they were considered married. A similar practice became popular in places such as Scotland in the 18th century, when young men and women were invited to choose partners at local festivals. If they were dissatisfied after living together for a year, they were free to part.

For couples who went through a formal period of engagement the once

CUPID'S ARROW *The statue of Eros in London's Piccadilly Circus represents the ancient Greek god of sexuality. Later he evolved into the Roman youth Cupid. His arrows of love were said to induce passionate desire.*

widespread custom of 'bundling', possibly dating back to ancient Rome, permitted them to spend one night together in the young woman's bedroom. Propriety was expected, but probably not observed.

Asking for a woman's hand on bended knee is one of the lasting legacies of chivalry and dates back to the Crusades when European knights were influenced by Arab culture. With her acceptance came the giving of a ring.

In Greece and Rome an engagement ring may have been originally slipped onto the third finger of the woman's left hand in the belief that a vein ran from this finger directly to the heart. Only

SAFE STORAGE *During her engagement, a 17th-century lady would collect and keep her wedding trousseau in a 'hope' or 'dower' chest. In the USA, this European tradition continued with beautifully painted pieces of wooden furniture.*

AMERICAN DOWER CHEST, 18TH CENTURY

STRAIGHT FROM THE HEART

The death of John Balliol of Barnard Castle, the wealthy 13th-century landowner and founder of Balliol College, Oxford, possibly gave rise to the use of the word 'sweetheart' as a romantic term of endearment.

Throughout the remainder of her life, Balliol's widow, Devorgilla, devotedly carried a silver and ivory casket containing her beloved's embalmed heart. When she died in 1290 the casket was buried beside her by the high altar of the Cistercian abbey in Dumfries she had founded just 17 years earlier. Henceforth it came to be known as Sweetheart Abbey.

much later, in Elizabethan times, did the wedding ring begin to assume a similar importance. By the 19th century the Church had changed betrothals into mere announcements of a wedding, and engagement rings became less important than the ring required for the matrimonial ceremony.

The now light-hearted Leap Year tradition, that on February 29 a woman may propose to her chosen man, was legally binding in Scotland in the 13th century. The Scottish parliament decreed in 1288 that 'olk maden ladye of bothe highe and lowe estait shall hae liberte to bespeke ye man she like'. If he refused, he could be fined—unless he was already betrothed.

Similar laws existed in France and some Italian cities. In Scotland a loophole used in medieval times stated that the female's proposal was valid only if she was wearing red flannel petticoats, making her more respectable than the original 'scarlet woman'—the Biblical whore described in Revelation.

THE DATING GAME
Making a match

According to Greek legend Aphrodite, the goddess of love, arranged a meeting between Paris and the lovely, but married, Helen. This, perhaps the first 'blind date', provoked the Trojan War. The term 'blind date' itself, coined in the 1920s, originated in the USA.

The world's first official marriage bureau was established in Threadneedle Street, London, in 1650. In a trailblazing prospectus, its founder Henry Robinson confidently announced: 'Such as desire to dispose of themselves or friends in marriage, may here likewise be informed what encounters there are to be had.'

On July 19, 1695, the earliest known British matrimonial advertisement appeared in the publication entitled *Collection for the Improvement of Husbandry and Trade*, announcing: 'A Gentleman about 30 Years of Age that says he has a Very Good Estate, would willingly Match Himself to some young Gentlewoman that has a fortune of £3000 or thereabouts. And he will make Settlement to Content.'

In 1958 two Americans, Shirley Sanders and Robert Kardell, became the first couple to be matched by computer, and were introduced to one another on a television show, *People Are Funny*. They were married in a church in Hollywood on October 18, and given a Honolulu honeymoon by the show's sponsors.

Computer dating was developed by a Harvard scholar, Jeff Tarr, who prepared and handed out some 10000 questionnaires to students living in Boston in 1965.

TYING THE KNOT

'We will have rings, and things, and fine array;
And, kiss me, Kate, we will be married o'Sunday.'

The Taming of the Shrew, ACT II, SC I, WILLIAM SHAKESPEARE, 1593-4

WEDDING WISH *Throwing grain, sweetmeats and fruit at the bride was an ancient Greek custom. Rice and confetti are today's symbolic missiles of fertility.*

The institution of marriage evolved in the first human societies to protect lines of descent and ensure that children were safely brought up. Well before 2000 BC the Sumerians had established laws concerning marriage, although free choice of spouse was not a feature of matrimony until modern times. Roman law was the first to introduce the requirement of consent to a union by both the bride and the groom.

Wife capture, practised among the early tribal Britons, proved unpopular with the Anglo-Saxon settlers of the 5th century, since women were a valuable family asset, spinning flax and wool for cloth—hence the word 'spinster'. Consequently, in the 6th century marriage by purchase became law. Family elders fixed the bride price and the term 'wed' arose, from the Old English for a pledge.

Child marriage was also common in Europe until at least the 18th century. In 1211, St Elizabeth of Hungary, then aged four, was carried in a silver cradle to the house of her 11-year-old bridegroom. Some 500 years later, Mary Villiers, a ward of Charles I, was seen climbing trees in her black mourning dress after being widowed at the age of nine.

At first Anglo-Saxons only visited the early Christian priests to have their weddings blessed, but, by the time of the Norman Conquest, what had once been purely a business alliance had become a religious rite. In the 16th century the Church decreed that every impending marriage should be announced by the public reading of banns, and that the wedding should be celebrated in church. This revived an early Christian custom: the 2nd-century theologian Tertullian noted that in Carthaginian society all marriages were considered clandestine and illicit unless announced in church.

In medieval Britain a costly alternative was available in the form of a special licence permitting a couple to wed privately and without having to announce the event in advance. The public calling of banns became a legal requirement with the English Marriage Act of 1754. Civil law retained the option of special licences, and these were considered more genteel.

WITH THIS RING...

The ring has proved an abiding symbol of marital fidelity, although other tokens, such as a halved coin, were common in Britain until the 17th century. In Sumeria around 10000 years ago rings probably evolved from the shackles placed on brides to subdue them. The Greeks were among the first to inscribe rings with such sentiments as 'mayest thou live'. And although the plain band of gold or silver has proved the most enduring design, there have been many alternatives, such as two hearts joined by a key, popular in Roman times.

Placing the ring on the third finger of the left hand originated with the ancient Greeks and Romans. From the 11th century in church ceremonies a priest placed the ring over the tip of the index finger 'in the name of the Father', then over the second 'in the name of the Son', before lodging it on the third finger 'in the name of the Holy Ghost'. But wedding rings were often worn on other fingers, and on the thumb, even in the late 1700s.

Anne of Brittany married the French king Louis XII in 1499 wearing

JEWELLED LINK *The Tudor gimmal ring, worn closed, was a golden sign of two interlocked lives.*

CHURCH AND CAKE *Tiered confections, marzipanned and iced, date from the 18th century, when a baker is said to have been inspired by St Bride's Church in Fleet Street, London. The ancient Greeks ate simpler cakes to ensure fertility.*

the first pure white wedding dress on record. By the end of the 16th century wearing white symbolised virgin purity, and in the 1700s white or silver wedding dresses were increasingly the choice of royal and aristocratic brides.

But the spectacular white wedding dates back no farther than Victorian times. Throughout Europe until the 19th century people got married in their best clothes, whatever the colour, or in their national costume.

When the first fashion plate of a white wedding dress appeared in the French publication *Journal des Dames* in 1813, the bridal gown was already becoming usual. The modest veil, which was worn in medieval times but had given way during the 18th century to a lacy cap or bonnet, also became an essential part of bridal wear in the early 19th century.

Decorative and symbolic flowers, first fashionable among the ancient Greeks and Romans, enjoyed a new

HEELS OVER HEAD *The ancient tradition of throwing shoes at the bridal pair to bring them good luck was revived in Victorian times.*

vogue in Victorian times. Denoting chastity and fertility, they were worn by Middle Eastern Saracen brides, and medieval Crusaders brought the custom to Europe. Fertility was also symbolised in ancient Greece and Rome by the entourage of female bridesmaids accompanying the bride.

Throwing the bouquet to onlookers echoes the reversal of a medieval frolic in which wedding guests tossed stockings at the bride and groom. If the groom's stocking, thrown by a woman, landed on his head it signalled that she would soon marry.

Some 3000 years ago in ancient Greece, fathers would pay for their daughters' marriage festivities. In 16th-century Britain the celebrations gave rise to the adjective 'bridal', from the 'bride ale' sold to raise money for the wedding feast.

The word 'honeymoon', from the honeyed wine that was consumed during wedding festivities, was probably coined in the 16th century. It evolved during the 19th century as a period of holiday and seclusion for the newlyweds.

NAMING AND CHRISTENING
A godly child

Adults, not babies, were the first people to be baptised as Christians. Initiated by the Church to symbolise spiritual rebirth, baptism marked the conversion of 'heathens' from paganism. 'Baptism', which derives from the Greek word meaning 'to immerse', reflects the common use of water in purification rituals before the advent of Christianity.

From about the 3rd century many newborn infants were baptised in a Christian ceremony that became linked to christening—receiving someone into the Christian faith. In the Middle Ages, when newborn babies had a tenuous hold on life, children were usually baptised on the day of their birth, but as the risk of disease faded during the 1800s the period before the christening took place lengthened to a few weeks. Initially godparents were simply known as 'sponsors', from the Latin verb *spondere*, 'to promise', since they vouched for the sincerity of an adult pagan in undergoing baptism.

The typical christening gifts of silver egg cups and saltcellars recall two ancient Roman traditions. Eggs were presented as symbols of fertility while salt was sprinkled on babies to protect them against evil. Gifts of coins were thought to ensure future wealth.

FROM THE FONT *Having been baptised in holy water, children emerge as members of the Church. Here the 10th-century Byzantine emperor Constantine VII is blessed in Constantinople.*

FOOD FOR GROWING INFANTS
Breast, bottle and wet nurse

Since Roman times, breastfeeding has evoked mixed feelings. Because they believed that sex would turn breast milk sour, Roman women tried to avoid sexual relations while they nursed their children (sometimes for up to three years). Nor have women always welcomed this maternal experience. Wet nurses, hired by parents to suckle their infants, were common in Roman Britain and still much in demand in the 18th century. Queen Victoria refused to breastfeed, calling it 'making a cow of oneself'.

The Greeks and Romans favoured an urn-shaped terracotta cup as an alternative to breastfeeding. Hollowed-out cows' horns were common in Britain from the Middle Ages until the 18th century, while 16th-century portraits depict infants with feeders made from

PEWTER SUCKING BOTTLE, 1750S

ALLENBURY FEEDER, 1930

CERAMIC CUP, GREECE, ABOUT 400 BC

CLAY CUP, CYPRUS, ABOUT 900 BC

POTTERY PAP BOAT, 1750S

FEEDING TIME *Infants have been bottle-fed for centuries. Spouted cups existed in Cyprus about 900 BC. Pap boats for mashed food were introduced in the 17th century and bottles appeared in the 19th century.*

wood or pressed leather. Pewter feeders and pottery containers were both made from the 18th century.

The india-rubber teat, patented in the USA by Elijah Pratt in 1845, encouraged bottle-feeding, although there was still little understanding of the health risks involved, and sterilising bottles by immersing them in boiling water was not widespread until the late 1800s. The British boat-shaped Allenbury feeder of 1900, with openings at both ends, marked an important change. Not only was it easier to clean, it was the first feeder to include a teat and valve to regulate milk flow.

Feeding cups of the 17th and 18th centuries often contained caudle or posset, a custard of milk and eggs flavoured with wine and sugar. From the 1850s evaporated and condensed cow's milk was produced, followed by substitutes made from dried and powdered cow's milk in the 1880s. Pap boats for weaning babies on to solids were used in the 18th century. The pap was a mixture of breadcrumbs or flour cooked in water or milk.

A BUNNY'S DELIGHT,
FROM THE BOOK
Little Grey Rabbit's Birthday
BY ALISON UTTLEY, 1944

MANY HAPPY RETURNS

Birthdays were marked with feasts and gifts in Egyptian and Persian households of the 5th century BC. But celebrating children's birthdays only became popular during the 19th century AD, when societies began to stress the importance of family values. Birthdays were initially seen as a time for passing on lessons of morality and behaviour.

The ancient Greeks are thought to have honoured the birthday of Artemis, the goddess of the Moon and fertility, with candles placed on temple altars. If the candles were blown out in one go, good favour from the goddess was ensured. Today the accomplishment is said to make a silent wish come true.

SAFE AND SECURE
Cradles, potties and playpens

The lullaby 'Hush-a-bye baby, on the tree top, When the wind blows, the cradle will rock...' reflects the age-old awareness that gentle rocking gradually quietens a crying infant. Tacitus, the 1st-century Roman politician and historian, recounts that some 2000 years ago Germanic peoples put their babies' cradles in tree branches to be rocked by the breeze. The word 'cradle' comes from the Old High German *kratto*, meaning 'basket'.

In the Bible, the infant Moses is saved from the Egyptians by being left to float down river in a basket. Rocking cradles made from hollowed-out tree trunks are mentioned in English manuscripts of the 9th century, and by medieval times most cradles

were either mounted on rockers or attached to fixed supports from which they swung from side to side.

Ancient Greek pottery bears images of young children sitting on 'potties', deep bowls with a hole in the side through which the legs could protrude. In Britain no furniture for potty-training existed until the small 'close chairs' of the 17th century, which had a hole in the seat to hold a chamberpot.

Ingenious methods have long been employed to keep tiny children safely in one place. In his *A Regimen for Young Children* of 1473, Bartholomew Metlinger suggested constructing a 'little pen of leather'. A 17th-century 'baby minder' consisted of an oak post embedded in the ceiling and floor, with a wooden arm protruding at right angles. An adjustable waistband secured the infant to the extension, so that he or she could then 'run around'.

SHAKE, RATTLE AND CHEW *A 17th-century child holds a wooden rattle in one hand and a coral 'gum stick' in the other. Traditionally coral had been thought to avert evil and bring good luck. Roman mothers hung strings of coral beads around their babies' cots.*

SNUG IN FRONT *Cradling a baby in the arms is instinctive, but tiring. The fabric baby sling, still used throughout Africa, leaves the mother's arms free. It is possibly one of the earliest human inventions.*

CLOTHES FOR A BABY
Dressing the very young

Until the 1700s most infants spent their first months of life tightly cocooned in linen swaddling bands. Swaddling was believed to encourage arms and legs to grow straight and had been practised in Europe at least since Roman times.

As babies were released from their bands during the 19th century, an increasingly large layette was required: shirts, vests, caps, bodices, barracoats (flannel wrappers), petticoats, gowns and shawls, bibs, socks and shoes. Changing customs in the 20th century shortened the list, but babies' clothing reached its ultimate simplicity with the American 'Babygro' stretch suit, patented in 1959 by Walter Arzt, a father frustrated with dressing his child.

From the early 1900s a popular trend developed for dressing boys and girls differently almost from birth. By the 1930s choosing blue for boys was well established, recalling the ancient belief recorded in the 5th-century *Book of Numbers* that blue granted protection against evil spirits. Girls, considered less important, needed no such aid; thus pink became the 'girls' colour' mainly to contrast with blue, but possibly also recalling the 11th-century belief that red clothing warded off illness.

APRIL FOOL
Joker's paradise

Because some people will believe almost anything, they are the perfect victims for practical jokes on the morning of April 1. April Fools' Day, also known as All Fools' Day, has no clear origin, but is often said to derive from Hilaria, a Roman spring festival of jollity and dissipation. An alternative suggestion, which is based on the Bible, is that this was the day on which Noah released a dove from the ark, on what seemed to be a fool's errand, to find land on an Earth that appeared to be completely flooded.

The fooling tradition may have come to Britain from France during the 16th century. There, April Fools' is known as *poisson d'avril* or 'April fish', *poisson* being a corruption of the word for passion and a reference to the mocking and tormenting of Jesus by the Romans on the day of his Crucifixion, remembered around this time of year.

One of the earliest known references to April Fooling in England comes in notes made in the 1680s by the antiquarian John Aubrey. A notorious practical joke involved a bogus 'Ceremony of Washing the White Lions'. In 1860 many Londoners were sent 'official' invitations to witness this ceremony at the Tower of London. They were to enter by the non-existent White Gate and many cab drivers repeatedly drove the length of Tower Hill looking for it. A similar trick is said to have been played at the Tower in 1698.

EASTER RESURRECTION
An annual rebirth

The long period of Lent ends on Maundy Thursday, which was named from the Latin *mandatum novum*, Christ's 'new commandment' that his disciples should love one another. In

SWEET SYMBOLS *Chocolate Easter eggs, such as this Victorian confection, were first enjoyed in the 19th century.*

ADORATION OF THE LAMB *Christ is often represented as the Paschal Lamb, named from the Jewish 'Pesach', 'Passover', when animals were sacrificed. Jesus was crucified during the Passover season, and celebrations of Easter were synchronised with this festival.*

ROYAL PENNIES *The traditional gift of specially minted silver Maundy money to the elderly poor dates back to medieval times.*

Britain the monarch gives Maundy money to several impoverished old people. Originally the monarch and the Church elders emulated Christ's humble act of washing his disciples' feet at the Last Supper, as well as making a charitable distribution of clothing, food and money to the poor. James II became the last monarch to perform the task in person—it passed to the royal almoner in the 1860s, before being dropped in

1754. By the beginning of Victoria's reign, the donation was of money only.

Easter Day is one of the Christian calendar's earliest festivals. Although it is not celebrated on a fixed date, Easter marks the start of spring. Its name comes from the fourth month of the pagan Anglo-Saxon year, *Eosturmonath* (April), said by the Venerable Bede to be named after the goddess Eostre, whose festival was celebrated then. In the 19th century Jacob Grimm, one of the Brothers Grimm, surmised that she was the goddess of dawn or spring. Others speculated that her emblem was the hare—the original Easter bunny.

The Easter egg is an ancient symbol of creation and rebirth. Murals on Etruscan tombs from the 6th century BC show it used in funerary rites, and the Greeks and Romans exchanged painted eggs at spring festivals. Zoroastrians, followers of a religion established in Persia around 600 BC, celebrate the new year on March 21 with gifts of painted eggs; new clothes are worn at this time, a custom echoed in the tradition of wearing something new on Easter Day.

By the 12th century Easter or Pace eggs, named from paschal eggs, were common to European Church rituals. They were boiled in dye and patterned with wax or flowers.

MAY DAY
The people's celebration

In contrast to many pagan celebrations, Beltane and other European spring festivals held at the beginning of May were never incorporated into the Christian calendar. Only in 1978 was May 1 made a bank holiday in Britain.

Other spring celebrations in Britain included 'bringing in the May'—the bringing home of flowering hawthorn, first recorded in 1240. Maypoles have their origins in ancient European tree cults, but the first recorded example in Britain of festivities taking place around a Maypole dates to the mid 1300s—a Welsh poem describes the Maypole as a birch tree. The first known example of an English Maypole dance in which ribbons suspended from the pole were plaited was in a performance of *Richard Plantaganet* by J.T. Haines in 1836.

The Puritans thought Maypoles to be phallic symbols and during the Commonwealth the 'stynkyng ydols' were banned. On the Restoration of the monarchy, Charles II commanded one of the tallest Maypoles to be put up on The Strand in London. About 40m (130ft) tall, it provided a focal point for May celebrations for some 50 years.

WHITE SUNDAY

Whitsun, also known as Pentecost, celebrates the coming of the Holy Spirit to Christ's disciples. The name derives from 'White Sunday', since on this day people wore white clothes for their baptism. From at least the 2nd century in England a week of festivities took place at Whitsuntide. One of the events was the Whitsun-ale, when villagers feasted and played games.

GREETINGS CARD, SENT TO MARK THE WHITSUN FESTIVAL

SUMMER SOLSTICE
The longest day

Although the summer solstice, the longest day, is on June 21, according to the modern calendar summer does not begin until Midsummer's Day, June 24. In pre-Christian times the solstice was celebrated with great bonfires, said to provide protection against evil spirits that could harm the growing crops.

From at least the 4th century, when the Church instituted the feast of the Nativity of John the Baptist to fall three days later, bonfires were lit to honour St John instead. In the Middle Ages and Tudor times it was believed that the fires of June 24 protected against bad weather, crop blight and diseases such as the plague, all of which commonly occurred at this time of year. Modern midsummer celebrations still take place at Stonehenge in Wiltshire. The alignment of the massive stones of the circular megalith give precise sight lines for the rising and setting of the Sun at the summer solstice.

RETURN OF THE SUN *In the early 1700s villagers celebrate the arrival of spring in northern Europe. Originally, adults rather than children danced around Maypoles.*

HARVEST FESTIVALS
Celebrating the crop

An abundant harvest has been cause for celebration since grain was first sown and tended. The precious crop provided food for the coming months, an essential ingredient for ale and other fermented drinks, straw for building and seed corn to sow for a new crop.

Superstitions and rituals of the harvest feature in most ancient cultures. In ancient Egypt the harvest was overseen by Renenutet, the snake-headed goddess of fertility. Corn dollies may have originated in ancient Greece. In Britain the final sheaf was believed to hold the corn's spirit. Remaining ears were plaited into a corn dolly, which was kept until spring. The last load of corn was also associated with the 'horkey', a feast to celebrate the harvest for those who had worked to bring it in.

Increasing mechanisation during the 19th century eroded these traditions and today's harvest supper is linked with the Church's Harvest Festival. Before the Reformation in the 16th century, crops were blessed by priests, but subsequently the Church largely ignored the harvest until the mid 1840s, when the Reverend Robert Hawker instigated a thanksgiving festival at his church in Morwenstow, Cornwall. Within 30 years harvest thanksgivings were being celebrated in most parishes. The Reverend Henry Alford's harvest hymn 'O come, ye thankful people, come, raise the song of harvest-home' was first published in 1844.

THE USA GIVES THANKS

In the autumn of 1621 at Plymouth, now in the state of Massachusetts, the newly arrived Pilgrim Fathers invited members of the neighbouring Wampanoag tribe to a three-day feast in gratitude for their help during the previous year of hardships.

By the mid 19th century a much reduced thanksgiving meal, featuring a roast turkey as its centrepiece, had become a yearly institution in New England. In 1863 the fourth Tuesday of November was declared a US national holiday, known as Thanksgiving Day.

SPIRIT OF THE CROP *The Greeks gave thanks to Demeter (left), the goddess of abundance. In Europe corn dollies (above) were later kept as charms and ploughed into the soil to bring good luck for the harvest.*

ALL SAINTS AND HALLOWEEN
In honour of the dead

For Celts and Anglo-Saxons the year ended when the herds were brought in from pasture at the end of October. The new year began in November, marked by the festival of Samhain, a celebration in which purifying bonfires were lit. On the night before Samhain, souls of the departed could return temporarily to their hearths, and ghosts and demons were free to roam the Earth.

To counter the influence of this pagan festival, during the 9th century the Church instituted the feast of All Saints or All Hallows on November 1. Thereafter, October 31 became known as All Hallows Eve, or Halloween.

In 998 the abbot of Cluny in France established November 2 as All Souls' Day, when prayers are said for the departed, thus completing the link between Samhain and Christian festivals. In the 16th century, as they imposed Catholicism in Mexico, the

colonising Spaniards took elements of local religions and incorporated them into their rituals. The Day of the Dead on November 1 remains one of the great celebrations.

In Britain most Halloween traditions died out with the rise of Puritanism in the 16th and 17th centuries, but games such as apple bobbing, in which apples floating in a bowl of water are caught in the mouth, are remnants of past rituals. When thrown over the left shoulder, the apple's peel would fall into a shape resembling the initials of a true lover.

The Halloween of today, in which children dress up as ghouls, ghosts and

HUBBLE, BUBBLE *Witches were traditionally set loose to cause mischief on Halloween, which heralded the return of winter. The Devil is said to have given them their supernatural powers.*

witches and light-heartedly demand 'treats' from neighbours under threat of a 'trick', has largely been reimported from the United States, where Irish immigrants introduced the custom in the 19th century. It is thought to stem from the idea that on Halloween all law is suspended. Dressing up in masks and costumes prevents people from being recognised by their own community. Being separated in this way allows the participants to play boisterous and often antisocial tricks.

The observance of saints' days, including All Saints, was banned by the English Protestants, but they soon created a new autumn festival in their place. In 1606 Guy Fawkes was hanged for his role in the Catholic plot to blow up the House of Lords on November 4, 1605. Parliament then passed an Act for the perpetual celebration of the failure of both this second attempt on the life of James I and the plan to destroy Parliament itself.

The Act ordered that everyone should attend church on the morning of November 5 as part of the Gunpowder Plot commemoration, which was soon popularly known as Guy Fawkes Day. By the 1630s the event was associated with bonfires and the burning of effigies. Initially these were of the pope or the Devil but from the 19th century they were often of Guy Fawkes himself.

LIGHTING UP THE SKY

Fireworks were invented by the Chinese. From the 3rd century AD they celebrated the New Year by throwing bamboo 'firecrackers' onto flames. As the trapped air in the stalks grew hotter, they exploded with a bang. Around 1050 gunpowder, developed for military purposes, was added to the bamboo to create 'modern' fireworks.

First mentioned in Europe in Vanuzzio Biringuccio of Siena's *Pyrotechnia* of 1540, fireworks were lit on the election of a new pope and the main feast days.

REMEMBER, REMEMBER... *By the 19th century effigies of Guy Fawkes were hanged and mocked by street crowds on bonfire night. Fireworks made Gunpowder Plot celebrations spectacular events from the 17th century.*

NEW YEAR'S DAY
The calendar starts

Throughout the world the new year has regularly been linked to the winter solstice or the vernal equinox. From 1155, when the English Crown first adopted the Roman practice of beginning the year in March, until the adoption of the Gregorian calendar in 1752, the English year began on March 25, a date set by the medieval Church as the Feast of the Annunciation or Lady Day.

Celebrations to mark this annual cycle were common in ancient Rome and continued over the centuries. In a masque by the English playwright Ben Jonson, which was presented to the court in 1616, a character appeared with an orange and a sprig of rosemary on his head to symbolise the season. In Scotland following the Reformation, the Church suppressed Christmas celebrations and New Year, or Hogmanay, became the main midwinter festival.

SECONDS TO MIDNIGHT *Revellers in New York in 1939 celebrate the 300-year-old Scottish tradition of Hogmanay.*

PANCAKE DAY
Preparing for Lent

Lent, a period of 40 days of fasting to symbolise the time Jesus spent alone in the wilderness, was instituted by the Church in the 7th century. Meat, eggs, dairy produce and wine were proscribed; the last of the meat was eaten on Collop or Shrove Monday, and the eggs and dairy produce made into pancakes on Shrove Tuesday.

The word 'shrove' comes from the period when, having made their pre-Lenten confessions, people received absolution, or were 'shriven'. Eating pancakes has been customary on Shrove Tuesday since the 14th century or even earlier, but the name Pancake Day was not noted until 1825. The practice of tossing pancakes probably began only in the 1840s.

After the Reformation, Protestant Churches took a disapproving view of celebrations at Shrovetide, the three days preceding Ash Wednesday. By the 1800s the making and eating of pancakes was one of the few continuing customs that still preceded Lent.

CHRISTMAS CHEER

*'Well do Christian people call this holy day, on which
Our Lord was born, the day of the new Sun.'*

ST AMBROSE, BISHOP OF MILAN, 340–97

As the dark closed in and the shortest day of the year approached, people in ancient Persia and later in the far-flung Roman Empire paid homage to Mithras, the Persian god of light and guardian against evil. From 300 BC followers of Mithras lit fires around the time of the winter solstice to celebrate what the Romans called *Dies Natali Invicti Solis*, the birthday of the unconquered Sun.

Worship of Mithras was one of the main rivals to early Christianity, but the Church was determined that celebration of the Nativity should prevail and by the 4th century AD December 25 had been firmly established as Christmas Day. Nevertheless, the modern Christmas retains elements of such pagan festivals as the Roman Saturnalia, which was celebrated around December 17.

Named after Saturn, the Roman god of plenty, Saturnalia lasted for seven days and involved much feasting, drinking and merrymaking; homes were brightly lit and decorated with evergreens. Normal roles and customs were reversed: men dressed as women and women as men, while masters waited on servants, and otherwise forbidden pastimes such as gambling were allowed. This topsy-turvy world lives on today in the traditions of the Christmas pantomime.

The pre-Christian tribes of northern Europe also celebrated the Yule, a midwinter festival similarly marked—for those who had the means to do so—with indulgent eating and drinking and the exchange of gifts. Fires were lit, from which the tradition of burning a large yule log is descended. Homes were decorated for Yule with evergreens such as holly and ivy, which are symbols of renewal and everlasting life, and also with mistletoe.

Epiphany on January 6 celebrates the visit of the Magi to the infant Jesus. In 567 the Church declared the 12 days between the Nativity and Epiphany a sacred season. By the time of the Norman Conquest in 1066, this period was established in England as the year's main holiday, a time to rest and make merry. To keep the year's luck, Christmas decorations were taken down on Twelfth Night.

FESTIVE TRADITIONS

Although Christmas celebrations are rooted in the past, they have evolved through the ages and continue to do so. Nativity plays, for instance, are 20th-century versions of medieval nativity pageants. Similarly, the medieval custom of carol singing in the streets was revived in the 19th century. Most modern carols date from that time, but one of the earliest, 'While Shepherds Watched Their Flocks by Night', was written as a hymn towards the end of the 17th century by the Irish poet and playwright Nahum Tate.

Today's Christmas is largely a Victorian invention embellished by commercial interests, but the first recorded Christmas tree was noted by a visitor to Strasbourg, then part of the Habsburg Empire, as early as 1605. The decorated fir is said to have been introduced into the British Christmas in the 1840s by Prince Albert. However, Princess Victoria, who was to become his wife, saw Christmas trees displayed at Kensington Palace in 1832, and in 1800 Queen Charlotte, the German-born wife of George III, had a tree put up for a party she held at Windsor on Christmas Day.

Electric lights for the tree made their Christmas debut in the United States in 1882. They did so at the New York home of Edward H. Johnson, an associate of Thomas Edison, who had created the first electric light bulb three years earlier.

The Christmas cracker, said to be the brainchild of the English pastry cook and confectioner Tom Smith, dates from the mid 19th century. Smith's idea was to wrap a sweet and a printed riddle in twists of brightly coloured paper, but he was inspired to add the 'bang' after sitting in front of a crackling fire. He proudly advertised his crackers as 'combining art with amusement and fun with refinement'.

Christmas traditions continue to evolve. The monarch's message, first broadcast to the people of the United Kingdom and the Commonwealth in 1932, was originated by George V.

GOLD, FRANKINCENSE AND MYRRH
The offerings to the infant Jesus were the original gifts of the three Magi, but presents were also given at pagan midwinter festivals. Before the 4th century AD Epiphany on January 6, marking the Adoration of the Magi, was the focus for celebrations. In the Eastern Church it remains so, but elsewhere marks the end of the Christmas season.

HERE COMES SANTA CLAUS *Patron saint of Europe's children since the 4th century, St Nicholas took on a new identity in 19th-century North America. Thomas Nast's portrait of 1863 firmly established Santa Claus as a rotund and kindly, white-bearded old man carrying a sackful of gifts to fill children's Christmas stockings.*

VICTORIAN STOCKING WITH BOXES OF CHOCOLATES AND A WOODEN DOLL

TREE FOR THE HOME *The Christmas tree was borrowed by the Victorians from medieval German midwinter celebrations.*

THE FIRST CHRISTMAS CARD *In 1843 Sir Henry Cole initiated the seasonal greeting with this design by J.C. Horsley. Only about 1000 copies were sold that year, but by 1880 the volume of cards was so great that the General Post Office had to ask people to post early for Christmas.*

LIGHT AND CHEER *A maid flourishes a flaming pudding, a distant reflection of the ancient pagan festival of light, at a stylish Victorian table. Christmas for the servants followed on St Stephen's Day, also called Boxing Day.*

CHRISTMAS CRACKER, LATE 19TH CENTURY

TIN CHERUB CANDLE HOLDER, 19TH CENTURY

CHRISTMAS CARDS, 1870s

SUPERSTITIONS, SIGNS AND OMENS

'He that hath understanding, let him count the number of the beast;
for it is the number of a man: and his number is Six hundred and sixty and six.'

THE DEVIL'S NUMBER SPELLED OUT, REVELATION, CH. 13, V. 18

OFF THE HOOF *Horseshoes were nailed on house doors with the ends uppermost to stop their good luck from running out.*

LUCKY LEAF *The rare four-leaved clover was thought to help its finder to recognise evil spirits and stay protected from wicked enchantments.*

GOOD MAGIC *Since ancient times people have worn amulets to ward off evil and illness, and to bring good luck. Worn around the neck, the mysterious word 'abracadabra' was also credited with magical powers and was inscribed on amulets. Charm bracelets became popular in the 19th century, bearing such trinkets as the saltcellar for luck, Noah's ark for safety and the key to happiness.*

WILD CAT *Black cats, classed as demonic familiars of witches by the 16th-century Church, are unlucky omens in most European countries and in the USA. But in Britain they are widely welcomed, especially if they cross a person's path or enter a house uninvited.*

For the millions of people who cross their fingers for luck or to avoid retribution for telling a lie, superstition exerts a strong grip. Like members of the earliest societies, who needed to control nature, they are seeking to ward off the random blows of fate.

Ancient peoples forged close links between superstition and religion. Crossing the fingers for luck resembles the sign of the Cross enacted by early Christians. Touching wood to prevent the thwarting of a plan, and holding a wooden crucifix when taking an oath, probably have a similar origin.

Many plants and animals, because they are free of human control, have

often been credited with supernatural powers. In the USA and much of Europe the four-leaved clover, a rare form of the three-leaved variety, is thought to bring luck. Its properties were first recorded in the anonymous *Gospelles of Dystaues* of 1507, where it is said that 'he that findeth the trayfle [trefoil] with foure leues [leaves]…shall be ryche all his life'.

Hawthorn, used in herbal medicine, is said to protect houses from being struck by lightning. It was long regarded as a protection against the evil spirits believed to roam the Earth, especially on the eve of great festivals such as May Day. In the 17th century the English essayist Francis Bacon noted the general belief that the plague could be detected by 'the smell of a mellow apple and (as some say) of May flowers'. This may explain the superstition that hawthorn flowers, or May blossom, invite bad luck if taken inside the house.

Like the hawthorn, the raven has associations both good and bad. Because this largest member of the crow family is a carrion feeder with jet-black plumage, it is often thought to foretell death and disaster. But the Spanish novelist Miguel de Cervantes relates in *Don Quixote*, published in 1605, that according to British tradition the legendary King Arthur had been transformed into a raven, 'for which cause it cannot be proved from that time to this, that any Englishman has ever killed a raven'.

In ancient Greek mythology the peacock was the sacred animal of the jealous goddess Hera. After the death of Argus, the guardian with the hundred eyes, Hera had his eyes transferred to the bird's tail so that they could witness the adulterous liaisons of her husband Zeus. In medieval Europe the bird's feathers were associated with a strong belief in the evil eye—the power of certain people or animals to bring bad luck to others simply by looking at them—and its

EVIL OMEN *A lone magpie is unlucky because, according to Christian legend, the bird refused to enter Noah's ark. Nor would it exchange its plumage for a full black mourning costume after the death of Christ.*

BIRDS OF THE REALM *The ravens of the Tower of London are Britain's national talismans; it is said that the Tower and the kingdom will fall if the birds should disappear. However, this tradition dates back no farther than the late 19th century.*

feathers are still thought to attract misfortune if taken indoors.

Good fortune is assured, however, to those who greet the first day of the month by saying 'rabbits'. A 1979 survey revealed that about 5 million rabbits' foot talismans were sold in Europe each year. Hares have a long pedigree. In ancient Rome they were associated with fertility and lust, and uncaged at the spring fruit and vegetable festival of Floralia. Because the hare was once thought to reproduce without the male, in Christian art it sometimes symbolised the Virgin Birth. This could explain the connection of the hare with Easter.

The iron horseshoe, once vital in transport, agriculture and warfare, has evolved into a good-luck symbol. In 17th-century England and North America people hung up horseshoes as an antidote to witchcraft. It is even said that Admiral Nelson had one nailed to the mast of his flagship, HMS *Victory*.

Opening an umbrella in the house is said to attract ill fortune. The origins of both the object, named after *ombrella*, Italian for 'little shade', and the superstition lie in China, where umbrellas were first made around 1000 BC. To avoid insulting the Sun, which the Chinese worshipped, they were only opened outdoors.

Sneezes have been blessed since the days of the ancient Greeks and Romans. This is probably due to a

ONE-WAY RUNGS *The superstition that it is bad luck to walk under a ladder may reflect an ancient fear of the gallows. The condemned commonly climbed a ladder to their execution.*

primitive belief that such explosions from inside the head were signs from the gods—for either good or evil.

ORDER OUT OF CHAOS

'Everything is disposed according to numbers,' said Pythagoras, the Greek philosopher and mathematician of the 6th century BC; and numbers have long been endowed with occult significance. The number three, now associated with the saying 'third time lucky' and with accidents being anticipated in threes, was considered a mystical number even before the Christian Trinity. The Anglo-Saxons believed in the powers of nine, being three times three, and used it to heal and to break spells.

Seven imparts mixed blessings. The 'seven-year itch', which according to popular tradition can bring the downfall of a marriage, reflects the widespread belief that life runs in seven-year cycles, thus the 'itch' is an indicator that life should change. There were also seven wonders of the ancient world, and Christianity identified seven deadly sins.

The Romans considered 13 the unluckiest number. The modern superstition that it is unlucky to seat 13 people at a table may reflect the story of the Last Supper, when Jesus, sitting at the Passover table with his 12 disciples, was betrayed by Judas.

ASTROLOGICAL FORECASTS
Written in the stars

Thanks to the brainwave of a British newspaper in 1930, thousands of popular publications across the world now carry astrological forecasts, and almost everyone knows the 'star sign' that corresponds with their date of birth.

In August of that year John Gordon, then the editor of the *Sunday Express*, commissioned the astrologer R.H. Naylor to cast a horoscope for Princess Margaret to celebrate her birth. As an afterthought, the piece also contained a few 'what the stars foretell' forecasts for people with birthdays in the following week. The reader response to these predictions was so enthusiastic that Naylor began a weekly column of horoscopes. This started a trend in British and American newspapers, and in 1936 the *New York Post* introduced the practice of running the horoscopes under the 12 signs of the zodiac.

Sumerian priests laid down the principles of astrology, a system of forecasting earthly and human events by observing the movement of heavenly bodies, in the 3rd millennium BC. Some 2000 years later, the Babylonians grouped stars into the constellations from which the signs of the zodiac take their names, and also divided the band representing the path of the Sun, the Moon and the principal planets into 12 equal segments.

In the 2nd century AD the Greek astronomer Ptolemy produced the first

TAROT CARD, DEATH, 15TH-CENTURY DESIGN

astrological textbook, *Tetrabiblos* (*Four Books*), stating that there were links between star signs and each of the four elements of earth, air, fire and water, and that these affected human destiny.

In subsequent centuries Roman, Arab and Renaissance scholars refined astrology, but its principles have endured. To obtain a true individual horoscope, the astrologer must know the date, time and place of someone's birth. The forecast is produced by a process based on the position of the Sun and planets at that moment, and on the qualities traditionally ascribed to them.

STAR-STRUCK Seeking to help people to understand themselves and predict their future, astrologers have studied the 12 constellations of Aries, Taurus, Gemini, Cancer, Leo, Virgo, Libra, Scorpio, Sagittarius (below), Capricorn, Aquarius and Pisces.

SIGNS AND DIVINATION
The clairvoyant's tools

Fortunetellers today are often Gypsies, nomadic descendants of a caste that once lived in India, where palmistry probably originated at least 3000 years ago before spreading to China, Tibet, Persia, Mesopotamia and Egypt. In ancient Greece, where fortunetelling was highly popular and developed the essentials of its present form, Aristotle declared the hand to be 'the organ of organs, the active agent of the passive powers of the whole system'.

The early Church held that palmistry was the stuff of pagans and heathens, and denounced it as a dangerous form of sorcery and witchcraft. During the Renaissance, however, palmistry again found favour in educated circles as a legitimate science.

The clouded crystal globe in which clairvoyants claim to divine the future may have evolved from the way seers of hunter-gatherer tribes 'read' reflections in water. A mirror or other polished surface may also have been used—a tradition reflected in the fairy-tale appeals of Snow White's wicked stepmother to the 'Mirror, mirror on the wall'. In Britain the crystal ball was established as a standard tool of the

LENDING A HAND *Palmistry followed strict rules first laid down in medieval scrolls. It might reveal an alarming destiny (below) or simply provide light-hearted amusement in a 19th-century French salon.*

MAP OF CONSTELLATIONS,
FROM PTOLEMY'S
2ND–CENTURY ORIGINAL

PALMISTRY HAND

CRYSTAL BALL

ASTROLOGICAL
BIRTH CHART

TEA LEAVES IN
CHINA CUP

TAROT CARDS (LEFT TO RIGHT):
TEMPERANCE, THE HERMIT, THE
MAGICIAN, THE FOOL AND
THE HANGED MAN,
15TH–CENTURY DESIGN

TELLING FORTUNES *People have tried to read the future in many ways: in a birth chart, in tea leaves, lines on the palm and from crystal balls and tarot cards. Ptolemy's all-embracing map of the heavens plotted the varied shapes and positions of the constellations in detail.*

occultist in the 17th century, when the favoured material was quartz or beryl.

Foretelling the future in the pattern of tea leaves displayed in a drained cup has no recorded origins, but the practice was introduced into Europe from China with tea itself some 300 years ago and was well known in the 18th century. Coffee dregs were read in a similar way, and an announcement in a 1726 edition of the *Dublin Weekly Journal* mentions the arrival of 'the Famous Mrs Cherry, the only Gentle-woman truly Learned in that Occult Science of Tossing of Coffee Grounds'.

Cartomancy, or fortunetelling with playing cards, has been practised since at least the 1700s. Using Italian cards from the game of *tarrochi*, French occultists claimed that Gypsies had brought the tarot to Europe and that it contained ancient secrets of Egyptian priests.

Tarot was played with 56 'minor arcana' or ordinary cards and 22 'major arcana' or trump cards, depicting various forces, characters, virtues and vices. For example, 'Temperance' was

shown as a winged woman pouring liquid between two large cups; she signified patience and moderation. Other cards included 'The Fool', signifying enthusiasm but also lack of discipline; and 'The Hanged Man', pointing to change and regeneration.

Elaborately painted packs appeared in Europe around 1415 in Milan, although they were not used for cartomancy at this time. Possibly inspired by variations of oriental packs brought to Venice by merchants, tarot cards may be named after the River Taro, a tributary of the River Po, which irrigates northern Italy.

Since 'reading the tarot' involves elements of myths and legends from many countries, including China, India and Egypt, its origins remain widely contested. Tarot may even derive from various mystic cults that were suppressed by the medieval Church, but which re-emerged later as occult magic.

PREDICTIONS AND DREAMS

Before amniocentesis—the scientific analysis of fluid from a pregnant woman's uterus—was developed in the 1930s, superstitions offered the sole means of predicting the sex of an unborn child. Around 4000 BC in Egypt, two types of wheat were watered with the woman's urine. The child's sex was determined by which sprouted first.

The Egyptians devised guidelines for interpreting the images seen in dreams around 2000 BC. A papyrus states: 'If a man sees himself in a dream looking at a snake—good, it signifies [many] provisions,' and 'If a man sees in a dream his bed on fire—bad, it signifies the rape of his wife.'

IN THE OLD TESTAMENT PHARAOH'S
DREAM OF SEVEN FAT AND LEAN
CATTLE IS INTERPRETED BY JOSEPH
AS PROPHESYING SEVEN YEARS OF
PLENTY, THEN SEVEN OF FAMINE

BURIAL AND CREMATION
The final journey

When someone dies, mourning and remembrance must be tempered with practicality. Burying bodies in pits or beneath mounds of earth or stones has long been accepted as a sensible and hygienic means of disposal that also allows the departed to be properly mourned. The world's oldest graves, found north of Beijing in China, date back at least 400 000 years.

To express concern for the deceased, and possibly also to ease their arduous

AT REST *Affluent families of the 19th century erected exquisite monuments to their loved ones, such as this finely carved column and scroll in Brompton Cemetery, London.*

passage from this world to the next, Neanderthal people buried their dead with a variety of domestic objects. In some Palaeolithic graves from around 5000 BC, bodies have been found curled into the foetal position, as though death were a form of rebirth. But most cadavers are laid out flat, fully displaying the face and clothing.

For the ancient Egyptians, whose mummy cases are among the earliest surviving coffins, preservation of the body was essential for prospects of an afterlife. The poor, who could not afford such a case, used matting, cloth or leather instead.

Jewellery discovered in tombs such as those of the Egyptian pharaohs

DEPARTED LONDONERS

In 1867 the Royal Society of Arts began displaying commemorative plaques on the London homes of deceased public figures as an 'instructive mode of beguiling a somewhat dull and not very rapid progress through the streets'. The first, to the poet Lord Byron, was at 24 Holles Street, since demolished.

The blue glaze finish introduced in 1937 became standard only after the Second World War. To qualify for a plaque a famed resident of London must be 100 years old or have been dead for 20 years.

OLDEST SURVIVING POTTERY PLAQUE, 1875, COMMEMORATING THE POET JOHN DRYDEN, WHO LIVED IN GERRARD STREET, LONDON

suggests that the dead were buried in their best clothes for their voyage to the 'other world'. In medieval Europe bodies were sometimes dressed in monks' habits to help to ensure the salvation of souls. For the same reason burial inside or close to churches was also popular. Best clothes are often favoured for dressing bodies, but night clothes are also used, emphasising the traditional belief that death is a form of sleep. Indeed, the word 'cemetery' has its roots in the ancient Greek for 'sleeping place'.

Food remains from prehistoric tombs suggest that funeral feasting is as ancient as burial itself. The Greeks celebrated funerals with meals and games. In Ireland, the traditional feast for survivors is called a 'wake', from a Germanic word for 'watch', and is held on the eve of the funeral.

Eating in the company of the dead may relate to a late medieval custom known as 'sin-eating', in which the sins of the dead were believed to be shared among the survivors. In most cultures the funeral feast takes place after the burial, with the mourners resuming everyday life in one another's company.

By around 1000 BC in Britain burial had been almost completely replaced by cremation, with the body placed on wooden pyres. The Greeks, Romans, Celts and Nordic peoples, from whom most of our modern customs originate, all used cremation as well as burial at various times. The Orthodox Jewish religion continues to forbid cremation, since it believes in the eventual resurrection of the body on the coming of the Messiah.

With the rise of Christianity, the belief in resurrection became widespread, and cremation virtually disappeared across Europe. But worries about the insanitary conditions caused by overflowing cemeteries in European towns led to its revival during the late 19th century.

COMMEMORATING THE DEAD
Mausoleums and monuments

The pyramids of Egypt, constructed from around 2600 BC to house the tombs of the pharaohs, are magnificent tributes to the dead. The great edifice that lent the mausoleum its name, however, was the tomb of Mausolos, ruler of Caria, at Halicarnassus (now Bodrum in Turkey), built in the 4th century BC. One of the Seven Wonders of the World, it was destroyed between the 11th and 15th centuries, probably by an earthquake.

Britain's earliest stone structures to contain the dead were communal burial

DARK DAY *Dressed in black, pallbearers of 1914 mourn the passing of a friend. Since the Middle Ages, coffins made of wood have been favoured over those shaped in stone or lead.*

sites such as the West Kennet Long Barrow in Wiltshire, which dates from around 3400 BC. At their simplest, memorials in British churchyards consisted of compact piles of earth marked by a wooden 'grave-rail', a board on two posts bearing the deceased's name.

Funerary monuments erected by the major roads leading to Roman cities featured portrait busts and inscriptions. Less eminent individuals were accorded more modest versions of these early headstones. Similarly, urban cemeteries built in Europe in the 19th century were laid out with large monuments on their main paths, less showy headstones behind and unmarked paupers' graves far from the eyes of the casual visitor.

THE COLOURS OF DEATH
Sombre black, pure white

The ancients thought that death was contagious. Wearing black helped to make mourners invisible to malevolent spirits that might seek them out. The Greeks wore black, while for the Chinese and Japanese white is the traditional hue of mourning, possibly because it is the colour of undyed cloth and therefore indicates humility and sorrow. In Iran, however, people believe that light blue will ward off the 'evil eye'.

In Europe, black has been a mourning colour since the late Middle Ages.

BLUE FOR YOU *Music reflects a mourner's sombre mood at a 'jazz funeral' in the French quarter of New Orleans and, as in ancient times, celebrates the deceased's life.*

Wealthy 19th-century families used it extensively, with black festoons hung at the threshold of the home, black coffins covered with black palls, and walls and beds draped in black cloth. Black mourning dress and veils were customary, often embellished with jewellery made of jet. Servants wore black, while carriages were garlanded with it. And not all was for show: Edwardian girls had black ribbons threaded through the edging on their underwear for months after a family bereavement. Poorer people wore 'favours'—ribbons on the lapel or bound around the arm—or other black accessories such as shawls.

The Christian dead are commonly buried in white, reflecting the belief that Jesus was entombed in a plain linen shroud. The practice was originally influenced by images of the medieval Dance of Death, showing bodies draped in white fabric. White, often associated in the Old Testament with innocence and purity, also symbolises hope for a joyful afterlife.

DEPARTURE SYMBOLS

• Until Victorian times Christians marked the site of a death by cutting a cross in the soil or turf—hence 'X marks the spot'. Since then, the traditional purifying presence of the cross has been supplied by funeral flowers.

• Across Europe from Roman times until the 18th century, the symbol of death was the skull and crossbones, or the skeleton of King Death with his dart and empty hourglass. Both indicated that a life had ended.

FOOD AND DRINK

Finding food was the most urgent daily need of early humans. To bring down game such as lions and mammoths, and to catch small birds and fish, humans developed inventive techniques and tools. Among the first to be learned were those of butchery, well refined by 5000 BC when, in what is now West Sussex, Boxgrove Man used flint knives to butcher rhino and wild horse.

People lived in small nomadic groups. While the men hunted, the women and children gathered nuts and seeds, berries, shellfish, honey and fungi. With fire came the discovery of cooking, first roasting, then slower cooking in the embers or on the edge of the fire until cooking pots were invented around 10000 BC in Japan.

At about this time the climate became milder, making plant life more variable. Hunter-gatherers began to supplement their diet with wild grasses such as wheat and barley. In the Middle East the first farmers were probably inspired to settle down and cultivate crops after noticing how discarded seeds and roots later germinated and sprouted. Stone Age farmers discovered pulses, which they ate as a kind of porridge, enlivened by plants such as dandelions. They learnt to domesticate sheep and goats, developing new, more docile breeds of these and other animals, and discovered how to use the fermentation process in brewing and bread-making.

The ancients found that yields declined if crops were always grown on the same ground. By the 1st century AD the Romans were alternating

crops with pasture to restore the soil's fertility. In medieval England, where fields were divided into strips, peasants planted legumes and cereals and left the land fallow one year in three. They realised that legumes invigorate the soil, without knowing how they capture nitrogen from the air.

Bread, cheese, beef and ale were the basic diet, ale being the drink of all ages and classes except for the aristocracy, who drank wine. With no root crops to feed animals in winter, creatures were killed in autumn and their meat salted. Even townspeople kept livestock : cows were shackled, but pigs wandered at will, feeding on rubbish.

By the 15th century the trade in precious spices was offering vast profits, particularly to Arab and Jewish merchants. European rulers wanting to master the trade routes financed voyages of discovery that opened up new worlds. Spanish and Portuguese explorers brought back to Europe exotic foods they had encountered in the Americas, including potatoes, tomatoes, maize, peppers and chocolate—although it sometimes took centuries for people to accept they were not poisonous. As empires were built, standards of living improved, and from the 1650s demand from the more prosperous classes for expensive goods such as coffee, tea and sugar burgeoned.

Between 1760 and 1820 Britain's open land was enclosed by the wealthy. Growing conditions were improved and new implements such as the seed drill dramatically increased agricultural productivity. As factories were established their workers, no longer able to grow their own food, increased the market for cheap produce. But the middle classes sought variety. From the 1840s railways revolutionised the quantity and quality of food available in the cities. Advances were made in food preservation and steamships brought in canned and frozen meat from around the world.

THE STORY OF FARMING
Tilling the soil

Farming began where wild wheat and barley grew abundantly—the Zagros mountains of Iraq, the Taurus ranges of Turkey and the valleys of Jordan. About 12000 years ago, farmers learnt to till the soil with simple draw-hoes made of hooked branches of wood, their points hardened in the fire.

In the fertile plains of Mesopotamia cereal crops brought prosperity. Instead of just supporting those who tilled it, the land could feed many. At Sumer, in the southern part of the region, farmers developed a seed drill for planting seed in rows—thousands of years before the birth of Jethro Tull, the English agriculturist credited with inventing it in 1701. The Sumerian device made a groove in the soil, the seed trickling into it through a funnel and tube.

After inventing the plough, probably during the 4th millennium BC, the Sumerians were able to break up and sow vast new areas. These first 'scratch ploughs' consisted of a heavy stick that dragged along the soil, scraping a shallow furrow. One person pulled the stick while another walked behind to guide the point, driving it as deeply into the ground as possible. By 3000 BC a more efficient plough had been devised which could be pulled by two oxen.

But heavier, damp soils required more powerful ploughs. These were in

AUTUMN TASK *With a basket full of seed, a medieval peasant sows next year's crop. Broadcast sowing required a steady pace and hand, otherwise the crop would be patchy.*

use in China around 200 BC, but only appeared in north-eastern Europe in the 6th century. They had three working parts: the coulter, which cut vertically into the ground; the ploughshare, which cut horizontally through the ground at grassroots level; and the mouldboard behind the two blades, turning the sods neatly over. Pulled by a team of six or eight oxen, they enabled farmers to clear virgin land for agriculture. As a result, food production and populations both increased sharply.

Centuries later the huge plains of the American Midwest inspired breakthroughs in farming equipment, which transformed the prairies into the granary of the USA. The English inventor Robert Ransome devised an all-iron plough in 1808, but the steel plough with an all-in-one share and mouldboard was the creation of an Illinois

MACHINE SOWING *From the mid 19th century the seed drill helped to revolutionise farming practices. Unlike the haphazard method of broadcast sowing, the drill dropped the seeds in straight lines and at regular intervals.*

HARD LABOUR *An Egyptian farmer of about 2000 BC pushes down on his simple wooden plough. The soil would still have been damp from the flooding of the River Nile.*

blacksmith, John Deere, in 1837. In 1892 John Froehlich of Iowa built the first successful petrol-powered tractor.

To cut their grain, early farmers used flint-toothed sickles made of wood or bone. During the 1st century AD farmers in Gaul devised a mechanical reaper, but the Romans preferred to put their slaves to work gathering the harvest. The reaper fell out of use and labourers persevered with sickles. The Reverend Patrick Bell of Scotland designed a mechanical reaper in 1826, but Cyrus McCormick, a Virginia farmer, built a more successful machine in 1840.

For thousands of years people beat the grain from the ears using a flail—a club-shaped head attached to a short handle by a chain or cord. The process of separating the grain from its surrounding chaff was a laborious one. In ancient Syria ears of wheat were toasted on flat, heated stones so that the chaff became brittle enough to be loosened by thrashing and rubbing.

A threshing machine to replace the flail was designed by the Scottish millwright Andrew Meikle in 1787. It consisted of a rotating drum shod with metal beaters, turning inside a metal

THROUGH THE MILL

• As a way of humiliating Samson while he was their prisoner, the Philistines forced him to grind grain using a stone quern—work normally carried out by slave women.

• Wheat was the driving force of the Roman Empire. North Africa was the empire's granary, and on two occasions Julius Caesar attempted to invade Britain for its wheat, which was already being cultivated in the south-east by 331 BC.

FURROW POWER *In the early 1700s Jethro Tull tried to improve the farmer's lot with a wheeled plough. Unlike the Egyptian model, Tull's had four sharp blades or coulters.*

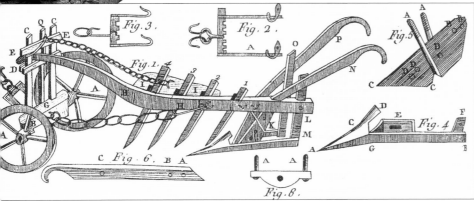

screen. The corn was fed between drum and screen. British agricultural workers opposed its introduction, destroying many machines during riots in 1830.

In 1836 J. Hascall and Hiram Moore of Michigan, USA, patented a machine to harvest, thresh, clean and bag the grain. Their horse-drawn 'combination harvester' did meet with some success, but it was almost a century before the combine harvester was established.

The All-Crop harvester, produced by the Allis Chalmers Company in 1935, was cheap to buy and could be pulled by a low-powered tractor. Self-propelled combines were developed in the 1940s. Together with grain dryers, combines removed much of the uncertainty from harvesting, eliminating the need to stack the harvested wheat in 'stooks' in the field to dry.

EARS OF WHEAT
The essential grain

All the 20000 varieties of wheat grown today descend from primitive grasses that grew wild thousands of years ago. Among these first wild wheats was *Triticum monococcum* or einkorn, 'one grain', which originated in Turkey. Another, emmer wheat, spread from present-day Iraqi Kurdistan to Egypt.

These were the first cereals to be domesticated, emmer probably around 7000 BC. Emmer was more robust, but

HARVEST TIME *Having cut the fields with sickles, English labourers of the early 1300s continue with the back-breaking work of stacking sheaves of corn.*

was neither very productive nor suitable for bread. Around 8000 years ago it interbred—by chance and by design—with another wild species to produce the high-yielding *Triticum aestivum*, or bread wheat, still in use today. Together with club wheat (*T. compactum*), a softer variety now used for cakes and pastries, it gradually replaced emmer in the Middle East and Europe, although in eastern Europe the growing season was too short for wheat production and rye became the major bread grain.

Flour was first made by hammering the grains between two stones. The result was coarse, gritty and wore down the teeth. Querns were used everywhere that wheat was grown and may have been invented in the Near East. The miller placed the grain in a lower, concave stone, laboriously grinding it with another round or cylindrical stone held in his hand. Around 1100 BC the large, flat upper stone of the quern was fitted with a handle that was rotated as the grain was fed between the upper and lower stones.

The rotary quern was the ancestor of the animal-driven millstones used in the Middle East from early Biblical times. By the 2nd century BC milling had become a profitable business in Rome. Donkeys were used, blindfolded so they would not be distracted, to turn the stones. When the Romans introduced the water mill throughout their empire, as far north as Hadrian's Wall, they made large-scale, cheap milling possible for the first time.

Wheat did not become a universal food until immigrants from the Crimea introduced the hardy Turkey Red strain—named for its place of origin—into North America in 1874. It adapted so well to the new climate that vast quantities were grown.

OUR DAILY BREAD
The first loaves

Bread has not always been the staff of life. From about 10000 BC Neolithic Britons made hearthcakes by grinding together weed seeds and wild emmer wheat, mixing the meal with water and cooking it on hot stones. Mixtures of flour and water gradually evolved into flatbreads such as Mexican tortillas and Indian chapattis. The first loaf of yeast-raised bread was probably created accidentally by mixing flour with ale rather than water to make dough, or from yeast spores in the air settling on dough before baking, particularly if the bakery was also a brewery.

In Gaul, Spain and Britain people developed liquid raising agents or leavens from beer, while in Greece and Italy, grape juice or white wine were

HOT WORK *Egyptian slaves bake bread in 2250 BC. By 2000 BC the Egyptians had learnt how to produce loaves with better keeping qualities by sprouting and drying grain before baking.*

used. Greek craftsman bakers took their skills to Rome, and by 30 BC there were some 300 bakeries in the city. Among the many breads produced in Roman bakeries was a flat bread topped with pickled fish and onions—the earliest form of pizza.

Enriched breads were also popular with the Romans, while toast may have its origins in an English medieval dish made by toasting white bread, which was then soaked in a white wine, reheated and served with almond milk. The croissant originated in Budapest in 1686. Night-shift bakers heard hostile Turks tunnelling into the city in preparation for an attack, and raised the

THE SANDWICH GAMBLE

The sandwich takes its name from the notorious British gambler John Montagu, Earl of Sandwich. In 1762, at the Beef Steak Club in Covent Garden, London, Montagu spent 24 hours gambling without a break. He asked for meat and slices of bread to be brought to him so that he could eat without interrupting his game. The convenient result appealed to London's fashionable society.

alarm. The bakers saved Budapest from invasion, and they baked the crescent-shaped roll to represent the symbol on the vanquished Ottomans' flag. The roll came to Paris in 1770 with Marie Antoinette, when she arrived for her marriage to the future Louis XVI.

By this time, new fermentation methods using milk, salt and barm, a yeasty foam from brewing beer, was producing finer loaves. In 1840, the secretary of the Austrian embassy in Paris established France's first Viennese-style bakery, where fine wheat flour, milk and water produced the long loaves that became classic french bread.

POPULAR PASTA
Food for the poor

The story that Marco Polo brought noodles from China to Italy 700 years ago is unlikely to be true. The Chinese and Italians probably developed pasta independently, and the Italian form may date back to the 7th century BC. Recipes for lasagne existed in Roman times, but pasta went out of favour with the fall of the empire.

In about the 8th century AD the Arabs reintroduced it, serving it with fish or vinegar-based sauces, and from the 11th century it was enjoyed with rich creams and cheeses brought to

GOLDEN OPPORTUNITY *A hungry family tucks into a pasta dinner at home in Naples in 1830. Three years earlier Giulia Buitoni, encouraged by the increasing popularity of pasta, had pawned her gold jewellery to start a pasta business.*

Europe by returning Crusaders. Shops in Italy sold pasta from 1400 and in 1824 the first commercial pasta factory opened. Pasta remained a southern dish until the country was unified. Soldiers of the nationalist leader Giuseppe Garibaldi, who captured Sicily and Naples in 1860, then persuaded northern Italians of its desirability.

Noodles have been used in Chinese and South-east Asian cooking from about 1100 BC, but in China they were also considered a food of the poor until AD 1500. The popular Chinese noodle dish chop suey did not come from China at all although it was named from the Cantonese *tsaap sui*, 'mixed pieces'. It was created in 1896 in New York by the chef of the Chinese goodwill emissary Li Hong Zhang, who was tired of serving American food at banquets.

ADVERTISEMENT FOR BUITONI PASTA, ITALY, 1930S

CULTIVATING RICE
The sacred grain

The most important staple food for the majority of the world's population is not wheat but rice, the seeds of another grass. The first known rice gatherers were the Neolithic Hoabinhian people, who lived in southern China and north Vietnam from about 10000 to 4000 BC.

Evidence of cultivated rice dates back to around 6000 BC: grains of that period were found in the remains of an ancient village at Hemudu in Zhejiang, China. By 4000 BC, cultivation of long-grain and short-grain rice had become well established in China and was just beginning in India, where rice and barley later became known as the 'two immortal sons of heaven'.

The word 'rice', derived from the Aramaic *ourouzza*, passed to European languages via the Greek *oruzon* and the Arabic *arozz*. The Arabs introduced rice into their Spanish territories from AD 711, but it did not spread elsewhere in Europe until 1468, when Spaniards planted arborio rice, the short-grain variety that became synonymous with

GATHERING THE GRAIN *In China rice has been harvested by hand for thousands of years. Leaving rice at the end of a meal is considered a sign of disrespect for the hard work required to gather the grain.*

risotto, at Pisa in Italy. Rice came to England in the Middle Ages, in the spice ships from the Orient, and was a precious ingredient, used mostly in puddings. The 19th-century colonial influence of Indian cooking and the expansion of tastes to embrace Eastern cuisine in the 20th century has made rice popular in Britain.

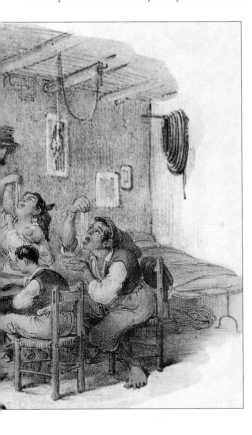

THE MYSTERY OF MAIZE
From corn on the cob to popcorn

The most plentiful cereal after rice, maize originated in about 7200 BC in Mexico, Honduras and Guatemala. Maize does not exist in the wild, and exactly how the ancient peoples of Central America managed to grow it is not known. However, the answer may lie in a wild grass known as teosinte, discovered in Mexico in 1973. Farmers may have tried to crossbreed teosinte

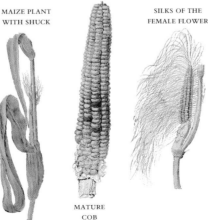

MAIZE PLANT WITH SHUCK

SILKS OF THE FEMALE FLOWER

MATURE COB

with other grasses to produce *Zea mays*, or maize, or it could have accidentally mutated from a plant that was already domesticated. In the 1940s, archaeologists working at Bat Cave, New Mexico, found 5000-year-old corn cobs. These early cobs—not kernels—were just 1 cm (½ in) long.

The first European contact with maize came in 1492. On his arrival in Cuba Christopher Columbus received two sacred gifts: tobacco and the grain known in Haitian as *maïs*. It was first eaten in Italy around 1650 as polenta, a dish previously made with wheat flour, which had sustained the Roman army.

Sweetcorn, one of the most popular varieties of maize, was grown by Native Americans from at least the early 17th century, but was not widely cultivated until after the American Civil War. The Native Americans also introduced popcorn—they believed that inside each kernel was imprisoned a tiny demon that made it pop when heated.

HEARTY OATS
Cheap and nutritious

Farmers first noticed wild oats as weeds growing in wheat fields. They were cultivated in Germany, Denmark and Switzerland in the 1st millennium BC, and reached Britain in the Iron Age. Oats thrived in such cold, wet, upland areas as Scotland. Long before the Romans arrived in Britain the grain became a staple, cooked as porridge.

Not everyone appreciated the grain. The Roman writer Pliny despised the Germanic tribes for eating what he and his contemporaries regarded as animal fodder. In his *Dictionary of the English Language* of 1755 the English writer Dr Johnson defined oats as 'a grain...fed to horses, fine live-stock and to men in Scotland'. James Boswell, Johnson's friend and biographer, responded: 'Yes, and that is why in England you have such fine horses and in Scotland we have such fine people.'

CORN ON THE COB *Since Guatemalan Indians first cultivated maize, or 'Indian corn', the plants have needed a little help to survive. The tough shuck around the ear must be unwrapped and the seeds—the kernels that we eat—then sown by hand.*

MEAT FROM THE WILD
Game birds and animals

Wild animals and birds, eaten raw, gave humans their first taste of meat. Two million years BC *Australopithicus* was an African scavenger supplementing a diet of roots, berries, nuts and termites by hunting small game or fishing. By 400 000 BC early humans may have been using fire to cook pieces of venison.

To hunter–gatherer societies, 'home' was where game such as woolly mammoth, long-horned buffalo and deer could be pursued. In Britain hunters relied on the red and roe deer, not only as a source of food, but also for their antlers, which could be made into tools. Elk, ox and pigs roamed the vast forests that covered the country, and ducks and geese were also plentiful.

The Romans introduced game parks to breed fallow deer, which had reached Europe from Anatolia. In England the least desirable parts of a deer, such as the tongue and offal, were used in a dish of mixed meats called 'umbles'—hence the expression 'to eat humble pie'. Originally from Spain, the rabbit was introduced into Britain by the Romans, who prized it as a delicacy. They raised

CATCHING A RABBIT
WITH A FERRET, EARLY 1300S

rabbits and hares in 'hare gardens', but these fell into decay with the end of the Roman occupation.

Left to fend for themselves, rabbits proved easy prey for wild animals and died out. But when they were reintroduced from France in the 12th century there were fewer predators, and rabbits that escaped from warrens established a flourishing wild population. Only the young were known as 'rabbits'; older animals were 'coneys'. Settlers named Coney Island near New York after its abundant colonies of the creature.

PLUMP POULTRY
Chicken and other birds

The wild red jungle fowl, the ancestor of our barnyard chicken, was probably domesticated in India around 2000 BC.

Originally a sacred bird and provider of omens, the chicken's culinary potential was discovered by the Greeks in the 5th century BC. Celts from Gaul probably brought the first chickens to Britain during the 1st century BC. Roman recipes were used, such as a stuffing for roast chicken which included ginger, shredded brains, eggs and pine nuts. The Romans also introduced the guinea fowl, but it disappeared from Europe in the Germanic invasions following the fall of Rome. It only returned in the 1530s, exported to France by merchants from the Guinea coast of Africa.

Around 1523 the turkey came to Europe from Central America. In Honduras, Spanish explorers bemused by the strange, dewlapped bird called it a 'guineafowl chickenpeacock'. The English confused its origins with those of the Turkish merchants who first brought it to northern Europe. While most other New World foods caught on slowly, by 1570 the turkey was already ideal Christmas fare.

HOME OF THE HAMBURGER

The medieval Tatar nomads of the Eurasian steppes tenderised slabs of beef by keeping them under their saddles. Before eating the meat raw, they added salt, pepper and onion juice—the original steak tartare.

In Germany this evolved into grilled Hamburg steak, a dish that emigrants took to the USA. In 1836 'hamburger steak' was on the world's first printed menu, at Delmonico's in New York. No one knows who thought of serving hamburgers in buns, but the dish was probably introduced at such fairs as the St Louis World's Fair in 1904.

MARKET DAY *Shoppers in London's Leadenhall Market in 1865 could not expect the choice offered there 500 years earlier, when swans were on sale. Wild or domestic, birds, rabbits and hares were the main source of fresh meat for most folk.*

BIG GAME *To subdue such a fiery creature as the aurochs, Neolithic people barely fed those they captured and kept them closely penned. Only then did they discover the powerful beast's potential for pulling ploughs as well as threshing grain.*

PRIME BEEF
On the hoof

The fierce horned aurochs, hunted down by prehistoric people with bows and arrows or spears, was the ancestor of today's placid Friesians, Herefords and Charolais. The massive beast was the last major animal to be tamed as a source of food, power and leather, but could be found wild in parts of eastern Europe until the mid 1600s.

Cattle, which were domesticated in about 6000 BC in Turkey or Macedonia, were probably only brought to Britain by farmers from northern Gaul in the 4th millennium BC. Beef was the country's favourite meat from the time of the Roman occupation. The long working lives and poor winter diets of cattle meant that their flesh was rather dry until crops such as Dutch clover were introduced in the 17th century. At this time the Yeomen of the Guard were nicknamed 'beefeaters'—a term first used for well-fed servants.

LAMB AND MUTTON
Middle Eastern meat

To the first farmers the wild sheep was an attractive prospect for taming. As well as being a source of wool and meat, it provided fat, which was useful for cooking, medicinal salves and as tallow for rushlights. Sheep were probably first domesticated in Iraq around 9000 BC, a process helped, no doubt, by their natural gregariousness.

Around 3500 BC—in the same period that sheep were introduced into Britain from Gaul—shepherds founded one of the world's oldest civilisations in Mesopotamia. The Sumerians had some 200 words for the creature, including fattened sheep, mountain sheep and fat-tailed sheep.

Middle Eastern methods of cooking lamb arrived in Europe during the Crusades. Shish kebab, Turkish for 'roast mutton on a skewer', reached the West from Turkey, where soldiers impaled chunks of lamb on their swords, roasting them over open fires.

SPRING LAMB *In the Middle Ages wool meant wealth and ewes' milk featured heavily in most people's diets.*

FRESH FIELDS *Roman shepherds move their flock, just as the first herdsmen had 8000 years before.*

REARING PORK
Fattened for the table

Because they need to be raised on those foodstuffs that were an important part of the human diet, such as acorns, nuts and cooked grains, pigs were tamed much later than sheep. The wild boar of Asia and Europe was first domesticated in Turkey around 7000 BC.

Britons were hunting wild pigs by 5000 BC. The more docile creatures we know today were originally bred

WINTER SLAUGHTER *Rich landowners could afford to feed their livestock all year round, but most people killed their animals in the autumn, then salted or smoked the meat.*

from domesticated boars in China and Iraq around 2900 BC, when Neolithic people began to have surpluses of food, enabling them to breed pigs for their succulent meat and valuable fat and skin. Their bristles, too, were made into brushes—it has been said that the only part of the pig not used is its squeak.

The Romans created extravagant dishes from their swine, including a version of foie gras made with the liver of pigs force-fed on dried figs and honey. But pigs were also the meat of the peasantry, and even city dwellers kept them. From ancient Greece to 19th-century New York, pigs roamed the streets feeding on refuse.

After the Norman Conquest the English adopted French derivative names for their meat. Once served on the tables of the ruling classes, animals were not known by their native Saxon names pig, ox, calf and sheep, but as pork, beef, veal and mutton.

COLOURFUL COLLECTION *An illustration from a 1920s seed packet shows the variety of vegetables available to the amateur American grower. Sealed seed packets date from 1816 and were first sold by the Shaker community, who guaranteed fresh seeds every year. Until then seeds were sold by weight.*

GARLIC, LEEKS AND ONIONS
The poor man's spices

The pungent tastes and odours of the onion or allium family have long been both praised and decried. One Turkish myth relates that when Satan first set foot on Earth, onions sprang up from his right footprint, garlic from his left.

In fact onions probably originated in northern Asia and the Fertile Crescent and have been cultivated for 5000 years. In Mesopotamia and Egypt raw onions and bread were the everyday diet. With their white bulbs and long green stems they were more like spring onions.

From the late Middle Ages onions were a mainstay of European cooking. They were probably introduced by the Romans, who were keen onion-eaters. The abundance of wild onions in North America is recorded in the name of a city, Chicago, derived from the Native American word for 'onion odour'.

The rations of the Egyptian slaves who built the pyramids included garlic as well as chickpeas and onions, but the bulbs probably originate from central Asia. The Romans, who called garlic the 'stinking rose', brought it to Britain in AD 43. Leeks are believed to derive from a Near Eastern variety of garlic. The first mention of their cultivation is in Mesopotamia in 2100 BC. They were adopted by the Welsh as their national symbol following a battle against the Saxons in AD 640. During the fighting, Welshmen wore leeks in their caps to distinguish themselves from the enemy.

ROOT VEGETABLES
Buried treasures

Because edible roots were among the first of mankind's foods, their origins are often obscure. The radish has been cultivated for so long that its true origins are lost and its wild ancestor has long disappeared, but from China to the Mediterranean it was grown as a staple food plant. Radishes came to Britain with the Romans. Larger, white varieties were commonly used in sauces for meat.

Domesticated in prehistoric times in its native Mediterranean region, beetroot was originally more like today's chard. The Greeks ate only the leaves, but turned the roots into a general tonic and blood cleanser. Beetroot as it is now known was first propagated in northern Europe during the 16th century.

The wild carrot of Afghanistan was small, thin and purple or yellow. Purple carrots may have been cultivated in Asia Minor in the 8th century BC. Neither the Greeks nor the Romans were impressed by the vegetable, although the Romans brought carrots to Britain.

The Arabs took carrot seeds to Spain, from where the vegetable reached the Netherlands during the Spanish conquests of the 15th century. There the

PERUVIAN TUBERS *The potato was so important to the Incas that they measured time by how long it took to cook one. Initially Europeans were more suspicious, blaming it for a multitude of evils from leprosy to wind.*

Dutch first produced a sweet-tasting orange variety by 1510. Around 1558 Flemish weavers escaping persecution by the Spanish brought orange carrots with them to England. At the court of James I their feathery tops were prized as decorations for hats.

High in the Andean mountains, where maize could not grow, the potato plant was first cultivated 5000 years ago. The starchy tubers were a staple food for the Incas, and Spanish conquistadores took the potato home with them in 1539. Its journey to Britain was more circuitous but began in 1586 when the English admiral Sir Francis Drake returned home from the Caribbean. He

CRIES OF LONDON *Having bought carrots and turnips from a market such as the one at Covent Garden, hawkers sell their wares to city folk.*

collected his provisions, including some potatoes, from the Colombian port of Cartagena, before picking up settlers from Virginia. One of these gave tubers to the herbalist John Gerard.

Gerard assumed the plant was from North America, though in fact it did not reach that continent until 1719, from Ireland. He called it the Virginia potato to distinguish it from the sweet variety, known in Britain since 1565 when it was brought back from the Caribbean by the admiral Sir John Hawkins. The word 'potato' comes from *batata*, the Taino name for the sweet potato.

As it was the first cultivated crop not to be grown from seed, and because it reached maturity underground, the potato was feared as the devil's work. It was also thought tasteless and became established in Europe only after the French Revolution, when French chefs adopted foods with proletarian flavours.

CABBAGES AND THEIR KIN
Green goodness

Native to the coastal regions of northern Europe, including Britain, the curly leafed wild or sea cabbage was first eaten in prehistoric times. Cabbages, named from the Latin *caput*, 'head', were much appreciated by the Romans. A high demand for the vegetable initially made it too expensive for all but the wealthy. The emperor Claudius

---

MYSTERIOUS MUSHROOMS

Wild fungi must have been a useful source of food for hunter-gatherers. Mushrooms and truffles were delicacies in Mesopotamia by 1800 BC and in Rome. The Romans were mystified by their natural history. The ancients thought that, being rootless, fungi grew where lightning struck or were an 'evil ferment of the earth'.

The Japanese were cultivating shiitake mushrooms some 2000 years ago, but Olivier de Serres, agronomist to the French king Louis XIV, began mushroom cultivation in the West, using species still common in supermarkets today.

---

once called upon the Senate to vote on whether there was a better dish than cabbage and corned beef. The Senate dutifully decreed that there was not.

All other relatives of the cabbage are variations bred to favour certain characteristics—hence Mark Twain's description of the cauliflower as 'nothing but a cabbage with a college education'. Originally from Cyprus, the cauliflower was known to the Romans but reached Britain from France only in the 16th century.

Brussels sprouts, first described by the Dutch botanist Dodonaeus in 1554, have more mysterious origins, although the Belgians believe Roman legions brought them to the Low Countries. The British did not discover brussels sprouts until the 17th century, when they quickly became popular.

LEAFY VARIETIES *Lettuces and cabbages were probably first bred to grow in tightly wrapped, rounded heads in monastery gardens during the late Middle Ages.*

GREEN LEAVES
Salad plants

Gardeners with plots full of lettuces that have gone to seed would recognise the plant grown around 710 BC by King Merodach-Baladan of Babylon. With its leaves sprouting from a tall central stalk, lettuce was known to the Greeks as 'asparagus', then the general term for stalk-like plants. Egyptian reliefs show pointed lettuces nearly 1 m (3 ft) tall.

The Latin name, *Lactuca*, 'milky', refers to the sap, which the Romans thought helped nursing mothers. They also believed in the vegetable's soporific effects—as did Beatrix Potter when she described the Flopsy Bunnies falling asleep after a surfeit of lettuce. The word 'salad' is derived from *sal*, 'salt'. The Romans liked to preserve their green leaves in brine, then wash them and pickle them in salt and vinegar.

Watercress, which Romans thought helped consumers to make bold decisions, made its first appearance on a European menu at the court of the French king Charles VI in the 14th century. The garden cress traditionally grown with mustard came from Persia and spread to the gardens of India, Syria, Greece and Egypt.

FORBIDDEN FRUIT
Appetising apples

The Book of Genesis does not identify which fruit Eve tempted Adam to eat in the Garden of Eden, but medieval Old Testament scholars presumed it was the familiar apple of orchards everywhere. Thereafter it became known in Latin as *pomum*, 'the fruit of fruits'. Before being renamed, many new fruits and vegetables, such as lemons, tomatoes, potatoes and aubergines, were called apples.

Pips dropped by travellers helped to spread apples from their native southeastern Europe and south-western Asia. Carbonised fruit found at Çatal Hüyük in Anatolia has been dated to 6500 BC, while dried apples were an important food for prehistoric Swiss lake dwellers.

Neolithic Britons picked wild crab apples, but sweeter, cultivated varieties were brought by the Romans. One of the earliest named apples was the pearmain, first recorded about AD 1200. Large, hard apples used for cooking were called costards, and the men who sold them in the street were soon known as 'costermongers'. During the 16th century a sharp increase in apple imports so alarmed Henry VIII that he dispatched his chief fruiterer, Richard Harris, to France to learn grafting techniques. On his return, Harris founded the first of Kent's apple orchards at Tenham Manor.

ABUNDANT HARVEST *Villagers gather the fruit from a French orchard of the late 15th century. At this time most fruit was considered indigestible unless cooked.*

THE PERFECT PEAR *In medieval England aniseed-flavoured roast pears were often served after a rich meal.*

A TASTE OF THE ORIENT

- Apricots first grew wild in China and were cultivated as early as 2200 BC. The ancient Greeks called them 'golden eggs of the Sun'. Peaches, which are also native to China, were known from the 5th century BC.
- The kiwi fruit was the original Chinese gooseberry, named after its place of origin. Farmers in New Zealand changed the name when they tried to introduce it into the anticommunist American market of the 1950s.

CHINESE PAINTING OF PEACHES, 1643

PEARS AND PLUMS
Orchard delights

Native to Asia Minor, pears have been cultivated for more than 3000 years. The Greeks and the Romans increased the number of varieties, but two of our most common pears are more recent introductions. John Stair, a Berkshire schoolteacher, raised a new type of pear in 1769, but it was named after the man who distributed it, a Mr Williams. The origins of the comice are grander: it was first grown in the gardens of Prince Louis-Napoleon Bonaparte in 1849.

The common European plum began as a hybrid of the tiny sloe and other forms native to Asia Minor. Pliny, the Roman writer, described a 'great crowd of plums' in Rome's orchards, including a Syrian variety known as the 'plum of Damascus' or damson. The Romans introduced improved varieties into Britain, as well as cultivated cherries.

In 1725 Sir William Gage brought back a French plum known as the *reine-claude* as a compliment to the wife of King Francis I. Thereafter it was known in English as the green Gage's plum, soon contracted to the greengage.

TROPICAL BOUNTY
Exotic flavours

When, in 1493, Christopher Columbus landed on Guadaloupe he discovered pineapples being cultivated extensively, as they had been in Central and South America from the 1st millennium BC. Carib Indians, who called the fruit *anana*, meaning 'excellence' or 'fragrance', hung them outside their huts as a sign of welcome, but also grew hedges of the spiky leaved plants to deter strangers.

The flavour and fragrance of the fruit 'astonished and delighted' the Spanish adventurers and those who received the *pinas de las Indias* that Columbus sent to Spain. A courtier to King Ferdinand described the reaction to the one fruit that survived the journey: 'In appearance, shape and colour, this scale-coated fruit resembles the pine cone; but in softness is the melon's equal; in flavour it surpasses all garden fruits. To it the king awards the palm.'

The first British-grown pineapple was presented to Charles II in 1672. Thereafter pineapples carved in stone became an architectural motif, gracing the gates and roof corners of the wealthy as symbols of hospitality.

Wild banana fruits are hard and full of seeds, so the palm was first cultivated for its fibrous leaves, useful for thatching and for wrapping food for cooking,

ADVERTISEMENT, EARLY 1900S

while the flowers and soft cores were eaten as vegetables. It is not known when the banana became edible and soft enough to be enjoyed as a fruit.

Grown in the Indus Valley before 3000 BC, the banana reached the Near East and Egypt by the 7th century AD, when the Koran identified it, not the apple, as the Biblical forbidden fruit. In 1482 Portuguese explorers encountered bananas growing along the coast of West Africa and adopted a version of their local name.

The first bunch of bananas seen in Britain came from Bermuda in 1633. Londoners marvelled at the sight of it ripening in a herbalist's shop. With the arrival of steamships in the 19th century, it became possible to import the perishable fruit from the West Indies.

A TASTE OF SUMMER
Berries and currants

The warm, dry climate that Britain enjoyed after 2500 BC allowed its early inhabitants to pick naturally sweet wild strawberries and raspberries, although the former were hard to gather, being even smaller than today's wild berries.

Strawberry cultivation began in the 13th century, but the large, modern fruit appeared only in 1819, the result of crossbreeding a small, sweet, scarlet fruit from Virginia with a pale Chilean variety tasting of pineapple.

Because the wild fruit is so full of flavour, raspberries were not cultivated in Britain until 1548. Gardeners also began to plant red and black currants, which they called raisins, thinking they were the fresh version of dried currants.

VEGETABLE FRUITS
Colourful ingredients

Cherry-sized tomatoes grew as weeds in the maize fields of Central America during the Stone Age. In 1519 Spanish explorers in Mexico came across a rich choice of varieties of Aztec *tomatl*. The first fruits to reach Europe in 1522 were probably yellow-orange, hence their Italian name *pomo d'oro*, 'golden apple'.

There is no record of their arrival in Britain, but in 1559 the Elizabethan statesman Lord Burleigh was growing tomatoes as ornamental plants. At first they were called love apples, from the French *pomme d'amour*, a corruption of *pomo dei mori*, 'apple of the Moors'.

Tomatoes were less appreciated as a food. In 1597 the English herbalist John Gerard wrote: 'They yield very little nourishment to the body, and the

ELEGANT EGGPLANT *Introduced to Spain by Arab traders in the Middle Ages, the eggplant or aubergine was thought to cause bad breath, madness, leprosy and even cancer.*

same naught and corrupt.' Tomato sauce crept into English cooking in the early 1800s, but tomatoes were not widely available until the 1880s, and did not become a salad ingredient in Britain until the 20th century.

The aubergine has been eaten in its native India for more than 4000 years. A small, pale brown variety arrived in England in 1587, when its French name, from the Sanskrit *vatimgana*, was adopted. In the USA it was called eggplant after a white, egg-shaped variety.

A PRICKLY PROBLEM *Before the canned fruit appeared in the 1800s, only the rich ate pineapples, which were grown in hothouses or brought by clipper from the West Indies.*

HARVESTING THE WATER

*'Let the waters bring forth abundantly
the moving creature that hath life...'*

GENESIS, CH. 1, V. 20

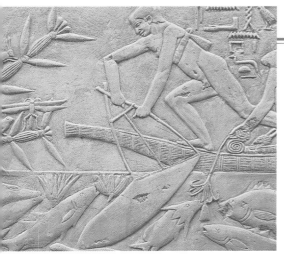

BOUNTY FROM THE NILE *Egyptian fishermen cast their net and barbed hooks, carved in stone relief during the 6th dynasty (2423–2263 BC). The Egyptians exported dried and salted fish to Syria and Palestine.*

Many nomadic peoples regarded fish as too sacred to eat. In some parts of India fish is said to be the food of ghosts; in others it is one of the eight symbols of Buddha. The ancient Celts believed the salmon had an immortal soul. In New Zealand the Maoris return their first-caught fish to the sea so that it can spread good reports about them to other fish, while the Tlingit of Alaska appoint the first halibut of the season as a mighty chief.

FIRST CATCH YOUR FISH

Before primitive peoples hunted or fished they gathered seafood such as oysters, mussels, whelks, crabs and lobsters from shores and shallows. The empty shells became the first coins, jewels and implements.

Bare hands were the earliest fishing 'tackle' until clubs and spears proved to be more effective. During the Palaeolithic era, people fished with barbed spearheads carved from antlers and bound to wooden shafts.

One of humanity's first tools was the gorge—the forerunner of the fish-hook. Used in the Dordogne in France by 25 000 BC, it was a piece of wood, bone or stone that wedged in the gullet of a fish and was attached to a line—initially a vine tendril, later a strand of leather or animal sinew. In about 2000 BC fish-hooks were among the first tools to be made from metal.

By attaching a line to a stick, early anglers invented the fishing rod. For thousands of years, fishing rods were less than 1 m (3 ft) long. The Romans were probably the first to make jointed rods, in the 4th century AD.

Harpoons were used in France and Spain from about 12 000 BC and the more practical bow and arrow followed in Europe around 8000 BC. Early fishermen also used the ancestor of the metal trident, the leister, a spear made from two or three barbed prongs of bone attached to a stick. In Estonia the skeleton of a Mesolithic fish was discovered with a leister prong still stuck in its back.

Basketwork fish traps, possibly the first baskets ever made, were also first fashioned in the Mesolithic period.

Funnel-shaped baskets with a wide entrance allowed the fish to swim in but not out again. Soon after 3000 BC the inhabitants of Oronsay and Oban in Scotland made baskets to take crabs and lobsters from deep waters, but also fished from coracles in inshore waters, using lines to catch sea bream, haddock and skate.

The first fishing nets were made from twisted plant fibre, hair or leather thongs. Inshore fishing with nets began around 8000 BC, but the Greeks were the first to make sturdy boats to

COD

MUSSELS

CRAB

OYSTERS

COCKLES

RAINBOW
TROUT

catch fish at sea, around 7000 BC. During the 4th century BC they also made the first steps towards oyster farming. Noticing that young molluscs attached themselves to pottery shards in the water, the fishermen of Rhodes threw more pieces into the sea.

The Romans were passionate about oysters and made an industry of rearing them. The first recorded oyster farmer was the Roman proconsul Sergius Orata, who laid out artificial beds near Naples in the 1st century AD. Oysters became so popular that they were imported from Britain, prompting the Roman politician and historian Sallust to comment: 'Poor Britons! There is some good in them after all. They have produced an oyster.'

In post-Roman Britain, seafish, which were sacred to the Roman goddess Venus, were customarily eaten on Friday, *Veneris dies*, the 'day of Venus'. As Christianity became more widespread, the Church introduced its own rites. Fish retained its association with Friday, which became a fast day in commemoration of Good Friday.

Fish could be eaten when meat was forbidden, for example during Lent and on fast days, because unlike meat, it was clean and bloodless, and considered to be purer. During the 16th century the reasons behind fast days became more economic than religious—they helped to preserve scarce meat animals and encouraged the ship-building trade.

FISH CUISINE

Parsley and fish were seen as a natural combination by the 12th century, when the writer Alexander Neckham recommended serving fish with a 'green sauce' of parsley, sage, costmary (a wild daisy), dittany (a type of oregano), thyme, garlic and pepper.

Later in the Middle Ages green sauces were associated with newly salted white fish, known as 'green fish'. A medieval recipe for *moules marinière* involved stewing mussels in wine, pepper and minced onion.

In the 19th century frying was seen as a way of masking the smell of stale fish and extending its keeping time. The result became popular as a cheap, handy food for the working poor, especially in London and the industrial North. The first reference to fried fish as a convenience food occurs in Charles Dickens's *Oliver Twist*, serialised in 1837-9, in which he describes a 'fried-fish warehouse' in a dismal alley near the City of London.

In the 1850s and 1860s, fried cod or flat fish was sold with a slice of white bread or a baked potato. Among the claimants to the title 'Oldest Fish and Chip Shop in the World' is Lee's in Manchester. It was established in 1863, but did not serve chips until after 1870, when they were introduced from France.

FISHY FACTS

- The first fish-like creatures appeared in the seas about 450 million years ago.
- Oysters were plentiful enough in Victorian Britain to be thought food for the poor until overexploitation and pollution exhausted the oyster beds.

EATING OYSTERS, 1734

- In the 18th century an overabundance of salmon led to a regulation in the Thames Valley protecting apprentices from having to eat it more than once a week.
- Caviar was once so inexpensive in the USA that in the mid 19th century saloons served it free at lunch counters because its saltiness provoked thirst and increased drinks sales.

CARP

LOBSTER

SPRATS

MACKEREL

PLAICE

HERRING

CATCH OF THE DAY *Town-dwellers in the early 1800s enjoyed few varieties of fish except pickled herring, although country folk could fish in trout streams or gather shellfish. With the advent of refrigeration in the 1830s and the steam trawler in the 1860s, fish could be packed in ice and delivered to local fishmongers.*

JASODA WITH THE
CHILD KRISHNA MILKING
A COW, INDIA,
ABOUT 1900

DAIRY FRESH? A decorous 18th-century milkmaid belies the fact that, until the 19th century, milk was generally dirty, contaminated with tuberculosis and diluted with water—or worse. It was often safer to drink beer rather than milk or water.

A DAILY PINT
The first milk drinkers

Mare's milk was the choice of the first milk drinkers, the nomads of central Asia. Cows were not yet domesticated when herdsmen first learnt to take milk from sheep, goats, asses and horses, soon after 9000 BC.

In Neolithic Britain, where cattle could easily fend for themselves in the forests covering most of the country, cow's milk was commonly drunk, but after the countryside opened up, in the Bronze Age, more sheep and goats were kept and milked.

The taste of sour milk—the result of hot weather and unhygienic containers—would have been familiar. Ancient Europeans drank whey and soured milk, and the Roman writer Tacitus referred to early Germanic tribes living on wild fruit, game and 'solid milk', which had been left to ferment.

Concentrating milk by evaporating it, then sweetening it with sugar, was one way of improving its keeping qualities. A British patent was taken out in 1838, but in 1852 an American named Gail Borden decided to develop his own condensed milk after a rough transatlantic journey during which the ship's two cows became too seasick to be milked. Initially the sweetened drink was unpopular with New Yorkers, who were used to milk whitened with chalk and made 'creamy' by the addition of molasses, but Borden's canned version gradually caught on, especially with soldiers in the American Civil War.

During his investigations into the souring process of wine and beer, the French biologist Louis Pasteur discovered that microorganisms from the air also soured milk, and that they could be destroyed by heating. In 1860 he 'pasteurised' milk for the first time by heating it to a temperature of 125 °C (257 °F), thereby caramelising the sugar to produce a dark-coloured milk. Pasteur later developed a method using lower temperatures and longer heating times, but the 'unnaturalness' of the pasteurisation process delayed its commercial introduction in Britain until the 1890s.

THE CHEESE BOARD
Milk transformed

At first cheese was simply the soft curds left behind after whey had been drained from sour milk before drinking. Cheese-making was revolutionised by the discovery of rennet, a digestive juice that is secreted in the stomachs of some mammals. Rennet curdles milk, producing enzymes that ripen cheese over a long period. It may have been accidentally discovered by Asian nomads who carried milk in bags made from animal stomachs.

The earliest reference to cheese made with rennet in western Europe dates to the Romans. In Britain cheese has probably been made for 4000 years. Julius Caesar found Britons preparing Cheshire cheese when he invaded in 54 BC. Cheddar, made from at least 1080, became famous in the 1600s, but was too expensive for most people. One 1727 recipe to make it at home may explain why: it recommends using curd made from milk with added cream and working in 1.5 kg (3 lb) butter.

Stilton was developed in the early 18th century. It was sold from a public house at Stilton, Cambridgeshire, but may have been made elsewhere. In 1724 the English writer Daniel Defoe gave a gruesome account of Stilton being 'brought to table with the mites or maggots round it so thick, that they bring a spoon with them to eat the mites, as you do the cheese.'

BIG CHEESE Medieval dairies made three main types of cheese: hard cheese from skimmed milk; soft cheese from whole or semiskimmed milk; and new or 'green' curd cheese, which was often flavoured with herbs.

YOGHURT MYSTIQUE
Health food

The beginnings of one of the world's first processed foods are a matter of controversy. Some experts say yoghurt was first eaten in the Balkans, others that it was first produced in the Caucasus. It was enjoyed by pharaohs and Israelites in Egypt, and was used medicinally by the ancient Greeks and Romans. The Persians took yoghurt to

India, where it was the diet of the yogi holy men 2000 years ago. The Turks claim its name derives from the Turkish *jugurt*, the Greeks from *ygeiarton*, 'food that brings health'.

Yoghurt was introduced into Europe in the 16th century, but did not catch on. In 1907 the Russian-French bacteriologist Elie Metchnikoff suggested that the vast quantities of yoghurt eaten by Bulgarians explained their longevity. It became popular in the 1950s, thanks to the German-American health-food promoter Gayelord Hauser.

BUTTER BEGINNINGS
A superior spread

Butter may first have been made when milk was 'churned' by the movement of the containers used by central Asian nomads on their journeys. The name comes from the Greek *bouturon*, 'cow cheese', but although the Greeks knew about butter, they used it as a medicinal salve rather than as a foodstuff.

The Romans thought butter a food for barbarians such as the Celts, who probably introduced it into Britain in the pre-Roman Iron Age. As the Celts knew how to preserve meat and fish with salt, they would soon have realised that it would also improve the keeping qualities of their butter.

But the salt was rarely added with a light hand: records from 1305 show 450g (1lb) of salt being added to every 4.5kg (10lb) of butter. Before the butter was eaten, the salt was removed by washing. The butter was then kneaded with water and the liquid pummelled out.

THE STORY OF ICE CREAM
Fit for royalty

Before ice could be easily obtained, water ices and ice cream were magical, luxurious dishes prepared for rulers. In the 1st millennium AD the Chinese used snow and ice to make fruit-flavoured drinks and desserts. They passed on their knowledge to the Persians and Arabs, who made syrups chilled with snow. These were called *sharbats*, from the Arabic *shariba*, 'to drink'.

Water ices appeared in Paris, Naples, Florence and Spain in the 1660s. When ice cream was first served in England, at Windsor Castle in May 1671, Charles II was presented with 'One plate of white strawberries and one plate of Ice Cream'. The hand-cranked ice-cream machine was invented in 1843 in the USA, and by 1850 ice cream was being sold commercially in Britain.

The invention of the ice-cream cone has been claimed by many, but the most appealing version concerns a Syrian pastry-maker named Ernest A. Hamwi, who sold wafer-like Persian pastries at the 1904 World's Fair in St Louis, USA. When the ice-cream seller at a neighbouring stall ran out of dishes, Hamwi rolled up a pastry, put a scoop of ice cream in it and called it a 'cornucopia'.

BEATING THE CREAM *By the time this dairy was operating in 1802, butter churns had evolved from primitive containers such as goatskins. The dash churn (far left), invented in the Middle Ages, used a plunger to agitate the cream. The barrel churn (right), with handles, was first thought of during the 18th century.*

FATTENED FOR THE POT *The Romans introduced the skills of rearing domestic fowl into Britain. A hen on a medieval manor farm was expected to lay 155 eggs annually.*

HENS' EGGS
Which came first?

Prehistoric food gatherers probably collected wild birds' eggs to bake or to eat raw straight from the shell. Geese were being raised for their eggs in the Middle East by 2500 BC. Although chickens were known in Egypt by 1350 BC, in Persia, ancient Greece and pre-Roman Britain they were valued mostly as sacred birds or for their fighting abilities.

In China, people were eating eggs as early as 1400 BC and had developed a method of preservation that involved burying them in soil—'thousand-year eggs'. But elsewhere hens' eggs only became an important part of the human diet during Roman times. Perfecting Greek techniques for raising domestic fowl, the Romans produced hens that laid far more eggs than any wild fowl. As a result, eggs became widely used cooking ingredients.

PRECIOUS HONEY
Liquid gold

Flying from flower to flower gathering nectar, it takes 300 bees some three weeks to make about 450g (1 lb) of honey. This wonderful source of sweetness and energy has been exploited by humans for thousands of years, and in ancient times symbolised all that was sweet in life. The Promised Land of the Old Testament was 'flowing with milk and honey'.

A Spanish cave painting provides the earliest evidence of honey-gathering. Dating to the late Palaeolithic era, it shows someone robbing a wild bees' nest on a cliff. The honeybee was probably semidomesticated in the Middle East in Neolithic times. Egyptian bas-reliefs of around 2600 BC illustrate bees being subdued by smoke—the first portrayal of beekeeping.

Wild bees only became plentiful in Britain once flowers began to bloom in the newly cleared pastures of the Neolithic period. Beekeepers of the late Bronze Age would carefully cut away sections of branches or hollow tree trunks where bees swarmed and take them home. Later, they made hives from bark or wickerwork, which they covered in honey and aromatic herbs in order to attract new swarms.

CAVE ART *A prehistoric inhabitant of Valencia, Spain, climbs a rope in search of honey, only to be attacked by a swarm of wild bees.*

LOAVES AND SYRUP *In the 15th century, European refineries crystallised sugar in cone-shaped moulds, producing loaves that weighed between 1.5 and 6kg (3 and 14lb).*

THE STORY OF SUGAR
Nature's bounty

During their invasion of India in 327 BC the soldiers of Alexander the Great discovered a 'solid honey not made by bees'. They were the first Europeans to taste sugar, which the Indians had been refining from 3000 BC. Some theories place the origins of sugar cane in the Bay of Bengal, others in the Solomon Islands of the South Pacific, but the Indians were the first to cultivate it.

From India, sugar cane spread to Indochina, Arabia and Persia, where it was being made into 'loaves' by the 5th century BC. Its expense meant that for centuries sugar was valued more as a medicine than as a foodstuff.

Sugar cane came to Europe around AD 800, during the Arab conquest of Spain, and was still used medicinally.

In medieval England, delicate children were given violet and rose-flavoured sugars to encourage good health.

From the 11th century more regular supplies were brought by Arab merchants and returning Crusaders, who had 'beheld with astonishment and tasted with delight…the cane growing in the plains of Tripoli'. Sugar entered the kitchens of the rich in the 13th century. It was often kept under lock and key and used to season savoury foods. In 1380 the French king Charles V sprinkled sugar and cinnamon over a dish of toasted cheese.

Although supplies of the precious commodity increased as the European powers planted sugar cane in their New World colonies, prices rose steadily after a tax was imposed in 1651. But the taste for sweetness was already well established. Noting the blackness of Elizabeth I's teeth, the 16th-century traveller Paul Hentzner thought it 'a defect the English seem subject to, from their too great use of sugar'.

By the 18th century even the poor felt unable to do without sugar, and each week would buy a few ounces scraped from a loaf. Sweetened meat

CUTTING SUGAR CANE IN THE ANTILLES, 1799

and fish dishes became rare as sugar was increasingly added to tea and coffee, puddings, cakes, biscuits and fruit pies. But not until the tax was finally removed in 1874 did sugar become the universal sweetener.

SWEETMEATS AND PRESERVES
All things nice

In the early Asian and Mediterranean civilisations, people satisfied their craving for sweetness by coating fruits, flowers, seeds and plant stems with honey. Honey-coated almonds were popular with the Romans and the Greeks, who called such confections *tragemata*, 'sweetmeats'. This may be the derivation of the name dragées for sugared almonds.

After the fall of Rome, delicate sweetmeats did not reappear until the Middle Ages, when they were made by caramelising spices and nuts, or by covering aniseed or caraway seeds in sugar to make 'comfits'. Sugar and spice were thought good for the digestion, and guests were given boxes of sweetmeats to be taken at night in their rooms.

Marchpane, or marzipan, from the Italian *marzapane*, originally a sweet

SPOILT FOR CHOICE *A Turkish sweetmeat vendor serves an eager clientele in 1851. Turkish delight, or* rahat lokum, *'giving rest to the throat', evolved from the sweet jellies popular throughout the Middle East.*

box but later its contents, came to England during the late Middle Ages. In medieval feasts, marchpane figures of people, animals and castles were presented at the end of each course.

Influenced by the Arabs, the Spanish and Portuguese brought the art of preserving fruit to Europe. Conserves of bitter oranges and lemons were shipped from Spain in the 13th century. Some 200 years later, Portuguese *marmelada* first reached England. Made from quinces—*marmalo* in Portuguese—it was a solid confection served in slices.

The English made marmalade with damsons or prunes, later with bitter oranges or lemons. Adding peel was an innovation of the mid 1600s. Soft fruits were bruised and boiled rapidly in sugar syrup without being sieved. The thick, reduced mass was vulgarly called 'jam'.

Modern marmalade originated when a Scottish couple named Janet and

A SWEET TOOTH *In 1899 a salesman for Bassett's confectioners spilled his samples in front of a wholesaler, who decided that he preferred the mix. As a result, Liquorice All-Sorts were born, and from 1926 were advertised by the figure of Bertie Bassett.*

John Keiller bought a consignment of oranges. Finding the fruit too bitter to resell, they converted it into an orange jam. It proved so popular the Keillers formed their own company in 1797.

SOLID CHOCOLATE
Sweetness to savour

The beans of the cacao tree were used to make drinking chocolate hundreds of years before Italian and French confectioners first produced eating chocolate—in Italy it was made into rolls and sliced. But it was not until 1819 that François-Louis Cailler of Switzerland had the idea of selling chocolate in blocks and making it on a factory scale.

The earliest reference to eating chocolate in Britain appeared in an 1826 advertisement for Fry's Chocolate Lozenges, 'a pleasant and nutritious substitute for food' when travelling.

Cadbury's marketed chocolate as confectionery from 1842, and in 1861 they introduced assortments, known as 'fancy boxes'. As Quakers who disapproved of alcohol and stimulants, the Cadburys and the Frys believed chocolate to be inoffensive and sustaining, although in fact it contains caffeine.

In 1875 a Nestlé worker together with a foreman at the factory of Daniel Peter, Cailler's son-in-law, had the innovative idea of adding condensed milk, thereby creating milk chocolate.

MOUTH-WATERING MOMENTS

• The inhabitants of Scandinavia, Germany and Britain chewed birch-bark 'tar' some 9000 years ago. Modern chewing gum was born in the 1860s, when Thomas Adams, an American businessman, began selling chicle, a gum from the sapodilla tree of Mexico's Yucatan desert.

• Pastilles were named after the Italian confectioner to the Medici family, Giovanni Pastilla, who accompanied Marie de Medici when she married the French king Henry IV. The royal children called Pastilla's sweetmeats *bonbons*, literally 'good goods'.

Spice labels (top illustration):

BLACK, WHITE AND GREEN PEPPERCORNS
GINGER ROOT
FRESH AND DRIED CHILLIES
VANILLA POD
TURMERIC ROOT AND POWDER
CLOVES
CINNAMON
SAFFRON
NUTMEG AND MACE
CORIANDER SEEDS
CUMIN SEEDS
BLACK AND GREEN CARDAMOMS

A PINCH OF SALT
The first seasoning

As farmers of the early Neolithic era began to eat less game than their hunting predecessors, they learnt to enhance the taste of their food. Unlike meat, vegetables and cereals contain little or no natural salt. At the same time, the invention of fire-resistant pots led to the discovery of a new cooking technique in boiling, which removes much of the salt in food. The white crystals also proved invaluable as a preservative.

The quest for more salt became a major preoccupation for early communities. It was obtained in many ways:

WHITE GOLD *From hollowed-out hunks of bread, containers for precious salt evolved into cellars such as this Georgian glass design. Medieval lords had fabulous ceremonial 'salters' in the form of dogs, lions or dragons.*

from natural surface deposits, by boiling seawater, by burning seaside plants and getting salt from the ash, or by mining underground deposits.

In Europe the earliest known salt mines were established in the Austrian town of Hallstatt, near Salzburg—both names mean 'Salt Town'—during the 1st millennium BC. Wealth from the mines founded a civilisation stretching from Spain to Yugoslavia. In Britain the deliberate production of salt was first practised in the early Iron Age by the Celts. Under the Romans, Droitwich, in the Midlands, became the site of a saltworks, 'wich' meaning 'a place where there is salt'.

The demand for salt quickly made it a powerful commodity in world economics and politics, a substance to be

SPICE WARS *The Dutch East India fleet returns from an early trading expedition. Determined to break the Dutch spice trade monopoly, merchants formed the British East India Company in 1600. The resulting trade wars eventually led to British rule in India.*

fought over, traded and taxed. Some of the world's earliest trade routes linked sources of salt to human settlements. The Via Salaria, 'Salt Road', one of the oldest roads in Italy, connects Rome with the port of Ostia and its saltworks.

The Romans gave salt rations, which they called a *salarium*, to soldiers and civil servants. Even when replaced by money it was still known as a *salarium*, hence the word 'salary' and the expression 'Not worth your salt'. Jesus called his disciples 'the salt of the earth'.

PEPPER AND SPICES
A taste of the East

The lucrative trade in pepper and spices began as early as 1450 BC, when Egypt imported cinnamon. From Malaysia and Indonesia, traders carried the spice across 7240 km (4500 miles) of open sea in canoes to Madagascar, then up the coast of East Africa to the Red Sea.

The first and most important of the oriental spices to reach Europe was 'Indian pepper', known in Greece by 431 BC. In ancient and medieval times 450 g (1 lb) of peppercorns could literally be worth its weight in gold. The Romans introduced pepper to wealthy Britons, along with ginger, named from the Sanskrit *sringavera*, 'horn-root'.

Saffron, the yellow stamens of *Crocus sativa*, grew wild in Italy. The Romans left the work of harvesting it to the Greeks, who had been cultivating the flower since ancient times. Such refined tastes lapsed after the fall of Rome until the Arabs planted *zafaran* in Spain in the 8th century AD. Nutmeg and mace were the last major spices to reach Europe, probably in the 12th century.

Strategically positioned between the East and West, Venice grew rich from

MINT

BAY LEAVES

PARSLEY

BASIL

THYME

ROSEMARY

CORIANDER

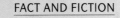

its monopoly of the spice trade. In the late 1400s other European nations set out to find new trade routes. In 1493 the Genoese explorer Christopher Columbus landed on Hispaniola (today Haiti and the Dominican Republic).

One local hot seasoning earned praise from Columbus, who described it as a 'better spice than our pepper'. The Spanish called it *pimiento*, the masculine form of *pimienta*, their name for 'black pepper'. In Mexico, where it had been valued since around 6000 BC, the Aztec word was *tchili* or *chili*.

The Portuguese took chilli peppers to India in 1525. Until then the Indian *kari*, 'sauce', was flavoured with cardamom, coriander seeds, turmeric and cumin, and made hot with black

HOT WORK *Pepper, the fruit of a climbing vine, is harvested in southern India in the early 1400s. Black pepper is made by drying the unripe green berries, white by drying the ripe red fruit and removing the outer skin.*

FACT AND FICTION

- Arab traders concocted stories to conceal the source of spices. Huge birds, they said, collected cinnamon and used it to make nests on cliffs.
- The Chinese imported cloves in the 2nd century BC, when courtiers chewed them to sweeten their breath for imperial audiences. They called them 'birds' tongues'. 'Clove' derives from the French *clou*, 'nail', which the spice is thought to resemble.
- Vanilla comes from the seedpods of a climbing orchid native to Central America. It was used by the Aztecs to flavour chocolate.

---

pepper. Dried chillies later became the basis of another hot sauce. Tabasco is a Native American word meaning 'land where the soil is humid', a good description of south Louisiana, where the seasoning was invented by the American Edmund McIlhenny in 1868.

HERBS FOR HEALTH
Ancient aromatics

When she caught the nymph Minthe with her husband Pluto, a jealous Proserpine threw her to the ground, turning her into an aromatic herb. As this Roman myth suggests, mint has been known since ancient times. It was much valued for medicinal purposes, particularly for stomach and digestive problems. The Romans often rubbed mint on their tables before a meal, perhaps to ward off indigestion.

Wreaths of wild olives were worn by successful Greek athletes at the Olympic Games while victors at the Pythian Games wore wreaths of bay leaves, from the Mediterranean tree

ADDED INTEREST *Early farmers from Britain to Mexico learned to flavour the bland cooked cereals that formed the staples of their diet by using the most aromatic herbs and spices growing wild around them. These plants were also prized for their medicinal qualities as well as for their fragrance.*

Laurus nobilis. The victorious Roman generals were crowned with wreaths of laurel, and from this tradition came the expression 'to rest on one's laurels'. For banquets, the Greeks preferred wreaths of parsley—named from the Greek *petroselinon*, meaning 'rock parsley', which may have been one of the five kinds known to the Romans.

The noble connections of basil are reflected in its name, which comes from the Greek *basilikon*, 'kingly'. It was a sacred plant in its native India, and the Egyptians combined it with myrrh and incense in their offerings to the gods. Used in the kitchen since 400 BC, basil reached England in the 16th century.

Roman settlers, whose cuisine relied on aromatic herbs, introduced thyme, sage, borage, chervil, dill, garden mint, fennel, parsley, rosemary and marjoram into Britain as garden plants. They also favoured coriander, perhaps the first Mediterranean herb to be imported to Britain, during the late Bronze Age, when it was added to pottages.

Rosemary, a native of Turkey and southern Europe and known in Latin as *rosmarinus*, 'rose of the sea', was a symbol of love and death. Also originating in southern Europe were sage, first used as a herbal remedy, especially to 'comfort' the heart, and thyme, named for its sweet aroma. The Greek *thymos* comes from *thyos*, 'incense'.

DRIED AND SALTED
Saved for tomorrow

Cave-dwelling hunter-gatherers of the Pleistocene epoch hung mammoth and bison carcasses to dry in the wind, then took them inside for cool storage. Although ignorant of the cause, the ancients nevertheless prevented decay by salting, drying or smoking food.

Cereals, lentils and peas, the most ancient dried foods, were used in Syria, Iran and Palestine by 8000 BC; grapes and figs were dried in ancient Palestine and Mesopotamia. And as the Old Testament relates, Joseph's foresight in storing up grain during years of plenty was instrumental in his rise to power.

Salt was first used to preserve fish and game birds in the Nile Valley during the 3rd millennium BC. Britons began salting food in the early Iron Age, when the climate was becoming colder and wetter, making it difficult to preserve food by wind-drying. Salt fish became an essential part of the diet where eating meat was forbidden on certain days by the Christian calendar.

The Egyptians pickled vegetables and meat by salting them in spiced brine. Among Europe's first vegetable pickles was sauerkraut, made by layering shredded cabbage leaves with salt and leaving them to ferment. Although known to the Romans, sauerkraut was 'lost' after the fall of Rome and reintroduced from China in the 13th century.

PICKLED ONIONS

GHERKINS

SALAMI

SHEEP'S CHEESE IN OIL

PEA SOUP, 1940S

PARMA HAM

CHORIZO SAUSAGES

PORTABLE PROVISIONS

• Hunter-gatherers sustained themselves on long journeys with dried salted meat similar to South American charqui, from the Peruvian *echarqui*, corrupted to 'jerky'.

• Potted meats or fish sealed with a substantial layer of spiced lard, butter or suet proved the ideal convenience food for Elizabethan sailors and travellers.

• H.J. (Henry James) Heinz began canning food in 1888, although his now famous baked beans were not test-marketed in Britain until 1905.

BRINGING HOME THE BACON
Curing, sausage-making and smoking

Preserving pig meat by salting or curing it of its propensity for 'going off' was a speciality of the Germanic tribes of Westphalia some 2000 years ago. Dry-salted and smoked, Westphalian ham from wild pigs or *Bachen*, from which our rashers may get their name, was popular with the Romans, who also favoured hams from the acorn-fed pigs of Gaul. Wiltshire hams, flavoured with molasses and kept pink with saltpetre, were known by medieval times.

All meat was so valuable that waste, even of the entrails, was anathema. Thus thrift explains the creation of the sausage. The ancient Babylonians and Greeks enjoyed sausages, and France and Italy have sausage-making traditions stretching back 2000 years. Black puddings were a Gaulish speciality.

Sausage type was originally linked to climate, so that in southern Italy dry sausages were favoured, while moister varieties were developed farther north. Names such as frankfurter (Frankfurt am Main) and romano (Rome) were acquired from their city of origin, but salami is from *salare*, Italian for 'to salt'.

SMOKED FISH

The Sumerians were the first people to combine drying and smoking flesh and fish. Later, red herrings became the mass-produced food of Britain during the Middle Ages. These whole, salted fish were dried and smoked until highly coloured, hard and so resistant to decay they could be eaten a year later. In fox hunting, the practice of 'drawing a red herring across the path' to destroy the scent led to the colloquial expression 'red herring' to describe a diversion.

The first kippers—flattened, salted herrings smoked or 'kippered' over an oak-wood fire—are said to have been produced in 1843 by a Northumberland fish curer. John Woodger was trying to develop for herrings the method used for smoking salmon since the 1300s.

SCOTTISH KIPPERS

FROZEN PEAS, 1940s

TOMATO SOUP, 1940s

PERFECT PRESERVES
The ancients knew how to save their harvests for days of hardship. Some 2000 years later, canning and freezing allowed large-scale food preservation for the first time. The results were cheap, convenient and brought consumers new tastes from around the world.

SUN-DRIED TOMATOES AND BASIL IN OIL

CANNED TOMATOES, 1940s

RASPBERRY VINEGAR

APRICOTS

PORCINI MUSHROOMS

MUSCATEL RAISINS

SUN-DRIED TOMATOES

FIGS

ADVERTISING THE LATEST FOODS, 1918

SHIITAKE MUSHROOMS

CANNED AND CONVENIENT
Long-term preservation

The Industrial Revolution brought a new victory over hunger. The enabling process was sterilisation, its executor a French confectioner named Nicolas Appert. As he boiled sugar for his sweetmeats, Appert tried to adapt the technique for perishable foods. In 1795 he arrived at the principle of canning. After much experimentation, Appert placed the food in loosely sealed jars, which he heated by boiling and then sealed tightly.

Appert's jars were soon superseded by canisters—shortened to 'cans'—of tin plate. These appeared in Britain at the beginning of the 19th century, and in 1811 the first canning factory was opened in Bermondsey, London.

Early cans were filled with food and sealed except for a small hole in the top. The contents were heated to boiling point before the hole was soldered. Then the cans were reheated, sometimes with fatal results: in 1852 one newspaper reported an occasion when 'steam was generated beyond the power of the canister to endure. As a natural consequence, the canister burst, the dead turkey sprang from his coffin of tin plate and killed the cook forthwith.' Once successfully sealed, cans had to be opened with a hammer and chisel.

COOL STORAGE
Refrigeration and freezing

Perhaps the Neanderthals, survivors of successive glaciations, discovered that food left in the ice stayed fresh. The Chinese stored snow in cellars before 1000 BC. Ice houses were rare in Britain until the late 1600s, although the principle was known. The English philosopher Francis Bacon is said to have died of a chill caught while collecting snow to stuff inside a chicken to keep it fresh.

Today's refrigerator stems from the work of the American Jacob Perkins, who patented his vapour-compression machine in 1834. A volatile fluid (ether at first) was compressed, evaporated to produce the cooling, then condensed and recirculated to the compressor. Some of the first commercial refrigerators were made by the Frenchman Charles Tellier. In 1877 they were used to transport meat from Buenos Aires to Rouen in a ship named the *Frigorifique*, meaning 'refrigerating'.

A technique to freeze-dry potato pulp was known in pre-Columbian South America, but Armour and Company of Chicago marketed the first freeze-dried food in the 1950s.

FROZEN ASSETS *The American Clarence Birdseye was inspired while on a trip to Labrador in 1912-15. He saw how fish that had frozen when lifted from the sea could be defrosted months later, still fresh.*

FULL OF BEANS
Ancient pulses

Highly nutritious and easily dried for winter storage, lentils, haricot beans, broad beans and chickpeas were some of the earliest vegetables to be cultivated. Lentils, probably native to the Middle East, were domesticated in around 8000 BC, while the various haricot beans native to the Americas were being grown by 7000 BC.

The Asian soya bean was first raised more than 4000 years ago. According to

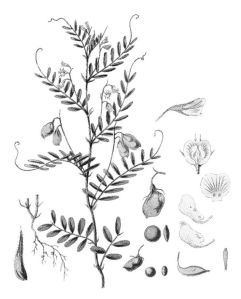

HEARTY FARE *Lentils and other pulses were an important food for the poor. In the Old Testament, the starving Esau sold his birthright to Jacob for a 'pottage of lentils'.*

Chinese legend, it was discovered by two bandits who survived being lost in the desert by eating the seeds of an unknown plant. Descriptions of soya sauce have been found in Chinese tombs dating to around 160 BC.

In ancient Egypt, Greece and Rome, chickpeas, broad beans and lentils were daily fare for most people. They came to be called 'pulses' after the Latin *puls*, a porridge made from bean meal. The humble origins, or frugal habits, of his ancestors were recorded in the name of the Roman statesman Cicero, from the Latin *cicer*, 'chickpea'.

Pulses were introduced into Britain from Europe in the pre-Roman Iron Age and used to make pottages, thick stews. Peas followed later, brought by the Romans.

A pulse known in Mexico as the *avacotl* was renamed the kidney bean by European herbalists after its shape—and in the belief that it strengthened this organ. In 1597 the English herbalist John Gerard described boiled kidney beans and pods served with butter as being 'excellent delicate meat'. The runner bean, a native of South America, first came to Britain in the early 1600s, but was grown only as an ornamental plant until the 19th century.

ADVERTISEMENT FOR BOSTON BAKED BEANS, 1911

BAKED GOODNESS

The first baked beans may have been the Egyptian dish *ful medames*, which in ancient times was made by burying broad beans overnight in hot ashes. In England, pork and beans was the staple fare of the Middle Ages. Settlers took the idea with them to North America, where they baked beans with pork and molasses. In 1875 the first canned beans were produced in the USA by Burnham and Morrill, but still with the original seasoned molasses sauce. Tomato sauce was introduced in 1891.

THE STORY OF THE NUT
Sustenance in a shell

According to the Roman author Pliny, 'the tree which first produced food for mortal man' was the oak. The acorn was the most important nut in the diet of prehistoric peoples, but the cave dwellers of northern Iraq in the Middle Palaeolithic era ate chestnuts, walnuts

FRIENDLY FACE *The coconut was known as the Indian nut until the late 1400s. Then the three dark spots on its base, like two eyes and a mouth, earned it the name* coco, *a Spanish and Portuguese word meaning 'grinning face'.*

and pine nuts. Once woodlands were razed to clear land for agriculture in the 5th millennium BC, the hazelnut took the acorn's place as the most widely eaten nut. Climatic changes also meant that both oaks and walnuts died out in Iraq and the Near East, leaving almonds and pistachios as the only nuts mentioned in the Bible.

The coconut, native to South-east Asia, India, South America and the Caribbean, fed and helped to build the earliest civilisations of the Indus Valley. The Sanskrit word for the coconut palm means the 'tree that furnishes all the necessities of life'. Its leaves were used for walls and roofs, its trunk for building and its shell as a vessel for eating and drinking. The hair of the mature nut made coir matting.

Walnut trees first grew on the shores of the Caspian Sea and in northern India. Because of the resemblance of the kernels to the two halves of the human brain, the ancient Greeks and Romans believed that they cured headaches. In the 17th century, early settlers in the North American colony of Virginia tried to stave off starvation with walnuts, acorns, roots and berries.

The peanut or groundnut is actually not a nut but in fact a pea-like legume. Originally from South America, it has been cultivated for at least 2000 years, and peanut-shaped pottery jars have been found in Inca tombs. Portuguese or Spanish navigators introduced it into China in 1538 and then to Africa, where peanuts became a cheap food for slaves.

For centuries Peruvian Indians and Africans ground peanuts by hand to make a paste—the original peanut butter. In 1890 a St Louis doctor named Ambrose Straub invented a peanut mill. He introduced the nutritious spread at the World's Columbian Exposition in Chicago in 1893, but its early popularity was due to Dr J.H. Kellogg, the American inventor of cornflakes, who prescribed it for convalescents.

PEANUT-BUTTER TIN, USA, 1920S

ESSENTIAL OILS
From seeds, nuts and fruit

For ancient peoples, oil was necessary for cooking, lighting and medicine. It was also used in religious ceremonies and for anointing the body. Following the advice of the Greek philosopher Democritus, who prescribed 'honey on the inside, olive on the outside', the Greeks and Romans oiled themselves after bathing, before and after exercise, and before and even during meals.

The oldest oil may be sesame, used in Egypt, Mesopotamia and Africa. The ancient Egyptians also extracted oil from radish seeds, while castor oil made a pungent choice for lamps. Almond oil was used in Asia Minor, coconut and soya in China and South-east Asia. Early American civilisations extracted it from peanuts, maize and sunflowers.

In Britain, as elsewhere in northern Europe, early farming communities used animal fat in their pottages and, when this was not available, linseed or the seeds of wild cabbage or native herbs. The Romans brought olive oil, but supplies dried up with the end of their occupation and butter became increasingly important. During the Tudor period Dutch immigrants cultivated rape extensively for its oil, and bright yellow fields became a familiar sight in south-east England.

It is not known who discovered how to extract oil from olives, or how to soak and brine the inedible raw fruit to make it palatable. What is known is that the olive tree was probably first cultivated in Syria and Palestine during the 4th millennium BC.

The olive seems to have reached Italy from Sicily in the 6th century BC and it was the Romans who spread it throughout Europe. With the screw press they also invented a method of making olive oil that has hardly changed.

The Romans produced virgin olive oil from the initial pressing. Second-quality and ordinary oils came from pressings of the pulp. Their oil did not keep and was often made just before using. The olives were preserved in jars with fennel, mastic (an aromatic resin) and brine, must or vinegar.

OLIVE HARVEST *Women of 19th-century Provence, France, pick olives by hand, a method familiar to the ancients. The Greeks considered olive groves sacred and only virgins and chaste men could cultivate them.*

BUTTER SUBSTITUTES
Margarine and other fats

ADVERTISEMENT FOR MARGARINE, ABOUT 1900

France boasts more about classic cuisine than about margarine, its other major contribution to modern eating. In 1867 Napoleon III launched a competition to find a substitute for butter that was longer-lasting and cheaper but just as nutritious. The only entrant was Hippolyte Mège-Mouriès, a chemist's assistant who had begun his experiments at the request of the French navy.

Starting from the premise that milk fat, the major ingredient of butter, was a type of body fat, Mège-Mouriès mixed

---

IN PURSUIT OF HEALTH

• In 1935 the Japanese physician Minoru Shirota created a fermented milk drink, Yakult, containing a lactic acid bacteria. His aim was to help people to maintain a healthy balance of bacteria in their intestines.

• Benecol, a full-fat Finnish margarine that reduces blood cholesterol levels, was introduced in 1996. Its key ingredient is sitostanol, a by-product of the wood-pulp industry, which inhibits the absorption of cholesterol.

• First marketed in 1985, Quorn is the protein produced by a mould that feeds on carbohydrates such as potatoes and rice.

---

animal organs with suet, a solid fat from around the kidneys, along with warm milk, minced pig's stomach and bicarbonate of soda. He called the opalescent mixture margarine, from the Greek word *margarites*, meaning 'pearl'. By 1874 it was selling 100 000 tonnes a year.

In Britain, margarine was first sold in the 1870s as 'butterine', a product created by the Dutch butter merchants Jan and Anton Jurgens who had improved on Mège-Mouriès' process. Despite its name, it contained no butter.

The modern margarine industry was born when the process of hydrogenation was discovered by the French chemist Paul Sabatier in 1903. Using this technique, liquid oils could be hardened by making them react with hydrogen in the presence of nickel. Hydrogenation also turns polyunsaturated fats in liquids such as sunflower oil into the saturated fats often linked with heart disease. In the mid 1960s soft margarines high in polyunsaturates were first marketed as foods to be included in a healthy diet.

Anxieties about the dangers of fat, especially the possible links between fat in the diet and obesity, heart disease and certain cancers, have also led manufacturers to develop a range of semiartificial and artificial products designed to taste like fat but without the calories or cholesterol. The simplest are mixtures of starch and water turned into emulsions and used in such products as low-calorie mayonnaise. Emulsified proteins from milk and egg whites are used in Simplesse, which became the first fat substitute approved by the American Food and Drug Administration (FDA) in 1990.

Olestra is a synthetic compound of sugar and fatty acids that tastes like fat but passes unabsorbed through the body and has no calories. It was discovered in Miami in the early 1960s by biochemists at Procter & Gamble looking for an easily digestible fat for premature babies. The FDA gave Olestra a limited licence in 1995 but concerns about its long-term effects remain.

ALTERNATIVES TO SUGAR
Artificial sweeteners

To satisfy their craving for sweetness, the Romans created sapa, an artificial sweetener made by concentrating grape must in lead-lined pots. It was sweet but also poisonous, causing miscarriages, headaches and anaemia.

While investigating the reactions of certain coal-tar derivatives in 1879 at Baltimore's Johns Hopkins University, the American chemist Ira Remsen and a German student, Constantin Fahlberg, synthesised the compound orthobenzoyl sulphimide, and stumbled across a synthetic alternative to sugar. Having eaten some bread at his bench and found it sweet, Fahlberg realised that he

SWEETER BY FAR
Discovered in 1879, saccharine was said to offer the benefits of sugar without the drawbacks. 'Hermesetas dissolve instantly, have no after taste, and give you all the sweetness you want without the calories you don't,' claimed this 1960s advertisement.

must have had some of the substance on his fingers. Later analysis showed it was 300 times sweeter than sugar. Fahlberg filed a patent claim and obtained financial backing for the new product, which he named 'saccharine'.

One-tenth as sweet as saccharine but without its bitter aftertaste, cyclamate was discovered in 1937. Michael Sveda of the American chemical company DuPont was smoking in his laboratory and put his cigarette down on the edge of the bench. When he next put it to his lips he was struck by its intensely sweet taste. James Schlatter of the drug company G.D. Searle was searching for an antiulcer drug in 1965 when he realised that aspartame, a mixture of two amino acids—aspartic acid and phenylalanine—tasted sweet. Some 200 times sweeter than sugar, it was marketed in 1981 as NutraSweet.

COLOUR AND FLAVOUR
Food additives

Adding colours to food is nothing new: medieval banquets could be brilliantly coloured affairs, with infusions of sandalwood used to dye foods red and saffron added to impart a vivid yellow. Today British food manufacturers add yellow colouring to low-fat spreads and margarines, which would otherwise be white or pale cream, because people expect these alternatives to be the same colour as butter.

In the 1960s consumers began to protest about additives in foods, but not for the first time. In 1762 the English cookery book writer Hannah Glasse warned her readers not to use artificial chemicals to colour pickles and desserts because they often contained harmful ingredients. At the time bread was whitened with chalk, alum and bone ashes, 'China tea' was often made from dried thorn leaves coloured with poisonous verdigris, and pickles were treated with copper to make them look green.

Even in 1904 some commercial tomato ketchups in the USA were still being coloured with coal tar. The food-processing industry fought attempts to regulate its methods, but in 1906 a Pure Food and Drug Act was passed—with the significant support of H.J. Heinz, whose name is synonymous with canned and bottled foods containing no artificial additives.

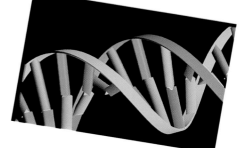

GENE POWER *The discovery of the spiral structure of DNA in 1953 offered scientists of the 1980s and 90s a means of altering the genes of plant or animal foods.*

DESIGNER FOODS
Selection and engineering

Since people first kept animals and grew plants for food they have been using controlled breeding to create meatier animals or crops with higher yields. In the 18th century agriculturists started to intensify the process, being more selective about the animals they chose. A Leicestershire farmer's son, Robert Blackwell, was one of the pioneers, and created distinctive breeds such as Longhorn cattle, Leicestershire sheep and Large White pigs.

When the Cambridge scientists Francis Crick and James Watson worked out the structure of the genetic material DNA in 1953, they paved the way for genetic engineering in the 1980s. The first genetically engineered food to go on sale was the Flavr Savr tomato, in the USA in 1994. The fruit had a shelf life of 50 days or more. This was made possible by blocking the action of the gene that allows rotting.

BREEDING A FATTER PIG *British pigs retained the long-legged, slim shape of the wild boar (above) until 1760, when they were crossed with the plumper, short-legged Chinese pigs. Through selective breeding, meatier animals, such as this 19th-century cottage pig (right), were then produced.*

ASSAM, INDIA

ROSE CONGOU, CHINA

JASMINE, CHINA

FRUITS OF EMPIRE *Tea has been cultivated in China (far left) since at least AD 350 and in the 19th century fast-sailing clippers raced to deliver their precious cargo to London, the centre of the world's tea trade. From the mid 1800s the British created tea plantations throughout their colonies. Variations in techniques and climate led to new flavours and*

EARL GREY, CHINA

THE STORY OF TEA
Precious leaf

One hot day more than 4500 years ago, the Chinese emperor Chen-nung was boiling water to refresh himself. A few leaves blew off a nearby shrub and landed in the water, and Chen-nung named the resultant brew 'tay', or 'ch'a'. The legend is an appealing one but in fact no one knows who first drank tea. However, the leaves came from the evergreen shrub *Camellia sinensis*, which is native to the foothills of the Himalayas.

The Chinese first gathered the leaves from the wild, and have cultivated the tea plant since at least AD 350. In time taking tea for its stimulating properties took on social and cultural significance throughout the Far East and India, which culminated in an elaborate tea ceremony in Japan, popularised in the 15th century.

Europeans first heard of tea in the 16th century from Dutch traders and Portuguese missionaries. Tea went on public sale for the first time in London around 1657, with many claims made for its medicinal value. In 1660 the diarist Samuel Pepys sent for 'a cupp of tee (a China drink) of which I never had drank before'.

It was the court of Charles II that established tea as the fashionable drink of the elite. His bride, the Portuguese princess Catherine of Braganza, was a dedicated tea drinker, and after she arrived in England in 1662 the habit soon spread. The 17th-century trend for taking afternoon tea in tea gardens

GENMAICHA GREEN TEA WITH RICE, JAPAN

TEA PLANT, *Camellia sinensis*

owed much to European adaptations of Oriental traditions.

The Chinese added heated milk to black, fermented teas, but not to green, unfermented ones. In 1665 tea was served with milk at a Dutch banquet in Guangzhou (Canton), and in 1671 the French brought the practice to Europe. As many teas were bitter-tasting, sweet-toothed Europeans also added sugar.

The ancient Chinese brewed up in unglazed red or brown stoneware pots and sent some of these to Europe with the first cargoes of tea. Dutch potters imitated the Chinese design, but soon gave their teapots more ornate and fanciful shapes, decorating them with coloured clays and glazes. The traditional, rounded British teapot is based on early Chinese pots.

NO MESS, NO FUSS *Tea bags were pioneered by the New York tea wholesaler Thomas Sullivan, who in 1908 sent silk-wrapped samples of tea blends to his customers.*

TEA ON TIME *The first tea makers appeared in the 1890s. When the alarm clock rang, a tiny spirit lamp was lit on this rather dangerous contraption of 1902, which in turn heated a copper kettle.*

DRINKING COFFEE
The invigorating bean

An Arabian legend tells of a goatherd making a drink from berries growing on strange shrubs, then experiencing extraordinary lucidity and wakefulness. The shrubs were said to have been planted by descendants of the Queen of Sheba, who had come from Kaffa in present-day Ethiopia, where the coffee plant *Coffea arabica* originates.

The ancient Ethiopians made food balls of crushed coffee beans and fat to sustain them on long journeys. The beverage was developed in Yemen during the 10th century, and from the 15th century coffee drinking became widespread throughout the Islamic world, including Turkey.

The beans were first sold in Europe after a consignment reached France in 1644. However, as early as 1637 the diarist John Evelyn mentions a Greek drinking coffee in England. Britain's

Madagascar. Coffee arrived in the New World in about 1723, when a French naval officer established a plant on the island of Martinique. A few years later, coffee was introduced into Brazil and burgeoned into a huge industry which was reliant on the slave trade of the 18th and 19th centuries.

In the ancient Arab world, milled coffee and water were heated several times to boiling point and the grounds left to settle before drinking. In Europe, coffee was made by a simple infusion until, in 18th-century France, a two-sectioned utensil was developed. The device separated the ground beans and hot water to produce a smoother drink, and came to be known as the cafetière. Count Rumford, the American-born Benjamin Thompson, devised the true coffee percolator—a coffee pot with a built-in metal sieve—in 1806.

THE SECRETS OF COCOA
The drink of the gods

When the Spanish explorer Hernán Cortés came home from Mexico in the early 1500s, he brought back with him the Aztec sacred drink. Made from the roasted seeds of *Theobroma cacao* or the *cacahuaquchtl* tree, *xcoatl* or *xocolatl* was flavoured with a pungent blend of chilli,

CUPS THAT CHEER

• Until the mid 19th century, tea was so valuable that it was kept in lockable containers, or caddies. The word caddy comes from *kati*, a Malaysian measure of weight.
• Soluble instant coffee was the invention of the Japanese-American chemist Satori Kato in 1901.
• In 1903 Ludwig Roselius, a German importer, first made decaffeinated coffee, calling it Sanka, from the French *sans* (without) *caffeine*.
• John Lawson Johnston, a Scot, began production of his Fluid Beef in Canada in 1874. Back in London in 1886, he renamed it Bovril, from the Latin *bos*, 'ox' and Vrilya, 'life force', invented by the novelist Edward Bulwer Lytton.

A BREAK FOR
TEA, 1939

OF ILL REPUTE *Like Arabian establishments of old, Britain's coffee-houses of the 17th and 18th centuries were considered hotbeds of sedition and scandal. Tea and cocoa also accompanied the gossip and the gambling.*

first coffee-house, The Angel, opened in Oxford in 1650, and coffee-houses appeared in London soon after.

Originally coffee of the best quality came from the Yemen's Mocha and Aden regions. However, in the early 17th century, plants were introduced from there into the Dutch colony of Java in Indonesia and into French colonies in the Indian Ocean, notably

musk and honey. Although Cortés had grown to like this brew, the Spanish eventually added sugar, vanilla and cinnamon to make the bitter drink more acceptable to European palates.

The Spanish and Portuguese, who controlled the areas where the cocoa tree grew, guarded the secrets of *xcoatl* production jealously, but by 1606 cocoa paste was being exported to Italy and Flanders. It seems to have made its first appearance in London around 1657. By 1765 cocoa made with West Indian beans was being drunk in the American colony of Massachusetts.

Cocoa powder was developed by the Dutch chocolate maker Conrad J. van Houten. In 1828 he patented a method for pressing cocoa butter from the roasted beans. This made possible the production of both instant cocoa and, with the addition of sugar and cocoa butter, chocolates.

WARRIOR'S BREW *The Spanish found more than gold in Mexico, and cocoa soon took the Old World by storm. At the feet of this 17th-century Amerindian are the traditional cup, whisk and cocoa-making pot.*

MINERAL WATER
The original health drink

The Romans appreciated the curative properties of mineral water, building spas from Bath in England to Tiberias in Israel. The idea of drinking, rather than bathing in, mineral water for its medicinal effects evolved more slowly, but was established by the Middle Ages.

For centuries scientists speculated about and tried to reproduce the therapeutic properties of naturally sparkling mineral water, especially its bubbles—known by chemists as 'fixed air' before being identified as carbon dioxide.

The pioneer of artificially carbonated water was the English clergyman and scientist Dr Joseph Priestley, who at first used carbon dioxide collected over vats of fermenting beer. In 1772 he demonstrated a carbonating apparatus in London. Three years later the English doctor John Mervin Nooth devised the 'gazogene', or soda siphon.

Artificially carbonated water was first produced for sale in Britain around 1781. But it was a jeweller from Geneva named Jacob Schweppe who, in 1790, established the first carbonated drinks company. After he moved to London in 1792, Schweppe's soda waters were sold by pharmacists for medicinal purposes and proved extremely popular. At the Great Exhibition of 1851, the company sold more than 1 million bottles.

Tonic water was born after doctors advised British colonists in Africa and India to take quinine to protect them against malaria. Erasmus Bond patented an aerated quinine tonic water in 1858. From 1880 it was made by Schweppes.

DRINKS DISPENSERS *The all-American soda fountain (left) was established in 1825 to sell carbonated water. Later this was mixed with syrups such as the original Coca-Cola recipe. For a more curative effect, people regularly visited spas such as Vichy in France, seen below in 1910.*

A GENTLE RESTORATIVE *A young woman is given a cup of lemonade, a drink that became popular in 17th-century Europe as West Indian sugar became increasingly available.*

CITRUS DRINKS
Lemon, orange and lime

The Mongols were drinking sweetened lemon juice preserved with alcohol in 1299—the first recorded people to drink lemonade. Northern Europeans had tasted their first citrus fruit only a century earlier, when the Crusaders came across the orange and lemon groves of Jaffa in 1191-2. Roman traders

had probably brought citrus fruits back from India, but they were not cultivated in southern Europe until the Arabs, who had discovered them in Persia, began to propagate them around the eastern Mediterranean.

Towards the end of the 13th century, citrus fruits arrived in Britain. Seven oranges and 15 lemons, as well as 230 pomegranates, were bought in 1289 for Eleanor of Castile, wife of Edward I, from a Spanish ship at Portsmouth.

In Europe, the taste for lemonade developed during the 1600s in France. Carrying metal containers on their backs, the *limonadiers* sold their wares on the streets of Paris. The European café began with the shops set up by lemonade, coffee and chocolate sellers.

Initially, English lemonade was a potent drink, the first recipes including brandy and sack, a fortified white wine from Spain. Lime juice, added to the newly fashionable punch, was imported from the West Indies from the 1680s. By the early 1700s lemonade was preserved with sulphur and bottled. Although non-alcoholic lemonade had become common, wine mixed with lemonade remained popular.

Orange juice, however, was still rare. In 1669 the English diarist Samuel Pepys described his first taste: 'I drank a glass…at one draught, of the juice of oranges…they drink the juice as wine, with sugar, and it is a very fine drink; but, being new, I was doubtful whether it might not do me hurt.'

FIZZ AND FLAVOUR
From ginger beer to Coca-Cola

People were already drinking soda water mixed with fruit syrups before the manufacture of prepared flavoured drinks began in the early 1800s. Ginger, popular since the late 18th century as the essential ingredient of ginger beer, was the first flavouring, added in 1820. Lemon followed in the 1830s. In 1850, ginger ale, developed by a Dr Cantrall in Ireland, revolutionised the soft-drinks market and was soon being sold in the United States.

Despite the flavourings and sugar, carbonated drinks retained their medicinal connotations. In the USA, a pharmacist named John Pemberton based in

Atlanta, Georgia, had had little success with such previous creations as Triplex Liver Pills and Globe of Flower Cough Syrup when he came up with a liquid cure for headaches and hangovers. The ingredients of his concoction included dried leaves from the coca shrub, from which cocaine is made (removed from the formula in 1905), extract of kola nuts and fruit syrup.

Advertised as an 'esteemed Brain Tonic and Intellectual Beverage', the syrup, now diluted with carbonated water, went on sale on a trial basis at Jacob's Pharmacy in 1886. One of Pemberton's partners, Frank Robinson, suggested the name Coca-Cola Syrup

LUCOZADE, LATE 1930S TIZER, 1930S GINGER BEER, ABOUT 1920

WHAT'S IN A NAME?

• Lithiated Lemon was the creation of Charles Griggs from Missouri, who introduced the lemon-lime drink in 1929. Four years later he renamed it 7-Up. Sales increased sixfold.

• When the daughter of Newcastle chemist William Hunter fell ill with jaundice, he formulated a carbonated drink flavoured with orange and lemon oils and plenty of glucose. This seemed to do the trick and the drink was marketed in 1938 as Lucozade.

• Tizer—derived from 'appetiser'— was launched in 1924 by Fred Pickup in Manchester. He had begun in 1907 selling ginger beer, changing from stone to glass pint bottles in 1920.

DISTINCTIVE LOOK *A 1923 advertisement omits the curvaceous Coke bottle. Cans were developed in the Second World War for the US armed forces serving overseas.*

and Extract, while his flowing script provided the drink's trademark.

Pemberton sold 25 American gallons (94 litres) of syrup at $1 a gallon, but spent $73.96 on advertising. In 1887 he sold two-thirds of his ownership to an Atlanta pharmacist named Asa Candler for $1200. After buying out Pemberton in 1891 for the sum of $2300, Candler began his successful marketing of Coca-Cola as a drink for the young. Two years later he registered the Coca-Cola trademark, although the battle to register 'Coke' was not won until 1945. Coke's success inspired hundreds of cola drinks, most famously Pepsi-Cola, first called Brad's Drink after Caleb Bradham, the pharmacist from North Carolina who created it in 1898 as a cure for dyspepsia.

Originally Coca-Cola was dispensed from soda-fountain pumps and mixed with fizzy water. It was first bottled in 1899, but in 1913 Benjamin Thomas of the Coca-Cola Company issued a challenge to manufacturers: he wanted an immediately recognisable bottle that would distinguish Coke from its rivals. The Root Glass Company produced a contoured design that was probably inspired by the humble coca bean, although it was said to imitate the hobble skirts worn at the time.

THE ART OF BREWING
From ale to beer

In 3000 BC a Sumerian poet praised the virtues of beer:
'I feel wonderful, drinking beer
in a blissful mood
with joy in my heart and a happy liver.'

Brewing only became possible once hunter-gatherers established organised, agricultural societies and began to cultivate cereals such as barley and wheat. Around 4000 BC the Sumerians learnt, probably accidentally, to make a crude ale, perhaps by noticing the effects of drinking gruel that had been left to ferment. The original ale was a weak brew made by soaking cakes of emmer wheat or barley in water and leaving them for about a day before draining off and then drinking the liquid.

Ale became more alcoholic once brewers malted the barley, a principle understood in Mesopotamia during the 3rd millennium BC. Germinating the grain, then drying and heating it so that the starch turned to sugar produced both a more powerful fermentation and a stronger flavour.

Fermentation itself was achieved by using the same vessels time after time.

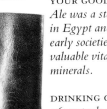

YOUR GOOD HEALTH *Ale was a staple drink in Egypt and other early societies, providing valuable vitamins and minerals.*

DRINKING CUP *In the 1600s tankards of hard 'jack' leather were known as black jacks.*

This allowed yeast—discovered by the French doctor Charles de La Tour in 1838 to be the microorganism responsible for the fermentation process—to build up in any cracks so that it could work on the next batch. Alternatively, the sediment from one brew was kept to start off the next, a basic version of the system used today.

The colour of the beer depended on whether the cakes were baked light or dark brown. Early brewers also balanced the sweetness of the malt by adding salt or perhaps mandrake, a plant with a leek-like flavour.

In northern Europe, where the art of growing wine grapes was not known but where barley and wheat flourished, brewing probably developed independently. The earliest evidence of brewing in Britain goes back to the Iron Age and a Celtic brew known as *curmi*. In

the 1st century BC, Saxons, Celts and peoples of Nordic and Germanic tribes were known for their ale. The Danes and Saxons who succeeded the Romans in Britain called their drink *öl*, which became the English 'ale'.

Beer was first brewed in Bavaria in the 9th century. It differed from ale by including hops, although in the 1500s these were also added to ale. Herbs had long been used to flavour and preserve ale, and by medieval times hops were the plants most commonly used.

Although native to Britain, hops were not used in local beers until the practice was introduced from Flanders in the 1400s. Bitter, well-hopped beer was preferred in southern England, sweeter ale in the north and Scotland. Both were drunk at all times of the day.

Most brewing was done during the winter. In Germany, beer that was kept cool in the summer with ice was called lager, from *lagern*, 'to store'. It only became commercially available when ice-making machinery was developed in the Industrial Revolution.

At the other end of the scale, porter, a dark, heavily hopped beer popular with market porters, was first brewed in London in the 1720s. It was exported to Ireland, but by the end of the century Irish porter was being imported to Britain, particularly porter, or stout, from the Dublin brewery established by Arthur Guinness in 1759.

ROLL OUT THE BARREL *Italian coopers of the 1400s followed a tradition that began in northern Europe during the Iron Age. The wooden casks made by the Celts for their ale impressed the Romans more than the drink.*

PUBLIC HOUSES
Social drinking

INN SIGN, BATH, 1756

Alehouses, taverns and inns were first established in Britain by the Romans. In the Middle Ages, many inns were set up for pilgrims—few braved the hardships of travelling without a good reason.

The influence of the Church was reflected in inn signs—necessary when most people were illiterate. The Lamb referred to Christ, the Crossed Keys to St Peter's insignia. During the Crusades the Saracen's Head appeared, while the title of England's oldest inn is claimed by Nottingham's Trip to Jerusalem. But rather than being a corruption of 'God Encompasses Us', the Goat and Compasses may refer to the arms of the Company of Cordwainers, in which a chevron resembling a pair of compasses is shown between three goats' heads.

Most publicans brewed their own ale. In the 1300s, government tasters tested an ale's strength by pouring some onto a bench and sitting on it. If their

AN EVENING OUT *The smoky intimacy of a tavern provides a welcome refuge for Italian card players in the 17th century.*

breeches stuck to the bench, the ale contained too much sugar. But from 1637 a royal edict required publicans to buy from a commercial brewer. In the 1700s brewers such as Bass, Courage and Tetley were founded and the 'tied house' was born.

CIDER DRINKING
The apple beverage

Apple and pear trees were not seriously cultivated before the 5th century AD, when cider became a drink for the poor. The cider-apple tree originated in Biscay. It reached Normandy in the 11th or 12th century, after which cider successfully competed with beer, since

using grain for alcohol could mean going without bread. Also known as 'apple wine', cider was brought to Britain by the Normans in the 1100s.

From the 1620s English settlers in North America planted apple trees, partly because they knew they would need cider to drink, as at home, in place of disease-carrying water. In the 19th century Horace Greeley, the American journalist and reformer, complained that: 'In many a family of six or eight persons, a barrel tapped on Saturday barely lasted a full week.'

PRESSING BUSINESS *Cider was made by crushing apples in a trough or a horse mill until John Worlidge, the English author of treatises on cider, made a special mill in 1676.*

FROM HONEY TO HOPS

• The earliest fermented alcoholic drink was mead, first made with honey well before the advent of farming.

• In Sumeria ale was also a currency and the name for it was *kash*—the origin of the modern synonym for 'money'.

• Kreuger Cream Ale, produced by the Kreuger Brewing Co of New Jersey in 1935, was the first beer in a can. In 1962 tab-opening, all-aluminium cans were the brainchild of Ermal Cleon Fraze of Dayton, Ohio, after he forgot his can opener and had to bash open a can of beer on his car bumper.

A WORLD OF WINE

'Wine is as good as life to a man, if it be drunk moderately:
what life is then to a man that is without wine?
for it was made to make men glad.'

ECCLESIASTICUS, CH. 31, V. 27

The pleasures of drinking wine began more than 7000 years ago in the Zagros mountains of Iran, where the wild grape *Vitis vinifera* grew. There, around 5200 BC, as Neolithic people founded the first settlements, they discovered the potential of grape juice. Ripening grapes naturally gather a bloom of wild yeasts. Breaking the skin allows these to mix with the juice, so starting the fermentation process by which grape sugar turns to alcohol.

To prevent the wine from spoiling, and to disguise any unpleasant flavours, the first winemakers added a resin called terebinth from the turpentine tree, *Pistacia atlantica*, which must have given the drink a powerful taste. By 2500 BC the Egyptians were also making retsina-like wines, which they classified as 'good', 'good good', 'good good good' or 'sweet'. After harvesting, they threw the grapes into wooden vats and trod them with bare feet. The juice was then fermented in

CHAMPAGNE BOTTLE, 20TH-CENTURY DESIGN

ROUND GLASS WINE BOTTLE, ABOUT 1690

SACK BOTTLE, 1658

PEWTER TANKARD, ABOUT 1700

WINE GOBLET, LATE 1600S

LEATHER JUG, LATE 1600S

SILVER CORKSCREW, 1700S

SERVING SUGGESTIONS *In early times wine was stored in wooden barrels and decanted as needed. Glass serving vessels were expensive, but were used by wealthier Romans. Leather or stone jugs and flasks remained more popular choices into the 18th century, while tankards were the affordable alternative to wine glasses until the 1800s.*

PRECIOUS CARGO *The Romans exported their wine in pottery amphorae. Italian wine was appreciated in Gaul, where the Celts drank it neat, a habit the Romans thought barbaric. They diluted theirs, adding spices, salt or rose petals to disguise spoilage.*

vats and filtered through linen. If not sold directly, the wine was stored in clay-sealed amphorae labelled with details of the vineyard and the year.

According to Greek legend, Dionysus, the god of wine, fled from Mesopotamia because its inhabitants drank mostly beer. The Greeks, who had a flourishing wine trade, planted grapes in their colonies from the Black Sea to Spain. Greek settlers took vines to southern France in about 600 BC.

The Greeks also encouraged the production of wine in Italy, where it had probably been introduced by the Etruscans. When the Romans took over the old Greek vineyards they began to produce high-quality wines such as Falernian, a much prized white wine, creating an industry centred on individual villas. Poorer people quenched their thirst with diluted vinegar, from the Old French *vinaigre*, 'sour wine'. Roman soldiers offered the drink to Christ on the Cross.

From the late 2nd century BC the Romans encouraged vine cultivation in their provinces, including Gaul. Viticulture slowly spread farther north, reaching the Rhône valley in the 1st century BC and then Bordeaux by the 1st century AD. Italian wine was imported to south-east Britain before the Roman occupation—it was popular among the Celtic Belgae tribes who had invaded in 75 BC. Under the Romans it was also locally produced.

After the collapse of the Roman Empire, Europe's wine industry was saved by the Church as monks planted vines to provide wine for Mass. The Dissolution of the Monasteries in 1536 was the final blow to English wine, in decline since Henry II married Eleanor of Aquitaine in 1152. Bordeaux had become part of the English Crown and

French vineyards had expanded to meet the English taste for claret, from the French *clairet*, a pale red wine or a mixture of red and white.

Most wines were consumed within a year; fortified wines such as sack from Spain or the Canary Islands kept longer. Roman connoisseurs had thought Falernian at its best after 15 to 20 years, but the taste for mature wines died out after the fall of Rome.

Vintage wines were rediscovered after British glass-makers learnt, in the early 1600s, to produce glass bottles strong enough to store liquid. At the same time the use of cork to keep them airtight—known in ancient Egypt, Greece and Rome—became more widespread. The corkscrew also became a necessity. The earliest reference to one dates to 1681, in a description of 'a steel worm used for the drawing of Corks out of Bottles'.

The practice of binning wines on their side began in the 1730s, helping

---

SPIRITED WINES

The English became port drinkers in the 18th century, when trade wars made drinking French wine unpatriotic. English wine merchants began to import strong Portuguese wines, which they fortified with brandy to help them withstand the journey.

At the same time fortified wines from Madeira were used as ballast for ships going to the East Indies. The discovery that subjecting them to extremes of heat and cold actually improved the wines led to them being matured in this way, a process called 'estufa', after the type of ship.

---

the ageing process by keeping the cork moist and stopping it from shrinking. It also led to a change in bottle style as the early onion shape gave way to cylindrical bottles in the 1760s.

These hardy new vessels played an important role in keeping the sparkle in champagne. At first the wines of the region were still. During the region's cold winters the fermentation process stopped, but it started again in the spring, giving off carbon dioxide. To winemakers the gas was a problem, as fizzy wines were thought inferior.

But British drinkers enjoyed the drink's delicate flavour, to which they

CHEERS! *The ancient Greek custom of handing a cup to the person being toasted, saying 'This to thee', exists in the modern habit of holding out a full glass of wine.*

were introduced in the early 1660s. It was imported in barrels and bottled on its arrival in the spring. Sugar was often added, which boosted its natural effervescence. By 1664 the English writer Samuel Butler was referring to 'brisk [sparkling] Champaign'.

A Benedictine monk, Dom Pierre Pérignon, cellar master at the Abbey of Hautvilliers near Reims from 1668 to 1715, mastered the art of blending wines from different parts of the region and of producing fine white wine from black grapes. He also introduced the cork tied down with string, and strong bottles, but even so most of them exploded.

The French first began to take champagne seriously after 1715, when it was favoured at the court of the Duke of Orléans. Jacques Fourneaux established the first firm to produce champagne in Reims in 1734.

THE WATER OF LIFE
The beginnings of distillation

After ale and wine came spirits. The process of distillation was understood by the ancient Egyptians, Greeks and Romans who used it to make solvents and salves rather than alcohol. In the 9th century the Arabs developed the art of distillation, making medicines, perfumes and elixirs by extracting the essences from fruits and flowers.

They also used the process to convert antimony, a metallic element, into an eye make-up called *al-kuhl*, meaning 'the powdered antimony'. This came into English as the word 'alcool', which was originally used to describe any fine powder or extract.

By the 1500s 'alcohol' had also come to mean the 'essence' of wine, but the word was not used solely for beverages until the 19th century. The names that were given to the first spirits reflected their fundamental importance to those who enjoyed them: the Latin, Russian, Swedish, Gaelic and French terms all translate as 'the water of life'.

STILL WORKING *German distillers oversee the process of making* aqua vitae *in 1532. The earliest stills collected the vapour in long, curling spouts, and were known as pot stills or alembics, from the Arabic word* al-anbiq, *'the still'. Distillation derives from the Latin* destillare, *meaning 'to drop or trickle down'.*

RECIPE FOR SUCCESS *The laborious process of distilling continues in a Danish castle around 1600. Scandinavian aquavit is made from grains, other spirits from fruit such as cherries.*

SPIRITED DRINKS
From brandy to rum

In the West, distillation was first used to isolate the essence of wine by apothecaries in the Italian town of Salerno in the early 12th century. They heated the liquid in earthenware vessels, and the rising vapours were then cooled, condensed and collected. Because alcohol boils at a lower temperature than water, the result was almost pure alcohol. As well as *aqua vitae*, 'water of life', this was known as *aqua ardens*, 'burning water'.

The apothecaries and doctors who practised distillation used wine or wine lees to make medicines. Monks distilled the juices of healing plants, evaporating them with water, or with wine, sugar and spices, to make the predecessors of liqueurs such as Chartreuse, made by Carthusian monks in Grenoble, France, 300 years ago.

During the Middle Ages *aqua ardens* became popular as a drink and by the 14th century it was being made by professional distillers. In Germany it was known as *Gebrandtwein*, 'burnt wine',

which became the Dutch *brandewijn* and eventually the English 'brandy', a word originally used for all kinds of foreign spirits apart from gin.

Cognac gets its name from the region of western France where it is made. Dutch immigrants were the first to decide to distil the area's harsh wine. Once it was realised that the process of double distillation made a particularly fine brandy, the great cognac houses were founded, the first by a Jerseyman, Jean Martell, in 1715. He was followed by a winegrower named Rémy Martin in 1724, and by Richard Hennessy, an Irishman from County Cork, in 1765.

GRAIN-BASED SPIRITS

The Celts called their 'water of life' *uisge beatha*, which evolved into *usquebaugh*, then *whiskeybaugh* and finally into 'whiskey' in Ireland and the USA, and 'whisky' in Scotland. Distillation may have reached Ireland from southern Spain, where it was introduced by the Arabs. By the 13th century, Irish religious houses were using barley to distil 'pot ale'—perhaps the earliest form of Irish whiskey.

Irish missionary monks travelling to Scotland took their knowledge of distilling with them. Although Scotch whisky had been made for some time before, the first written reference to it dates from 1494, when the Scottish Exchequer recorded that Friar John Cor bought 'eight bolls' of malt, which was enough to make 1500 bottles.

Most whisky was made at home, using surplus barley which was malted then dried over a peat fire, giving the drink its smoky taste. Blended Scotch may have originated when barley farmers from the Borders took a cask or two of whisky to a local merchant who then combined them with other casks. The Chivas brothers, John Walker and George Ballantine all began as licensed grocers making 'house blends'.

The Poles claim to have been making vodka since the 8th century, 400 years before it was recorded in Russia. In Russia the term *zhizennia voda*, 'water

of life', evolved into *vodka* or *wodka*, 'little water'. The original recipe probably arrived by way of trade routes linking Russia and Poland with the Middle East. Most vodka is distilled from grains, but early makers used any available surpluses, including molasses, fruit and potatoes.

Gin, the drink that earned the name of 'Mother's Ruin' in the 1700s from the drinking habits of wet nurses and mothers, was first thought of as a medicinal preparation. A type of gin was made in Amsterdam by 1575. However today's gin was the creation of a 17th-century Prussian-born physician named Franciscus Sylvius. He distilled a

ADVERTISEMENT FOR JOHNNIE WALKER WHISKY, 1829

pure spirit alcohol from rye, which he then redistilled with crushed juniper berries. The name of the spirit, 'jenever' or 'geneva', comes from the Dutch word *jineverbes*, 'juniper'.

In the late 1500s, English soldiers fighting with the Dutch for the Protestant cause learned to appreciate a shot of 'Dutch courage'. They called the drink itself 'Hollands' or 'gin'. Dry gin came onto the British market in the 1870s and was first made by Booth's in London. The drink was lighter and less aromatic than Dutch gin and proved popular when mixed with soda water, bitters or tonic.

The West Indies gave the world rum, distilled from the sugar cane planted there by the Spanish from the late 15th century. The name may derive from the Devonian word 'rumbullion', whose meaning is unknown. One account of

Barbados written in the mid 1600s describes 'rumbullion, alias Kill Devil', as 'hot, hellish and terrible'.

From 1655 the Royal Navy replaced beer rations with rum, which lasted better on long voyages and doubled as an anaesthetic. After Admiral Edward Vernon, nicknamed 'Old Grog' for his grogram (grosgrain) cloak, began diluting the rations in 1740, rum gained the new name of 'grog'. Those suffering from drunken dizziness were 'groggy'.

White rum was made in Jamaica by 1825. From 1862 it was produced by Emilio Bacardi, first in Cuba and from 1960 in Florida. The Cuba connection is still celebrated by two cocktails: the Cuba Libre, made from rum and Coca-Cola and created by a Florida bartender in the Spanish-American War of 1898, and the Daiquiri, consisting of rum, lime juice and sugar, which originated with American engineers working in Cuba's Daiquiri iron mines.

SHAKEN, NOT STIRRED

Xochitl, daughter of an Aztec noble, served a drink of cactus juice to the emperor, who was so impressed that he married her and named the drink after his new wife. Another account traces the cocktail to Betsy Flanagan, an American barmaid who in 1776 decorated her bar with tail feathers from roasted poultry. When asked by a drunken patron for 'a glass of those cocktails', she served him a mixed drink garnished with a feather. Or mixed drinks may be named after the *coquetier*, 'egg cup', in which they were first made by a New Orleans apothecary named Antoine-Amadé Peychaud in 1795.

BRITISH COCKTAIL RECIPE BOOK, 1930

HIGH SPIRITS *In imperial Russia vodka was the drink enjoyed by peasants and royalty alike. The House of Smirnoff was founded in Moscow after the city was burnt by Napoleon in 1812. By 1886 Smirnoff was the only vodka allowed on the imperial table.*

FASHION AND BEAUTY

More than 40 000 years ago the inhabitants of western Europe adorned themselves with jewellery of ivory and bone. Clothes, worn to protect their bodies from the elements or to provide covering for modesty's sake, came much later. The people of northern Europe probably first slung animal skins around themselves as protection from the cold in about 25 000 BC. In the Mediterranean and Middle East, fibres from plants such as flax, and the hair of goats and sheep, were woven to form lightweight fabrics that not only afforded protection against the Sun's rays but also signified social status. The earliest of these textiles, made in Anatolia in Turkey, date to about 6500 BC.

As civilisations developed, so styles of dress also evolved. In Egypt, Greece and Rome, clothes were draped, while the people of northern Europe and the East wore stitched, tubular garments. In the classical world the toga, worn not only by rulers but also by philosophers and teachers, was regarded as a symbol of civilisation. Breeches and tunics, by contrast, were considered typical of barbarian, tribal societies.

But the idea of fashion, with its ever-changing cycles of styles and trends, first took hold in the mid 1300s in Paris, London and the Italian city-states, when the elite rejected their flowing garments for tight-fitting clothes decorated to show the latest tastes. Men's robes, which had previously been ankle-length, now reached above the knee, while female dress was transformed by lacing, buttons and the introduction of the décolletage. As people desired to change their silhouettes at regular intervals—a trend that coincided with a growing international textile trade—so cutting and tailoring developed.

Early fashion belonged to the elite, who tried to preserve their social superiority with 'sumptuary laws' forbidding tradesmen and yeomen from wearing expensive and lavishly embroidered fabrics. But the French code of dressing, based on a fixed social hierarchy and courtly etiquette, was overturned by the Revolution of 1789. Elaborate wigs and powdered hair were abandoned, men's clothes were no longer embellished with embroidery and lace, and women adopted the simple Empire gown. Style became a mark of individual freedom, adopted for its own sake. No longer the preserve of the aristocracy, it soon became associated with the avant-garde, Romantic writers and artists, political activists and dandies.

In Britain affordable, mass-produced printed textiles and fashion accessories were made available by the Industrial Revolution. These were popular with the middle classes, who saw them as a means of expressing their new confidence and success. For men power now lay in business, not the court. The dark suit became a male 'uniform', while women paraded the family's status through their own and their children's dress. Fashion and femininity were inextricably entwined. Women were weighed down by petticoats and their mobility restricted by delicate shoes.

In the late 1800s attempts began to make female dress more 'sensible'. But ideals of beauty and fashion held sway, with department stores offering ready-made copies of the newest styles featured in magazines, society photographs and, from the early 1900s, the cinema. From these beginnings the consumer-orientated 20th-century fashion and beauty industries were launched.

MAX FACTOR
MUSEUM OF BEAUTY

HOLLYWOOD

LEATHER WARES
A Native American woman follows the age-old practice of decorating hide that has been prepared and tanned. Her ancestors prized buffalo and deerskin for making clothes and blankets.

FUR, LEATHER AND FELT
Nature's materials

The earliest fabrics were formed from large leaves and grasses pounded or joined together to make utilitarian clothes such as rain capes. In colder climates early humans learned to utilise gut thread and bone needles to sew animal skins into garments.

At first they used fish bones and thorns to hold the furs together at the shoulder, but by about 20000 BC they were sewing garments similar to those worn by the Inuit today, with the fur on the inside. Fur appeared on the outside of clothes only from the Middle Ages.

Once people learnt to domesticate wild animals, the skins of sheep, goats, donkeys and cattle were commonly used for clothing. In Mesopotamia, the traditional costume of the Sumerians was a sheepskin kilt.

Clothes were made from rawhide during the Palaeolithic era, but they were stiff to wear and perishable—in hot weather the hide dissolved into a glutinous mess. Possibly as early as 20000 BC people discovered how to treat rawhide to make it into leather. In Sunghir in Russia, burial mounds from that time have revealed skeletons clad in hats, shirts, trousers and moccasins made from leather or fur.

To create leather, the hair had to be removed from the hide and the skin softened with a mixture of oils, fat and brains. Inuit women wore their teeth to the gums by chewing the skins to make them supple. Then, after the fat layer had been scraped away, the inner layer was preserved by salting, smoking or tanning. Developed by the ancient Egyptians, tanning is a lengthy process that uses tannin-rich oak bark and galls—swellings on oak trees caused by

insects or microorganisms—to soften the leather permanently.

According to legend, merchants leading caravans along Middle Eastern trading routes lined their shoes with soft camel hair, and the heat, sweat and pressure produced felt. It was certainly one of the earliest materials, probably predating woven cloth. Made from compressed animal hair, it did not fray and was impermeable, making it useful in cold, damp climates. In Bronze Age Germany and Denmark people wore felt clothes, while Siberian nobles of the Iron Age sported fine felt stockings.

LEG WORK *Ancient Greek women roll wool before spinning it. Spinning was thought suitable for unmarried women, or 'spinsters'.*

WARMTH FROM WOOL
Spinning and weaving

Before wool can be woven into cloth it must be drawn out into a continuous thread. Spinning probably began in the Zagros region of Mesopotamia, where sheep were first domesticated around 9000 BC. The wool fibres would have been rolled between the hands, but from about 7000 BC the spinster put the

combed wool on a distaff, drew out the fibres and hooked them onto a spindle.

The Sumerians were raising woolly white sheep by 3000 BC, a practice continued by the Greeks and Romans. Sheep were domesticated in Britain by 700 BC, but the Romans began wool weaving there only around AD 80. Yarns such as worsted, which originated in the East Anglian village of Worstead in the 1100s, helped to build the British wool and weaving industries.

The laborious process of spinning was speeded up by the invention of the spinning wheel, which turned the spindle mechanically. It arrived in Italy from India via the Middle East around 1300, reaching Britain 40 years later.

In 1733 the English weaver John Kay invented the 'flying shuttle'. This device, which shot automatically back and forth across the material, enabled workers to weave varying widths of cloth so quickly that spinners could not supply yarn fast enough.

In 1761 the Royal Society of Arts offered a prize for a machine that could spin six threads at a time and be operated by only one worker. The winning entry, invented in 1766 by a Lancashire

RAG TRADE *The woman in red spins with a distaff and spindle while her coworkers benefit from such medieval innovations as the treadle loom and wire brushes for untangling wool.*

weaver called James Hargreaves, spun eight threads at a time. It came to be known as the spinning jenny after a common colloquial term for a machine.

Looms have existed in one form or another since 5000 BC. The most basic type of loom was strung around the waist of the weaver and attached to a tree, but this was soon followed by models with wooden frames to hold the threads in place. Thereafter looms became more complex, but using them remained labour-intensive until the invention of the power loom by a Leicestershire rector named Edmund Cartwright in 1785.

Often using two or more colours, Scottish weavers made a type of twilled

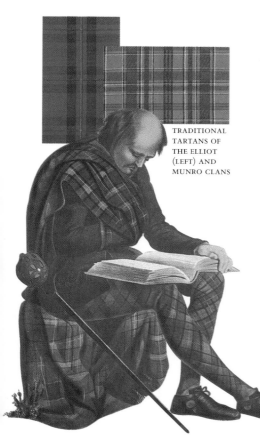

TRADITIONAL
TARTANS OF
THE ELLIOT
(LEFT) AND
MUNRO CLANS

SCOTTISH SPLENDOUR *The full glory of the Campbell tartan is demonstrated by this member of the clan in 1845. Earlier Scottish tartans were simpler, using only two or three colours to make a pattern.*

PAISLEY PATTERN *The original design was based on the pine cone or the cashew, ancient symbols of fertility.*

cloth with a diagonal weave from the 1400s. Around 1826 a London clerk making out an invoice for tweels, the Scottish spelling of 'twill', misread it and wrote the word 'tweed', a name that has stuck ever since.

Tartans have existed for centuries in both India and South-east Asia. Originally a coarse material known in Old French as *tertaine*, tartan was made in Scotland from the late Middle Ages. Scottish clans began to adopt individual tartans as interest in a mythical past grew following the defeat of Bonnie Prince Charlie in 1746. But it was British Army regimental dress, together with the monarchy and aristocracy, that popularised clan tartans, during the 19th century.

The elaborate, swirling patterns of paisley originated in the Indian region of Kashmir, where for centuries colourful shawls were woven from Pashmina wool, later known as cashmere after the Kashmir goat from which it comes.

These shawls were introduced into Britain by the East India Company in the 1760s and their immense popularity meant that copies were being reproduced by the late 1700s. In the early 19th century, paisley shawls were being made in Norwich, Edinburgh and the town of Paisley, near Glasgow.

COOL LINEN
The first textile

Deep inside a cave in the Judaean desert, preserved by the dry air, the oldest examples of woven fabric yet discovered proved to be pieces of linen dating from around 6500 BC. Linen is made from *Linum usitatissimum*, the fibrous flax plant, which in Egypt was used some 2000 years before cotton.

The ancient Egyptians collected wild flax plants from the banks of the River Nile, bound them into bundles,

then dried them. The seeds were removed before the plants were soaked in water, which separated the fibres in the stems from the hard core, after which they could be beaten, washed, spun and woven.

Cloth made from flax was strong, yet cool and light to wear. It could be wrapped or folded simply around the body. The Egyptians used sunlight to bleach their linen, which in its natural state is a dull grey-brown. White linen became a symbol of purity and divinity for the Egyptians and for the Greeks, Romans and the Christian Church.

FIGURE HUGGING *The long linen skirt of a high-ranking Egyptian nobleman reveals the favoured style of around 1400 BC, when elaborate pleating became fashionable.*

COLOURFUL CLOTH *In the 17th century cottons from India and the Middle East were so costly that wealthy and fashionable Europeans prized them above silk.*

ANCIENT ART *Chinese workers wind and dye lengths of silk in 1840. The Romans so identified the country with the material that they called China* Sericum, *from the Latin word* serica, *meaning 'silk'.*

LUXURIOUS SILK
China's best-kept secret

Around 2640 BC the mythical emperor Huang Ti asked his wife, Xi Lingshi, to discover what was eating the leaves of the mulberry trees in the palace garden. When a silkworm cocoon accidentally fell into some hot water, the empress pulled it out, only to discover that it was made from one long, delicate thread.

The origins of silk are shrouded in such legends. Certainly, however, it was the Chinese who discovered, in about 3000 BC, that the silkworm, which feeds on the leaves of the white mulberry tree, wraps itself up in a cocoon made from a single, continuous silk filament some 600-900 m (2000-3000 ft) long.

The Chinese carefully guarded their highly profitable secret: smuggling silk cocoons out of the country was punishable by death. Silk first appeared in the eastern Mediterranean around 500 BC. East and West were linked by trade, and the routes along which the material travelled was known as the Silk Road.

By 206 BC Chinese silk was being exported to Asia and the Middle East.

Industries for weaving and dyeing silk developed in Syria, Greece and Rome, but only small quantities of raw material were used. Most silk cloth from the East was unravelled and reworked.

Then, around AD 552, on behalf of the Byzantine emperor Justinian I, two Persian monks smuggled mulberry seeds and silkworm eggs out of Persia in bamboo canes, thereby founding the European silk industry. England's own industry was established from 1685 by French weavers who settled in London.

KING COTTON
The versatile fabric

On his return from India in 445 BC, the Greek historian Herodotus described 'a wool exceeding in beauty and goodness that of sheep'. Early civilisations prized cotton for its softness and whiteness. In the city of Mohenjo-Daro in the Indus Valley, people were weaving it into fabric from 3000 BC.

By 63 BC cotton was being exported to Europe from India and Egypt as a luxury material. It was introduced in Spain in the 10th century by the Moors,

PICKING COTTON *From 1815 North America rivalled India as a source of cotton, but slaves paid the price for the falling costs that brought cheaper clothes.*

and 300 years later the first of Europe's cotton industries was underway in Barcelona, mainly producing sailcloth.

These fabrics still exist in the form of denim and jean. *Serge de Nîmes*, contracted to denim in the 1500s, was made in Nîmes, France, where it was used as sailcloth. Jean, which unlike denim is dyed in solid colours or bleached, was first made in Genoa in Italy as a lining material for clothes and furnishings. It gained its present name in the 1560s, from the Genoese sailors who wore trousers made from the textile.

In England, cotton was known by the early 1200s, but no one had seen it growing. The English explorer Sir John Mandeville, returning from India in 1350, claimed that 'There grew there a wonderful tree which bore tiny lambs on the endes of its branches. These branches were so pliable that they bent down to allow the lambs to feed when they are hungrie.'

From 1612 the British East India Company began to import colourful Indian cottons such as calico, which was named after the Indian port of

WORKING ENGINE *By inventing the cotton gin in 1793, a young American named Eli Whitney speeded up the laborious process of deseeding cotton bolls by hand.*

Calicut, and brightly painted chintz, from the Sanskrit *chitra*, 'variegated' or 'spotted'. At first cotton, particularly fine muslin from Al-Mawsil in modern-day Iraq, was prized for its rarity, but the increasing mechanisation of the cotton trade made it less expensive than wool by the early 19th century. European fashions were transformed. Women of all classes began to wear printed cotton dresses—the first time popular and fashionable tastes coincided.

THE SYNTHETIC REVOLUTION
From rayon to Lycra

In 1664 Robert Hooke, Curator of Experiments to the Royal Society, first suggested the possibility of making an 'artificial glutinous composition much resembling' the substance produced by silkworms. If this solution could be formed into thin fibres, then they could be woven. Yet it was not until 1883 that the first man-made silk was created by the British inventor and physicist Sir Joseph Swan while searching for a filament for his electric lamp.

But Swan failed to exploit his new process commercially, leaving the Frenchman Comte Hilaire de Chardonnet to found the first factory for manufacturing artificial silk, or rayon, in 1890. His method was dangerous, however, and some of his early factories blew up. It was the British chemist C.S. Cross who, in 1892, patented the safer viscose process of making rayon, which is based on cellulose, the constituent of plant cells that gives fibres such as linen their strength. The earliest British maker of artificial-silk hosiery was the Wardle and Davenport company in 1912, but rayon was not widely used for clothes until the 1920s.

The first all-synthetic fibre was developed by Wallace Carothers of the American chemical company Du Pont. In 1938, after dismissing names such as Duparooh ('Du Pont pulls a rabbit out of a hat'), the company chose 'nylon'.

Initially the new material was used to make toothbrush bristles. In the USA, women had to wait until 1940 for nylon stockings, which were greeted with enthusiasm, despite rumours that they melted on contact with exhaust fumes. Delayed by wartime austerity, nylons first went on sale in Britain in 1946.

The principles used in nylon were soon adapted to create other synthetic fibres. Acrylic was sold in the USA from 1951 under the trade name Orlon. The British chemists James Dickson and Rex Whinfield discovered polyester in 1941, but it was declared secret by the Ministry of Supply until after the

HAPPY AT LAST *Despite early promises of stockings 'as strong as steel', the strength of nylon fibres, shown here magnified, ensured the material's success. In the USA, the return of nylons after shortages during the war led to the 'nylon riots' of 1945 as thousands mobbed the stores (above).*

war. Patented as Terylene in Britain, it appeared in the form of ties in 1955. In the USA it was marketed as Dacron from 1953, when Du Pont demonstrated its crease-resistant qualities with a suit that had been worn for 67 days.

But some of the most successful of the new fibres were the ones that could stretch. Lycra, marketed by Du Pont in 1959, could increase up to eight times in length and still contract to its original size, making it ideal for underwear.

WASTE NOT, WANT NOT

• In China the bark of the paper-mulberry tree was used to make not just writing paper, but clothes and even armour. Surviving examples include a paper hat, belt and shoe dating from AD 418.
• Asbestos, which was known in China from the 3rd century AD, was called by the Chinese 'cloth washable in fire' and was even, on occasion, used to make suits.

FINE WORK *By the 1300s England was famous throughout Europe for its accomplished stitchery.*

PINS AND NEEDLES
The tools of the trade

Twenty-seven thousand years ago, people protected themselves against the cold with furs they had stitched together using bone needles pierced with a hole. Pins were made from fish bones, as well as from long thorns. Later, bone, horn and ivory were used, the needles having a round hole at one end or in the middle. From 4000 BC the Egyptians were fastening clothes with copper pins. Metal needles and pins, the wire bent over to form the head, were made in Europe during the Bronze Age.

By the Middle Ages pins of the best quality were bronze, but iron or brass pins were also luxury items, hence the term 'pin money', originally the spending money given to a woman by her father or husband. To protect their delicate points, pins were being stored in cases from the 1300s; pincushions appeared in the mid 1500s. Pins continued to be made by hand until the 1820s, when Lemnel Wright, an American, developed a machine to do the job.

Steel needles were brought to Europe in the 14th century from the Middle East. The first European steel needles, which were produced in Germany in 1370, held the thread in a hook at one end. Metal needles with closed 'eyes' were being made in the Netherlands by the 15th century.

VICTORIAN NEEDLE AND THREAD CASE

Thread, too, had been transformed by this time. Early sewers had used leather thongs, gut and grasses until technology provided linen, wool, silk and cotton yarns. In Britain thread of silk or linen, thought superior to cotton, was sold loose in hanks until spools were introduced in the mid 1700s. In 1844 the mercerisation process to strengthen cotton threads and give them a sheen was invented by John Mercer.

Thimbles were worn on fingers or thumbs, hence the Old English name *thymel*, 'thumb stall'. The first thimbles were conical and fashioned from leather, but later simple bands that left the fingertip exposed were also made—examples of these have been found in the Roman ruins of Herculaneum and Pompeii. The English were making dome-shaped thimbles from the early 1500s.

A STITCH IN TIME *Singer's sewing machine, patented in 1851, was soon aimed at the mass market. As a result fashions were introduced that called for more sewn details such as ruffles.*

THE SEWING MACHINE
A servant in the house

The sewing machine brought affordable ready-made clothes within the reach of many, but at first few people wanted it. The English cabinet-maker Thomas Saint, who took out the first British patent for a sewing machine in 1790, probably never built one. Barthélemy Thimmoniers, a French tailor, created the prototype for the first commercially produced model in 1830, but his machines were destroyed by rioting tailors afraid for their jobs.

In 1834 Walter Hunt, an American inventor, created the lock stitch, the first true sewing-machine stitch. But his daughter persuaded him not to patent it because it would be 'injurious to the interests of handsewers'. Although all later machines used his lock stitch, Hunt failed to profit from it.

Nine years later, a Boston mechanic, Elias Howe, developed a machine after watching his wife's arm movements while sewing. He patented it in 1846, but was unable to find backing and in 1849 travelled to England. Howe sold the British rights for £250 to a corset manufacturer, but returned home destitute to find his patent infringed by the new manufacturers. These included Isaac Singer, who produced one of the first truly practical sewing machines in 1851. Howe successfully sued Singer, but the manufacturers subsequently decided to share ideas in one of the first patent 'pools'. It was Singer who forged ahead, however, introducing the home sewing machine in 1856.

In the 13th century a French tailor created the first pattern from thin wood, but his idea was discouraged by the tailors' guild until the 16th century. Help came for amateur sewers during the 19th century, when some women's magazines began offering their readers one-size patterns for embroidery, lace and dressmaking.

Packaged paper patterns, sized and with instructions, were the brainwave of Ebenezer Butterick, an American tailor. He created his first pattern, for a man's shirt, in 1863. Within a decade millions of his patterns were being sold across the USA and Britain, making fashion accessible to the middle classes.

NEEDLECRAFT *Samplers embroidered with pictures and letters show the skill of the sewer but they have also been used to commemorate such important life events as the birth of a child, as celebrated on this linen cloth of 1598.*

STITCHING TECHNIQUES
The art of necessity

Quilting and patchwork were skills born of necessity and thrift. Both the Egyptians and the Chinese knew how to quilt by about 3400 BC, while the oldest known piece of patchwork in the world was put together around 980 BC in Egypt using the dyed and shaped hide of a gazelle.

The Chinese donned quilted clothes as protection against the cold, but quilting was also useful against a more deadly enemy: in 490 BC Persian soldiers at the Battle of Marathon had

PRECIOUS ART *Embroiderers used threads of silver, gold or silk to work such decorative designs as this simple chain-stitch pheasant created in China in the 5th century* BC.

quilted armour. In the 11th century the Crusaders wore quilted clothing under their armour and brought the technique back to western Europe. By 1563 the trade in quilted bedding was established in London. In North America, English settlers of the 1600s recycled scraps of fabric to make patchwork quilts.

Simple oversewing to mend and patch skins and fabrics gradually developed into more complicated stitches and designs. Embroidery seems to have originated in China, Japan, Arabia and Mesopotamia before 1200 BC. In Britain the first reference to a specific embroiderer dates to AD 679, when Thomas of Ely described how St Etheldreda, the abbess of Ely, offered vestments worked in gold and jewels to St Cuthbert.

As it is known today, lacemaking, the most expensive of textile techniques, is European in origin. Bobbin lace evolved from weaving in early 16th-century Flanders. It uses a pillow, a pattern and numerous threads, each of which is weighted by a bobbin. Needle lace, which began in Italy in the late 1400s, is created with a single thread and needle and is worked using thousands of buttonhole stitches to cover a web of threads.

AN EYE FOR DETAIL *The exquisitely delicate work of bobbin lacemakers was first used in modest trimmings for underlinen, but by the 1600s lace had become a luxury item for both men and women, fashioned into cravats, cuffs, headdresses and gowns.*

SKIRT AND DRESS
Fashion essentials

The earliest styled garments were draped around the body, accentuating its contours while marking the wearer's status and gender. In Egypt this form of dress developed before 1500 BC from the *schenti*, a belted loincloth that was more like a pleated, knee-length skirt. For women, the skirt finished under the breasts, secured by shoulder straps.

The styles adopted by the classical Greeks and Romans were looser. The chiton, which formed the basis of the Greek wardrobe from 700 BC, fell from the shoulders and waist in folds. The man's chiton was shorter, but otherwise there was little difference between the sexes. In Italy, the early Etruscans used ties to create close-fitting dresses, but contact with Greek civilisation led to the adoption of a draped

BEAUTY AND STYLE *A tunic gown adorns an Etruscan statuette of Aphrodite from the 6th century BC.*

TAKING A STROLL *The classically inspired Empire-line gowns of the early 1800s were lighter than any seen since ancient times. White was the colour of choice.*

chiton for Roman women and a flowing, semicircular toga for men.

In the 5th century AD the draped look was abandoned as the influence of northern Europe grew, spread by the Germanic tribes who invaded Gaul and raided Britain. From about 450 to 1300 the dress was a sewn, T-shaped garment belted at the waist. A flared skirt helped to accentuate the bust, waist and hips.

Around 1350 the rise of competitive court societies in Italy and France introduced the idea of a fashion cycle. The dress now became the focus for the tailor's skill and the wearer's sophisticated taste. Lacing, buttoning and the

cutting of fabric across the grain all contributed to a fitted look.

The floor-length gown became an exclusively feminine item in the early 16th century. From 1530 female costume was composed of the bodice and the skirt or 'kirtle'; the one-piece outfit remained as a long undershift. This form of dressing was worn for ceremonial occasions until the 18th century. For more private moments, the one-piece gown had re-emerged by 1700 as the loose, open-fronted 'mantua', which was often worn in the mornings.

In the 1800s advances in the technology of clothing production and materials led to a wider variety of styles suitable for particular occasions. The width of the crinoline dictated the fashion for skirts, blouses and jackets in the 1860s, but from 1870 princess-line dresses were cut in one length.

By the turn of the century the new pursuits of cycling and tennis had hastened the fashion for tailored skirts and blouses. The trend for sensible rather than symbolic

ENGLISH LOOK *Lifting her gown from the ground, a well-to-do woman of 1540 reveals the stylish cut of its pinned-up skirt, cut separately from the bodice.*

forms of dress—part of the movement towards emancipation—underpinned the simplification of female dress. From 1925 the short, shift-like dress encouraged the switch to mass production. It was left to designers such as Coco Chanel in the 1920s and Christian Dior in the 1950s to introduce stylistic features that reflected the mood and taste of the time.

WOMEN'S WEAR *A blouse and skirt made a practical outfit for work or sports. In 1906 these elaborate confections were also available.*

THE SHIRT
Buttoned up

Evolving from the simple T-shaped undergarment of the Middle Ages, the linen shirt with embroidered front, cuffs and collar formed a distinctive and expensive part of the male wardrobe by 1530. By 1600, collars and cuffs had become such elaborate displays of lace and starch that they were separated from the body of the shirt and tied on.

This practice continued until the early 20th century, when stiffened cuffs and collars were attached by studs. The main part of the garment changed little, although the rise of the three-piece suit during the 18th century meant that less of the shirt was visible.

From about 1720 comfort, fit and respectability dictated the introduction of pleated sleeves, neck gussets and longer shirt tails. Completely open-fronted, buttoned shirts only became common after 1900, when stripes and colours provided some choice. By this

time the blouse was acceptable as both day and evening wear for women.

During the 1920s American shirts with buttoned cuffs and attached collars announced a greater informality in male dress, with exotically patterned shirts designed for leisurewear. But in Britain the business shirt retained unbuttoned cuffs until the early 1960s.

FASTENED UP
Safety pins, buttons and zips

In the 2nd millennium BC in Greece, Italy or Sicily, the original safety pin was created by doubling a straight bronze pin and hooking one end into the other. The Romans wore safety pins as brooches, known as *fibulae*, using them for fastening their cloaks and robes. But the safety pin then seems to have disappeared until it was reinvented in 1849 by the prolific American inventor Walter Hunt.

Finding himself $15 in debt to a draughtsman, Hunt spent just 3 hours one afternoon

BREATHE IN *Belts have been used since earliest times to hold in place clothes, tools or weapons. A buckle such as this 6th-century bronze one added style.*

twisting pieces of wire. The resulting 'Dress Pin' had a coil spring and a concealed point. His colleague paid him $400 for the rights, and the modern safety pin was created.

Buttons existed long before there were buttonholes. First seen by the 3rd millennium BC in the Indus Valley civilisation of Mohenjo-Daro, buttons were made from wood, bone, shells, stone, horn or pottery, and were more decorative than useful. The Romans, however, used them as fasteners by inserting them into loops sewn onto the edge of a garment.

Buttons were known in Britain from the 2nd millennium BC, but they were

valued as fashion accessories. Girdles, sashes and clasps secured the loose clothes that were generally worn before fashions became more fitted during the 14th century, after the appearance of the buttonhole.

Hand-made from precious metals, glass or even gems, buttons became symbols of rank and wealth for the fashionable in the 14th and 15th centuries. It was around this time that women's clothes began to be buttoned differently from men's. One explanation is that the buttons on women's gowns were sewn on the side that suited the right-handed action of the servant facing her mistress. Another suggests that men's coats were designed to fasten so that they could draw their swords more easily.

Buttons became popular during the 18th century, when they began to be mass-produced from sheet metal. Even ankle boots were fastened by rows and rows of tiny buttons, thereby making the button hook an indispensable item.

STATUS SYMBOL *The Celts made rich use of gold for jewellery and other ornaments, including buttons.*

In 1893 a Chicago inventor named Whitcomb L. Judson patented a 'clasp locker or unlocker' for boots and shoes, but his invention was as clumsy as its name.

Not until 1913 was the first practical 'hookless fastener' patented, by a Swedish-born American engineer named Gideon Sundback, who was employed by the Automatic Hook and Eye Company. The Talon Slide Fastener, as it was called, was used by US armed services in the First World War.

W.L. JUDSON'S SHOE-FASTENING PATENT, 1893

In 1923 the fastener was adopted by the American B.F. Goodrich Company for its brand of galoshes, originally called Mystik Boots. The enthusiastic president of the company renamed the boot the Zipper, and the name quickly caught on for the new fastening.

A SUIT OF CLOTHES

*'In this month his Magestie and whole Court changed the fashion
of their clothes…a close coat of cloth…reached the calf of the leg, and upon that
a surcoat… The breechs [were] of the same colour as the vest or garment.'*

Rugge's Diurnal, OCTOBER 11, 1666

When, in the 14th century, the accounts for Edward III's Great Wardrobe itemised several 'suits of clothes'—probably the first recorded use of the expression—they simply meant outfits of between three and six garments. From 1600 the masculine costume of a close-fitting jacket known as a doublet, breeches and hose made up a form of suit, especially when all of one colour.

Although the individual elements existed, the idea of a suit of matching coat, waistcoat and breeches was not established until the 1660s. In England it was Charles II who introduced the suit, following a fashion set by the French king Louis XIV. The London

ROYAL FASHION *The suit—and French tastes—began to dominate European fashions in the 1660s under Louis XIV, seated here in 1711 in a suit of flared coat, vest and breeches.*

diarist Samuel Pepys described the new mode on October 15, 1666: 'This day the King begins to put on his vest…being a long cassocke close to the body, of black cloth, and pinked with white silke under it, and a coat over it, and the legs ruffled with black riband like a pigeon's leg.'

Buttoned the length of the front, the vest was the forerunner of today's waistcoat, although until the 1750s it often had sleeves. Like the coat, which replaced the doublet, it was collarless, knee-length and loose-fitting. The coat was left open to reveal part of the rich fabric of the vest, but cheaper material was often used for the back, hence the vest's early name of 'cheat'.

The 18th-century man of fashion had informal, dress and court suits, but the difference between them was more in the fabric than the cut, with court

suits usually made of white, red, green or pink silk or velvet. But in England and France from the 1760s there was a move towards a simpler English style based on the clothes worn by the aristocracy for country pursuits. In dull shades of brown, blue or black, these wool suits were more informal.

By the second half of the century, the coat's full skirt had been trimmed

COUNTRY CLOTHES *The plainer English style of the late 18th century, worn here by the son of a rich cotton manufacturer, consisted of a long coat, vest and knee breeches.*

MAROON AND BLACK *In his jerkin, doublet and trunk hose, an Italian nobleman of 1526 wears the sombre Spanish style of matching clothes that preceded the three-piece suit.*

to create the tailcoat and morning coat. Around 1770 the small coat collar appeared. As turned-down coat collars grew higher, wigs and hairstyles grew shorter. By 1780 the vest had reached waist level. In fashionable circles the unsightly expanse of shirt that was now exposed by the shorter waistcoat was bridged by braces.

THE AGE OF RESPECTABILITY

Trousers have been worn since ancient times: the Chinese dressed in trousers tied at the waist and often at the ankles to protect them against the cold, while Asian nomads wore similar garments for riding. In Persia they were traditional for women as well as for men, spreading to central Europe by 400 BC. Celtic peoples adopted trousers in the following century. Englishmen wore ankle-length *braies* or breeches until the 1100s. Thereafter braies became undergarments and were replaced by knee breeches.

English sailors and soldiers wore wide-legged trousers from the 1730s, but trousers only became fashionable after 1807, at first for informal daywear. Initially they were almost identical to close-fitting pantaloons, which replaced knee breeches from 1790. Beau Brummell, the dandy and champion of simple English style

and tailoring, initiated a trend for wearing tight black trousers.

By 1817 trousers were shoe-length. Popular with George IV, they were accepted as standard daywear by 1825. They were worn with a waistcoat and a full-skirted frock coat—first seen in the late 1700s—for the day, but with a tailcoat for the evening. The favourite

CASUAL WEAR *By 1905 the lounge suit, soon to be known as the business suit, no longer retained the short, square look of the sack jacket, and had become longer and leaner.*

patterns for trousers were strong plaids, stripes and checks. The loose, tubular cut was established in the 1860s. Trousers with front creases appeared in the 1880s and by 1913 had become common garb.

Not until the 1850s did the jacket become fashionable for casual wear. At first known as the sack coat, and later as the lounge jacket, its ancestor was

the short suit jacket worn by boys and working men. In the age of the sewing machine, mass production and the first ready-made suits, the jacket's simpler, more box-like structure was easier to make than the tailored coat.

By the 1860s the lounge jacket was being worn with matching trousers in plain materials, stripes or even checks. The lounge suit was adopted for informal daywear by the middle classes keen to present a respectable exterior, but businessmen kept their frock coats until the 1920s. Ties, worn since the 1830s, added a splash of colour.

In the 1860s the Norfolk jacket, a version of the lounge jacket, appeared, worn with matching knickerbockers for outdoor pursuits, one of a number of garments influenced by the growing enthusiasm for sports. Used for sports and summer wear from the 1880s, the blazer was said to have been created in the mid 1800s on HMS *Blazer*. The ship's captain, irritated by the sight of his ragged crew, ordered them to wear blue serge jackets with navy buttons, or so the story goes.

For women, matching jackets and skirts appeared as holiday wear in the 1850s. By the 1890s tailor-made costumes were smart and practical everyday garments for young working women. The first trouser-suit to be worn by a woman was modelled by the French actress Sarah Bernhardt in Paris in 1876, but it was not until the late 1920s that women began to wear beach 'pyjamas'. Thereafter trousers were quickly accepted for holidays, sports and country walking.

STARCHED COLLAR, 1925

COATS AND MACKINTOSHES
Against the elements

To keep out the cold, prehistoric people fashioned cloaks out of animal skins held to their bodies with a leather thong. The basic design, used in ancient cultures and in the early centuries AD, was bell-shaped with a hole cut for the head—'cloak' comes from the Old French *cloke*, 'bell'. For ordinary men and women cloaks were doubly useful, serving as clothing and bedcovers. More luxurious Egyptian capes were made of fine linen and hung from a decorative neckband.

The caftan, a sleeved garment worn crossed over in front and tied with a sash, originated in Asia in ancient times. It reached eastern Europe during the 13th century, when it was worn over trousers and fastened with a belt.

In western Europe the first true overcoat appeared in the late 16th century in the form of a calf-length coat with a fitted body and gathered skirt. Often blue, it was worn by apprentices, servants and those belonging to educational institutions such as Christ's Hospital in London. As a result, Christ's Hospital students were called bluecoat boys—and gentlemen avoided wearing the colour blue.

Only in the 1700s did the outdoor coat become a fashionable and practical

PRACTICAL STYLE *The greatcoat of 1753 was characterised by its shoulder capes and wide, buttoned cuffs. French by design, it was abandoned by the fashion-conscious from the 1830s, but survived as the coachman's box coat.*

a round armhole extended in one piece to the neckline.

The trench coat also had military origins. Manufactured in 1910 as the Tielocken by Thomas Burberry of London, it acquired its present name in the First World War, when a version that had rings attached to the belt for carrying grenades was made for army officers.

During the Second World War the British navy developed a warm, short coat that fastened with wooden toggles. It was made from a thick woollen material known as Duffel after the Belgian

BURBERRY'S ADVERTISEMENT, 1910

BURBERRY'S ADVERTISEMENT FOR THE TIELOCKEN, 1910

GRIPPING STUFF

While hunting, Georges de Mestral, a Swiss aristocrat, was inspired to create an alternative to the zip by the burs that attached themselves to his clothes and to his dog. Examining the burs under a microscope, he realised they were covered in thousands of hooks and tried to reproduce the effect. The result, patented in 1956, was two strips, one with tiny loops to which the little hooks on the other clung. Although his fastener was made from nylon, de Mestral named it Velcro, from the French *velours*, 'velvet', and *croché*, 'hooked'.

alternative to the cloak and the cape. Initially men's coats were either top coats, styled identically to their indoor equivalents but made of a heavier fabric and considered suitable for walking, or capacious, heavy-duty greatcoats for travelling.

Coat styles proliferated during the 1800s. Around 1830, fashionable men adopted the knee-length waisted wool coat with a black velvet collar. The Raglan overcoat of 1857—named after Lord Raglan, commander of British forces in the Crimean War—was distinguished by the cut of its sleeves, which instead of being stitched into

town where it was first made commercially in the 19th century. After the war, large quantities of surplus coats were sold off cheaply, making duffle coats a new 'uniform' for students.

The search for waterproof clothing began when ancient peoples tied water-repellent leaves to a net base, or sewed strips of animal intestines together to create capes and head coverings. The Inuit made a type of waterproof hooded coat from strips of seal intestine or from seal or reindeer skin; this was known as a *parka* in the Aleutian Islands and an *anoraq* in Greenland. With the growing fashion for winter sports, 'anorak' was adopted by the Scandinavians in the 1920s for a lightweight, wind and rain-resistant sports jacket, while the heavier windcheater became known as a parka.

The first raincoat was created in 1747 in French Guiana by an engineer named François Fresnau, who water-proofed an old overcoat by smearing it with latex from rubber trees. Fox's Aquatic Gambroon Cloak was manu-factured in London in 1821 using 'gam-broon', a water-repellent twill, but the first man to exploit the commercial potential of waterproof fabric was the Scottish chemist Charles Macintosh.

Macintosh sandwiched two pieces of cloth tightly together with a solution of

WARM AND DRY *The traditional anorak worn by Inuit women (left) allows the wearer to carry her baby on her back. A Murgatroyd raincoat demonstrates the 1950s taste for artificial fabrics.*

India rubber, but although waterproof, the resulting fabric was almost too stiff to tailor. Then a medical student named James Syme discovered a better method for dissolving rubber. In 1823 Macintosh patented the process using woollen cloth and began to make the waterproof coats that bear his name.

Still, early mackintoshes had some disadvantages. In 1839 the *Gentleman's Magazine of Fashion* remarked that 'a Macintosh is now become a trouble-some thing…on account of the offen-sive smell.' Until Charles Goodyear's vulcanisation process was applied to the cloth in 1843, it melted in hot weather.

In 1851 the Aquascutum company of London produced a chemically treated fabric that repelled water and could also be styled into the latest fashions. The name comes from two Latin words meaning 'water shield'.

Aquascutum coats established their reputation in the Crimean War, helped by the tale of one General Goodlake and his sergeant, who, finding them-selves surrounded by the enemy, were able to escape because the Russians mis-took the Britons' grey raincoats for their own uniform.

GLOVES AND SCARVES
Protection and ornament

In ancient Egypt, Greece and Rome, gloves were worn for protecting the hands from hard work, for hunting and by soldiers. Among the treasures dis-covered in the tomb of Tutankhamun was a pair of white linen gloves dating to the 14th century BC.

From the 6th century AD a pair of gloves was given to a bishop at his con-secration to signify that his hands were clean for God's work. By the Middle Ages jewel-encrusted gloves were also symbols of power. Despite his disguise, Richard the Lionheart is said to have been taken prisoner on his way back from the Crusades because he could not bear to part with his costly gloves.

Leather gauntlets used for hawking and falconry were associated with the medieval knight, who would challenge another knight by striking him with his gauntlet or throwing it to the ground.

Only after 1834, when the cutting die was invented by the Frenchman

Xavier Jouvin, based on detailed studies of hands in a dissecting room, did gloves become everyday wear for all. The die, which could cut out six gloves at once, enabled gloves of a standard size and shape to be mass-produced for the first time.

The origins of the headscarf and the handkerchief lie in the Anglo-Saxon headrail. Later known as the coverchief, from the Old French *couvrechef*, 'head

CASUAL ELEGANCE *A woman of the 1880s wears the long gloves that were essential items of feminine full dress from 1640. Before 1640, gloves were virtually the same for both sexes.*

covering', it covered the head and shoulders, hanging down the side of the face. After the upper classes abandoned it in the 1400s, the kerchief, as it was then known, was worn by peasant and working-class women until the 1800s.

Flowing scarves were an essential part of the feminine wardrobe around 1790 to 1830, reappearing in the 1880s with two American dancers who took Europe by storm. Dancing with the Folies Bergères in Paris, Loie Fuller used lengths of material stitched to batons, while Isadora Duncan incorpo-rated yards of flowing drapes into her unique 'free-form' dancing. After the Russian Ballet also used scarves to sen-suous effect from 1910, the possibilities of the scarf were quickly recognised.

EVENING WEAR
Dressing for dinner

The evening dress code was set by the Englishman George 'Beau' Brummell. He perfected his sober style between 1800 and 1817, introducing the tailored black coat and black pantaloons as fashionable dress for evening engagements. Until then 'full dress' for a man had simply meant a more elaborate version of the suit he wore during the day.

This change coincided with a trend for dividing the day—and fashions—into neat sections based on mealtimes. The concept of evening dress was in place by the 1820s, and in 1838 the Parisian paper *Le Dandy* noted that 'the black English suit with silk buttons is always required' for important occasions.

By the 1850s men's evening wear had become a uniform of black tailcoat and trousers with a braid stripe on the outside seam, waistcoat, white shirt and white cravat. The waistcoat was either black or white until the end of the century, after which white was established as *de rigueur*.

The dinner jacket was greeted with shock by society commentators. Its place of origin is claimed as Monte Carlo, London and New York, where in 1886 the millionaire Griswold Lorillard wore it to a

BEAU BRUMMELL, 1805

ball at the Tuxedo Park Country Club. In the USA it is still a 'tuxedo'.

Derived from the lounge jacket in the 1880s, the early 'dress lounge'—the term 'dinner jacket' was coined only in 1898—was worn with a black waistcoat and a black tie. By about 1914 it was fastened with one button, and by the 1920s it was double-breasted.

But evening dress was expensive. In 1897 Charles Pond, an impoverished entertainer, asked to borrow a dress suit from Moss Bros, a secondhand clothing shop in London established by Moses Moss in 1860. Moss's son Alfred lent

TIMELESS APPEAL *Designing for the Chanel label in 1995, Karl Lagerfeld re-created a look worn by Coco Chanel in the 1930s. Now the epitome of haute couture, her first designs were made to be worn for exercise and sport.*

Pond a dress suit without charge several times before the men agreed on a fee, thereby establishing the earliest dresswear hire firm.

The first designer whose name was as familiar as her work was influential was a Frenchwoman named Rose Bertin. In the 1770s she was dressmaker and milliner to the French queen Marie Antoinette, but died in poverty in 1812, her fashions out of date.

Until the mid 1800s fashionable women visited dressmakers who would custom-make outfits for each client in their workshops. The idea of the luxury haute-couture salon, where a designer showed his creations, emerged with the establishment of the first fashion house in Paris. But although France was the acknowledged arbiter of fashion from

FASHION FOR ALL

• The Reverend William Lee, who lived near Nottingham, developed the first knitting machine in 1589. Trying to attract a woman who was a keen knitter, he devised a frame to knit worsted stockings.

• Dungarees take their name from a poor-quality Indian calico that came from the Dungri area of Bombay.

• In 1963 the invention of the plastisol transfer allowed people to choose their designs, reinforcing the T-shirt's status as a consumer classic.

the mid 17th century, the first haute couturier was an Englishman.

Born in Lincolnshire in 1825, at the age of 12 Charles Frederick Worth was apprenticed to a firm of drapers. Eight years later he left for Paris to become a designer, setting up the House of Worth in 1858. Although he took credit for the demise of the crinoline in 1870, his skill was not so much in revolutionising fashion as in marketing it. Worth introduced the designer label and the idea of using live mannequins to model his creations. These innovations helped to make him the first fashion tycoon.

It was a woman, however, who realised that couture clothes could be both elegant and comfortable. Gabrielle 'Coco' Chanel opened her first dress shop in Paris in 1910, but was forced to close her second during the First World War. She reopened in 1919 and by 1924 was leading the fashion world. Taking her inspiration from men's clothing, she introduced a relaxed way of dressing based on wool jersey or cotton dresses, trousers, cardigans and fake jewellery. Practical, modern and stylish, her designs revolutionised women's fashion and were soon copied the world over.

LA BELLE PERSONNE

ELEGANCE AT A PRICE *Worth's successors maintained the label's fashionable status with designs such as this evening dress of 1924 to 1925, the first season of calf-length dresses. Parisian fashion houses introduced 'le cocktail dress' with the cocktails vogue of the 1920s.*

THE CASUAL LOOK
Everyday clothes

When designers such as Chanel made casual clothes fashionable in the 1920s and 1930s, knitwear became essential items in a woman's wardrobe. The origins of knitting remain obscure: it was possibly developed by Arabian nomads around 1000 BC, or in Egypt from the 7th century AD. The earliest examples date to the 1100s. By the 13th century knitting had reached Europe, where its popularity was reflected in the 'knitting Madonnas' painted in the late 1300s.

The people of the Channel Island of Jersey were known for knitting high-quality stockings by the 1580s. Jersey was the name for all knitted garments until, in the late 1600s, it was associated with the blue fisherman's jersey. Men adopted striped jerseys for winter sports in the second half of the 19th century.

DESIGNER LABEL *Added in 1886, the Levi's patch illustrates the garment's strength. The stitching on the back pockets, dating to 1873, symbolises the wings of an eagle and freedom.*

In the 1890s American college athletes coined the word 'sweater' to describe the garment's effect on their bodies.

Hoping to strike it rich in the Gold Rush, in 1853 a 24-year-old Bavarian named Levi Strauss left New York for San Francisco. But instead of prospecting, he saw a future in outfitting miners and established a wholesale business selling materials and other dry goods.

In 1872 a Nevada tailor named Jacob Davis wrote to Strauss telling him of his own method of placing metal rivets to fasten pocket seams and the base of the fly. Davis asked if he would finance a patent with him. Strauss agreed and the patent was granted in 1873.

Made in denim with braces buttons, a back pocket and a watch

pocket, the 'waist overalls' proved so popular that two factories were built. When, around 1890, lot numbers were given to the products, the overalls with copper rivets became lot '501'.

A 'lightweight short-sleeve white cotton undervest' was regulation uniform in the US Navy from 1899. Still, American men only abandoned the all-in-one union suit after coming across the more comfortable French sleeveless cotton vest during the First World War.

Undershirt sales plummeted when Clark Gable appeared vestless in the 1934 film *It Happened One Night*. Then, in 1942, the US Navy made the 'T-type' shirt regulation underwear. But it was Marlon Brando's T-shirt-clad performance in the 1951 film *A Streetcar Named Desire* that transformed the T-shirt into outerwear for men. Women followed suit after the French film stars Brigitte Bardot and Jean Seberg were pictured wearing T-shirts from 1960.

THE WILD ONE *By giving the T-shirt 'rebel status', the film star Marlon Brando helped to transform a plain white undershirt into the most widely worn garment this century.*

NEXT TO THE SKIN

*'In olden days a glimpse of stocking was looked on as
something shocking. Now, heaven knows, anything goes.'*

'ANYTHING GOES', FROM THE SHOW OF THE SAME NAME, COLE PORTER, AMERICAN COMPOSER, 1934

Many items that would now be considered undergarments, worn for modesty, warmth or to shape the silhouette, were once outerwear. In ancient Egypt the basic and often the only item of clothing for men was the linen *schenti* or loincloth. Children and servants often went naked, while dancers were scantily clad in girdles. Higher ranks wore draped robes in public, but, like the Greeks, they did not distinguish between outer and undergarments.

Nevertheless, it was the Greeks who, in about 400 BC, introduced the forerunners of the bra and corset, although neither seems to have been common. A breast band flattened the bust, while the figure was shaped by a *zoné*, a band of linen or kid worn around the waist and lower body.

Roman women wore similar items under their tunics. For Roman men a linen loincloth was the original and sole undergarment. During the winter, emperors wore *femoralia*, knee-length drawers; these were adopted by soldiers during the 2nd century BC and by civilians in the following century.

Then, in the 4th century AD, the loincloth was replaced by the *camisia*. At a time when it was difficult to keep clothes or bodies clean, it usefully protected outergarments. For men it took the form of a loose shirt and for women a longer smock or shift. Later known by the Norman term *chemise*, this was the essential undergarment for both sexes until the 19th century.

By the Middle Ages, influenced by the Germanic tribes who overran Europe after the fall of Rome, men's outerwear consisted of a short tunic

MENSWEAR *A late-15th-century portrait of St Roch, who devoted his life to caring for plague victims, shows how hose were cut from cloth and tied to the tunic with laces.*

and breeches called *braies*. But with the Norman fashion for longer tunics, braies became undergarments, growing shorter until, by about 1500, they resembled trunks.

As braies shrank, leg coverings grew longer. Roman *fascia* were lengths of cloth wrapped around the leg, but were thought effeminate and suitable only for old people. Nevertheless, it was men who first wore knee-length stockings, or *chausses*, in western Europe in the 9th century. From about 1340, when they were renamed 'hose',

COVERING UP *The fashionably tiny waist of the 1830s was achieved by whalebone or steel corsets and emphasised by layers of petticoats. Underneath is a voluminous chemise.*

meaning 'leg covering', they fitted the leg tightly from foot to crotch. Women, too, began to wear stockings, but until the 1960s only ballet dancers and actors wore tights.

In the 16th century men's hose were divided into trunk hose, which covered the seat, and 'netherstocks', which covered the lower legs and from the mid 1500s were called stockings.

FRENCH SWIMWEAR, 1908

BATHING BEAUTIES

In the late 1700s women adopted chemise-like gowns for sea bathing, then newly fashionable. Most men swam naked until the mid 1800s, but in 1870 the all-in-one suit appeared. A knee-length skirt made the one-piece costume acceptable for women by 1914, but by the 1920s it reached the hips only. In 1946 the French couturier Jacques Heim designed a two-piece outfit whose impact was compared with the atom-bomb tests on Bikini Atoll. But Sicilian mosaics from the 4th century AD show female athletes wearing the very first bikinis.

Socks were known in Britain from Roman times, and Charles I wore them for ball games, but ankle socks were first introduced, along with trousers, in the early 19th century.

BURDENSOME LAYERS

Although clay figurines made in Minoan Crete around 2000 BC show snake-goddesses dressed in flounced skirts and corsets, the slim waist became the foundation of European fashion only in the 14th century.

At first the new look was achieved by lacing, but the Elizabethan 'body' or 'pair of bodies', from which the word 'bodice' derives, was made of rods or busks of bone or wood. 'Body' gave way to 'stays' in the early 1600s and to 'corset'—from the Old French *cors*, 'body'—in the late

MODERN MISS *During the 1920s, the age of the boyish figure, bras simply covered the breasts, but in the 1930s they were designed to uplift and shape. Cup sizes were introduced in 1935.*

1700s. By then it was a separate garment, usually made of whalebone, rather than part of the dress itself.

The petticoat's name reflects its 15th-century origins as a man's 'petty coat', from the French *petit cote*, 'little jacket', the precursor of the waistcoat. But in the 1500s 'under-petticoat' came to refer to an undergarment tied to the bodice of the dress with laces.

In the late 18th century petticoats were unsuitable under the Empire-line sheath dresses made of flimsy new materials such as muslin. As a result, a trend for pantalettes or drawers began among young girls, and was later adopted by their elders. At the same time, wax or cotton 'bust improvers' helped to shape the figure.

Respectable Victorian women were weighed down by layers of underwear, but in the 1870s came combinations—chemise and drawers in one. Men had been wearing one-piece garments combining undervest and drawers from the early 1860s. In the 1880s concerns about health and hygiene brought innovations such as the German doctor Gustav Jaeger's woollen underwear, which allowed the body to 'breathe'.

With the new century, underwear became lighter and simpler. After 1910 men's combinations often consisted of a short-sleeved top and shorts, while in 1935 the American underwear manufacturers Coopers patented the Y-Front. At first called 'Brief Style 1001', it was inspired by a magazine photograph of a man wearing a pair of swimming trunks on the French Riviera. On its

SHOP DISPLAY FOR Y-FRONTS, 1950s

launch in Chicago, the entire stock of 600 pairs sold out on the first day. Y-Fronts were made in Britain from 1938, but by the late 1940s were facing competition from boxer shorts, worn as US army issue during the war.

For women, the revolution began around 1910 when the S-shaped figure of Edwardian fashions gave way to a more natural line. Even so, early brassieres—the term is first recorded in American *Vogue* in 1907, although why a French name for a baby's vest was adopted is unclear—were rigid affairs that also covered the midriff.

But in 1913 an American debutante named Mary Phelps Jacob (later Mrs Caresse Crosby) rebelled. One evening before a dance she asked her maid to tie two handkerchiefs to a length of ribbon, thereby creating the modern brassiere. Jacob's friends loved the idea, which she patented in 1914, but after failing to market it successfully she sold her patent to Warner Bros for $15000. By this time the brassiere was already a success story. With the introduction of synthetic fibres, the reign of restricting steel, whalebone and canvas finally came to an end.

BACK TO BASICS *By the late 1920s, women were free of the tyranny of bulky, constricting underwear. The streamlined silhouette demanded nothing more than a bra and girdle.*

EVERYDAY HATS
Headwear for all occasions

Animal skins, leaves and straw were transformed into the earliest head-gear, while animal skulls covered in fur became the first helmets. These functional items afforded protection from the weather or from aggressors, but hats were also status symbols. In both ancient Greece and Rome, only freedmen were entitled to wear them.

Being easy to make, variations of the cap were worn in most early civilisations. The ancient Greek model was the close-fitting felt *pilos*. These were early berets, perennially fashionable in the traditional Basque form popularised by the French in the 1920s.

It was the women of Minoan Crete who, around 2100 BC, sported what may have been the first 'smart' hats: pointed hats, berets, turbans and three-cornered constructions with ribbons or plumes. Greek women shaded themselves from the sun with the wide-brimmed *petasos*. But from about 1200 BC feminine head-wear consisted of scarves, hoods, veils or headdresses—hats for women did not reappear until the 16th century.

From Roman times until the Middle Ages most men wore caps or hoods. Ways of draping hoods grew increasingly intricate, however, and by the early 1400s the 'fashioned hood' was in effect a hat, kept in shape with a padded ring and wicker hoops. Thereafter, men of fashion donned hats.

Both sexes wore bonnets in the 1500s, but these soft, velvet affairs bore

TRILBY, 1930s

BOWLER, 1910–20

BERET, 1920s

BOATER, ABOUT 1910

HOMBURG, 1920–30

BONNET, 1840s

PANAMA, ABOUT 1910

TOP HAT, 1890s

FLAT CAP, 1880s

SIGN OF THE TIMES *During the 16th century the soft black cap was regulation wear for tradesmen and artisans. Gentlemen adopted the flat peaked cap for country pursuits in the late 19th century, but made sure never to wear it 'in Town'.*

HATS OFF *From earliest times hats symbolised social status. Tall, stiff headgear such as the top hat made the wearer more imposing, while Victorian women always wore a modest cap or bonnet. The enthusiasm for sports in the late 1800s brought casual styles such as the boater.*

GAINING AN ADVANTAGE

• In ancient Greece, courtesans wore sandals with nails studded into the sole so that their footprints would leave the message 'Follow me'.

• Roman charioteers wore the first peaked caps—made of bronze—to shield their eyes from the sun's glare.

• The expression 'hat trick' dates from a cricketing practice of the late 1850s, when bowlers who got three batsmen out in successive balls were rewarded with a new white hat.

no relation in style to the rigid bonnets women adopted in the Victorian era. There was also an Elizabethan bowler with a hatband made of crepe, silk and pearls, or silk and spangles.

The traditional men's bowler was designed by the London hatters Lock's of St James's in 1850, at the request of William Coke, a Norfolk landowner who wanted a hard, close-fitting hat for his gamekeepers. Although sometimes still called a 'Coke', it is more generally known as a bowler after Thomas and William Bowler, the firm of feltmakers who manufactured it. The grey, flat-brimmed version named after the Earl of Derby caught on in the USA, where men's clothes were more informal.

The other great hat of the 1800s was the top hat, although tall hats had been a feature of Puritan dress in the 1600s. Until about 1830 it was known as a high-crowned beaver hat, after the material from which it was made. The

silk top hat was the invention of John Hetherington, a London hatter. In 1797 he provoked a riot and was charged with 'a breach of the peace for…wearing upon his head a tall structure having a shining lustre and calculated to frighten timid people'. But by 1850 the topper was being worn by all classes.

From the 1870s smart Englishmen sported Panamas, made since the 1600s from strands of leaves from a palm-like plant in Ecuador and Colombia. Men and women adopted the boater in the 1880s, while in the 1890s the stiff felt homburg was popularised by the Prince of Wales, one of whose favourite spas was the German town of Homburg, where the hat was made. A new style made its debut in George du Maurier's 1895 play *Trilby*, in which the actor Beerbohm Tree played the character of Svengali in a soft-framed black hat.

FASHIONABLE FEET
From fur boots to stilettos

Hunters were probably the first people to think of protecting their feet by wrapping them in animal skins—the earliest surviving examples date from the 2nd millennium BC. Knee-high boots were known by 13000BC, when a Spanish cave painting depicted a man and a woman wearing boots of fur and animal skin. Gradually, however, they became the essential footwear for men, while leisured women wore decorative but impractical shoes. Only in the 1830s did ankle boots—considered suitably modest—become fashionable.

In the 1820s the hero of Waterloo, the 1st Duke of Wellington, gave his name to a tall, slim-cut leather boot. It reigned supreme until the 1860s, when it lost out to the elastic-sided boot, invented in 1837 by Queen Victoria's bootmaker, J. Sparkes Hall, and reinvented in the 1950s as the Chelsea boot.

HEIGHTS OF FASHION

During the pre-Roman era, northern Europeans made shoes from rawhide. Using a single piece of animal skin for each shoe, they pierced the edges with holes, then threaded through a leather thong. This was pulled tight and tied on top of the foot. The Native American buckskin version, the *maxkeseni*, came to England in the 17th century as the moccasin and was briefly in vogue until it fell victim to an import tax.

The brogue, too, started out as a rough shoe of undressed leather tied on with thongs in 16th-century Ireland

SOLE PROVIDER *Sandals of papyrus, woven palm leaves or plaited leather made cool foot coverings for Egyptians around 1500BC and were standard footwear in Greece and Rome.*

TYING A SANDAL, GREEK AMPHORA, 5TH CENTURY BC

and Scotland. Holes allowed bog water to drain out while the wearer was walking. The shoe proved so practical that British gamekeepers and their masters adopted it, although the version of the late 1800s was heavier and more square-toed. It became more refined until, in the 1930s, the Prince of Wales shocked conservative society by wearing suede brogues with a lounge suit.

In the late 11th century shoemakers began to stitch together the sole and upper. Previously shoes had been made in one piece. Silk and velvet began to be used, while buttons and buckles became alternatives to laces.

From the early Middle Ages wooden clogs or pattens protected feet from Europe's filthy streets. The Venetian *chopine* of the 1500s, whose clumsy wedged sole raised its female wearer as much as 50cm (20in), was an extreme

response to urban grime. In the late 1500s a more practical solution was made by building up layers of leather to form a wedge at the end of the sole, but by 1600 shoes had recognisable heels. As a result it became more economical to make 'straights', which were worn on either foot, and left and right shoes disappeared until the late 18th century.

Both men and women wore heels. The French king Louis XIV added an extra 12.5cm (5in) to his small stature, while ladies at the court of Louis XVI could not tackle stairs unaided. Heels did not reach such extremes again until the stiletto appeared in Italy in 1953.

Comfort was a necessity as interest in sports grew. Canvas and rubber shoes for playing croquet were introduced in the USA in 1868. Similar British shoes made in 1876 were dubbed plimsolls after the Merchant Shipping Act sponsored by Samuel Plimsoll MP. The join between the shoe's upper and sole was thought to resemble the compulsory 'Plimsoll line' indicating the depth to which merchant ships could be loaded.

GREAT STRIDES *Boots, shoes and sandals were all known in ancient times, the choice of footwear dictated by climate and terrain. In the 20th century, practicality and comfort led to the popularity of unisex sports shoes.*

OXFORD BROGUE, 1920S
CLOGS, ABOUT 1910
STILETTO, 1980S
CHELSEA BOOT, 1960S
PLIMSOLL, 1960S
BASEBALL BOOT, 1960S
LEATHER RIDING BOOT, 1800S
UTILITY SANDAL, 1940S

HIDDEN TREASURE *Made in about 2300 BC this gilded silver earring was found among the ruins of Troy excavated in the late 1800s.*

PRECIOUS JEWELLERY
The art of adornment

Long before they wore clothes, people adorned themselves with necklaces bracelets and pendants fashioned from seashells, fish bones, pebbles, mammoth tusks or wood. These objects were valued not only for their beauty, but also as status symbols and amulets.

In western Europe the idea of body ornaments began around 38000 BC. An industry in bone and ivory that was flourishing 4000 years later in France produced pierced or grooved animal teeth and ivory rings. By 5000 BC the jewellery-makers of northern Iraq were able to drill the tiny holes necessary to make necklaces out of obsidian, cowrie shells and stone.

Gold was probably discovered in Mesopotamia before 3000 BC, and the jewellery of Sumeria is among the most extraordinary ever made. When the Sumerian queen Pu-abi died in about 2500 BC, she was buried with a cloak of beads made from gold, silver, lapis lazuli, carnelian, chalcedony and agate. On her head gold flowers rose above three diadems. The Sumerians mastered many of the techniques still used by jewellers—metalworking, filigree, stone-cutting and enamelling. But it was the Egyptians

FINE ACCOMPANIMENTS *Foppish men used fans in the 18th century, but these elegant accessories were mostly carried by ladies of fashion. Parasols helped them to maintain the ideal pale complexion.*

138

who mastered the art of making glass beads, in the 3rd millennium BC. They were first manufactured for a commercial market in Egypt around 1400 BC.

Turquoise and lapis lazuli were among the gems prized and worn by the ancients, while emeralds were found in Upper Egypt around 1650 BC.

KEEPING COOL

Feathers attached to a handle were used as fans around 3000 BC by the Chinese. They soon created flat hand fans by stretching silk, bamboo or palm leaves over wooden frames.

The Japanese discovered in the 6th century AD how to make fans fold. They used painted or embroidered paper, silk or lace for the mount, and ivory, carved wood or mother-of-pearl for the blades. In the 16th century these became status symbols for women in Europe, where feather fans had been used from the Middle Ages.

Emeralds were first brought to Europe in the late 1500s from South America, where they were worn by the Incas.

Diamond deposits, discovered in the streambeds of India, were also known by the ancients. They were valued for their rarity rather than for their sparkling beauty as until the late Middle Ages no one knew how to cut them—diamonds are 85 times harder than sapphires or rubies. Their full glory was revealed in the 17th century, when a Venetian lapidary named Vincenzo Peruzzi developed the 'brilliant' cut.

Because gemstones were so valuable, the Romans built up a large industry in fakes. Their craftsmen were particularly skilled in making artificial emeralds from coloured glass that had been heated with copper or iron-containing chemicals, but also fashioned artificial rubies, sapphires and pearls. In the 1600s a new method using a brilliant glass was developed in Paris to make gem-like stones. Known as paste jewellery, it came to be prized in its own right, and was the precursor of the costume jewellery of the 20th century.

FAN OF OSTRICH
FEATHERS,
19TH CENTURY

SILK PARASOL
WITH IVORY
FOLDING
HANDLE,
19TH CENTURY

SHOT SILK
PARASOL,
19TH CENTURY

PURSES AND BAGS
For personal possessions

Until the Middle Ages personal effects were wrapped in a piece of material, which was hidden inside the clothes. By the early 13th century this fabric enclosure had developed into the pouch, bag or purse, made for both men and women in leather, fur or cloth.

Bags were larger than pouches or purses, but all three were worn attached to the belt or girdle by a cord or thong that could be cut from behind—hence the expression 'cutpurse' for a thief. In fact, purses rarely contained money since few people had any to carry. Men used them for their documents and women for sewing implements.

In the 16th century men's hose became so voluminous that vertical pockets could be sewn into the seams. The suit, introduced in the late 1600s, had horizontal pockets in the waistcoat

and coat, making men's bags things of the past until the 1830s, when the briefcase appeared. The purse, small enough to be carried in the pocket, was used only for coins.

In the mid 17th century women wore pairs of cloth bags tied or taped to their undergarments. Access to these pockets was by way of slits in the skirt. With the slimline Empire styles of the late 18th century, however, French women carried small bags called reticules or, more sarcastically, 'ridicules'.

The modern handbag, in the form of a framed leather bag, was born in the 1850s. But it was not until the hobble skirts of 1909-10, and the flimsy fashions of the 1920s, that the handbag came into its own. Shoulder bags appeared during the Second World War for women in the forces, who were unable to salute smartly while carrying a handbag.

MAN WITH BAG TIED TO HIS BELT, 1440

LEATHER HANDBAG, ABOUT 1920

MAPLE WALKING STICK WITH HORN HANDLE, 19TH CENTURY

KNITTED PURSE WITH BELT HOOK, 19TH CENTURY

EVENING BAG, 1920S

EMBROIDERED BAG, 1920S

RETICULE, EARLY 1800S

BLACK MALACCA CANE WITH SILVER TOP, 19TH CENTURY

STYLE IN HAND
Umbrellas and walking sticks

Prehistoric chiefs carried with them sticks decorated with emblems, or staffs with carved antlers. In ancient Egypt sticks of various forms were carried by everyone from shepherds to pharaohs. Swordsticks, with a blade hidden in the hollow handle, were among the 132 sticks found in Tutankhamun's tomb dating to 1325 BC.

On a monument built in 2400 BC the Assyrian king Sargon of Akkad is shown being protected from the sun by a servant holding a parasol. The Roman *umbraculum*, meaning 'shady place' or 'bower', was a sunshade made of cloth stretched over a wooden frame. The idea of a device for protection against the rain first appeared in China, where silk umbrellas were used by the nobility from 1000 BC. Waterproof versions appeared between the 4th and 6th centuries AD, constructed of paper made from mulberry bark and then oiled.

The modern umbrella was first seen in Italy in the late 16th century, and spread to France and England in the 1630s. The English adapted the Italian name *ombrella*, 'little shadow', but the French chose the more accurate *parapluie*, 'against the rain'. Initially umbrellas were made of leather or heavy oiled canvas, supported by whalebone ribs, but in 1829 a Parisian factory began to manufacture fine umbrella silk. Henry Holland of Birmingham patented the first successful metal ribs made from steel tubes in 1840.

Probably the first man in London to carry an umbrella regularly was the English philanthropist Jonas Hanway. From 1750 he defied his critics—who thought it was the godly purpose of rain to make people wet—for some 30 years before his habit caught on.

YESTERDAY'S BAGGAGE *Pouches, bags and purses, originally made to be attached to a belt, have been used since the Middle Ages. Walking sticks and canes were popular from the early 1700s. Hollow ones made useful hiding places for valued items.*

ROYAL PROFILE *The Egyptians emphasised their eyes—the windows of the soul—with black kohl or eye paints of vivid green or blue.*

PAINTS AND POWDERS
The changing face of beauty

Shades of white, black, orange, yellow and red were only a few of the 17 colours prehistoric peoples mixed to paint their bodies (and their cave walls). Their intent was not mere ornamentation. A decorated body was believed to give protection from the forces of evil.

From around 4000 BC the Egyptians wore cosmetics as a defence against eye diseases and the blazing sun. Kohl, a black paste made from lead sulphide, soot, burnt almonds or ground ants' eggs, was applied around the eyes and to the lashes and brows.

In the 14th century BC the Egyptian queen Nefertiti painted her nails red with henna, but it was the ancient Chinese who created nail polish from gum arabic, egg white, beeswax and gelatine. A lipstick from a Babylonian tomb dating to about 4000 BC is the oldest cosmetic found in the Middle East. It may have belonged to a man.

The Greeks were less approving of cosmetics, a term that comes from their word *kosmetikos*, 'skilled in arranging'. But it was the Greek physician Galen who, in the 2nd century AD, is said to have transformed water, beeswax and olive oil into one of the first skin preparations, which he named 'cold cream'.

Roman women ensured a lily-white complexion by using either chalk or a poisonous, even deadly, cream of white lead, developed in the Indus Valley in the 3rd millennium BC. Poppaea, wife of the Roman emperor Nero, tried to imitate the translucent quality of youthful skin by painting her veins blue.

Until the 18th century cosmetics were mostly the preserve of royalty, the

Clear Red

LIPSTICK BY MAX FACTOR, 1951

PAN-CAKE CASE AND BOX, 1939

THE BEAUTY FACTOR *Once it was discovered that Technicolor film turned faces red and blue, Max Factor and his son created Pan-Cake foundation in 1935. Camouflage shades were developed for commandos during the war.*

wealthy and prostitutes. Only in the 1880s did perfume and toiletry firms such as Eugène Rimmel and Boots make face preparations more widely available. Painted nails became all the rage after the introduction of the first liquid nail polish in 1913. During the First World War factory work provided many women with more money to spend on such luxuries.

Hollywood revolutionised make-up, a term that was used only for theatrical products until it was made respectable from 1920 by Max Factor, a Polish immigrant wigmaker. After emigrating to the USA Max Factor developed film make-up in 1914. In 1918 his 'Society' range became the first make-up for the general public.

HEAVENLY SCENTS
Perfumes ancient and modern

Frankincense and myrrh were valued so highly that the Magi offered them to the infant Jesus. Before it was discovered how to dissolve flower oils in alcohol, only these fragrant gum resins gave long-lasting scents. The ancients used perfume mostly in the form of incense, a practice reflected in the origins of the word, from the Latin *per*, 'through', and *fumus*, 'smoke'.

On public occasions the Egyptians placed on their heads cones of scented fat that melted in the heat, perfuming their hair, faces and bodies. Although the Egyptians began to distil perfume from the madonna lily around 1350 BC, the art of distilling rosewater and other floral scents was perfected in the Islamic world in the 9th century AD. By the late 1100s perfumes were a central part of European culture, but were not widely used in England until the 1500s. Sweet lavender water, distilled in Surrey from the early 17th century, was Britain's first commercially produced scent.

In the early 1700s, two Italian silk dealers based in Cologne began to sell a family recipe for aqua admiralis, a refreshing blend of oils of neroli, rosemary and bergamot. Renamed eau de cologne in 1709, its fame spread during the Seven Years' War of 1756-63 thanks to its popularity among the soldiers who were stationed in the city.

One of the first perfumes to contain synthetic odours was created in 1923 by the Frenchman Ernest Beaux. He submitted samples to Coco Chanel, who chose the fifth, naming it Chanel No.5, allegedly after her lucky number.

DECANTING PERFUME, ROME,
ABOUT 1ST CENTURY BC TO 1ST CENTURY AD

HAIR ON HEAD AND BODY
From shaving to perming

Men have been shaving for some 30 000 years, originally with sharpened flint blades, clam shells or shark's teeth. In India and Egypt copper and gold razors were used in the 4th millennium BC. Mesopotamian towns often had a street of barbers' shops where clients were shaved with a razor and pumice stone. Whereas Indian women shaved their legs with razors in the 4th century BC, strong-nerved Greek women singed their skin smooth with a lamp.

The dangers of the cutthroat razor remained until a razor with a toothed

guard along one edge appeared in Sheffield in 1828. But it was an American travelling salesman, King Camp Gillette, who invented the modern safety razor with a removable, replaceable blade in 1895. He wrote to his wife, 'I stood before that mirror in a trance of joy.'

In 1900 the American Samuel L. Bligh thought up his 'beard grinder', but it needed a sewing machine to work. By pedalling hard, the shaver forced the machine's driving-wheel belt over an emery-coated roller, wearing away his stubble. It was only in 1931 that a former US army colonel named Jacob Schick successfully manufactured an electric razor.

To keep cool the Egyptians often kept their hair very short or even shaved it, but protected themselves from the effects of the sun with elaborate wigs of human hair, sheep's wool or horsehair.

GILLETTE SAFETY
RAZOR, 1904

PORTRAIT OF A LADY *A pale complexion was as essential to the beauty of the 1700s as it had been in the 3rd millennium BC. Only in the 1920s did white skin lose its social status and the tan become fashionable.*

Grass or vegetable fibres sufficed for the cheapest versions. Alternatively, they dyed their locks red, blue or green. In ancient Greece those not naturally fair used yellow flower petals or coloured powders as lighteners. The Romans first used soap as a hair dye. Made of goat's fat and beechwood ash, it gave the hair a sandy-red colour.

Throughout the Near East, women set their hair in waves by coating it in wet clay and then drying it in the sun before combing out the curls. The women of ancient Greece wore their hair in long ringlets created with tongs. Ladies had their hair dressed by maids. Only after the Parisian hairdresser Marcel Grateau invented the waving iron—and the 'marcel wave'—in the 1870s did women frequent 'hairdressing stores'.

The 'permanent' wave was first seen in London in 1906. Karl L. Nessler, a German hairdresser, applied borax paste and then 12 brass curlers, each of which weighed almost 1 kg (2 lb). The method took 6 hours. Cheaper and faster was the cold perm of 1945. Its French inventor, Eugene Schueller, had introduced synthetic hair colorants in 1907 and launched Dop, the first mass-market shampoo, in 1934. Shampoo, from the Hindi word for 'massage', dates to 1877 when English hairdressers boiled up soap, soda water and herbs.

BEAUTY TIPS

• The 'Iceman' found in the Similaun glacier in Italy had the oldest tattoos ever seen. Powdered charcoal and needles were probably used to make the marks some 5300 years ago.

• In 840, Blackbird, a singer from Baghdad, opened the world's first beauty school in Spain. He taught hairdressing, how to use cosmetics and how to make deodorant.

• Wigs became fashionable in western Europe from 1624, after the French king Louis XIII lost his hair and beard through illness.

DESIGN FOR LIVING

Two million years ago, chipping stone with stone, our ancestors made the first tools. But technology really began around 8000 BC, when nomads settled down to grow crops and domesticate animals. Then people started to use the Earth's materials and its sources of energy to control their world, finding new ways to make the most of their own muscle power, and later enlisting the great forces of water and wind.

Baskets were woven for carrying and storing food in the Middle East at around this time, although nets for fishing had been cast in the Mediterranean around 11000 BC. Once settlements were established and more food was produced life became more than a basic struggle for survival. And because one tool could be used to make another, increasingly sophisticated versions were devised, such as an axe blade made by striking metal with a hammer stone. In the first attempt to change material with fire, pottery was produced in Japan in about 10000 BC. Copper knives were made in the Near East by 6000 BC, about the same time that bricks were baked in Jericho. By 3500 BC potters' wheels were spinning in Mesopotamia.

In warm climates, successful agriculture required irrigation. Oxen or camels were harnessed in ancient Egypt to the *saqiya*, a device for transmitting drive through primitive gears to a series of buckets that raised water from the Nile. The Romans instigated treadwheels powered by animals or men to raise water, and ground their

grain with 'hourglass' mills in which an upper stone was turned by the labour of asses or donkeys against a stationary lower one.

In about 25 BC the Roman architect Vitruvius described an 'undershot' waterwheel rotated by water flowing beneath that could rotate millstones to grind corn. In the 4th century AD the Romans began to harness water energy in this way, but from the 14th century power was provided more efficiently by an 'overshot' wheel. In this, water was channelled to the top of the wheel, driving it around to power such devices as water-raising piston pumps in mines. Only from the late 1700s was this wheel surpassed by steam—the driving force of the Industrial Revolution.

In China and Japan, windmills may have existed by 2000 BC, but the oldest documented machines that could exploit the force of the wind were constructed in the 9th century AD in the Seistan region of Iran. There, windmills with horizontal sails were used for milling grain and raising water from wells. The European windmill, with vertical sails, appeared in England and France in the 1180s.

Metal-smelting changed human lives for ever. Bronze was alloyed from copper and tin and worked in Mesopotamia in about 3500 BC, but it was another 2000 years before iron was smelted. In modern times, steel was manufactured in bulk from the 1860s, other strong materials such as aluminium from the 1880s. These transformed everyday goods, as did plastic in the 20th century.

When the English physicist Michael Faraday discovered a way of generating electricity from rotary motion in 1831, the foundations for modern living were laid. A century later, when the first true computers used electricity to transform the processing and storage of information, and thus the organisation of work, they effected the electronic revolution that made Moon landings possible.

CIRCULAR MOTION
The wheel

It is difficult to think of a world without the wheel, but 5000 years ago the pharaohs of Egypt had no knowledge of it when they built the great pyramids. And about 1500 years later the ancient Britons constructed Stonehenge using wheel-less technology.

Wheels can easily be imagined to have originated from rollers—tree trunks used to move heavy loads. However, a thinner slice cut from a large tree and used as a wheel would have been weak and quick to split. The first wheels clearly recognisable as such appeared about 3500 BC in Sumeria (now Iraq), made from three planks of wood clamped together with wooden struts. Dating from about this time, a sketch on a clay tablet survives from Uruk in Mesopotamia and shows a

SKETCH OF A WHEELED CART, MESOPOTAMIA, ABOUT 3200 BC

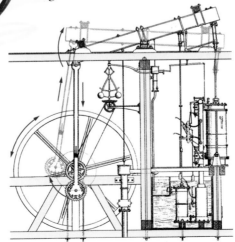

ROLLING BY *The Egyptians were introduced to the wheel by Middle Eastern invaders in 1600 BC, and by 1475 BC were making wheels with four spokes for carts and chariots, such as those on this barque-carrying model. The number of spokes was increased to eight for the light chariots of the pharaoh Tutankhamun.*

sledge adapted for easier use on varied terrains by the addition of four wheels. Potters' wheels in the form of simple turntables were also employed in Mesopotamia during this period.

In central Asia by 2500 BC, and in Crete by 2000 BC, copper nails were hammered in around the circumference

of a wheel to improve its wear on the carts, wagons and chariots of the day. Ancient spoked wheels that were carved from wood usually had iron tyres put around their rims to increase strength and durability, a basic design used well into the 19th century. Generally, elm was cut for the centre, or nave ; ash for the rim, which was made up of several felloes (curved wooden pieces). For firmness, 'Johnny Oak made the spoke'.

But spoked wheels proved too weak to bear the heavy steam-driven vehicles developed in the 19th century. In the 1820s a steam bus operator, Walter Hancock, removed the nave and shaped the ends of the spokes into wedges that fitted together at the centre. This stronger 'artillery wheel', named from its adoption for gun carriages, was used in the first cars of the 1880s.

Two meshed wheels, with teeth or cogs around their edge, were the gears first employed in around 200 BC in North Africa, for raising pots of water from wells. In the 4th century BC the Greek philosopher Aristotle mentioned what seem to be gears, and 150 years later Ctesibius of Alexandria used a toothed rack and wheel (a rack and pinion gear) to turn the cogs in a water clock.

GEARED UP *In 1781 the Scottish engineer James Watt invented a gear to convert a steam engine's 'straight line' motion into rotary motion. A gear wheel moved around another like a planet around the Sun.*

ENDURING TECHNOLOGY

- The power of scissors, pliers and nutcrackers depends on the lever, as does that of the winch and the oar.
- A crane combines the principles of the pulley and the lever.
- The axe and chisel are wedges that are used to split wood. Nails are a type of wedge used to hold pieces of wood together.
- A camshaft opens and closes the valves that control fuel flow in a car engine.

SEESAW, A SIMPLE LEVER BALANCED ON A FULCRUM

PRIME MOVERS
From the lever to the pulley

Using simple levers, Stone Age people were able to move heavy loads long before the wheel was invented. In the 3rd century BC the Greek mathematician Archimedes explained how levers worked when he showed that a simple lever multiplied force in proportion to its length on either side of its fulcrum, or its point of support. The potential power of the lever was, Archimedes realised, almost infinite : 'Give me but a place to stand and I will move the Earth,' he declared.

The Greeks also used the winch, a combination of a roller and a lever, to raise heavy weights during the construction of such great buildings as the Parthenon in Athens. A rope wound around a roller exerted a greater pulling force, they discovered, when the roller was fitted with long arms to turn it. In ancient building work, winches were often driven by men walking inside a vertical wheel which turned the device.

Cranks were used by the Chinese as winding handles on their winnowing machines some 2000 years ago, and in

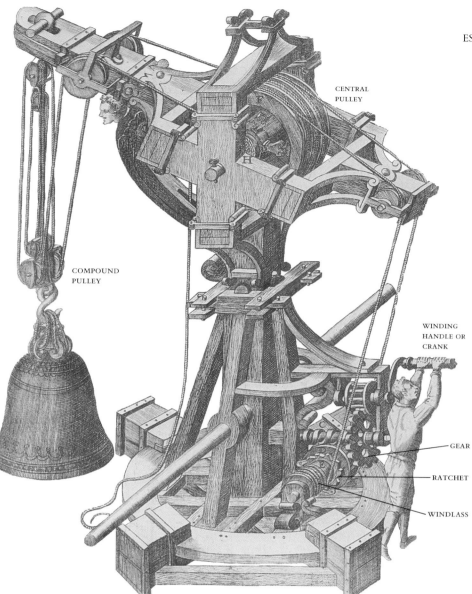

CENTRAL PULLEY

COMPOUND PULLEY

WINDING HANDLE OR CRANK

GEAR

RATCHET

WINDLESS

RAISING AGENTS
Wedge, screw and cam

To raise boulders far enough to insert levers, Stone Age people used wedges more than 300 000 years ago. Much later, Egyptian quarrymen hammered home wedges made of bronze or wood to split huge blocks of stone. Axes, first shaped in flint by *Homo erectus* more than 250 000 years ago and used to cut wood, use the principle of the wedge. From around 35 000 BC stone axe heads were being fitted to wooden handles to make more effective weapons and tools.

A screw thread works as an extended wedge with its lifting surface arranged in the form of a spiral. Screws described by Archimedes in the 3rd century BC were used for pumping. A continuous spiral screw, made of wood and turning inside a tube, raised water for irrigation. But the Archimedean screw was old by the time its namesake noted it, having been invented in ancient Egypt and used along the Nile. The Greeks and Romans employed the screw to press grapes and olives.

For breaking open the tough husks of rice grains the Chinese of 2000 years ago used hammers released by 'trip' devices—protrusions or cams fitted to a turning handle. Cams became widely used in the West only in the 11th century and were used in pounding woollen material to clean it, operating hammers in smithies and beating rags in the paper-making process.

the Middle Ages they were employed for turning grindstones. In the early 17th century, cranks with connecting rods, or crankshafts, began appearing in hand-operated mills and pumps.

Pulleys, which essentially consist of a wheel with a grooved rim through which a rope or chain is pulled to lift heavy objects, can also multiply force. Although the Egyptians did not use true pulleys, they almost certainly ran their ropes over smooth timbers to alter the direction of movement when raising blocks of stone for the pyramids.

The first mention of a true pulley occurs in the *Mechanica*, which was written in Greece in the 4th century BC, while compound pulleys, or block-and-tackle, were described before AD 100 by the Greek scholar Hero of

TURN AND RAISE *Using this 15th-century combination of moving devices, a single man could lift a heavy bell. As he turned the handle, the meshed gears rotated. This motion was then translated through a right angle to rotate a windlass. Ropes transferred the force from the windlass to the central pulley, then to the compound pulley. The ratchet on the windlass was a safety device.*

Alexandria. When pulleys are linked together, people can lift objects weighing far more than themselves. Like the lever, the compound pulley acts as a form of gear to multiply force while proportionally reducing the distance that the objects move. The Romans used compound pulleys in cranes, and 15th-century sailing ships had hundreds of them for hoisting and trimming sails.

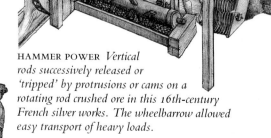

HAMMER POWER *Vertical rods successively released or 'tripped' by protrusions or cams on a rotating rod crushed ore in this 16th-century French silver works. The wheelbarrow allowed easy transport of heavy loads.*

FLINT, BONE AND WOOD
Early tools and weapons

By hurling weapons of flint or bone at ibex, mammoths and bison, the people of the Stone Age brought down their prey 500 000 years ago. With tools of the same natural materials, flesh was cut from bones, hides stripped for leather, and antlers and tusks removed for fashioning into missiles and cutting implements. Animal sinew was also used to lash pieces of wood together for spears.

Some 400 000 years ago Europeans carved wooden spears, but it was the development of chisels in Europe in around 8000 BC that made true joinery possible. Carved wooden handles for the axe and adze (a tool like an axe but with a curved blade at a right angle to the shaft and swung between the legs) were made in the Middle East from 5500 BC. Adzes were the basic tools for shaping wood until the 1700s.

By 2500 BC the ancient Egyptians were producing richly carved and decorated furniture inlaid with ebony and ivory. Using lathes, which had already existed for nearly 1000 years, the ancient Greeks created turned furniture. The lathe was used to rotate the wood steadily against a cutting tool, such as a chisel, held by a craftsman. In the design devised by the Greeks for

CREATIVE CARVING *Sharp flints, the first tools, were used to create such realistic ancient sculptures as this mammoth-tusk horse. After about 8000 BC, more detailed work was made possible by the introduction of tough-edged stone chisels and fine metal chisels, which were kept sharp with honing stones.*

WORKING WITH WOOD *The brace, used by St Joseph in this 14th-century painting, was rare until the Middle Ages. But most of his carpentry tools, including the hammer, saw and pincers, were invented in the Stone and Bronze Ages and remain unchanged today.*

making bowls and vases, a cord attached to the top of a springy vertical pole was wound around the wood, which was spun by a craftsman operating a treadle to pull the other end of the cord. When the treadle was released, the pole spun in the opposite direction.

FIRED EARTH
Making pottery

People living in caves in Kyushu, Japan, around 10 000 BC discovered that when clay was heated in a fire it formed a hard waterproof material. So began the recorded history of practical pottery, although small clay figures in animal shapes found in eastern Europe may have been made for religious purposes as long ago as 25 000 BC.

As hunter-gatherers across the world settled down into farming communities, they needed vessels to store water,

PROGRESS ON A PLATE *The first potter's wheel, used in 3500 BC in Mesopotamia, was a simple turntable. In 1500 BC the Greeks attached a disc to the base of the turning shaft allowing the potter to turn the wheel with his foot. The simple wheel shown here probably evolved from the Greek design.*

oil and food. By 7500 BC the potter's craft, which was then well established in China, was becoming widespread in both Africa and the Middle East.

The first pots were shaped by hand, or made by coiling lengths of rolled-out clay on top of each other, and then smoothing out their surfaces. Pots could be hardened by being left in the sun, but they emerged stronger if brushwood was piled around them and set alight. By 5000 BC the kiln, a clay oven heated by fire, had been invented in Asia. Its higher temperature produced a molten paste that ran into any cracks, with the result that pots became more waterproof.

Because most natural clays contain iron, which turns rust coloured when heated in air, pots are naturally red and were later named terracotta from the Italian for 'baked earth'. The Egyptians added charcoal and oil to the clay to

BY DESIGN *The colourful decoration on this Mesopotamian plate of about 5000 BC was painted on before it was fired. Slips of clay water drizzled onto the surface, or patterns incised with metal or wooden tools, were also used by early potters to enhance their wares.*

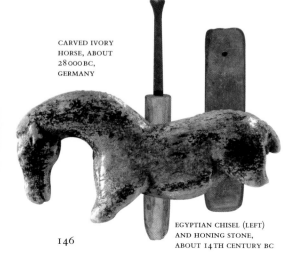

CARVED IVORY HORSE, ABOUT 28 000 BC, GERMANY

EGYPTIAN CHISEL (LEFT) AND HONING STONE, ABOUT 14 TH CENTURY BC

A SIMPLE POTTER'S WHEEL DEPICTED ON A CERAMIC MAJOLICA PLATE, 16TH CENTURY

CHINESE GLAZED STONEWARE POT, 6TH CENTURY

SMOOTHLY SUPERIOR *Stoneware, a pottery that was watertight even without glazing, was made by firing clay at high temperatures in China from about 1500 BC.*

make black pottery. Searching for a way of re-creating the deep blue hues of lapis lazuli, the Mesopotamians covered the surfaces of their pots with copper ore before firing them. Glazes were created in around 1600 BC, when potters found that ores of tin produced a white finish. Soon more effective waterproofing was achieved with a lead glaze that turned to glass during firing.

It was the practical genius of the Chinese that gave us porcelain. Using kaolin, a clay that forms a glassy material when it is heated, together with a feldspar rock known as petuntse, and firing at temperatures that reached 1400°C (2552°F), potters of the early Tang dynasty (AD 618-906) produced a

translucent, hard, white material that had a ring like a bell. Arriving in Europe in the 16th century aboard Portuguese ships, porcelain was first called 'China-ware', or Chiney, from the Persian word *chini* and later became known as china.

A soft-paste porcelain, so called because it could be fired at a much lower temperature than true porcelain, was developed in Italy in 1575 by mixing kaolin with glass. But it was not until 1707 that Johann Böttger, as alchemist to Augustus II, the ruler of Saxony and Poland, worked out how to make the real thing. The first true Western porcelain was made at a factory set up by Augustus at Meissen, near Dresden, in 1710.

Bone china appeared in the 1750s, when potteries at Bow and Chelsea in London added bone ash to soft paste. Easier to make and stronger than true porcelain, it became the standard English porcelain. At the same time Josiah Wedgwood began producing a lead-glazed white earthenware. From then on his Staffordshire potteries turned out high-quality goods at affordable prices.

THE STORY OF GLASS
A brilliant discovery

A happy accident probably gave us glass. Around 3000 BC Middle Eastern nomads camped on the sandy shores of a lake discovered tiny droplets of glass in the places where they had lit their fires. What they did not realise was that the glass had been formed by chemical and physical changes created when sand (silica), containing significant amounts of soda (sodium carbonate) deposited from the waters of the lake, was heated.

Glass beads were used as common currency in the ancient world. In about 1500 BC the Egyptians made hollow glass by forming a core from a bag of sand or a lump of clay, attaching it to a metal rod then covering it in molten glass. When the glass had cooled the bag or clay was removed.

Glassworking became simpler after about 300 BC when, in Alexandria, molten glass was poured into a mould, a second mould pressed down on it and the glass shaped between the two. Nearly three centuries later, a glass-maker in Syria, then under Roman rule, discovered that a blob of glass on the end of a tube could be blown into a vessel of almost any shape, then manipulated to create handles or spouts.

CLEAR ADVANCE *Once they had mastered the technique of glass-blowing (below), discovered around 30 BC, the Romans mass-produced glass. The objects they made ranged from simple jars to this jug, with its hexagonal body and funnel neck, fashioned in about AD 500.*

PENNY MADE OF
97 PER CENT
COPPER,
BRITAIN, 1970

BRONZE COIN,
GREECE, ABOUT
4TH CENTURY BC

FROM COPPER TO BRONZE
Precious and practical

More than 9000 years ago the people of south-eastern Turkey discovered that copper could be cut from the shiny rocks of the region with stone tools. However, copper's name comes from Cyprus, which supplied much of the metal to the ancient world.

Pieces of copper were soft enough to be beaten and shaped into pins and other jewellery, while malachite, a bright green copper ore, was a perfect material for making beads. Copper-working has continued uninterrupted since these early times, but the metal's value appreciated considerably in the 17th century when it was found to be an effective conductor of heat, and yet

SHOWING THEIR WORTH So revered was their craft that Egyptian metalworkers were probably treated like magicians. The processes that they used, such as forcing the forge fire with blowpipes, were enshrined in the reliefs, hieroglyphs and wall paintings created to decorate ancient tombs.

more so when, in the 19th century, experiments with electricity proved it to be the most efficient conductor of electric currents after silver.

But it was lead that spurred the major breakthrough in metal production. In about 5000 BC, at both Çatal Hüyük in Anatolia and Yarim Tepe in northern Mesopotamia, rocks rich in lead ores were smelted (heated so that the ores convert to pure metal) and the resulting lead made into necklaces and bracelets.

Tin was extracted in Egypt from about 3500 BC. Smelted with copper over wood fires, it was used to create bronze, an alloy that was ideal for hard-edged heads for axes and spears. Bronze objects, from weapons to jewellery and ornaments, are highly resistant to decay

IN THE MONEY Prized for their intrinsic value, metals have been used for settling deals since about 600 BC.

BRASS COIN, CHINA, ABOUT 1600

10-PFENNIG IRON COIN, GERMANY, 1916

NICKEL SHILLING, BRITAIN, 1970

and are still found in ancient sites around the world. They were included in collections of goods buried with the bodies of the rich and powerful; the tomb of Tutankhamun, which was completed in about 1350 BC, contained bronze knives, pins, razors and swords and a bronze trumpet.

For many centuries bronze objects remained more precious than practical, probably because stone was more available and easier to work, but around 1700 BC the people of the Aegean discovered that bronze did not always have to be heated before it could be worked. By 'cold hammering' alloys containing about 10 per cent tin, they crafted a wide range of tools and weapons.

IRON AND STEEL
Industrial production

Pure iron came from outer space. The ancient Egyptians and Aztecs first encountered it in fallen meteorites. In Egypt they called it 'the metal from the sky', and in Mexico 'the gift of heaven'. Since iron usually occurs on Earth in impure ores, meteoritic iron was considered more valuable than gold.

The Iron Age began when, around 1500 BC, the Hittite people of western Asia occupied Anatolia and discovered a way of smelting iron from local ores. They built clay-lined furnaces, and put iron ore and wood in them. On firing,

MEN OF STEEL Workers of 1893 endure the intense heat of an early foundry. By this time, the success of the Bessemer converter meant that steel had largely replaced iron for both industrial construction and household objects, such as scissors and cutlery.

the wood turned to charcoal, and the carbon in it combined with the iron ore to produce metal mixed with 'slag', a glassy residue. Repeated hammering beat most of the slag out of the mixture, leaving relatively pure iron which was then 'wrought', or beaten when hot, to produce blades. Something close to steel—iron containing less than 1 per cent of carbon—was created when charcoal was hammered into the surface. The Hittites called it 'good iron'.

Cast iron was made by the Chinese around 600 BC by melting iron containing phosphorus, which liquefied at a lower temperature than other iron ores. The molten metal was then poured or cast into moulds. This technique transformed Chinese life by making possible the production of such basic implements as cast-iron ploughshares and cooking pots.

In the West, the first cast iron was a 14th-century material. A blast of air from a furnace, called a 'blast furnace', heated it to a temperature of 1200°C (2190°F). When fired with charcoal the iron absorbed significant amounts of carbon, which lowered its melting point. Cast into cannons, medieval iron changed the face of warfare.

In Britain iron from blast furnaces was known as pig iron because, cast from large troughs into smaller moulds, it resembled a sow feeding her piglets. By the 17th century cast iron was being used for water pipes and a century later,

during the Industrial Revolution, it was fashioned into railway tracks.

Until the 18th century, a vast area of woodland was felled to make charcoal—some 4000m² (4800sq yd) for every tonne of iron fired. In 1709 an English iron manufacturer, Abraham Darby of Coalbrookdale in Shropshire, turned coal into a more efficient fuel known as coke by heating it in an airless chamber. He then used the coke to smelt iron. The results were increased production and less pollution.

Pig iron was too brittle for most heavy industrial uses, but strong wrought iron was needed for the steam-driven machinery, railways and bridges destined to cover the new industrial landscape. In 1784 the English iron manufacturer Henry Cort invented the 'puddling process', a faster method of turning pig iron into wrought iron in a specially designed furnace. Although the first iron bridge had already been built over the River Severn at Coalbrookdale in 1777-81, it was the puddling process that made possible widespread iron construction.

Mass-production of steel, a stronger, more malleable material than iron, began after the English inventor Henry Bessemer devised a way of converting pig iron to steel in his 1856 Bessemer converter. By oxidising the carbon in iron and burning it away as carbon monoxide and dioxide gases, mild steel (iron containing about 0.25 per cent carbon) could be manufactured.

Specialist steels were devised in the 20th century. The car manufacturer Henry Ford pioneered the use of high-tensile sheet metal—a low-carbon steel combining strength with good welding performance—for car bodies in 1908. From the 1920s this steel was used in refrigerators and washing machines.

Stainless steel was invented in 1913 by Harry Brearley, a Sheffield metallurgist and cutlery maker, who discovered that any steel containing 15 per cent chromium does not rust. Brearley made Sheffield synonymous with stainless steel, although not without such opposition as the comment that 'rustlessness is not so great a virtue in cutlery, which…must be cleaned after each using.'

WEATHERPROOF *Galvanised zinc-coated steel, corrugated for extra strength and used since the late 1830s as a rust-resistant building material, contrasts with the steel shell of a car abandoned in Queensland, Australia.*

ADAPTABLE ALUMINIUM *The German designer Hugo Junkers quickly recognised the potential of aluminium in aircraft and used it in his Junkers trimotor of the 1920s. Light, strong and resistant to rust, it also proved, from the 1880s, to be ideal for kitchenware.*

officer, in 1842. By immersing a cheap metal such as steel in a solution containing molten nickel and passing a current through it, a coating of nickel was laid onto the steel.

Zinc ore was heated with copper to form brass around 1000 BC in Turkey, but was not extracted as a metal until the 16th century. This development was spurred by the interest of alchemists who were searching for ways to turn base metals into gold. Noticing that adding zinc to copper gave it a golden hue, they imagined it might lead to the real thing. In fact brass, as the zinc-copper alloy became known, proved to be more decorative than precious and became popular in horse brasses, household ornaments and such musical instruments as trombones.

Using zinc, nickel or chromium—a steel-grey metal discovered in 1795 by the German chemist Martin Heinrich Klaproth in the mineral crocoite—bright, hard-wearing surfaces could be produced at a modest cost. Now cutlery, pots and other household utensils could be mass-produced and made widely available at affordable prices.

Although it constitutes 8 per cent of the Earth's crust, aluminium was not extracted in any quantity until 1854 when a French chemist named Henri Étienne Sainte-Claire Deville separated the metal from its ores in his laboratory. The method was complex and expensive. Commercial production did not begin in earnest until Charles Hall in the USA and Paul Héroult in France simultaneously discovered in 1886 that aluminium could be manufactured relatively simply by passing an electric current through the mineral cryolite, already heated until it was molten.

METAL DISCOVERIES
Nickel, zinc and aluminium

Nickel's name means 'Devil's copper', a translation of the German *Kupfernickel*. It comes from the experience of 15th-century miners who failed to find copper in the hills around Saxony in Germany and instead were poisoned by arsenic. Only in 1751 did Axel Cronstedt, the Swedish mineralogist and chemist, extract the new silvery metal nickel from the deadly ore.

Nickel proved its particular worth in the electroplating process, invented by Werner von Siemens, a Prussian army

DIGGING DEEP
Mining for coal

Between 200 and 300 million years ago, plants that had carpeted the Earth died, decayed and were compressed layer upon layer to form coal. This 'fossil fuel' was first found by Bronze Age people across Europe in seams exposed to view by movements of the Earth's crust. They gathered it up by hand or chipped it out with sharp flints.

From the 5th millennium BC coal was excavated in western Europe with flint axes. Shafts were hacked into chalk and limestone, tunnels or galleries were extended with picks made from flint or deer antlers, and debris was removed with the shoulder blades of cattle. About 2000 years ago, coal was also burned in China and India. In the same era the Romans extracted 'the stone that burns' in Britain to heat their villas and to smelt copper, zinc and tin. They even transported it in large quantities to Hadrian's Wall, where, around AD 300, a Roman guardhouse at Housesteads Fort was converted into a coal shed.

In the 12th century 'bell pits', named for their shape, were dug around the bases of shafts sunk down to 12 m (40 ft) deep, but once their roofs had reached the point of collapse pits would be abandoned. When the increasing prosperity of Elizabethan England led to a rising domestic demand for coal, mining methods advanced in response. Bell pits were dug, then extended into a series of 'rooms', with pillars of coal acting as roof supports. Horses walking in circles to drive a windlass or gin hauled the coal to the surface.

Longwall mining, so called because coal is removed from a long coalface and the adjoining area protected by wooden props, was introduced in the Shropshire coalfield in 1770. This technique avoided the wastefulness of using pillars of coal to prevent roof collapse.

WELL OUT *Using a 1500-year-old Chinese technique and pulverising the rock in a hole 21 m (69 ft) deep with an iron tool at the end of a wire, Edwin L. Drake struck oil in 1859, a year after releasing this less productive 'spout'. The first true gusher was hit in Texas in 1901. Petroleum or motor spirit, refined from crude oil, revolutionised 20th-century transport.*

UNDERGROUND RICHES

• Coal from Somerset was burned by the Romans in the 3rd century AD to replace wood to fuel the sacred flame at the Temple of Sulis in Bath. They also took it to their villas in Wiltshire and Buckinghamshire.
• Pit ponies were brought into mines from 1749 at Tanfield Moor Colliery, Yorkshire. They replaced women and older children who had been hurriers, hauling piles of coal on wheeled carts to the base of the shaft.
• Offshore drilling rigs, such as those in the North Sea, were first used in the 1940s in the Gulf of Mexico.

DRILLING FOR FUEL
Gas and oil

The remains of single-celled organisms such as plankton, which thrived hundreds of millions of years ago before being buried beneath sea-floor sediments, form our resources of natural gas and oil. While drilling for brine the Chinese, who had first attempted to penetrate the Earth's surface around AD 300, hit gas by accident. Taking advantage of their good fortune they burned the gas, boiled the brine and produced salt. Gas seepages also occurred naturally. To the Greeks and Romans they signified divine intervention and sacred flames for religious rites were lit from them.

Methane gas released during coal mining first led to speculation about its potential for lighting. John Clayton, the rector of Crofton, near Wakefield, noted in the 1680s that when he heated coal 'the spirit which issued out caught fire at the flame of a candle'. In 1794 the inventor William Murdoch lit his house in Redruth, Cornwall, with coal gas. Naphtha, an oil burned in lamps, was distilled from coal tar in 1822, and by 1859 was being produced on a large scale from rocks known as oil shales.

From the 9th century BC people of the Middle East burned tarry bitumen, which they found seeping from the Earth's surface. But only in 1857, when the German prospector G.C. Hunäus struck oil and gas near Hanover, was oil encountered by drilling. In 1859 Colonel Edwin L. Drake made a much larger find at Titusville, Pennsylvania.

A simple oil refinery was built in Pennsylvania in 1860, but in 1900 an efficient system was developed to separate useful 'fractions' such as petrol. The demand for petrol, whose usefulness had previously been scorned, increased after 1885 when Gottlieb Daimler adapted the internal-combustion engine to run on petrol and Karl Benz built a three-wheeler driven by a petrol engine.

EDWIN L. DRAKE

RICH PICKINGS *At the 15th-century silver mine in Kuttenberg, Germany, ore was excavated and then piled into baskets and dragged to teams of crushers. The extracted silver metal was graded and sold to merchants.*

adhered. This may have inspired the Greek legend of Jason, who underwent a series of arduous adventures to win the golden fleece and so become king.

When the Roman Empire spread to Spain at the dawn of the Christian era, gold and silver mines began to be sunk. In England, coinage was minted from such metals in the 8th century AD by Offa, King of Mercia, and Edward I enacted the world's first consumer protection laws. His hallmarking system of 1300, which stamped gold and silver with a leopard's head, the king's mark, ensured that precious metals mixed with alloys were not passed off as pure.

GLITTERING GEMS
Mining for diamonds

India is the home of the diamond. Here, before the 4th millennium BC, people first discovered this compressed, crystalline carbon. Its name comes from the Greek *adamas*, meaning 'impenetrably hard'. Valued as gems as well as for cutting, diamonds were traded between India and Mesopotamia, where they were worn to bring success from the 3rd millennium BC, if not earlier. Until 1870, the year they were discovered in volcanic rock in Kimberley, South Africa, all diamonds had been found in sand and gravel.

The craft of cutting diamonds to create reflective facets began during the 15th century. Until then stones were simply polished or shaped into a dome known as a cabochon. In 1477 Maximilian I, the future Holy Roman Emperor, gave the first known diamond engagement ring, to Mary of Burgundy.

STONE OF OFFICE *The world's largest diamond was set in the British monarch's Sceptre with the Cross in 1910. It was cut from the Cullinan Diamond, mined in South Africa in 1905.*

PRECIOUS METALS
Gold and silver

At the beginning of time, declared the Greek writer Hesiod, the Olympian gods created men of gold who lived like gods in true happiness. Gold's lustre, and its malleability and immunity to decay, first inspired the peoples of the Middle East about 6000 years ago. The ancient state that extended from Aswan in Egypt to Khartoum in Sudan was called Nubia, meaning 'the land of gold'. The golden statues in the tombs of the pharaohs, including Tutankhamun, attest to gold's value in decoration and ritual.

The first prospectors found gold in tiny grains deposited on riverbeds. They separated them from alluvial sand with sheepskins to which the gold

GENERATING POWER

*'It was not until about seven o'clock, when it began to grow dark,
that the electric light really made itself known and showed how bright and steady it is.'*

THE *New York Times*, SEPTEMBER 5, 1882, AFTER ITS OFFICES WERE CONNECTED TO THE PEARL STREET POWER STATION

BRIGHT LIGHTS *Electricity brought the night to life, and by 1895 the theatres and shops of the Bowry, New York, were aglow. A steam-driven dynamo (inset) provided electricity to a few private homes in London in 1882.*

At the flick of a switch, electricity lit and empowered homes and factories, and also made possible new means of communication and entertainment. The seeds of this revolution were sown in China, where the magic of magnetism, the force that was destined to unlock the door to electricity, was probably discovered in the 2nd or 3rd millennium BC. The Chinese found that the mineral magnetite, an iron ore also known as lodestone, has powerful magnetic properties. The Greeks also knew of it, and the philosopher Thales thought that 'the magnet has life in it because it moves the iron'. Because he experimented with lodestone from

Magnesia, Thales described it as Magnesian, hence the word 'magnet'.

Both the Chinese and the Greeks knew that if amber, a fossilised resin used to make jewellery, was rubbed, it attracted small pieces of material, rather like a magnet. Centuries later, William Gilbert, physician to Elizabeth I, experimented with both magnetism and this static form of electricity. He concluded that the invisible 'effluvium' responsible for both of them was widespread and gave the name 'electrics' from *elektron*, Greek for 'amber', to all substances that had electrostatic properties.

The next challenge was to produce electricity in larger, regular quantities. In 1660 the German physicist Otto von Guericke managed to accumulate electricity in a melon-sized ball of sulphur by rotating it against his hand, and the 18th-century American scientist Benjamin Franklin showed that electricity would flow through metal rods.

But it was the battery that made electricity available in a continuous flow. In 1800 the Italian physicist Alessandro Volta placed a circle of cardboard soaked in brine between two metal discs. To his delight a current of electricity flowed from this 'voltaic pile', and the more layers he added the greater the current became.

THE VITAL LINK

Hans Christian Oersted, a Danish physicist, discovered in 1819 that a wire with a current flowing through it would make a compass needle move—because the electricity had created a magnetic field. In 1821, in the first of many influential experiments, the English physicist Michael Faraday used an electric current to make a wire move around a magnet immersed in a bowl of mercury.

By using electricity to create movement, Faraday had hit upon the phenomenon that became the key to the electric motor. Returning to his investigations ten years later, Faraday used magnetism to create a series of 'momentary currents' that were

AMBER WITH INSECTS, ABOUT 200 MILLION YEARS OLD

brought about by magnetism. These currents, which he described as 'induced', were destined to be used in the electricity industry from its earliest days.

Faraday's discoveries also led to the invention of transformers, which could change the voltage of electricity and make it cheaper to transmit over long distances. And in 1831 he designed the first dynamo, in which a magnet is used to convert mechanical energy into electrical energy without the need for a battery.

ELECTRICITY TO USE

The advances in electricity were adapted for practical purposes. From the 1840s electrical systems were used for sending telegraph messages and, in 1858, for powering arc lamps in

MICHAEL FARADAY

FATHER OF ELECTRICITY

Michael Faraday was born in 1791, in London. At the age of 13 he started work as a bookbinder and in 1812 copied out and bound some lectures he had attended and sent them to the lecturer, the chemist Sir Humphry Davy, together with a letter asking for a job. The next year he was taken on as an assistant.

Faraday's discoveries, achieved through a combination of brilliant intuition and painstaking research, made possible the modern electricity industry. He neither sought nor accepted honours, and in 1867 died 'plain Mr Faraday', as he wished.

lighthouses. But it was not until 1881 that electricity first went on public supply, in Godalming, Surrey. A small generating plant driven by a water wheel on the Wey river provided electricity for street lighting and a few private houses.

A dynamo was installed at Holborn Viaduct in London in 1882, by the company whose American founder, the inventor Thomas Alva Edison, was among the many people instrumental in realising the practical uses of electricity. The dynamo lit the electric lamps in a post office, a church and a public house. Later that year a version six times more powerful was installed by Edison's company at Pearl Street, New York.

Conventional steam engines were used for the first coal-burning power stations between 1882 and 1884, when the Irish-born engineer Charles Parsons invented a turbine which converted steam into rotary motion by forcing it past a series of fan-like blades. The first power station using steam turbines opened in 1888 in Newcastle upon Tyne.

In 1895 the first hydroelectric station was completed in the USA at Niagara Falls. This incorporated water turbines modelled on the ones invented by the French engineer Benoît Fourneyron in 1827—themselves updated versions of the water wheels which the Romans had pioneered for power production.

ON LINE *High above ground, Chicago linemen of 1921 connect the 33 000-volt power cables taking electricity across the country. Britain's National Grid was begun in 1927.*

FIXING COLOURS
Dyes and paints

Nature endowed the ancients with a rainbow of colours for painting and dyeing. Plants provided many of them: red from madder, blue from indigo or woad, black from oak apples and myrtle, and yellow from saffron. Wood smouldered to charcoal also made an effective black. Local minerals were another rich source of colour, with reds from iron oxides, yellows from clays or ochres, blues and greens from ground lapis lazuli and malachite, and whites from ground seashells.

The oldest surviving dyed fabrics are Egyptian, dating from 2000 BC, but the invention of dyeing is probably much older. The Egyptians certainly understood the use of mordants, metallic salts used to fix the dye to the cloth. Indigo alone requires no mordant and is probably the oldest dye of all. Its name comes from the Spanish word for India, where the plant grows prolifically.

At the beginning of the Christian era Tyre in the eastern Mediterranean was famous for its purple dye and its smell. Tyrian purple was produced by pounding the bodies of the molluscs *Purpura* and *Murex* and then boiling them for three days in a salt solution. Only part of the mollusc was used. The rest was left to rot—hence the foul smell. Tyrian purple was known to the Minoans from at least 1600 BC. Due to its rarity, it was used to dye the robes of emperors and popes.

ARTIST'S PAINT PALETTE AND GRINDER, EGYPT, 1250 BC

Such traditional dyes were used until Victorian times. But in 1856 William Perkin, an 18-year-old student at the Royal College of Chemistry, London, made the first synthetic dye, a brilliant mauve, from coal tar. Perkin's 'mauveine' was such a success that the following year he set up a factory to make it at Greenford, Middlesex.

Other man-made dyes appeared but the most significant was a synthetic version of alizarin, the red pigment found in the root of madder, by Heinrich Caro at the Badische Anilin und Soda-Fabrik (BASF) in Germany in 1869.

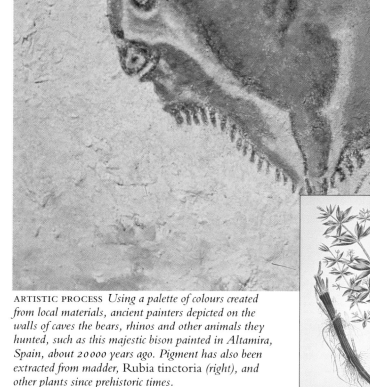

ARTISTIC PROCESS *Using a palette of colours created from local materials, ancient painters depicted on the walls of caves the bears, rhinos and other animals they hunted, such as this majestic bison painted in Altamira, Spain, about 20000 years ago. Pigment has also been extracted from madder,* Rubia tinctoria *(right), and other plants since prehistoric times.*

Caro's new process spelt the end of madder dyes and the birth of the modern chemical industry.

Paint requires both a pigment to give it colour and a 'binder' to make it stick to a surface. Since Stone Age cave 'paintings' were generally applied without using such binders they were, strictly speaking, made with dyes or pigments. In the 3rd millennium BC gum arabic, a resin obtained from the acacia tree, was employed in Egypt as a binder. Egg white or

DESERT HARVEST *A Mexican worker collects 'cochineal insects' feeding on cactuses in 1777. The bodies of more than 200000 were crushed to produce 1 kg (2 lb 3 oz) of a brilliant red dye, brought to Europe by Spanish conquistadores in the 16th century.*

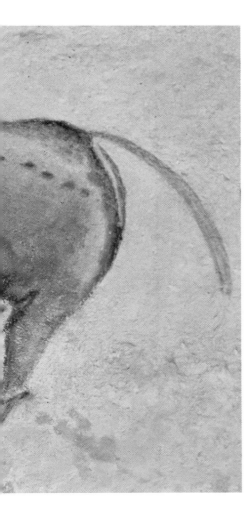

beeswax were also widely used for this purpose until the Middle Ages, but both ingredients made paint expensive.

Paint did not become widely used until the 18th century, when linseed oil from flax and zinc oxide, a white pigment, became increasingly available as an alternative to white lead, which was not only toxic but had a yellowish tinge. Mixed together they composed the new paints. A cheaper, safe and much whiter pigment, titanium dioxide, came into use after the First World War.

FERTILISING THE LAND
Spurring crop growth

Egyptians farming in the Nile Valley more than 4000 years ago appreciated their fertile soil. After the annual flood, when the river carried down minerals and spread them across the land, crops were prodigious. The ancient Greeks noticed that plants flourished where cattle had been grazed, and by the 4th century BC were using manure to fertilise vineyards.

Organic materials such as wood ash, bones, dried blood and sea-bird droppings were the main fertilisers until the 19th century. In 1840 the notion of chemical fertilisers was proposed for the first time by Justus von Liebig, a German chemist. Liebig argued that farmers had to replace those chemicals, particularly nitrogen, phosphorus and potassium, which plants took from the soil to enable them to grow. Two years later Sir John Bennet Lawes, an English landowner, produced superphosphate, the first artificial fertiliser, by treating coprolites (the fossilised excrement of prehistoric animals) with sulphuric acid to make them soluble in water.

Synthetic nitrogen fertiliser was invented in 1898 by Adolph Frank and Nikodem Caro, two German scientists working at BASF. But the decisive development came in 1910 when the German chemist Fritz Haber devised the process, which still carries his name, for converting nitrogen in the air to ammonia, which could be used, in turn, to produce fertiliser. In Britain, Imperial Chemical Industries (ICI) began combining nitrogen, phosphate and potash to manufacture synthetic fertilisers in 1926.

NATURALLY BRIGHT *These intensely coloured pigments, including ultramarine, China yellow, Venetian red and raw sienna, belonged to the painter J.M.W. Turner. Also in his box are tubes of ready-mixed paints, introduced in the 18th century.*

CONTROLLING PESTS
Chemicals for crops

In the 8th century BC the Greek poet Homer recommended burning sulphur to fumigate plant pests. And in the 1st century AD the Roman writer and natural historian Pliny the Elder suggested killing cabbage-white caterpillars with a wormwood compound.

Most early forms of chemical pest control came, as Pliny had suggested, from substances extracted from plants. In France a solution of nicotine, from tobacco leaves, was used to kill aphids in 1763. Pyrethrum, from a type of chrysanthemum, also proved successful.

More poisonous insecticides were introduced in the 1880s, including Paris Green, an arsenic compound. DDT, or dichlorodiphenyltrichloroethane, was synthesised in 1939 by Paul Muller, a German chemist.

POWER SPRAY *Disease-spreading fleas, mosquitoes and lice were killed by DDT and its derivatives. It saved millions of lives during and after the Second World War, but its lethal effects on wildlife led to a widespread ban in the 1970s, when less toxic alternatives had been developed.*

POTENT MIXTURES

- The ancient Britons painted themselves with woad, a blue dye extracted from the leaves of *Isatis tinctora*, to scare their enemies.
- Greasepaint was invented by Ludwig Leichner, a German opera singer, and independently by Carl Baudin of the Leipzig City Theatre in the 1860s.
- In 1885 the weed-killing properties of Bordeaux mixture, a combination of copper sulphate and lime used to treat a mildew ravaging the vineyards of Bordeaux, were discovered. It was the first chemical weedkiller.

THE STORY OF RUBBER
Waterproof and flexible

In the 6th century AD the Aztecs of Mexico took a substance they called *olli*, which oozed from the trunks of trees, and made it into bouncy balls. They also invented the game *tlachtli*, knocking the balls around a long court, the object being to throw them into two large rings mounted on the walls.

In 1530 the Italian geographer Pietro Martire d'Anghiera described rubber in his book *De Orbe Novo* (*From the New World*). 'From one of these trees a milky juice exudes,' he wrote. 'Left standing it thickens to a kind of pitchy resin.' By 1615 Spanish troops in South America were using this 'resin' to waterproof their cloaks. After the English chemist Joseph Priestley noted in 1770 that it was useful for rubbing out pencil marks, it became known as rubber.

Rubber was used in the early 19th century to make a variety of waterproof clothes, but it was prone to become sticky in warm weather and rigid in the cold. The Scottish chemist Charles Macintosh solved this problem in 1823 by placing a layer of rubber between two layers of cloth, thereby inventing the raincoat that still bears his name.

Charles Goodyear, an American inventor, started on a series of complex experiments to harden rubber in 1834. After a succession of failed attempts he accidentally reached his long-sought goal in the early 1840s when he spilt some rubber and sulphur on a hot stove. The substance that resulted was both waterproof and pliant.

Synthetic or Buna rubber, which is made from butadiene, a chemical extracted from petroleum, was created after experiments had been carried out by German chemists in 1927. In 1931 a team led by Wallace H. Carothers at the American chemical company Du Pont came up with neoprene, a stronger and flame-resistant synthetic rubber.

TOP HAT
COVER

TENT

WATERTIGHT
Charles Macintosh's partner Thomas Hancock patented the process of vulcanisation, which Charles Goodyear had invented, in 1843. In The Origin and Progress of the Caoutchouc or India Rubber Manufacture *of 1857, Hancock illustrated the many novel waterproof articles the pair had produced.*

DRIVING
GLOVES

MUD-RESISTANT
BOOT

TUBING FOR
GAS SUPPLY

INFLATABLE
BOAT

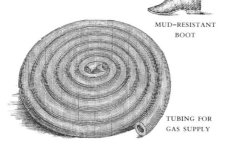

THE PLASTICS REVOLUTION
Shaping objects

The word 'plastic' stems from the Greek word *plastikos* meaning 'fit for moulding'. Materials with naturally plastic qualities, including horn, tortoiseshell and shellac, have been used for thousands of years to make ornaments and the handles of tools. But the modern plastic age began in 1862 when the English chemist Alexander Parkes made imitation ivory combs and hairslides. Parkes first added nitric acid to cellulose, a substance abundant in the woody parts of plants. He then used camphor to shape the resulting material, cellulose nitrate, into a pliable form, which he called 'Parkesine'.

In 1869 a similar product was made by the American engineers John and Isaiah Hyatt to replace ivory in billiard balls. They named their plastic 'celluloid', and commercial success followed, despite the material's flammability, with the manufacture of toys and dressing-table sets. The American businessman

MAN-MADE FIBRES

• Earl Silas Tupper was working for Du Pont in the USA when, in the 1930s, he transformed a lump of black polythene slag, a by-product of oil refinery, into a lightweight, nonbreakable plastic. He used it to make the airtight food containers known as Tupperware from 1938.

• In 1913 Herbert Faber and Daniel O'Conor, a salesman and an engineer respectively, applied for a patent for an insulation material for electric wiring to replace mica. The first Formica came in black only and was used in car parts and radios. Marble patterns were introduced in 1925, and in the 1940s it was used to decorate public places and shops.

George Eastman created a new flexible celluloid film for cameras in 1889.

Unlike celluloid, which contained some natural materials, Bakelite was entirely synthetic. Patented in the USA in 1907, it was the result of the Belgian-born chemist Leo Baekeland's search for a shellac substitute. Baekeland's winning formula was a mixture of the chemicals phenol and formaldehyde.

Bakelite was a resinous material that could be moulded by heat and pressure. It was both durable and popular since, once heat-set, it could not be softened or pushed out of shape. Made into telephones and radios from around 1929, its distinctive look—dark colours, often blended to create imitations of marble and onyx—helped to define the 'modern' style of the interwar years.

The 20th-century plastics industry was not truly launched until 1922, when the German chemist Hermann Staudinger proved that rubber consisted of long chains of a basic molecule repeated in a structure now known as a polymer. He also discovered that styrene, an oily liquid component of crude oil, could be turned into a polymer when heated. During the 1920s polystyrene was developed in Germany as an alternative to rubber and patented by the company I.G. Farben in 1929. Objects were fashioned by injection moulding it into predetermined shapes.

Perspex was developed in 1930 after chemists working in Britain, Canada and Germany discovered that methyl acrylate could be 'polymerised' to create a clear, strong plastic. In 1936 this Perspex was used in the windshields and cockpits of the new Spitfire aircraft.

An English chemist named Reginald Oswald Gibson had already invented polyethylene, or polythene, in 1933. Easily moulded and water-repellent, it was used from 1939 as a cable insulator and in radar components. The first polythene household product was a washing-up bowl made in 1948.

INCREDIBLE FIBRES
Strands of strength

In 1963 Royal Aircraft engineers at Farnborough in Hampshire discovered that when fibres were heated their molecules changed into strong chains of pure carbon. The result was carbon fibre, exploited in the construction of lightweight performance cars, tennis rackets and golf clubs.

Strands the diameter of a human hair are the basis of fibre optics. In 1955 Dr Narinder Kapany of Imperial College, London, showed that light could travel down a fine fibre made of two types of glass. The different glasses made the light 'bounce' to the end of the strand. Fibre optics was used in the endoscope, a medical device for looking inside a patient's body, by the American surgeon Basil Hirschowitz in 1958. In 1966 the scientists Charles Kao and George Hockham, who were working at the Standard Telephone Laboratories in Essex, proved that such fibres could also carry telecommunications signals.

BAKELITE TELEPHONE, 1930S

BAKELITE ELECTRIC BED WARMER, 1930S

BAKELITE SALTCELLAR, 1930S

CELLULOID DOLL, 1920S

BAKELITE 'MICHELIN MAN' ASHTRAY, 1950S

BAKELITE CAMERA, 1930S

VINYL RECORD, 1960S

BAKELITE CIGARETTE BOX, 1930S

BAKELITE SHAVING STICK, 1930S

NYLON STOCKING, 1960S

CELLOPHANE PACKAGING, 1960S

MATERIAL WORLD *During the 20th century plastics have made possible the creation of dozens of affordable and durable everyday objects. Since 1948, when the American company CBS made the first black vinyl records, plastics have hugely increased the availability of music in the home.*

MAGNIFYING THE MINUSCULE
The microscope

Without the microscope the amazing world invisible to the human eye, including cells and bacteria, would still be a mystery. At many ancient sites across the world, including some such as Gordion in Turkey that date back to the 9th century BC, pieces of transparent rock crystal with curved surfaces have been found. But whether these crystals were actually recognised and used as lenses, or merely regarded as decorative jewels, is unknown.

If the ancients had understood lenses they would probably have invented spectacles, but these did not appear in Europe until the 13th century AD. It was the Dutch spectacle-makers Hans and Zacharias Janssen who devised the compound microscope, which combined two lenses, in 1590. However, imperfections in the lenses meant only a blurred image was produced.

Some 90 years later Anton van Leeuwenhoek, the Dutch naturalist, used a single, perfectly ground lens to magnify bacteria hundreds of times. Awed by such sights, the naturalist Henry Power proclaimed:

'In the wood-mite or -louse you may behold
An eye of trellis-work in burnisht gold.'

During the 18th century, lenses gave sharper images as chromatic aberration, the presence of coloured fringes produced by the division of white light into its colours, was progressively reduced. But not until 1830 did the English microscopist Joseph Jackson Lister successfully remove the distortion, which resulted from greater bending of light at the edge of a lens than at its centre, known as spherical aberration.

About a century later the electron microscope revealed more detail, providing magnification that was some 100 000 times greater than that of a standard microscope by focusing electron beams in a magnetic field.

FORTIN BAROMETER, ABOUT 1809

VORTICELLA, A SINGLE-CELLED ANIMAL

MINIATURE WORLD *In 1674 the single lens in a microscope like this revealed to Anton van Leeuwenhoek hitherto unknown organisms, which he described as 'animalcules'. He was the first person to see spermatozoa.*

HUMAN SPERMATOZOA

WEATHER REPORT *In the early 1800s Jean Nicolas Fortin produced his highly accurate mercury barometer, which is still used today.*

NEW HORIZONS *From 1600 the quest to understand the Universe was aided by the development of telescopes and binoculars.*

UP AND DOWN *In this sealed thermometer, made to a 1640s design, the glass balls sink one by one as the temperature rises and rise as it falls.*

TELESCOPE, 1650S DESIGN

IVORY BINOCULARS, ABOUT 1840

DISTANCE VIEWING
Telescopes and binoculars

Credit for the telescope's invention is still contested, but a Dutch spectacle-maker named Hans Lippershey is the most likely candidate. He applied for a patent for his 'looker', consisting of a concave and a convex lens in a tube, in 1608. However, his discovery may have been predated by those of the English mathematician Leonard Digges or the Italian physicist Giambattista Della Porta, both of whom hinted at similar instruments in the previous century.

In 1609 the Italian scientist Galileo made his own telescope, turning it towards the heavens. Having identified the moons in orbit around Jupiter, Galileo deduced that the Earth was not the motionless centre of the Universe. The first images of stars seen in early telescopes were surrounded with coloured fringes, which

LOOKING UP *A 14th-century illustration suggests that even 200 years before the telescope was invented people were gazing up at the heavens through tubes (left). After looking at the Moon through his true telescope, Galileo drew a detailed picture of its surface (above).*

resulted from chromatic aberration. In 1668 the English astronomer Isaac Newton solved this problem in a design that remains essentially unchanged. His reflecting telescope used curved mirrors to focus light from the heavens.

Binoculars, first seen in Paris in 1823, consisted of a small telescope for each eye. They were improved towards the end of the 19th century when Ernst Abbe, assistant to the German scientist and instrument maker Carl Zeiss, discovered that by putting two triangular glass prisms in each telescope a magnification similar to that of much longer telescopes could be achieved.

MEASURING TEMPERATURES
The thermometer

In 1592 temperature was probably first measured when Galileo devised an instrument consisting of a glass bulb attached to a slender glass tube, which he immersed in water. Any decrease in the temperature of the bulb lowered the pressure of the air within and sucked the water higher into the tube. But because it was sensitive to changes in atmospheric pressure the instrument was unreliable.

In 1624 the French scientist Jean Leurechon used *thermomètre* to mean 'measurer of heat'. The first thermometer to be sealed

ON FULL BEAM

As he sat in a park in Washington DC one morning in 1951 the physicist Charles Townes dreamed up the laser's precursor. Planning to amplify microwaves (electromagnetic radiation beyond the visible spectrum) for use in radar, he decided to use high-energy atoms in ammonia molecules to produce 'microwave amplification by stimulated emission of radiation'. An acronym made its name 'maser'. Theodore Maiman, another US physicist, applied the same idea to light and built the first laser, emitting red light from a ruby crystal, in 1960.

from the air, and stay unaffected by atmospheric pressure, was made in 1641, by Ferdinand II, Grand Duke of Tuscany. Ferdinand also used coloured alcohol, but later in the century Tuscan scientists replaced it with mercury.

In 1724 the German physicist Gabriel Fahrenheit described a temperature scale. He set zero (at the time the lowest temperature considered obtainable) as the freezing point of a mixture of ice, water and sea salt, and 96° as body temperature, which he worked out by placing the thermometer bulb in either the mouth or the

BODY HEAT *Santorio Santorio, a professor of medicine in Padua from 1616 to 1636, measured body temperature with this 'thermoscope', an adaptation of Galieo's earlier device.*

armpit. On the Fahrenheit scale, water freezes at 32° and boils at 212°.

In 1742 the Swedish astronomer Anders Celsius suggested a temperature scale in which the freezing point of water would be 100° Celsius and the boiling point 0° C. This illogical scale was inverted by the French scientist Jean Pierre Christin the next year.

More than a century passed before doctors started systematically measuring body temperature to aid diagnosis. In 1868 a German professor of medicine, Karl August Wunderlich, published *The Temperature in Diseases*, based on measurements of 25000 patients. His research required great dedication since his clinical thermometer was some 30cm (1ft) long and it took about 20 minutes to register each reading.

But help was at hand. In 1852 a thermometer with a constriction in its narrow glass tube to prevent the mercury falling back was patented and in 1867 Clifford Allbutt improved this with a shortened version. Supported by Wunderlich's data, this thermometer became invaluable to physicians.

EVALUATING AIR PRESSURE
The barometer

In 1643 the Italian physicist Evangelista Torricelli announced that people live 'submerged at the bottom of an ocean of elementary air'. He concluded this by using the first barometer, a glass tube 1.2m (4ft) long, sealed at one end, filled with mercury and inverted into a bowl containing more mercury. Torricelli found that some of the mercury stayed inside the tube, supported by atmospheric pressure. He also noticed that the level rose in fine spells and dropped when it rained, an observation which soon spurred systematic research into the weather across Europe.

Greater accuracy was achieved by the French physicist Jean Nicolas Fortin with his barometer of 1809, and with the banjo-shaped aneroid barometer invented in 1843 by the French scientist Lucien Vidie. The latter consists of a metal box from which air has been extracted. One side of the box moves when barometric pressure changes, an alteration transmitted to a needle pointing to a description of the weather.

DRIPPING AWAY *In a water clock built by Ctesibius of Alexandria in the 3rd century BC, time was shown by a model fighter pointing to the falling water level.*

WEIGHTING TIME *By the late 15th century wall clocks were being built by artisans across Europe. They functioned through a series of wheels driven by a falling weight on a cord. The pendulum improved the accuracy of clocks in the mid 17th century.*

MACHINES TO MARK TIME
Clocks and timepieces

Noticing the way that shadows moved as the Sun advanced across the sky, the Egyptians were inspired to make the first sundials as long ago as 2000 BC. A crossbar was sited so that its shadow moved over a series of marks on the ground as the day progressed.

The Egyptians measured time after sunset by charting the movement of the stars or with water clocks. The earliest known of these clocks dates from the 14th century BC during the reign of Amenhotep III. Standing in the temple of the god Amun-Re at Karnak, it consisted of a vessel with a small hole in the bottom through which water dripped, marking time as the liquid's level fell.

Water clocks, or clepsydras (from the Greek word *klepsudra*, meaning 'water stealer'), continued to mark time until the Middle Ages. Many of these clepsydras were ornately engineered, and some sounded bells or moved hands to indicate the hour. So widely used did they become that Aristotle, the Greek philosopher, grumbled that 'the length of a tragedy should not be judged by the clepsydra, but by what is suitable for the plot'.

Mechanical timekeeping, so written accounts record, began in about AD 1090 when the Chinese astronomer Su Sung devised a water-powered clock controlled by a form of escapement, a notched wheel that was driven by a falling weight on a cord. In Europe the earliest mechanical clocks were made in the late 13th century—one was erected at Dunstable Priory in 1283.

The oldest surviving clock in Britain was built for Salisbury Cathedral in 1386. It has no hands and strikes the hours on a bell. Indeed, the word 'clock' comes from *glocke*, German for 'bell'. Similar clocks, some striking the quarters as well as the hours, were built throughout western Europe. But they

AT A STROKE *This German wall clock of about 1520 had metal figures which struck a bell on the hour. Weights (not shown) turned the crown wheel of the verge escapement, a mechanism which controlled the wheel's rotation and, ultimately, the progress of the single hour hand around the clock dial.*

were not accurate, and a loss or gain of several minutes a day was the best that could be expected.

In the mid 15th century clockwork timepieces driven by the power of a coiled spring appeared. The rate at which the spring turned the driving wheels was kept steady by a fusee, a spiral groove cut on a cone-like form, connected to the mainspring drum by a gut line. Spring power meant that clocks no longer needed external weights and did not have to be hung on walls. This made possible the development of portable clocks and watches, clocks small enough to be worn.

Galileo was the first to understand how the pendulum worked after seeing lamps swinging in Pisa Cathedral in 1581. But it was not until 1641, the year before his death, that the then blind Galileo asked his son Vincenzio to construct a pendulum clock. Vincenzio never finished his task, and it was left to Salomon Coster and Jan Van Call to produce the first pendulum clocks, to a design created by the Dutch physicist Christiaan Huyghens in 1657.

The anchor escapement appeared around 1670, possibly the invention of the London clock-maker William Clement. The mechanism rocked one 'tick' with each swing of the pendulum, and made accurate timekeeping possible for the first time. In 1675 Huyghens and the English physicist and architect Robert Hooke independently invented the hairspring, a fine spiral balance spring that bought similar accuracy to portable timekeepers such as watches.

PORTABLE CLOCKS
The birth of the wristwatch

Until clocks small enough to be carried were invented, sundials were the only portable timepieces. Some of the earliest watches were made at the beginning of the 16th century by Peter Heinlein of Nuremberg in Germany. These watches were housed in drum-shaped cases. Heinlein also made watches that resembled pomanders, small, pierced metal balls filled with sweet-smelling herbs or scent and carried to ward off infection or mask foul smells.

Possibly the first watch worn on the arm was 'an armlet of gold, all fairly

PUNCTUAL SIGNALS

Radio time signals were initially broadcast in the USA from the Navy Yard at Boston, Massachusetts, in 1905. The BBC later transmitted the first hourly 'pips' from the Royal Observatory in Greenwich in 1924, switching in 1990 to an atomic clock in Broadcasting House.

Telephone announcements of the time began with a speaking clock in France in 1933. A similar service was introduced in Britain in 1936.

garnished with rubies and diamonds and having the closing thereof a small clock'. It was presented by the Earl of Leicester in 1571 to Elizabeth I.

A 'watch to be fixed on a bracelet' was recorded in the 1790 accounts of the watchmakers Jacquet Droz and Paul Leschot of Geneva, Switzerland. However, wristwatches remained extremely rare. Both men and women continued to wear fob or pocket watches attached to ribbons or chains.

The change began after the German navy issued wristwatches to all its officers in 1880, on the basis that they were easier to consult on a storm-tossed ship. But resistance persisted until the First World War when lightweight and easy-to-read wristwatches proved more practical for use in the trenches than pocket watches.

The Rolex company, which was founded in Geneva in 1905 by Hans Wilsdorf, introduced a waterproof watch, the Rolex Oyster, in 1926. Even after it had been immersed in water for three weeks, it kept excellent time. The

REINFORCED *The Ingersoll 'Midget' wristwatch for men was manufactured between 1911 and 1917. Its metal grill protected the glass from breakage.*

year after its launch, an Oyster was worn on a cross-Channel swim by the London typist Mercedes Gleitz, again without suffering any damage.

Electronic watches took the USA by storm when the Bulova Accutron was introduced in 1960. Using a vibrating tuning fork to set the time, it proved to be far more accurate than any mechanical watch. Further innovation followed in 1967 with the development of quartz watches by the Swiss Horological Electronic Centre. Powered by batteries, they contained quartz crystals that vibrated more than 8000 times a second and made possible the most precise watches to date. Nor did they need to be wound.

Digital watches arrived in 1971. Developed by the American engineers George Theiss and Willy Crabtree, they presented a light-emitting diode, or visual number display, and were called 'Pulsar' watches.

AWAKENED BY BELLS
Alarm clocks

WINTER TIME *From the 14th century monks in Europe marked time by the hourglass as well as the water clock, rendered ineffective by the freezing temperatures of winter.*

The Greeks may have been the first to use clepsydras as alarm clocks. Ctesibius of Alexandria invented one clock with ringing bells around 270 BC. From the 6th century AD water clocks served as alarms in Europe's monasteries—the clock-keeper would ring a bell when it was time for the monks to pray. These developed into clocks that would set off the monastery bells automatically. Some of the early mechanical clocks were also used by monasteries to wake monks from their slumbers so that they could pray at matins.

THE COMPUTER REVOLUTION

'We used to have lots of questions to which there were no answers.
Now, with the computer, there are lots of answers to which we haven't thought up the questions.'

PETER USTINOV, ACTOR AND RACONTEUR, *The Illustrated London News*, 1968

To help them with calculations that were too difficult to work out on their fingers, the ancient Romans invented an aid to calculation—a flat slab covered in sand for marking out values, with pebbles as counters. By about 450 BC these pebbles, or *calculi*, had been strung on separate wires for units, tens, hundreds and thousands to create the abacus. This device, which may also have been known to the Babylonians, made addition and subtraction easy.

Centuries later, following the scientific advances of the Renaissance, the Scottish mathematician John Napier speeded up increasingly complex calculations using 'bones'—sets of rods engraved with numbers and placed side by side so that answers could be read from them. Logarithms, first described by Napier in 1614, were printed tables which enabled numbers to be multiplied or divided by adding or subtracting their 'powers' (9, for example, is 3 to the power of 2).

MATHEMATICAL MACHINES

Soon mechanical calculating devices appeared. In 1642 the French philosopher and mathematician Blaise Pascal constructed one of the first, to help his father, a tax official. It consisted of chains of gears with the numerals 1 to 9 on their circumference. A more efficient machine, which was made in the 1670s by the German mathematician Baron Gottfried von Leibniz, spawned many imitations.

The British mathematician Charles Babbage brought the theory of mechanical calculation to maturity with his 'difference engine' proposed in 1822 and his 'analytical engine' of 1840. Babbage's prototype for the latter (neither machine was ever actually built by him) possessed the

MATHEMATICIANS COMPETE FOR SPEED WITH
DECIMALS AND ABACUS, GERMANY, 1504

first separate memory and logic components, which he named the 'store' and the 'mill'.

In 1936 the British mathematician Alan Turing produced a specification for a machine that could work with logical statements and shorthand symbols as well as numbers. In the same year a young German engineer, Konrad Zuse, built his first prototype computer, the Z1, on a table in his parents' apartment.

Using electrical relays (switches) to combine numbers in binary form—using the digits 0 and 1, to represent 'off' and 'on'—Zuse constructed Z3, the first fully operational, program-controlled digital computer in 1941. Strips of old movie film were punched with holes to provide Z3 with data. Zuse thought of substituting electronic for mechanical relays, which he estimated would speed calculation 1000 times. But his idea remained unrealised for want of investment.

Meanwhile a team at Bletchley Park in Buckinghamshire, making use of

Turing's advances, were incorporating electromechanical devices in their machines. A group led by Tommy Flowers, a Post Office engineer, used 1000 valves to build Colossus, which was completed in 1943. Colossus analysed coded German messages in a way that made it possible to work out the specifications of the machine that had generated them. The key to the success of Colossus was its processing speed. Now it took only 2 hours to

BRILLIANT CAREER *Lady Ada Lovelace, daughter of the English poet Lord Byron, helped Charles Babbage to work out how to use punch cards to feed information into his 'analytical engine'. She was later claimed as the first true programmer, and the computer language ADA is named after her.*

decode a message that had previously taken three experts six weeks to interpret. The Colossus worked using valves, which had first been incorporated in logic circuits in the USA in the 1930s. And it proved conclusively that computers were logical machines, not mere calculators.

Also in 1943 the US Ballistics Research Laboratory commissioned the engineers John Mauchly and John Presper Eckert of the University of Pennsylvania to build a computer to produce tables of ballistics data, such as the trajectories of artillery shells. The result, completed in 1946, was ENIAC (Electronic Numerical Integrator and Computer). But it was cumbersome and had no internal memory. This last barrier was surmounted by a team at Manchester University in 1948, which constructed the Small Scale Experimental Machine, a computer with a stored program.

The computer's commercial potential was not immediately appreciated, but in Britain the management of J. Lyons and Co, owners of popular tearooms, set up the team that built LEO (the Lyons Electronic Office) for data processing in 1950. The US company IBM (International Business Machines) made its first computer in 1953.

COMPUTER GENERATIONS

In this first generation of computers, valves were used as switches— registering 'on' or 'off', that is, 1 or 0 in the binary system. But they were expensive, bulky, consumed large amounts of power and also required incessant cooling.

The potential of replacing valves with more efficient components had been glimpsed in 1947 when William Shockley, Walter Brattain and John Bardeen, all scientists at the Bell Telephone Laboratories, discovered that tiny fragments of the substance germanium, a semiconductor, could do the same job, only much faster. Germanium was used in the first transistors, named from a combination of the words 'transfer' and 'resistor'. In 1953 the first transistor-based second-generation computer was built at Manchester University and from the mid 1950s the use of components made from silicon (which is, after oxygen, the most abundant element in the Earth's crust) increased performance dramatically.

Progress towards the 'computer on a chip' began at about this time. By 1959 the American companies Fairchild and Texas Instruments had manufactured 'integrated circuits' with all the components sharing a slice of silicon. Used from the early 1960s in third-generation computers, they powered the US systems which, in 1969, made the Apollo 11 Moon landing possible.

In the same year Ted Hoff, a Stanford engineering professor, put all a computer's functions on a single programmable chip, or central processing unit, which he called a 'microprocessor'. By 1971 Intel and Texas Instruments in the USA were manufacturing microprocessors for the first handheld calculators. Compact, desktop machines were soon on sale. The Altair, the first microcomputer, was marketed as a kit in 1975.

NUMBER CRUNCHING *A real version of Babbage's 'difference engine' was finally built in 1991 to celebrate the bicentenary of his birth. In his original concept of 1822, Babbage also included a printer, whose purpose was to generate tables of numbers automatically.*

NO HANDS *The storage capacity of the transistor (below, left) has vastly reduced computer size. This 1980s computer-operated robot welded intricate car parts.*

QUICK CALCULATIONS *The ENIAC (Electronic Numerical Integrator and Computer) used 18 000 valves, 70 000 resistors, 10 000 capacitors (which stored electrical charge) and 6000 switches. It was 30 m (100 ft) long, weighed some 30 tonnes and performed 5000 additions a second.*

HIGH SPAN *Simply built wooden truss bridges were widely used by the military during the American Civil War. The Potamac Creek Bridge was up in just nine days.*

BRIDGING PLACES
Crossing the water

When Neolithic people settled down they often chose to be close to rivers and streams. The need for dry crossings quickly became apparent and the first, basic bridges of 10000 years ago consisted of one or more tree trunks laid across the water, with a large stone or wooden pier added for support at the centre of wide rivers. Flat stone bridges, such as the medieval Post Bridge which survives in Devon over the East Dart, were suitable for shorter spans.

In the 5th century BC, the Greek historian Herodotus described a bridge he had seen in Babylon with 100 stone piers linked by 1.5m (5ft) wooden beams. For greater spans in stone the Romans were the first to make use of the arch, though for speed of construction wood was commonly used.

Interest in Roman bridges revived during the Renaissance. The Italian scholar and architect Andrea Palladio studied Roman designs before inventing the truss, an open structure of light wooden struts linked by angled cross-beams, in 1570.

The box girder, a variation on the truss, was invented in the 19th century by the Newcastle engineer Robert Stephenson. The girder of his Britannia Bridge of 1850, spanning the Menai Strait in north Wales, owed its strength to being a closed tube, or box, through which trains ran.

The first cast-iron bridge, of 1779, crossed the Severn at Coalbrookdale in Shropshire. This elegant arch inspired the song-writer Charles Dibdin to remark: 'Though it seems like network wrought in iron, it will apparently be uninjured for ages.' Built without any screws, the bridge was held together by dovetail and mortice-and-tenon joints.

The Winch footbridge, the original suspension bridge, was built to span the River Tees in England in 1741. A concrete roadway 21m (70ft) long was introduced in 1801 by the American engineer James Finlay for the Jacob's Creek Bridge in Pennsylvania. The first bridge suspended from steel cables, Brooklyn Bridge in New York, was completed in 1883.

BUILDING ACHIEVEMENTS

- By using suspension wires, the world's longest bridges make practicable spans more than 1410m (4630ft) long. Their origins lie far back in Neolithic times when short rope or vine bridges were strung across streams.
- The Romans first used concrete to build a theatre at Pompeii in 55BC.
- Persecuted Christians in Rome dug tunnels for use as secret underground burial galleries, or catacombs, from the 2nd to the 5th centuries AD.
- The first tunnel beneath the Alps, 73m (240ft) long, was built in 1707. But a major passage under Mont Cenis, measuring 13km (8 miles), was not bored until the 1860s.

PASSAGES UNDERGROUND
Tunnels and tunnelling

The ancient Egyptians constructed tunnels leading to their pharaohs' tombs. The earliest, dug through solid rock in about 1220BC in the Valley of the Kings, gave access to the tomb of Merneptah (the son of Rameses II). A tunnel 107m (350ft) long led to a shaft opening on to another tunnel of 91m (300ft). At the end of it lay the king's burial chamber.

By the 8th century BC Persians and Armenians were digging extensive *qanats*, or irrigation tunnels, to carry water 32km (20 miles) or more from rivers to towns. But attempts to tunnel under water proved unsuccessful until relatively modern times.

In 1818 a box-shaped iron casing, or shield, was devised by the British engineer Marc Isambard Brunel to support the roof of the first tunnel to be dug under the River Thames. As miners within shovelled through the soft clay the shield was pushed forward with screw jacks, and the tunnel gradually lined with a brick carapace. Digging continued in this painstaking way for more than two decades.

SAFE PASSAGE *The first underwater tunnel, opened in 1843, covered 1100m (3600ft) below the Thames between Rotherhithe and Wapping in London. Queen Victoria knighted its celebrated engineer, Marc Isambard Brunel.*

FEATS OF CONSTRUCTION
Advances in building

The oldest known form of construction is the post and lintel—two vertical supports with a horizontal crossbeam. This probably dates back to prehistoric times, when tree trunks served as posts and branches as lintels. From about 2500 BC the burial chambers within Egyptian pyramids imitated this style in stone, but such monumental structures had limitations because they allowed only short horizontal spans.

Wider openings became possible with the arch, invented by the Assyrians and Babylonians in the 6th century BC,

ARCHITECTURAL GLORY *Roman amphitheatres employed the principle of the arch on an unprecedented scale. Completed in AD 80, the Colosseum in Rome showed how it could support a huge weight of masonry and inspired architects for more than 1000 years.*

which was used in such gateways as the Ishtar Gate of Babylon. Because a single arch transmitted loads outwards and downwards, it could bear a far greater weight than the post and lintel.

The round arch used by the Romans created gloomy buildings with small windows. Not until about AD 1050 was it superseded by the vault, a much steeper arch used to magnificent effect in Gothic cathedrals such as those at Chartres in France and Canterbury in England in the 12th century.

The elegant dome is, in structural terms, a series of arches meeting at a single point. Domes capped tombs from about 2500 BC in the Mesara Plain in Crete, but the world's first great dome, with a diameter of some 44 m (144 ft), appeared in AD 124 on the Pantheon in Rome. Its size was made possible by a thinly applied layer of concrete, which enabled the surface weight to be minimised. Later domes, such as the one that was created by Sir Christopher Wren for St Paul's Cathedral in the City of London, completed in 1710, have chain ties around their bases to contain outward pressure.

BUILDING UPWARDS
Skyscrapers

Concrete and steel, which combine strength with lightness, made skyscrapers possible. Equally important was the lift. The first lift had been installed on the outside of Louis XV's Palace of Versailles in 1743 to allow him easy access to his mistress's second-floor apartment. However, safe and speedy transport up and down was not devised until 1854, by the American engineer Elisha Otis. His 'safety hoister', a lift supported by a cable, boasted a mechanism that held it in place even when the cable was severed.

After Chicago's great fire of 1871, Otis's invention proved invaluable as the city was rebuilt upwards. The ten-storey Home Insurance Building,

GOING DOWN *To reassure people that his lift was safe, Elisha Otis ordered an assistant to cut the supporting cable. Held in place by a spring with a ratchet and a pawl, which fitted into a notch in the ratchet, the lift was halted.*

completed by William Jenney in 1885, was the first tall structure to use cast iron and steel in a supporting frame. By the mid 1930s skyscrapers had multiplied in American cities. The word itself was far older, having been used since 1794 to describe tall items ranging from top hats to ships' sails.

THE CANAL NETWORK
Inland waterways

The oldest man-made waterway is a canal still navigated today. It is China's Grand Canal, a 1609 km (1000 mile) link between the Yellow and Yangtse rivers, started in the 6th century BC. Some 5 million men, employed over about 600 years, were needed to dig it. In AD 984, two watergates were installed to give temporary control of the water level, and qualify as the first locks.

The Romans built the first canal in Britain, between Lincoln and the River Trent 17.5 km (11 miles) away, in AD 65. Known as the Fossdyke, it is still in use today. But canals only spread across Europe after the development of the pound lock in Italy around 1370, which allowed a stretch of water to be isolated and gradually lowered or raised.

Such locks proved essential to the network of canals that transformed the face of Britain in the Industrial Revolution. The first of these was the Duke of Bridgewater's Canal, completed by the wheelwright James Brindley in 1761 to link the duke's collieries at Worsley, Lancashire, with the heart of industrial Manchester.

MOVING ABOUT

Humans had travelled the world and colonised every continent save Antarctica by 40 000 BC. While much of their exploration was on foot, many journeys must have been made in boats, although no trace remains of these original craft. A paddle made in 8 500 and found in Star Carr in Yorkshire and a dugout canoe from Pesse in the Netherlands fashioned in 7400 are the earliest tangible evidence of such endeavours.

For millennia canoes and rafts remained the most effective means of travelling or carrying loads, and were probably used by the Beaker Folk who erected the stone circles at Stonehenge in 2200. The stones were brought from south Wales by river and sea lashed to wooden rafts. Once on land they were probably transferred to sledges and pulled along the ground with ropes—the method used by the Egyptians at about this time to build the pyramids. Light craft made of skins stretched over a wooden framework, the forerunners of the Irish currach and the Welsh coracle, may be equally old. Buoyant and easily paddled, these were the vessels in which medieval Irish monks embarked to explore the Atlantic.

The first tracks on land were designed to give access to waterways; they were built on higher ground to help travellers to see around them and avoid attack. Because they were used only by people or pack animals, gradients mattered less than dry footing. The Romans built their roads along the chalk ridges of England, avoiding the forests and the valleys. This pattern continued for

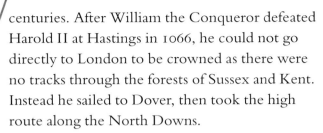

centuries. After William the Conqueror defeated Harold II at Hastings in 1066, he could not go directly to London to be crowned as there were no tracks through the forests of Sussex and Kent. Instead he sailed to Dover, then took the high route along the North Downs.

The first wheeled wagons were made in Sumeria in about 3500, drawn by oxen or, later, horses, but without adequate roads these vehicles had limited use as cargo carriers. Early carts had a single shaft passing between two animals and attached to a breast harness. Horses were used more efficiently as draught animals after Chinese farmers invented the horse collar in about the 3rd century AD. By removing pressure on the animal's windpipe, the padded collar, used in Europe by early medieval times, allowed these creatures to pull much heavier loads.

Strong, solidly built horses for carrying heavily armed knights into battle were first bred in France in the 13th century and proved equally suited to hauling carts and towing boats along rivers and canals. By the 16th century wagons were generally fitted with wheels up to 30 cm (1 ft) wide, and needed at least eight horses to pull them. Coaches were built to the same design, but only the rich could afford the necessary huge teams of horses.

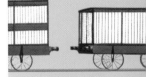

Roads improved greatly in the 18th century, leading to the era of the mail coach. The first, between London and Bristol, started in 1784. The second half of the century also saw a fever of canal-building, inspired by the successful Bridgewater Canal linking Manchester and Worsley, completed in 1761. A similar boom followed the success of the first railways in the 1830s. The steam locomotive began the shrinking of journey times that has continued with the motor car, invented in 1885, and the aeroplane (1903), both made possible by the internal-combustion engine.

THE DRAISINE IN USE, 1817

EASY RIDING *Propelled by a rider driving his feet against the ground in a running motion, the wooden Draisine was a crude but surprisingly effective machine.*

PEDAL POWER
The beginnings of the bicycle

The bicycle is a simple machine but its design was not easy to perfect. In fact the development of the 'iron horse', which enabled thousands of ordinary men and women to escape from the grime of Victorian towns and discover the joys of the countryside, occupied most of the 19th century.

The first person to realise that it was possible to construct a balanced two-wheeled vehicle was Baron Karl Drais von Sauerbronn, a German engineer who showed his wooden Draisine in 1817 in Paris's Luxembourg Gardens. The following year an English coach-maker, Dennis Johnson, copied the design to produce an iron model.

More than two decades later, a Scottish blacksmith called Kirkpatrick Macmillan developed swinging pedals that operated cranks driving the vehicle's rear wheel. But his design failed to catch on and the next breakthrough did not occur until 1861, when the French coachbuilder Pierre Michaux and his son Ernest produced a *vélocipède*, named from the Latin for 'swift-footed'. The large front wheel had revolving pedals attached to its hub, while a simple brake acted as a control on the rear wheel.

With this principle of construction, the bigger the front wheel the farther the velocipede could travel for each turn of the pedals. The concept was taken to an extreme by James Starley, foreman at the Sewing Machine Co. of Coventry. His 1870 model had the rider perched precariously on a wheel measuring up to 1.5 m (5 ft) across, with a diminutive rear wheel trailing behind. Nicknamed the penny-farthing from the sizes of the wheels, it created the first cycling boom. Tricycle versions were made for those of a nervous disposition and for women, who found it hard to manage with their long skirts.

'The horse that never says neigh', as the penny-farthing was dubbed in the USA, was used for outings, racing and a round-the-world trip. The adventurer Thomas Stevens set off on his machine from California in April 1884 and covered 21725 km (13 500 miles) before returning in December 1886. By this time, the penny-farthing's popularity was being challenged by the Rover 'safety' bicycle, which

FREEDOM FOR ALL *Even before the bicycle took on its modern shape (above), the penny-farthing (left) had made cycling all the rage as a convivial form of exercise as well as a mode*

was first produced in 1885 by John Kemp Starley, James Starley's nephew. The Rover laid the foundations for the modern bicycle: two wheels of equal diameter, with the rear one driven by a chain that was turned by pedals set between the wheels, and a diamond-shaped steel frame.

The final element was the pneumatic tyre, an instant hit on its launch in 1888 when it was advertised with the boast 'vibration impossible'. With the application of gears, developed in France in 1889 to minimise the effort needed to pedal over varied gradients and terrains, 'bone shakers' were things of the past.

The bicycle also played a part in emancipating women's clothing. In the late 19th century some female cyclists adopted loose trousers gathered at the ankle, named 'bloomers' after their advocate Amelia Jenks Bloomer of New York. Cycle racing began in 1868, with the Englishman James Moore winning a track race at the Parc St Cloud in Paris. He won the first road race, a 134km (83 mile) trek between Paris and Rouen, the following year.

JOHNNIE DUNLOP ON THE FIRST BICYCLE WITH PNEUMATIC TYRES, 1888

A SOFTER RIDE

One day in 1887 the Irish vet John Boyd Dunlop watched his son Johnnie bounce uncomfortably on a tricycle. Dunlop fashioned a tyre from a garden hose, filling it with water. He improved the design by using rubber inflated with air. The pneumatic tyre was a great success but the idea was not new—the civil engineer Robert Thompson had first patented it in 1845.

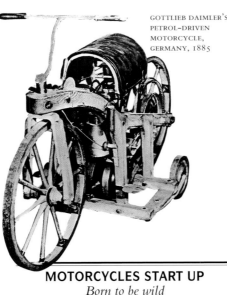

GOTTLIEB DAIMLER'S PETROL-DRIVEN MOTORCYCLE, GERMANY, 1885

MOTORCYCLES START UP
Born to be wild

The bicycle is the most fuel-efficient mode of transportation yet invented, but the cyclist cannot escape the necessity of exerting muscle power. In 1868, just a few years after they had developed their rotary-pedal velocipede, Pierre and Ernest Michaux attempted to resolve this drawback by attaching a small steam engine to its rear.

However, the first bicycle powered by a petrol engine was built in 1885 by the German engineer Gottlieb Daimler, whose main attention was focused on the invention of the motor car. The

motorcycle acquired its classic layout, an engine low in the frame midway between the wheels and controlled by twist grips on the handlebars, at the instigation of two Paris journalists, the brothers Eugene and Michel Werner. Their *motocyclette* was exhibited at the 1897 Paris Salon.

Development of the motorcycle was rapid, and was accelerated considerably by the establishment of such races as the Tourist Trophy (TT), first held on public roads on the Isle of Man in 1907. At the first motorcycle race, a 152km (94 mile) course from Paris to Nantes and back, organised by the Automobile Club de France in 1896, all but one of the competitors rode three-wheeled models. But the two-wheeled variant soon proved best for manoeuvrability, and the invention of the sidecar in 1903 by a W.G. Graham killed off the trikes, which had often been built for more than one person.

In the early 1950s the NSU company in Germany produced mopeds, small-engined machines started by pedalling. Motor scooters, which had more powerful engines and 'skirts' around the front to provide protection from the weather, had first appeared in Italy in 1946 when the Piaggio company introduced its Vespa. The Lambretta was launched by a rival company in 1947. By the 1960s 'mods', who favoured scooters, and 'rockers', who preferred motorcycles, had become distinct, and often violently opposed, youth groups in Britain.

AGE OF INDEPENDENCE
Aimed at the youth market, mopeds were affordable and became popular with fashionable Europeans in the 1950s.

of transport. The tandem first took to the roads in 1869, while a tricycle for two and a 'sociable' for three were produced in 1883. By this time the Cyclists' Touring Club of Great Britain, established in 1878, had some 10000 members. 'The world revolves around the bicycle,' enthused new recruits to the craze.

PEOPLE ON THE MOVE
Coaches and buses

Journeys were painfully slow for the travellers and exhausting for the horses pulling the stagecoaches that began to link Britain's major towns in the 17th century. Travelling between infrequent stops or stages, at which they were replaced, the teams of horses that plied the rutted highways might cover no more than 25 km (15 miles) in a day.

In the early 19th century, passengers on the newly established fast mail coaches could reach Bath from London in 15 hours instead of three days, but road travel was still, in the words of the

novelist Charles Dickens, 'a very serious penance'. Scheduled public transport was now at least reliable and increasingly affordable, provoking the Duke of Beaufort to complain of sharing cramped space with heavily loaded old ladies 'sure to have a canary bird or parrot in a cage'.

The early experiments in urban public transport, such as the scheduled service in Paris started by the French mathematician and philosopher Blaise Pascal in 1662, were no more than briefly fashionable with the aristocrats on whom their success depended. By the 19th century, however, the expansion of towns and cities meant that many more people had to travel long distances to reach their places of work.

The linking of the word 'omnibus', Latin for 'everything' or 'everybody', with a public transport vehicle began in Nantes in Brittany in about 1823.

Stanislas Baudry began operating his 16-seat horse-drawn vehicle to a regular timetable, taking customers from the centre of town to his bathhouse in the suburbs. If space allowed, Baudry would carry other passengers, and he used the word 'omnibus' to emphasise his service's universal appeal. The bathhouse soon shut down but the service remained hugely successful.

In London the first omnibus route was launched in July 1829 by George Shillibeer, who had worked as a coachbuilder in France. The vehicles, which ran from Paddington Green to the Bank of England, had seats for 20 passengers. Staff were uniformed and courteous, and the passengers were offered free

TRAVELLING IN STYLE *Passengers embark on a journey on one of Shillibeer's popular omnibuses (left), drawn by three horses abreast.*

newspapers and magazines to help them to pass the journey. The vehicles were called 'Shillibeers' because 'omnibus' was considered a vulgar word. When rival operators painted his name on the sides of their vehicles, Shillibeer began calling his own 'Shillibeer's Original Omnibuses', and the word became part of polite vocabulary. Double-decker horse-drawn buses were introduced in 1847. They became widespread when the Great Exhibition of 1851 led to a vast increase in passengers.

Early attempts at motorbuses were failures. Steam coaches, which were introduced in the 1830s, were heavy and damaged road surfaces. They faced opposition from the operators of turnpike roads, as well as heavy charges. The first petrol-driven buses, which operated in London from 1899, proved unreliable. However, there was a breakthrough when the London General Omnibus Company introduced its dependable B-type in 1910. In 1913 B-type buses lost only 0.02 per cent of their scheduled time to breakdowns.

PEARS

SLOANE STREET & ALBERT HALL

KENSINGTON, KNIGHTSBRIDGE, HYDE-PARK-CORNER JA B
LONDON GENERAL OMNIBUS COMPANY LIMITED
HAMMERSMITH & PICCADILLY-CIRCUS

NESTLÉ'S MILK
HUDSON'S SOAP

THE OMNIBUS COMES TO TOWN *Although early models, such as this 1904 double-decker, frequently broke down, motorbuses proved popular with the public and by 1916 had replaced London's fleet of horse buses. In the same year, female conductors were employed for the first time in the city to issue and punch tickets, replacing male conductors who had joined the armed forces.*

BELL PUNCH AND TICKET RACK, 1890S

LINING UP *Renault taxis, introduced into Britain in 1907, await their passengers in Trafalgar Square, London. A permanent stand was first established in the Strand in 1633 by a Captain Bailey, who set fixed rates for journeys by hackney carriage.*

TAXI!
Transport for hire

London's black-cab drivers, who must pass the rigorous test known as The Knowledge and become licensed before they can ply their trade on the street, continue a tradition that was established in 1662. Needing funds for road improvements, Charles II introduced licensing in that year under an Act of Parliament which included regulations for hackney coachmen.

The light, two-wheeled cabriolet, named from the French for a 'playful leap' and introduced in 1823, gave rise to the generic term 'cab'. Other specialist hire coaches included the hansom, a two-seater with an enclosed carriage patented in 1834 by the Leicester architect Joseph Hansom. The brougham, built for Lord Brougham by the London coachbuilders Robinson of Mount Street, was introduced in 1839.

Arguments over fares were finally laid to rest in 1891 with the invention of the taximeter by Wilhelm Bruhn of Hamburg. A fellow German, Friedrich Greiner of Stuttgart, was the first to operate motor cabs with taximeters, taking his first fare in May 1897.

In London the motorised taxi only caught on after 1907, when the reliable two-cylinder Renault was imported from France. As with horse-drawn models, designs for motorised cabs proliferated. The introduction of a mass-produced model, the FX3, in 1946, gave rise to the now familiar black cab.

DRIVING FORCES

• Horse-drawn wagons running on rails, called trams after the rail carts used in mines, appeared in New York in 1832, in Paris in 1855, and in Birkenhead in 1860. Electric trams were used in Germany from 1884 and in Leeds from 1891.

• The Paris Automobile Club hired out the first rental cars in 1896. Britain's first hire service, begun by James Edward Tuke of Harrogate and Bradford, Yorkshire, opened for business in the same year.

• The first motorised hearse was used in Buffalo, New York, in 1900. Britain's first was a Daimler used in 1901 to transport the body of William Drakenford, a Daimler Motor Car Company employee.

FRENCH HORSE TRAM, ABOUT 1880

THE BIRTH OF THE PRAM

The forerunner of the perambulator or pram, named from the Latin for 'walk about', was the baby carriage. England's earliest known example was shaped like a scallop shell and featured a canopy roof and carriage lamps. Designed to be pulled by a dog, the wooden vehicle was created for the 3rd Duke of Devonshire by the architect William Kent in 1733.

By 1850 all four-wheeled vehicles had been banned from footpaths so both perambulators and pushchairs, introduced around that year, were made with three wheels. The first pushchair to allow a baby to lie flat as well as sit up appeared around 1876.

THE FIRST PERAMBULATOR, 1733

HOME ON THE ROAD
The caravan

The circus proprietor Antoine Franconi owned one of the first caravans, which appeared in France in the 1830s. His elaborately decorated nomadic carriage or *voiture nomade* contained a built-in kitchen, dining room and bedroom. Such vehicles were also known in Britain. In his novel *The Old Curiosity Shop*, which was published in 1840, Charles Dickens describes in detail the fictional caravan of Mrs Jarley, the owner of a travelling waxworks.

The concept of caravans may have been new in the 19th century, but the word caravan, from the Persian *karwan*, 'company of travellers', was not. The term had been used to refer to a basic stagewagon for 200 years. However, decorated Gypsy caravans did not become familiar sights on British roads until the 1870s. The explorer Sir Samuel Baker pioneered the idea of the caravan pleasure tour when he and his wife purchased a Gypsy caravan and toured Cyprus for six months in 1879, pulled by a team of oxen.

THE CAR IS BORN

*'Glorious, stirring sight!' murmured Toad… 'The poetry of motion,
the real way to travel… O bliss! O poop poop! O my! O my!'*

The Wind in the Willows, KENNETH GRAHAME, 1908

It looked like a rickety tricycle, but the contraption tested out by the German engineer Karl Benz in the grounds of his Mannheim workshop in the spring of 1885 was destined to change the face of the world. The following summer, the motor car covered about 1 km (⅔ mile) at a speed of 15 km/h (about 9 mph) in a public demonstration. This epoch-making event was reported in a local newspaper under the heading 'Miscellaneous'.

KARL BENZ,
1844-1929

While Benz was busy in Mannheim, Gottlieb Daimler, another German engineer, was assembling his first motor car, a four-wheeled carriage. After many false starts, the time was ripe for the birth of the car.

Steam engines had been used to drive road vehicles since the late 1700s, but they were heavy and inefficient. Motor cars needed a new prime mover. It was found in the internal-combustion engine, in which fuel is burned inside the engine rather than in an external furnace, such as in a steam engine.

The first practical version of such an engine, running on coal gas, was developed in 1860 by Jean Joseph Etienne Lenoir, a Belgian engineer working in Paris. Lenoir ran a vehicle from Paris to Joinville-le-Pont, a journey of some 9.5 km (6 miles), which took about 3 hours.

In 1862 the French scientist Alphonse Beau de Rochas proposed a more efficient system for the internal-combustion engine known as the four-stroke cycle, but his idea came to nothing. More than a decade later the German engineer Nikolaus August Otto effectively reinvented the engine with his four-stroke gas-powered version, manufactured in 1876.

POWER ON WHEELS *Introduced in 1899, the state-of-the-art British Daimler was one of the first models to be steered by a wheel rather than a tiller.*

Daimler and Benz used Otto's four-stroke cycle to make engines that could run on petrol and were about nine times more powerful than Lenoir's. Although both produced their cars in 1885, Benz was the first to offer his vehicles for sale, in 1887.

From its early days in Germany, the motor car was destined to progress fastest in France. In 1895 a car designed by the engineers René Panhard and Emile Levassor, with features providing the pattern for the modern car, including a wheel on each corner, the engine at the front and a pedal clutch, won the first motor race. Levassor took just under 49 hours to complete the course from Paris to Bordeaux and back, at an average speed of 24 km/h (15 mph).

He finished 6 hours ahead of the second car, a Peugeot which sported the first pneumatic tyres to be used on a car. The Peugeot might have won the race had its driver not exhausted his stock of 22 inner tubes for puncture repairs. Barely a decade after its invention the car had proved itself much more than a toy.

A SLOW START

In Britain the development of the motor car was severely held back by the Highways and Locomotives Act, which was introduced in 1865 to control the heavy steam-powered traction engines of the time. Mechanical vehicles were restricted to a maximum of 4 mph (6.5 km/h) and had to be preceded by a person carrying a red flag.

The first British road motorist was a Henry Hewetson of Catford, who imported a Benz from Germany in

ALL BLACK *By 1921 Main Street in Henderson, Texas, was packed with Model T Fords, and horse-drawn carriages were rare. Mass production had made motoring affordable for many, but at the cost of choice: Henry Ford offered his 'Tin Lizzie' in 'any colour...so long as it's black'.*

November 1894. He hired a young man to cycle ahead of the car and warn him if he spotted a policeman.

Despite the restrictions on driving, some people accurately foresaw a profitable future for the motor car. One of them was the entrepreneur Frederick Simms, who bought the patents to Daimler's engines in 1893. When the 'red flag' Act was amended in 1896 to allow 'light locomotives' to be driven on the roads, the Daimler Motor Car Company became the first car manufacturer in Britain. It completed its first car in 1897.

Building each of these early cars took three months of skilled craftsmanship by a few dedicated individuals. In 1913 the American car manufacturer Henry Ford installed a conveyor-belt assembly line at his factory, perfecting a technique used since 1901 by a rival company, Oldsmobile. A single car could now be put together in about 90 minutes.

In contrast to other cars of the time, which were far beyond the means of the average family, Ford's Model T, introduced in 1909, was designed as a 'car for the multitude' and priced accordingly. This was the car that launched the era of popular motoring, and in 1920 it became the first car to sell a million.

Mass production reached Europe after the Second World War. The first British model to sell a million was the Morris Minor, launched in 1949. Drawings of the car by its designer Alec Issigonis were sold at auction for nearly £26000 in 1996, a tribute to the place of both Issigonis and the Morris Minor in car design innovation.

The early motorists were dedicated enthusiasts, and needed to be since cars were both uncomfortable and unreliable, and journeys were plagued by burst tyres, oil and water leaks and other mishaps. As more people

SEEN AND HEARD *Gas lights and hand-pumped horns were optional extras until the mid 1920s when electric versions became standard.*

acquired cars, they needed to be taught how to use them. The first dedicated driving school was opened in Birkenhead by a William Lea in 1901. Driving tests and licences became compulsory in Paris in 1893. In Britain licences were required after 1903, but were issued annually on request regardless of competence. Driving tests were introduced in 1935.

THE QUEST FOR SPEED *Competitors in this 1903 race from Paris to Madrid were among the first to top 100 mph (160 km/h). The dust was blinding and the many fatalities included these two entrants, whose Renault crashed soon after this photograph was taken.*

THE DEVELOPING CAR

Many features of the car originated early on and became standard only after being 'reinvented' years later. Milestones in the development of the car include:

- 1891 Front engine, Panhard and Levassor, France.
- 1899 Windscreen, Amedée Bollée, France.
- 1902 Seat belt, Baker Electric, and air conditioning, Franklin, USA. Disc brakes, Lanchester, UK.
- 1904 Automatic transmission, Sturtevant, USA.
- 1905 Pneumatic bumpers, Welbeck, UK.
- 1911 Windscreen wipers, Benz, Germany.
- 1912 Electric ignition, Cadillac, USA.
- 1921 Reversing lights, Wills St Claire, USA.

ACETYLENE HEADLAMP, ABOUT 1910

BRASS HORN, ABOUT 1920

HIGHWAYS AND BYWAYS
How roads were made

Throughout history rulers have needed good roads to ensure control of their empires. To this end the first great thoroughfares were built in China during the 9th century BC. By the end of the Han dynasty in AD 220 approximately 32 000 km (20 000 miles) of imperial highway existed.

The Romans built roads throughout their empire, including Britain, from the 1st century AD. After the fall of the empire, these roads were left to decline. Britons went back to using roads that were little more than dirt tracks, waterlogged in winter and dusty in summer. Often the roads were so steeply cambered that carriages were in constant danger of toppling over. Only a few had a paved causeway, or 'causey', alongside for pedestrians and pack animals.

At the other extreme were the 'hollow ways', which are still found in some parts of England, notably Devon and Cornwall. Streams or rainwater could be diverted onto these concave roads to wash the mud and rubble to the lowest point, from where it could be

THE ROYAL WAY *Still in use in the 1800s, the King's Road was built in the 6th century BC. It ran from Susa, the capital of Persia, to Sardis on the coast of Turkey.*

EMPIRE BUILDING *The Romans had unrivalled expertise in road construction, and built their highways on solid foundations. To improve drainage, they gave roads, such as this stone-block one, convex surfaces so that rain could run off easily. Any gaps left between the stones were filled with gravel.*

cleared away easily. Gradually these roads sank lower and lower. 'The stag, the hounds, and the huntsmen have been known to leap over a loaded wagon in a hollow way without any obstruction from the vehicle,' commented the Irish educationalist and inventor Richard Edgeworth in his *Essay on the Construction of Roads and Carriages* in 1817.

From the 18th century the streets of some British towns were often 'paved' with naturally rounded cobblestones collected from a beach—some of these streets still survive in Rye, Sussex. Blocks cut from large hunks of hard stone, usually granite, were also used. Gaps between

HEAVY TRAFFIC *With large teams of horses pulling goods vehicles across the land, new road construction was becoming essential to the smooth flow of commerce throughout Britain by the 18th century.*

the stones were filled with earth. This quickly became so compacted that water could not penetrate, producing a reliable, if bumpy, surface.

MAKING PROGRESS

Road building was transformed by three men. The first of these was Pierre Trésaguet, a French road engineer. In the 1760s he created a more stable structure by having three layers of successively smaller stones on a cambered earth base. Similar methods were applied by the Scottish civil engineer Thomas Telford in the early 19th century. In his roads, grit produced by wheels rolling over a top layer of broken stone filled any gaps, making the surface watertight.

Telford's methods were simplified in the 1820s by his compatriot and fellow engineer John McAdam, who dispensed with foundations. So long as it was waterproof, he asserted, a single layer of graded stone laid on the earth would suffice. McAdam told his workmen to select only stones small enough to fit into their mouths. One day he came across a stretch covered with larger stones. When the workman was admonished, so the story goes, he grinned, revealing a huge toothless mouth. After that, the surveyors were given a 5 cm (2 in) ring gauge or a pocket balance and a 170 g (6 oz) weight for checking stone sizes.

But the demands of the motor car called for a more impervious surface, not least to suppress the clouds of dust created by the suction of the tyres. The solution was to seal the surface with tar. Spread hot then compacted with a roller and top-dressed with gravel, 'tarmacadam', from the word 'tar' and McAdam, or 'tarmac' makes a smooth

surface. A section of the London to Nottingham road was the first to benefit from this material, in 1845.

The first motorway was the 10km (6¼ mile) Avus Autobahn, on the outskirts of Berlin, opened in 1921. Its instigator was the racing enthusiast Karl Friedrich Fritsch, who provided a loop at each end so that the road could double as a racing track.

CELEBRATING SPEED *Posters extolled the virtues of autobahns, built in the Depression of the 1930s to stimulate Germany's construction and manufacturing industries.*

RULES OF THE ROAD
Codes, signs and signals

Regulation of traffic did not begin with the invention of the motor car. As early as 45 BC Julius Caesar limited the number of wheeled vehicles allowed to enter Rome—exceptions were granted for those 'bringing materials necessary for building temples to the gods or public works' or those carrying priests or vestal virgins.

The Romans also introduced the custom of keeping to the left, a habit that was reinforced in medieval times when riders throughout Europe passed oncoming strangers sword arm to sword arm. An increase in horse traffic

---

UNDER CONTROL

• One-way traffic systems were used in some of London's narrow lanes in 1617 to regulate 'the disorder and rude behaviour of Carmen, Draymen and others using Cartes'.
• Speed limits of 4 mph (6 km/h) in the country and about half that in towns and villages were introduced in Britain in 1865 to control vehicles powered by steam. In 1896, after the motor car had become established, it was raised to 12 mph (19 km/h).
• A study to evaluate different reflective road studs was set up by the Ministry of Transport in 1937. After two years, the cat's-eye invented by the road repairer Percy Shaw was the only type in perfect condition. It is still used today.

---

towards the end of the 18th century meant that the convention gained strength but it was not enshrined in British legislation until 1835.

Until the Revolution of 1789, French carriages had habitually kept to the left, which forced pedestrians onto the right side of the road. However, when they were faced with oncoming crowds of hostile *sans-culottes*, or republicans, the aristocrats wisely moved over. Maximilien Robespierre, the revolutionary leader, ordered all Paris traffic to drive on the right in 1791. The following year the first 'keep right' law in the USA was applied to the Pennsylvania turnpike, after visits by Marie Joseph La Fayette, the French soldier and liberal reformer.

Gas-lit traffic lights, using the colours red for 'stop' and green for 'caution', were placed near Parliament Square, London, in 1868. Cleveland, Ohio, had the first electric traffic lights, in 1914. The three-colour system of red, amber and green was introduced into New York in 1918, and London in 1926.

Milestones installed by the Romans along major routes were the earliest incarnations of road signs. The prototype of the modern traffic sign was erected near Lausanne in Switzerland in 1790 to warn of a steep hill. In Britain the Bicycle Union placed the first road signs on dangerous hills, in 1879. Throughout Europe a plethora of signs followed until 1903, when the French pioneered the concept of nationally standardised symbols.

Restrictions on parking were needed in Paris as early as 1893 but reached Britain only in 1930, when they were imposed in London's Mayfair. Parking meters were the brainchild of Carlton Magee, editor of an Oklahoma City newspaper and chairman of a committee charged with finding ways to control parking. The first meters were installed in 1935. In London, meters appeared in 1958, again in Mayfair.

The first island at the centre of a road was built in Liverpool in 1862. In 1864 a Colonel Pierpoint had one sited in London's St James's Street so that he could reach his gentlemen's club safely. But this did not prevent him from being knocked down by a cab at that very crossing. It is said that the accident happened as he stood in the road admiring his handiwork.

DANGER SIGNALS *The first traffic lights exploded a few months after being installed, in 1868, injuring a policeman operating them. Speed-limit signs were erected from 1904 in Britain, but crashes, such as this 1907 accident (below), caused 22 deaths a day.*

FIRST-CLASS PASSENGER COACHES

PRIVATE CARRIAGE

FULL STEAM AHEAD
The birth of locomotion

'You can't imagine how strange it seemed to be journeying on thus, without any visible cause of progress other than the magical machine, with its flying white breath and rhythmical, unvarying pace…' recorded the actress Fanny Kemble on August 25, 1830, after her specially arranged railway trip from Liverpool to Manchester. The age of the railway had begun.

Grooved stone pathways to guide vehicles were used by the Babylonians in around 2000 BC, but it was the wagonways of the medieval mines in Europe that led directly to the railways.

MOVING ALONG *The wooden wagonway of this 16th-century French silver mine was built to transport ore. In 1604 horse-drawn vehicles were pulled along the first British wagonway, in a mine near Nottingham; more wagonways were added to transfer loads to the ports.*

In the 1st century AD the inventor and mathematician Hero of Alexandria had experimented with steam, the motive power of the railway revolution. He played with a wind ball, or aeolipile, in which a hollow sphere connected by pipes to a sealed cauldron of heated water rotated as steam escaped.

Only in 1698 was steam used for a practical purpose. The English engineer Thomas Savery invented a pump that used vacuum power produced by condensation of the steam. But it was Thomas Newcomen, the Devonshire ironmonger, who built the first practical steam engine, in 1712. Like Savery's pump, it was used for draining mines. In the 1760s the Scottish instrument-maker James Watt improved the power

and efficiency of the steam engine by introducing a separate condenser.

By the 1780s both British and French pioneers were experimenting with the idea of using steam to drive heavy-wheeled road engines. A breakthrough came in 1804 when the Cornish engineer Richard Trevithick developed a high-pressure engine compact enough to operate on a tramway. After a few days the rails on which the locomotive was run cracked under its weight and the engine was converted into a pump.

Unable to obtain financial backing for his engines Trevithick left Britain to work in the silver mines of Peru. The challenge was then taken up by William Hedley of Newcastle upon Tyne. In 1813 he built the *Puffing Billy*, a locomotive christened for its exhalations of steam. It was George Stephenson, a mine mechanic, who

was most tenacious in pursuing the development of the locomotive. In 1825 his *Locomotion* was used to pull the first engine-driven freight and passenger service along the 16km (10 miles) of the Stockton & Darlington Railway. Stephenson's son Robert built the *Rocket*, victor in the 1829 trials to decide the form of motive power for the Liverpool to Manchester line.

The German engineer Werner von Siemens designed the first successful electric train, drawn by a locomotive picking up current from a live rail, in Berlin in 1879. Four years later electric trains were introduced in Brighton and Northern Ireland.

Diesel power, which did not involve the huge costs of electrification, made its debut in 1912, in a locomotive built by the Swiss firm Sulzer. However, credit for the technology lies with the German engineer Rudolf Diesel, who perfected the engine in 1897.

STRONGER THAN A HORSE *Richard Trevithick's powerful 'tram wagon' made its first journey in February 1804, pulling 10 tonnes of iron at an average speed of 8km/h (5mph) along the Merthyr tramroad in south Wales. It 'worked exceedingly well', a proud Trevithick wrote to a friend.*

LUGGAGE COACH

LIVESTOCK CARRIAGES

TAKE A RIDE *Early rail passengers sat in coaches similar to those used on the roads, while the rich enjoyed the luxury of private carriages. Separate coaches were provided to transport the luggage.*

CLASSICAL CONCOURSE
Designed to celebrate the railway age, Euston station opened in 1837, the year of the first season ticket. Its imposing Great Hall (below) was built in 1849.

London & Greenwich Railway Company.

THIS TICKET WILL ADMIT

William Bebe Esquire

from 19 January 1837 to 19 April 1837.

NOT TRANSFERABLE

Nº 60 *Third Class*

Secy

EARLY SEASON
TICKET, 1837

second-class passengers. A booking clerk named Thomas Edmondson, who worked on the Newcastle & Carlisle Railway, invented preprinted tickets in 1837 to save him writing out the same details for each traveller. For passengers unable to read, some railways issued tickets with pictures that represented major towns: a sack of cotton for Manchester, a fleece for Leeds, after their main industries.

As more rail services were set up, timetables became necessary. The first was published in 1838 by the London & Birmingham Railway. In 1839 George Bradshaw, a Manchester printer, produced the first timetable of all services. The growth of timetabled railway operations led to standard time being adopted throughout the UK. However, they gave 'no guarantee of punctuality', as the South Yorkshire Railway admitted in 1851.

TICKETS, PLEASE
Passenger travel

In its early days horse-drawn rail was used almost exclusively to carry freight, but passengers rode on the Swansea to Oystermouth rail service shortly after it began operating in 1807. As train travel developed, it quickly became a matter of class. Panelled coaches, which had well-padded seats, allowed first-class passengers to relax in comfort. Second-class coaches were simpler in style but usually had seats, while passengers in third-class open wagons were showered with soot spewed out by the engine.

The first railway station opened at Liverpool Road, Manchester, in 1830, complete with a waiting room and separate booking halls for the first and

ON THE RIGHT TRACK

• Sleeping cars were introduced in the USA in 1836. Passengers had to supply their own bedding.
• The American George Pullman leased his first carriage in 1859. The drawing-room-cum-sleeping Pullman cars were the inspiration behind the luxurious Orient Express, established in 1883 by the Belgian entrepreneur Georges Nagelmackers.
• The American Union Pacific and Central Pacific Railroads completed the first transcontinental railway, running from coast to coast, in 1869.
• One of the earliest films set around trains or a station was *The General*, a 1926 silent comedy based on an incident in the American Civil War. Buster Keaton played a Confederate train driver chasing his train after it had been stolen by Union soldiers.

GOING UNDERGROUND
Tunnels and underground railways

Building the railways generated a huge amount of tunnelling. In 1830, passengers journeying between Canterbury and Whitstable had the first experience of tunnel travel as their train passed under Tyler Hill. The Metropolitan Railway, a 6km (3¾ mile) London line which linked the Paddington and Farringdon mainline stations, was the first railway to operate entirely underground. Its locomotives were fitted with special equipment to divert the exhaust steam they generated back into their water tanks.

On January 9, 1863, its debut day, 700 invited guests travelled the length of the line without mishap. The journey took 33 minutes. Thousands of people massed the next day for the public opening, when two employees, who were forced to spend more time underground than the passengers, were overcome by fumes. Electrification finally came to the rescue after 1890, the year that the City & South London Railway opened for business.

Britain's first 'moving staircase' or escalator, an American innovation that dated from 1899, was installed at Earl's Court underground station in 1911. To quell passengers' fears, a man with a wooden leg, 'Bumper' Harris, was engaged to ride up and down and show how easy it was to get on and off.

BELOW THE STREETS *London's Metropolitan Railway had seven stations including Baker Street (below). It was an insult, one newspaper said, 'to suppose that people…would prefer…to be driven amid palpable darkness'.*

OAR AND SAIL
On river and sea

As the Egyptians built the pyramids they used large barges, drifting with the Nile current, to transport heavy blocks of stone for journeys of more than 800 km (500 miles). Woven papyrus and reeds were their favoured boat-building materials. However, they also made ships from wood, binding the planks together with leather or papyrus thongs passed through holes made in their edges. A 43 m (142 ft) ceremonial river boat which was found buried near the Great Pyramid of Giza is the earliest known example of a ship made from planks of wood. It was built of cedar and sycamore in about 2600 BC.

Oars were used for propulsion in Egypt by 3000 BC, although sails may have been auxiliary sources of power. For steering, the Egyptians used oars at the stern. Rudders appear to have been invented in China, where they were certainly known by the 1st or 2nd century AD, although they did not appear in Europe for another 1000 years.

In the relatively calm waters of the Mediterranean, the oar was the ruler of the sea for centuries. However, it could

not provide sufficient power for exploring other continents. That was achieved in the slow but seaworthy caravels, 15th and 16th-century sailing ships which weighed around 100 tonnes.

The caravel had square sails, three masts and a simple deck below which a mid deck ran like a shelf around the inside of the hull. When he embarked on his journey westward in 1492, the Genoese explorer Christopher Columbus had two caravels. But his flagship *Santa Maria* was a *nao*, a cargo vessel which measured a mere 24 m (80 ft). Some 27 years later, the Portuguese explorer Ferdinand Magellan's *Vittoria*, the first ship to sail around the world, was no larger.

The sailing ship reached its peak between the 17th and 19th centuries in the form of the bluff East Indiaman, used for trade between southern Asia and Europe, and the elegant sailing clipper, which was built for speed and could be driven hard. At night clipper sailors did not reduce sail and 'snug down', but pressed on in the race to be first home with the new season's crop of tea from China. Port to port they made an average speed of about 6 knots.

Racing became a competitive sport in the early 17th century, when an annual event was set up in Amsterdam. The competitors in Britain's first race, held in 1661, were Charles II and his brother James, who raced their yachts *Katherine* and *Anne* between Greenwich and Gravesend.

RULING THE WAVES *The Portuguese and the Dutch built the first of the heavy three-masted East Indiamen in the 16th century. But English vessels, such as the one above, were dominating the trade routes by the 1720s.*

ALONG THE NILE
Discovered in a tomb dating from 1900 BC, this model of an Egyptian river craft has both oars and a mast. The first sails may have been made from palm leaves or mats of woven reed stretched between poles. However, drawings show that the Egyptians hoisted sails woven from cloth from around 2000 BC.

SHIPPING NEWS

• In 1624 James I watched the first demonstration of a submarine. Built in London by the Dutch physicist Cornelius Drebbel, the craft had a wooden framework covered with greased leather. It was powered by 12 oarsmen whose oars extended through sealed ports.

• Of the many barges used in Britain, the best known is the narrow boat, developed in the 1760s by the land agent John Gilbert and the canal builder James Brindley. This versatile craft was made to fit Brindley's canal lock and measured 22 m x 2.1 m (72 ft x 6 ft 10 in).

• The first boat to be powered by a diesel engine was a French canal boat, the *Petit Pierre*, in 1902.

CRUISING THE OCEAN *'Getting there is half the fun'* *boasted an advertising slogan of the shipping line Cunard, which offered luxury cruises from the 1920s. By this time the journey between Britain and the United States had been reduced from the two weeks taken by the Great Western to just five days.*

DRIVEN BY STEAM *Launched in 1802 the wooden tug* Charlotte Dundas *was the first motorised vessel to achieve commercial success. It pulled barges and ships along the Forth and Clyde canal.*

POWERING THROUGH
Motorised boats

Steamboats driven by paddle wheels were the first motorised craft. They included an experimental model built in France in 1783 and an American ship used to ferry passengers along the Delaware river in 1790. For long sea crossings bigger ships, which could carry sufficient coal, were needed.

The *Great Western*, an ocean liner built by the British engineer Isambard Kingdom Brunel, was the first steamship to cross the Atlantic regularly, and took just over 15 days to complete its maiden voyage in 1838. It was 72 m (236 ft) long and the 23 m (75 ft) saloon was far grander than that of any previous vessel. The 240 passengers were divided almost equally between first class and steerage.

In 1835 a Kent farmer, Francis Pettit Smith, invented the screw propeller, first used by the 237 tonne *Archimede*, built in 1839. Brunel's iron-hulled *Great Britain*, launched in 1845, was the first screw-propelled transatlantic passenger ship. At 3270 tonnes and 98 m (322 ft) in length, the ship was huge by the standards of the day but was later dwarfed by Brunel's 1858 liner the *Great Eastern*, which was nearly 213 m (700 ft) long and weighed 18 914 tonnes.

The steam turbine, in which highly pressurised steam is directed against or through vanes on a rotor, was designed by the engineer Charles Parsons. It made its debut at the 1897 Spithead naval review, fitted to his tiny launch, aptly named *Turbinia*. Capable of 34½ knots, the *Turbinia* caused astonishment when it outpaced some of the Royal Navy's finest steamships.

In 1901 the first big ship, the Clyde passenger steamer *King Edward*, was fitted with a turbine. Three years later the first ocean liner, the *Victoria*, was built, closely followed by the Cunard ships *Carmania*, in 1905, and the *Lusitania* and *Mauretania*, both in 1907. The *Mauretania* set the standard of ocean-liner luxury for a generation, with accommodation for 2145 passengers and interior fittings of mahogany, maple and oak, and crystal chandeliers. 'If ever there was a ship which possessed the thing called soul, the *Mauretania* did,' mourned the American president Franklin D. Roosevelt when the ship was scrapped in 1936.

The principle of using underwater 'wings' to lift the hull of a boat clear of the surface as the craft moves through the water, reducing drag and improving speed and fuel efficiency, was established by the British engineer Thomas Moy in 1861. The first commercial hydrofoil, built in the late 1930s, was used for trips along the Rhine. The hovercraft was held above the water on a cushion of air, a principle patented by the British engineer Christopher Cockerell in 1955. It was first used for cross-Channel journeys in 1968.

SAFETY AT SEA
Lighthouses and lifeboats

A flaming beacon at the top of the world's first lighthouse could be seen from a distance of 48 km (30 miles). One of the seven wonders of the ancient world, the 107 m (351 ft) tall tower was constructed around 270 BC on Pharos, a small island off the port of Alexandria in Egypt. A lighthouse at Dungeness on England's south coast was the first to have an electric lamp, installed in 1862.

The overburdening of cargo ships in the 19th century led to huge loss of life, prompting the radical politician Samuel Plimsoll to press for reforms. In 1876 a law was passed requiring the painting of a circle bisected by a horizontal line at the safe loading level—the mark still known as the Plimsoll line. The idea was not original: medieval Venetian traders had drawn similar marks on their cargo vessels.

A series of wrecks, culminating in the loss of the *Titanic* in the North Atlantic in 1912 with the death of more than 1500 passengers, resulted in legislation making it compulsory that lifeboats be provided for all. The first purpose-built shore-based lifeboat was the *Original*, built in 1790 by Henry Greathead, a Newcastle shipwright.

SAVED FROM DROWNING *Henry Freeman was the only survivor from the Whitby lifeboat which capsized in 1861. He owed his life to his cork life jacket, devised by a Captain John Ross Ward in 1854.*

FIRST FLIGHT

'…the motion was wonderfully smooth—smoother yet—and then! Suddenly there had come into it a new, indescribable quality—a lift—a lightness—a life!'

GERTRUDE BACON, THE FIRST BRITISH WOMAN TO FLY AS A PASSENGER, AUGUST 1909

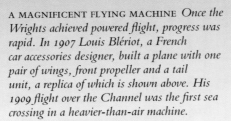

Men first took to the skies lashed to kites. The date was around 1000 BC and the place China, but whoever thought of attaching a person to this primitive 'flying machine' remains a mystery. However, records show that condemned men were used as test pilots for man-bearing kites by the Chinese emperor Wen Hsuan Ti in AD 559. In one of his vivid descriptions of Chinese life in the 13th century, the explorer Marco Polo wrote: 'They find someone stupid or drunk for no wise man, or undepraved would expose himself to that danger.'

Icarus, in Greek legend, personified classical fantasies of flying. He soared into the sky, but flew too close to the Sun and plummeted into the sea after the wax used to make his wings melted. Early attempts at gliding

A MAGNIFICENT FLYING MACHINE *Once the Wrights achieved powered flight, progress was rapid. In 1907 Louis Blériot, a French car accessories designer, built a plane with one pair of wings, front propeller and a tail unit, a replica of which is shown above. His 1909 flight over the Channel was the first sea crossing in a heavier-than-air machine.*

turned dreams to reality, but injuries and fatalities were frequent. Eilmer, the 11th-century 'Flying Monk' who broke his legs after fitting himself with wings and jumping from Malmesbury Abbey, was luckier than most.

The Italian Renaissance artist Leonardo da Vinci sketched many imaginary flying machines, including a clockwork helicopter and machines designed to imitate the flapping of a bird's wings. Far ahead of their time, they did not progress beyond the drawing board.

UP, UP AND AWAY

A breakthrough came in 1783 when two paper-makers, the brothers Etienne and Joseph Montgolfier, demonstrated the first hot-air balloon, made of cloth and lined with paper. A burner, fuelled by straw and wool, heated the air, which rose as it warmed, filling the balloon and lifting it upwards. It flew about 2.5 km (1½ miles) before crashing and bursting into flames.

A few months later, after a second experiment in which a sheep, a rooster and a duck survived a short flight and a bumpy landing, a young physician, François Pilâtre de Rozier, and a nobleman, the Marquis d'Arlandes, became the first men to make a

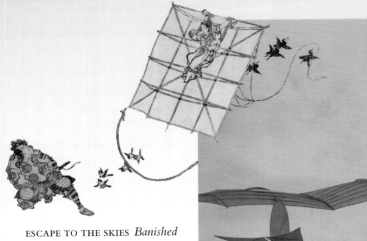

ESCAPE TO THE SKIES *Banished to an island off Japan, the 12th-century samurai Minamoto no Tametamo is said to have tied his son to a kite (above) and flown him to the mainland. By the 19th century the pioneers of flight had taken to gliders, with often fatal results; Otto Lilienthal (right) was killed when his glider crashed in 1896.*

Gleanings in Bee Culture, whose editor Amos Root had been present.

By the outbreak of the First World War, the flying machine was firmly established. The hostilities led to the construction of purpose-built fighters and bombers, and in 1919 the English pilots Captain John Alcock and Lieutenant Arthur Whitten Brown used a Vickers Vimy bomber for the first nonstop flight across the Atlantic. The journey, from Newfoundland to Ireland, took 16½ hours.

Propeller-driven aircraft reached their limits of speed in the Second World War. The gas turbine, a type of

SPEEDING AHEAD *The first jet aircraft, the Heinkel He 178, was demonstrated in 1939. Its designer, Hans von Ohain, realised that exhaust gases from a gas turbine could be fed through a nozzle forming a jet that would drive an aircraft far faster than propellers.*

THE HELICOPTER STORY

The French bicycle maker Paul Cornu built the first helicopter to achieve free flight, but 20 seconds was the longest it stayed in the air. The first entirely successful helicopter was the German Focke-Wulf Fw61, which made its maiden flight in 1936. Fitted with two rotors, it established many records, including an endurance record of more than 80 minutes and a speed record of 122 km/h (76 mph).

Igor Sikorsky, a Russian-born engineer working in the USA, designed his XR-4 in 1942. This helicopter had a single main rotor, and a tail rotor to prevent the body whirling around uncontrollably.

balloon ascent. In 1783 they took off from the grounds of the Château de la Muette in the Bois de Boulogne west of Paris. They remained aloft for 25 minutes and landed safely, having travelled about 8 km (5 miles). Finally human beings could fly.

Much was achieved in balloons, including the first aerial crossing of the English Channel in January 1785 by the French balloonist Jean-Pierre Blanchard and the American Dr John Jeffries, and a parachute descent in 1797 by the French aeronaut André Jacques Garnerin. Balloons were also used for reconnaissance flights by the French Republican Army in 1794.

Powered airships were pioneered by Frenchman Henri Giffard in 1852, but the future lay in the technology of heavier-than-air machines. From basic principles described by the British engineer Sir George Cayley in an 1809 paper *On Aerial Navigation*, the German engineer Otto Lilienthal produced a series of hang-gliders of increasing sophistication in the 1890s.

POWERING ON

Inspired by the glider pioneers and the recent introduction of the internal-combustion engine, two American bicycle manufacturers, the brothers Wilbur and Orville Wright, experimented with powered flight. With each design breakthrough, the Wrights checked their advances against their knowledge of bird flight. They made four flights in 1903 on their first aircraft, the biplane *Flyer*, at Kitty Hawk in North Carolina. The longest lasted just under a minute and covered 259.6 m (852 ft).

The following year the brothers not only built an improved version of the plane, *Flyer II*, but also proved that they were truly in control of the machine by completing a circular route. Yet the sole report of this feat appeared in a beekeepers' magazine,

internal-combustion engine which was developed independently by Frank Whittle in Britain and Hans von Ohain in Germany, offered a new source of power. Although Whittle was the first to patent the gas turbine, in 1930, it was von Ohain who was given the necessary support to develop the jet, from the German aircraft designer Ernst Heinkel.

By the end of the war both Britain and Germany had jet fighters in service; the Royal Air Force's Gloster Meteor 1 and the Luftwaffe's Messerschmitt 262 first flew in 1944. Supersonic flight, where an aircraft travels faster than the speed of sound (about 330 m/1100 ft a second), was achieved by the American Air Force's rocket-propelled Bell X-1 in 1947.

THE SKY'S THE LIMIT
Passenger aircraft

Conflict in the air made possible the airline business that thrived in peaceful skies. During the First World War the combatants produced almost 200000 aircraft. After the 1918 armistice, planes could be bought cheaply and military pilots found employment providing air displays or offering demonstration rides to thrill seekers: in June and July 1919 alone, some 10000 'joy-riders' flew over Blackpool. Others decided that the future lay with commercial travel.

Germany's Deutsche Luft-Reederei established the world's first passenger airline in February 1919. The following month the French started a route from Paris to Brussels. In the same year the first daily international service was set up by a British company, Air Transport and Travel, linking London and Paris from Mondays to Saturdays. On its inaugural flight the plane carried consignments of newspapers and leather, several brace of grouse, some cream and a single passenger, George Stevenson-Reece of the London *Evening Standard*.

By the end of 1919, little more than a decade after powered flight had become a reality, Britain had five infant airlines, Germany had seven and France eight. Passenger services did not begin in the USA until 1926, but by 1929 more people were travelling by plane across that country than any other.

Converted bombers were used as passenger aircraft, but purpose-built airliners were soon made, starting with the British de Havilland DH16 in 1919. The 1926 American Ford Trimotor and 1930 German Junkers 52 were made entirely of metal, a novelty at the time.

Most notable of the interwar designs was the American Douglas DC-3, put into service in 1936. The aeroplane had seats for 21 passengers, retractable landing gear, two powerful engines, a maximum speed of 320km/h (200mph) and an immensely tough structure. By the end of 1947, more than 13 000 had been built, most for military purposes.

The first pure jet airliner was the de Havilland Comet, introduced by the British Overseas Airways Corporation (BOAC) in 1952. It provided smooth flights at 805km/h (500mph) for 36

EXPRESS DELIVERY *William Boeing (below, left), the founder of the Boeing Airplane Company, and the pilot Eddie Hubbard were among the pioneers of international airmail services in 1919.*

LUFTHANSA PASSENGER TICKET, 1926

WRAPPING UP *Early travellers with Deutsche Luft-Reederei travelled in open cockpits (top); they were given flying suits, helmets and goggles to wear on the daily service between Berlin and Weimar. The company's emblem was a crane rising in flight, the logo still used by Lufthansa.*

passengers but it was withdrawn after metal fatigue led to the loss of two aircraft over the Mediterranean.

The Boeing 707 set the standard for long-haul airliners after 1958. It had 179 seats and a cruising speed of about 910km/h (565mph). Greater capacity was possible with 'jumbo jets', such as the 1970 Boeing 747. Seating around 500, it ushered in an era of mass plane travel.

ALL THE COMFORTS *Passengers on a 1930 Air National flight are offered sandwiches and tea, coffee or milk to sip from paper cups. American Airlines provided greater luxury after 1933 with the first full sleeping berths, advertised above.*

COME FLY WITH ME
In-flight service

Flights on the first airliners were bumpy, cold and noisy—but offered no end of adventure. Passengers were advised to wear gloves and heavy coats and to put cotton wool in their ears. Bad weather and mechanical failure made forced landings commonplace.

Nevertheless, attempts were made to maintain standards of service and comfort. In-flight meals, in the form of prepacked lunch boxes, were available

on cross-Channel flights almost from their inception, while hot meals, accompanied by champagne, wine and coffee, were introduced in 1925 by the French Air Union. From 1927 Imperial Airways' luxury 'Silver Wing' flights to Paris also offered hot food, which was served by male stewards from a galley at the rear. No food was served on the cheaper, second-class flights.

The company had already thought of offering entertainment to help its passengers to pass the time during long journeys. Then, in 1925, it pioneered

the in-flight film with a dramatisation of Arthur Conan Doyle's classic adventure story *The Lost World*.

In 1930 women flight attendants were employed for the first time after Ellen Church, a registered nurse and private pilot, wrote to the American company United Airlines offering her services. She was taken on and then instructed to recruit seven other registered nurses as her colleagues. Swissair followed suit by hiring Europe's first stewardess, Nelly Diener, in 1931, but in Britain jobs in the air remained

AT YOUR SERVICE *Ellen Church (below, third from left) and her team of stewardesses wait to begin their duties in 1930. These included carrying luggage on board, checking that seats were screwed down properly, helping with refuelling and pushing planes into hangars at the end of the flight.*

BETWEEN CONTINENTS

The seaplane enjoyed a brief heyday for intercontinental flights. Frequent refuelling stops and the lack of airfields in Latin America, Europe and Asia gave the advantage to an aircraft that could land on a lake or harbour.

In 1937 Pan American used the Sikorsky S-42 Clipper (above) for transatlantic trial flights, launching a regular service in 1939 with the 70-seater Boeing 314 Clippers. Its New York-Lisbon flight took 29 hours. From 1938 Imperial Airways flew the Short S-23 C class Empires from Southampton to the Far East.

strictly 'for the boys'. In May 1936 Daphne Kearley was employed on a cross-Channel service in order to type letters for travelling businessmen. She was an exception, however, and it was only in 1943 that BOAC introduced women flight attendants.

HAPPY LANDINGS
Airports and their safety systems

The early pilots flew by observation, following rivers, railway lines and other landmarks, and their light aircraft could land on no more than a level field. A First World War training aerodrome at Hounslow Heath, London, became Britain's first 'customs' airport in the summer of 1919. By then airworthiness certification, licensing of pilots, rules of

THE PEOPLE'S PLANE *Reliable and cheap to build, the Douglas DC-3 (above) was introduced in 1936 and used by airlines all over the world. Instrumental in popularising flying, the plane became affectionately known as the Dakota.*

PAPERWORK *Although tickets and tags were produced by the earliest airlines, it was the travel company Thomas Cook who, quick to realise the appeal of flying, issued the first air travel brochure in 1919.*

BAGGAGE LABEL, 1920S

AIR TRAVEL BROCHURE, 1919

UNDER COVER
Hounslow Heath airport offered passengers only a shed-like waiting room; in 1946 this tented area at nearby Heathrow provided travellers with armchairs, a bookstall and facilities for sending overseas cables.

the air, signals, and arrival and departure procedures had been established for only a few months.

In the 1930s instruments based on gyroscopes were developed to help pilots to fly level, even in fog or cloud. At the same time, the primitive method of using beacons as a guide to American mail pilots coming in to land was replaced by radio ranging. This system, based on narrow radio beams emitted by the beacons along which the pilots could fly to their destinations, made all-weather flying possible.

FINDING THE WAY

'So geographers, in Afric-maps,
With savage-pictures fill their gaps;
And o'er unhabitable downs
Place elephants for want of towns.'

On Poetry, ANGLO–IRISH SATIRIST JONATHAN SWIFT, 1733

Using sticks or stones, nomadic tribesmen sketched out in the sand or traced on rock journeys completed, indicating tracks taken and the whereabouts of freshwater sources and neighbouring tribes. No definitive evidence of these maps exists but the achievements of early peoples in finding their way across vast landscapes would surely have been impossible without them.

The world's oldest surviving map was drawn on a small clay tablet in 2300 BC, and discovered at Yorgan Tepe in modern-day Iraq. It shows an area bounded by hills and divided by a waterway, and names the owner of an area of land. Marked on its edges are the four cardinal points, north, south, east and west.

From the same area is the first known attempt to map the world, in around 600 BC. At the map's centre is Babylon, straddling the River Euphrates, and a ring of ocean forms an outer boundary. More practical is a map surviving from ancient Egypt, a papyrus of 1150 BC showing the layout of gold mines near the Red Sea coast and routes for getting there.

FROM HEAVEN TO EARTH

By 600 BC Phoenician explorers were using the positions of the brightest stars to guide them on their journeys. The ancient Greeks produced maps of the constellations, and Homer, the Greek poet of the 8th century BC, relates that the legendary hero Odysseus was told by the nymph Calypso to keep the constellation of Great Bear, or Ursa Major, on his left as he voyaged home

PTOLEMY'S WORLD *Relying on the positions of 8000 known places, Ptolemy plotted the shape of the world in AD 150. Because he underestimated the circumference of the Earth, the parts of the world he knew, roughly from the west coast of Europe to India, occupied a disproportionately large part of the globe. This 15th-century copy is bound in an atlas, so called after the representation of the Greek giant Atlas holding the heavens aloft, then common in books of maps.*

ASTRONOMER WITH GLOBE
AND DIVIDERS, GERMANY, 1568

to Ithaca through the Ionian Sea. Using their knowledge, observations and imagination, the Greeks also speculated about the nature of the Earth. By the middle of the 4th century BC they knew the Earth was round, and had devised the lines of latitude forming parallel horizontal bands north and south of the Equator.

Lines of longitude, the meridians that run vertically from pole to pole, were added piecemeal until in AD 100 the geographer Marinus of Tyre developed a grid with regularly spaced intervals in which locations could be described mathematically by means of the grid's coordinates.

Building on Marinus's work, the astronomer and geographer Ptolemy of Alexandria produced the first great map of the world in about 150. Ptolemy greatly influenced the development of geography, and more than 1000 years later European navigators were only just beginning to correct his calculations. The beautifully drawn *mappae mundi*,

from the Latin for 'maps of the world', produced in Europe in the Middle Ages when the Church had a near monopoly on learning, often placed the holy city of Jerusalem at the centre of the world. Unknown lands were added around the periphery.

Sailors needed something more practical, and in the 13th century developed the portolan, a form of navigational chart which recorded the distances and bearings between landmarks, sea depths and tidal variations. When the Genoese navigator Christopher Columbus

CHARTING A COURSE *Drawn on hide, this earliest surviving portolan or navigational chart was probably used by 13th-century sailors journeying through the Mediterranean. The accuracy of portolans was helped by the compass, introduced from China, where it may have been used since the 1st century AD.*

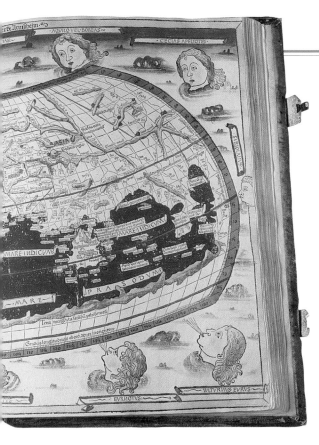

set off on his first great voyage across the Atlantic he was convinced he would reach Asian 'islands and mainlands in the Ocean'. Instead, in 1492, he landed in the Bahamas and revealed the existence of the Americas to Europeans.

Thanks to his explorations and those of other navigators, maps became increasingly accurate in the 16th century. The foremost map-maker of the era was the Flemish Gerardus Mercator, who devised a method of displaying the curved surface of the

COMPASS, ITALY, 1580

Earth on a flat map. This enabled navigators to plot bearings as straight lines.

The introduction of the telescope in the early 1600s made it possible for astronomers to chart the positions of stars and other celestial bodies with considerable accuracy. This stimulated interest in the heavens, and led to the establishment of the first modern observatories.

The Royal Observatory at Greenwich, built in 1675 by Charles II, was instructed to record the positions of all stars. Sailors then calculated their longitude by observing the motion of the Moon against the fixed background of stars. But the method was not sufficiently accurate.

Latitude had long been estimated by observing the height or elevation of the stars above the horizon. The problem of estimating longitude while on the move was solved in 1761 by the English clockmaker John Harrison. He devised an accurate chronometer which would keep precise time at sea. By working out local time from the elevation of the Sun, and comparing it with the chronometer reading, which was set to Greenwich time, sailors could calculate how far east or west they were of the observatory.

The Sun's elevation could be measured with the reflecting quadrant, invented by the English astronomer John Hadley in 1730, and with the

BREAKING A TREND *In the 1930s the simple-to-follow London Underground map dispensed with scale and used only vertical, horizontal or 45-degree diagonal lines. Its creator was an engineering draughtsman named Harry Beck. He was paid just 5 guineas for his graphic masterpiece, which has been used as a model for underground railway maps all over the world.*

sextant, introduced by Captain John Campbell, after 1757. The Greenwich Meridian was accepted internationally as the prime meridian, zero degrees of longitude, in 1884.

DETAIL AND ACCURACY

Ancient map-makers used depictions of hills, valleys and rivers to hint at topography, the shape of the land. The first contour lines, linking points of the same elevation, were used in 1584, by the Dutch surveyor Pieter Bruinsz to indicate the depths of the Het Spaarme river. It was not until 1791 that land contours were used, on a map of France by the cartographer Jean Louis Dupain-Triel.

The 18th century also saw the first truly accurate maps created using triangulation, in which distances are calculated by measuring angles to a distant point from each end of a baseline. The French cartographer César François Cassini de Thury produced the first, mapping France between 1744 and 1783 at a scale of about 2.5 cm to 1.2 km (1 in to ¾ mile).

In 1791, the Duke of Richmond established the Ordnance Survey to produce a set of maps covering Britain for the military; the first was a map of Kent, at a ratio of 2.5 cm to 1.6 km (1 in to 1 mile). The cartographer John Carey published a 'road atlas' showing distances between towns in 1809.

PROTOTYPE FOR THE LONDON UNDERGROUND MAP (RIGHT) AND HARRY BECK'S ORIGINAL SKETCH, BOTH 1933

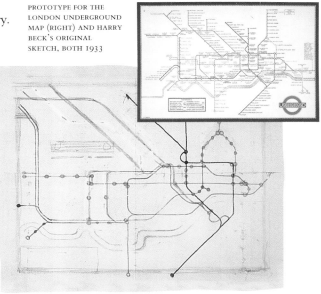

LIVING TOGETHER

Creatures can survive together in groups only by obeying sets of rules. But the human attributes of consciousness, language and logic have made possible societies far more sophisticated than the ant hill or the lion pride. As hunter-gatherers, in an era that began about 1.5 million years ago, our ancestors lived in loose family groups. About 400 000 years ago they began to settle down, if only for a season. By the 4th millennium BC some stable groups were established in Sumeria, in the fertile plains between the Tigris and Euphrates rivers. Here, with the advent of irrigation, year-round farming and organised labour replaced subsistence living.

Other rivers had a similar influence on the development of civilisations. Settlements sprang up along the Nile in Egypt during the 5th millennium BC, while the Yellow River in China and the Indus in Asia became sites of civilisations from the 4th and 2nd millennia BC. In the same period the society of the Mayas' forebears began to evolve in Central America.

As they grew and expanded, early civilisations developed their own social, religious and political systems to bind diverse peoples into coherent and governable societies. Myths telling how the gods had determined the destinies of their earthly subjects also had a crucial influence on the politics of early city-states. In times of crisis, assemblies were convened to elect military chiefs to counter external aggression from neighbouring communities. Eventually such leaders were retained in peacetime and, like Sargon who ruled Sumeria in about 2350 BC, became kings.

Many early warrior leaders were elected, but most civilisations eventually developed hereditary systems of monarchy. The outcomes of battles were often seen as divine judgments, and rulers taking power after military conquest could claim the right to govern and their subjects' obedience. To endorse their authority, many rulers claimed direct descent from the gods. Egyptian pharaohs were regarded as incarnations of the sky-god Horus and the sun-gods Ra, Amon-Ra and Aton.

Christian kings and queens also became seen as agents of God. Pépin le bref ('the Short'), crowned King of the Franks in 751, was the first sovereign to have his authority reinforced by divine power at a Christian coronation. In Britain a coronation service was devised by St Dunstan, Archbishop of Canterbury, in 973 for King Edgar's investiture at Bath Abbey. Its elements—recognition of the right to rule; an oath of allegiance; investiture; anointment with holy oil; homage from his subjects—formed the basis of future coronations.

In early communities priests dispensed judgments while the king tended the temporal needs of his people, including raising and equipping an army and building defences—endeavours financed by taxes. Many means of doing business, including money and trade, existed in ancient times. For most, work was poorly rewarded, if at all. By the 15th century most peasants were allowed to consume what they produced in return for services and dues paid to their lords. Craftsmen, and markets where they sold their wares, flourished in towns and cities from the 16th century, but our modern ways of living stem largely from the Industrial Revolution. By 1914 most people worked in factories and offices rather than in the fields or small workshops.

THE FIRST TOWNS
Society takes root

Humankind was slow to settle down. Although recognisably modern humans had evolved by 100000 years ago, it is only in the past 10000 years that they have rooted themselves in villages, towns and cities. Jericho, in the Jordan Valley, has been occupied almost continuously since 8000 BC, making it the oldest town in the world. Its foundation, in a spot near fertile land and with

WALLED CITY *Massive fortifications some 4m (13 ft) thick protected Jericho as early as 7000 BC. This similarly impressive wall surrounded the town in the late Middle Ages.*

a freshwater spring, coincides with the shift from nomadic hunting and gathering to a settled form of life centred on agriculture. One thousand years after people built the first houses there, Jericho had 2000 inhabitants.

Communities have practical reasons for their locations, the most important being water supply. Many settlements sprang up alongside rivers, which also provided the easiest form of transport before roads were built. River crossing points were particularly favoured: in about AD 43 the Romans established Londinium at the most convenient bridging point of the Thames.

Other sites include natural harbours, such as at New York, founded in the 1620s by Dutch settlers as New Amsterdam, and easily defended high ground. Jerusalem, for instance, grew around a citadel built in about 24 BC, just as Edinburgh did around its castle in the 11th century. Islands are also easily defended, explaining the location of Paris, which the Romans founded on the Ile de la Cité in the River Seine, and Venice, built from the 6th century on the islands of a lagoon in the Adriatic. The proximity of established trade routes, or of natural resources such as coal or minerals, have also been key factors in the evolution of settlements.

If agriculture provided the first great revolution in human affairs, the growth of towns prompted the second. The word civilisation comes from *civis*, Latin for 'citizen', and the rise of the first great civilisations certainly coincided with the building of cities. Uruk in Mesopotamia (modern-day Iraq) may have been the first and by 3000 BC had reached a population of 50000.

Cities of this size were prosperous enough to afford great buildings such as palaces and temples, and to support a priestly class liberated from the daily struggle for survival. Soon cities were springing up independently in many parts of the world, creating distinct patterns of language, culture and architecture. Hunter-gatherers, it is tempting to suppose, were all much the same; but city dwellers quickly developed the diversity typical of human societies.

CITY PLANNING
Order out of chaos

Demands of defence or religion often influenced the shapes of cities. In some places, such as the early Mesopotamian city of Uruk, streets radiated outwards from religious buildings, with the well-to-do living in large houses on the main thoroughfares. The homes of the working people were tucked in between or behind them, and were accessible only through narrow alleys. The grid pattern that dominates almost all cities in the USA is equally ancient, first appearing in the Indus Valley. The earliest known example, Rahman Dehri in Pakistan, dates from about 3500 BC. The main thoroughfare in these early grid cities often aligns with the course of the Sun in the sky, suggesting that initially the guiding force behind the grid pattern may have been religious.

The grid was later adopted for military purposes, as the layout allowed the rapid movement of soldiers to vulnerable points of the rampart. Alexander the Great, the Macedonian king who in the 4th century BC conquered an empire that covered much of Asia, imposed a grid on many of the numerous cities he founded, including Alexandria in Egypt. In the USA, the grid pattern was adopted for management purposes. It made the vast expanse of 'new' land easily divisible into standardised plots for surveying and sale.

Other cities enlarged around small settlements, with the roads and tracks that predated them creating a series of major thoroughfares linked by smaller ones. London and many other European cities fit this pattern, growing as individual villages were swallowed up by urban sprawl.

While some cities have grown organically, others have been planned from scratch. In about 400 BC the Greeks constructed a city in the Peloponnese designed to collect together

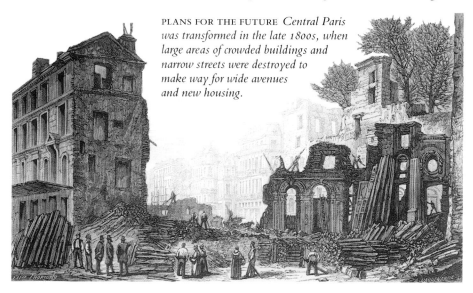

PLANS FOR THE FUTURE *Central Paris was transformed in the late 1800s, when large areas of crowded buildings and narrow streets were destroyed to make way for wide avenues and new housing.*

THE PAST UNDER ASPHALT *Even a pattern as formal as New York's, laid out on a grid from 1811, contains historical remnants of ancient thoroughfares. Broadway, one of the main avenues on Manhattan Island, follows the course of an old Native American track.*

the populations of previously isolated villages and hamlets. They called it Megalopolis, or 'Great City', a term more recently used to describe the closely grouped cities of the American eastern seaboard: Boston, New York, Philadelphia, Baltimore and Washington DC. Together, they comprise some 800km (500 miles) of almost continuous urbanisation.

As cities grew, their rulers became preoccupied with civic management. The emperor Nero enforced one of the earliest examples of municipal restrictions when he forbade buildings in Rome to be more than 21m (70ft) high. His pronouncement, which followed the devastating fire of AD 64, aimed to prevent the construction of ramshackle tenements.

By this time Rome and other big cities were full of apartment buildings, often built above shops in city centres. The ruins of Herculaneum, buried by the eruption of Vesuvius in AD 79,

---

A PLACE TO LIVE

• The earliest identifiable village street in England runs between the well-preserved ruins of eight 2000-year-old houses at Chysauster in Cornwall.

• Houses were first numbered in Paris in 1463. In Britain numbering did not appear until 1708, on a street in London's Whitechapel area.

• Britain's first municipal park was Preston's Moor Park, which was enclosed from common land by the corporation in 1834.

---

include apartment buildings of at least four storeys. The collapse of populations after the fall of Rome in the 5th century AD reduced the pressure on housing. But by the 13th century, five-storey apartment buildings were being built in the eastern Mediterranean port of Acre by the Crusaders, who had won control of the area.

Before the rise of industry, city centres were occupied by members of the mercantile, political and religious

elites, surrounded by craftsmen such as metalworkers, weavers and potters. The poor lived on the periphery, often outside the city walls. But in the 1800s, when factories built in town centres started to create pollution and squalor, the wealthy tended to move out, often to higher ground, leaving the central areas to factory workers. In London, where the prevailing winds blow north-eastwards, the wealthy tended to move west. The middle classes found a new environment on the edges of the city—the suburbs.

NEW TOWN *Bournville, a town built in the late 1800s by the Cadbury brothers to house their Birmingham chocolate-factory workers, greatly influenced suburban development.*

HOUSING THE PEOPLE
Modern building initiatives

The Industrial Revolution changed the face of Britain, creating an exodus from rural areas to the new factories as well as severe overcrowding in towns and cities. By the mid 19th century insanitary slums were a feature of most large towns. To improve the conditions of the poor, charities and municipalities began to build better housing. The first municipal housing in Britain was provided by the City of Liverpool, which completed six blocks of flats, misleadingly called St Martin's Cottages, in Silvester Street in 1869.

At about the same time, industrialists led the way in creating entirely new communities, building model villages for workers at their factories. In 1898 the town planner Ebenezer Howard proposed the establishment of a series of small cities in previously rural land. The first such garden city, Letchworth in Hertfordshire, was approved in 1903.

DEMOCRATIC RULE
Government by the people

The word 'democracy', defined today as government by all the people, comes from the Greek *demos*, 'common people', and *kratia*, 'power'. During the 6th century BC all Athenian citizens were expected to vote and participate in government. But franchise was far from universal. Excluded from citizenship, and voting, were women, minors, slaves and those who did not have Athenian parentage;

CASTING VOTE *Early Greek voters used stones or shells to register their choice; by the 4th century BC they were given official ballot tokens.*

together they accounted for some 90 per cent of the population.

The Roman Republic, established in 509 BC, was governed by the Senate, a representative body whose members were elected by a hereditary aristocracy and headed by two consuls who ruled jointly. The plebeians, the vast numbers of people not of high birth, were eventually allowed to be elected as senators and from 367 BC it was compulsory for one of the consuls to be a plebeian.

After Rome adopted imperial rule in 27 BC democratic government was for centuries the exception rather than the rule. It re-emerged in medieval city-states of Italy and Flanders such as Florence, Pisa and Bruges, where men qualifying for citizenship elected a ruling town council.

The United States of America was the first modern democratic republic, but only white, property-owning males were eligible to vote in the inaugural presidential elections of 1788. In Britain the right to vote in early 14th-century parliamentary elections was based on qualifications of property and wealth, and most men, as well as all women, were disenfranchised.

By the 19th century the great changes in society and the growth of large cities had produced some glaring anomalies: in 1830 Cornwall's sparse population returned 44 Members of

A QUESTION OF DIPLOMACY

Rulers have relied on diplomats since the time of ancient Egypt, when representatives of the pharaohs travelled to neighbouring states. Modern diplomacy began in the medieval Italian city-states, where rules governed the appointment and conduct of ambassadors. In 1455 Milan established the first permanent embassy, in Genoa. The concept of diplomatic immunity was first applied in Britain in 1708 following the arrest of a Russian ambassador for a debt of £50.

Parliament, while the City of London, which had a population exceeding 100 000, was represented by four. By the end of the century successive Reform Acts had reorganised the distribution of seats and also increased the size of the male electorate.

The first woman to vote in a British parliamentary election was Lily Maxwell, a shop owner who as a ratepayer had mistakenly been placed on the electoral register. She cast her vote for the Liberal candidate in November 1867, but the following year female suffrage was declared illegal. Supporters of this exclusion argued that women were unsuited to the rowdiness that frequently accompanied the open voting customary at this time.

In 1856 the modern secret ballot was introduced in the colony of Victoria in Australia. Its use in Britain passed into law in 1872, despite opposition from landlords, who feared that they would no longer be able to influence the voting behaviour of their tenants.

The first country to grant suffrage to women was New Zealand in 1893. Despite the increasingly militant activities of Britain's 'suffragettes', a term coined in 1906 in the *Daily Mail*, it was not until 1918 that some women over the age of 30, along with those who

VOTES FOR ALL *The first clear demand for political equality for women was made by the British feminist Mary Wollstonecraft in her 1792* Vindication of the Rights of Women. *But it was the campaigners of the Women's Social and Political Union, founded in 1903, who put women's suffrage on Britain's political agenda.*

held a university degree, were granted the right to vote. The Finnish parliament was the first to elect women members, in 1907. Britain followed suit in 1918, when Constance, Countess Markievicz, was elected as Sinn Féin member for a Dublin ward, although she never took her seat in the Commons. The first woman to sit in the Commons was the American-born viscountess Nancy Astor, who won a by-election for the Conservatives in Plymouth in 1919.

SILVER AND ENAMEL PIN, EARLY 1900S

CUP AND SAUCER MADE FOR 'THE WOMEN'S EXHIBITION', LONDON, 1909

ROSETTE, EARLY 1900S

SMOOTH-TALKING
A late Victorian parliamentary candidate attempts to canvas for votes. The general election of 1874, the first to be conducted by secret ballot, proved to politicians that they needed popular support, not just the approval of the rich and powerful.

IN PARLIAMENT
Governing bodies

The world's earliest parliament was Iceland's *Althing*, which convened from the 10th century. The island's 36 local chieftains would assemble once a year to discuss the business of the island.

Britain's Parliament evolved from the early medieval Curia Regis (King's Court), an advisory body to the monarch consisting of the chief lords, landholders and Church leaders. In 1264 the Earl of Leicester, Simon de Montfort, summoned the 'commons'—knights of the shires and representatives of large towns. These evolved into the House of Lords and the House of Commons.

The word 'parliament', from the Old French *parlement*, meaning 'talk', dates to 1246, but the Model Parliament, the first in which 'commoners' were elected and not merely called on arbitrarily, came into being in 1295. By the 15th century Parliament had acquired the right to make laws.

Parliament based itself in the Palace of Westminster, founded by Edward the Confessor in the 11th century, in 1547. The present Houses of Parliament were designed by Sir Charles Barry and constructed between 1840 and 1867 after a fire destroyed most of the old palace in 1834.

The origins of Britain's oldest political parties, the Tories and the Whigs, can be traced back to 1679 and the demand for Parliament to be convened to exclude Charles II's Roman Catholic brother James (later James II) from the succession. His supporters were nicknamed Tories, probably from the Irish *toraighe*, 'runaway', used as a term of abuse against Irish Catholic royalists; their opponents, who favoured James's exclusion, were called Whigs, after a group of Scottish Presbyterian rebels known as Whiggamores (from *whig*, 'to drive', and *mere*, 'mare').

During the 19th century the Tories developed into the modern Conservative Party, while the Whigs evolved into the Liberal Party. The first party committed to secure parliamentary representation for the working class was Australia's Political Labor League of Victoria, founded in March 1859. Its first MP was elected later that year. Britain's inaugural 'labour' MPs were both miners, who were returned at the 1874 general election. The modern Labour Party, founded in February 1900 as an offshoot of the trade union movement, did not acquire its name until 1906. Only in 1924 did James Ramsay MacDonald form the first Labour government.

RAISING TAXES
Money for the state

When Henry III first summoned his panel of 'commoners', he did so to win their support for the raising of additional revenue to meet such emergencies as a foreign war. An early form of tax in Britain was the poll tax, a set amount payable by all adults and first collected in 1379. Its great unpopularity led to the Peasants' Revolt of 1381, when officials were killed by a mob in London, and the tax was seldom reimposed before being abolished in 1698. It made a brief, and equally unpopular, return as the community charge, levied between 1989 and 1993.

The principle that British monarchs could not raise taxes without the assent of their council was established in the Magna Carta (Great Charter) in 1215, but the need for rulers to raise revenues from the population was ancient, illustrated by the Sumerian proverb 'You can have a Lord, you can have a King, but the man to fear is the tax collector.' As early as 2500 BC Sumerian priests required farmers to hand over a set proportion of all their produce, a system perpetuated in the tithe collected by the medieval Church. The Romans established import duties and a head (poll) tax, as well as taxes on consumption, sales, property and inheritance.

Tax on income was initially levied in Florence in 1451. In Britain, income tax was brought in as a war measure by William Pitt the Younger in 1799.

BURNING ISSUE *The killing of Wat Tyler by the Lord Mayor of London, Sir William Walworth, is shown in this 15th-century illustration. Tyler led the Peasants' Revolt of 1381 against Richard II's poll tax. The tax again provoked a violent response when it was reintroduced some 600 years later (top).*

MAKING A LIVING
From farm to factory

Work began, and remained for millennia, confined to the land. Even in great civilisations such as those of Egypt, Greece and Rome where men were employed by the thousands to create colossal monuments and public buildings, the majority of people worked in agriculture. In Britain, even during the Roman occupation, when workers were used in such major construction projects as road networks, aqueducts, public baths and harbours, farm work remained the most common means of subsistence.

By early medieval times most land in western Europe was owned by hereditary lords. Under the system known as feudalism, a lord parcelled out his land to peasants to farm and provided them with common grazing ground, justice and safety from attack. In return the lord received payment in the form of money, crops or services. People worked close to their homes, and the whole family, including young children, contributed to making a living. Those involved in crafts such as weaving operated at home on a small scale, hence the term 'cottage industry'.

From these modest beginnings craftspeople began to sell their wares. Many freed themselves from their dependence on the land to become the first town dwellers. As their trades expanded, from the 12th century they formed themselves into specialist guilds.

A DAY'S PAY The workers who built Europe's medieval cities were among the few to receive a salary for their labour and skills.

IN CONTROL Until mass production became widespread in the 19th century, craftsmen such as this 14th-century Italian metalworker were masters of their trade.

These regulated working practices and conditions and rates of pay. Among the earliest British examples are the Company of Merchant Taylors and the Company of Goldsmiths, both of which were founded in 1327.

Working systems were refined in the late Middle Ages, with specific tasks such as spinning wool being 'put out' to nonguild workers before the yarn was woven into cloth. The textile industries of the 16th and 17th centuries foreshadowed the transformation in working practices that was to come with the Industrial Revolution. Guilds were bypassed by employers, and larger working units— in essence the first 'factories'—set up.

Work now became more centred on the factory, which was often far from the home. Here new machines could repeat tasks endlessly and people were required just as operators. The English entrepreneur Richard Arkwright established one of the world's first powered factories in 1771, when he concentrated his cotton-spinning machines in a single, water-driven mill at Cromford in Derbyshire.

Advances in technology meant that manufacturing and processing could be broken down into a series of repetitive tasks, each of which was completed or supervised by an individual worker. Credit for the introduction of the assembly line goes to the American Oliver Evans, who in 1784 opened a mechanical grain-milling factory near Philadelphia in Pennsylvania.

Mass production was pioneered by the French-born British engineer Marc Brunel, whose son Isambard Kingdom went on to make major contributions in shipbuilding and in bridge and tunnel construction. Marc Brunel's proposals for a system to make pulley blocks for Royal Navy ships at Portsmouth were approved in 1803. When the machinery was installed three years later, work previously done by 100 workers could be carried out by as few as ten men. But the assembly line was greatly refined by the American Henry Ford, whose 1913 car assembly line slashed production times.

MIDDLEMEN The great markets of the 15th and 16th centuries brought rich pickings for town merchants, who purchased produce such as wool from local farmers and sold it on to brokers from other parts.

CITY GENTS *The day's figures were entered and updated manually by teams of office workers in the 1920s. Their occupation had changed little since the scribes of ancient Egypt first recorded crop yields for taxation.*

SETTING UP OFFICE
Keeping records and doing business

The thousands of scribes spread across ancient Egypt, employed by the royal banks developed by the Ptolemaic kings around 250 BC, were probably the world's first 'office workers'. Their labours were coordinated from the capital, Alexandria. Egyptian sculptures dating from as early as 2400 BC show scribes squatting with their papyri resting on their knees. In about 1500 BC the scribe and satirist Khety listed the disadvantages of other professions and then described his own as 'the most important of all occupations', for 'there's no job without an overseer, except the scribe's'.

Khety had ample justification for his views: as transcribers of literary texts and recorders of accounts, inventories, work attendance, regulations and court proceedings, Egyptian scribes needed to be both literate and numerate, and were part of an educated elite. Scribes were usually the sons of scribes, and thus engaged in a secure profession.

Much later, literate Norman clerics who administered law and justice became Europe's first clerks. The term persisted with the predominance of clerics among the scribes of medieval Europe. With the introduction of typewriters in the 1870s, more women were brought into offices to operate them. In Britain, women made up one-third of clerical workers by 1911.

The late medieval office, named from the Latin *officium*, 'performance of duty', would have been no more than a room in a private house at which a scribe carried out his work. In the 16th century the German painter Hans Holbein the Younger painted the merchant Gerg Gisze sitting in his study surrounded by the tools of his trade: scales, pens, ink and a seal. Gisze works alone.

In London in the early 18th century the coffee-house became established as a place where people could meet, discuss business schemes and do deals. This was the beginning of the modern office: the East India Company, founded in 1600 to trade in Asian spices, operated from a private house in Leadenhall Street, London, until it relocated to commercial premises nearby in 1726. By the end of the 18th century it was accepted that the place of business was essentially outside the home.

WORKERS' RIGHTS
Associations and the law

The early history of trade unions in Britain is characterised by attempts, such as the Combination Act of 1799 passed by the Tory government, to outlaw these organisations. (The Act was repealed in 1824.) Groups of skilled workers began to control the hiring of apprentices and bargain with employers for better working conditions in the late 18th century, but as the movement grew the trade unions sought to create an alliance among themselves. This culminated in the first meeting of the Trades Union Congress in Manchester in 1868, at which 34 delegates represented 118 000 trade unionists.

Trade unions were finally legalised in an Act of 1871, and by the end of the century more than 1.5 million workers were members. Levies were introduced in 1901 by the Miners' Federation; members contributed one penny each month towards a parliamentary fund to elect their own MPs.

Until the 19th century workers were given little or no protection: child labour was commonplace, as were long hours worked in unsafe conditions for minimal pay. After campaigns by social reformers such as Robert Owen, who from 1800 created a model community for his workers in New Lanark, Scotland, governments introduced a series of Acts to regulate conditions.

The first such legislation, the Health and Morals of Apprentices Act of 1802, restricted apprentices from working more than 12 hours a day, while Lord Shaftesbury's Factory Act of 1833 prohibited the employment in textile factories of children under the age of nine. The National Insurance Act of 1911 provided insurance against 'loss of health and for the prevention and cure of sickness', but only in 1974 did Britain introduce legislation governing the health and safety of all employees.

WITHDRAWAL OF LABOUR *European workers made increasing use of strikes from the late 1800s to improve working conditions. But late payment of wages to Egyptian labourers in about 1165 BC precipitated the first ever strike.*

AIMING TO PLEASE *Ladies select gloves at the department store Au Bon Marché in Paris in 1889 (left). By this time the idea of stores retailing a wide variety of items was well established. 'Anything from a pin to an elephant' was the slogan of Whiteley's, one of Britain's first, opened in 1863.*

TRADING PLACES
Markets, shops and stores

No money passed hands in the trading exchanges that first took place more than 10000 years ago. Instead neighbours swapped items ranging from pots to lumps of precious metal, used to make tools or jewellery. Plants or objects that were thought to have medicinal properties were also exchanged, as was food in times of surplus.

By about 6000 BC, when agricultural communities had become established in ancient Egypt, food and livestock were being traded for such necessities as clothing, furniture and even coffins in regularly used sites or markets. Traders displayed their goods on the ground or on temporary market stalls, a practice used in Britain until the Middle Ages.

European stallholders began setting up more permanent shops from about the 12th century. Each sold a specific

selection of items, from baskets to bread. This set the pattern of shopping for centuries: shopkeepers were specialists and their wares were fetched for customers by clerks and packaged on the premises.

A chain of pharmacies was set up in Japan in 1643, but the modern multiple retailer was the child of the Victorian consumer boom. W.H. Smith & Son began selling books and periodicals at London's Euston Station in 1848, after winning the bookstall concession for all stations on the London & North Western Railway. By the end of the

FOR SALE *Cloth merchants display their wares in a Roman forum. After metal coins with set values were produced around 700 BC trade became much easier. Most ancient Greek and Roman towns had marketplaces where people came to buy household goods.*

CHAIN LINK *Some of today's best-known British retailers set up shop in Victorian times and were among the earliest chain stores. Marks and Spencer began as a stall in Leeds market in 1884, offering goods for a penny.*

century, W.H. Smith had 800 outlets, while the Nottingham chemist Jesse Boot, who had opened his first store in 1877, owned 181 shops.

The idea of the department store, selling many different types of goods, was pioneered in Paris with the opening of the Belle Jardinière in 1824. As shops became larger a new breed of retailer began to emerge. Among them was the American Harry Gordon Selfridge. In 1879 he began working as a stock boy for the store owner Marshall Field in Chicago, and made rapid progress within the company.

Among Selfridge's many innovations were annual sales, the bargain basement, gift tokens and the now universal practice of placing perfume and cosmetics stands near the main entrance to attract women customers into the store. In 1906 Selfridge moved to London, where he opened his Oxford Street department store in 1909.

SERVE YOURSELF
The shopping revolution

Self-service shopping began in 1912, when two independent stores opened for business in California. In 1916 Clarence Saunders established Piggly Wiggly in Memphis, Tennessee. This self-service grocery had a turnstile entrance and check-out system, and proved so successful that within seven years Saunders was managing some 2800 small shops.

Michael Cullen, the man credited with inventing the large modern supermarket, opened the first of his King Kullen outlets in New York State in 1930. It offered around 300 cut-price items to attract customers. Britain was slow to follow suit. Its first supermarket chain, Premier Supermarkets, did not open a branch, in London, until 1951.

The Army and Navy Co-operative Society Ltd, founded in London in 1871 to supply Britain's servicemen and

PLEASE TAKE A BASKET HERE *SELECT YOUR GOODS and* PAY AT THE CASH DESK

DELIVERING THE GOODS

• London was the site of the world's first advertising agency, established in 1786 by William Tayler. He charged a commission for placing advertisements in provincial papers.
• Shopkeepers' lives were made easier with the introduction of the cash register, patented in 1879 by a US saloon owner, James J. Ritty.
• Neon lighting made its debut in an illuminated sign over a barber's shop in Paris in 1912.
• Sylvan Goldman designed the first shopping trolleys in 1937. He had to hire people to push them around his Oklahoma City store to encourage customers to use them.

---

their families, was the first store to offer a mail-order service. It produced its first catalogue, 112 pages of items ranging from gout remedies to hare soup, in the following year.

To increase sales of their sewing machines in the 1850s, the Americans Isaac Singer and Edward Clark devised the concept of hire-purchase or payment by instalments. Buying on the 'never-never', a term first used during the 1920s, made expensive items instantly obtainable and gave a boost to the manufacturing industry.

In the 'honesty boxes' found in English taverns in the 1600s, the insertion of a penny released the lid of a tobacco box. Customers were relied upon to take only enough to fill their pipes and to close the lid. Modern vending machines appeared in the 1860s. Among the successful developers was Percival Everitt, who installed a machine to dispense postcards at Mansion House underground station in London in 1883.

AT YOUR SERVICE *In 1950 the concept of self-service was still new to the British, although Romford Co-operative Society introduced the system in 1942. Shops had signs explaining what to do.*

THE ADVERTISING AGE
Selling the product

Hawkers calling out their wares in the streets of ancient cities were the world's first advertisers. But modern advertising did not begin until the mid 15th century when the invention of movable type made it possible to print many copies of a single notice. In 1479 the first British publisher and printer, William Caxton, produced an advertisement for his books in this way.

The French *Journal Général d'Affiches*, published from 1612, pioneered newspaper advertising. By 1758 the English author Samuel Johnson was reporting: 'Advertisements are now so numerous that they are very negligently perused, and it is therefore become necessary to gain attention by magnificence of promise and by eloquence sometimes sublime and sometimes pathetick.'

In the 20th century radio proved an ideal medium for communicating the

NEW BRANDS *As factory-made products became more widely available, distinctive logos and packaging were needed to make them identifiable. The Heinz slogan '57 varieties' is among the most enduring. The number was chosen in 1896 by the company's founder simply because he liked the sound of it.*

messages of manufacturers. The word 'commercial' was used from 1922 when a New York station broadcast the first radio advertisement, for apartments.

Television took advertising into new realms. Its first true commercial, a picture of a Bulova clock ticking, was screened by a New York station in 1941. In Britain the first was an advertisement for SR toothpaste, shown on the inaugural day of ITV in 1955.

CASH IN HAND
Minting and printing

Using a reed the scribes of ancient Mesopotamia scratched onto clay tablets the value of quantities of barley, wool, sesame oil and other essential goods. Their calculations were made by comparing each commodity with a standard weight of silver, which is how this precious metal became the first 'money' 4000 years ago.

A wide variety of scarce items were used as tokens that could be exchanged for life's necessities or luxuries. In China goods were 'bought' with strings of cowrie shells from at least 1500 BC. In comparatively recent times tobacco was used as cash by 17th-century American colonists.

Coins of set value, which allowed payment to be made by count rather than weight, were introduced in Lydia, in western Turkey, in about the 7th century BC. Standardised slugs of electrum, a naturally occurring alloy of gold and silver, were stamped with images of animals or gods to indicate their value. The Persian emperor Darius I became the first person to issue coins bearing his own portrait, in the 5th century BC.

The words 'money' and 'mint' are both derived from the name of Juno Moneta, the Roman goddess of, among other things, prophecy. Her temple became an official site of coin production for the Romans, who imposed a rigid currency system throughout their empire from the 1st century AD.

Named after an early Germanic word meaning 'pledge', the penny was introduced in the 8th century by Egbert of Kent and, more widely, by the Mercian king Offa. Later in the century 240 Saxon coins, known as sterlings,

THE MONEY MAKERS *Coins of the realm are struck in 1809 at the Tower of London. The city's first mint was used by Romans at the end of the 3rd century BC but it was only one of many sites, including Canterbury, where coins were produced. London achieved a monopoly in the mid 16th century.*

ANGLO-SAXON DINAR, 8TH CENTURY

PAPER PROMISES *'All these pieces of paper are issued with as much solemnity and authority as if they were pure gold and silver,' the explorer Marco Polo commented on 13th-century Chinese paper money (left). Britain did not introduce banknotes until the late 1600s, some 40 years after the first cheques or 'drawn notes' were issued.*

CHINESE BANKNOTE, 1287 EARLY ENGLISH CHEQUE, 1659

EAST ANGLIAN COIN, 8TH CENTURY

ROMAN *solidus*, 4TH CENTURY

CHANGING TIMES *Struck by Celtic tribes in the 1st century BC the first British coins were superseded by a standard Roman currency. This was replaced in its turn by local coinages, such as the silver penny and the gold dinar introduced by Offa and other Anglo-Saxon kings.*

were minted from a pound of silver, hence the pound sterling. In medieval Latin documents the English pound, shilling and penny were denoted as *libra* (pound), *solidus* (a Roman gold coin) and *denarius* (a Roman silver coin). This led to the use of the symbols £, s and d. After decimalisation in 1971 the new penny was written simply as 'p'.

The Chinese invented paper money around the 7th century AD, although their early notes were really certificates of deposit that could be exchanged for cash. By the 11th century notes of fixed denominations were being used.

Sweden issued Europe's first paper money, with fixed denominations, in 1661. Early British banks, including the Bank of England, which was founded in 1694 to raise money for William III's war against the French, issued certified

and numbered notes made out for the amount deposited. The handwritten notes were made payable to the named depositor or the bearer. Note holders could cash these in full or make part withdrawals, in which case the new balances were duly noted on them.

In the early 18th century the Bank of England introduced fixed denominations. By 1745 notes were being part-printed with face values ranging from £20 to £1000. Fully printed banknotes appeared in 1855. A move towards giving the Bank a monopoly on note issue in England was made in 1844 with the passing of the Bank Charter Act. But the last private bank to issue its own notes, Fox Fowler and Company, ceased doing so in 1921.

Early banknotes could be exchanged for their face values in gold. But cash payments were suspended from 1797 to 1821 because of the drain on the gold reserves caused by wars with France and again after the outbreak of the First World War. The first £1 and £2 notes were issued in 1797.

CASH AND CREDIT

CREDIT CARD,
1960S DESIGN

- The Babylonian business interests of the 7th-century BC 'Grandsons of Egibi' included pawnbroking.
- In 1951 the US Diners' Club issued the first general-purpose credit card. In the decade that followed, more than 300 000 people signed up for it.
- Barclays Bank's Enfield branch became the site of the world's first cash dispenser in 1967, when £10 was the maximum single withdrawal.

FIGHTING THE FORGERS
The lure of easy money

Because they contained a set amount of silver, gold or other precious metal, early coins had an intrinsic value. This made forgery difficult but not impossible—a counterfeit Greek silver coin with a copper core was produced in the 6th century BC. Much more common-place, however, was the debasing of coins—slivers would be shaved off the edge then melted down and sold.

One method of protecting coins from being degraded in this way was by milling or grooving the edges, a technique first adopted in England in 1663 at the instigation of John Evelyn. The diarist and founder member of the Royal Society had encountered the idea in France, where the world's first milled coin had been produced in 1639.

Unlike his 12th-century Chinese predecessor-in-crime, who was given the death penalty for producing false notes, Daniel Perrismore, Britain's first recorded counterfeiter of paper money, was merely fined and pilloried in 1695. Counterfeiting was made punishable by death in 1697—a sentence that remained unchanged until 1832.

In another attempt to deter forgers in 1697, the Bank of England introduced the watermark, a translucent design impressed on the paper during manu-facture and visible when the note is held up to the light. In 1940 metallic thread was introduced as an additional device.

THE BUSINESS OF BANKING
Loans and deposits

Priests in the wealthy Mesopotamian temples were the first bankers, lending sums of money for an agreed period and charging interest on their loans. This system became increasingly widespread during the 1st millennium BC, and the loan agreements were recorded on clay tablets, which were smashed once the debt had been paid off. The temples also instituted the idea of holding an item of value, usually property, as secu-rity against debts.

Modern banks developed in Venice in the late 1100s, when a state tax was levied to help to pay for war expenses. The committee that was responsible for accounting for the fund later became a bank. In Britain the first such institution was founded by Lawrence Hoare, a London goldsmith, who began accept-ing cash deposits in 1633.

Building societies originated in the industrialised regions of the north of England and the Midlands in 1775. They were set up to provide homes for groups of working people, the societies' members. These houses, which were paid for from a pool of weekly savings, were allocated by ballot. Once each member was housed the society was dissolved. The first permanent society was the Woolwich Equitable Benefit Building and Investment Association, founded in 1847.

SMALL BEGINNINGS *Penny banks encouraged the poor and the young to save what little they could spare. The first was opened in 1847 in Clyde, Scotland. Once a pound was deposited the account was transferred to the town's Provident Bank. Within four years penny banks run by schools, Sunday schools and clubs were operating all over Britain.*

CAPITAL GAIN *By 1915 London was the world's leading financial centre, used by many foreign corporations, such as the Russian Tobacco Company, to handle share issues.*

SHARES AND SHAREHOLDERS
Raising finance

The framework of company finance was established in the 13th century, when French stock markets traded bills of exchange, orders specifying sums of money to be paid to individuals on par-ticular dates. Introduced in Florence in 1408 the concept of limited liability made investors liable only for their own stake should the company get into debt.

Priced at £25 each, 240 shares were issued in 1553 to raise capital to finance a search by the merchant adventurer Sebastian Cabot for a north-east passage to the Orient. Cabot's voyage ended in Russia but led to the creation of the Muscovy Company, the first joint-stock company, members pooling their stock for the purpose of trade.

By 1695, 140 joint-stock companies were operating in Britain. Stock and share trad-ing took place in coffee-houses such as Jonathan's, off Threadneedle Street. In 1773 this became London's first dedicated stock exchange.

CRIME AND PUNISHMENT

'My object all sublime
I shall achieve in time—
To let the punishment fit the crime—
The punishment fit the crime…'

The Mikado, WILLIAM GILBERT, LIBRETTIST, 1885

BABYLONIAN STONE STELE
INSCRIBED WITH
HAMMURABI'S CODE,
ABOUT 1750 BC

A slack builder found responsible for the death of his employer's son is to sacrifice his own son; but the owner of an ox that damaged property cannot be penalised, as the animal had shown no sign of being violent. Thus are recorded two of the 282 judgments made by Hammurabi, who ruled Babylon for 40 years from 1792 BC. His Code, the most complete collection of early laws, was based on custom and previous verdicts, and was designed to integrate the peoples of his empire.

Britain's legal code, divided into common law and statute law, is shaped by historical developments. Common law, influenced by Roman and Norman practices, is, like Hammurabi's Code, based on custom and principles established by the precedent of previous cases. It can be said to date from the 12th century, when Henry II replaced local and ecclesiastical law with a 'common law' for all.

Statute law is enshrined in legislation passed by Parliament, which first won the right to pass laws in the 1300s. Among its early Acts were the Statutes of Provisors of 1351 and 1390, which limited the papacy's right to appoint clergy over the heads of local patrons.

FAIR TRIAL *A case is heard at the Old Bailey, the Central Criminal Court for the City of London, around 1850. A court had been in use at the site since 1539; the adjoining Newgate prison was demolished in 1902-3.*

The Bill of Rights, an Act passed in 1689, established Parliament as Britain's primary governing body.

Medieval Britain made much use of trial by ordeal, a form of justice used in a few of Hammurabi's Codes. Guilt or innocence was decided by the accused undergoing a dangerous test, and the result regarded as a divine judgment. A more objective approach began with the spread of common law, and in 1275 Edward I declared that criminal cases should be tried by a jury of 12 men.

The jury system, introduced into Britain by the Normans, is based on a Germanic custom in which conflicts were adjudicated by a group of local people familiar with the case in hand, rather than by an impartial panel. But the idea of trial by jury goes back to ancient Greece, where every citizen had the right to sit in judgment on his fellows. Jurors were chosen at random from those who presented themselves at the court, and the size of the jury varied according to the severity of the charge. A jury of 500 was selected in 399 BC to try the philosopher Socrates, accused of impiety and the corruption of youth. Having been found guilty by a simple majority, he was sentenced to death by drinking a potion of hemlock.

In many early civilisations, local rulers were also the decision-makers and highest judges, delegating ordinary cases to deputies. Judges were first appointed in England by William the Conqueror in the late 11th century. In the 12th century graduate practitioners became recognised as having special knowledge and skills in the law, giving rise to the legal profession. The division between barristers, who pleaded litigants' cases in the king's courts, and solicitors, concerned with property and financial work, was established by the 14th century but became rigid in the 1600s. Magistrates, usually unpaid lay people also known as justices of the peace, were first appointed in 1361 when they replaced judges in trying less serious offences.

SOCIETY'S RETRIBUTION

Throughout history, death has been reserved as the punishment for the worst crimes, although offences warranting the death penalty have varied greatly. Capital punishment is found in Hammurabi's Code for offences ranging from robbery to adultery. In early-16th-century England the death penalty could be imposed for treason, murder, larceny, burglary, rape and arson, and by the late 18th century there were more than 200 capital offences.

In 1826 Russia became the first country effectively to abolish capital punishment, when Tsar Nicholas I

LEGAL EAGLES

• Itinerant judges of the 12th century held their trials outdoors, where a barrier or 'bar' separated them from the public, the accused and lawyers. Newly qualified barristers are still 'called to the bar'.
• Solicitors have been so named since the 13th century, when they won the right to 'solicit' the court into resolving long, drawn-out cases.
• That barristers cannot sue for their fee is based on tradition: in the 13th century barristers did not work for a fee, relying instead on a voluntary payment from their clients.

commuted all such sentences, except for treason, to exile in Siberia. In Britain capital punishment was abolished in 1965, except for treason.

Imprisonment is a relatively recent means of punishment. The Old Testament refers to Joseph being jailed in the pharaoh's prison, but in most ancient civilisations jails served as labour camps or places of remand for people awaiting trial. Custodial sentences were introduced in AD 890 by Alfred the Great for breaking a pledge, but throughout the Middle Ages jail was mainly for debtors and those awaiting trial or sentencing.

In the 1500s attempts to reform minor offenders led to the creation of houses of correction holding both men and women. Some 200 years later the philanthropist John Howard—whose suggestion that jailers should be paid wages rather than fees extracted from prisoners became law in 1774—was among the reformers campaigning to improve appalling conditions. This led to the building of 'convict prisons' where inmates, now segregated by sex, served a set term in prison as punishment for their crimes. The City prison for women at Holloway was built between 1849 and 1851.

SHORT, SHARP SHOCK *A monk and his mistress pay for their sins by being publicly humiliated in stocks, a common medieval punishment. More degrading was the pillory with a hole for the sinner's head.*

A HANGING OFFENCE *In Britain executions of major criminals or repeat offenders were carried out in public until 1868 to deter and warn others.*

HOLY HEALING *In the 13th century religious orders were set up solely to provide nursing care for the sick. The word 'nurse' comes from the Latin* nutrire, *meaning 'to nourish'.*

CARE AND THE COMMUNITY
Hospitals, nurses and national health

In the infirmaries attached to their monasteries, monks treated the sick with herbal medicines prepared from plants tended in their well-stocked gardens. These healing havens, which survived in the plague-ridden, war-torn Europe of the 5th to 16th centuries AD, were the forerunners of hospitals.

The Church also established the first hospitals, which offered food, rest and prayers to the sick and dying. Few of the staff had any medical training and conditions could be primitive—up to six patients had to sleep in each bed at the Hôtel Dieu in Paris, established in 651 by Bishop Landry.

In Britain advances in health care remained sporadic until Public Health Acts were passed in the 19th century. These appointed boards of health as well as medical officers who researched and reported on sanitary reform and the incidence of disease. At the same time the need for skilled nursing care began at last to be recognised. In 1836 Pastor Theodor Fliedner and his wife opened the first

A CLEAR VIEW *In 1951 this boy became an early beneficiary of the National Health Service Act when he received a new pair of spectacles. Masterminded by the Labour Minister of Health Aneurin Bevan, the Act made health services freely available to all for the first time.*

A HELPING HAND

- In 1937 the emergency 999 telephone service was established in London. More than 13 000 genuine calls were made in the first month.
- Alice Stebbins Wells, who worked in Los Angeles from 1910, was the first policewoman with full powers of arrest. Grantham was the first town in Britain to see policewomen on active duty, in 1914.
- Until 1601 when Elizabeth I's Poor Relief Act ruled parishes must provide for them, the destitute turned to the Church, the wealthy and charitable individuals for food and shelter.
- A French military surgeon, Baron Larrey, devised the world's first ambulances—light horse-drawn carts mounted on springs—for Napoleon's Italian campaign of 1796.

nurse training school in Kaiserwerth, Germany. The Quaker philanthropist Elizabeth Fry was so inspired by a visit there that she opened Britain's first nursing school, in London in 1840.

One of the women who trained at Kaiserwerth was Florence Nightingale. Only after she revolutionised the care of wounded and sick soldiers during the Crimean War between 1854 and 1856 was the value of good hospital management and nursing care fully appreciated. Some of her earliest actions on arriving at the Crimea were to requisition 200 scrubbing brushes and to arrange for her patients' clothes to be washed. By insisting on these and other hygienic measures she was able to reduce the death rate in the Scutari field hospital from 42 to 2 per cent.

Germany became the first country to introduce a sickness benefit scheme, in 1883. In Britain the National Health Service Act, passed in 1946 and implemented two years later, gave people access to comprehensive health services funded by the government for the first time.

FIRE! FIRE!
Dousing the flames

To fight fires more effectively the Greek inventor Ctesibius, who lived in Alexandria in the 3rd century BC, devised a pump to replace buckets of water. This was bettered four centuries later by the inventor Hero whose hand-powered pistons forced water through a pipe and a nozzle. Emperor Augustus created the world's first fire brigade in Rome in AD 6, with 7000 *vigiles*.

Coordinated fire-fighting was rare in Roman and medieval Britain. But from the 13th century some towns required householders to own equipment—after 1574 the inhabitants of Winchester had to bring their buckets of water to quench fires. The Great Fire of London

LONDON'S BURNING *Firemen of 1883 tackle a blaze in the streets of London, using a steam engine. Britain's first full-time brigade had been formed in the city in 1833, funded by a consortium of fire insurance companies.*

in 1666, which left more than 100000 homeless, showed the need for a more effective system.

The City of London council made provision for men to patrol the city looking for blazes, but did not see the need to organise fire-fighting. That was left to insurance companies, who established private fire brigades. The first, set up by the Phoenix Fire Office in 1684, was probably staffed by watermen.

A lever-operated pump mounted on a carriage was built in Germany in 1518, and by 1632 there was a fire engine in use in London. In 1712 John Grey and Nicholas Mandell patented a pump fitted with an air vessel, which produced a continuous jet. Long hoses, used from 1672 in Holland, were introduced into England in 1688.

John Braithwaite and John Ericsson increased the force of the jet with their 1829 steam fire engine. It was cumbersome and slow, and manual pumps continued to be used until motorised fire engines were invented in 1910.

POLICE POWERS
Keeping public order

At the beginning of the 1st century AD the emperor Augustus appointed three cohorts, each comprising 1000 men, to police the streets of Rome. They were one of the first forces of law and order to be controlled by a civilian authority.

The Anglo-Saxons developed a type of community policing with the frankpledge system. People were grouped into tithings of around ten families and were held responsible for each other's conduct. The Normans required these groups also to prevent crime, and punished those that failed. They introduced constables, who gradually took over the duties of the groups' spokesmen and became responsible for keeping the peace.

Increasingly rewards were offered to individuals who caught criminals or restored stolen goods, but this system led to corruption. In the 17th century

LONG ARM OF THE LAW *A pickpocket is apprehended in 1830 by a 'bobby', as Robert Peel's uniformed policemen were nicknamed.*

such criminals as London's 'thief-taker general' Jonathan Wild were arranging to have goods stolen specifically to sell them back to their owners.

In 1667 the first police force was established in Paris; its men were given uniforms in 1829 'to compel them to intervene and restore order instead of vanishing into the crowd for fear of being noticed as often happens'. Henry Fielding, the novelist and Chief Magistrate of Bow Street, London, employed a privately funded force of six constables from the mid 1700s. This was continued by his brother Sir John Fielding and in 1797 the Bow Street Runners were a force of 68 men.

The Metropolitan Police, founded by the Conservative Home Secretary Robert Peel, became Britain's first statutory police force in 1829. Its crime prevention duties included lamplighting and watching for fires. When the Criminal Investigation Department (CID) was set up in 1842, crime investigation was added to its brief.

The first police car, used in Akron, Ohio, in 1899, was an electric wagon with a maximum speed of 25km/h (16mph). But British forces continued to use horse-drawn vehicles until 1920 when the Metropolitan Police Mobile Patrol Experiment acquired its first cars. Within a few days the patrol had been christened the 'flying squad' by W.G.T. Crook, the crime reporter of the *Daily Mail.*

RELIGIOUS AWAKENINGS
In awe of spirits

The oldest religious response to the realities of life and death can probably be seen in the way the ancient dead were laid to rest. Between 100000 and 50000 years ago Neanderthal people were buried with tools beside them and their skulls dyed a red ochre colour, suggesting some belief in an afterlife. Personal objects left in a grave may have been intended for the use of the deceased during their next 'existence'.

Nature's mysterious and powerful forces were controlled, so our early ancestors believed, by supernatural beings. Drawings on the walls of caves at Lascaux in France created between 20000 and 8000 years ago include a creature half-man and half-stag and men disguised as animals. The figures may represent ancient kinship with the nonhuman world.

These depictions of 'special' humans suggest that ancient people had begun to conjure in their minds gods who personified the sacred nature of life. Female figurines unearthed in the Middle East and the Mediterranean area are thought to represent the Mother Goddess, a

EARTH MOTHER *The ancients' awe at the powers of human fertility was personified in the* Maltese Lady, *now headless, carved in limestone in about 3400 BC.*

fertility deity common in ancient civilisations. In Egypt she was Isis, in Sumeria Inanna and in Greece Aphrodite.

Soapstone seals about 4000 years old found at Mohenjo-Daro in the Indus Valley possibly reflect the roots of Hinduism. One seal shows a figure sitting cross-legged, suggesting the practice of yogic meditation, and may be an embryonic representation of the Hindu god Siva. The oldest scripture of the Indo-European world, the Rig-Veda, is a collection of hymns written down in the 4th or 5th century AD but thought to have originated in about 1500 BC. The hymns give accounts of creation and of the battles and marriages of the gods, such as Vishnu and Siva, who became deities central to Hinduism.

DAILY PRAYER *The Jewish religion goes back to the 2nd millennium BC, but the skullcap, or yarmulke, worn by men as a mark of reverence before God, dates from the 1600s.*

WORSHIPPING ONE GOD
The Jewish faith

As human societies developed, so the relationships with their gods and goddesses multiplied. But around 2000 BC in the Near East a seminomadic Semitic farmer named Abraham embraced the worship of one all-powerful God. Led by God to Canaan, an area roughly corresponding with modern Israel, Abraham made a pact with God that he and his sons would live faithfully in God's presence. In return Jewish people believe that God promised Abraham and his descendants 'the entire land of Canaan, to own in perpetuity'.

About three centuries later Abraham's descendants became enslaved in Egypt, but were led to freedom on a great Exodus to Canaan, the 'Promised Land', by the prophet Moses. The Bible relates that before reaching Canaan Moses received the Ten Commandments from God. These divine laws reminded the Israelites of their obligations and stressed the sanctity of human life. Eventually the Commandments were set down in the Torah, the first five books of the Bible, and became pillars of the Jewish faith.

Several religious symbols still unite Jews worldwide. The menorah, a candelabrum with a branch for each of the seven days of the week, was first used in the Temple of King Solomon in

FAITH AND WORSHIP

• Jews came to Britain during the Norman Conquest of 1066, but were expelled in 1290 and only readmitted in the 1650s by Oliver Cromwell.
• After Henry VIII was refused permission by Pope Clement VII to divorce his first wife, Catherine of Aragon, in order to marry Anne Boleyn, a lady of the court, he severed connections with Rome and in 1534 declared himself head of England's national Church.
• The rosary used in prayer by Roman Catholics is known in Sanskrit as 'the muttering chaplet'. It was originally a string of beads or gems used by Buddhists and Hindus to keep count of their prayers.
• The first bells were tolled in Christian churches in the 8th century.

Jerusalem around 970 BC. During the 6th century BC the six-pointed Star of David came to symbolise the saviour or Messiah who was a descendant of the Israelite king David and would come to bring salvation to the Jewish people. David's shield was also traditionally thought to be shaped like the Star.

Following the destruction of the Temple by the Babylonians in 586 BC, the Israelites were deported to Babylonian cities. There the synagogue, from a Greek word meaning 'assembly', arose as the Jewish place of worship.

JESUS AND CHRISTIANITY
Following the Messiah

Early in the 1st century AD Judaea was the Roman province of ancient Palestine and here Jesus, a carpenter's son, preached the imminent arrival of the Kingdom of God foretold by the Jewish prophets. Jesus saw himself as the Messiah or, in Greek, the Christ—but one who would deliver people from sin, not the political and military saviour foretold by the Jewish tradition.

Jesus arrived in Jerusalem in about AD 30 with 12 disciples for the festival of Passover, the ancient celebration of the Exodus from Egypt. Accusing him of

THE RISEN JESUS Belief in the resurrection of Jesus Christ, witnessed here by his follower Mary Magdalene, and later by his disciples, became central to Christianity. Jesus's conquest of death is seen by Christians as the key to personal salvation and everlasting life.

emperor Constantine had converted to Christianity; by 400 it was the Roman Empire's official religion.

The first public churches, simple buildings that were known as basilicas and based on a rectangular Roman design, were built at this time. Over the next 100 years cross-shaped, round and polygonal churches were constructed, with worshippers called to services by trumpet blasts.

Christianity arrived in the British Isles with the Roman occupation in the 1st century, but widespread conversion only followed the 5th-century mission of St Patrick in Ireland. In the next century St Augustine established the English Church, and in 597 became its first Archbishop of Canterbury.

ORIGINS OF ISLAM
Culmination of faiths

In Arabic 'Islam' means 'submission to God'. The prophet Muhammad ibn Abdullah, its founder, a trader from Mecca, now in Saudi Arabia, is said to have received in AD 610 a vision of the angel Gabriel. These and other revelations were transcribed during and after his lifetime, and within 24 years of his death in 632 the Koran or Qur'an, emphasising the oneness of God, was completed. Muslims regard it as the culmination of all holy scriptures.

Faced with hostility to his teachings, Muhammad left Mecca in 622 on a *hijra*, or emigration, to Medina, also in modern Saudi Arabia. Using tree trunks for walls and palm leaves for a roof, he built the first mosque, named from the Arabic for 'a place of prostration' and symbolising submission to God.

GOLDEN CITY *Peoples of three great faiths meet in Jerusalem, where Christians worship beneath the onion domes of the church of St Mary Magdalene. Jews offer prayers at the crenellated Wailing Wall, the holiest remnants of the Hebrew Temple (centre right). In the distance on Temple Mount, site of Solomon's Temple, stands the 7th-century Dome of the Rock, one of Islam's holiest shrines.*

blasphemy, and fearing that he would provoke a riot, the Jewish priests handed Jesus to the Roman prefect Pontius Pilate, who sentenced him to death. Jesus died a martyr, nailed to a cross, but on the third day after the Crucifixion his tomb was found to be empty. His followers' belief that Jesus had risen from the dead confirmed their view that he was indeed the Messiah promised in the Hebrew Bible.

Paul, a Jewish convert, spread the Christian message to the Gentiles of the eastern Mediterranean and his letters, written in the two decades from AD 50, are the earliest existing Christian teachings committed to paper. The four evangelists' Gospels recounting Jesus's life followed: Mark's in about 70, Matthew's and Luke's during the 80s, and John's in about 100.

By the 3rd century Christianity had an established canon or code of law incorporating 39 books of Jewish scripture, the Old Testament, and the 27 books of the New Testament. The Church's popularity and influence spread. Before his death in 327, the

203

TEACHING AND LEARNING

'The fellow in charge of Sumerian said: "Why didn't you speak Sumerian?" [He] caned me.
My teacher said: "Your handwriting is unsatisfactory." [He] caned me. I began to hate the scribal art…'

ANONYMOUS MESOPOTAMIAN ON HIS SCHOOLDAYS, ABOUT 1700 BC, RECORDED ON A CLAY TABLET FROM NIPPUR, IRAQ

As knowledge, skills and customs passed from one generation to the next, so human societies evolved and developed. But formal educational systems emerged with the development of writing in Mesopotamia and Egypt from about 3500 BC. In both these civilisations, institutions were set up to train the sons of the wealthy and ruling classes for the all-important jobs of scribe, administrator and priest. School discipline was severe, as it was in most other early civilisations—the Hebrew word *musar* means both 'education' and 'corporal punishment'—but a diligent student's career was assured.

The Greeks evolved a three-tiered educational system, introducing the concept of primary, secondary and higher education later adopted by the Romans. Schools were set up in towns throughout the Roman Empire, often contributing to diplomatic efforts: Gnaeus Julius Agricola, governor of Britain from AD 37 to 93, won over many local chiefs by providing education for their sons.

After the fall of Rome the Church became the main provider of education. It set up schools attached to monasteries and cathedrals throughout western Europe to teach Christian doctrine and Latin, then an international language, to those destined for the priesthood or clerical occupations. Guilds, based on the Roman *collegia* through which

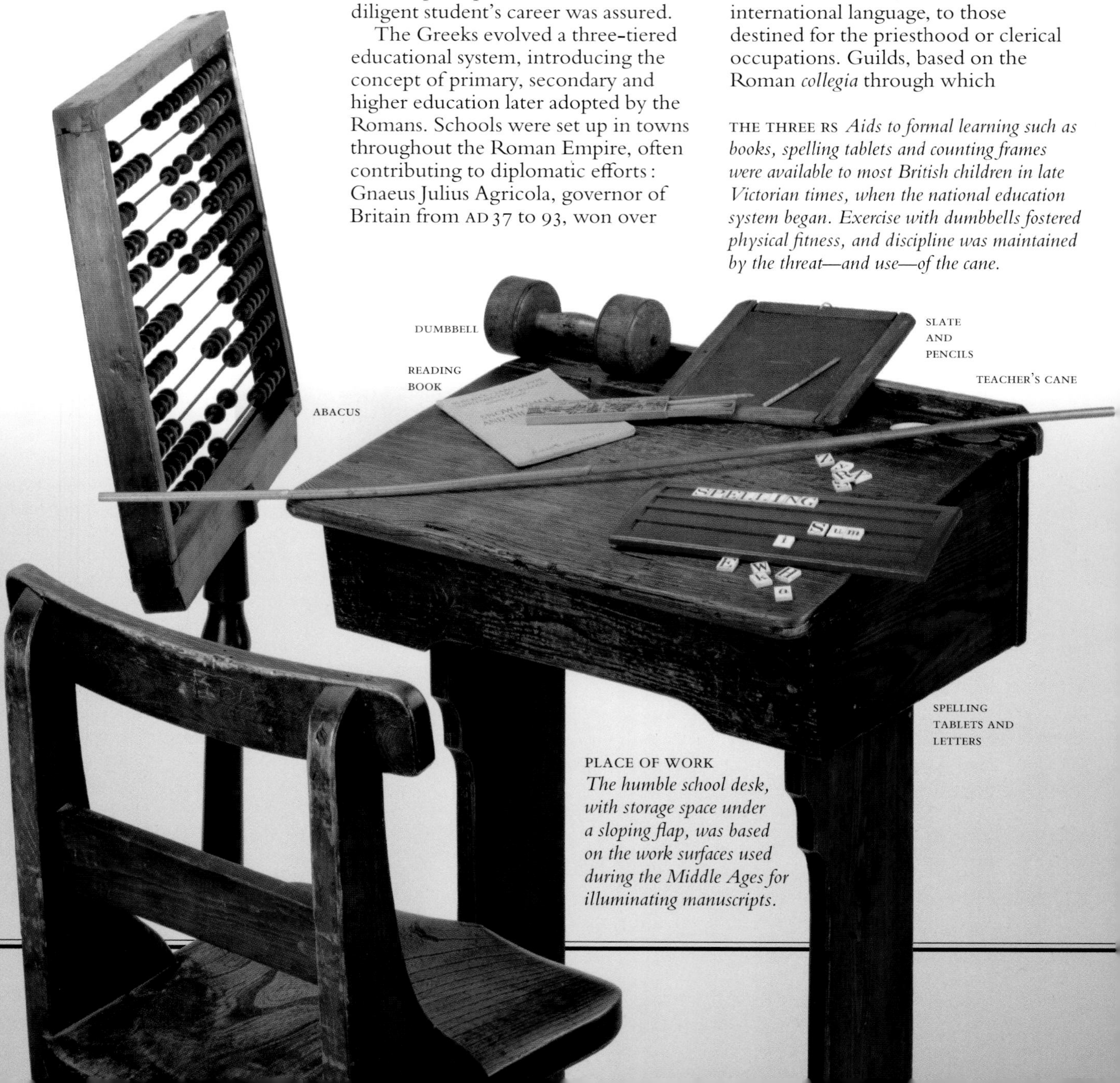

THE THREE RS *Aids to formal learning such as books, spelling tablets and counting frames were available to most British children in late Victorian times, when the national education system began. Exercise with dumbbells fostered physical fitness, and discipline was maintained by the threat—and use—of the cane.*

DUMBBELL

READING
BOOK

ABACUS

SLATE
AND
PENCILS

TEACHER'S CANE

SPELLING
TABLETS AND
LETTERS

PLACE OF WORK
The humble school desk, with storage space under a sloping flap, was based on the work surfaces used during the Middle Ages for illuminating manuscripts.

GREEK BOWL, DETAIL,
ABOUT 500 BC

PRIVILEGED PURSUITS *The word 'school' derives from the Greek skhole, 'leisure': only children of rich families, such as those above being supervised by their tutor, had the time to devote to studies.*

craftsmen regulated their own trades, also helped to promote basic literacy through apprenticeships. But in the late 16th century, despite the growing availability of printed books, education was still largely confined to the privileged few.

By the time free village schooling was introduced in parts of the Netherlands in 1618, earlier Protestant reformers such as the German Martin Luther

TEACHER'S PET *Throughout the Middle Ages, only those licensed by the Church were allowed to teach. Vocational teacher training was introduced in the 17th century.*

had already promoted the idea that all children should go to school and learn to read the Bible. Influenced by a scheme for universal education put forward by the Czech educational reformer John Comenius, the German duke of Gotha introduced compulsory schooling to his state in 1642.

In Britain until the early 1800s education was provided by a hotchpotch of voluntary and private enterprises. Many boys' grammar schools, such as the one at Stratford-upon-Avon attended in the 16th century by the future playwright William Shakespeare, were funded by royal endowments. Some establishments became so well known beyond their area that they started taking some fee-paying residential pupils. By the 19th century these had become known as public, rather than

local, schools. Sons of the wealthy, once educated at home by governesses and tutors, now went away to school.

Rich individuals might provide a school for their district; the first Sunday school was probably that instituted by the Gloucester newspaper publisher Robert Raikes in 1780 to teach basic literacy skills to working children. Little provision was made for educating girls until the establishment of North London Collegiate School in 1850, inspiring a network of girls' day schools around the country.

The first step in creating a national system of education was taken in 1839, when a committee was formed to administer state grants to the various educational societies and set up a system of inspections. By the early 1880s primary education was compulsory—and free—throughout

Britain. Secondary schooling, received by only one child in 70 in 1900, was mandatory by 1945.

Third-tier education, developed by the Greeks, disappeared with the fall of the Roman Empire. It re-emerged when a school of medicine at Salerno, Italy, established by the 10th century, rekindled the study of medicine.

By the 11th century Bologna in northern Italy had a thriving school of law. With other *studia generalia*, places of learning visited by scholars from all parts, it became one of the first 'modern' universities, named from the Latin for 'society' and conferring universally valid teaching licences. Oxford University, a *studia generalia* from the late 12th century, founded the first residential college, University College, in 1249.

Queen's College, London, set up in 1848 to improve the educational standard of governesses, was the first women's college. In 1877 the University of London admitted women to all faculties, producing female graduates in 1880. The first women's college to gain university status was the College for Women, Hitchin, Hertfordshire, in 1869. It moved to Girton, Cambridge, in 1873, and is now Girton College.

SIMPLE LESSON *Education for village children in early Victorian Britain was often limited to dame schools such as the one below, run by a woman who charged a small fee for minding local youngsters. In towns, poor families relied on charity schools. In the 1500s these had been the first to take girls as well as boys.*

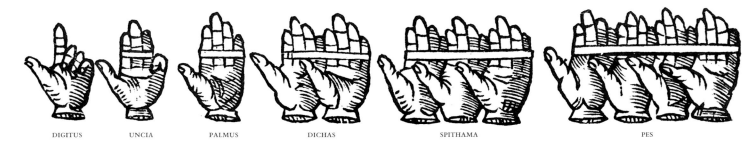

DIGITUS   UNCIA   PALMUS   DICHAS   SPITHAMA   PES

MEASURE FOR MEASURE *A 16th-century Flemish guide shows how to use the fingers and hands to measure short lengths. Local variants of all measures proliferated throughout Europe until the 19th century.*

WEIGHTS AND MEASURES
Setting a standard

When early peoples needed to measure something, they used their bodies to provide dimensions. The Egyptian cubit, employed from about 3500 BC, was based on the distance from a man's elbow to the tip of his index finger (about 21 in/52 cm) and subdivided into further units the width of a finger.

By about 1000 BC the Greeks were using a modified cubit in which one of the subdivisions was based on the length of the average man's foot—roughly 12 in (30 cm). The Romans adopted the foot, splitting it into 12 *unciae*, 'twelfth parts', or inches.

The British imperial system of weights and measures evolved from a mix of Roman, northern European and improvised units. The mile originated in the Roman *mille passus*, or 'thousand paces'. It was set at its current 5280 ft (1.6 km) in the late 16th century. Yards originated in Anglo-Saxon times. The first standard for the measure was set around 950, when King Edgar defined the yard as the 'measure of Winchester', a reference to a rod kept at the city that was his capital. The current lengths of the yard, foot and inch, roughly established by the late 1300s, were confirmed in the Weights and Measures Act of 1855.

Pounds take their name from the Roman *pondo*, a weight of about 12 oz (340 g), but another Roman weight, the *libra*, is the origin of the abbreviation lb. The first English standard was established in the 13th century. The avoirdupois pound now in general use, equal to 16 oz (453 g) and named from Old French *aveir de peis* or 'goods of weight', was adopted in the late 1500s.

The idea of using the dimensions of the Earth as a basis for measurement was first suggested by the French cleric Gabriel Mouton in 1670. Only after the French Revolution of 1789 was a commission established to 'bring to an end the astounding and scandalous diversity in our measures'. The metre, from the Greek *metron*, 'measure', was defined as one ten-millionth of the distance from the North Pole to the Equator.

In 1799 a platinum rod exactly 1 m long was established as the standard and deposited in the National Archives. All other lengths were derived from it in multiples of ten,

TIME, PLEASE *Decimal time, a French experiment of the early 1800s, was a failure.*

using the prefixes kilo (from the Greek for 'one thousand'), deci, centi and milli (from the Latin words for 'one-tenth', 'one-hundredth' and 'one-thousandth'). The unit of volume, the litre, was set at 1000 cubic centimetres and the unit of weight, the gram, was defined as the weight of 1 cubic centimetre of water.

The metric system became the French legal standard in 1840 and was soon adopted throughout Europe. In Britain the slow process of metrication began only in 1965.

COUNTING THE DAYS
Calendars and standard time

In agricultural societies, the calendar was important because it determined the right time for sowing and harvesting. The farmers of ancient Egypt, who divided the year into three seasons (Nile flood, sowing and harvest), developed a 12-month year based on lunar cycles. But the rhythmic waxing and waning of the Moon does not relate to the solar year, the time the Earth takes to orbit the Sun. By the time Julius Caesar came to power in Rome in AD 46 the seasons were three months out of step with the calendar.

The Julian calendar, devised by the Alexandrian astronomer Sosigenes and named after Caesar, closed the gap by adding an extra day every fourth, or leap, year. This close approximation was still wrong by some 11 minutes a year, and by 1572 this had built up to a 'loss' of ten days. In a revision ordered by Pope Gregory XIII, it was calculated that the value of a solar year differed from the Julian calendar, used throughout Western Europe, by just over three days every 400 years. Consequently, in 1582 ten days were 'lost'—October 5 became October 15—and it was decreed that leap years should occur

MAKING A DATE *A committee meets in 1582 to discuss the Gregorian calendar. When it was adopted in Britain, in 1752, 11 days 'disappeared', and many people feared they were being cheated into paying too much tax.*

AS TIME GOES BY *Before accurate clocks were made, in the late 17th century, the hourglass was the everyday means of keeping time.*

STEELYARD SCALES, ROMAN DESIGN

HOURGLASS, ANCIENT GREEK DESIGN

BELL WEIGHTS, LATE 1700S DESIGN

BAROGRAPH, LATE 19TH CENTURY

GUINEA SCALE, LATE 1700S

DISPENSARY'S BEAMSCALE AND WEIGHTS, ANCIENT DESIGN

HOW MUCH? *Middle Eastern merchants of 4000BC knew the beamscale, still used as a symbol of justice. Many other systems were later created to weigh money and objects. The barograph, or self-recording barometer, devised in the 1860s to record changes in atmospheric pressure, helped develop weather forecasting.*

only 97 times in 400 years; practically, this means that century years are leap years only if they can be divided by 400.

The Gregorian calendar was adopted in France, Italy, Spain, Portugal and Luxembourg, but elsewhere in Europe there was a reluctance to accept a change dictated by the Roman Catholic Church and the new calendar was not introduced into Britain until 1752. The system of consecutively numbering the years of the Christian era, with dates marked BC (before Christ) or AD (*anno Domini*, Latin for 'in the year of the Lord'), was devised in the 6th century.

That the day is divided into two periods of 12 hours each also dates back to the ancient Egyptians. Their 'seasonal hours' varied in length according to the Sun's course, a system still in use in Europe when mechanical clocks became established in the 14th century. Standard time zones were adopted in 1884 by an international conference, which set the zero meridian at the Royal Observatory, Greenwich.

FORECASTING WEATHER
Red sky at night, shepherd's delight

Babylonian tablets dating from the 12th century BC record early observations of weather lore, such as 'When a cloud grows dark in the sky, a wind will blow.' Formal records of the weather began to be kept in China in 1066BC. For millennia, weather forecasts were based on the observation of natural phenomena and related through such homespun sayings as 'If croaking frogs drone in the swamps, drenching rain shall fall from the clouds' (recorded by the Greek physician Aratus in 278BC), and the 16th-century English proverb 'Christmas on the balcony, Easter by the fireside.'

Scientific meteorology began in 1854, when the French astronomer Urbain Le Verrier was asked to investigate why a French warship and 38 merchant ships had sunk near Balaklava, Ukraine, during the Crimean War.

Le Verrier was able to show that the ships had been engulfed by a 'sudden' storm that had swept across western Europe, thus proving that storms travel around the Earth. This opened the way to weather forecasting of a kind, as did the confirmation by the Dutch meteorologist Christoph Buys Ballot a few years later that windflow follows isobars, lines drawn on charts to connect points of equal atmospheric pressure.

In 1861 Admiral Robert Fitzroy, Superintendent of the Meteorological Office, coined the term 'weather forecast', deeming it to smack less of soothsaying than 'prophecy'. On August 1, 1861, *The Times* broke new ground and printed a Meteorological Office forecast predicting fine weather across the country, but after criticism from the Royal Society no forecast was published for another 11 years.

WATER AND WASTE

'It's limpid and clear from all mud
This water I sell for the public good
Its excellent virtues no mortal can tell
So sweet is the water from Union Well.'

DOGGEREL ON THE SIDE OF A 16TH-CENTURY WATERCART, MONKWEARMOUTH, SUNDERLAND

SPREADING DISEASE *The deepening of the Fleet Street sewer in 1845 and other efforts to improve London's sewerage system failed to prevent cholera epidemics killing 20000 city-dwellers. A total overhaul of the system, completed in 1875, led to a dramatic improvement in the health of Londoners.*

To preserve and channel precious water, early Bronze Age settlers in Europe encased springs in wooden holding tanks. Where the water table was deep below the ground, they dug wells, lined them with wood, stone or brick, and scooped out the water with hollowed gourds, leather bags, clay jars or wooden buckets.

The wells of cities of the ancient Near East were so deep and sturdy that one built in the 9th century BC at Nimrud in modern-day Iraq still held water when it was discovered in 1951. In the 1st millennium BC the peoples

of this area made huge stone cisterns to hold rainwater, some hewn from stone blocks and others hollowed out from the rocky land.

The Egyptians seem to have thought of damming rivers and wadis, water channels that drain dry outside the rainy season. The oldest surviving dam, a wall of masonry some 80m (270ft) thick and 110m (370ft) long, was built around 2000 BC to contain the spate waters of Wadi Gerrawi, about 40km (25 miles) south of Cairo.

Settlers in the Indus Valley, covering eastern Pakistan and part of western

India, were among the first to pipe water into the home. It flowed through clay pipes around 2000 BC. An ambitious water system constructed by the Minoans in Crete at about the same time included overground aqueducts to carry water from the mountains to the palace at Knossos,

LIFTING WATER *By 2000 BC the shaduf was being used to help to irrigate crops. Each operator scooped river water into a bucket attached to one end of a pole. A counterweight on the other end of the pole brought the bucket back to waist level so water could be poured into a channel to flow across the land.*

ASSYRIAN SHADUF,
7TH CENTURY BC

IN THE PIPELINE

• Copper pipes were first used in an Egyptian temple around 2450 BC. Cast-iron pipes, tried out in Germany in the 1400s, were first used on a large scale around 1680 at the Palace of Versailles in Paris.
• Some of the first standardised items were water pipes, calibrated by the Romans so they could calculate and charge for the volume of water used. The standard pipe was 9 cm (3½ in) wide.
• When his legions faced drought in Egypt in 49 BC, Julius Caesar may have extracted salt from seawater using a 300-year-old method devised by the Greek philosopher Aristotle.

11 km (7 miles) away. Their terracotta pipes were tapered at one end so they could fit together easily.

Public waterworks scaled the heights with the magnificent arched aqueducts built by the Romans, but the first of their water channels, the Aqua Appia,

FLUID TRANSPORT *Animal skins, such as the one carried by this young Arab in 1901 Jerusalem, have been used since the earliest times to transport water.*

constructed in about 300 BC to service Rome, was in fact an underground conduit. This system had first been developed in the Near East, and was used in Persia by the 6th century BC.

Lead pipes were commonly used in Rome, causing some physicians concern about contamination. The Greeks had already experimented with wool, wick and tufa (a porous rock) as filters, and the Romans added wine to the list of purifiers. Water was also filtered by being percolated through layers of progressively finer sand.

With the fall of the Roman Empire the superbly organised waterworks system collapsed, and plumbing survived in the West only in large public buildings and the great monasteries. Attempts to supply cities were not resumed until 1190, when a network of lead pipes was laid down in Paris. London's first public water conduit was built in 1236; water was

taken from the Tyburn stream at what is now Stratford Place in Oxford Street then carried to the City in lead pipes. But such ventures were few until the growth of cities in the mid 18th century led to the creation of private water companies.

SEWERS AND WASTE

At Skara Brae in the Orkneys, the oldest known British Neolithic settlement, villagers living in simple stone huts around 2800 BC built a drainage system and used rudimentary lavatories. The Greeks and Romans drained waste into cesspits and sewers. The cesspits were rarely emptied, and open sewers gave off such a stench that they were eventually covered over.

The same problems affected European city-dwellers up to the 19th century, when the discharge of effluent into streams and rivers, and the overspill of cesspools, led to pollution and the spread of diseases. The first large-scale underground sewers were built in Hamburg,

Germany, when the city was rebuilt after a fire in 1843.

London's sewers were redesigned by Sir Joseph Bazalgette, appointed Chief Engineer to the Metropolitan Board of Works in 1845. His sewers, which are still in use, intercepted the city's streams and carried the waste to outfalls north and south of the capital. Pumping stations lifted the sewage up to a higher level to aid the flow.

CLEARING THE STREETS *From the Middle Ages Europe's cities reeked of rotting rubbish tipped from windows and doors. After the Great Fire of 1666, scavengers were appointed to clean London's streets. By the mid 19th century huge quantities of rubbish were collected by dustmen (below) and deposited at sea, dumped on waste ground or burned.*

THE WRITTEN AND SPOKEN WORD

From facial expressions, gestures, grunts and shouts, our distant ancestors developed systems of signs and symbols, which soon became resources essential to survival. The noises made by babies are probably remnants of early people's vocal signals, while the way they learn to speak reflects the human instinct for speech and our ability to learn language. What cannot be explained is why humans, scattered around the world, seem to have developed the faculty of speech at about the same time, some 100 000 years ago.

Until 3500 BC, when the Sumerians traced the first pictographs, no records exist of early human language or its development. And why as many as 3000 different languages are spoken throughout the world remains a mystery. Common links exist between apparently different language groups; every language might be traced back to a single, unknown language family.

Around 3100 BC Egyptian hieroglyphs were first engraved on monuments. Some 2000 years later the Chinese began to preserve their history and customs in pictographs. Number symbols evolved from the 3rd century BC in India. This system reached Persia in scientific tracts in the 9th century AD, becoming known as 'Arabic' after being copied in Middle Eastern manuscripts.

In Europe at this time scholarship was mainly religious: Biblical narratives were recorded in

books inscribed and copied by hand for use in abbeys and monasteries. Such books were beautiful rarities unseen by the illiterate masses.

Attempts to create printed pages were similarly labour-intensive. In China raised images on wooden blocks were transferred with ink onto paper possibly as early as the 7th century. Only in the 1450s, when, in Germany, Johann Gutenberg synthesised the two processes of printing, did books become available to a wider readership.

The invention of the printing press generated an unparalleled spread in scholarship, as well as a new interest in everyday languages. In Europe it also shifted the emphasis from oral traditions to the visual transmission of ideas in books, making such ideas more widely available.

Weekly newspapers appeared in the early 1600s in the Netherlands, but with improvements in printing technology a century later daily papers provided ordinary people with a relatively inexpensive means of learning about politics and society. From the late 1830s trains transported books and newspapers over long distances. There was also a regular postal service and the electric telegraph. By 1875 the telephone was operational, and 20 years later Guglielmo Marconi transmitted the first message using a 'wireless'.

In the USA the typewriter, marketed from 1873, revolutionised office printing methods. Later its keyboard was used in the first word processor, created by IBM in 1964. It was also an integral part of the most important communications invention since the printing press: the personal computer, marketed in 1975 as the Altair kit in California. Within 20 years the Internet, developed in the 1970s by the US government, military and university computer systems, re-established the principles of 15th-century publishing: to free people from ignorance and illiteracy.

THE MAKING OF LANGUAGE

*'Therefore is the name of it called Babel; because the Lord did there confound the language of all the Earth:
and from thence did the Lord scatter them abroad upon the face of all the Earth.'*

GENESIS, CH. 11, V. 9

According to the Out of Africa theory of human evolution, *Homo sapiens* left its birthplace in Africa and began to roam the world about 100000 years ago. Fossils cannot tell us about the capacity of early humans for speech, but scientists speculate that by this time *Homo sapiens* was communicating in some form of language. Over the next 60000 years prehistoric people settled in the eastern Mediterranean, across large tracts of Asia and in New Guinea and Australia. The languages they took with them changed all the time—a process that continued when, between 40000 and 16000 years ago, Asian migrants crossed the Bering Strait to settle in the Americas.

Farmers from eastern Nigeria and Cameroon moved out to central and southern Africa around 5000 BC, after which languages evolved with common characteristics derived from their shared source. Similarly, the Sino-Tibetan group of languages, which includes Chinese, spread with the cultivation of cereal crops along the Yellow River from about 4000 BC.

Proto-Indo-European, the ancestor of all Indo-European tongues—the group to which English belongs—was probably first spoken about 6000 years ago. Indo-European is thought to have spread to Greece from its birthplace north of the Black Sea around 2000 BC.

The roots of Indo-European were first identified in the 18th century, when scholars began to notice that many of the world's languages share significant similarities. In 1786 the British Orientalist and amateur philologist Sir William Jones detected links between Greek, Latin, Gothic, Persian and ancient Sanskrit. The word 'brother', for example, has similarities to the Greek word *phrater*, the Latin *frater* and the Sanskrit *bhrater*.

Invasion and conquest also spread some languages and displaced others. Military victories by the Chinese Empire in the early centuries BC brought Chinese to southern China, where a vast array of languages existed.

Spearheaded by Roman invasion and settlement, Latin spread through much of Europe over some 800 years. French, Italian, Spanish and the other Romance languages sprang from Latin as regional dialects during the 1st millennium AD. A pocket of resistance to Romanisation, and to later linguistic and

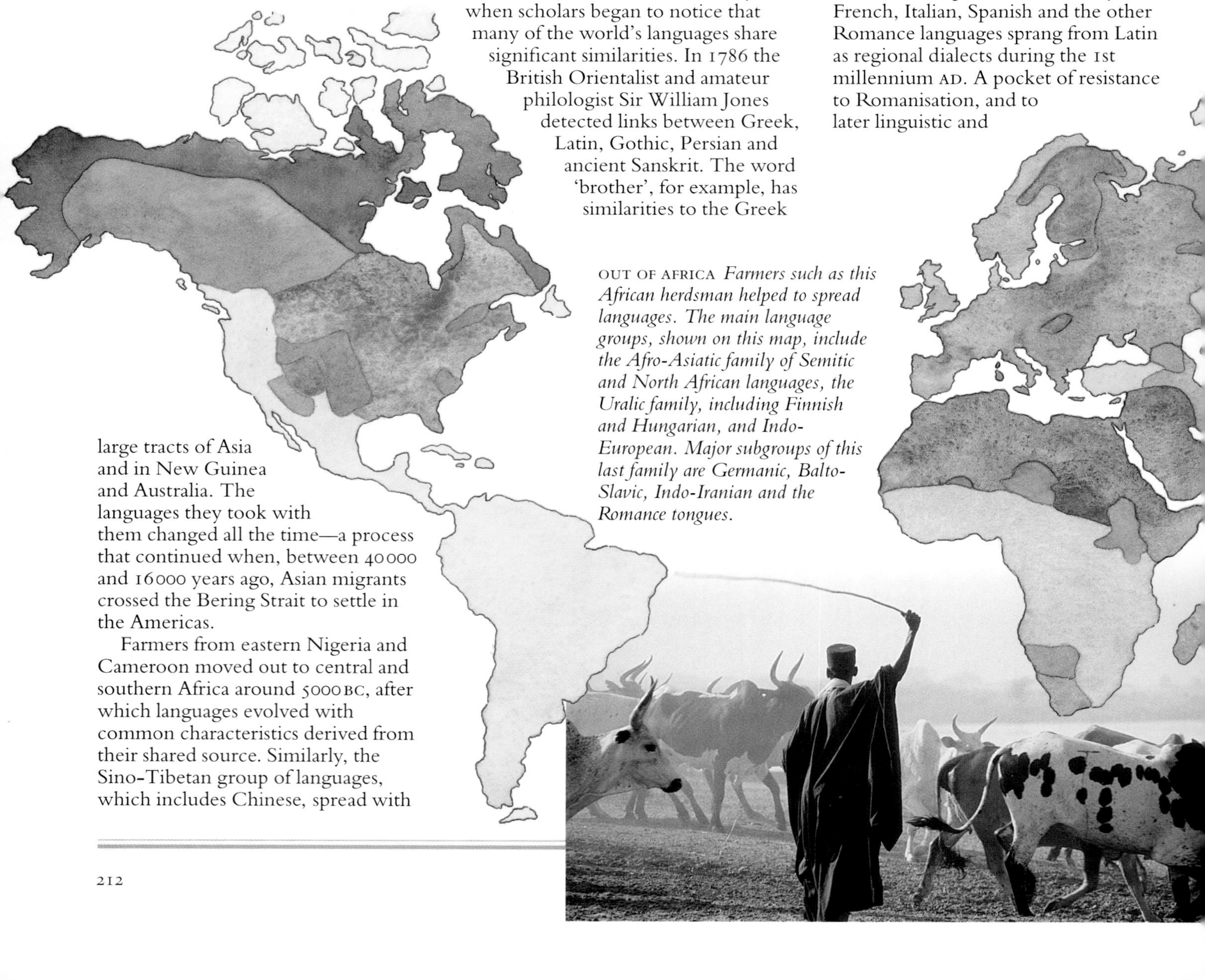

OUT OF AFRICA *Farmers such as this African herdsman helped to spread languages. The main language groups, shown on this map, include the Afro-Asiatic family of Semitic and North African languages, the Uralic family, including Finnish and Hungarian, and Indo-European. Major subgroups of this last family are Germanic, Balto-Slavic, Indo-Iranian and the Romance tongues.*

cultural incursions, still exists in the Basque area of the western Pyrenees. But whether Basque resembles the earliest spoken languages, surviving from human migrations across Europe 35 000 years ago, remains a mystery.

After Mandarin Chinese, English is the most widely spoken language, with an estimated 427 million native speakers. The earliest known languages of the British Isles were those spoken by the Celts. These northern European farmers had migrated across France, Spain and the British Isles by about 500 BC. Their languages, forming another branch of the Indo-European group, dominated much of this area until Christian times.

New linguistic influences reached Britain after the departure of the

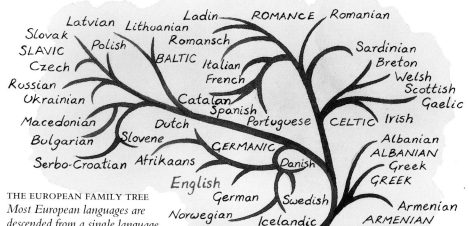

THE EUROPEAN FAMILY TREE
Most European languages are descended from a single language, Proto-Indo-European, which seems to have split into a number of dialects by the 3rd millennium BC. These developed into separate languages, spread by conquest, trade and farming.

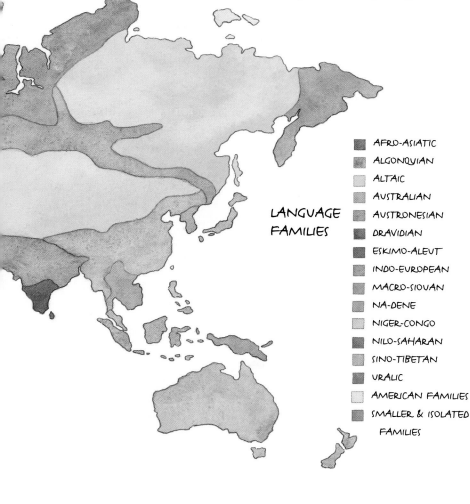

LANGUAGE FAMILIES

- AFRO-ASIATIC
- ALGONQUIAN
- ALTAIC
- AUSTRALIAN
- AUSTRONESIAN
- DRAVIDIAN
- ESKIMO-ALEUT
- INDO-EUROPEAN
- MACRO-SIOUAN
- NA-DENE
- NIGER-CONGO
- NILO-SAHARAN
- SINO-TIBETAN
- URALIC
- AMERICAN FAMILIES
- SMALLER & ISOLATED FAMILIES

Romans in about AD 410. Angles, Jutes and Saxons from the North Sea coasts of Europe introduced Germanic dialects belonging to the Indo-European mother-group. In the 6th century, Anglo-Saxon, or Old English, resembled German. Almost all of the 100 most frequently used modern English words, including 'you', 'here', 'there', 'English' and all the numeral names, are of Anglo-Saxon origin.

French was imported into Britain with the Norman Conquest of 1066, and within 200 years English had incorporated many French words. A large number—'treasurer', 'treaty', and 'court', for example—related to administration, but French names for everyday items such as 'chair', 'money', 'flower' and 'robe' also became common currency. As exploration took merchants to new lands, words were absorbed from other languages, and by the late 15th century English had largely lost its elaborate Germanic inflection.

From the 17th century Britain's conquest and colonisation of many parts of Africa, Asia and North America, as well as Australia and New Zealand, ensured that over the next 300 years English became spoken around the globe. In return, it adopted words from colonised countries, ranging from 'jodhpurs', riding breeches named after a town in India, to 'cooee', an Australian Aboriginal call used to attract attention.

MEANINGS IN PICTURES
From pictographs to cuneiform writing

Sumerian scribes were carving the first pictographs, words in pictures, into limestone tablets by 3500 BC. The earliest symbols were used for accounts and inventories, but over time scribes combined symbols to make ideograms that represented their language more fully.

When, around 2900 BC, the scribes began to use soft clay tablets, it became

CHINESE ORACLE BONE, 2ND MILLENNIUM BC

TELLING FORTUNES *A bone (above) reveals the inscriptions used by ancient Chinese priests to divine the future, while the pictographs on a Sumerian clay tablet show trees, sacks of grain and farming implements.*

difficult to draw curves. Instead they used the ends of their reed styluses to make wedge-shaped signs that became increasingly abstract until they no longer resembled the original objects.

Thus cuneiform—named from the Latin *cuneus*, meaning 'wedge'—became the first system of writing to contain no recognisable pictorial elements. From about 2800 BC scribes stopped drawing in vertical columns. Perhaps because it was easier, especially for those scribes who were right-handed, they turned the symbols on their sides and wrote in horizontal rows from left to right and from top to bottom.

Cuneiform proved so adaptable that it was borrowed by other peoples for more than accounting purposes. The

PRIDE IN HIS WORK *An Egyptian scribe awaits his instructions. As well as accounts, scribes recorded Egypt's history and works of literature, geography, cookery and astronomy.*

Persians, Assyrians and Babylonians all used it to record their own languages.

By about 3100 BC the Egyptians had developed their own complex system of hieroglyphs, so called after the Greek words for 'sacred carvings' because they first appeared on monuments to the pharaohs. The hieroglyphic system contained about two dozen alphabetic signs representing individual consonants, but no vowels; a number of signs that represented particular sequences of two and three consonants; and various picture-signs.

Some of these picture-signs were true pictographs, pictures of things represented, while others simply provided a clue as to the meaning, such as a stick-picture of running legs to indicate a verb of motion.

SUMERIAN PICTOGRAPHIC TABLET, ABOUT 3100 BC

EGYPTIAN SCRIBE, ABOUT 2600 BC

There were some 4500 signs in all, which were used and combined in a variety of ways. Sound pictures, for example, spelled out the words: a tree and the Sun could be combined to make the word 'treason'.

Hieroglyphs could be written in any direction, but were commonly written from right to left. Only the chosen few—royalty, priests and scribes—had the skills to read and write hieroglyphs.

The earliest Chinese inscriptions that can be identified as writing were made from around 1400 BC, although the system may have begun several centuries earlier. Early Chinese pictographs were carved on tortoiseshells or pieces of animal bone.

ALPHABETS AND SCRIPTS
Systems for writing

The alphabet made it possible for people to read and write as long as they could learn the small number of characters representing the basic sounds of their spoken language. The first alphabet was a North Semitic script known as Canaanite. Other northern Semitic scripts that developed after 1050 BC are known as Phoenician.

Canaanite was used from about 1700 BC by people living in Syria and Palestine and was spread by traders throughout the eastern Mediterranean.

Each of the 22 characters had a name to make it easier to remember: the first, which was represented by an ox's head, was called *aleph*, the second, a house, *beth*. These became the Greek *alpha* and *beta*, from which 'alphabet' is derived.

The earliest Hebrew alphabet was an offshoot of Phoenician known as Old Hebrew. A later version of it is still used by the Samaritans, a Jewish sect, but the Hebrew script most commonly known today dates from the 3rd century BC.

The Arabic alphabet is descended from a South Semitic script that broke

HOLY WRITING *Each chapter of the Koran begins with the words 'In the name of Allah, the beneficent, the merciful', printed here in a modern Kuwaiti edition.*

from the northern scripts very early on. The first Arabic inscriptions date to AD 512-13. The alphabet was used to transcribe the Koran, the Muslim holy book, after which the Arabic alphabet spread to Africa and Asia with the rise of Islam during the 7th century.

The alphabet used by the ancient Greeks derived from the Phoenician system, but around 750 BC the Greeks added extra consonants and vowels to suit the sounds of their own language. They also standardised the direction in which the lines were written and read, from left to right, in about 500 BC. By the 5th century BC their alphabet had 17 consonants and 7 vowels.

Around 700 BC the Greek alphabet was used by the Etruscans of central Italy as the model for their own. The Romans adapted the Etruscan alphabet for themselves, Latin first appearing

DISTINCTIVE STYLE *Roman carvers developed the script known as 'monumental capitals' for stone inscriptions, as on the base of Trajan's Column built in Rome around AD 106-13.*

around 600 BC on the 'Black Stone' of the Roman Forum. The Roman alphabet was made up of 21 letters until the 1st century BC, when Y and Z were taken from the Greek alphabet to represent sounds in words and names borrowed from Greek. Today's 26-letter alphabet was completed in the Middle Ages when J, V and W were added.

Recent research has challenged the belief that the Cyrillic alphabet was devised in the 9th century by the Greek saints and missionaries Methodius and Cyril, the founders of the Russian Orthodox Church. Instead, scholars suggest that to write Slavic languages Cyril invented the Glagolitic alphabet, and that this was eventually replaced by the Cyrillic script.

THE CALLIGRAPHER'S CRAFT
The development of handwriting

Before the invention of the printing press in the 15th century, sacred texts and government documents were laboriously copied by hand. As the calligrapher's craft grew more sophisticated in the Middle Ages, traditional writing practice changed. Whereas the Greeks and Romans used capital letters for stone inscriptions and lower case on papyrus and wax tablets, 8th-century calligraphers began to set upper and lower-case letters together.

Calligraphy led to elaborate styles of joined handwriting perfected by scribes in Europe's monasteries. Carolingian script developed in the 8th century, named after the dynasty from which the Holy Roman Emperor Charlemagne was descended. The predominant style in western Europe, its capitals were

FAST WORK *Written around AD 830 in Carolingian script, a piece from the Stuttgart Psalter shows the small, linked letters used by scribes so that they could work more quickly.*

regular while its lower-case letters combined straight lines and curves.

Gothic script, also known as 'black letter', first appeared in Germany in the 13th century. Its heavy, angular style reigned until the Renaissance. Then, in the early 1500s, the Venetian printer Aldus Manutius developed the more rounded *littera antiqua* script, as well as an elegantly slanting font, which he introduced in the Aldine Virgil, dedicated to Italy. The script came to be known as italic and thereafter all slanted letters were called italics.

TEACHING TYPE *As the invention of the printing press led to an increase in literacy, so the demand grew for people who could teach writing. A page from one of the first manuals, published in 1522, displays the graceful style of the Italian calligrapher Lodovico Arrighi.*

THE MAGICAL RUNES

In the 2nd century AD Germanic peoples inscribed the angular shapes of the runic alphabet in wood, stone and bone, even in manuscripts. They may originally have used the runes for magical rituals, but in Britain, where the runic alphabet became the first used to write Old English during the 6th century or earlier, the Anglo-Saxons used runes mainly to mark the owners or makers of caskets, jewellery and weapons.

SCANDINAVIAN RUNE STONE, 7TH CENTURY AD

CONSTANTINE CROSS, COMBINING THE LETTERS X AND P, BRITAIN, 4TH CENTURY AD

SACRED SYMBOLS
Ancient and modern

The Assyrian people of around 2000 BC represented their sky-god Anu with a cross, while for the Chinese of the same period it symbolised the fertile earth. The Romans celebrated the festival of Diana, the goddess of the Moon, with small, cross-marked cakes—the quarters represented the quarters of the Moon. Similar cakes are said to have been eaten by the early Saxons and were the precursors of hot cross buns. In 692 the Council of Constantinople adopted the Crucifix as the official emblem of Christianity, but originally this took the form of the figure of Christ with his arms outstretched, without the Cross.

The first Christian symbol may have been the fish, adopted by early followers when Roman persecution forced them to worship in secret. As an image it signified Christ's feeding of the 5000, and that his disciples were fishermen. Also, Greek was the original language of the New Testament, and *ichthus*, the Greek for 'fish', provided an acrostic for the words *Iesous Christos Theou Uios Soter*, meaning 'Jesus Christ, the Son of God, the Saviour of man'.

Formed by superimposing the Greek letters chi (X) and rho (P), the chi-rho monogram at first represented good luck among pagan peoples, apparently because it contained the first two letters of the Greek word *chrestos*, 'auspicious'. It may have been used as a secret symbol of Christianity by early worshippers, but became a public emblem in the 4th century after being adopted by the future Roman emperor Constantine I.

From the earliest times the circle has represented wholeness and eternity. For the Romans it often symbolised the Universe. In the hand of the goddess Fortuna, the 'wheel of Fortune' became an emblem of life's inconstancy and the impotence of individuals confronted by the randomness of fate.

Since the 1930s the swastika has been associated with the German Nazi Party. Yet this Greek cross with the ends of its arms bent at right angles is an ancient emblem of prosperity and good luck, its name derived from the Sanskrit *svastika*, meaning 'well-being'. It was used in Mesopotamia around 2000 BC, while in ancient China it represented the 'four regions of the world'.

The six-pointed star, also known as the Star of David, was adopted as the emblem of Judaism and has been found as a symbol on Jewish tombstones dating to the 3rd century AD. According to legend, David was carrying a shield in the shape of a hexagram when he killed Goliath.

MAGICAL CREATURES
Symbolic animals

The lions, horses, rhinoceroses and bison drawn on cave walls across France and Spain some 15 000 years ago were probably symbols of danger, speed and strength in the hunt. More recently, in the 17th century, Native Americans erected totem poles, decorating them with carvings of animals, spirits and

ZODIAC MAN *The 15th-century English* Guild Book of the Barber Surgeons *used the zodiac symbols to illustrate the ancient belief that each sign rules a different part of the body. Aries, for example, governs the head, making Arians susceptible to headaches, while Pisceans suffer from problems with their feet.*

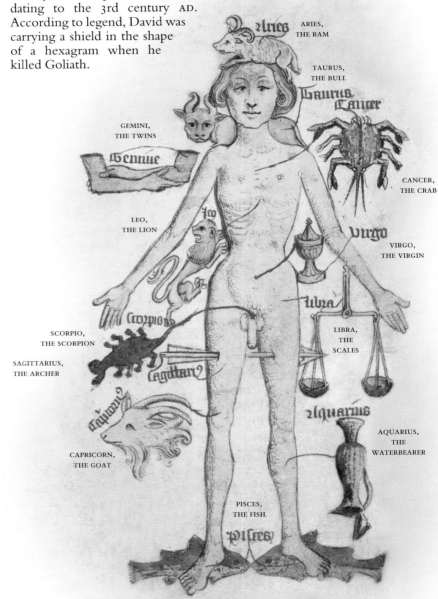

ARIES, THE RAM

TAURUS, THE BULL

GEMINI, THE TWINS

CANCER, THE CRAB

LEO, THE LION

VIRGO, THE VIRGIN

LIBRA, THE SCALES

SCORPIO, THE SCORPION

SAGITTARIUS, THE ARCHER

AQUARIUS, THE WATERBEARER

CAPRICORN, THE GOAT

PISCES, THE FISH

other sacred symbols. These carvings not only identified a tribe or family but also narrated its history and signified its wealth and social status.

Since ancient times astrologers have associated certain animals with individual signs of the zodiac. Although the precise origins of the signs remain mysterious, they were devised in ancient Babylon and Egypt. The Egyptians thought the stars in the constellation of Leo resembled a lion—the Babylonian equivalent was the Great Dog—but the reasons behind other choices were more arbitrary.

The 18-sign zodiac used by the Babylonians from the 6th to the 3rd centuries BC included the Bull of Heaven representing Taurus. From about 650 BC Capricorn was symbolised by a fishtailed goat, a reference to Ea, god of the waters, who taught men how to live. Before Scorpio became a sign of the zodiac, a terrifying scorpion man appeared in a Babylonian

POSTER FOR FINNISH PEACE COMMISSION, ABOUT 1980

epic from before 2000 BC. In the Egyptian zodiac the constellation of Aries was originally identified with both the ram and the goose.

A dove bearing an olive branch was an emblem of the renewal of life associated with the Greek goddess Athena, while in the Old Testament it brought Noah the message that the Flood had subsided. In the New Testament the Holy Spirit descends in the form of a dove at Christ's baptism.

In St John's Gospel, Christ is the sacrificial Lamb of God who 'taketh away the sins of the world', but the lamb also represents his innocence and gentleness. Matthew, Mark, Luke and John, the evangelists, often appear in medieval texts symbolised by, respectively, a man (Christ's humanity), a lion (royalty and the Resurrection), an ox (sacrifice and the Passion) and an eagle (grace and the Ascension).

After opponents called the US presidential candidate Andrew Jackson a jackass in 1828, he defiantly adopted the donkey as his political emblem and it became the Democratic Party's official symbol. The Republicans chose the elephant after the American cartoonist Thomas Nast portrayed the party as an elephant crushing inflation in 1874.

During the Second World War the British 7th Armoured Division adopted the desert rat as its sign. Its 'scurrying and biting' tactics symbolised the strengths of the British soldiers fighting in North Africa.

A CLOSE SHAVE *Until 1745 barbers were also surgeons and their duties included bloodletting, used for a variety of ailments. The red-and-white stripes of the barber's pole represent blood, bandages and the staff gripped by a patient to make the vein swell.*

SELLING SITES
Commercial signs

Shopkeepers in ancient Egypt, Greece and Rome advertised their premises with signs, hoping that the publicity would attract customers. In the town of Pompeii, preserved in volcanic ash after a volcanic eruption in AD 79, signs painted on the whitewashed walls of buildings included bushes or branches of ivy to publicise a tavern—the ivy bush was sacred to Bacchus, the god of wine, and a symbol of revelry. Both the tavern and its sign were introduced into Britain by the Romans after AD 43.

Signs became more common in Europe during the Middle Ages, and by the 14th century English merchants were obliged to place them outside their shops. However, the large, swinging signs that proprietors displayed so enthusiastically sometimes led to accidents, and in the 17th century a ruling required English shopkeepers to mount their signs flat against the walls of their premises, out of harm's way.

The three golden balls above a pawnbroker's shop probably come from the coat of arms of the Medicis, bankers, patrons of the arts and rulers of Florence during the Renaissance. The balls are thought to represent the two-to-one odds against the pawned object being redeemed by its owner.

GIANTS OF THE HILLS

Great figures are incised into the turf of chalk hillsides in many parts of Britain. Some, such as the Uffington Horse in Berkshire (below), were probably created by Celts around 1000 BC. The horse may represent a god or be the badge of a tribe that worshipped horses.

The male figure at Cerne Abbas in Dorset, long associated with fertility, is thought to be some 1500 years old. According to local lore it is the outline of a giant who terrorised the area, stealing sheep, until the people killed him while he slept, preserving his shape by cutting a line around his body.

217

BANNERS OF ALLEGIANCE
Flags and heraldic emblems

Some 5000 years ago the Egyptians and Assyrians carried standards. These poles were topped with metal figures of animals or gods that were thought to give speed or strength. One of the earliest references to a fabric flag dates to the 12th or 11th century BC, when a white flag symbolised the Chinese emperor Zhou's power. From China flags travelled to India, where they were also used in warfare and for signalling. A white flag is first known to have been used to signal a truce in AD 1542.

The first known flag of the Western world, the *vexillum*, was used by Roman soldiers from about 100 BC to replace the standard. A square of either red or purple tasselled cloth decorated with a symbol or inscription, it was designed to be hung from a lance and was carried

FRIEND OR FOE? *When, in the early 1100s, visored helmets made them unrecognisable, soldiers displayed emblems on shields and later on tunics, after which these were known as coats of arms. These became so popular in tournaments that heralds had to regulate their use, hence the term 'heraldry'.*

on horseback. Today the study of flags is known as vexillology.

Flags with symbols were more commonly used from the 12th century, at the time of the Crusades, when the cross was one of the most popular. The Danish white cross on a red field, the oldest flag in continuous use, is said to have fallen from heaven to Valdemar II during the Battle of Lindanisa in 1219.

In the Middle East the crescent sign, originally an ancient Egyptian symbol of the waxing Moon, first appeared on Turkish banners in about 1250. Some 200 years later it became the official symbol of Islam.

When national flags were established in medieval Europe, many rulers chose the flag of their country's patron saint. The red cross of St George was adopted

BATTLE SIGNS *A British ship (left) flies the Red Ensign at the Battle of Camperdown in 1797. From 1864 the Red Ensign was reserved to the Merchant Fleet.*

for the English flag in the 13th century. In 1606, after England and Scotland were united under James I, the Union Flag combined the St George's cross and the white cross of St Andrew, the patron saint of Scotland. Following the union of Great Britain and Ireland in 1801 a redesigned flag incorporated the red cross of St Patrick.

Introduced as a maritime flag, the Union Flag of 1606 came to be known

by the British Navy as a 'Jack', possibly used by sailors as a nickname. The term was well established by the late 1600s.

The first American flag had 13 stripes representing the 13 American colonies, and had the British Union Flag in one corner. In 1777 Congress officially replaced the Union Flag with a blue field containing 13 stars. According to George Washington, the country's first president: 'We take the stars from heaven, the red from our mother country, separating it by white stripes, thus showing that we have separated from her, and the white stripes shall go down to posterity representing liberty.'

SIGNS AND MIMES
Shorthand and manual alphabets

FINGER-SPELLING *An engraving of the 18th century shows the British two-handed manual alphabet used by deaf people. It evolved from systems first published in the late 17th century.*

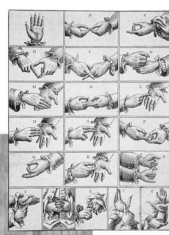

BREAKING THE SILENCE *The French priest Charles-Michel de l'Epée, founder of the first free deaf school in 1760, takes a lesson of young deaf people. He is said to have devised his sign system after meeting two deaf sisters who had their own system of hand signs.*

The ancient Greek writer and soldier Xenophon was said to have devised a form of shorthand while writing memoirs of the philosopher Socrates in the 4th century BC. The first Latin shorthand was invented in 63 BC by a Roman slave, Marcus Tullius Tiro, who needed to record the notoriously long speeches of the politician Cicero. One survivor of his system is the symbol '&', known as the Tironian Sign or ampersand.

Tiro's system flourished in Europe until the medieval Church associated it with sorcery and it was abandoned. In 1588 Timothy Bright, an English doctor, published a 'shorte and new kynde of writing by character' that paired meaning-signs and sound-signs in a manner reminiscent of Egyptian hieroglyphs. Some 200 others followed over the next 250 years, but most were too complicated to be successful. In 1763 Phillip Gibbs introduced the first system to use only phonetic characters.

It was not until 1837, when the English teacher Isaac Pitman published his *Stenographic Soundhand*, that a practical system for everyday use became available. In 1888 competition came from a system published by the

PROTEST AND LIBERATION

The peace cross of the Campaign for Nuclear Disarmament (CND), used since 1958, combines the semaphore signs for N and D in a circle symbolising global unity. In the 1970s feminist and gay liberation movements adopted female and male biological symbols respectively. These were first used in the 1700s by the Swedish taxonomist Carolus Linnaeus. The female symbol ♀ represented Venus, the Roman goddess of love, the male sign ♂ Mars, the Roman god of war.

PEACE CROSS,
20TH CENTURY

Irish-born John Gregg in 1888. Gregg's system still predominates in the USA.

Manual alphabets are another way of representing a language. The simplest is finger-spelling, in which there is a sign for each letter of the alphabet. The earliest recorded two-handed alphabet was devised in 1680 by George Dalgarno, a Scottish teacher. But most deaf people today use a true sign language, which has its own grammar and vocabulary unrelated to any spoken language.

MARKS OF QUALITY
From trademarks to international relief

Under a law of 1266 introduced by Henry III, English bakers were obliged to mark their bread with a seal—the original trademark. In late medieval Europe it became common practice for craftsmen, merchants and others to put their individual marks on products.

When the International Committee of the Red Cross was created in Geneva in 1863 it was proposed that workers should wear white armbands. But perhaps because of the possibility of confusion with signs of truce, a red cross was added. In Muslim countries a red crescent was chosen when, in 1876, the sultan of Turkey objected to the cross's Christian connotations.

ALL SHAPES *The red triangle of Bass is the oldest registered trademark, dating to 1876. Edouard Michelin created the Michelin man in 1898, inspired by a pile of tyres and a sketch of a large man.*

BASS & CO'S PALE ALE
Bass 1/o
IN BOTTLE

SHOWCARD FOR
BASS PALE ALE,
ABOUT 1895

THE MICHELIN
MAN, LATE
20TH CENTURY

219

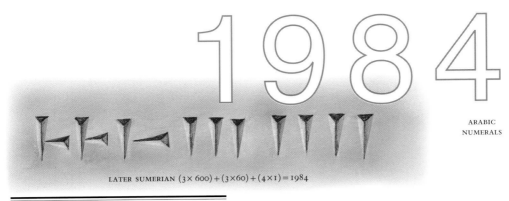

LATER SUMERIAN (3 × 600) + (3×60) + (4×1) = 1984

ARABIC NUMERALS

A YEAR IN NUMBERS *In the Sumerian system, written in cuneiform script and based on the number 60, the positioning of each group of symbols, left to right, denotes its value in hundreds, tens and units. The same is true of the Arabic numerals we use today. Egyptian symbols denote simple additions, while Roman numerals mix addition and subtraction.*

EGYPTIAN NUMERALS

1000×1   + (9×100)   + (8×10)   + (4×1)

ROMAN NUMERALS

MCMLXXXIV

1000 + | (1000 - 100) | + 50 | + (3×10) | + (5-1)

COUNTING UP
Early mathematics

People counted on their fingers long before the 16th century BC when the practice was first recorded by the Egyptians in *The Book of the Dead*, a volume of spells and formulas intended as an aid to the afterlife. Decimals, based on the number ten, evolved from the habit of counting in this way, and 'digit' comes from the Latin *digiti*, 'fingers'.

In about 8000 BC, in the Middle and Near East, arithmetic began. By this time it must have been apparent that for a number to be useful it needed both a name and a means of combining it with other numbers in regular sequences. In the 3rd millennium BC the Egyptians, who counted in tens, worked out a system using different hieroglyphs for units, tens and larger number groups.

From the 3rd millennium BC the Sumerians used a system based on 60—which is 10 multiplied by 6, the number of constellations then known. In this system the wedge-shaped symbol ⟨ represented both 1 and 60, which made the order of the symbols in any written number critical to its interpretation. A modified symbol, a small wedge representing 10, could also be added on, so that ⟨ meant 11 and ⟨ 600.

An ancient table of square roots incised in clay revealed that from about 2000 BC the Babylonians, who inherited their mathematics from the Sumerians, retained the base-60 system for astronomy and pure mathematics, but used a base-ten system for the sums of trade.

Their interest in astronomy led the Babylonians to divide the hour into 60 minutes of 60 seconds. Based on the time the Sun took to circle the heavens (about 360 days), they also devised the 360° circle. From 500 BC the Greeks and Romans used letters of the alphabet as numerals. Roman mathematics was based on the number ten, but involved cumbersome arithmetic.

COUNTING UP *At harvest's end Egyptian scribes of 1400 BC record the amount of garnered grain, on which taxes were based. The Egyptians wrote units, tens and so on, using hieroglyphs read in groups from left to right. They also devised simple fractions.*

ONE AND ZERO
The modern system

Although described as Arabic, the numerals we use today derive, in fact, from a Hindu system developed between the 3rd century BC and the 6th century AD. The earliest record of these numerals, written in Sanskrit, appears on an Indian plate made in about AD 595, featuring the digits 346 in decimal notation. The first known zero was chiselled into a monument in Gwalior, India, about 876. In the 9th century the Hindu system reached Persia, written in scientific tracts. It became known as

SANSKRIT NUMERALS

1   9   8   4

Arabic after being copied in Middle Eastern manuscripts at this time.

In Europe, despite knowledge of the superior Arabic system from Latin works of the early 13th century, Roman numerals were still in use until the late 1500s. So vehement was European hostility to Arabic numerals that in the city of Florence they were banned from all accounting in 1299.

Fractions, which had been familiar to the Babylonians, were adapted to the decimal system by the Austrian mathematician Christoff Rudolff in 1530. Simon Stevin, a Dutch army quartermaster, popularised them in 1585 in his book *De Thiende* (*The Tenth*), but only in the early 17th century did the Scottish mathematician John Napier first use the decimal point as it is employed today to mark the divide between whole units and tenths, hundredths and thousandths.

Mercantile Arithmetic, by Johann Wildman, published in Leipzig in 1489, contains the first recorded use of the symbols + and -, which denoted 'excess' and 'deficiency'. While teaching Rudolff, Heinrich Schrieber used them in 1518 to mean 'add' and 'subtract', and Rudolff included them in his algebra text *Coss* in 1525.

The Greeks wrote their fractions by placing one number over another. The horizontal bar was probably added by the Arabs. Robert Record, an Oxford University mathematician who said that 'no two things can be more equal than a pair of parallel lines', devised the equal sign in the 16th century. The multiplication sign was first used by William Oughtred in England in 1631.

THE BINARY CODE

In 1679 Gottfried Leibniz, the German polymath, published the first description of number systems. This included the binary system, which has a base of two. The idea of base two was not new. In 1605 the English philosopher Francis Bacon had expounded a secret code which used only the letters 'a' and 'b'.

In his *De augmentis scientiarum* of 1623 Bacon wrote that a man 'could express and signify the intentions of his mind by objects…provided those objects be capable of a twofold difference only.' Bacon anticipated by more than 300 years the binary code of computer programs, which use 0 and 1, not a and b. In binary, reading from the right, 10110 is no units, one 2, one 4, no 8, and one 16—making 22 in decimal notation.

SHAPES AND SYMBOLS
Geometry and algebra

Long before it was reformulated in the 6th century BC by Pythagoras, the Greek mathematician, the Babylonians understood the geometry of the right-angled triangle. But the Greek teacher Euclid, who died in about 275 BC, was the first geometrician. In Alexandria, Euclid wrote *Elements*, in which he set out such axioms as 'a straight line is the shortest distance between two points'. When asked by Ptolemy I of Alexandria to make his proofs easier to follow, Euclid, believing he had stated eternal truths, uttered the rebuke: 'There is no

royal road to geometry.' *Elements* later became the most successful textbook ever, running to over 1000 editions after the invention of printing in the 1450s.

Algebraic calculations were made in about 1700 BC by the Egyptian mathematician Ahmes. Two millennia later, in about AD 275, the Greek mathematician Diophantus devised a series of symbols to represent unknown quantities and invented quadratic equations.

The word 'algebra' stems ultimately from the Arabic text, *Hisâb al jabr w'al muqâbalah* (*The Science of Reunion and Opposition*), published in AD 830. *Al-jabr* was translated into Latin and came into English as 'algebra'. In the 16th century the French mathematician François

MATHEMATICAL RECORD *The first printed book on geometry was written by Luca Pacioli of Venice in 1494, illustrated here with the tools of his profession.*

WRITTEN EVIDENCE *The Greek mathematician Euclid's proof of Pythagoras' theorem of the right-angled triangle, completed in the 6th century BC, was translated in the 13th century AD in this Arabic manuscript.*

Viète used a series of letters as symbols for unknown numbers, but favoured the Latin term 'analysis' over 'algebra'.

In the century that followed, Viète's compatriot René Descartes combined algebra and geometry, showing in 1637 that any point on a two-dimensional surface could be located by two numbers, each representing distances along straight lines drawn at right angles to each other. These coordinates were soon being used for graphs, then maps.

SKINTIGHT A 12th-century monk stretches hide on a frame before scraping it smooth to make parchment.

WRITING SURFACES
Papyrus and paper

According to legend a Chinese courtier named Ts'ai Lun discovered paper in AD 105. Noticing scraps of rotting rag and tree bark floating on water, Ts'ai picked up the pieces on a screen, drained off the water and proceeded to write on the dried material. In fact, paper may already have been produced for two centuries, replacing both wood and silk as writing surfaces in China.

Papyrus, made from dried reeds, was used as a writing material in ancient Egypt from about 3000 BC. Parchment and vellum (made from processed animal hides) were used in the 2nd century BC at Pergamum, in modern-day Turkey, and gradually replaced papyrus in Mediterranean countries over the following centuries. Paper made from linen rags, and hemp and flax cords, appeared in the Middle East during the 8th century, although parchment remained the preferred material for religious works and legal documents. Paper reached Europe from Muslim Spain in the 10th century AD.

Following the fall of the Spanish Umayyad dynasty in the 11th century, paper continued to be used by the Christian conquerors. As it became more common across Europe, paper-mills were built, the first in England dating from about 1494. These mills

KEEPING A RECORD From steel-nibbed Georgian varieties to the plastic ball-points of the 20th century, modern pens have left traditional quills far behind. Portable inkwells and propelling pencils first appeared in the 19th century, when wood and straw began to be used to make paper.

REED OF KINGS This papyrus, from about 1200 BC, was produced under a monopoly of the pharaohs. The word 'paper' comes from 'papyrus', an Egyptian term for 'the royal'.

struggled to obtain enough linen to meet the demand for paper. Many countries therefore banned the export of this raw material, and in 16th-century England it was made illegal to bury the dead in linen shrouds.

With the rise of both literacy and newspapers, the demand for paper increased further in the 17th century. The continued use of rags and cloth made large-scale production impossible, until in 1800 Mathias Koops, a

Dutchman, patented a paper made from straw and wood. Three years later the first functional paper-making machine was built at Frogmore, Kent, by the engineer Bryan Donkin. The principle of his machine—pouring a suspension of fibre and water onto a vibrating wire mesh conveyor belt to produce a continuous sheet of paper—remains in use.

HARMONISED PRODUCTION *A team of 3rd-century BC Chinese workers manufacture paper. Wood and straw are gathered, ground and beaten, boiled in water, then left to dry.*

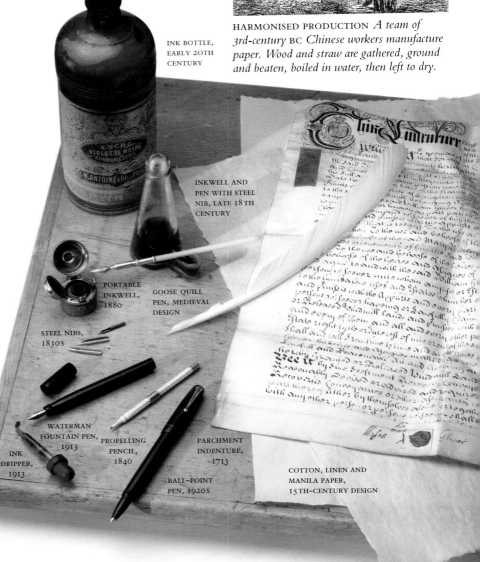

INK BOTTLE, EARLY 20TH CENTURY

INKWELL AND PEN WITH STEEL NIB, LATE 18TH CENTURY

PORTABLE INKWELL, 1880

GOOSE QUILL PEN, MEDIEVAL DESIGN

STEEL NIBS, 1830S

WATERMAN FOUNTAIN PEN, 1913

PROPELLING PENCIL, 1840

INK DRIPPER, 1913

BALL-POINT PEN, 1920S

PARCHMENT INDENTURE, 1713

COTTON, LINEN AND MANILA PAPER, 15TH-CENTURY DESIGN

TOOLS FOR INSCRIPTION
Pen and ink

Words in pictures, or pictographs, were drawn on cave walls with ink. Prehistoric people used both black pigment made from charcoal and iron oxide in shades between bright yellow and dark brown, mixed with animal fat, to form viscous writing materials. Ink got its name from the Greek practice of fixing colours by heating them. It derives from the word *enkaiein*, which means 'to burn in'.

The ancient Egyptian scribes worked with a palate holding two 'ink cakes'. Black (from carbon) and red (from ochre) were mixed with gum, dried, then rubbed with a wet brush made from rush stems to make a liquid. In 2000 BC Chinese scribes used a durable ink made from soot mixed with gum solution, writing on wooden strips using a bamboo pen. In the 3rd century BC the Romans used the same method of writing as the Egyptians, and also scratched text with a stylus, a sharp

VICTORIAN LETTER *Having dipped the nib of her pen in an inkwell, a young lady sits down to write. In the mid 1800s the English inventor Joseph Gillot introduced three slits into the nib, making it more flexible.*

WRITING WITH 'LEAD'

A large oak tree in Borrowdale, Cumbria, is said to have been uprooted during a fierce storm in 1564, revealing a deposit of 'black lead'. No one knows who first realised that graphite made an ideal marking substance, but in 1565 the Swiss-German naturalist Conrad Gesner described a stylus of graphite encased in wood.

In 1858 the American Hyman Lipman had the idea of producing a pencil with a glued-in rubber. Four years later he sold the patent for his implement for $100 000.

---

pointed tool, into a wax-coated tablet. The advantage of writing on wax was that the tablet could be easily smoothed over and reused.

Two new inks appeared in medieval Europe. One was prepared by combining iron salt and oak galls, producing a liquid that became dark brown with age. The other was made by suspending carbon from soot in a mixture of gum and water, but this needed constant stirring to stop it solidifying.

By the 13th century quill pens, made of sharpened goose feathers, were used throughout Europe. Such quills had been used by the Romans from about 500 BC, reappearing in Spain in the 7th century AD.

Metal pens were made at least from the late 16th century but these were rare and largely ornamental. A steel nib was developed in 1803 by Bryan Donkin, but it proved less flexible than the quill and was corroded by the ink.

By the late 1820s nibbed pens were commercially available. In 1832 a John Joseph Parker became the first to overcome successfully the difficulties of producing a pen that had its own reservoir of ink. But fountain pens did not catch on until, in 1884, the American inventor Lewis E. Waterman developed the first

---

practical version using the noncorrosive inks that were newly available.

Various designs of ball-point pens appeared after the first was patented in 1888 by the American inventor John L. Loud. But they did not become commercially successful until 1938, when the Hungarian brothers Ladislao and Georg Biro produced a model using quick-drying ink. Launched in 1943, it sold by the million.

KEYBOARD PRINTING
The typewriter

DESKTOP MACHINES *By about 1900, typewriters were providing many women with a 'respectable' profession. Female typists in Britain made their debut in 1887, at the Inland Revenue Office, London.*

Handwriting continued as the mainstay of offices until typewriters usurped calligraphy's monopoly. Henry Mill, the English inventor, had patented an artificial writing machine in 1714, but the earliest typewriter was not built until 1808. It was designed for the blind Italian Countess Carolina Fantoni to write her letters, but its mechanism remains unknown.

In 1866 two Americans, Christopher Latham Sholes and Carlos Glidden, produced a workable typewriter. Seven years later Sholes signed a contract with E. Remington and Sons, the New York gunmakers, who made the first mass-produced typewriters. One early buyer was Mark Twain, the first author to submit a typewritten manuscript, of *Life on the Mississippi*. The electric typewriter was invented by Thomas Alva Edison, the American scientist, in 1872, and first sold by a Connecticut firm, Blickensderfer, in 1902.

PRINT SPREADS THE WORD

'He who first shortened the labour of copyists by device of Movable Types
*was disbanding hired armies, and cashiering most Kings and Senates,
and creating a whole new democratic world: he had invented the art of printing.'*

Sartor Resartus, THOMAS CARLYLE, HISTORIAN AND ESSAYIST, 1833-4

MARK OF THE ENGLISH PRINTER
WYNKYN DE WORDE, 16TH CENTURY

The first prints were woodcuts, made by the Chinese from at least the 7th century AD. They cut spaces around an image on a flat wooden surface to make a raised 'negative' and then applied ink to it and transferred the image onto paper. This process of relief printing is thought to have evolved either from 'chops', ornately designed seals of Chinese characters used for stamping documents, or from the common practice of making inked rubbings from inscriptions. Like paper, relief printing spread west towards Europe at a snail's pace. It was not until the 14th century that designs were printed on European textiles, and playing cards made from pieces of printed paper.

The development of typography—printing which used movable pieces of metal, each with a raised letter—made possible the mass production of letters, words and phrases on pages. Because the Chinese language consists of many thousands of characters and symbols, China was not the ideal place for movable type to evolve. The new process of typography developed, instead, in medieval Europe.

In about 1450 Johann Gensfleisch, known as Gutenberg, perfected the art of printing in Mainz, Germany. He discovered a relatively soft alloy made of antimony, lead and tin. With this

Gutenberg was able to cast letter shapes and found that they were durable enough to withstand repeated use. He also devised an ink made of boiled-oil varnish and lampblack, to coat the metal, and adapted presses used for making wine and paper to imprint ink on to a page.

Modern books have their origins in Gutenberg's productions. Among his first volumes were the Donatus *Latin Grammar* created in about 1450, the 42-line Latin Bible (so called from the number of lines in each column), completed by 1455, and in 1460 the *Catholicon*, an early encyclopedia. No more than 200 copies of each book were printed. The pages were decorated with hand-painted illuminations. Printed books began to spread rapidly across Europe. By 1500, more than 9 million copies had been published.

Although the printing process remained basically unchanged for 400 years, different styles of lettering or 'typefaces' evolved. Gutenberg's first typeface imitated the handwriting styles of local scribes. *The Origins of Everyday Things* is printed in Bembo, designed in the 1490s by Francesco Griffo of Bologna. Its name derives from the Italian cardinal Pietro Bembo, whose tract *De Aetna* appeared in the new typeface.

Modern typefaces, which are designed on computers by creating letters on grids consisting of small squares called 'pixels', trace their origins back to 17th-century France. A committee of scholars was established by Louis XIV in 1692 to develop a new typeface based on

SET TO LAST *Printers prepare to print pages in a 17th-century workshop. One uses ink pads to ink the type in an iron frame, the 'chase'. This will then be covered with paper and put into the hand press, which will press the paper onto the inked type.*

TYPECASE

'scientific principles'. By dividing a page into more than 2000 tiny squares, the scholars proceeded to design a precise typeface, Romain du Roi, in a similar manner.

Lithography, named from the Greek words for 'stone writing', was invented in about 1796 by Aloys Senefelder, a Bavarian playwright, and used to print his dramas. In this technique a greasy crayon was used to draw on a polished limestone surface. The stone was then wetted and, since grease repels water, the greasy areas remained dry. Greasy ink was then applied, which adhered only to the crayon grease. Paper laid on the stone then picked up ink, creating a reproduction of the image on paper. From the 1870s limestone was replaced by metal plates.

The Linotype machine was patented in 1884 by Ottmar Mergenthaler, a German-born American inventor who was working in Baltimore. It cast lines of type from molten metal, and was controlled by a typesetter operating a keyboard. Complete pages of lines of type could be created in this way, without the need to arrange letters individually by hand. Two years later early models of the Linotype machine were used to print the *New York Tribune.*

In 1939 the American physicist Chester Carlson patented the first copying machine, which was operated by a process he called 'electrophotography'. It was later named 'xerography', from the Greek for 'dry writing'. Documents placed on a glass screen were copied by having their image focused on an electrically charged plate dusted with a negatively charged powder. The powder then stuck to the positive charge left by the image, which was transferred, with the help of heat, to a blank sheet of paper.

The Haloid Company in New York welcomed the invention in 1947 after 20 other companies had shown Carlson the door. In 1949 the Xerox Copier Machine Model A was launched and three years later the trademark Xerox was registered. Subsequently the name became synonymous with the photocopier.

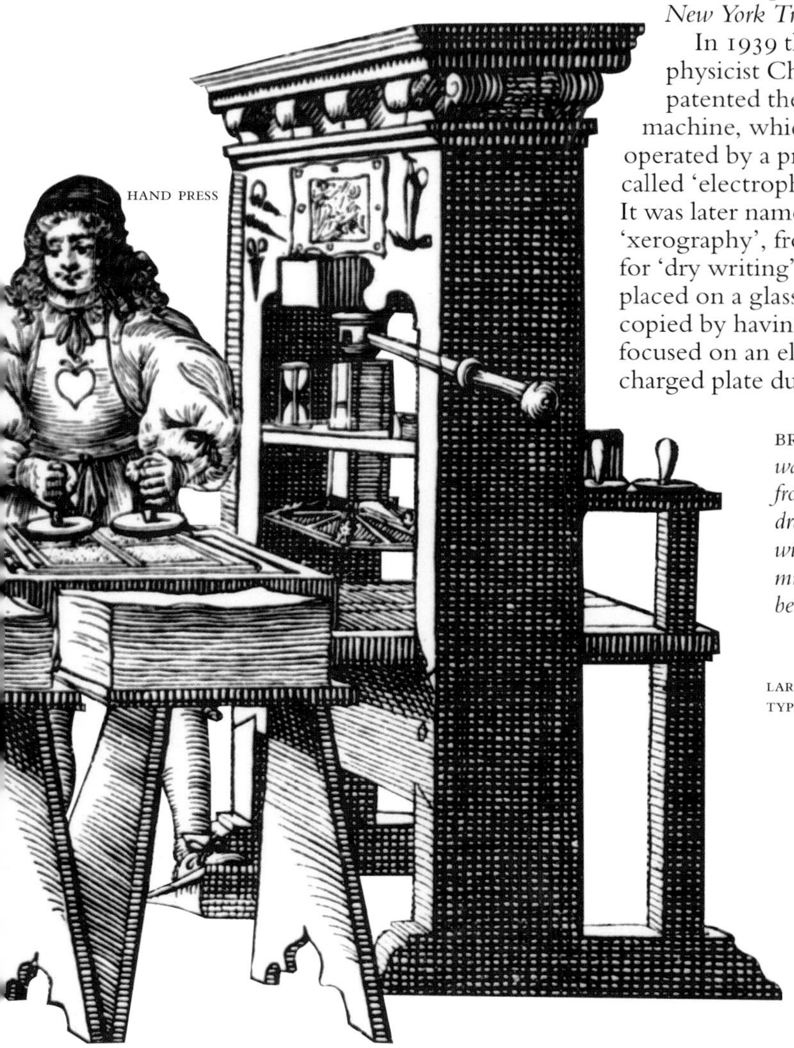

HAND PRESS

BRIGHT TINTS *Lithography was used for printing posters from the 19th century. By drawing on separate stones with several pigments, a multicoloured image could be produced.*

LARGE WOODEN TYPE, MID 1900S

SPELLING IT OUT *From the 15th to the 20th century printers have kept movable metal type in a 'typecase'. From here selected letters were made into words on a 'composing stick', adjustable to a column width by a screw or lever. Once the stick was full, the block of type was put on a tray, a 'galley'—the name still given to a printed page proof.*

WOODEN TYPECASE WITH SMALL CAST-METAL TYPE, MID 1900S

METAL GILL SANS TYPE, 36-POINT

METAL COMPOSING STICK, LATE 1800S

FOLIES-BERGERE

La Loïe Fuller

ILLUMINATED
MANUSCRIPT
LETTER, FRANCE,
12 TH CENTURY

form long scrolls, and rollers were attached at either end. As readers progressed through the text, they furled one roller while unfurling the other.

In China narrow strips of wood or bamboo inscribed with text were lashed together with cords to create small works from about 1300 BC. Wax tablets bound into books appeared in the

BOUND IN BOOKS
From clay to parchment

As the first civilisations developed they needed to record information so that it could be circulated and preserved. The Sumerian system of writing known as cuneiform evolved from simple pictographs around 3500 BC and was later used to inscribe royal annals, legal codes and epic stories on rectangular clay tablets. Particularly important ones were cased singly in clay 'envelopes'.

Papyrus, the main alternative to clay, was first used in ancient Egypt. Individual sheets were stuck together to

---

EPOCHS OF INFORMATION

- The oldest surviving 'cookery book' was inscribed on stone tablets in Mesopotamia around 1700 BC. The recipes were mainly for meat stews, usually boiled in milk and blood.
- Book tokens, like paperbacks, were a product of the 1930s Depression. They were launched in 1932 by the English bookseller Harold Raymond.
- CD-ROMs, introduced in 1982, enhance the written word with video sequences, graphics and sound on a computer. A disk can store as much data as about 200 000 book pages.

8th century BC in Assyria. Each of the beeswax 'sheets', dyed yellow with an arsenic-based pigment known as orpiment, was contained in a frame of ivory or wood and inscribed with a bone or bronze stylus. Hinged along one side, the frames made a fan-folded book.

Around the 1st century AD a Roman *codex*, mainly used for inscribing laws, appeared. Consisting of parchment leaves fastened together, this was the direct ancestor of the modern book.

By the 4th century papyrus, which grew only in certain places, had been superseded throughout Christendom by more widely available parchment. To create a book a large sheet of parchment or vellum (made from calfskin) was folded into a folio of two pages, a quarto of four or an octavo of eight pages. Grouped together into sets of leaves or quires, they were first cut, then sewn together with cords before being attached to a backing of leather.

READY REFERENCE
Encyclopedias and dictionaries

One of the earliest printed books was Johann Gutenberg's *Catholicon* of 1460, which continued a tradition of encyclopedias dating back to the ancient Greeks. In the 4th century BC the philosophers Aristotle and Plato had planned a cultural survey of society, incorporating philosophy and natural history. Fragments of their project, the first encyclopedia, survive in the work of Plato's nephew, the scholar Speusippos. By the 1st century AD encyclopedias had taken their modern form as vast anthologies of facts, such as the Roman author Pliny's *Historica Naturalis*.

In 18th-century Europe the encyclopedia once again assumed a position of importance. Edited in 35 volumes by the French philosopher

Tom Jones, NOVEL BY HENRY FIELDING, FOUR VOLUMES, 1750 EDITION

A POLITICAL COMMENTARY BY GEORGE BATE, 1652 EDITION

PAN'S PAPERBACK EDITION OF JACK KEROUAC'S NOVEL, 1963

The Pickwick Papers BY CHARLES DICKENS, 1850S

STRAIGHT-TO-PAPERBACK EDITION OF HAROLD NICOLSON'S ANALYSIS, 1940

TRACT AND FICTION *As literacy spread in 17th-century Britain, political books increased in number. The novel, invented in the 18th century, found a mass audience with Charles Dickens. The mid-20th-century paperback put literature in the pocket.*

Denis Diderot between 1751 and 1780, the *Encyclopédie* offered a complete review of the arts and sciences of the day. It was a far more ambitious project than the publisher intended when he commissioned Diderot to translate the Englishman Ephraim Chambers's *Cyclopaedia*, the first edition of which appeared in 1728. The *Encyclopaedia Britannica*, first published in 1768, was created to bring some objectivity to Diderot's highly personal work.

Reference information was also compiled in ancient dictionaries. The Akkadians of Mesopotamia produced a list of words in the 7th century BC—the oldest known dictionary. But only in the early 18th century was a definitive work on the English language completed. In 1707 Humphrey Wanley, a member of the Royal Society, requested a work to 'fix' the English language. Samuel Johnson, the English writer, responded, and with six assistants recorded 43 500 words and 118 000 illustrative quotations by 1755.

The Philological Society was established in 1842 to prepare the first English dictionary to be based on historical principles. After several decades of research the dictionary was completed in 1928. Five years later the 13 volume, 16 400 page work was published under its new title, *The Oxford English Dictionary*.

ALDUS MANUTIUS'S LOGO, 16TH CENTURY

MATCHING PICTURES *The philosopher Denis Diderot's 18th-century* Encyclopédie *included 12 volumes illustrating the text. This plate shows the mechanism of a cannon.*

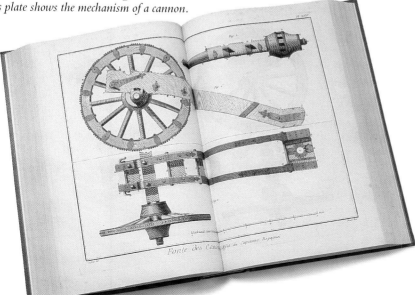

POPULAR READING
Books for all

Popular paperbacks have their roots in 16th-century Italy, where small, portable and relatively inexpensive texts were first published in Venice by Aldus Manutius in 1501. To make his scholarly titles accessible to a wider audience, Manutius printed runs of 1000, instead of the usual 250 copies, and used an italic typeface to fit more words onto each page. Since his methods were widely imitated he devised one of the first publisher's logos, a dolphin and anchor, to protect his editions against unauthorised copying.

The novel, the only literary genre to appear after the invention of mechanical printing, revolutionised reading habits. Prose fiction had been available since the 1650s, but it was *Robinson Crusoe*, Daniel Defoe's novel of 1719, that brought secular books to a mass audience.

By the 1820s cloth cases around stiff covers began to replace leather, so that in the 1850s George Routledge's Railway Library of novels could be sold for just one shilling (five pence). But the true paperback was not created until 1935 when Allen Lane launched his Penguin series. As a travelling salesman weighed down with casebound books, Lane had decided that the future lay in paper covers.

HOLY SCRIBE *A saint illustrated in a medieval manuscript copies a text in a 'scriptorium', or writing room. Until the advent of printing in the 1450s, all books were laboriously produced by hand.*

LIBRARY COLLECTIONS
Books to consult and borrow

Libraries existed in both Babylonia and Egypt before 2000 BC. Founded in the 3rd century BC, at Alexandria in Egypt, the largest Greek library was reputed to have held as many as 700 000 scrolls. Private libraries became popular in the Roman Empire, and bookshops traded from the 1st century BC.

In England in 1602 the diplomat Sir Thomas Bodley restored a medieval library in Oxford. Eight years later the government's publishing body, the Stationer's Company, resolved to give the Bodleian a copy of every new book made in Britain. The British Museum Library, now the British Library, was awarded the same privilege in 1753.

During the 18th and 19th centuries subscription lending libraries flourished. Some still survive, such as the London Library, founded in 1841. Free public libraries were established by Act of Parliament in 1850.

...tion ruin. It was as much as our Heavy Cavalry Brigade could do to cover the retreat of the miserable remnants of that band of heroes as they returned to the place they had so lately quitted in all the pride of life. At 11 35 not a British soldier, except the dead and dying, was left in front of these bloody Muscovite guns. Our loss, as far as it could be ascertained, in killed, wounded, and missing at 2 o'clock to-day, was as follows:—

	Went into Action. Strength.	Returned from Action.	Loss.
4th Light Dragoons ...	118	39	79
8th Hussars ...	104	38	66
11th Hussars ...	110	25	85
13th Light Dragoons ...	130	61	69
17th Lancers ...	145	35	110
	607	198	409

It is not certain that all these were killed, wounded, or missing; many may still come in, and about 80 wounded have already returned. Captain Nolan was killed by the first shot fired, as he rode in advance of the Hussars, cheering them on. Lord Lucan was slightly wounded. Lord Cardigan received a lance thrust through his clothes. Major Halkett, of the 4th Light Dragoons, was killed. Lord Fitzgibbon, of the 8th Hussars, was desperately wounded, and has since, I fear, died. Cornet Houghton, of the 11th Hussars, is killed. Captains Goad and Oldham and Cornet Montgomery, of the 13th Light Dragoons, are killed. Captain White and Lieutenant Thomson, of the 17th Lancers, are killed. Captain Charteris, 92d Foot, Aide-de-Camp to Lord Lucan, is killed. Captain Morris, who was ...

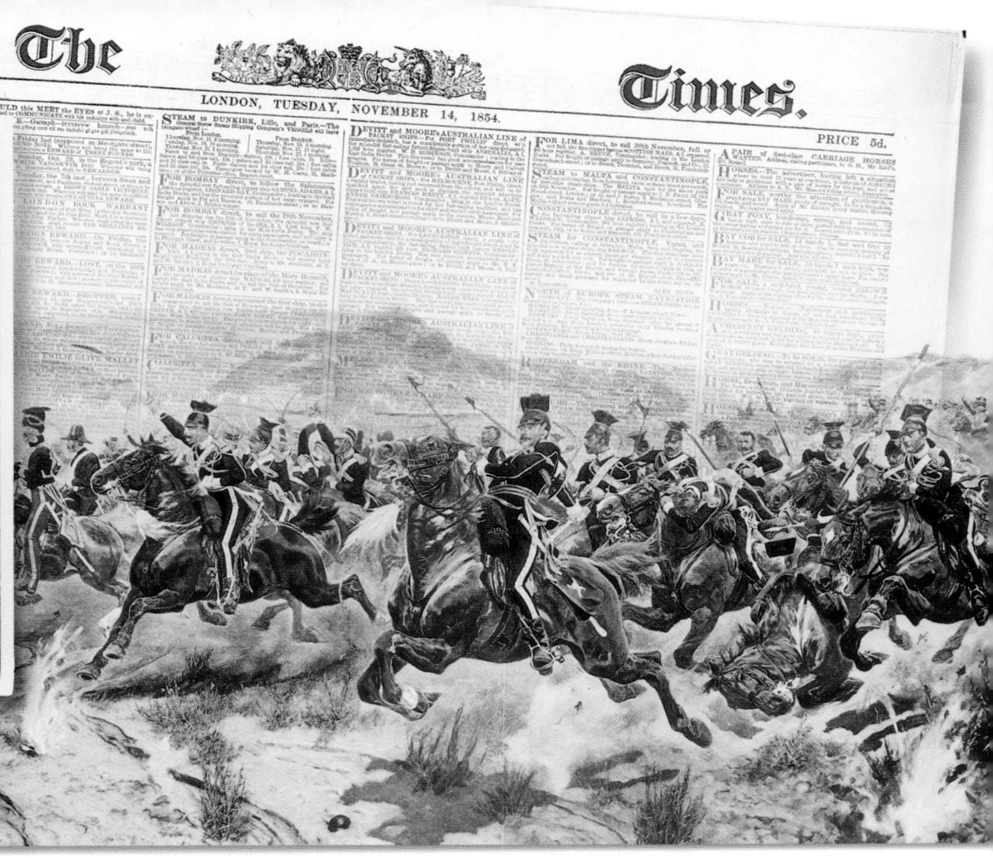

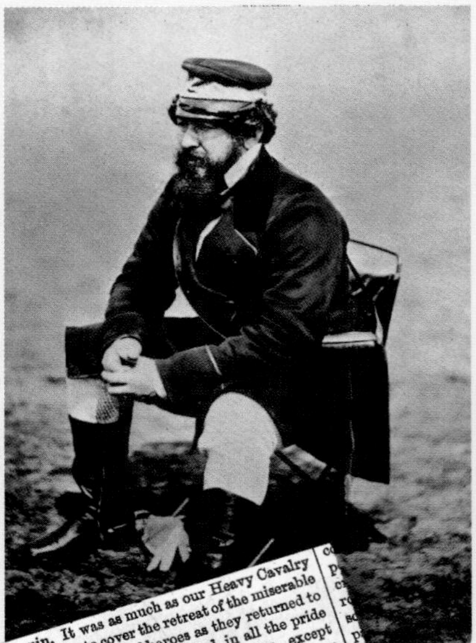

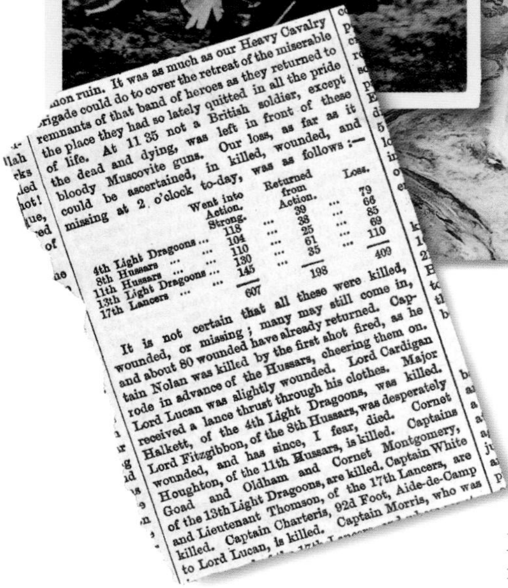

FROM THE VALLEY OF DEATH *Among the earliest full-time war correspondents was William Howard Russell (above, left), who reported on the Crimean War for* The Times. *Russell wrote about the Charge of the Light Brigade on October 25, 1894, recording the huge number of dead and wounded (left).*

REPORTING EVENTS

Current affairs

In the public meeting places or *fora* of ancient Rome, in about 60 BC, the first news reports were posted on walls to keep the public informed. A government gazette, the *Acta Diurna* or *Daily Events*, featured official announcements together with reports of battles, gladiatorial games and astrological omens.

A system of mass news reportage was also developed in China during the Han dynasty (202 BC to AD 220). Summaries of events written by postmasters in distant parts of the empire would be delivered back to court. The *Pao*, or *Peking Gazette*, a sheet distributed to civil servants, appeared during the Tang dynasty (618 to 906) and provided the latest court news.

'Broadsheets' were originally single pages published in late-15th-century Europe by the Church and state. They mixed propaganda with sensationalised reports of such events as floods and mystical visions, and were illustrated with woodcuts to aid the illiterate.

A short pamphlet of 1513, entitled *The True Encounter*, is the first known published account of a contemporary event by an eyewitness. Describing the Battle of Flodden, in which the English army defeated the troops of James IV of Scotland, it was written and printed by an Englishman, Richard Faques.

In the 17th century single-page news sheets printed with 'relations' of events were read by an educated elite some time after the events had taken place. There were also 'diurnalls' (weekly reports) in book form, political 'mercuries' (named after the Roman messenger of the gods) and government news 'intelligencers'.

Dutch *corantos*, 'currents of news', appeared in the 1620s. They provided news of the week's political events in Europe, printed for the first time on folded sheets of paper, the form used by today's newspapers. The first daily was *The Daily Courant*, which reported on international affairs to a small London readership from 1702. The *Evening Post*, first printed in 1706, was aimed at a wider audience and was published three times a week to coincide with the mail coaches leaving London.

Not until 1779 was a Sunday paper launched—Elizabeth Johnson's *British Gazette and Sunday Monitor*, which contained a summary of the week's news and a religious column. 'It kills a few hours of this dull morning and pleads an excuse for a preference of a coffee-house box to a chapel-pew,' quipped William Davies in his satire of 1786, *News the Malady*.

GENTLEMEN OF THE PRESS

'News' writers were plying their trade by the 1600s in Japan. They compiled single-page gossip sheets, containing information collected by traders who travelled around the country. News gatherers in 18th-century London congregated around the Royal Exchange and St Paul's Cathedral. After gleaning business and political news from men of affairs, they would rush to sell information to publishers. Full-time reporters were first employed by newspapers in the 19th century.

MASS CIRCULATION
Headlines and tabloids

Headlines to catch readers' attention evolved from the 17th century. By the 1770s the events of the American War of Independence merited such punchy titles as 'Detroit is Taken'. In Britain taxes on paper meant editors avoided such an extravagant use of space. Only after taxes were abolished in 1855 were headlines truly exploited.

The Times, the oldest surviving title, was launched by a bankrupt coal merchant, John Walter, to pay off his debts. It was originally published as the *Daily Universal Register* in 1785. Appealing to an educated readership, it

prospered as *The Times*, the enduring name it was given in 1788. It was also known as 'The Thunderer', a nickname it lived up to when it published an article on the Reform Bill in 1831, urging people to 'thunder for reform'.

The first tabloid—with half-size pages—was produced by the British editor Alfred Harmsworth on January 1, 1900, as a special millennium issue of New York's *The World*. He relaunched the *Daily Mirror*, his ailing newspaper for 'gentlewomen', as Britain's first tabloid in 1904, with immediate success.

PERIODIC DIVERSIONS
The magazine business

The Gentleman's Magazine, published from 1731, was one of the first magazines to use the word, derived from the Arabic *makhzan*, meaning 'storehouse'. Periodicals had made their appearance in the previous century. The edifying *Monthly Discussions* was the first, published by the German theologian Johann Rist in 1663. Nine years later in France a more frivolous type was launched with *Le Mercure Galant*, containing poetry and court gossip.

In England the similarly lightweight *Athenian Gazette* (retitled the *Athenian Mercury* after only one issue) began publication in 1690. Made anxious by an extramarital affair he was conducting, its publisher John Dunton had the idea of the 'problem page' in 1691. The advisers, the original agony aunts, were in fact men. Rising literacy levels among women led Dunton to launch *The Ladies' Mercury*, the first magazine for women, in 1693.

Literary magazines appeared in the 18th century. Among the first was the *Museum* of 1746, which mainly printed book reviews. In the 19th century magazines were used as forums for serialised novels. Several works of Charles Dickens were printed in magazines that he himself edited, including *The Old Curiosity Shop* which appeared in 1840-1 in *Master Humphrey's Clock*.

BULLETIN BOY *By 1914 sensational stories, boldly advertised on street newsstands, had pushed the sales of popular daily papers to over a million a day.*

FUNNY PICTURES
Caricatures, cartoons and comic strips

Caricatures parody, often cruelly, a person's distinctive features. The word derives from the Italian *caricatura*, meaning 'exaggeration', which was used in the 17th century. In the 1740s the English printer Arthur Pond published the first collection of caricatures to be bound in a volume. Using punning titles to identify his subjects while also avoiding libel actions, Pond's comic portraits appeared in *The London Magazine* and *Town and Country Magazine*.

Comic strips have their roots in 16th-century Germany where religious tales were printed from woodcuts in a series of images, following a 'strip' format, onto a single piece of paper. The first regular comic-strip character in a newspaper was Richard Outcault's 'Yellow Kid'. He appeared in *The New York World* after its owner Joseph Pulitzer introduced a comic-strip page in 1894. Such was the bald, flap-eared boy's popular appeal that the rival press baron William Randolph Hearst poached him for a supplement to his *New York Journal*.

FIRST ISSUE OF
Punch, 1841

JOURNALISTIC MILESTONES

• 1621 The printer Nathaniel Butter published an English newspaper in London. It had no fixed title and appeared, more or less, weekly.
• 1711 Mary de la Rivière became the first female newspaper editor, of England's *The Examiner*.
• 1841 *Punch*, a magazine dedicated to satirising the British way of life, was launched.
• 1885 *Good Housekeeping*, which tested consumer goods, was published in the United States.
• 1888 Britain's *Financial Times* appeared, printed on pink paper to distinguish itself from its rivals.

GERMAN
LETTER
CARRIER,
16TH
CENTURY

BY POST
Conveying letters

The original role of mail systems was to bind together the outposts of empires. The ancient Egyptians had postal services from about 2000 BC. A thousand years later the Zhou dynasty in China probably used horses for carrying mail between post houses.

In Greece the small city-states relied on local, fleet-footed messengers from about the 8th century BC, but it was the Roman Empire that developed a postal system which, by the 1st century BC, was so efficient that it remained unrivalled until the 19th century. With post houses set at regular intervals along an extensive road network, distances of more than 270 km (170 miles) were traversed by letter carriers in 24 hours.

In medieval Europe the post, which had lapsed with the demise of Rome, was revived for business correspondence, allowing traders and merchants to maintain contacts with customers. Demand for postal systems for private letters increased from the late 1400s as more people learned to read. One of the most successful systems belonged to the Thurn and Taxis family, patronised by the Habsburg emperors and based in Bergamo in Italy. By the 1500s up to 20000 of their couriers were delivering post over most of Europe.

Two government-controlled postal systems were also established at this time. In 1477 Louis XI of France set up a royal service with 230 couriers, and in 1516 Henry VIII of England appointed a Master of the Posts to ensure a regular service for official letters.

REGULAR DELIVERIES
From mail coach to postcode

In 1680, to meet London's increasing volume of letters, a merchant named William Dockwra created an urban postal service. His 'penny post' proved an immediate success. Letters were pre-paid and stamped with their place and time of posting and delivered by post boys. Two years later the Master of the Posts shut the service down, then reopened it under government control.

By the 18th century speedier systems were needed to satisfy Britain's growing industries. In 1782 John Palmer, the manager of a Bath theatre, suggested using mail coaches along the London to Bath route. Subsequently horse-drawn coaches reduced the journey from three days to 16 hours, and were quickly adopted countrywide.

Demand reached mass proportions in the 19th century. In 1840 the British administrator Rowland Hill saw his proposal for a uniform postage rate of one penny on letters weighing ½ ounce (14 grams) adopted. Simultaneously Hill introduced 'a bit of paper just large enough to bear the stamp, and covered at the back with a glutinous wash'—the adhesive stamp.

In the 11 months from May 1840 that Penny Blacks were on sale, some 68 million were printed. Until 1847, when a machine was invented for perforating sheets of stamps, clerks were obliged to cut them up manually. Stamp collecting began almost immediately.

In 1842 *The Times* published a personal advertisement from 'a young lady being desirous of covering her dressing-room with cancelled postage stamps'. In 1864 a French collector, George Herpin, coined the word 'philately', from the Greek 'to love what is tax-free', referring to the fact that stamps made letters free to the receiver for the first time.

Clay envelopes existed to protect texts in Mesopotamia around 1900 BC,

COLLECTION POINTS *Fifteen years after the launch of the Penny Black stamp in 1840 the Post Office placed six pillar boxes on the streets of London. The boxes were so popular that by 1900 there were 32 593 across Britain.*

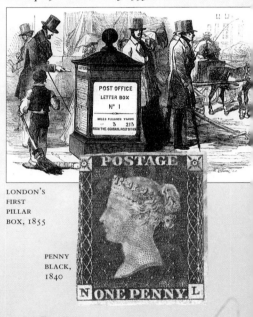

LONDON'S
FIRST
PILLAR
BOX, 1855

PENNY
BLACK,
1840

FIRST BRITISH
ILLUSTRATED
POSTCARD, 1894

WISH YOU WERE HERE *British postcards did not carry pictures until 1894. Once small scenes or 'vignettes' appeared, postcards ceased to be prepaid, and the sender was required to attach a halfpenny stamp on the reverse side.*

THROUGH THE MAIL

• Because birds carrying messages were often killed in flight by hawks, medieval Arabs made a habit of sending important messages twice.

• George Gerard devised the 'Jiffy' bag with his son in the 1960s after hearing a story of how a mouse made itself a nest by tearing old newspapers to shreds. The name referred to the fact that goods could be packed quickly, 'in a jiffy'.

• Postcodes were originally used in war-torn Germany in 1944. To aid with mechanised sorting, postcodes that could be read by machines were introduced in Britain in 1959.

• The General Post Office's express service, introduced in 1891, allowed for living creatures to be sent by post. In 1909 two suffragettes, campaigning for women's voting rights, were sent by express post to 10 Downing Street after Prime Minister Herbert Asquith refused to meet them. The police were powerless to intercept the post, but the Prime Minister's butler refused to accept the delivery.

GERMAN WOODCUT
OF THE MIDDLE
EASTERN PIGEON
POST, ABOUT
14TH CENTURY

but until the Penny Black, packaging for letters proved unpopular because it added to their weight and therefore to the expense of postage. Instead, letters were folded, sealed with wax and then addressed. Hill's uniform penny charge heralded the return of the envelope.

Pillar boxes appeared in Italy in 1850 and two years later were experimentally introduced in St Helier in Jersey by the novelist Anthony Trollope, who was a Post Office employee for 33 years. In 1853 Botchergate in Carlisle boasted

BY EXPRESS *Post Office stagecoaches pass on the road to Leeds in about 1830. Such was the speed of the service that letters posted to London from the north of England were generally delivered the next day.*

the first pillar box on mainland Britain, coloured bronze-green. Two years after France established a nationwide parcel post in 1881, a similar service was set up in Britain, and 'letter carriers' became known as 'post men'.

The postcard was patented in the USA in 1861 by John P. Charlton of Philadelphia and was soon on sale, bearing several distinctive patterned borders. Popular success only arrived with the prepaid postcard, first printed by the Austrian post office in 1869, which sold nearly 3 million in its first three months of issue. The idea was adopted in Britain in 1870, where the halfpenny stamp on the card was its cost.

Trained birds have carried messages at different periods since pigeons were first sent to the cities of ancient Greece to deliver the results of the Olympic Games in the 8th century BC. Hot-air balloons carried emergency messages during the Prussian siege of Paris in 1870, and a regular service by aeroplane started in 1918 in the United States. A year later the first international air mail began between London and Paris.

CODED MESSAGES
Signals and semaphore

Palaeolithic peoples sent long-distance messages in visual and aural codes. A fire could signal in flame or smoke the sighting of animals or an enemy's approach, as could simple log drums or animal horns. The ancient civilisations of China, Egypt and Assyria all used smoke signals to convey news.

A kind of semaphore began around 300 BC when the Greeks devised a way of arranging large vases on two low walls to spell out different letters of the alphabet. Similar systems persisted during the Middle Ages, and in the 16th century the Italian mathematician Gerolamo Cardano spelled out letters in code with flaming torches.

After the invention of the telescope in the early 17th century, visual messages could be detected from greater distances. However, a universal system emerged only when the semaphore telegraph was devised in 1791 by the French engineer Claude Chappé. He set movable wooden crosses, with tilting arms at both ends of a horizontal beam, on a chain of hilltop towers. Each of 49 possible positions of the arms indicated a letter or symbol.

VOICES THROUGH CABLES
Telephone messages

In 1849 the inventor Antonio Meucci rigged up an electrical device that, so he claimed, allowed conversation with his bedridden wife from different floors of their home in Havana, Cuba. But the first authenticated telephone call was made in 1860 by a German teacher, Johann Philipp Reis, who considered his invention, *das Telephon*, a 'philosophical toy' not worthy of a patent.

From 1872 to 1875 the Scottish-born American inventor Alexander Graham Bell and the American inventor Elisha Gray attempted to transmit messages along telegraph wires. Both filed American patent applications in 1876, but it was Bell, a professor of elocution trying to make an instrument that would help deaf children to speak, who made the decisive breakthrough.

On March 10, 1876, Bell's assistant, an electrical engineer named Thomas Watson, was in another room when he heard Bell's voice over the telephone saying, 'Mr Watson, come here, I want you.' According to Watson's autobiography, Bell summoned Watson after spilling acid over himself. In the same year, Bell and Watson demonstrated the telephone at the Centennial Exhibition in Philadelphia, where the Emperor of Brazil assured it public attention by exclaiming, 'My God, it talks!'

The success of Bell's telephone lay in its vibrating metal discs. These could convert speech into electrical frequencies representing the human voice, then transform them back to audible vibrations. Early telephones consisted of two wall-mounted boxes made of wood. The user listened to the call through a receiver that was hooked onto the side by a cable, and spoke into an opening in one of the boxes. Anyone wanting to make a call alerted the operator by turning a crank to ring a bell.

The first telephone switchboard was set up in 1877 at the Holmes Burglar Alarm company in Boston. The following year the first commercial public exchange, which linked 21 telephones, was opened in New Haven, Connecticut. Thousands of switchboards were built during the next decade, with electric light bulbs indicating busy lines.

Operators, most of them female, gradually became redundant after 1889 when Almon Brown Strowger, a Kansas undertaker, patented an automatic switchboard that was destined to become known as the 'girlless, cussless telephone'. Strowger's invention was spurred by his discovery that the local switchboard operator, the wife of his main rival, was redirecting calls to her husband's funeral parlour.

ACROSS THE USA *The first New York-to-Chicago call was made in 1893 by Alexander Graham Bell. The line was opened as part of the celebrations at Chicago's Columbian Exposition Fair.*

CONNECTED CALLERS *The earliest telephone of 1875 was a purely experimental apparatus, but by the 1880s telephones were practical devices with tubular earpieces. Many variations on the first 'candlestick' model of 1905 were made over the next three decades.*

MAKING NOTES *Invented in the USA in the 1920s, the 'Holdaphone' raised the earpiece on the shoulder, leaving the telephone user's hands free to take messages.*

TWIN TUBE WALL TELEPHONE, 1880s

CANDLESTICK TELEPHONE WITH DIAL, 1934

BELL'S FIRST TELEPHONE, 1875 DESIGN

OVER THE AIRWAVES
Radio broadcasting

Radio waves, theorised the Cambridge physicist James Clerk Maxwell in 1864, could not only be artificially created but would travel at the speed of light. Maxwell was correct, and in about 1888 Heinrich Hertz, a German physics professor, transmitted such 'radiation' (the source of the word 'radio') from a spark generated between two metal balls.

Practical radio was made possible by the Irish-Italian Guglielmo Marconi. In 1894 he used Hertz's spark generator to send a telegraph message across a room in the family home near Bologna. Marconi soon discovered that by using aerials and connecting an earth to both transmitter and receiver radio range could be increased. In 1895 he transmitted a message to his brother Alfonso, unseen on the opposite side of a hill.

Marconi moved to London in 1896. In 1897 his Wireless Telegraph & Signal Company opened a wireless station for shipping, and in 1901 picked up the first transatlantic radio signal, sent from Cornwall to Newfoundland.

Radio buffs also made progress with homemade sets that relied on the detection qualities of crystals such as silicon, discovered in the early 1900s. These were incorporated into 'cat's whiskers', receivers named after the thin wire that was used to connect the crystal with an electric circuit.

In 1922 the Operadio, portable but weighing 10 kg (22 lb), was invented by the American J. McWilliams Stone. Radios were miniaturised after the transistor was invented in 1947 by John Bardeen, Walter Brattain and William Shockley, scientists for Bell Telephone Laboratories in the USA. The Sony TR-55 was launched in 1955, quickly followed by other transistor radios.

TUNING IN The valve wireless was the most popular source of home entertainment in the 1930s. From 1923, programmes were listed weekly in Radio Times. *After 1947, transistors made portable, then miniature, radios possible.*

VALVE MAINS
WIRELESS,
1930

POSTWAR
ENTERTAINERS,
1946

POCKET-SIZED
TRANSISTOR
RADIO, 1950S

PORTABLE BATTERY-
OPERATED TRANSISTOR
RADIO, 1950S

TELEPHONE BOX

• Written messages with pictures were first sent down telegraph lines by the British inventor F.C. Bakewell on his 'copying telegraph' of 1850. The modern version of the fax—short for 'facsimile'—was sent to target offices by Xerox in 1964.

• The Connecticut Telephone Company installed a public call box in 1880 at their New Haven offices.

• The mobile phone was first put to commercial use in Sweden in 1981. Low-power radio transmitters covering a designated area, known as a cell, enabled users to make calls directly to other cells linked by a computer network.

RADIO ENTERTAINMENT
Broadcasting services

Beginning with 'O Holy Night', which he played on the violin, the Canadian-born Reginald Aubrey Fessenden broadcast carols on Christmas Eve 1906 from Brant Rock, Massachusetts. His tunes were gladly received by sailors 8 km (5 miles) out at sea.

But radio entertainment was slow to develop. The American Lee de Forest transmitted live opera from New York in 1910. Later, in 1917, the German army broadcast radio entertainment for its troops. The first regular radio station was KDKA, founded in Pittsburgh, USA, in 1920.

Once the British Broadcasting Company was established in 1922 radio finally became available to the British public. (The BBC became a public corporation in 1927.) The inaugural BBC programme, a news broadcast, was transmitted in November.

The Light Programme (now Radio 2) was launched in 1945, followed by the Third Programme in 1946. Pop first came on air with Radio 1 in 1967. The station's disc jockey Tony Blackburn inaugurated the station by playing 'Flowers in the Rain' by The Move.

233

LEISURE AND SPORT

To celebrate moments of relief from the arduous business of survival, prehistoric peoples—so their cave paintings reveal—sang and danced, played musical instruments and organised games. The people of the Ukraine were using mammoth bones as percussion instruments 20 000 years ago, and in 2600 BC an Egyptian recorded on papyrus the oldest known joke: 'How do you entertain a bored pharaoh? You sail a boatload of young women dressed only in fishing nets down the Nile and urge the pharaoh to catch a fish.'

For the Egyptians, leisure activities were available only to the privileged few, but the pursuit of leisure dominated the lives of rich Greek and Roman slave owners. The Greek word *mousike* described a fusion of music, poetry and drama, and young Greeks were said to spend as much time learning to dance as learning to fight. Although the words 'theatre', 'arena' and 'circus' are Latin in origin, the oldest surviving playhouse, built in the 4th century BC, is the ancient Greek settlement of Epidaurus, now in Greece. Within the roofed Roman theatre at Pompeii, gladiatorial combats, military exercises and games took place. Some vestiges of these entertainments survived in the tournaments of the Middle Ages.

Play, which evolved in mammals to teach their young how to survive, has been developed by humans into a huge range of games and pastimes. A simple board game was carved onto a roof slab in an Egyptian temple in 1400 BC, at about the time that Hercules is said to have inaugurated the

Olympic Games. These included chariot and bareback horse-races as well as athletic events.

Music and dance, means of communication that also kept enemies and animals at bay, soon gained a role in religious practice. Egyptian wall paintings of the 2nd millennium BC probably show dancing girls and musicians entertaining guests at banquets. After the Roman emperor Constantine was converted to Christianity in 312, Christians introduced dance and drama into church services.

From medieval times until the Industrial Revolution, leisure reverted to a minority pursuit. But the peasants who abandoned farming to labour in the new towns and cities needed time off for rest and fresh air. Football, cricket and other team games were soon taken up by workers as well as by the gentry, and the great national museums and art galleries were established to provide education in addition to pleasure.

Mechanisation also began to influence leisure. Labour-saving devices in the home allowed housewives time to enjoy such sports as tennis and golf, while the invention of photography in 1839 brought within easy reach the art of picturing the world—which was previously only possible by drawing and painting. The invention of sound recording in 1857 also made music more accessible. The American inventor Thomas Alva Edison, who 20 years later made sound recording a practical proposition, was equally involved with what he called 'motioned pictures'.

The completion of the entertainment revolution began in 1923, the year after the British Broadcasting Company had made its first radio broadcasts, when the visionary Scots engineer John Logie Baird carried out his earliest successful experiments with instantaneous moving pictures. 'What's the good of it?' asked one scientist after a demonstration of early television in 1926.

VOCAL EXPRESSION
A song for every occasion

The human voice was central to all forms of ancient music. The Book of Psalms, which instructs the faithful to 'sing unto the Lord a new song', contains some of the earliest references to Jewish singing. Chanting is also mentioned in the Rig-Veda, the first of a collection of Hindu sacred verses known as the Vedas, written in the 4th or 5th century AD but which may go back to the 2nd millennium BC. In ancient Greece, music was believed to have a significant influence on character, and instrumental sounds were considered incomplete without vocals.

The early Christian worshippers sang their prayers in unison, with their simple melodies rooted in Greek and Hebrew musical tradition. Plainsong was the name given to this ritual melody, used by clergy and choirs to recite psalms and prayers. A later form of plainsong was known as Gregorian chant after Pope Gregory I, who ordered a review of Church music in the late 6th century.

Folk songs, some of which originally had a religious significance, flourished in the Middle Ages, passed down orally from generation to generation. Both folk songs and ballads were meant

LULLABY ILLUSTRATED BY KATE GREENAWAY WITH MUSIC BY MYLES FOSTER, LONDON, 1880

to accompany dancing. The ballad 'Greensleeves' was first referred to in 1580, when a licence to print 'a newe northern Dittye of ye Ladye Greene Sleves' was granted to Richard Jones.

Roman nurses used the soothing sounds of *lalla, lalla, lalla* to hush their charges. The oldest English lullaby to have survived—'Lollai, lollai, litil child, Whi wepistou so sore?'—was written by an Anglo-Irish friar around 1315. But 'Hush-a-bye, baby' is probably no older than 17th century.

Most of the nursery rhymes known today date from the 1600s or later. The majority were not composed for children, but are the remains of ballads, folk songs, poems ('Wee Willie Winkie'), ancient ritual ('Ladybird, Ladybird') or prayers ('Matthew, Mark, Luke and John'). The expression 'nursery rhyme' was not used in print until 1824, in *Blackwood's Edinburgh Magazine*.

CHURCH SINGERS *The Book of Psalms provided early Christian worshippers with the text for the first songs of praise sung in church. Under the influence of St Ambrose, Bishop of Milan, hymns became an essential element of public worship in the 4th century.*

WIND INSTRUMENTS
Flutes, trumpets and horns

The straight, pipe-like flute is the oldest known musical instrument. The earliest surviving example, found in Slovenia, was made from a bear's thighbone with fingerholes drilled into it and is about 50000 years old. It is likely that at least some later Stone Age instruments, also made from animal bones, had a reed inserted in the mouthpiece to produce a richer tone.

Sculptures, paintings and pottery created from about 3000 BC show a range of wind instruments, including an oboe-like reed pipe depicted on a Mesopotamian vessel that was carved around 2600 BC. These instruments were popular in the Near East and were later adapted by the Greeks into the double-reeded aulos, the ancestor of the oboe and clarinet. The modern clarinet was developed in about 1690 by Johann Christophe Denner, a German instrument-maker who was trying to improve upon the *chalumeau*, a simple French wind instrument.

PLAYING A DOUBLE FLUTE, ROMAN, ABOUT 465 BC

Tubes of graded lengths tied together were named after Pan, the Greek god of woods, fields and flocks who was said to have invented them—according to the Greek shepherds who played panpipes. But the oldest examples of the instrument, dating to about 2000 BC, were discovered in the Ukraine.

The transverse flute, in which air is blown sideways across the mouthpiece, was first known of in China in the 9th century BC. It reached Germany in the 12th century—hence its old English name of the German flute. Originally made of wood, it had one thumbhole and four to eight fingerholes. Keys to cover the airholes were added from 1677. In the 1800s the flute changed from a conical to a cylindrical shape.

Most trumpets in antiquity were straight, but throughout the ancient world curved animal horns were used to send men into battle and to spur them on while fighting. Long trumpets with a cylindrical tube and flaring bell were sounded by Egyptian priests and soldiers by 1400 BC. Two trumpets, one bronze and gold, one silver, were found in the tomb of Tutankhamun, the pharaoh who died in about 1340 BC.

The Romans called straight trumpets *tubas*, but also had a J-shaped model, the *lituus*, and the G-shaped *cornu*, both thought to have originated with the Etruscans, who lived in central Italy in the 7th and 6th centuries BC. Around AD 1400 instrument-makers learned to bend the trumpet's tubing into an S shape, later folding it back on itself to form a loop.

Until the end of the 18th century European horns and trumpets produced a restricted range of notes. Valves that controlled air flow more precisely were invented in about 1815. The first

valved horn was patented in 1818 by the German horn player Heinrich Stoelzel. New brass instruments followed in quick succession, including the bass tuba, which was invented in 1835 in Berlin. In 1846 the saxophone was patented by the Belgian instrument-maker Adolphe Sax, who had developed it some six years earlier.

MAKING STRINGS SING
Harps, guitars and violins

The idea of stretching a string over a hollow box so that it could be strummed and plucked probably originated in Mesopotamia. Simple bow harps can be seen in tablets from the Sumerian city of Ur around 2800 BC.

Triangular frame harps, a European invention, were first shown on Celtic manuscripts of the 9th century. In about 1720 a German musician named Jakob Hochbrucker created a harp with pedals that raised the pitch of

HIGHLY STRUNG *The harp played by a Sumerian musician around 2500 BC is an ancestor of the one seen in the 18th-century French workshop below. Many of the instrument-makers' skills have not changed for 200 years.*

the strings by a semitone. Advances made around 1810 by Sébastien Erard, a Parisian instrument-maker, led to the greater range of tone found in the modern classical harp.

Lutes, which have strings running over a sound box and along the arm, were depicted on Babylonian seals in about 2300 BC. 'Lute' comes from the instrument's Arabic name *al-ud*, 'the wood'. A family of guitar-shaped lutes known as gitterns were the forerunners of the guitar, which was being played in western Europe by the late 1300s. At first guitars had four or five strings, but from the late 1700s they had six.

Made of horsehair strung on wood, the bow appeared in the Byzantine Empire around the 10th century. It was used to play the pear-shaped vielle, the ancestor of the two main kinds of viol that developed in the 1500s: the viola da gamba, held between the legs, and the viola da braccio, played on the arm.

The violin, which evolved from the medieval fiddle, developed in Italy in the late 1500s as an instrument to provide music for dancing. The first great violin-maker was Andrea Amati. One of the pupils at his workshop was Antonio Stradivari, who before his death in 1737 perfected the art of violin-making, creating more than 1000 instruments.

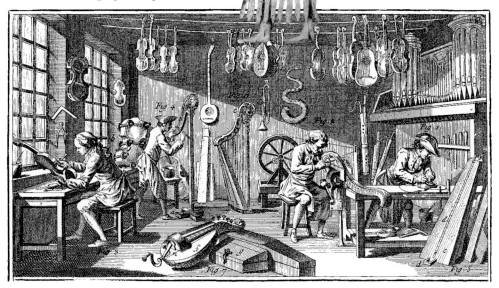

FIT FOR ROYALTY *King David plays the psaltery in a 13th-century illustration, accompanied by musicians on the rebec, cymbalum, organ and tuba.*

FINGERS ON THE KEYS
Organs and pianos

Working in his father's barbershop in Alexandria in the 3rd century BC, the future engineer Ctesibius accidentally dropped a lead weight down a pipe and noticed that the compressed air was pushed out with a squeak. He adapted the idea into the hydraulis, a small organ built along the same lines as a set of panpipes, incorporating a series of tubes of different lengths. Air was pumped into the internal chamber, where water stabilised the air pressure; sliders controlled the release of air through individual pipes. Perfected in the late 1st century BC by the architect Vitruvius, the organ came to be played throughout the Roman Empire.

The craft of organ-building almost disappeared from Europe after the fall of Rome, but was preserved in the Middle East. Instruments occasionally arrived in the West as gifts, such as the organ that was offered to the Frankish king Pepin by the Byzantine emperor Constantine Copronymus in AD 757. By the 10th century organs had been adopted to provide church music, but it was only in the following century that the unwieldy sliders were replaced by levers and then by keyboards.

Rudimentary stringed instruments that were precursors of the piano were played before Biblical times. The psaltery, played by plucking, had strings stretched over a sound box of four unequal sides. This gave birth to the Middle Eastern dulcimer, in which the strings are struck with hammers.

The first person to combine the action of the dulcimer with a keyboard was Bartolommeo Cristofori, an Italian instrument-maker. His invention is listed—under the name *arpicembalo*—in an inventory from 1700 of the Medici family's instruments; a few years later it is referred to as a *gravicembalo col piano e forte*, or 'harpsichord with soft and loud'. The earliest known composer to have written pieces for the piano was the Italian Lodovico Giustini, who published 12 piano sonatas in 1732.

KEEPING TIME

• The first reliable metronome was devised in Amsterdam in 1814 by the German organ-maker Dietrich Winkel, but produced by the musician Johann Nepomuk Maelzel, who patented it in his own name. Winkel sued successfully, but Maelzel had retired to the USA with the profits.
• Karaoke machines are generally believed to have originated in Japan in 1976, but Roy Brooke of Cheshire claims to have sold a similar machine to some Manchester clubs in 1975.

DRUMMING OUT A RHYTHM
Percussion instruments

The first drumbeats may have been sounded out on mammoth skulls and animal skins stretched over mammoth bones in the Ukraine around 14000 BC. The oldest drums to have survived intact are 'waisted' clay examples from about 3000 BC found in Germany and the Czech Republic. Vases and pots of the same period reveal that drums were played in the Near East; crocodile-skin drums of a similar age have been unearthed in graves in China.

Kettledrums—single-headed drums shaped like a bowl—were introduced into Europe from the Near East by the Crusaders in the early 1100s. These 'nakers' as they were known, from their Arabic name *naqara*, survive as modern timpani. In the 19th century the addition of a handle enabled rapid tuning, and allowed pitch to be altered during play, making the timpani central to the orchestral percussion section.

UNIVERSAL LANGUAGE *Today's musical instruments have evolved over thousands of years from shells, bones or gourds. Ancient peoples modified these, for example by making holes, to create instruments that produced just one note each.*

WOODEN CLARINET, GERMANY, EARLY 18TH-CENTURY DESIGN

BODHRAN (IRISH DRUM), TRADITIONAL DESIGN

BENT-NECK LUTE, 10TH-CENTURY EUROPEAN DESIGN

ALTO SAXOPHONE, BELGIAN DESIGN OF ABOUT 1840

SONG SHEET *Early music scores, such as this English example from the 1200s, were handwritten. The information shown under a note indicated simply its pitch and the syllables of the words.*

MUSICAL NOTATION
A lyrical alphabet

When cuneiform tablets unearthed in the Babylonian city of Ur in the 1920s were analysed, it became clear that one, from the late 1st millennium BC, held the earliest known representation of a musical scale. Another tablet of 1400 BC, found in Syria, contained the notes and text of a song—the oldest known sheet music. Ancient music had been thought to consist of one melody, but the tablet showed several harmonies.

Ancient Greek musical theory was the starting point for modern musical notation. The existence of fixed ratios between intervals of sound was discovered by the mathematician Pythagoras in the 6th century BC. This led to a systematic means of depicting notes. Using alphabetic and pseudo-alphabetic characters, by 450 BC scores were being written for plays such as Euripedes' *Orestes*.

The modern system of notation evolved from church music in the 9th century, when plainsong was written using dots and squiggles known as neumes, from the Greek *neuma*, 'gesture'. Neumes were not a scale system, but appeared above a text to indicate changes in pitch.

A six-note scale and the stave, a set of horizontal lines on which the note symbols were placed, was invented in the 11th century by an Italian monk, Guido of Arezzo. By the late 1600s his scale had been replaced by a seven-note one.

Notation became more sophisticated after 1260, when the musician Franco of Cologne created a series of shapes to denote the duration of sounds. Scores became more precise with the introduction of breves and semibreves in the 13th century, and minims and crochets in the 14th. Quavers and semiquavers appeared in the 15th century.

THE ORCHESTRA
Instruments in concert

One of the earliest depictions of a group of musicians is on a Sumerian seal made around 4000 BC, which shows a small orchestra based on kettledrum, harp and horns. Musicians flourished in the Near East. The orchestras that entertained the pharaohs during the 2nd millennium BC were often made up of Near Eastern musicians, many of them women. Most musicians earned a living by playing at banquets. Harps, lyres and lutes were played alongside oboes, flutes, tambourines and rattles.

The Western orchestra is rooted in the Renaissance. Because orchestras were needed to accompany the singers, the development of opera in the 1600s stimulated polyphonal instrumental music, combining two or more melodic parts. By 1800 the baroque ensemble or orchestra was established, founded on string instruments, recorders or flutes, oboes, bassoons, keyboard, trumpets, horns and cello or bassoon.

Conductors first stepped out from the orchestra in the early 1800s. Until then a leading member of the orchestra gave the beat. The French composer Hector Berlioz was one of the first to conduct from a full score.

CHAMBER MUSIC *A group of 18th-century musicians enjoy an informal concert in the home of the German-born composer George Frideric Handel. Public concerts paid for by subscription helped composers such as Mozart.*

FRENCH HORN, 19TH-CENTURY DESIGN

CORNET, AUSTRIAN DESIGN OF 1820

PENNY WHISTLE, 19TH-CENTURY IRISH OR US DESIGN

VIOLIN, ITALIAN DESIGN OF ABOUT 1550

WOODEN FLUTE, 12TH-CENTURY GERMAN DESIGN

CAVE PAINTING OF DANCERS,
TANZANIA, LATE STONE AGE

THE RITUALS OF DANCE
Rhythms of life

To ancient peoples dancing was an important means of expression, first depicted in cave paintings in Africa and southern Europe some 20000 years ago. They danced to show their delight at a birth, to court a marriage partner, to appease the gods, to guarantee success in the hunt or as a way of expressing social unity. The slow, repetitive and hypnotic movements of war dances helped to tone muscles, heighten emotions and focus minds in preparation for battle. These were the forerunners of military drills and marches.

Descriptions dating to 1800 BC relate that the Egyptians danced to Osiris, the god of vegetation, to ensure the fertility of the Nile plains. Wealthier families entertained their guests with slave girls who danced to the accompaniment of cymbals, tambourines or clapping. To the ancient Greeks, dance was a pastime of the gods and a vital part of education and military training.

Folk dancing is a purely recreational pursuit rather than a ritual performance. Nevertheless it has roots in religious traditions. Dancing around a sacred object was an ancient form of religious observance later incorporated into folk dances. In Europe, for example, dancing around a maypole recalls the ancient rituals of tree worship.

As religious calendars were set, days of celebration often coincided with pagan festivals, as with Christian Easter and the rites of spring. Morris dancing, associated with Whitsun, probably evolved from ritual sword dances, which were widespread throughout Europe and had their origins in nature worship. The swords are exchanged for sticks or handkerchiefs, and there are ritual disguises including an animal character and black-faced figures whose perceived resemblance to the Moors may have given the dance its name.

In Europe folk dancing was largely an entertainment for peasants until the 14th century, when people from all classes began to join in. English country dances originate from various May Day ceremonies. They took the form of 'round' dances for any number of couples, line dances and set dances for two to four couples.

In the early 1700s social dances began to develop national identities, as with Scottish jigs, reels and strathspeys. From English dance steps and the French quadrille, pioneers who emigrated to the New World created American square dancing.

Andalusian gypsies were performing flamenco professionally in the 1800s, when it was given its name, from the word for Flemish gypsies. However, the evocative dance had probably developed by the 16th century, after the Gypsies arrived in Spain. But whether it derived from their Hindustani origins or from Spanish folk dances is unknown.

CHAIN REACTION *By the 15th century the stately steps and gestures of court dances were far removed from their more unrestrained folk-dance predecessors. The shift away from group formations to couples was a gradual one.*

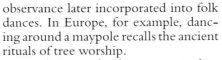

AT THE BALLET
Formalised steps

Ballet had its origins in the 14th century when more formal versions of folk dance were developed in the royal courts of Europe. For anyone attending the courts of the Italian and French Renaissance, dancing skills were compulsory. Grand families had their own dancing masters, one of the most famous being Guglielmo Ebreo da Pesaro, who taught at the court of the

ROLE REHEARSAL *The longer tutus worn by these dancers in 1874 were introduced by the ballerina Maria Taglioni in* La Sylphide *in 1832. A shorter form appeared in the 1880s.*

Medici in Florence. Dancing masters also began to publish books—the earliest was *De arte saltandi et choreas ducendi* (*On the Art of Dancing and Conducting Dances*) by Domenico of Piacenza. Published around 1420 it was the first work to distinguish between a *danza*, with a uniform rhythm, and a *ballo*, with more varied rhythms.

Many formal dances were performed as interludes in operas or plays. Known as ballets de cours, French for 'court ballets', their steps and sequences descended from folk dances and court processions and were performed by aristocratic amateurs.

The first true ballet de cour was *Circé ou le ballet comique de la reine* (*Circe or the Comic Ballet of the Queen*), which was shown in Paris in 1581. When the

French king Louis XIV founded the Académie Royale de Danse in Paris in 1661 in order to 're-establish the art in its perfection', he emphasised the divide between refined court and peasant dance. But it was not until 1672 that Louis recognised the need for purely professional dancers.

Initially male dancers predominated, and it was thought unseemly for ladies of the court to dance with them. The first professional ballerina, the French Mademoiselle de Lafontaine, appeared in *Le Triomphe de l'amour* (*The Triumph of Love*) in Paris in 1681. With music by the Italian-born French composer Jean Baptiste Lully, it was the first ballet to tell a tale through dance and gesture.

By 1713 the first fully professional dance school had been established at the Paris Opéra, and steps such as the entrechat and chassé formalised and named. The first ballet dancers to perform the pas de deux, or 'step for two', were also the first to dance on pointe in a staging of Charles Didelot's *Flore et Zéphyre* in London in 1796. They were attached to mechanical lifting devices, but such equipment was soon dispensed with as unnecessary.

In the 1820s dancing on full pointe became established, with ballerinas using cotton wool to pad their shoes and give themselves some stability. 'Blocked' shoes, which have their toes stiffened with glue, only appeared during the 1860s.

FROM BALLROOM TO DISCO
The pleasures of dancing

Popular dance was dominated by circle and line formations until the *danse à deux*, 'couple dancing', became standard in the 1300s. Thereafter, countless varieties of dance emerged. The waltz, named from the German word *walzen*, meaning 'to rotate', appeared in the 18th century. It developed from the Ländler, a traditional dance for couples from southern Germany and Austria with the familiar 1-2-3, 1-2-3 rhythm. When first performed by twirling embracing couples, the waltz sent shock waves through polite society.

More shocking yet was the tango, born in about 1880 from a marriage in the slums of Buenos Aires between a Spanish dance based on the flamenco and the raunchy Argentine *milonga*. By the outbreak

CRAZY FOR YOU *African slaves took the tango's beat to Argentina. There, polite society thought the dance uncivilised until it caught on in Paris in the early 1900s. In London the approval of Queen Mary finally ensured it respectability by 1914.*

TAP DANCING
Homesick African slaves, shuffling barefoot in time to work songs and blues, may have put metal bottle tops in between their toes as a way of adding sound to their rhythms. Tap dancing, an American form of theatrical dance that added elements of ritual African foot stamping, Irish jigs and European clog dances, was performed by black Americans in their 19th-century minstrel shows. From 1925 metal taps were attached to dancers' shoes, but tap first took the world by storm in the 1930s and 1940s, when it was transformed for the big screen by such maestros as Fred Astaire and Gene Kelly.

FRED ASTAIRE IN *Top Hat*, 1935

of the First World War the tango had become a craze throughout Europe. The foxtrot also originated around this time, probably named after the comedian Harry Fox in 1913. His act in the extravagant American revue known as the Ziegfeld Follies included a series of trotting steps.

The dominance of couple dancing was broken by jazz dance, based on rhythms taken to the USA by West African slaves. At the turn of the century such dances as the black bottom appeared in the black American dance halls of Atlanta, in Georgia. During the 1930s these evolved into the acrobatic jive and jitterbug, in which dancers improvised freely on a few set steps.

By 1962 'disco', from the French *discothèque*, 'record library', referred to dimly lit Parisian dance halls where people danced the twist. Devised in the USA in about 1958, the twist was initially banned in dance halls, but went on to gain widespread popularity.

Discos had arrived in Britain by the mid 1960s, playing mostly Tamla Motown or soul music. Music created with discos in mind, and the dancing style that accompanied it, originated in the 1970s, encouraged by films such as *Saturday Night Fever*.

THE ORIGINAL GLOBE
THEATRE, LONDON, 1600S

ON THE STAGE

'If a play does anything—either tragically or comically, satirically or farcically—to explain to me why I am alive, it is a good play.'

Tynan Left and Right, KENNETH TYNAN, THEATRE CRITIC, 1967

Religious ritual inspired the world's first dramas. In the 4th millennium BC Egyptian players dressed in lion face masks and other costumes to pay homage to the god Bes, protector of pregnant women. While Egyptian ceremonies were also 'theatrical' occasions, the first dramatists in a modern sense were the ancient Greeks, whose plays addressed such human emotions and failings as passion, the lust for power, and self-destruction.

Greek tragedy evolved from the choral lyric, a poem, often religious, sung and danced by a chorus. In the 6th century BC an essential part of the festival honouring Dionysus, god of wine and fertility, was the dithyramb, a hymn sung by a male chorus.

Dialogue and dramatic action are said to have been introduced by

Thespis, probably an actor and playwright. He added a single actor who stood out from the chorus, playing several parts and addressing the chorus directly. Direct exchanges between characters began when the playwright Aeschylus added a second actor. His tragedy *The Suppliant Women*, written in about 490 BC, is the earliest play to have survived complete.

Thespis was also the first known recipient of a theatrical award, presented at the Athenian Dionysia in 534 BC, as well as the source of the word 'thespian'. 'Tragedy' comes from the Greek *tragos*, 'goat', a reference to animal sacrifices made at festivals or to the practice of giving a goat as a prize, and *oide*, meaning 'song'.

Comedies first entered theatrical competitions in 486 BC. Derived from the Greek *komos*, 'revel', and *oide*, comedy developed from the revels associated with fertility rites. By the 3rd century BC comedies were mostly political satires and burlesques featuring some 30 stock characters such as the lover, the bounder and the virtuous woman.

The great theatres built by the Greeks were inspired by the arenas of Bronze Age Crete, where the Minoans enjoyed spectator sports in amphitheatres with stepped seating. In the palace at Knossos, a fresco of about 1400 BC shows rows of women seated on a large grandstand. In the 6th century BC

the Greek theatre of Thorikos consisted of wooden benches set in the hillside looking down on a rectangular *orkhestra* where the chorus danced. A century later the benches were replaced by stone steps.

By the mid 5th century BC the theatre of Dionysus near the Acropolis in Athens included a *skene*, a wooden façade with three doors. This provided the background for the actors—and also the derivation of the word 'scene'. The Greek playwright Sophocles introduced the idea of showing the location of the action by fitting painted canvasses onto the *skene*.

The Romans dispensed with the *orchestra* and the chorus, presenting their comedies on a high stage across which a curtain could be drawn. But Roman theatre was diminished by popular taste. In the 1st century AD serious drama declined in favour of bawdy pantomimes and mimes.

The early Church condemned entertainment of this kind, closing all

THE WORLD'S A STAGE *The Globe theatre, where many of Shakespeare's plays were first presented, was built in 1599 using timbers from Burbage's 1576 Theatre. A reconstructed Globe opened in London in 1997.*

TRAGIC ACTOR
HOLDING HIS MASK,
ITALY, 4TH CENTURY BC

theatres in the 6th century before later realising the potential of drama to encourage moral behaviour. In western Europe the earliest recorded drama dates to the mid 10th century, when plays based on the life of Jesus formed part of the liturgy, the Church's system of public worship. From the 13th century medieval mystery and miracle plays related stories from the Bible and the lives of the saints, while morality plays personified vices and virtues.

Secular theatre survived in Europe in the itinerant groups of entertainers who performed at markets and fairs, as well as in the minstrels employed by lords. From the late 15th century in England, small companies of actors were hired to give 'interludes'—short dramatic sketches—between the courses of banquets held in the great houses of the nobility.

Professional actors and, later, actresses emerged in Europe from the mid 16th century. In Italy they were first seen in the commedia dell'arte, semi-improvised satires and comedies in which masked actors played a standard cast of characters, including Columbina, a flirtatious servant girl,

the miserly Pantalone and Arlecchino (Harlequin), a quick-witted servant.

After Henry VIII broke with the Catholic Church in 1532, English writers satirised the old religious plays and explored a wider range of both social and political issues. By the end of the century professional playwrights such as Christopher Marlowe, Ben Jonson and William Shakespeare were writing for companies who performed in purpose-built theatres rather than inn yards.

England's first playhouse was erected in 1576 by James Burbage, leader of a company of actors under the patronage of the Earl of Leicester. At a time when theatre was regulated by the city council, Burbage signed a lease for a piece of land in Shoreditch, east of London's city walls. Here he constructed a timber-framed structure with a thatched roof and three galleries, naming it the Theatre.

Although actresses appeared in Britain in the 1570s with the Italian commedia dell'arte players, women first began to appear on the British stage after the Restoration of Charles II in 1660. Previously they were seen only in court masques.

Acting became increasingly popular after the founding of the first amateur dramatic society, the Shakespeare Club at Cambridge University, in 1830. Miss Kelly's Theatre and Dramatic School, the first in Britain, opened in 1840. In the early 1900s the new repertory theatres performed a different play almost every week.

CHARACTERS FROM THE COMMEDIA DELL'ARTE, ITALY, 1600s

PLAY-ACTING *The English actor-manager Sir Beerbohm Tree, seen here in* The Merry Wives of Windsor, *founded the Royal Academy of Dramatic Arts (RADA) in 1904.*

endured by knights of the Order of St John in 1522 and was set to music by a committee of composers. It was the first time movable perspective scenery was used in a British theatre, and also the first dramatic performance to feature a woman, Mrs Edward Coleman.

But the British continued to prefer 'semi-opera'—an amalgam of spoken dialogue and singing. In 1693 *The Gentlemen's Journal* still felt that 'Operas abroad are plays where every word is sung; this is not rellished in England.' Through-sung opera caught on in the early 1700s, and in 1710 the Queen's Theatre, Haymarket, became London's first opera house. The German-born George Frideric Handel staged his opera *Rinaldo* there the following year.

MAKING A SONG AND DANCE OF IT

Tavern-keepers of the mid 1600s had an eye for a good deal. So when organs were banished from churches by the Puritans many of them were bought by publicans, who then employed

halls were rebuilt as theatres, without supper tables. Renamed 'palaces of variety', they became homes to stars such as Marie Lloyd and, later, Gracie Fields.

The American equivalent of music hall came to be known as vaudeville, a term introduced by French immigrants possibly from the words *vau* or *val de Vire*, referring to the valley of Vire in Normandy, known for its popular songs. The first vaudeville show, which offered eight acts, including comics, singers and dancers, was devised in 1881 for family audiences by the American manager and performer Tony Pastor.

From the late 1800s music hall and vaudeville faced competition from musical comedies and revues. William Gilbert and Arthur Sullivan had been delighting audiences with their light operas since collaborating on *Thespis; or, the Gods Grow Old* in 1871. But in 1892 Osmond Carr's *In Town*, the first English musical comedy, was staged in London. As plots grew stronger and were integrated more with the music, the word 'comedy' was dropped. The American musical gained its first major London success in 1898 with Gustave Kerker's *The Belle of New York*.

A music-hall entertainer had just one turn in a programme, but a revue player appeared in several numbers. In the USA, revues brought fame to Al Jolson and Fanny Brice, who starred in the *Ziegfield Follies* from 1910. The revue format was revived by Jonathan Miller, Peter Cook, Dudley Moore and Alan Bennett of the Cambridge Footlights Club to create the satirical revue *Beyond the Fringe* in 1961.

SET TO MUSIC
Opera and musicals

The idea of telling a dramatic story in words set to music originated in Italy in the late 1500s. Inspired by the essential role that music played in ancient Greek tragedies, the Camerata, a group of musicians, poets and aristocrats in Florence, helped to create a new form of musical drama called *opera in musica*, or 'work in music'.

The first true opera was written by two leading members of the Camerata, the librettist Ottavio Rinuccini and the composer Jacopo Peri. *Dafne*, a short work based on the Greek myth of the nymph who was turned into a bay tree to escape being raped by Apollo, was originally performed in public as part of the Florence Carnival in 1597.

'Through-sung' opera, in which all or most of the libretto is set to music, reached London in 1656 with one of the few theatrical performances of the Commonwealth period. Sir William D'Avenant's *The Siege of Rhodes* told the story of the six months' privation

LIGHT WORK
From 1881 most of Gilbert and Sullivan's operettas were first staged at the Savoy Theatre, built by the impresario Richard D'Oyly Carte.

organists to entertain their customers. By the early 1800s taverns and 'song-and-supper rooms' provided patrons with food, drink and a lively succession of comedy turns, singers and acrobats, all under the auspices of a chairman.

This form of entertainment proved so popular that in 1852 an English publican named Charles Morton built the first of London's great music halls, the Canterbury. In the late 1800s the music

LOOK BEHIND YOU!
Punch, Judy and pantomime

The crotchety nature of Punch may have evolved from the ungainly, deceitful country bumpkin who was a stock character of Greek and Roman mimes. Puppet shows were also enjoyed in Greece in the 6th century BC.

When, in the 1550s, the commedia dell'arte, 'comedy of art', developed in Italy, one of its stock characters was Pulcinella, a sly, braggardly servant who always managed to escape punishment. In the early 1600s Pulcinella became a favourite of Italian marionette shows.

In 1662 the diarist Samuel Pepys noted Pulcinella's arrival in England. Renamed Punch, he took characteristics from the English clown while gaining a nagging wife called Joan and, probably, his humped back. English morality plays were also the source of Punch's fight with the Devil—replaced by a crocodile in the mid 19th century.

But in the late 1700s his popularity declined. With all their paraphernalia, marionette shows became uneconomical, so Punch was reborn as a glove puppet—a form first seen in England in the 1400s, when puppet shows were based on mystery plays. By 1820 his looks and his habit of beating his wife, now called Judy, were established, as was the expression 'pleased as Punch'.

The pantomime, named from the Latin *pantomimus*, meaning 'complete mime', was established in Roman times as a light entertainment in which a chorus narrated the plot while actors mimed the action. Its modern British form was adapted from harlequinades, comic antics popular in 17th-century France, by the British harlequin John Rich in the early 1700s. The tradition of basing story lines on fairy tales began in the late 18th century, but the Victorians introduced the convention of a woman playing the principal boy.

CONJURERS FORM THE LETTER 'H', FRENCH MANUSCRIPT, 1100S

THAT'S THE WAY TO DO IT! The text of Punch and Judy shows was established around 1800. Some characters have come and gone, but the basic story remains the same.

Come to the
PUPPET EXHIBITION
VICTORY HOUSE,
LEICESTER SQUARE,
October 24th to 29th, 1938
11 a.m. — 10 p.m.
Many Demonstrations.

TICKET FOR A PUNCH AND JUDY SHOW, LONDON, 1938

PUNCH AND JUDY

IT'S MAGIC
Tricks of the trade

The first of the great illusionists were the sorcerer-priests of ancient Egypt, Persia and Greece, who bedazzled congregations into seeing 'miracles' that were produced by mechanical devices. The opening of temple doors by hot air emanating from an altar fire, the projecting of voices down tubes opening into the mouths of statues, and mechanically produced trumpet sounds were just a few of the tricks up their sleeves. The word 'magic' comes from the Old Persian *magus*, meaning 'sorcerer'.

An ancient Egyptian papyrus relates how the pharaoh Cheops, who ruled around 2600 BC, was entertained by a magician who could 'put on again a head that hath been cut off', proving it with a goose. Sword swallowing, neither an illusion nor a trick, was known in ancient Greece and Rome. A Roman physician noted in the 2nd century AD that *abracadabra* worked as a charm to cure fevers, but it may have originated as the Greek *abrasadabra*, a magic word used by some early Christian sects.

One of the earliest sleight-of-hand tricks was the cups and balls. Medieval jugglers and itinerant performers at fairs and in taverns confused their audiences by making three cork balls appear and disappear under three metal cups.

In the 1700s the terms 'conjurer' and 'magician' lost their supernatural associations and performers began to play in theatres and music halls. Mind-reading was introduced as a trick in 1781 by Philip Breslaw. Sawing a woman in half was first performed in London by the British magician P.T. Selbit in 1921.

PHOTOGRAPHY

'From today painting is dead.'

FRENCH PAINTER PAUL DELAROCHE, 1839,
ON HIS FIRST SIGHT OF PHOTOGRAPHS

NIEPCE'S ORIGINAL PHOTOGRAPH,
TAKEN IN SAINT LOUP DE VARENNES,
FRANCE, 1826 OR 1827

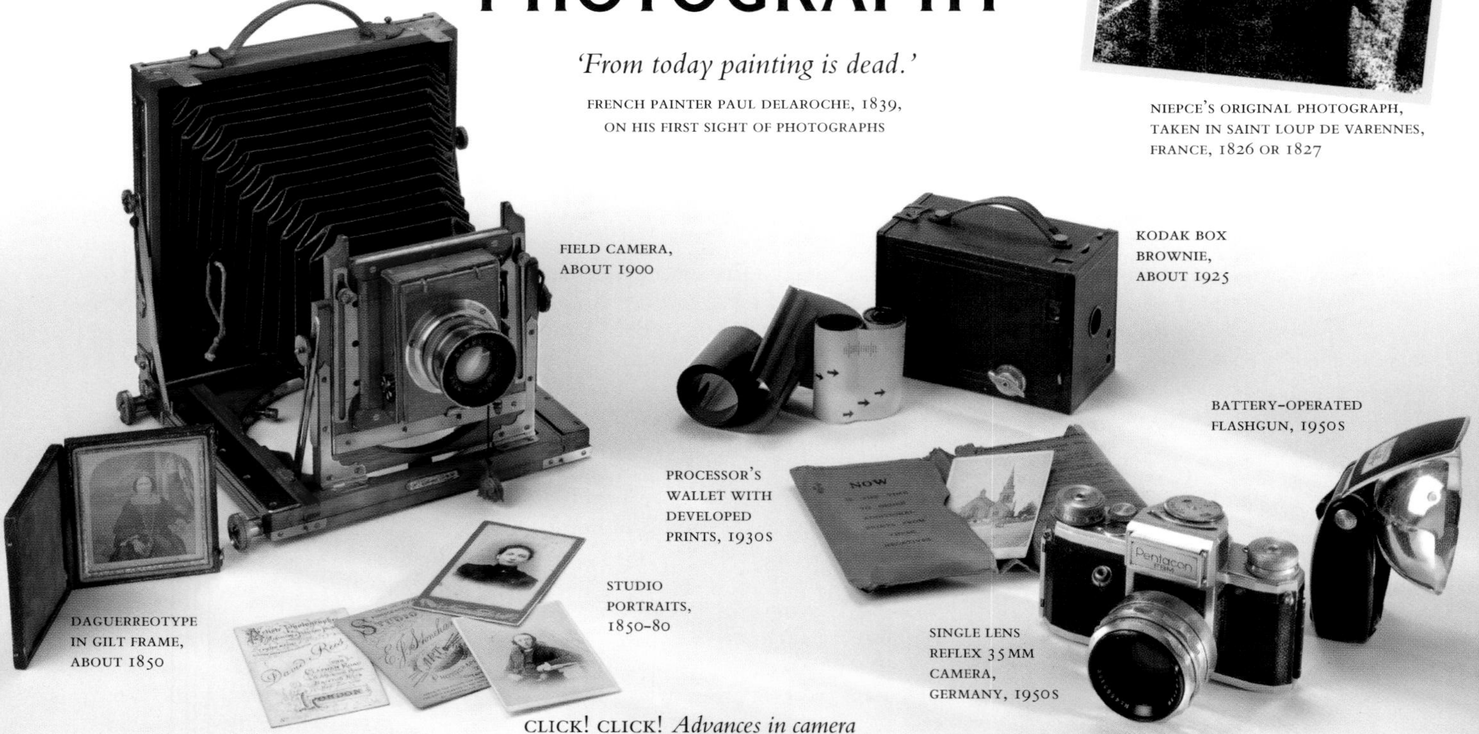

FIELD CAMERA,
ABOUT 1900

KODAK BOX
BROWNIE,
ABOUT 1925

BATTERY-OPERATED
FLASHGUN, 1950S

PROCESSOR'S
WALLET WITH
DEVELOPED
PRINTS, 1930S

STUDIO
PORTRAITS,
1850-80

DAGUERREOTYPE
IN GILT FRAME,
ABOUT 1850

SINGLE LENS
REFLEX 35 MM
CAMERA,
GERMANY, 1950S

CLICK! CLICK! *Advances in camera technology, including the introduction of 35 mm film and the flashlight, freed photographers from the restrictions of the studio and natural light. From 1936 colour was available on 35 mm, but had earlier been possible with glass-plate Autochromes, sold by the French Lumière brothers from 1907.*

Since prehistoric humans first drew wild animals on cave walls some 30000 years ago, their descendants have strived to reproduce three-dimensional reality on a flat surface. In the 19th century photography seemed to bring that quest to an end.

The story of the camera began about 1000 years before this. Arab astronomers of the 9th century knew that a beam of light reflected from an illuminated object and entering a darkened room through a small hole would project the image of the object upside-down on the opposite wall. They used this principle to observe sunspots and eclipses without damaging their eyes. The *camera obscura*, named from the Latin for 'dark

LIGHT PAINTING *By the 1860s a typical camera obscura projected a scene onto a white-topped surface using a mirror and a lens mounted on a rotating tower. The ephemeral images produced were widely used by artists as drawing aids.*

chamber', was little known in Europe until the 15th century, when it was described by the Italian artist and scientist Leonardo da Vinci. In the 17th century the room became a movable tent, then a portable box.

What had been missing was a way of recording the images. The key to

progress lay in the way that silver nitrate darkens on exposure to light, a phenomenon discovered in 1727 by the German physicist Johann Heinrich Schulze. Thomas Wedgwood, son of the pottery-maker, and the chemist Humphry Davy were probably the first to make use of this phenomenon later in the century. But they could not 'fix' the images, which turned black when exposed to more light.

In the 1820s the camera, light-sensitive chemicals and a method of stabilising the image were brought together by Joseph Nicéphore Niépce, a French chemist. He took the oldest surviving photograph from the attic of his house in Burgundy. The rather indistinct view is captured on a pewter plate coated with pulverised bitumen of Judaea (a type of asphalt), which hardened white in the light to give the image of rooftops and a barn. From the positions of the shadows, it is clear that the exposure time was about 8 hours.

Niépce went into partnership with the theatrical scene-painter Louis Jacques Mandé Daguerre. It was

SHOOTING HIGH *Photographers such as the American W.H. Jackson, seen here in 1873 on the Yosemite Observation Point, soon discovered how to record the wonders of the landscape—and took enormous risks to do so.*

Daguerre who, in 1837, succeeded in using common salt to fix a silver image on a polished and silvered copper plate. Each of the solid metal plates used by Niépce and Daguerre was a 'one-off', with a mirror-reversed image.

Two years earlier Daguerre had realised that an image was forming on the plate before it was visible to the eye. His discovery is said to have happened after he left an underexposed plate in a cupboard, planning to repolish then reuse it. To his surprise, when he took the plate out an image was visible. He repeated the 'accident' until he discovered that a chemical had brought out, or developed, the hidden or 'latent image': it was apparently mercury vapour, which had seeped into the cupboard from a broken thermometer.

With this chemical acceleration Daguerre realised exposures could be reduced to 2 or 3 minutes, a reasonable time to expect humans to keep still. Probably the first person to be photographed was a man having his boots blacked on a Paris boulevard, at whom Daguerre pointed his camera in 1839. Taking pictures of people

became so important that more than 90 per cent of all daguerreotypes were portraits.

In the autumn of 1839 the new medium crossed the Atlantic. The first American daguerreotype, taken by D.W. Seager, was of St Paul's Church in New York. Within a year, the daguerreotype, which the American essayist Oliver Wendell Holmes dubbed the 'mirror with a memory', had swept through the USA.

At the same time as Daguerre was developing his process, the English scientist William Henry Fox Talbot was also experimenting with photography. It was he who invented the negative-positive process, enabling copies to be made. The earliest surviving negative is of a diamond-latticed window in Fox Talbot's family home, Lacock Abbey in Wiltshire. Probably exposed for 1 or 2 hours, it was taken in August 1835. His process was unveiled at the Royal Society, London, at the end of January 1839, a few weeks after Daguerre's.

Fox Talbot discovered the latent image for himself and, modifying his process, patented the resulting calotype, named from the Greek *kalos*, 'beauty', in 1841. The process was unable to rival the daguerreotype

for its precision of detail, but was capable of much subtler effects with more gradation of tones. A friend of Fox Talbot's, the English astronomer Sir John Herschel, coined the word 'photography' in the 1840s from the Greek *photos*, meaning 'light', and *graphein*, 'to write'.

In 1844 Fox Talbot set up a printing establishment in Reading, Berkshire. He published *The Pencil of Nature*, the first commercially produced book to be illustrated with photographs. Fox Talbot's text prophesied the future of photography as an art form, as a printing system and as a documentary record. He even foresaw infrared and ultraviolet scientific photography.

By the 1850s the calotype and daguerreotype had been superseded by new processes. Glass plates, used instead of paper to receive negative images, made both fine detail and multiplication of prints possible for the first time. However, photography remained in the hands of professionals who had the necessary knowledge of chemicals as well as the skill to perform often complex manipulations.

George Eastman, an American bank clerk who became a photographic manufacturer, revolutionised photography in 1888 with his Kodak camera, which could be used by amateurs. Once the owner had used up the 100 frames on its paper-backed roll film the whole camera was usually sent back to the Kodak factory for the pictures to be processed and a new film to be put in. However, it was Kodak's affordable Box Brownie, priced at 5 shillings (25p) in Britain, which brought photography to the masses when it was introduced in 1900.

HOLIDAY SNAPS *The truth of the original Kodak marketing message: 'You Press the Button, We Do the Rest', is demonstrated by this young photographer in 1910 (left). In a typical 1920s advertisement (above) Kodak promoted amateur photography as a leisure pursuit.*

MOVING PICTURES

'By its means historical events can henceforth be preserved just as they happened and brought to view again not only now, but also for the benefit of future generations.'

OSKAR MESSTER, GERMAN INVENTOR, PRODUCER, DIRECTOR AND PROPAGANDIST, 1897

FAST FORWARD *Eadweard Muybridge used 24 cameras to record the actions of a woman leaping over a stool, among the thousands of images he took in the 1880s. The Lumière brothers' sequence of family pictures (above) comprised the first true film, in 1895. Louis Lumière is said to have been inspired by a sewing machine when he invented a means of holding each frame still for a split second.*

The principles behind photography, first demonstrated in 1839, led directly to the birth of motion pictures, but two other essentials of cinematography came before it. In its simplest form projection, the first of these, involved using lights to cast shadows onto a screen or wall. Elaborate shadow puppet entertainments originated in the Far East in the 14th century. In 17th-century Europe the same principle was used in the 'magic lantern' to project painted images.

The second vital ingredient of film, persistence of vision—the retention by the brain of a luminous image on the retina for a split second after the image disappears—had been appreciated since the 17th century. It seems to have been scientifically demonstrated for the first time in 1824 by the English physician Peter Mark Roget, whose name is more often associated with his later thesaurus. Soon the zoetrope and other optical toys used this phenomenon. After 1839, attempts were made to use

photographs in these toys, but because of the lengthy exposure times needed, the process of taking the images proved to be painfully slow. Only after the 1870s did film-making finally become a practical proposition.

In the late 1870s Eadweard Muybridge, an English photographer who had moved to the USA in the 1850s, was commissioned by Leland Stanford, a railway tycoon and former governor of California, to photograph a racehorse in action, apparently in an attempt to prove that as a horse galloped all its hoofs were, for brief periods, clear of the ground. Muybridge's black and white photographs, taken by a series of

SEEING IS BELIEVING *Movement is perceived when the revolving images on such toys as the Phenakistoscope are seen through a series of slits or holes.*

PHENAKISTOSCOPE
DISC, FRANCE, 1835

MAKING MOVIES *On location in sunny California in the 1920s the director Charles Ray consults his team (above). The British-born comic genius Charlie Chaplin (right) worked as a film actor, producer and director in the USA from 1910.*

cameras operated by trip wires set off by the horse as it ran past, showed that this was indeed the case.

Etienne Jules Marey, a French scientist, used a single camera—his 'photographic rifle'—to take pictures of birds in flight in the 1880s. But only celluloid film and projectors could enable long sequences to be taken and viewed in a way that gave a realistic impression of motion. Meanwhile the best results came from mounting sequences of pictures and running them in mechanical 'flicker books'. Many were viewed in machines such as the Mutoscope, a freestanding, 'penny in the slot' peepshow invented in 1894.

In 1891 the American inventor Thomas Alva Edison patented the Kinetoscope, mainly devised by his assistant W.K.L. Dickson. This viewing box used images captured on celluloid roll film, introduced in 1889 by the American George Eastman. The first Eastman Kodak film was 70 mm wide. Edison split it down the middle so he could join the pieces together and make longer lengths. In 1907, 35 mm film became the cinematographic standard.

With roll film it was possible, at last, to record photographic sequences in continuous form. The Kinetoscope used 15 m (50 ft) looped rolls, each with some 20 seconds of playing time.

The films were recorded at a specially built studio at the Edison Laboratories in West Orange, New Jersey. They featured vaudeville turns and sketches by 'stars' such as the frontiersman William Cody, better known as Buffalo Bill.

Kinetoscope parlours containing coin-operated machines sprang up in the USA and Europe, but the pictures could be viewed by only one person at a time. The film screening acknowledged as the world's first was a public showing in the converted basement of the Grand Café, Paris, on December 28, 1895.

The event had been organised, and the films shot, by the brothers Auguste and Louis Lumière, whose family owned a factory making photographic equipment in Lyons. Their Cinématographe incorporated both camera and projector and was named from the Greek *kinema*, meaning 'motion'. It used a claw mechanism to hold each frame motionless in front of the lens for a split second before moving the film on.

The public premiere consisted of ten 1-minute films, including workers leaving the Lumière factory, a family mealtime, a gymnast, and a blacksmith at work. Many viewers were so

frightened by seeing a locomotive steaming towards them that they hid under their seats. 'It is life itself, movement taken from the living,' marvelled the journal *La Poste*.

Cinema was taken up most enthusiastically in the USA. *The Great Train Robbery*, often considered the first true movie, was a narrative western lasting 11 minutes and made in 1903. It was shot in Edison's studio by Edwin S. Porter. By 1907 film-makers were starting to find the sunshine and scenery of southern California ideal for their purposes. Nestor film studios was the first to make a permanent base in Hollywood.

Sound and pictures were incorporated into Edison's Kinetophone, a combination of his phonograph and Kinetoscope, of about 1895. Synchronised dialogue first accompanied projected film at the 1900 Universal Exhibition in Paris, where films included scenes from such dramas as Shakespeare's *Hamlet*, and featured famous stage actors such as Sarah Bernhardt. However, tone quality was generally so bad, and the synchronisation so difficult, that most films were 'silent' until sound-on-disc and sound-on-film systems were introduced in the 1920s.

In 1929 the American Academy of Motion Pictures made its first awards. *Wings*, a First World War flying adventure, was judged Best Picture, the German Emil Jannings Best Actor, and the American Janet Gaynor Best Actress. The name 'Oscar' was first used in 1931, reputedly after the academy's librarian, Margaret Herrick, commented that the winners' statuettes resembled her uncle Oscar.

AL JOLSON IN *The Jazz Singer*, THE FIRST FEATURE FILM TO INCLUDE SPOKEN DIALOGUE, USA, 1927

MUSICAL MACHINES
The birth of the gramophone

HAND-CRANKED
GRAMOPHONE
WITH HORN, 1900

DANSETTE
RECORD
PLAYER,
1950S

PLASTER MODEL OF
NIPPER, 1908

REEL-TO-REEL TAPE
RECORDER, GERMANY, 1950S

Edouard-Léon Scott de Martinville, the Parisian painter, connected a megaphone to a stylus made of a hog bristle which rested on a revolving drum. When he made a noise, a wavy line was etched into the smoke-blackened paper covering the drum. His Phonautograph had produced the first visual trace of sound waves, in 1857.

Scott had no interest in playing back recorded sounds, but two decades later the American inventor Thomas Alva Edison, working on a device to translate Morse code signals into marks on paper, succeeded in doing so. On December 6, 1877, his mechanic, John Kruesi, built the first phonograph to Edison's design.

Turning the handle of its cylinder, Edison shouted the rhyme 'Mary had a Little Lamb' through a tube attached to a diaphragm which vibrated to the sound. This caused a stylus to make indentations in the aluminium foil that covered the cylinder. A stylus attached to a listening tube was then used to reproduce the sound.

Edison predicted his machine would 'be used largely for music, either vocal or instrumental, it will sing a child to sleep, tell us the time, preserve the voices of our greatest men and enable future generations to listen to speeches by a Lincoln or a Gladstone.' Indeed

LISTENING IN Electric record players were first produced in 1925. Like hand-cranked gramophones they used 78rpm discs, some with labels of Nipper in front of a horn, until the advent of LPs in the late 1940s. By then tape recorders were also in production.

recordings made in 1878 included a speech by a US president, Rutherford B. Hayes. But these soon wore out.

Recordings that could be played again and again were first made on a machine patented in 1886 by Alexander Graham Bell, the inventor of the telephone, his cousin Chichester Bell and

IN THE ROUND Recordings on cylinders for the Edison phonograph lasted for 2 minutes. Most cylinders were sufficiently hard to be played about ten times.

WAX CYLINDER
FOR THE EDISON
PHONOGRAPH,
1887

EDISON'S
PERFECTED
PHONOGRAPH,
1887

the inventor Charles Sumner Tainter. The Graphophone's cylinder was covered in wax, which was engraved by the stylus. Edison immediately made his own wax-cylinder version. The rivals then joined forces, producing Edison's Perfected Phonograph in 1887.

CAPTURED ON DISC
Short and long play

Emile Berliner, a German migrant to the USA, also harboured an ambition to 'etch the human voice'. Working on an idea originated ten years earlier by the French scientist and poet Charles Cros, Berliner used a stylus to trace a wavy line on a glass disc covered with lampblack and linseed oil. He hardened the trace with shellac, a purified resin, and used it as a 'master' negative to transfer the pattern to a flat metal disc. The grooves on the second disc could play back the recorded sound.

Berliner demonstrated a disc-record player, the hand-cranked Gramophone,

in May 1888. In 1897 the Berliner Gramophone Company produced their first shellac discs for playing on a 78 rpm (revolutions per minute) turntable.

On Berliner's early recordings titles were engraved at the centre. Printed paper labels were the brainchild of Eldridge Johnson, first issued in 1900 by his Consolidated Talking Machine Company, New Jersey. Johnson had had the idea of using a long, flared horn to amplify sound in 1898. Depicted on every label was the 'dog and trumpet' trademark, adapted from a painting called *His Master's Voice* by the English artist Francis Barraud. In the original painting, a fox terrier, Nipper, listened to the horn of a phonograph, but this was substituted with a gramophone in the trademark illustration.

Recording quality improved with the advent of electrical recording systems. Edison and Berliner had both developed microphones for converting sound into electrical energy, but the resulting sound needed amplification. Solving the problem in the 1920s, the Western Electric Company combined a microphone with public address amplifiers, and in 1925 the Brunswick Panatrope, the first all-electric record player with loudspeakers, was launched.

The US company RCA-Victor was the pioneer of long-playing records, producing a 33⅓ rpm shellac recording of Beethoven's Fifth Symphony in 1931. But not until 1948, when shatter-proof plastic records were launched by Columbia Records (CBS), was the 78 rpm disc made obsolete. Etched with 100 microgrooves per centimetre (254 per inch) for high-quality sound,

MELODIES FOR SALE

The original jukebox, an electrically operated Edison phonograph, was installed at the Palais Royal Saloon in San Francisco, USA, in 1889. Its four listening tubes came into action when a nickel was placed in the slot.

The name 'jukebox' comes from a 1939 article in *Time* magazine reporting that 'Glenn Miller attributes his crescendo to the "jukebox" which retails recorded music at 5 cents a shot in bars.' In US slang, the word 'juke' means 'to dance'.

and providing 23 minutes' playing time on each side, LPs were a great success.

Opera was a popular choice for early recordings. In 1878 the French soprano Maria Rôze used an Edison phonograph to record an aria from Gounod's *Faust*, and by 1896 cylinder recordings of operatic favourites were on sale.

As gramophones and discs became more readily available, sales of popular music soared, and in April 1935 'The Lucky Strike Hit Parade', featuring the week's most popular songs, began on US radio. The first 'number one' was George and Ira Gershwin's *Soon*. After his 1941 hit *Chattanooga Choo-Choo* sold a million, the American bandleader Glenn Miller was presented with a copy of the recording sprayed with gold—the first true gold disc.

WAR RECORD *Glenn Miller conducted the American Band of the Allied Expeditionary Forces in Britain in 1944. Many concerts were recorded, and four recording sessions were held at Abbey Road studios in London.*

To record telephone conversations Valdemar Poulsen, the 'Danish Edison', devised the Telegraphone, in effect the first answering machine, by capturing sound on piano wire with magnetic recordings in 1898. By 1920 the search had begun for new recording surfaces, and in 1929 Dr Fritz Pfleumer filed for a patent in Germany for a flexible tape with a magnetic coating.

Pfleumer joined forces with AEG of Berlin, launching the Magnetophon, the first modern tape recorder, in 1935. German models recovered by the Allies at the end of the Second World War inspired the development of high-quality tape recorders in Europe and the USA in the late 1940s.

Wishing to listen to music when he was travelling, the founder of the Japanese company Sony, Masura Ibuka, had the idea of adding a pair of light-weight headphones to a small tape recorder. The Sony Walkman went on sale in 1979.

FIRST SONY WALKMAN, 1979

DIGITAL TECHNOLOGY
From music box to compact disc

Musical watches made in the Vallée de Joux, Valley of Toys, in Switzerland in the 18th century gave birth to the music box of the 1790s. When the lid of the box was opened, a cylinder with raised indentations turned against a small metal comb to play a tune.

The original music box was digital in concept—with each indentation representing a single piece, or 'bit', of information. Modern digital recording began with the compact disc (CD), which stores sound data as microscopic pits on its surface. The CD was developed by the Dutch company Philips in the 1970s, and demonstrated at the Salzburg Festival of 1980 by the Austrian conductor Herbert von Karajan. The first CD players, using laser beams to scan the discs, were sold by Sony in Japan in 1982.

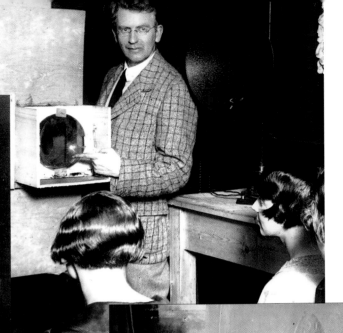

TELEVISION PICTURES
Seen on 'the box'

In March 1930 Ramsey MacDonald, the British prime minister, was presented with a television receiver for use in 10 Downing Street by the Scottish electrical engineer John Logie Baird. After watching *The Man with the Flower in his Mouth*, by the Italian playwright Luigi Pirandello, MacDonald wrote to Baird on April 5: 'You have put something in my room which will never let me forget how strange is this world and how unknown.'

Baird's name is indelibly linked with the invention of television, but no one person was responsible for this 20th-century marvel. It developed from a series of discoveries and innovations, starting from the discovery in 1862, by Abbé Castelli, an Italian-born priest working in France, that variations of light could be transmitted down a telegraph wire as electrical impulses.

The first real step forward came in 1884 when a German student, Paul Nipkow, had the idea for an 'electrical telescope'. It had a rotating disc pierced with holes which 'dissected' images mechanically into a series of separate lines of varying light intensity. The light was converted into an electric current then projected onto a screen through a second rotating disc.

By 1897 a second German, the physicist Karl Ferdinand Braun, had solved the same problem in a different

THE GREAT INVENTOR *In his experimental television system (above) John Logie Baird used a revolving disc to create a picture of a doll's head. Inset next to Baird's 1926 demonstration (top) is a close-up of a living face he reproduced on a screen. The image consisted of a series of narrow vertical lines—produced from the disc's rotation.*

way. He developed the cathode-ray tube, inside which streams of high-energy electrons passed through a vacuum and created spots of light when they hit a fluorescent screen at the far end of the tube. This method of scanning electrically, rather than mechanically, was the technological basis of modern television.

No further progress was made until the development of the first television camera, which could scan an image using an electron beam. Its inventor was Vladimir Kosma Zworykin, a

Russian-born American, who applied for a patent for his iconoscope in 1923, and spent ten years perfecting it.

John Logie Baird had built his first, but unsuccessful, apparatus on an old tea chest, with a disc made from a hatbox lid, mounted on a knitting needle and driven by a motor from an electric fan. The clarity of the images produced by his later working mechanical systems was poor. He sharpened the images by breaking them up into more lines. Later, in an attic above a Soho restaurant in London, with equipment which included a Nipkow's disc, Baird produced the first image of a living face. Early in 1926 he used his Televisor to show such images to members of the Royal Institution.

Baird went on to produce a colour transmission system which he demonstrated in 1928. In the same year he made the first transatlantic television broadcast, transmitted from London to Hartsdale in New York. Baird had secured his place in television history, but his crude mechanical system was destined to be overtaken by electronic imaging based on Zworykin's iconoscope. Zworykin was later hailed as the father of modern television.

HOME ENTERTAINMENT
Programmed broadcasting

John Logie Baird's enthusiasm, and his genius for publicity, led to the realisation of television's potential for mass entertainment. The Baird Company opened a television studio in London in 1928. Later that year the world's first scheduled television service was launched in the USA by the General Electric Company's Station WGY Schenectady, New York. Their first transmissions were of the faces of men talking, laughing and smoking.

Baird's approach made use of singers and other performers. His company dominated early programme making in Britain, operating a daily broadcast service after securing the use of the BBC's transmitter, in 1929. But it was not possible to broadcast pictures and sound

BRITAIN'S FIRST OUTSIDE BROADCAST THE DERBY, JUNE 1931

simultaneously from one transmitter. Pictures of singers mouthing words alternated with a black screen over which the sound was broadcast. On the day Ramsay MacDonald acquired his receiver a second transmitter came into use; Annie Croft and Gracie Fields sang on the first simultaneous sight and sound broadcast.

In Tokyo in 1931, Japanese engineers broadcast a baseball game on closed circuit television. That June British viewers experienced their first outside broadcast—Baird's transmission of the Derby, live from Epsom. Most such programmes were received by enthusiasts who built their own sets using diagrams presented in *Television*, a new specialist magazine.

Many popular programme formats originated early in television history. *Spelling Bee*, the original game show,

was screened by the BBC in 1938 while *Faraway Hill*, the first soap opera, was shown in Washington and New York for 30 minutes every Wednesday from 1946 onwards. The world's inaugural commercial television station, WNBT New York, opened in 1941.

THE VIDEO REVOLUTION
Recorded on tape

In 1927 John Logie Baird became the first person to attempt to create a video. Images were recorded on 78 rpm discs which could then be played back on a gramophone linked to his Televisor. However, Baird never succeeded in playing recognisable pictures back from his Phonovision discs.

Baird's experiments became obsolete with the rise of electronic recording, which synchronised images with sound recordings on magnetic tape. The US company Bing Crosby Enterprises first

demonstrated video recording in 1951, and by 1953 the first video recorder had been built by RCA, but the playback quality in both of them was very poor.

Ampex, the Californian company named from the initials of its founder, Russian-born Alexander M. Poniatoff, plus 'ex' for 'excellence', produced the first commercial video recorder. The Ampex VR 1000, which was over twice the size of a wardrobe, was launched at a broadcasting exhibition in Las Vegas in 1956 and caused an uproar. It was initially intended for use by television stations but soon led to the development of video recorders for home use.

The Ampex VR 1000 ran on tapes 5 cm (2 in) wide and 800 m (875 yd) long. The first video recorder aimed at the domestic market, Telcan, also used reels of tape and was first sold in Britain in 1963 by the Nottingham Electronic Valve Company. It was not until the 1970s, however, that neatly packaged videocassette recorders went on sale.

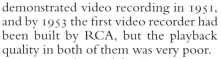

FAMILY VIEWING *In the 1950s television was watched in darkened rooms; colour remained experimental in Britain until the late 1960s. From 1948 the BBC's revolving logo (left) introduced its popular newsreel.*

Bohemian Rhapsody BY QUEEN, THE FIRST POP VIDEO, SHOWN ON 'TOP OF THE POPS', 1975

IN VISION

- The BBC officially adopted the word 'televiewers' in 1935. Audiences had previously been known as 'lookers'.
- The first purpose-built television station, in Berlin, was opened in 1935 in readiness for the 1936 Olympics.
- ITV, Britain's first commercial channel, was launched in 1955.
- The first live transatlantic television programme was shown in 1967. Britain's contribution included the live world premiere of 'All You Need is Love' by The Beatles.
- Britain's first television licences went on sale in 1946, priced £2 each.
- Betamovie, the first camcorder for making home videos, was launched by Sony in 1982.

THE FIRST FERRIS WHEEL, 77 M (250 FT) ACROSS, USA, 1893

HOLIDAY HABITS
Relaxation and celebration

On the first holidays, or 'holy days', people stopped their work for religious devotion. To allow time for worship, the Egyptian pharaohs forbade work on about 70 days of the year, while in ancient Rome more than 100 feast days were dedicated to gods and goddesses. Work days were known as *dies vacantes*, or vacant days, from which, through a reversal of meaning, 'vacation' derives. Both the Jewish Sabbath and the Christian Sunday began as religious rest days based on the Biblical Creation story in which God 'blessed the seventh day' and 'rested from all His work'.

The early Church absorbed pagan feast days into its religious calendar. In the Middle Ages working on a public holiday without official dispensation

was a punishable crime equal to murder. The celebration of saints' days lapsed in England and other Protestant countries following the Reformation of the 16th century. In many places they were eventually supplanted by such national holidays as the Fourth of July, commemorating the American Declaration of Independence in 1776.

By 1830 the Bank of England shut for 18 days a year, giving its workers holidays. In 1834 these were reduced to just four: Good Friday, May Day (May 1), All Saints' Day (November 1) and Christmas Day. In 1871 the banker and Liberal MP Sir John Lubbock helped to pass the Bank Holidays Act. It obliged all banks in England and Wales to close on Christmas Day and Boxing Day, Good Friday, Easter Monday, Whit Monday and also on the first Monday in August.

When Europe began to change from an agrarian, rural society to an industrial, urban one in the late 18th century, manual workers were granted little time away from their jobs. Britain's first employees to benefit in the long struggle for paid leave worked at the South Metropolitan Gas Company in London. In 1872 they were granted annual leave with pay 'as a mark of appreciation of their conduct'.

TIME OUT *In medieval times a summer fair (left) would be held in conjunction with sales of sheep and wool. Public holidays, which allowed Londoners the chance to picnic on Hampstead Heath (below), were eagerly anticipated by Victorian families. The first official bank holiday to be celebrated was Whit Monday, May 29, 1871.*

THE FUN OF THE FAIR
Entertaining the crowds

All over medieval Europe people made merry at the fair. Acrobats, stilt walkers and jesters entertained the crowds, and trinkets could be won as prizes. But although most of these carnivals coincided with religious occasions, fairs evolved from livestock sales and the annual hiring of labourers. Here craftsmen and merchants sold their wares, as the Romans had done at the trade fairs they established at business venues.

A merry-go-round operated in 1620 in Turkey, but roundabouts had existed in Byzantium in the 5th century. In Britain a hand-powered carousel was set up in London in 1729 at Bartholomew Fair, a cloth fair instigated in 1120 by Rahere, the jester of Henry I. Big wheels appeared from the 15th century. They became known as Ferris wheels after George Ferris, the American owner of a company that produced big wheels, built a huge steam-powered version holding more than 2000 people for the World's Columbian Exposition in Chicago, in 1893.

TAKING THE WATERS
Spa and seaside

According to legend, the West Country town of Bath was founded on the spot where Bladud, the father of King Lear, was cured of leprosy in 836 BC by immersing himself in steaming swamps. The ancient Romans appreciated Bath's waters, and drank them for their health-giving properties. In the Middle Ages pilgrims would visit Bath and other such European sites to be healed.

In the 16th century watering-places, including Vichy in France and Baden-Baden in Germany, became popular resorts. One of the most stylish was Spa. Since the 14th century the Belgian town had been visited by invalids who

TAKING THE WATERS IN THE PUMP ROOM, BATH, LATE 18TH CENTURY

sipped its mineral-rich spring waters in the hope of a cure. In the 17th century the wife of Charles II, Catherine of Braganza, visited Tunbridge Wells in an attempt to cure her childlessness. Spas, as they were now known, then became an upper-class vogue.

The sea, said a Dr Wittie in 1660, kills 'all manner of worms'. However, not until the following century were the merits of the seaside more widely appreciated. Scarborough in Yorkshire, known for its medicinal springs, led the way in the 1730s. Sea bathing, regarded as shocking by many, was sanctioned by the medical profession, including the physician Richard Russell. He also recommended that sufferers of all complaints from gonorrhoea to gout drank seawater, mixed with milk or port.

Advances in engineering combined with the Victorian love of promenading resulted in the conversion of the boat jetty to the seaside pleasure pier. The first was effectively a large suspension bridge, designed by Captain Samuel Brown, a naval architect, for Brighton. A song composed for its opening in 1823 proclaimed:
> 'But of all the sweet pleasures that
> Brighton can boast,
> A walk on the Chain Pier
> delighted me most,
> That elegant structure, light,
> airy and free,
> Like a work of enchantment
> hangs over the sea.'

The first iron pier, with a frame sunk into the seabed, was constructed at Herne Bay in Kent in the 1860s.

ON VACATION

• William Wordsworth and other Victorian Romantic poets fostered interest in the natural beauty of such areas as the Lake District and Scotland, which became holiday destinations.
• Rules were strict at Joseph Cunningham's Young Men's Holiday Camp, opened in 1894 at Douglas, Isle of Man. Alcohol and gambling were forbidden and holidaymakers, who slept in rows of tents, were fined for returning after 11.45 pm.
• The principle behind dodgems, using a metal floor and electrically charged ceiling to power 'cars', was patented in 1890 by a New Yorker named James Adair, but the idea was not realised until the 1920s, in rides called Gadabouts.
• In 1932 the New Yorker Hotel installed a television set in every bedroom.
• The South African-born Billy Butlin opened his first venture in 1936 near Skegness, Lincolnshire. Facilities at the 600-chalet holiday village included a theatre, recreation hall, swimming pool and tennis courts.

PEDALLING AROUND CAMP, CLACTON, 1937

LONDON STYLE *At the Carlton and other grand hotels many guests first experienced such innovations as electric lights.*

A ROOM FOR THE NIGHT
The birth of the hotel

Accommodation for travellers sprang up along ancient trading routes. In ancient Persia inns, which were usually built around a central courtyard, were known as caravanserais. During the early Middle Ages travellers lodged at monasteries. From the 11th century the advent of the Crusades and pilgrimages, as well as the development of trade, meant increasing travel and the opening of many lodging houses. These short-term resting places offered few facilities; guests often had to share rooms, or sometimes even beds.

The oldest known hotel, the Hōshi Ryokan, was founded in Japan in AD 717. The Hotel, named from the French for a large private mansion, opened in Exeter, Devon, in 1770 (it is now the Royal Clarence). David Low began business at his Grand Hotel in London in 1774. Low had been a hairdresser, but most early proprietors had a background of serving the aristocracy.

Hotels, unlike royal palaces, swiftly embraced the innovations contrived to make life more comfortable. Early standards were set in the USA: Tremont House, the 'palace for the people' opened in Boston in 1829, was the first hotel equipped with internal plumbing.

HOLIDAYS ABROAD

*'We would venture anywhere with such a guide and guardian as Mr Cook,
for there was not one of his party but felt perfectly safe when under his care.'*

MATHILDA LINCOLNE AND HER SISTERS, *The Excursionist* (THOMAS COOK'S TRAVEL NEWSPAPER), 1855

Until Christian pilgrims began to visit Jerusalem from AD 66 to enrich their faith, the purpose of foreign travel was to explore, conquer and trade with neighbouring lands. Money also made possible the 'Grand Tour' of the Continent from the mid 16th century. The sons of British aristocrats, who were the first people to be described as 'tourists', were sent on journeys around the capitals of Europe. Travelling in the charge of a tutor, the purpose was to complete their education.

As well as knowledge of foreign cultures many young men returned with works of arts or archaeological remains as souvenirs. They were not

both travel and accommodation provided, was a Mr B. Emery, the son of a Swiss watchmaker who had settled in England. Following the end of the Napoleonic Wars, from about 1816, Emery arranged for groups of up to six people to travel from London to Switzerland by stagecoach on 16-day trips costing 20 guineas.

The first tourist travel agency was set up by Thomas Cook, a temperance advocate and wood-turner, who ran his first excursion, a day trip from Leicester to a temperance meeting in Loughborough, in 1841. The cost of the journey was 1 shilling (5 p). By the time Cook opened a permanent office in London in 1865, his horizons had

broadened. A decade earlier he had led a trip to Paris via Cologne. The highlight was an excursion down the Rhine re-enacting the journeys that had inspired poets such as Lord Byron. When Cook died in 1892 his agency was the world's largest and boasted that it could send customers to any part of the globe.

Travel by sea was an integral part of Thomas Cook's long-haul itineraries. From the late 19th century passengers travelling to India aboard the liners of the Peninsular and Oriental Steam Navigation Company (P&O) discovered that the best cabins were those protected from the sun's glare. Wealthy travellers became accustomed

TRAVELLING MONEY *'Circular notes' enabled 18th-century travellers to obtain set amounts of cash from foreign banks, a system used until 1891 when American Express introduced its 'traveller's cheques'. Package holidaymakers were issued with coupons to 'buy' accommodation as well as tickets for the journey.*

CIRCULAR NOTE, 1874

INNOCENT ABROAD *An 18th-century Grand Tourist, pressed by his tutor, practises his French on an innkeeper. He is clasping* Letters to his Son *by Lord Chesterfield, who claimed that, despite their opportunities, young travellers went 'into no foreign company, at least none good'.*

the first to do so. The Cretans had brought back ivory and precious metals from Syria and Egypt during the 2nd millennium BC to adorn their mighty Minoan palaces.

Journeys for pleasure, which were affordable to the new industrial magnates as well as the aristocracy, burgeoned in the 19th century. The pioneer of the package holiday, with

TRAVELLER'S CHEQUE, ABOUT 1910

HOTEL COUPON BOOKLET, 1873

EGYPTIAN RAILWAY TICKET, ALEXANDRIA TO SUEZ, 1870S

to asking for a 'posh' ticket: port (side) out, starboard home.

In 1844 a P&O ship departed from Southampton for a four-month trip cruising around the Mediterranean. On board was the noted writer William Makepeace Thackeray, granted a free passage in return for a chronicle of the journey intended to popularise cruising. Despite Thackeray's efforts—he particularly enjoyed the concerts and stargazing on deck at night—such seaborne holidays only became fashionable after 1918 when redundant warships were put to enterprising use.

The Greek writer Philostratos recommended in about AD 170 that 'those of advanced years should bask in the warm sun without moving'. But to

the Victorian and Edwardian tourists who visited the Mediterranean to enjoy its mild winters, pale skin was *de rigueur*. The vogue for sunbathing is thought to have originated with the American expatriates Gerald and Sara Murphy. After the 1922 winter season they persuaded the owner of the Grand Hôtel du Cap at Antibes on the French Riviera to remain open. From this otherwise deserted hotel they ventured

each day to sunbathe on the beach. Two years later the Murphys bought a villa in Antibes and invited such friends as the American writer F. Scott Fitzgerald to join them in their new-found pleasure. The Riviera soon became a playground for the rich.

GUIDES AND PASSPORTS

Herodotus, the 5th-century BC Greek historian and voyager, was the first author to describe the places he visited. He wrote of the Babylonians who had 'long hair and cover themselves with perfume' and marvelled at 'beasts in Libya that go without water'. The oldest known printed guidebook, Benedict's *The Wonders of Rome* of 1473, advised on notable sites to visit.

The Grand Tourists had hired guides to conduct them around Europe, but the 19th-century sightseer needed a cheaper alternative. The publisher John Murray's first guidebook for English tourists abroad, *Travels on the Continent*, appeared in 1820. In Germany a guide to Koblenz was compiled in 1829 by

TRAVEL GUIDE, 1904

COOK'S BAGGAGE LABEL, ABOUT 1950

PASSPORT TO THE WORLD *Letters of safe conduct were used by travellers in Britain by 1215 but passports did not become compulsory until 1914, with the outbreak of the First World War. Booklet passports were introduced two years later.*

BRITISH PASSPORT, 1919

BRITISH PASSPORT, 1895

COOK'S WORLD TRAVEL SERVICE

MAKING LIFE SIMPLER *Travel agents offered package tourists every possible service, from transporting their baggage to the hotel to providing interpreters. Independent travellers relied on guidebooks to identify the outstanding attractions to be seen in foreign countries.*

INTERPRETER

INTERPRETER'S BADGE, ABOUT 1930

Karl Baedeker, who was the son of a bookseller and printer. A decade later his guides included 'stars' awarded to outstanding hotels, restaurants and attractions. The idea was so popular that all guides became known as 'Baedekers'.

To afford travellers safe passage the Egyptian pharaohs issued them with cartouches, oval frames enclosing an engraving of the ruler's name. In the 2nd century BC the Greeks used 'letters of confidence' as early 'passports'.

HOTEL CHATEAU GÜTSCH LUCERNE

FLASHMAN'S HOTEL RAWAL PINDI

HOTEL LUGGAGE LABELS, ABOUT 1930

SUN TAN OIL

SUNTAN OIL, 1950S

FUN DAYS *In 1910, when winter sports holidays (right) were in their infancy, most tourists enjoyed the cool mountain air in summer. Sunbathers of the 1920s put olive oil on their skins, but in 1936 the French company L'Oréal launched the first mass market suntan lotion, Ambre Solaire.*

ROMAN DICE,
1ST CENTURY BC

THROWING GAMES *For 5000 years gamesters have played with dice made of wood, stone or bone. In ancient Greece animal knucklebones were used in simple games (above) or adapted into rudimentary dice. Values were assigned to four sides of the uneven, oblong bones, with numbers of opposite faces adding up to seven.*

ROLLING THE DICE
The lucky throw

Dice-playing was so popular in ancient Greece that triple six, the best throw of all, became synonymous with good fortune. The Romans too were keen players and even had professional associations for those who made their living from gambling. The emperor Claudius wrote a book on the subject of playing dice in the 1st century AD.

Such discoveries as a set of bone dice and the box in which they were stored, found in Glastonbury, Somerset, show that playing dice also spread through Iron Age Europe. By this time dice had been around for thousands of years—they have been found in 5000-year-old Sumerian graves and in the ruins of cities in India and Pakistan built in around 2300 BC.

In western Turkey the Lydians used dice to amuse themselves from about 1300 BC. Herodotus, the Greek historian, reported in the 5th century BC that during a long famine King Atys of Lydia allowed his subjects to eat only on alternate days. On fasting days 'the game of dice, the game of knuckles, games of ball and other games were invented' to help to pass the time.

FRAUD AND FORTUNE

• Playing for money has encouraged deception from early times: digs at Roman sites have unearthed loaded dice weighted with spots of mercury.
• In Roman times dice-playing was illegal outside the midwinter festival of Saturnalia but soldiers took dice on campaigns for all-year amusement.
• Premium Bonds, in which investors forgo interest in exchange for a chance of monthly cash prizes, were launched by the British Government. ERNIE (the Electronic Random Number Indicator Equipment) drew the first winning numbers in 1957.

THE CASINO
Playing palaces

In 1713 the first recorded gambling establishment was opened at the Duc de Luxembourg's Paris home, the Hôtel du Perron, by Ferencz Rákóczy II, Prince of Hungary and the exiled ruler of Transylvania. Drunken brawls were commonplace and winners could spend their money on the services of the resident prostitutes.

The first legal casino, the Promenade House at Baden-Baden, in south-west Germany, opened in 1765. It moved to its present location in the ornate Kurhaus in 1827. The Flamingo was the first of the grand casino-hotels for which Las Vegas, Nevada, is famed. Built in 1946 by the gangster Benjamin 'Bugsy' Siegel, it lost $100000 in the first two weeks of operating. When Bugsy was killed in 1947 another gangster, Gus Greenbaum, took over the casino. He made a profit of $4 million in his first year alone, which encouraged other crime syndicates to establish casinos in the town.

The invention of roulette is often credited to Blaise Pascal, the 17th-century French mathematician who developed many devices to illustrate chance. But it is more likely that the roulette wheel derives from the 18th-century game of hoca, in which a ball is spun into a circular plate that contains 40 pockets around its edge.

A slot machine, whose mechanism was driven by coins, was invented in the 1st century AD by Hero of Alexandria to dispense holy water. But coin-operated gambling machines did not appear until the late 19th century. In 1890 a British patent was issued for a mechanism with multiple dials and a window for viewing symbols. The design was adopted in 1895 by the Bavarian-born Charles Fey of San Francisco whose 'Liberty Bell' was the world's first one-armed bandit.

HITTING THE JACKPOT *American gamblers of 1950 try their luck on one-armed bandits. The alternative name 'fruit machine' derives from 1908 when, to beat a gambling ban imposed in some states, winners were given sticks of fruit gum rather than cash.*

WHEEL OF FORTUNE *A convoy of English soldiers escorts a lottery wheel to the City of London for a draw in 1805. The draws were held publicly in an attempt to prevent accusations of fraud. However, opponents of the lotteries claimed that some dishonest operators were able to obtain tickets cheaply and then sell them on to their customers at a vast profit.*

ENGLISH LOTTERY
TICKET, 1800

LOTTERY LUCK
Drawing numbers

After the Hebrews conquered Canaan, the Lord said to the prophet Moses 'the the land shall be divided by lot'. The idea of a lottery was first developed into a game by the Chinese, who invented keno some 2000 years ago. This was a highly popular amusement in which the players selected their own numbers.

The funds raised may have been used to finance such major construction projects as the Great Wall of China.

Keno eventually reached the United States in the 19th century where it gradually took on a different character. Players no longer chose their numbers, instead buying cards with randomly preselected numbers printed in a grid. To win, every number printed on one row of the grid had to be matched by the card holder with those drawn at random from a collection of numbered balls. The game was first patented under the name of Bingo—a word chosen for its exclamatory sound—in 1930 by an Edwin Lowe.

The first public lottery of more modern times was organised by the widow of the painter Jan van Eyck in Bruges on February 24, 1466, to raise money for the poor. A public lottery started in Florence in 1530 was the first to give cash prizes, and the idea was quickly adopted by other Italian cities.

In 1566 Elizabeth I established the first English national lottery, as a method of raising money for harbour repairs. Lotteries continued to be held in the country until 1826 when corruption by the organisers led to a ban. Britain's first regular state lottery was organised in 1994 by the Camelot consortium under government control.

A SPORTING CHANCE
Gambling on a result

Private wagers on two-horse races were commonplace among the aristocracy when horse-racing became a popular sport in medieval times. At the race-track betting against odds set by a bookmaker began in the 19th century. Such gambling remained 'on course' until 1886 when a Harry Schwind and a Mr Pennington set up a partnership at Ladbroke Hall in Worcestershire to act as 'Commission Agents and Bookmakers to the Aristocracy'. Odds were available to punters on the horses that Schwind trained there.

Six years later Ladbrokes was bought by the entrepreneur Arthur Bendir, who moved it to London. Guards officers employed as commission agents helped to ensure Bendir's success in cultivating the rich and famous. From 1913 clerks took bets at small curtained-off desks, ensuring total discretion.

John Barnard, a former officer in the Coldstream Guards, set up Pari-Mutual Pools in 1922, issuing coupons on which punters could bet on the outcomes of six football matches. In the first year of operating Barnard could

POSTER FOR LITTLEWOODS
POOLS, 1950

not even cover his postage costs, but his idea gradually found favour and the coupons started flooding back during the following year.

Inspired by Barnard, John Moores, a telegraphist at the Commercial Cable Company's Liverpool office, started a rival operation with two of his colleagues in 1923. To keep their identities secret from their employers the trio printed coupons under the name 'Littlewood', the original surname of one of them, Harry Askham. Starting with capital of £150, and hiring boys to distribute the first 4000 coupons outside Manchester United's stadium, their first season's accounts showed a loss of £600. Two of the partners lost their nerve and withdrew, but Moores persisted and by 1930 he was a millionaire.

ADMISSION TICKET
TO THE BRITISH
MUSEUM, 1790

TREASURES ON DISPLAY
Art galleries and museums

As proof of their status the rich and powerful of ancient Egypt, Babylonia, China and India amassed precious objects. And although the Greeks were probably the first to collect and display art for its beauty, it was the Romans, by systematically plundering the nations they colonised, who stimulated a wider interest in artistic accomplishments.

In medieval Europe art was not collected other than by churches and monasteries, and it was only during the 15th century that noble families such as the Medicis in Italy began buying art and displaying it in their own homes. The first art exhibition on record was held at the Palais Royal in Paris in 1667.

Private collections of unusual items were put together in the 15th century, when they were known as 'cabinets' from the Italian *gabinetto*, meaning 'cage' or 'basket'. In 1523, as the beneficiary of the brothers Domenico and Antonio Grimani, the Venetian Republic became the first public body to inherit and exhibit such a cabinet. A similar bequest to Oxford University by the explorer and collector John Tradescant led to the opening in 1683 of the Ashmolean Museum. On view were exotic objects ranging from stuffed animals and birds (including a dodo, a flightless bird from Mauritius that would be extinct by the end of the century) to weapons, armour and coins.

The British Museum, which grew from several cabinets, including that of the physician and explorer Sir Hans Sloane, was the first national collection. After Sloane's death in 1753 the British Government accepted responsibility for maintaining the 100000 paintings, as well as for the books and specimens, not only for 'the learned and the curious, but for the general use and benefit of the public'. In 1759 the museum was opened in Montagu House, Bloomsbury, and admission was free. The

THE GREAT EXHIBITION

The first industrial exhibition of manufactured goods was sponsored by Britain's Society of Arts in 1756. In the following century Prince Albert, Queen Victoria's husband, suggested boosting British industry by inviting exhibitors to display their technological wizardry, and in 1851 'the Great Exhibition of the Works of Industry of all Nations', the world's first international exhibition, opened in Hyde Park, London. The event was housed in a huge structure of glass and iron designed by Joseph Paxton, gardener to the Duke of Devonshire, and dubbed by *Punch* magazine 'the Crystal Palace'. The exhibition, described by Victoria as 'magical...so vast, so glorious, so touching', provided the nucleus of the collections for both the Victoria and Albert Museum, founded as the Museum of Manufactures in 1852, and the Science Museum, which opened in 1857.

'GLADIATORIAL TABLE' WITH STATUE OF ATLAS, 1851

THE GREAT EXHIBITION CATALOGUE

SILVERWARE, 1851

MACHINERY SECTION OF THE GREAT EXHIBITION

GOODS NEWS
More than 100000 objects were shown at the Great Exhibition. They were arranged in categories, which included machinery, textiles and cutlery, with examples illustrated in a catalogue.

museum was rebuilt on the same site between 1823 and 1852.

In 1776 the Earl of Pembroke opened his home, Wilton House near Salisbury, to the public free of charge. The idea was immediately popular and that year the house received some 2500 visitors. When the Earl of Leicester granted access to Holkham Hall in Norfolk a year later, 'noblemen and foreigners' were allowed to visit from Mondays to Saturdays. 'Other people' were allowed on Tuesdays only. But it was financial necessity, not generosity, that led the 6th Marquis of Bath to open Longleat in Wiltshire to the public in 1949, making it the first stately home to be run as a commercial enterprise.

LIVING WONDERS
Botanical and zoological gardens

In the early 15th century BC Queen Hatshepsut of Egypt imported frankincense trees and other exotic plants from Somaliland, which she displayed with leopards, monkeys and other wild animals to impress visiting dignitaries and suitors. But it was her successor, Pharaoh Thutmose III, who extended the botanical collection with plants and seeds from Palestine and Syria.

Pleasure parks for entertainment, planted with ornamental trees, were built by both the Greeks and Romans, and similar parks existed in India by the 3rd century BC. The first modern European botanical garden, founded in Pisa, Italy, in 1543, was greatly influenced by contemporary discoveries in the New

World, such as the Aztec gardens of Montezuma I at Huaxtepec in Mexico.

Solomon, the Israelite king of the 10th century BC, kept menageries. In the 4th century BC the 300 creatures collected by the Macedonian king Alexander the Great became the subjects of Aristotle's *History of Animals*. When the Roman Empire fell, zoos disappeared and were not revived in Europe until the Middle Ages.

Henry I of England put the animals presented to him by other monarchs in a small zoo at Woodstock, Oxford, around 1100. In the 13th century three leopards given by Frederick II of Sicily to his brother-in-law Henry III became the first residents of London's Tower Menagerie. They were soon joined by 'a white bear', a polar bear from Norway, which was regularly observed fishing in the Thames.

The French king's menagerie at Versailles, where animals were kept for research and education, became a modern zoo in 1665. In London the royal tradition of housing wild animals at the Tower continued until 1828, when all the creatures were moved to the Zoological Gardens in Regent's Park under the management of the Zoological Society of London. Here the world's first reptile house opened in 1849, and the first insect house in 1889.

Fish were kept in captivity by the Sumerians about 4500 years ago, while the Chinese bred carp for food around 1000 BC. Goldfish, brightly coloured

FEEDING TIME *The Zoological Society of London was founded in 1826 for scientific purposes, but it also managed London's zoo as a place of popular public entertainment.*

AIR POWER *In the 1760s Philip Astley discovered that if he stood on the back of a horse while it galloped in a circle, centrifugal force helped to keep him balanced. In the following century Jules Léotard (inset) swung through the air on a trapeze in the skintight garment that was to be named after him.*

varieties of carp, were kept as pets during the Song dynasty (AD 960-1279). In 1596 the first book on aquarium management was written in China.

Goldfish in bowls were introduced into England in 1711, but larger aquariums were not possible until scientists had discovered how plants produce oxygen and how animals use it. By 1853 the first public aquarium had opened at London Zoo.

CIRCUS ACTS
Travelling wonders

The original circus was the racetrack of Roman times, with long straight sides and semicircular ends, but today's version was devised in England by a former cavalry officer, Philip Astley, in 1768. It gained the name 'circus' in 1782, when rival horseman Charles Hughes opened his Royal Circus in London.

By 1777 Astley, who was considered one of the best horsemen of his day, had created a show that incorporated 'The Little Military Learned Horse', a strongman named Signor Colpi, clowns and acrobats. A monkey was soon added, and in 1832 a lion, a tiger and some zebras were led around the ring.

Acrobats, jugglers and clowns all performed in ancient times, as did animal tamers. Alfred the Great, the 9th-century king of Wessex, was once entertained by a wild-beast show. But the first of the modern animal tamers, the Frenchman Henri Martin, performed with lions, an elephant and a boa constrictor in 1831 at the Cirque Olympique in Paris. Morok the Beast Tamer, born the American Isaac Van Amburgh, claimed to be the first person to put his head inside a lion's mouth. In 1838 he entered the ring of Astley's Amphitheatre.

The flying trapeze was born out of the daring of the Frenchman Jules Léotard, who first performed with the Cirque Napoléon in Paris in 1859 at the age of 21. Initially a pile of mattresses was the only protection against dangerous falls for Léotard and other circus performers. The safety net was introduced by a Spanish acrobatic troupe, the Rizarellis, at the Holborn Empire in London in 1871.

OLYMPIAN IDEALS
The victors

Athletic sports, including running and ball-and-stick games, were popular among the ancient Egyptians. But in Greece sporting ability also took on a religious dimension. At certain sacred sites dedicated to the gods events grew in prominence, drawing athletes and spectators from the various city-states. Most renowned of these were the Pythian Games at Delphi; the Nemean Games held at Nemea or Argos; the Isthmian Games at Corinth; and the Olympic Games, held in honour of Zeus, the father of the gods, every four years at Olympia. All four events comprised the Crown Games, named from the crowns of leaves given to winners.

The original Olympic victory was recorded in 776 BC when Coroebus of Elis, a cook, won the *stadion*, a track race of approximately 185 m (200 yd), which gave rise to the word 'stadium'. According to legend, this was the farthest that the hero Herakles (known to the Romans as Hercules) could run in a single breath.

By 500 BC the games were attracting some 40 000 spectators. As part of the religious ritual athletes, accompanied by their trainers, would arrive a month in advance for a strictly supervised pre-games ritual. Athletes would compete naked for the three days of the games, probably because the Greeks were proud of their bodies, which they regarded as divine gifts, and wished to display them. Only winners were honoured—no recognition was given to those who came second or third. From the beginning contenders competed for money and bribery was commonplace.

THE RACE *With a high-stepping gait, Greek runners compete in the 6th century BC. When revived in 1896 the Olympics took place in Athens, in a stadium constructed to an ancient Roman design. More than 300 male athletes from 13 countries took part in nine sports.*

SPORTING DEEDS

• Leonidas of Rhodes won the foot-race in four Olympiads between 164 and 152 BC.

• In 1812 sportsmen competed at the first modern athletics contest, held at the Royal Military College, Sandhurst, England.

• Judo, whose name means 'easy way', was developed in Japan in the 19th century. It derived from the ancient martial art of jujitsu, which had fallen into disrepute by this time because of its dangerous techniques. Judo's inventor was Dr Kanō Jigorō, who opened his first *dojo*, 'training hall', in 1882.

UNITED ENDEAVOUR
The interlocking Olympic rings represent competitors' homelands: Europe, the Americas, Africa, Asia and Oceania.

The Roman emperor Theodosius, who banned all pagan festivals, ended the games in AD 394.

In Britain the Cotswold Olympics were held in 1604, nearly 300 years before the modern Olympic Games began. Between 1859 and 1889 the Greeks tried to reintroduce the games. But their efforts were thwarted by rioters protesting that only wealthy athletes could afford to travel to Athens to train. At about this time Baron Pierre de Coubertin, a French educationalist, suggested to his country's government that it should find a way to improve the physical condition of France's youth.

Coubertin's plan for reviving the Olympic Games, not just for the French but for young people from other lands, was accepted, and the International Olympic Committee was formed in 1894. It resolved that 'sports competitions should be held every fourth year on the lines of the Greek Olympic Games'. The modern Olympic Games were inaugurated in Athens in April 1896. The first winter games were held at Chamonix, France, in 1924.

The symbol of the Olympics—five interlocking rings—was designed by Coubertin in 1913. It was first used for the Antwerp games of 1920, accompanied by the motto *Citius, Altius, Fortius,* 'swifter, higher, stronger', written by Father Henri Didon, a Dominican friar. The Olympic flame, which burns constantly throughout the games, was first used in 1928 at Amsterdam. It may recall the relay races run in ancient times (although not at Olympia) using torches, not batons.

IN COMPETITION
The earliest events

Although by 3800 BC organised races probably took place in Egypt, the Greeks were the ancient masters of athletics. The *daiulos,* a race to the end of the track and back, was added to the one-length *stadion* in the Olympics of 724 BC. It was followed four years later by a *dolichos* or endurance race.

After the demise of the ancient games, track and field sports were rare until the 12th century and even then were often banned for being distractions from military archery. The marathon, a 42.195 km (26 mile 385 yd) race, dates back to the 1896 Olympics. It commemorates Pheidippides, who ran from Athens to Sparta with a plea for help after the Persians, en route to attack Athens, reached Marathon in 490 BC.

In 708 BC the pentathlon, comprising the five disciplines of long jump, discus, javelin, running and wrestling, was introduced. Long jumpers often held weights to provide extra momentum.

BRONZE DISCUS,
GREECE, 6TH CENTURY BC

BODY CONTACT
Wrestling, boxing and the martial arts

Throws, headlocks, strangleholds and other skills of unarmed combat gave rise to wrestling, a pastime depicted in Egyptian wall paintings at Beni-Hasan in around 3400 BC. The Babylonians, Assyrians and ancient Chinese also wrestled, but the Greeks made the sport their own, crediting the mythical hero Theseus, who slew the Minotaur, with having laid down the first rules of 'scientific wrestling' in about 900 BC.

Greek wrestlers oiled their bodies. They then sprinkled powder or sand

FAIR SPORT *From the 4th century BC Greek boxers protected their hands with wrappings of leather strips. Centuries later, in 1743, the English boxer Jack Broughton laid down the first set of rules (above, right) for less dangerous modern contests.*

over the oil to provide a 'second skin' and to help the body to stay warm. Wrestling was an Olympic sport from 704 BC. Its most fearsome and often fatal version was the *pankration,* introduced in 648 BC, which combined elements of boxing and wrestling. Only biting and gouging were forbidden.

Hieroglyphs drawn by the Egyptians in the 4th millennium BC suggest that boxing reached them from Ethiopia, then spread north to Greece. The physical intensity of combat was typified by Epeius, a boxer who in Homer's epic 8th-century BC poem the *Iliad* declares: 'With one mighty blow I will tear this fellow's flesh to ribbons.'

From 688 BC boxing was included in the Olympics, but despite its violence deaths were rare. The sport, which was adopted by the Romans, was later revived in 17th-century England. The first recorded bare-knuckle fight was between a butcher and his footman. It took place in 1681 to entertain the Duke of Albemarle. In 1719 James Figg, who had won so many fights that he was acclaimed as the champion of England, set up the first modern school of boxing in London. On his business card he described himself as 'Master of the Noble Science of Defence'.

DERBY COUNTY
GOALKEEPER,
FA CUP FINAL, 1899

FOOTBALL SCORES
Going for goal

Four thousand years ago the Egyptians played catch or casual kicking games with leather or linen balls stuffed with reeds or straw, and a kind of football may have begun in ancient China around 200 BC. Here *t'su chu*—literally, 'to kick a stuffed leather ball'—was enjoyed by players who attempted to kick the ball through a hole in a silk net.

Two teams were needed for *episkuros*, a popular ball game in ancient Greece and later in Rome, where it was known as *harpastum* or *pila pedalis*. One Roman stone tablet from the 2nd century AD and discovered at Sinj in modern-day Croatia shows a man holding a football made up of hexagonal sections.

Roman legions may have brought football to northern Europe; certainly by the 12th century a lawless, violent type of football was common in Britain. The ball was an inflated pig's bladder encased in leather. Shrove Tuesday was a traditional day for football, and in such Roman cities as Chester the game was said to have been played to commemorate the Romans' departure.

Feuds between football teams and their fans concerned medieval monarchs, starting with Edward II in 1314 who proclaimed: 'Forasmuch as there is a great noise in the city caused by hustling over large balls, from which many evils may arise, which God forbid, we command and forbid, on behalf of the King, on pain of imprisonment, such game…' The name of the game first appeared in an Act passed in 1424 forbidding the game of 'fute ball'.

Football remained a brutal game which, according to the Puritan Philip Stubbes in his *Anatomie of Abuses*

ELBOWED OUT *A blue-shirted Scottish defender elbows aside an English attacker as his teammate dribbles the ball downfield. The first official soccer international was played in Glasgow in 1872.*

of 1583, 'causeth fighting, brawling, contention, quarrel picking, murder, homicide and great effusion of bloode'. A century later a violent version was still being played at schools such as Eton and Winchester and only in 1848 did Cambridge University attempt to standardise rules for a safer 11-a-side game.

The Football Association (FA) was set up in 1863, when representatives of clubs and schools began the task of establishing a set of rules. By 1871 FA membership consisted of 30 clubs from London and the Home Counties. The following year the first FA Cup final was held at the Oval cricket ground, London: Wanderers beat the Royal Engineers 1-0. The desire for regular matches and payment for players led a dozen clubs to form the Football League in 1888. The word 'soccer' is derived from 1890s' Oxford University student slang for 'Association'.

CHINESE FOOTBALL BOOTS,
18TH-CENTURY ILLUSTRATION

SPORTING MILESTONES

- 1497 A football was bought for James IV of Scotland. Its price was 2 shillings.
- 1681 Charles II attended a football match between his servants and those of the Duke of Albemarle.
- 1744 The first known golfing trophy was awarded in Edinburgh.
- 1764 The course at St Andrews, Scotland, was the first with 18 holes.
- 1871 England played Scotland at rugby for the first time.
- 1875 The first known football programme was prepared for a match at Hampden Park between Queen's Park and Wanderers.
- 1887 Molesey Ladies, the first women's hockey club, was founded.

PLAYING RUGBY
Catch and try

In one version of their game of football Greek players attempted to throw or carry a ball over a line marking the end of the playing field, despite the resistance of the opposing team. The modern game of rugby, which has similar aims, derives from ancient ball games but was not played until 1823. In that year, so sporting legend relates, William Webb Ellis, a student at Rugby School in Warwickshire, caught the ball during a game of football and ran with it. In other versions of the traditional tale, the first handling of the ball is dated to 1838 or 1839 and the instigator is said to have been a boy named Mackie.

Whatever the truth, from 1841 'running-in' with the ball was permitted at Rugby and a few other public schools. In 1846 *The Laws of Football as Played at Rugby School* were published, establishing the first rules for scrummaging. It also stated that 'All matches are drawn after 5 days or after 3 days if no goal has been kicked.' Points were not scored for a touchdown, but for a subsequently successful 'try' at kicking the ball over the crossbar.

In 1871 the Rugby Football Union (RFU) was created as the governing body of the sport in England. The size of teams remained fluid until 1875, when

PASSING MOVE *One of the running moves of rugby, developed from about 1875, is played out in a match between Yorkshire (with the ball) and Lancashire in 1895. The shape and size of the oval ball was fixed in 1892 (top).*

sides of 15 players were introduced in a match between the universities of Cambridge and Oxford.

A dispute in 1895 over financial compensation for rugby players' unpaid, or 'broken', time spent away from their jobs led 22 clubs from the north of England to form the breakaway Northern Football Union. The NFU developed its own rules, and in 1906 stipulated that sides should consist of only 13 players. It renamed itself the Rugby Football League in 1922.

A ROUND OF GOLF
The game of clubs

Hockey may be the most ancient of all ball-and-stick games. A drawing in an Egyptian tomb at Beni-Hasan, created in about 2000 BC, shows two youths with sticks contending for a ball. And a Greek marble carving from about 500 BC also shows young men with bent sticks and a ball.

From the 1750s hurley, shinty and bandy were played in Ireland, Scotland and Wales. Hockey, probably named from *hoquet*, an Old French word for a shepherd's crook, developed into an organised sport in the Victorian era. At a club founded in 1861 at Blackheath in southeast London, a game said to be unsuited to 'weakly or timid players' was played with a 200 g (7 oz) rubber cube.

The modern game, which is played with a ball and incorporates the bully, began in 1871 at Teddington, south-west London. It became popular among the upper classes after it was taken up by the Duke of Clarence in the 1870s.

Many cultures boast games similar to golf. In the 10th-century Chinese game *chiuwan*, bamboo-shafted clubs were used to hit hardwood balls into holes in the ground marked with flags. Traders may have brought the game to the West, but similar European games such as the Dutch *kolven* or *kolf*, in which a ball was aimed

at posts placed at each end of a short course, probably arose independently from the Middle Ages.

The object of the golf that was played from the 15th century on the east coast of Scotland, from which the modern game originates, was to hit the ball into a distant hole. By 1457 the game was well established and was soon taken up by women. Mary, Queen of Scots was censured by the Church in 1568 for playing the game so soon after the murder of her husband, Lord Darnley, the previous year.

Early courses were rough, with narrow fairways, but from the middle of

CLUB PRACTICE *At Blackheath, where golf was introduced around 1610, a pensioner from the Royal Naval Hospital, Greenwich, carries the clubs. 'Caddie', from the Old French* cadet, *a page at court, dates from the 1790s.*

the 19th century they gradually began to take on their modern look with clipped greens. The first golf balls were probably made of wood. Leather featheries, balls that were filled with as many compressed, boiled feathers as 'would fill the brim of a top hat', succeeded them in the early 17th century. In 1898 the modern rubber-cored ball was invented by the American golfer Coburn Haskell, assisted by the rubber engineer Bertram Work.

THE CRICKET MATCH
Leather on willow

No one knows when countrymen of the Weald in southern England began using stones and sticks to play the game destined to become cricket. What is certain is that a county sport developed from a custom of shepherds. One stood in front of a wicket-gate with a stick, while another hurled a stone to hit the 'bail', or crosspiece, on the gate top. 'Bail' is Old French in origin, going back to *baillier*, 'to enclose', or even farther back to the Latin *baculum*, 'stick'.

'Cricket' probably comes from *crok*, an Old English word for a shepherd's crook or curved staff. Another possible early name for the game was 'creag'. In 1300 the royal wardrobe accounts recorded 100 shillings being laid out for

VICTORIAN HERO *Dr William Gilbert 'W.G.' Grace was the greatest cricketer of his day. In a career lasting from 1865 to 1908 he played in 22 Tests, scored 126 centuries and took 2876 wickets.*

GENTLEMEN'S PURSUIT *Cricketers of about 1740 enjoy a game at the Artillery Ground in London, while the umpire keeps score by cutting notches in a stick. Enthusiasts played the game in their everyday clothes, with hats and tailcoats removed for ease of movement.*

Prince Edward to 'play at creag'. The word 'cricket' was in use by 1550, when, as 'a scholler in the free school of Guldeford', John Derrick, later to become a coroner, 'and several of his fellowes did runne and play there at crickett and other plaies.'

The laws of the game were not laid down until 1744. Cricket was becoming widely popular, particularly in southern England, by the time that Thomas Lord, the Yorkshire-born entrepreneur and a keen cricketer, opened his ground in 1787. It was in Dorset Fields (now Dorset Square), part of the Marylebone estate.

Lord had been attached to the White Conduit Club where he met the Earl of Winchelsea. The earl and a number of other aristocrats encouraged Lord in his venture, and the Marylebone Cricket Club (MCC), which became responsible for the laws of the game, was born. Lord's ground and the MCC moved to their present location in north-west London in 1814.

Cricket travelled all over the world with the British Empire, and was introduced into Australia by a ship's crew in 1803. In 1877 Australia beat England in the first Test (international) match, held in Melbourne. After an 1882 match, played at the Oval in London, in which England lost again to Australia, the *Sporting Times* commented that English cricket would be 'cremated and its ashes taken to Australia'. This led to the Ashes games between Australia and England, whose trophy is an urn (which remains permanently at Lord's) containing the ashes, probably of a bail burned on England's tour of Australia in 1882-3.

ANYONE FOR TENNIS?
Rackets and royalty

A French handball game, *jeu de paume* or 'game of the palm', played from the 12th century in French monastery cloisters, became so popular that Paris had at least 13 manufacturers of balls for the game by 1292. Its modern name, tennis, comes from the French *tenez*, a word probably called out by the server before hitting the ball and shortened from the expression *tenez-vous prêt*, or 'get ready'. The game was first recorded in English as 'tenetz' by the poet John Gower in 1399.

Early players hit the ball with their bare hands. They soon devised large gloves and eventually, to make them lighter, the centres were replaced with a taut, elastic rope weave. By about 1500, short-handled rackets appeared, and both hands and rackets were used to hit the ball.

Tennis was popular with the French kings, who did much to introduce the game to the rest of Europe. When Henry V received some balls from the future Charles VII of France in 1414, he started a tradition of aristocratic play in Britain. The first tennis world championships, the oldest of all sporting world championships, was won by the French player Monsieur Clergé in about 1740. He held his title for nearly a decade.

The game at which Clergé excelled was what we now know as real tennis. Played in an enclosed court, the ball is allowed to bounce off a wall. The modern game of tennis is a direct descendant of real tennis. The inventions of the rubber ball, which could bounce on grass, and the lawn mower, used to create a smooth playing surface, meant that tennis began to be played regularly on grass in the mid 19th century. More powerful rackets with longer handles appeared at about the same time. But the first lawn tennis club was not founded until 1872, at Leamington, Warwickshire.

In 1874 Major Walter Clopton Wingfield of Wales published the rules for the game, played on an hourglass-shaped court. The following year he took out a patent for what he called 'Sphairistiké' (from a Greek word for 'ball game'). The game, he explained, could 'be played in any weather by people of any age and both sexes'.

In 1875 J.M. Heathcote, a real tennis player who had started to play lawn tennis, asked his wife to cover a ball in flannel to make it easier to hit on wet grass, and the idea quickly caught on.

GIRL WITH SHUTTLECOCK
AND BATTLEDORE, 18TH CENTURY

THIS SPORTING NATION

- Baseball is first mentioned in *A Pretty Little Pocket Book*, an English book of games published in 1744.
- Squash was probably invented by boys at Harrow School, and was being regularly played there by 1850.
- In about 1879 the Duke of Beaufort adapted the ancient children's game of battledore and shuttlecock, playing it over a net at Badminton, his Gloucestershire home.

Lawn tennis became so popular that the All-England Croquet Club at Wimbledon, in London, was persuaded to set aside a lawn for tennis. In 1877 it became the All-England Croquet and Lawn Tennis Club and as such instituted the first Wimbledon Tennis Championships, in which a rectangular grass court was used. Only 22 players, all of them men, entered the championship, which was won by Spencer Gore. The first winner of the women's championship, inaugurated in 1884, was Maud Watson.

WINNING PLAY *In the Wimbledon women's final of 1914, Dorothea Lambert Chambers's unflagging determination and skill in placing the ball led to her victory over Ethel Larcombe.*

HITTING HARD *Medieval real tennis players whacked the ball with bound hands in a walled court. When lawn tennis became established in the 1800s, wooden rackets strung with sheep's intestines (left) were used.*

ON HORSEBACK

*'His colour is Bay, and his near foot before with both his hind feet
have white upon them, he has a blaze downe his face, something of the largest. He is
about 15 hands high, of the most esteemed race among the Arabs.'*

THOMAS DARLEY, WRITING ABOUT THE DARLEY ARABIAN COLT, 1703

A DAY AT THE RACES *A racecard from the
Roodee at Chester details the horses running
on May 2, 1791, and the prize monies to be
won. Such cards were first printed during the
18th century but the Roodee, where racing still
takes place today, had become the site of
Britain's first permanent racecourse by 1540.*

In the steppes, the grasslands that
extend from the Ukraine to
Mongolia, horses were first corralled
for food in around 4300 BC. Here, too,
where horses had roamed wild for
centuries, someone was first inspired
to jump up on horseback. This lasting
partnership predated the wheel as a
form of transport by 500 years.

Riding spread through both
trade and war, but migration was
slow and horse-drawn chariots did
not appear in the Middle East until
about 1800 BC. Horses made their
sporting debut at the Olympic Games
in Greece where four-in-hand chariot
races were run from 680 BC.

Early riders sat bareback or on
blankets, but saddles made balancing
much easier. Leather saddles were

AT A GALLOP *The Derby, like all Classics a
race for three-year-olds, began in 1780 as an
annual contest of 1.6 km (1 mile) across Epsom
Downs in Surrey. In 1784 the distance was
extended to 2.4 km (1½ miles).*

developed by the Scythians, nomadic
warriors of central Asia, between the
3rd century BC and the 1st century AD.
The saddle was further improved in
medieval Europe to hold heavily
armed knights more securely in place.

Scythian horsemen also devised the
first stirrups, pictured on a vase of
the 4th century BC from Chertomlyk
in the Ukraine, and the horse collar.
Scythian stirrups of iron are said to
have been introduced to Europe by the
Asiatic chieftain Attila the Hun,
who repeatedly invaded the Roman
Empire in the mid 5th century AD.

ROPE BIT WITH ANTLER CHEEKPIECES, UKRAINE, 4000 BC

IRON BIT, BOHEMIA, 6TH CENTURY BC

CONTROLLED POWER *Wear marks on teeth from equine skeletons 6000 years old suggest that Ukrainians restrained their mounts with a rope bit placed in the horse's mouth and attached to cheekpieces carved from antlers. An extension of the bit formed the reins. By the Iron Age, metal bits were in use.*

Such stirrups were certainly being used in China and Japan by AD 600.

Horseshoes were fitted in Eurasia by the 2nd century BC. Nailed iron horseshoes probably arrived in Europe around the 5th century AD, introduced by invaders from the east, although they may also have been independently invented by the Romans.

Bareback horse-riding became an Olympic event as early as 648 BC, but the modern sport of horse-racing was developed by the Arabs. Horses had already been raced long before the first hippodrome, or racing track, was built in Baghdad in the 8th century AD.

When the Crusaders returned to Europe between the 11th and 13th centuries they brought Middle Eastern horses home with them. These were raced as a way of showing off their speed to prospective buyers. The secretary to Thomas Becket, the Archbishop of Canterbury, wrote in about 1160 that 'jockies, inspired with thoughts of applause, and in the hope of victory, clap spurs to the willing horses, brandish their whips, and cheer them with their cries.' The first record of a financial prize occurs some 30 years later, when £40 was offered by Richard I to the winner of a 4.8 km (3 mile) race contested by knights.

In the early 15th century races were initiated in Europe at Sanlúcar de Barrameda in Spain. Britain's most ancient race is most probably the Kiplingcotes Derby, at Market Weighton, Yorkshire, which has been run on every third Thursday in March since its inception in 1519.

Racing in Britain became more organised in the 17th century when Charles II established the spring and autumn meetings at Newmarket, Suffolk, which remain pivotal to the racing calendar. For many of the races the king donated prizes of 100 guineas' worth of silver plate. Two or sometimes three horses would take part in each race, probably because no more were available locally. To win, a rider had to be victorious in two heats. For 'sweepstakes' the prize was a purse to which each owner had contributed beforehand.

As racing became more fashionable, fields grew larger and new racecourses were established, including Royal Ascot, founded by Queen Anne in 1711. But modern racing did not begin until the inauguration of the English Classics—the St Leger in 1776, the Oaks in 1779 and the Derby in 1780.

Unless they owned their mounts, the successes of early jockeys were not recorded. In 1822 Weatherby's *Racing Calendar*, which had existed since 1773, began publishing the names of some winning jockeys at major courses. The oldest racing publication is *Cheny's Horse Matches*, a record of all the stakes wagered in races, which was launched at Newmarket by John Cheny in 1727.

The first woman jockey on record is 22-year-old Alicia Meynell, the mistress of a Colonel Thornton. In 1804 Meynell rode sidesaddle on her lover's 20-year-old horse Vingarillio against a Captain William Flint, over a 6.4 km (4 mile) course at York. Meynell started favourite at 5-4 on, but lost the race.

BENT ON VICTORY *Polo was played in China by the 8th century AD. According to the 11th-century Persian poet Firdausi, the game was invented in ancient Persia around 600 BC. Its name comes from 'pulu', the Tibetan word for 'willow root', from which the balls were made. Polo was brought to Britain by British army officers who first encountered it in India in the 19th century.*

EQUESTRIAN EXCELLENCE

• The English thoroughbred racehorse is descended directly through the male line from Arabian stock. It was bred from 43 'royal' mares and three stallions, the Darley Arabian, the Byerly Turk and the Godolphin Barb, brought to Britain between 1690 and 1730.

• Steeplechases, run over a course provided with artificial obstacles, probably originated in Ireland in the 18th century. Riders would mark a course through countryside, using church steeples as landmarks.

• The Grand National was first run at Aintree, near Liverpool, in 1839.

• Showjumping became popular from the mid 19th century at agricultural shows, which from 1875 staged leaping, or 'lepping', contests.

SKIER, ROCK PAINTING, NORWAY, 2000 BC

ON SKIS AND SKATES
Sports on snow and ice

The god of winter, so Norse legend relates, walked the world on skis. Pine and spruce skis 5000 years old have been found in Scandinavian bogs, and skiers depicted 4000 years ago in Norwegian rock paintings resemble their modern counterparts. In such sub-Arctic areas as Siberia short, wide snow boards were worn, sometimes with animal pelts attached to their undersides to prevent dangerous slipping.

Skis began as curved frames covered with leather, and lengthened in northern Europe; examples about 4000 years old found at Kalvtrask, Sweden, measured more than 2 m (6 ft). The mobility and sure-footedness that skis confer is

probably reflected in Roman legends that describe the northern Europeans as *hippopodes* or 'horse-footed'.

By the 15th century most of the armies in northern Europe were using skis. Skiing was recorded in parts of Slovenia in the late 17th century, but was unknown in France, Italy or Switzerland until it was introduced by British and Scandinavian travellers in the 19th century.

Downhill and competitive skiing started after 1840, when a Norwegian farmer's son named Søndre Norheim replaced the usual loose leather strap (which made sharp turns impossible) with a firm binding made from birch roots soaked in hot water. This binding held the heel and instep of the boot to the ski.

The first ski races were held near Oslo, Norway, in 1866 and by the turn of the century competition was widespread. International downhill slalom racing, named from the Norwegian for 'sloping path', began in 1927, but piste skiing still involved

arduous climbs. In the Swiss Alps trains used by summer visitors were adapted for skiers, and in 1932 the Parsenn cable car opened at Klosters in Switzerland.

Two thousand years ago skates were fashioned from the bones of elk, ox and reindeer. But although the word comes from the Old North French *escace,* meaning 'stilt', skating probably originated in Scandinavia. By the Middle Ages, it was widely enjoyed as a pastime on the frozen canals of Holland. A Dutch engraving of 1498 depicts the patron saint of skating,

ICE DANCERS, USA, ABOUT 1910

VILLAGE FREEZE *Ice-skating was a means of winter travelling for these 17th-century Dutch villagers, who also enjoyed ball-and-stick games on the ice (below, centre right). By the 20th century skating was almost exclusively a leisure pursuit.*

WINTER LEISURE *A poster from 1905 advertises sporting holidays on Mont Blanc at the fashionable resort of Chamonix, France. Leisure skiing began in the 19th century and soon became popular among wealthy city-dwellers.*

St Lydwina of Schiedam, who when she was 16 in 1396 broke a rib in a fall. It is the first known illustration of the sport.

If not before, British skaters certainly took to the ice in the Great Frost of 1662. On December 1 of that year the diarist Samuel Pepys recorded seeing people in St James's Park, London, 'sliding with their skeetes, which is a very pretty art'. In 1683, during another Great Frost, Pepys danced on the ice with Charles II's mistress, Nell Gwyn.

In about 1740 the first skating club was founded in Edinburgh and 30 years later the first skating manual, written by Captain Robert Jones, an officer in the Royal Artillery, was published. Knowledge of the sport travelled to North America, where in 1848 E.W. Bushnell of Philadelphia invented an all-iron skate that clipped onto a boot. The first mechanically refrigerated ice rink, the

GLIDING AHEAD *Viking invaders brought their skates to Britain in the 10th century. This pair, made of bone, was found in York.*

Glaciarium, opened in London in King's Road, Chelsea, in 1876.

The Dutch developed competitive speed skating in the early 19th century, and it became popular in the Fenlands of Britain where a contest was first held in 1814. Half a century later Jackson Haines, an American dancing master, demonstrated a skating technique that used dance movements; through such innovations, figure skating evolved.

TAKING AIM
Archery and darts

LONG SHOTS *When shooting in the village butts, during compulsory practice, these Tudor crossbowmen left a record of their accuracy on a piece of paper attached to the target.*

The original arrows, wooden sticks with stone heads attached, were hurled for survival, not sport, about 50000 years ago in North Africa. Here also, by 15000 BC, flexible sinews and sticks had been combined into bows. The ancient Egyptians were the first to make archery a peaceable pastime, a custom continued by the Greeks, whose legendary hero Odysseus won the hand of Penelope in an archery competition.

For millennia the bow and arrow remained man's most lethal weapon. To ensure their bowmen's skills were well honed, 13th-century English monarchs kept bows and arrows available for practice. Sporting archery grew as the gun gained military supremacy and in 1537 Henry VIII endorsed the foundation of the Fraternity of St George, which conducted both archery and firearm shooting. In his educational book *Toxophilus, the Scole of Shooting*, dedicated to his monarch in 1545, Roger Ascham, tutor to Princess (later

Queen) Elizabeth, recommended it as excellent exercise and recreation.

At competitions Tudor archers took aim from a distance of some 144-216m (160-240yd), targeting a straw mark 45cm (18in) across with a wooden peg placed at its centre. Archers attempted to 'make a length' by shooting all their arrows the same distance—this being the object in battle. In butt shooting, a paper disc was mounted on a butt, a mound of earth, sited some 90-126m (100-140yd) from the bowman.

In the 18th century the foundations of modern archery were laid by Sir Ashton Lever of Alkrington Hall, Manchester, with the assistance of his secretary Thomas Waring, a skilled bowmaker. Lever founded the Toxophilite Society in 1781, after which archery became widely popular.

By the 17th century French children were playing a game called *les dards* using a square piece of paper marked with a bull's-eye and four-feathered darts. The game became an adult favourite, often played in public houses, from the early 20th century. It spread rapidly after the *News of the World* promoted a darts competition in 1927.

TABLE AND TARGET
Billiards, snooker and skittles

Mary, Queen of Scots, who ruled from 1542 to 1567, enjoyed a game of billiards, which was probably known from the 15th century. When billiards was described in 1598 by John Florio, an Anglo-Italian writer, as 'a kind of play with balles upon a table', the cue was flattened into a spoon shape at one end for hitting the ball. It became a tapered rod in the 19th century. In 1875, officers of the Devonshire Regiment invented snooker, named from the slang word for a new cadet at the Royal Military Academy, Woolwich, London.

A game similar to ten-pin bowling has been found in an Egyptian child's grave of around 5200 BC. Skittles originated in Germany. There peasants first threw stones at flat-bottomed clubs in the 3rd century AD.

BOARD GAMES

*'It takes too long to play, there's no winning post, no finishing line, the rules
are too complicated and the players just keep going round and round.'*

REJECTION LETTER FROM PARKER BROTHERS TO CHARLES DARROW ABOUT HIS MONOPOLY GAME, 1933

Their rules are lost, but board games were first played for entertainment nearly 9000 years ago. Boards with parallel rows of holes—perhaps for a counting game or one involving a race to the finish—have been found in Syria and Israel, and date back to about 7000 BC. From such entertainments our modern board games evolved.

Chess, a game of skill that mimics battlefield strategies, probably originated in north-west India as *chaturanga*, a two-handed game without dice in which real battles were replayed in miniature using pieces representing the fourfold division of the Indian army: infantry, chariotry, cavalry and elephants.

The first mention of chess, as the game *shatranj*, is found in the Persian *Karnamak-i-Artakshatri-i-Papakan*, a romance written in the early 7th century AD about Ardashir, the 3rd-century founder of the Sassanid dynasty. Chess travelled, it seems, from India to Persia, perhaps during the reign of King Khusrau Nushirwan, from 531 to 578, or that of King Khusrau II Parwiz, from 590 to 628.

Then, with the Arab conquest of Persia in the 7th century, it went west to Europe by a variety of routes. By 1000, court chess players in Baghdad were solving complex problems. By the 15th century European chess allowed a first pawn move of two squares, and increased the queen's powers.

In 1996 a board with 8 by 12 squares was discovered in a grave at Stanway in Essex which dates to the 1st century AD. Each player had 12 identical pieces, and a thirteenth that was different. The game is probably a local version of the Roman game of *latrunculi*—a strategic contest that involved trapping the enemy's pieces. This may be a forerunner of draughts, a game of strategy that seems to have been invented to play on a chessboard in the 12th century in southern France. However, Polish

FALL FROM GRACE *The first English version of snakes and ladders, with snakes representing punishments for bad behaviour, was produced in 1892 by F.H. Ayres. His original board was unconventionally circular.*

draughts, played on a board of 10 by 10 squares, appeared in Paris around 1725.

Ludo's predecessor, which came from India, was *pachisi*, or *chaupat*, usually played by four players on a cross-shaped board of cloth with arms 30 cm (12 in) long. Dice or cowrie

PEACEFUL CLASH *Two Arabs pursue the strategies and tactics of the battlefield in a game of chess in 13th-century Spain.*

shells were thrown to determine each move. Pachisi, often called the 'national game of India', is certainly centuries old, although the earliest evidence of it dates to the 16th century when the Mughal emperor Akbar favoured play on an outdoor court in his palace at Fatehpur Shikri—using 16 beautiful maidens as his playing pieces. The Popular Game of Parcheesi, widely played by the British under the Raj, was registered in London in 1863.

Gyan chaupar, devised in India as a moral lesson for children, was the forerunner of snakes and ladders. Boards date back to the 18th century, but the game itself is probably much older. The Tibetan form of the game, according to tradition, originated in the 12th century AD. The goal—the last square on the board—was Nirvana, the Hindu state of perfect bliss. Each square was inscribed with such concepts as kindness, arrogance or charity. Ladders led from 'good' squares upwards towards Enlightenment, while snakes led downwards from 'bad' squares.

Monopoly, named from the Greek for 'owning everything', originated as The Landlord's Game. Patented in the USA in 1903 by the Quaker Elizabeth Magie, it was designed as propaganda against dishonest capitalist landlords. Handmade copies of the game circulated in the 1920s. By 1924, when houses and

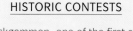

IVORY CHESS PIECE, INDIA, 17TH CENTURY

HISTORIC CONTESTS

• Backgammon, one of the first races to a finish involving a roll of a dice, probably comes from ancient Rome.

• The chess expression 'checkmate' comes from the Arabic *al shāh māt*, meaning 'the king is dead'.

• Allied POWs in Nazi-occupied Europe were sent specially designed Monopoly sets, with compasses, maps and blades hidden in them.

• IBM's Deep Blue was the first computer to win a chess competition. It beat the world champion Gary Kasparov in 1997.

---

hotels had been added, its moral message was lost.

In 1933 Charles B. Darrow, an unemployed heating engineer from Pennsylvania, redrew the board on the oilcloth covering his kitchen table to depict Atlantic City. For counters he used charms, including a top hat, an iron and an old boot borrowed from his wife's bracelet. Darrow patented his version. After an initial refusal, based on '52 fundamental playing errors', Parker Brothers finally bought the rights in 1935.

An adapted English version based on the streets of London was manufactured in the same year by John Waddington, but the game's true origins were suppressed until exposed by a legal investigation in the 1970s. Earlier, in 1959, Cuba's communist leader Fidel Castro

had banned Monopoly and ordered all sets to be burned, claiming the game was immorally capitalistic.

Scrabble seems to have been invented in its finished form at the first attempt. In 1938 an American architect, Alfred M. Butts, submitted for patent the game Criss-Cross, which he had devised in 1931 while he was unemployed during the Depression. Butts determined the values of individual letters by counting the number of times each was used on the front page of the *New York Times*.

In 1946 handmade Scrabble sets with plywood letter squares, fashioned in his garage by Butts' partner James Bruno, a retired government official, went on sale as Lexico. Bruno was already turning out 200 sets a week by the time the US firm Selchow and Richter bought the rights in 1948 and mass production began in earnest— they sold it as Scrabble from the early 1950s. The British version, which was made by J.W. Spear and Sons, appeared in 1954.

Two Canadian journalists, Chris Haney and Scott Abbott, invented Trivial Pursuit one evening in 1979. Finding that their Scrabble set was incomplete, they came up with ideas for a new game. Trivial Pursuit sprang, said Haney, from 'one burst of creative energy'. Most of the questions were devised in England by Haney's brother John, who trawled the shelves of his public library in Weymouth, Dorset.

IN THE MONEY *By 1940—when Parker Brothers had manufactured Monopoly for five years—Charles Darrow was a millionaire.*

CHINESE 'MONEY CARD'

GERMAN COURT CARD, ACORN SUIT, BASED ON DESIGN OF 16TH CENTURY

MAMELUKE
FIVE OF POLO STICKS,
15TH CENTURY

HOLDING THE CARDS
Packs and suits

Enjoyed by both rich and poor, playing cards became all the rage in Europe in the 14th century. Some 400 years earlier, in AD969, the Chinese emperor Mu-tsung was said to have spent New Year's Eve enjoying card-like games. These were played with tokens marked with spots to indicate their values, rather like today's dominoes. Chinese 'money cards', which may also originate from the 10th century, were copied from banknotes. Although the first packs to have suits, they did not have court cards.

The Egyptian Mamelukes were making cards by the 13th century, and the oldest surviving fragment is from one of their sets. A Mameluke set of the 15th century comprised 52 cards in four suits: coins, which were similar to those of Chinese cards, polo sticks, swords and cups. Each suit had three court cards: the *malik* (king), *na'ib malik* (deputy king) and *thani na'ib* (second deputy).

Playing cards like those in the Mameluke set have been discovered in Spain where cards, or *naipes*, were known by 1371. Nine years later cards had also reached such cities as Basle, Paris and Florence. Aristocrats amused themselves with hand-painted cards. Other players used cards printed from wood blocks with colour applied with stencils or fingertips. These cards were the first printed materials to be mass-produced.

Names and symbols for the suits varied from country to country, as did the number of cards in a pack. Today's standard British pack originated from France in 1470. French

KING OF HEARTS, 17TH-CENTURY DESIGN

FOLLOWING SUIT *Islamic players kept the idea of suits, used in the Chinese card system, and introduced the world's first court cards into their packs. European countries created their designs on Islamic principles after the 14th century.*

KING OF HEARTS, 18TH CENTURY

TRADITIONAL VALUES *The English court cards and suits, accepted as the international standard since the 1930s, have altered little since their introduction in 15th-century France.*

PLAYING THE JOKER *The joker made his debut as the top card in euchre, a game played in the USA since the mid 19th century.*

playing cards were the first to contain a queen rather than the deputy king used elsewhere in Europe. Of the suits, *carreaux*, 'paving tiles', became our diamonds, *trèfles*, 'clover leaves', clubs, and *piques*, 'pikeheads', became spades, named from the Italian or Spanish word for 'sword'. The final suit of *coeurs* or hearts, remained constant.

Games in which 'tricks' are won by the highest card have been played ever since cards arrived in Europe. Two-handed whist was a game of rank first played in the 17th century. It developed from English triumph or trump, played by 1522 and the first game to feature a trump suit outranking the others for the duration of the game. Bridge or biritch, the four-handed game of rank destined to become the world's most popular card game, is derived from whist. The first set of rules was compiled around 1885 by a John Collinson.

Primero was fashionable at the court of Elizabeth I. William Shakespeare certainly knew it, and has Henry VIII playing it on the night of Elizabeth's birth. Three players bet on their hands, with pairs, three of a kind and three of the same suit sought-after combinations. From primero developed such five-card games as brag and French *poque*, based on betting and bluffing. Old poker, which was played with 20 cards, was being enjoyed in Mississippi by 1829, possibly after poque was introduced by French immigrants.

The father of rummy games is *conquian*, which was much played in Mexico before it moved north as coon-can into the USA around the 1850s. Gin rummy was first played in New York in 1909 and canasta was introduced around 1940 at Montevideo, Uruguay. Using two packs, including jokers, canasta became a worldwide craze in the 1950s.

PAIRING UP *Originally played by the lower classes, who called their game whisk, whist was being enjoyed by high society gamesters in coffee-houses and private homes by the 18th century.*

LEARNING AS FUN *Cards were used as aids for students from the 17th century, and in such educational games as French for Beginners from the 1800s.*

Carottes
Car-rot

Butcher

Boucher
Boo-sha

Tomb

A PERFECT FIT *This puzzle of Europe, made by John Spilsbury in 1766, is one of the oldest surviving 'dissected maps'. The term 'jigsaw puzzle' was first coined in the United States in the 20th century from the jigsaw, a vertical saw produced in 1793 for cutting sharp curves.*

name, the *stomachion*, meaning 'the problem that drives one mad'.

In a Chinese woodcut of 1780, two courtesans play with *chi-chiao*, 'seven clever pieces', later the Chinese tangram. Each *tan* represented a celestial body, the Sun, the Moon, Mars, Jupiter, Saturn, Mercury or Venus. The pieces could be arranged into hundreds of forms, from a triangle to a bird in flight.

Solving Rubik's Cube, patented in 1976 by the Hungarian Erno Rubik and designed to help architecture students to think three-dimensionally, was a global craze in the 1980s. In 1984 Larry Nichols, a Massachusetts chemist who had patented a similar puzzle in 1972, won a ruling invalidating the patent. But by then the craze had peaked and Rubik's association with the cube was on its way into the dictionaries.

SINGLE-MINDED *Solitaire, in which a player moves pegs step by step to leave just one in the centre of the board, was played in France by the end of the 17th century. Marbles were first used for the game in the 1850s.*

PUZZLE PARTS
Jigsaws and conundrums

An 18th-century London engraver and map-maker, John Spilsbury, devised the first jigsaw puzzles to help children to learn geography. Spilsbury made some 30 different versions of his 'map dissections', gluing prints onto thin sheets of mahogany before cutting them into segments. By the end of the 18th century puzzle pictures had become more amusing, but jigsaws remained an expensive rarity until the late 19th century, when a die was invented which could stamp the shapes out of a sheet of card. This, and the development of colour lithography, allowed cheap and cheerful jigsaws to be produced.

However, the *loculus*, a 14-piece puzzle devised in the 3rd century BC by the Greek mathematician Archimedes, is the oldest known puzzle comprising a number of pieces. The difficulty of moving the pieces to form a square is described by the puzzle's alternative

HIDDEN MEANINGS

• Puzzle rings, made of interlocking pieces, are the descendants of gimmal rings, which were used as betrothal and wedding rings from the early 15th century.
• In Denmark, Norway and Iceland the card game patience is called *kabal*, meaning 'secret knowledge', which suggests that it may be related to telling fortunes.
• A flourishing trade in secondhand cards sprang up in Britain after taxes were levied on packs in the early 17th century. After 1765 aces of spades were printed by the commissioner of stamps and used to show the amount of extra tax paid. This created a market for forgeries.
• Chinese cards from the Ming dynasty (1368-1644) bore portraits of characters from the *Water Margin*, a popular novel.

WORD POWER
Crossword puzzles

The Victorian parlour game of magic square or double acrostic, in which groups of words were arranged so that the same words read vertically and horizontally, inspired the crossword puzzle. Arthur Wynne, who was born in Liverpool but worked on *The New York World*, remembered his grandfather playing magic square and adapted it to include clues and blanks. In 1913 the newspaper published the world's first crossword. 'Torquemada' compiled the world's first cryptic crossword, which was published in 1925 in Britain's *Saturday Westminster*.

CHILD'S PLAY
A world of toys

In Mohenjo-Daro in the Indus Valley about 4000 years ago a child pulled along a model cart and its team of oxen. Other discoveries reveal that Egyptian children played with cats with movable tails, miniature snapping crocodiles and figures of bakers kneading dough. To a child from antiquity, a modern toyshop would contain many familiar favourites.

Parents and the children themselves fashioned toys from everyday materials until a German toy industry developed

PICTURE OF FUN *Youngsters at play are commonly shown on children's pottery from ancient Greece. This illustration of a child enjoying Kottabos ('Sink the dummy duck') is shown on a 5th-century BC toy cup.*

in the 16th century. It was so successful that most toys owned by the children of Europe in the next 300 years were made in that country. Typical toys were wooden animals, often made as sets to furnish farms and Noah's arks.

German craftsmen also applied their skills to metalwork. Miniature soldiers were made in the 13th century—woodcut prints show boys playing with model jousting knights. Most of these early figures were cut-outs from metal sheets. They became rounded only in 1893 when a London firm, Britains, used a hollow-cast moulding process to make model soldiers from the Life Guards cavalry.

Coaches and horse-drawn transport were common toys in the 18th century,

GIFT HORSE *Wooden horses are among the oldest surviving toys, dating back to the 5th century BC. This pull-along model of about AD 200 would have been an Egyptian infant's treasured companion.*

and model trains, including some that were propelled by steam, followed in the 19th. American companies became the first to produce clockwork train sets in 1855, and electric models in 1884. Pedal cars for children appeared in 1905, less than 20 years after motor cars were first manufactured. Construction sets for aeroplanes were available from 1913, a decade after the Wright brothers' first flight.

In the 19th century, an appreciation of the importance of play to child development led to the creation of construction toys. Wooden blocks that could be assembled into towns and castles were produced in Germany from 1800, and by 1850 American parents could buy 94-piece miniature log cabins for children to build.

In 1901 a Liverpool meat importer's clerk, Frank Hornby, patented a system based on interchangeable parts, thin strips of perforated metal held together with nuts and bolts. Marketed at first as 'Mechanics Made Easy', the system became even more popular in 1908 when it was renamed Meccano. One of the most successful construction toys was the Lego bricks system, named from the Danish *leg godt*, 'to play well'. It was devised in 1955 by the Danish carpenter and toy-maker Ole Kirk Christiansen.

HELLO DOLLY
Making figures

The earliest known doll-like figures, including the *ushabti* made by the ancient Egyptians, were not children's playthings but religious talismans which were used as funeral figures. From around 2000 BC these ushabtis represented servants who, in earlier times, would have been buried alongside their dead masters to serve them in the afterlife.

Small girls in ancient Greece played with jointed dolls made of baked clay. On reaching marriageable age at around 12, a girl would ritually abandon

MODEL PROGRESS

• Talking dolls, who could say *mama* and *papa*, were introduced in Paris in 1823 by the German musician Johann Maelzel.
• William Harbutt, an art teacher in Bath, invented a putty-like modelling material called Plasticine in 1897 after his students complained that clay dried too fast for easy working.
• In 1932 Meccano Ltd produced six miniature vehicles as accessories to its Hornby train sets. The cars were so popular that the range was relaunched in 1933 as Dinky cars, from the Scottish slang for 'tiny'.

such toys and dedicate them to Artemis, goddess of the Moon and of fertility, a custom later adopted by Roman girls.

Little is known about dolls in the Europe of the Middle Ages, but they were certainly commonly used as playthings by the 15th century. German woodcut prints of 1491 depict dollmakers at work fashioning figures out of wood, and some of the dolls even have movable limbs.

The earliest known doll's house, built in 1558, was commissioned by

WOODEN BUILDING BLOCKS, USA, ABOUT 1890

MECHANICS MADE EASY, 1901

Duke Albrecht V of Bavaria. Although the house was originally intended as a gift for his daughter, the duke found it so fascinating that he kept it on show in his private art collection. In Britain the oldest surviving doll's house dates from the 1690s and was given to Ann Sharp, daughter of the Archbishop of York, by Princess, later Queen, Anne, who was her godmother.

In the late 17th century the habit of dressing dolls in elaborate copies of the day's fashions was established. One early example, a jointed wooden doll made in about 1690, is said to have been owned by the family of James Edward Stuart, pretender to the British throne.

Dolls were known as 'toy babies' or 'babies' until the 18th century, when the word 'doll', a diminutive of Dorothy, first came into use. However, the first dolls to be fashioned in the image of an infant did not appear until about 1850, when wax models

OUT OF THE TOYBOX *Many of the most enduring toys satisfy children's natural instincts to imitate. Models of animals and people have been used in play since ancient times and replicas of such recent innovations as the car and train were instantly popular. Educational toys, including Meccano, bricks and modelling clay, cement the link between learning and play common to mammals.*

were made in England by Augusta Montanari and her son Richard.

'Wax dolls', with wax heads attached to wooden or cloth bodies, had been introduced in Germany during the 17th century. Mass-production techniques were first used for making dolls in the 19th century, when moulded heads made of papier-mâché or ceramic were turned out in their hundreds.

Dolls moulded from Celluloid, an early form of plastic, appeared in the USA in 1863. Twentieth-century additions include 'teenage' dolls such as Mattel Toys' Barbie. Named after 17-year-old Barbara Hondler, the daughter of the company's founder, she was launched in 1959. Barbie's first outfit was a zebra-striped swimming costume.

SOFT AND CUDDLY
Rag dolls and stuffed animals

A stuffed doll found in a Roman child's grave from the 3rd or 4th century BC is probably the earliest surviving rag doll. The person credited with first producing rag dolls on a commercial scale is Margarete Steiff, the German seamstress, who began a mail-order business selling felt elephants in 1880. The Steiff firm also claimed to have introduced plush bears, a cuddly version of the clockwork bears that were popular in the 19th century, at the Leipzig Fair of 1903.

Although Steiff bears, which from 1905 featured a button in one ear, were immediately popular, teddy bears were first created in 1902 in the USA. Morris Michtom, a sweetshop owner, and his wife began making stuffed bears after seeing a newspaper cartoon of a hunting incident in which Theodore Roosevelt, the American president, spared the life of a bear cub. They named their bear 'Teddy' after the president's pet name.

WOODEN DOLL WITH CONTEMPORARY CLOTHES, ABOUT 1750

STEIFF BEAR WITH EAR BUTTON, GERMANY, 1907

CLOCKWORK TRAIN, GERMANY, ABOUT 1895

DINKY TOYS, 1950S

PLASTICINE, ABOUT 1900

FLAT TIN SOLDIERS, FRANCE, 1920S

PAINTED WOODEN ARK ANIMALS, GERMANY, 1880S

REPLICA OF FIRST BARBIE, USA, 1995

PLAYGROUND GAMES
Children's favourites

In 1560 the Dutch artist Pieter Bruegel the Elder created *Children's Games*, a complex oil painting in which he depicted children amusing themselves with some 55 different pastimes of the day. Most of these games are still enjoyed by children today, from tree-climbing and blowing soap bubbles to playing hide-and-seek, king of the

A STEADY HAND *Children from ancient Greece and Rome enjoyed playing marbles. Early games used balls made of stone such as marble, hence the name.*

castle and games of marbles and jacks. A remarkable number of the games were ancient even in Bruegel's time. The children of ancient Greece played versions of pig in the middle (*chytrinda*), tug of war (*dielkustinda*) and hide-and-seek (*apodidraskinda*).

Many of these games have been recorded around the world. Blindman's buff was played in ancient Greece and in Rome, where it was called *chalke muia*, or 'brazen fly'. The English name comes from the Old French *buffe*, a 'buffet' or 'blow', and betrays its once more physical aspects.

Hopscotch was enjoyed in ancient Greece, where it may have been based on the myths surrounding labyrinths and mazes. These were symbols of the perplexities of human life. Hopscotch was later adopted by the Church as an allegory of the soul's hazardous journey from Earth to Heaven.

Chasing games, variously called tig, tag, he or it, are linked to ancient fears of being touched by evil or the devil. The idea that players are safe if they touch iron, thought in pagan times to guard against evil spirits, or wood, representing the Crucifix, clearly has religious connotations.

The first conkers were empty snail shells suspended on strings. They were only replaced with horse chestnuts in the 19th century. The name of the game may well stem from 'conqueror', referring to an unbeaten conker.

The children's singing game that begins 'Ring-a-ring o'roses', continuing 'A pocketful of posies, a-tishoo!, a-tishoo!, we all fall down,' may date to the Great Plague of London in 1666. Ringing bells called people to bring out

FUN TIME *Childhood pastimes have changed little since the Dutch artist Pieter Bruegel the Elder painted* Children's Games *in 1560. The detail shows a game of tug of war.*

their dead, the 'roses' were red spots, and posies of herbs were believed to ward off the disease. Sneezing was one of the symptoms of the disease.

At the climax of the rhyme 'Oranges and lemons', children chant 'Here comes a chopper to chop off your head…'. These words were not in the earliest written version of 1744, appearing only in the 19th century, but one theory is that they refer to the executions of Anne Boleyn and Catherine Howard, wives of Henry VIII.

ACTIVITY TOYS
Invention and exercise

Roller skates made a dramatic debut at a London masked ball in 1760 when Joseph Merlin, a Belgian instrument-maker, glided into the room on his contraptions playing a violin. Merlin promptly smashed into the opposite wall, breaking both his instrument and a mirror, and seriously injuring himself.

Not until 1823 was the idea of roller skates revived, by Robert John Tyers, a

HOP TO HEAVEN *When hopscotch was used by the Church to help to explain its teachings the last square was often called 'paradise'.*

London fruit merchant. Tyers had some success with his Volitos, which had five small wheels arranged in a line, much like the Rollerblades launched by the Canadian ice hockey player Scott Olsen in 1980. The traditional four-wheeled design was adapted by American surf-shop owner Bill Richards in 1958 to create the skateboard.

The Frisbee owes its invention to William Russell Frisbie, who in 1871 founded the Frisbie Pie Company in Connecticut. His pies were popular with students at Yale, the local university, who had fun throwing the empty saucer-shaped metal containers to each other. In 1948 Fred Morrison, a Los Angeles building inspector, produced a plastic version. Originally he named it Morrison's Flyin' Saucer, but later changed it to Frisbee, altering the spelling of the creator's name to avoid legal difficulties.

In 1957 Wham-O Manufacturing bought the rights to the Frisbee. Then, in 1958, it launched the plastic Hula-Hoop

THE HULA-HOOPING CRAZE BEGAN IN 1958

ANCIENT AND MODERN

• Variations on noughts and crosses were known in ancient Egypt, Greece, Rome and China, where the game was played by at least 500 BC. It was introduced into Britain by the Normans in the 11th century, when it was known as 'three men's morris'.
• Skipping, using a piece of rope which has handles attached to each end, probably dates back only to the 19th century.
• Yo-Yos were first mass-produced in the 20th century by the American David Duncan, who in 1929 bought the rights to what was then a popular toy in the Philippines. But such toys were also widespread in ancient Greece and China.

and created an instant craze. But hoops are ancient toys, featuring in Egyptian tomb paintings of 2500 BC.

The kite, named in English after the bird of prey, was being flown in China as early as 1080 BC, when it may have been used to frighten away evil spirits. Archytas of Tarentum, a Greek scientist, built kites in the 5th century BC, but the idea did not reach Europe until the late 16th century, when they were brought from the East by Dutch traders.

BOOKS FOR CHILDREN
A good read

'What is the use of a book,' thought Alice, 'without pictures or conversations?' When Lewis Carroll put these words into the mind of his heroine in *Alice's Adventures in Wonderland*, published in 1865, such thinking was still quite new. Books written specifically for children were rare before the mid 18th century. The earliest example in the English language, an eight-page collection of rhymes entitled *A Booke in Englyssh Metre, of the great Marchante Man called Dives Pragmaticus, very preaty for Children to reade*, was produced by Alexander Lacy in 1563. Almost a century later the Czech educationalist John Comenius introduced the first picture book, *Orbis Sensualium Pictus (The Visible World in Pictures)*, in 1658, published in Latin and German.

Increasing literacy among the young made specialised children's publishing commercially viable. The publisher John Newbery launched his business in 1744 with the games book *A Little Pretty Pocket Book intended for the Instruction and Amusement of Little Master Tommy and Pretty Miss Polly* and was responsible for many innovations.

In 1751 Newbery introduced the first children's magazine, *The Lilliputian Magazine; or the Young Gentleman and Lady's Golden Library*, a miniature monthly journal containing stories, jokes and songs. In 1765 he published the first novel written specifically for children, *The History of Little Goody Two-shoes*. The anonymous author of this rags-to-riches story is thought to be the novelist and playwright Oliver Goldsmith, an associate of Newbery.

SICKNESS AND HEALTH

Our ancestors attributed most disabling or fatal diseases to supernatural causes. Vengeful gods and spirits were believed to implant malevolent objects in their victims or to rob them of their souls. To cure the sick, spells were chanted, and potions concocted from plants and animals were given to entice back lost souls or dispel evil intrusions.

The preserved remains of human skeletons show evidence of ancient surgery. A right arm bone of a 40-year-old man who lived more than 45 000 years ago in what is now Iraq bears cut marks suggesting it was amputated above the elbow. Other simple surgical procedures such as lancing abscesses were recorded in the Babylonian Code of Hammurabi in the 18th century BC. Advice on herbal medicine and the treatment of wounds were included in this and other manuals, such as those written in Egypt in about 1500 BC.

Treating the whole patient was fundamental to early medicine. In the 4th century BC Hippocrates, the Greek 'father of medicine', stressed the importance of diet and exercise to good health. For about another 2000 years Western physicians largely accepted the ancient Greek belief that illness resulted from an imbalance of the four humours—blood, phlegm, black bile and choler (yellow bile). Treatments were devised to correct any imbalances, and many patients judged to have 'too much blood' were bled so severely that they only narrowly escaped death.

As the ancient Egyptians embalmed their dead they carefully sorted the different organs from

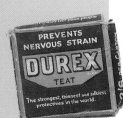

PREVENTS
NERVOUS STRAIN
DUREX
TEAT
The strongest, thinnest and silkiest
protectives in the world.

WILLS'S CIGARETTES.

TRIANGULAR BANDAGE
FOR THE SCALP

each other. In China and India, mutilating dead bodies was prohibited on religious grounds, but from about the 3rd century BC the Greeks, who learned their medicine from the Egyptians, began to dissect cadavers. Gradually the complex web of body systems and functions became clear, but no major advances were made until the 1500s, when surgeons such as the Frenchman Ambroise Paré performed dissections and recorded their findings.

Even in the 17th century most doctors believed, like the Graeco-Roman physician Galen in the 2nd century AD, that blood was made from the ingredients in food and drink, then destroyed as it was used. Regarding such views as mistaken, the British physician William Harvey conducted experiments that involved constricting human arm veins. He concluded that veins contain one-way valves to keep blood flowing towards the heart, which pumps blood 'constantly in a circular manner' around the body. Although he was declared 'crack-brained' by his peers after he published his theory in 1628, Harvey changed the course of medical history.

Despite such advances, epidemics remained rife in the 17th and 18th centuries. Most at risk were the inhabitants of crowded, insanitary towns and cities. Once the English physician Edward Jenner's work on vaccination during the 1790s had been accepted, the control of epidemics became possible, but improvements in public hygiene in the 1800s proved just as vital in preventing disease.

Surgery continued to be hazardous. Even if patients survived it, death from sepsis was likely until the English physician Joseph Lister introduced his antiseptic techniques in 1865. The diagnostic breakthroughs made possible in the late 1800s by the discovery of X-rays and the means of measuring blood pressure also helped to secure the foundations of modern medicine.

THE FIRST DISEASES
Infections and their origins

Some of the bodies that the ancient Egyptians preserved by mummifying bear witness to such deadly diseases as tuberculosis, smallpox, bilharzia and poliomyelitis. The Egyptians also made note of deaths from the 'plague', a word that was then used to describe a variety of fatal epidemics.

Ever since humans have been on Earth, they have suffered from infectious diseases caused by viruses, fungi, bacteria, protozoa and parasitic worms. Some of the first human diseases were caught from the other primates with whom our early ancestors shared their tropical habitats. Malaria and yellow fever are two of our oldest killers and were spread by flying insects. They became infected by feeding on primate blood, then presumably passed on the infection to humans by biting them.

About 250000 years ago humans began moving to temperate regions. Here there were no other primates from which diseases could be caught, but as humans huddled in caves for warmth and shelter they became hosts to parasites such as bed bugs, which had previously only infected cave-dwelling bats. Those infections able to spread themselves by physical contact or in the spray of coughs and sneezes now had a perfect opportunity to proliferate. Such diseases became even more successful from about 12000 years ago, when, with the beginning of agriculture, more humans began living at close quarters.

Crowded conditions also proved the breeding grounds of tuberculosis and typhoid. Rats and their fleas became vectors of bubonic plague, a disease which was first described by the Roman physician Rufus of Ephesus during the 2nd century AD.

UNDERSTANDING INFECTIONS
Cause and effect

Until the 19th century most illnesses were attributed to divine displeasure or to low-quality air—malaria was named from the Italian for 'bad air'. But diseases such as leprosy were known to be 'catching' from Old Testament times, when all lepers were declared 'unclean' and forced into isolation.

In the 1st century BC the Roman encyclopedist Marcus Terentius Varro speculated that disease might be caused by minute particles entering the body, and in the 6th century AD the Hindu doctor Suśruta suggested that malaria might be spread by mosquitoes. But the realisation that people or things could transmit 'plagues' was not accepted until the Middle Ages. From about 1380, after the plague or Black Death had exterminated nearly a quarter of Europe's population, ships carrying

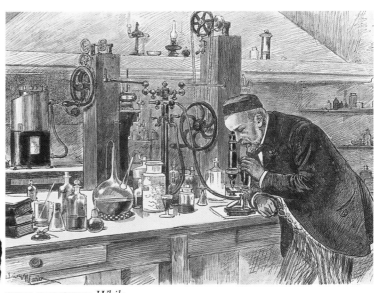

GERM DETECTIVE *While investigating why beer and wine spoil, the French chemist Louis Pasteur discovered that airborne organisms are responsible and that they can be destroyed by heat. In 1885 he produced a rabies vaccine by heating bacteria. Thus weakened, they could be injected into patients to make them immune.*

infection were refused entry to Venice. At Ragusa on the Adriatic, immigrants and traders had to remain outside the city for 40 days to prove they were not infected. This was known as *quarantinza*, from the Italian *quaranta*, 'forty', hence the word 'quarantine'.

Epidemics, suggested the Italian physician Giraolamo Fracastoro in 1546, were caused by 'seeds' wafted through the air or carried in water. Much later the microscope would help

BENT OVER *The humpback of a gardener depicted in an Egyptian tomb painting of about 1500BC was probably caused by Pott's disease, a tuberculosis of the spine.*

to confirm this principle, but as early as 1683 the instrument's Dutch inventor Anton van Leeuwenhoek probably viewed bacteria from his teeth by means of its powerful lens. In 1850 Casimir Davaine showed that anthrax could pass in the blood from infected to uninfected sheep and cattle, and detected rod-shaped anthrax bacilli in newly infected animals.

Even the most powerful microscopes could not detect viruses, the minute agents responsible for diseases such as polio. In 1892 the Russian bacteriologist Dmitry Ivanovski discovered that the agent of tobacco mosaic disease, which affects tobacco leaves, was not filtered out by a fine mesh that trapped bacteria. In the late 1930s, when the electron microscope was invented, viruses were finally observed directly.

PREVENTING INFECTIONS
Vaccination and cleanliness

In a practice that may originally have come from India, the Chinese of the 11th century AD put the scabs from pustules of smallpox victims into the nostrils of nonsufferers to give them a mild form of the disease and so prevent a severe attack. Although fatalities numbered 1 in 50 at best, this 'elective infection' quickly became widespread after being introduced into Britain in 1720.

By the 18th century it was well known in country districts that milkmaids who caught cowpox did not succumb to smallpox. Using a cobbler's needle, a farmer named Benjamin Jesty 'injected' his wife and family with pus from the udder of a cow infected with cowpox in 1774.

True vaccination was first achieved by the British physician and naturalist Edward Jenner. In 1796 Jenner encountered a dairymaid with fresh cowpox lesions on her finger. A few days later he inoculated eight-year-old James Phipps with pus from the dairymaid's pustules. The boy developed cowpox symptoms.

After a few weeks Jenner risked injecting Phipps with part of a human smallpox scab. To Jenner's relief and delight the child remained well. In 1798, after further successes, Jenner

published his results to public acclaim. Further vaccines—named later from *Vaccinia*, the cowpox virus—followed.

Louis Pasteur produced an anthrax vaccine in 1881. Crucially, he discovered how to reduce the deadly virulence of these bacteria before they were injected. The British anaesthetist John Snow showed that cholera was spread in water, and in 1854 stopped a cholera outbreak in London by removing the pump handle of a polluted public well.

THE CURE *The cowpox pustules on the hand of dairymaid Sarah Nelmes were used by Edward Jenner in 1796 for his pioneering inoculation. By the 1850s free smallpox vaccination was available in large cities.*

THE SEARCH FOR A CURE
Killing the enemy

Discovering a 'magic bullet' to quash disease was the German biochemist Paul Ehrlich's aim when, in 1909, he successfully synthesised Salvarsan, an arsenic-based compound. 'Sulpha' or sulphonamide drugs, patented in 1932 by the German bacteriologist Gerhard Domagk, cured some cases of meningitis and septicaemia, but there was no

DEADLY ANGEL *Advances in public hygiene in the 19th century, and the knowledge that diseases spread in dirty water, were hugely effective in preventing much-feared epidemics.*

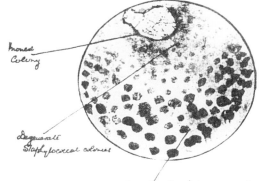

KILLERS KILLED *On his original drawing Alexander Fleming noted where groups of infective staphylococcal bacteria had been debilitated by the growth of penicillin mould.*

reliable cure for bacterial infections until after the discovery of penicillin.

Before leaving for a holiday in 1928 the bacteriologist Alexander Fleming left on a bench in his laboratory at St Mary's Hospital, London, some culture dishes of *Staphylococcus aureus* so that they could be disinfected. On his return he noticed that in one dish a growth of the green mould *Penicillium notatum* had wiped out the bacteria.

Fleming, unaware that the ancient Egyptians put moulds on wounds to prevent infection, discovered that *Penicillium* could kill many bacteria. In 1929, after treating his assistant for a staphylococcal infection, he published his findings. But only after 1940, when the German-born biochemist Ernst Chain and the Australian Howard Florey purified penicillin at Oxford University, was it put to practical use.

COOK'S SECRET *In his journeys of the 1770s, which included a landing in Tahiti (left), Captain Cook preserved the health of his men by insisting that they ate orange extract, sauerkraut and cress. Citrus fruits were later discovered to contain large amounts of vitamin C.*

VITAL INGREDIENTS
The story of vitamins

In 1912 Casimir Funk, a Polish-born American biochemist, coined the word 'vitamine' for a group of substances he thought to be 'vital' to life. Funk also believed these vitamines to be 'amines', chemicals derived from ammonia. The first part of Funk's theory was proved correct, the second partially so, which is why 'vitamin' lost its final 'e'.

Scurvy was an occupational hazard for sailors, although from the 1500s Dutch seamen benefited from including citrus fruits in their diet on lengthy voyages. Even if it did not kill him, scurvy made a sailor's teeth fall out, weakened his bones and prevented his wounds from healing.

By the time the British naval surgeon James Lind wrote his *Treatise of the Scurvy* in 1753, more British sailors succumbed to the disease than died in action. When Lind's advice that British sailors' diet should contain fresh citrus juice or fruit was adopted by the Royal Navy in 1796, scurvy vanished. What Lind did not know was that scurvy is caused by lack of ascorbic acid, or vitamin C, which citrus fruits contain.

Beriberi had been known in the East for millennia until in 1901 Gerrit Grijns showed that polishing rice removed an essential nutrient. Eating brown rice, with some of the husk left on, could prevent the disease, which results in fatal paralysis, emaciation and anaemia. It was named from *beri*, a Singhalese word for 'weakness'.

The English biologist F. Gowland Hopkins discovered in 1906 that animals, including humans, need to eat 'accessory substances' that the body cannot make for itself. In 1912, Casimir Funk discovered the antiberiberi substance, which was indeed an amine.

LIFESAVERS *Charles Best (left) and Frederick Banting injected insulin into dogs suffering from diabetes in order to conquer the disease.*

HORMONE TREATMENT
Understanding diabetes

In the Ebers papyrus, written during the 16th century BC, the Egyptians included prescriptions 'to drive away too much urine'. One recommended medicine was a liquid strained, after four days, from a mixture including cakes, wheat grains, green lead, soil and water. Aretaeus of Cappadocia, a physician of the 2nd century AD, was the first to describe diabetes accurately. Because of sufferers' frequent urination, he named it after the Greek word for 'siphon'. Aretaeus also recognised the thirst 'as if scorched by fire' and 'dreadful emaciation' typical of diabetes.

For another 2000 years diabetics continued to waste away because their pancreas glands were not releasing insulin, the hormone essential to the control of energy-supplying glucose from their blood. Thomas Willis, physician to Charles II, made a step towards identifying the cause in 1674 when he described the urine of diabetics as 'wonderfully sweet'. Thereafter the adjective *mellitus*, from the Latin 'honey-sweet', was added to the name.

In 1869 a German student named Paul Langerhans discovered the existence of thousands of minute tissue clusters in the pancreas. These were later named the islets of Langerhans in his honour. In 1889 two Germans, Oskar Minkowski and Joseph von Mering, discovered that the islets had some connection with diabetes, and from 1909 the term 'insulin', from the Latin *insula* ('island'), was being used for the islets' secretions.

Various attempts were made to extract insulin from the pancreas, but it was the pioneering work of Charles Best and Frederick Banting in the Toronto Medical School in Canada that made insulin treatment possible for diabetics. Banting and Best isolated insulin in 1921, and in January 1922, having injected each other to ensure the safety of their procedure, they administered it to their first patient, 14-year-old Leonard Thompson. The boy, who had been close to death, made a total recovery—and headline news. Thereafter he took regular doses of insulin.

MENTAL ILLNESS
Diseases of the mind

Divine displeasure and the power of evil spirits were, until the 19th century, the usual explanations for mental illness. Sufferers were routinely exorcised, banished, punished or locked up. But Greek physicians recognised a disease they named *apoplexia*, described by the Roman Caelius Aurelianus as a 'sudden collapse, as if from a deadly blow…in general without fever, and it deprives the body of all sensation.'

In about 400 BC the Greek physician Hippocrates linked apoplexy with black bile or melancholy, one of the four humours, and noticed that it was prevalent in rainy weather. As well as associating mental illness with an imbalance of body physiology, he and his successors prescribed a regime of calm and 'occupation', plus hellebore and other purgative drugs. But such sympathetic attitudes had disappeared in Western Europe by the Middle Ages, when witchcraft and demonic possession

SIGMUND FREUD, 1936

were again deemed the only reasonable explanations for insanity.

From the 8th century Muslim Arabs set up asylums for 'retreat and security'. The first hospital for the mentally ill had been founded in Spain by 1409, but by the 17th century most of Europe's mental patients were chained to the walls of dark 'dungeons'. The French physician Philippe Pinel, director of the Bicêtre asylum for men from 1793, removed patients' shackles and talked to them about their problems.

The idea of 'talking cures' became, in the late 19th and early 20th century,

IN THEIR MADNESS *'Bedlam', from William Hogarth's series of pictures* The Rake's Progress, *highlighted the indignities endured by mental patients in the 18th century.*

ANIMAL MAGNETISM *In treating patients under hypnosis, Freud was influenced by 'animal magnetism'. This was induced by Franz Anton Mesmer in the belief that it 'drew out' symptoms of 'hysterical fever'.*

central to the work of Sigmund Freud, the Viennese neurologist. In his *Studies on Hysteria* of 1893–5, regarded as the first written account of psychoanalysis, Freud described how nervous diseases, typified by symptoms such as paralysis and 'fits', could be linked to such drives and emotions as sexual desire and guilt buried deep in the unconscious mind.

Many of Freud's patients were analysed under hypnosis, a treatment practised by the ancient Egyptians to change states of mind. The term 'hypnotism', from the Greek *hupnos*, 'sleep', was coined in 1843 by the Scottish surgeon James Braid to describe trances induced by the Austrian physician Franz Anton Mesmer.

ILLS AND AILMENTS

• Arthritis has been detected in Neanderthal skeletons 50 000 years old. The ancient Egyptians called it 'hardening in the limbs'.

• Epilepsy is named from a Greek word meaning 'a taking hold of'. Sufferers were thought to be seized by mysterious powers.

• When sailors' daily supplies of lemon juice were replaced by lime juice in the mid 1800s, American sailors called their British counterparts 'limeys'.

• Vitamins with similar functions were first grouped by code letters in the early 20th century.

• In 1943 the Dutch physician Willem J. Kolff treated a patient with the first artificial kidney, a cellophane filter immersed in a water bath that was linked to the patient's bloodstream.

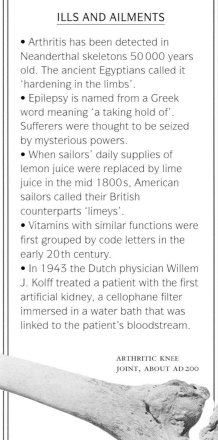

ARTHRITIC KNEE JOINT, ABOUT AD 200

GUARDIANS OF HEALTH

'I swear by Apollo the physician, and Asclepius, and Health, and All-heal, and all the gods and goddesses…
I will follow that system of regimen which, according to my ability and judgment,
I consider for the benefit of my patients, and abstain from whatever is deleterious and mischievous.'

FROM THE HIPPOCRATIC OATH, 4TH CENTURY BC

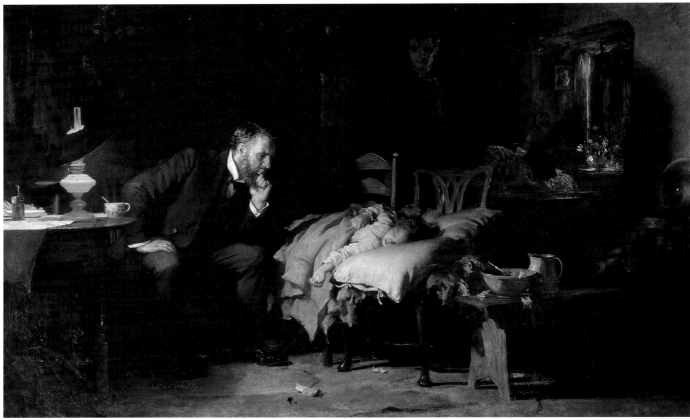

In early societies shamans renowned for their religious rituals, spells and incantations were the first guardians of health. Healer priests, whose methods interwove medicine and astrology, practised in Sumeria and Babylonia, but according to the Greek historian Herodotus, who was writing in the 5th century BC of an era probably 2500 years earlier than his own, Babylonia had no specialist physicians. Herodotus described how the sick would be taken into the marketplace and passers-by asked, on the basis of their experience, to give advice on treatment. 'No one', he said, 'is allowed to pass the sick

man in silence without asking him what his ailment is.'

The Code of Hammurabi, a set of Babylonian laws carved on a stone pillar in the 18th century BC, encompassed recommended legal practice for doctors that had been current for many centuries. Penalties for malpractice were severe. 'If the doctor, in opening an abscess, shall kill the patient his hands shall be cut off,' it decreed. Fees were determined according to tables set out in the code.

The 110 pages of the Ebers papyrus, written in Egypt in about 1550 BC, describe the medical practices known

BEDSIDE MANNER *By the late 19th century medical education had been standardised in Britain, but many diseases remained incurable. The compassion of a doctor's home visit was as important as prescribed drugs.*

at the time. Imhotep, the work's central character, is the first physician in the historical record. Chief adviser in the Egyptian court of Zoser, who reigned from 2630 to 2611 BC, Imhotep was so revered for his healing powers that he was worshipped as a god. The papyrus also revealed that specialists were common in ancient Egypt. Although he also took on cases of eye and belly disease, Iry, a court physician of about 2500 BC, was given the title 'Keeper of the King's Rectum'.

From about 1200 BC the Greeks worshipped Asclepius, the god of medicine who was identified with Imhotep. In life, Asclepius was thought to have been a physician who made some miraculous cures. Throughout Greece temples were built in his honour where the sick would gather to sleep, hoping that Asclepius or one of his priests would visit them in their dreams and effect a cure or impart the knowledge to make one possible.

As Greek civilisation advanced, philosophers started searching for rational explanations of illness. In about 460 BC, when such scientific approaches were in their infancy,

TRADITIONAL WOODEN SHAMAN'S CHEST FOR HOLDING HEALING CHARMS, WESTERN NORTH AMERICA

Hippocrates was born in the Greek island of Cos. The 'father of medicine', Hippocrates taught and practised in Cos, which had a medical school, and in other parts of the Mediterranean area. He proposed that illness was caused by malfunction of the body rather than the malign effects of supernatural interference.

Medicine advanced rapidly after Hippocrates' time, and a medical school was established at Alexandria in 300 BC. The Greek physician Galen, whose teachings influenced medical practice for more than 1500 years, gained his first experience of medicine in around AD 140, when, as a boy, he visited the medical school in his home town of Pergamum (now Bergama in Turkey) to study how wounded gladiators responded to treatment.

Like Galen, Greek and Roman physicians received no formal education, and 'apprentices' learned their skills on the job. Before the 3rd century AD, when under the

SKILLED MANIPULATION *Turkish doctors of the 15th century attend to a patient with a skeletal problem. Knowledge of Eastern medicine first reached the West with the returning Crusaders in the 11th century.*

emperor Severus formal training and bedside lessons were introduced, anyone could set up as a physician.

After the fall of Rome, European medicine was kept alive by the Church, with monks gaining some medical knowledge in new hospitals such as St Bartholomew's in London, founded in 1123. Formal medical education probably began in the first medical school, set up in Salerno, Italy, between the 9th and 11th centuries. Until the

TOY ΙΠΠΟΚΡΑΤΟΥΣ

BEST PRACTICE *Observe all; study the patient; evaluate honestly; assist nature. These were Hippocrates' fundamental principles of treatment and are reflected in the Hippocratic oath of medical ethics.*

1600s the *Canon of Medicine*, by the Persian philosopher and physician Avicenna, remained the basis of medical teaching in Western hospitals and universities. Written in about 1010 it drew on a 9th-century translation of Galen's works.

A WOMAN'S PROFESSION
Like Antiochis, whose skills were honoured by her home town of Tlos, women in ancient Greece practised medicine. It was one of the few male occupations open to Roman women, while in China the first record of a female doctor dates to about 160 BC.

Throughout medieval Europe some women 'leeches' practised as healers, including Euphemia, the 13th-century abbess of Wherwell in Hampshire. In Italy, Germany and Korea women were allowed medical training from the 14th century, but elsewhere the total exclusion of women persisted.

The modern pioneers faced huge public opposition, but in 1849 Elizabeth Blackwell became the first woman to qualify as a doctor in the USA. Elizabeth Garrett Anderson, inspired by a meeting with Blackwell, passed the exams of the British Society of Apothecaries in 1865.

FINGER ON THE PULSE
Taking pulse and blood pressure

The pulse's throb has been felt since ancient times to assess people's health, and in about AD 1100 the Greek doctor Archimanthaeus wrote in *The Coming of a Physician to his Patient*: 'The fingers should be kept on the pulse at least until the hundredth beat in order to judge of its kind and character...'.

The 17th-century Italian professor of medicine Santorio Santorio, a pioneer of thermometer development, timed the pulse against a 'pulsilogium', an instrument incorporating a pendulum. But only after 1707, when John Floyer of England made use of his 'pulse watch', were rates regularly or accurately timed.

To measure blood pressure, the Italian doctor Scipione Riva-Rocci wound an inflatable bag around the arm of his patient to constrict its main artery. He then used a column of mercury to measure how much pressure in the bag would completely stop the blood flow—as detected by feeling

LISTEN AND SEE *The oldest diagnostic instruments, a doctor's senses, were enhanced by the stethoscope from the early 19th century. Sphygmomanometers had become standard for measuring blood pressure by the 1920s. Recording heartbeats as 'waves' began in the early 1900s.*

the patient's pulse at the wrist. The device was named a sphygmomanometer, from the Greek word *sphugmos*, meaning 'pulsation'.

Riva-Rocci's invention dates back to 1896. However, it had been preceded 20 years earlier by an instrument combining an aneroid barometer with a bulb that was pressed against the wrist to constrict the circulation. The refinement of using a stethoscope to listen to the sounds in the artery as the blood overcame the pressure in the cuff was added in 1905 by the Russian physician Nikolai Korotkoff.

LISTENING TO THE BODY
The stethoscope

By tapping a patient's chest and listening to the sounds produced, Leopold Auenbrugger, an Austrian physician of the 18th century, realised he could gain vital clues about the heart and lungs. Auenbrugger's technique was popularised by the Frenchman Jean Nicolas Corvisart after 1801.

The only other way of detecting internal sounds was to place an ear to the body. In 1816, however, the French physician Theophile René Hyacinthe Laënnec invented the first listening aid—essentially a paper tube. He called it the stethoscope, from the Greek *stethos*, meaning 'chest', and is said to

have thought it up to avoid having to put his ear to a young woman's bosom.

Laënnec later used a wooden tube 30 cm (1 ft) long as a listening device. He wrote a book about his work in 1819, offering purchasers free stethoscopes. The flexible, twin earpiece design of the 1850s used Laënnec's principles.

THE VITAL SMEAR
Early warnings

In 1923, in a New York medical school, the Greek-born cytologist George Nicholas Papanicolaou made a chance discovery that has saved countless lives. While investigating how vaginal cells change during the menstrual cycle Papanicolaou examined a smear sample from a woman with cancer of the womb. He noticed some of the cells were unusual, an observation he later described as 'one of the greatest thrills I ever experienced'.

In 1928 Papanicolaou published his results, and his conclusions that smear samples could be used to discover the stages of cervical cancer. But it was over a decade before his findings were taken seriously, and the smear or Pap test was only adopted worldwide in 1948.

TUBERCULOSIS CLINIC, PENNSYLVANIA, USA, ABOUT 1930S

ELECTROCARDIOGRAM (ECG), 1980S

BINAURAL STETHOSCOPE, ABOUT 1860

SPHYGMOMANOMETER, WITH CUFF, 1910

MONAURAL STETHOSCOPE, ABOUT 1830

THE INSIDE VIEW
X-rays, endoscopes and ultrasound

Before the end of the 19th century a doctor could detect changes inside the body only by cutting it open. But diagnosis was revolutionised by the German scientist Wilhelm Roentgen. While passing electrical discharges through vacuum tubes on November 8, 1895, he discovered that a nearby piece of paper that was painted with the substance barium platinocyanide glowed with a bright fluorescence.

Roentgen then found that invisible rays from the tube, which he called X-rays because he did not know what they were, blackened photographic plates. He used these plates to show that when the rays passed through the body they were blocked to different extents, most of all by bone. Roentgen created the first permanent X-ray image, of

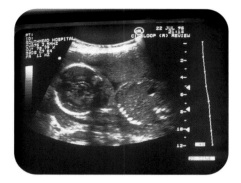

HELLO BABY *Ultrasound, first employed by Ian Donald in Glasgow in 1956 to estimate the size of abnormal growths in the ovary, was soon being used for viewing and measuring unborn babies in the womb.*

were clearly outlined if the birds drank a fluid containing bismuth. The barium meal, with barium sulphate performing the same role, was later administered to humans.

A tube lit by a candle formed the first endoscope, named from the Greek *endon*, 'within'. It enabled 18th-century physicians to look into the rectum to detect disease. In 1868 Adolf Kussmaul, the German physician, passed a rigid tube into the stomach of a sword swallower

THE FIRST X-RAY, OF
FRAU ROENTGEN'S
HAND, 1895

the bones inside his wife's hand, on December 22, 1895.

Within weeks an astonished world was shown X-rays. One London newspaper reported how they passed through wood, wool and flesh to create pictures of Frau Roentgen's hand bones and ring. 'They are', it said, 'ghastly enough in appearance, but from a scientific point of view they open up a wide field for speculation.' X-ray diagnosis of bone fractures became widespread, and the diagnosis of diseases of soft tissues, such as the lungs, was also revolutionised by Roentgen's work.

Walter Cannon, then a Harvard physiology student, showed in 1897 that the intestines of geese, which were poorly shown up with X-rays,

BONE DANCE *The ability of X-rays to make the skeleton visible quickly caught the imagination of the public, and was expressed in cartoons such as this German example from the early 1900s.*

but he was unable to see anything because the tube was unlit.

The first endoscope fitted with a lens for viewing the stomach was made by the Polish surgeon Joseph von Mikulicz in 1881. It was lit with a modified light bulb. However, the endoscope's potential was only truly realised after 1955 when the Indian physicist Narinder S. Kapany, working in London, used bundles of minutely thin glass fibres to carry light down a tube into the body and send back clear fibre-optic images to the viewer.

BEATS AND WAVES
Electricity from heart and brain

That electric signals were involved in muscle contraction was discovered by the 18th-century Italian physiologist Luigi Galvani. Ordinary electric currents had been measured with galvanometers since the 1820s, but in 1903 the Dutch physiologist Willem Einthoven devised a galvanometer sensitive enough to pick up on the body surface electric signals from a beating heart. These were translated into movements of a needle, which traced an electrocardiogram (ECG). Einthoven then worked out how heart defects were shown in the traces.

In 1924 Hans Berger, a German psychiatrist, discovered how to detect on the skin of the scalp electrical signals made by the brain. His first 'brainwave' or electroencephalograph (EEG) trace came from his son.

FIRST AID

EDWARDIAN
HEAD BANDAGE

To bind wounds, the Egyptians used linen bandages spread with honey and myrrh (a mild antiseptic). By 2500 BC they were also using palm tree fibres as splints.

Modern sticking plaster was being made in the USA by Robert Shoemaker by 1838. Band-Aid was produced in the 1920s by the US company Johnson & Johnson. The idea came from an employee, Earle Dickson, who had laid sterilised gauze inside a roll of sticking plaster to create ready-prepared bandages for his accident-prone wife.

NEW PARTS FOR OLD

'Only a few months ago I lay in hospital, a dying man with a stricken heart.
Then came the miracle. I was given a new lease of life. Today, I am the second man
since the Creation to live with the heart of a dead man beating in his breast.'

PHILIP BLAIBERG, SOUTH AFRICAN DENTAL SURGEON, SECOND HUMAN HEART TRANSPLANT PATIENT, 1968

Hegesistratus, a Persian soldier and renowned fortuneteller, was the first person known to have worn an artificial limb. In the 5th century BC, Herodotus, the Greek historian, described how Hegesistratus cut off his foot to escape imprisonment by the Spartan enemy. Equipped with a wooden replacement he then fought against them.

To replace a hand severed in battle the Roman soldier Sergius Silus possessed an 'iron hand', so Pliny recorded in his *Natural History* of the 1st century AD. And a skeleton excavated in central Italy of around 300 BC had a wooden leg covered with realistically modelled bronze sheeting between knee and ankle.

Simple artificial limbs, such as peg legs or false feet or hands with or without 'hooks', were worn largely for cosmetic effect. They provided some support, but no movement, and changed little for centuries until a 16th-century French

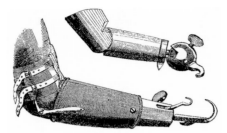

ARTIFICIAL JOINTED ARM AND HAND, 1851

military surgeon, Ambroise Paré, started to make hands fitted with holders for quill pens and even with fingers made individually mobile by a series of minute levers. Paré also created ingenious legs of wood or metal. Their pivoting knee joints and sprung feet were designed for wounded soldiers. Some of Paré's elbow joints moved with the help of ratchets.

Replacement surgery, initially used for badly damaged and arthritic hips,

is a 20th-century advance pioneered in 1905 by the Chicago surgeon J.B. Murphy. Progress was slow until the early 1930s when the potential of vitallium, a noncorrosive metal, for oral rebuilding in dentistry was discovered. Knowledge of vitallium's possibilities reached two US surgeons named Venable and Stuck who in 1932 employed it for joint repair.

In 1979 a patient with burns over more than half her skin was the first to be treated with Silastic, an artificial skin made from treated shark's cartilage and cowhide developed in Massachusetts by the surgeon John Burke and Ioannis Yanna, a chemist. Within three weeks the patient's own skin had started to grow into and over the Silastic matrix, which was eventually absorbed by her body.

PEG LEGS *Long before Pieter Bruegel painted these beggars in the 16th century, amputees fitted with wooden limbs had been shown in Roman mosaics.*

Artificial ligaments made of Goretex, a porous form of Teflon better known as a sportswear fabric, were approved for use in the USA in 1988. Although rarely used as total replacements these are invaluable aids to recovery.

IMPLANTS, GRAFTS AND TRANSPLANTS

The English surgeon W.H. Walshe suggested in 1862 that if a heart stopped beating it could be 'shocked' back into action with electricity. Duchenne de Bologne, Walshe's French colleague, pursued the idea and in 1872 described *le main électrique*, an electric hand which could administer impulses to the patient's chest and effect resuscitation.

The artificial pacemaker, which gives a lifesaving boost to an ailing heartbeat, was named by A.S. Hyman, an American cardiologist who in 1932 devised a bulky apparatus weighing

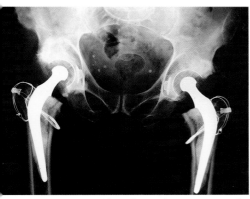

NEW HIPS *Modern-day replacement joints for hips affected by arthritis owe much to the English surgeon John Charnley who, in the 1960s, used stainless steel to replace the 'ball' at the top of the thigh bone and tough polythene to remould sockets in the pelvis.*

7.2 kg (16 lb) to deliver regular electrical stimulations to the heart. By 1960 a team from New York had inserted the first pacemaker, which was charged from a small unit attached to the outside of the chest.

During the 1950s the first artificial hearts were built in laboratories, but it was not until 1969 that one was implanted, by Denton Cooley of Texas. This air-powered plastic device was a temporary replacement to keep

patients alive until hearts became available for transplant. In 1982 an American dentist named Barney Clark survived for 112 days after receiving the first artificial heart intended as a permanent fixture. Clark's new heart, a pump known as the Jarvik-7 designed by the American physician Robert Jarvik, worked using compressed air.

By the 6th century BC the Hindu surgeon Susruta was practising plastic surgery in India. He created new ear lobes from cheek flesh, and new noses, complete with bamboo nostrils, out of skin taken from the forehead, to replace noses cut off as a punishment for crimes such as adultery. Susruta's knowledge passed to the Arabs and to the Greeks and Romans.

The art of grafting was revived in the 16th century by the Italian surgeon Gaspare Tagliocozzi, who recorded his attempt to 'restore the appearances of patients who had lost their noses' in a book that included 22 woodcuts of facial operations. Although he had no knowledge of tissue rejection, Tagliocozzi realised that only tissues from the same individual would 'take'. But the medieval Church was so opposed to such interference with nature that Tagliocozzi was denounced after his death as a sorcerer.

In 1823 a G. Bunger of Germany rebuilt part of a nose with skin from a patient's own thigh. Experiments with bone and skin grafts advanced in the following century, and the first transplant of a major body organ took place in 1950 when a patient was given a new kidney by the American surgeon

MAKING IT BETTER

- Ancient Egyptians were buried with false limbs supplied by embalmers for use in the afterlife.
- Before syphilis could be cured with penicillin it was a common reason for nose rebuilding because the disease eats away the tissues.
- The Romans used plastic surgery after cutting away the brand marks on freed slaves.
- In 1905 the first successful corneal graft was carried out by Eduard Konrad Zirm in Moravia.
- A 2300-year-old woman's skeleton, with two rams' bones replacing a missing left foot, was discovered in Kazakhstan, central Asia.

Richard H. Lawler. Four years later an American team led by Joseph Murray transplanted a kidney from one identical twin to another. Such successes highlighted the significance of rejection, identified in the 1950s by the US physician Emile Holman as a reaction of the body to 'alien' tissues. The identical twins' tissues were accepted as 'self' because they shared the same genetic make-up.

Throughout the 1950s and 1960s the essentials of rejection were gradually worked out. Now the way was clear for the first liver and lung transplants, which took place in 1963. But public emotions were truly aroused when, on December 3, 1967, the South African surgeon Christiaan Barnard gave a new heart to 55-year-old Louis Washkansky at the Groote Schuur Hospital in Cape Town. Washkansky lived for 18 days.

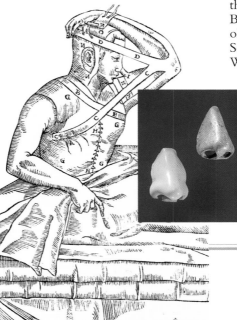

SAVING FACE *The 16th-century Italian surgeon Gaspare Tagliocozzi was renowned for his nasal reconstructions which grafted skin from the arm onto the face. Tagliocozzi based his techniques on those that gardeners used on trees. In the 18th century replacement noses made from ivory (centre) and metal (right) were implanted for facial repair.*

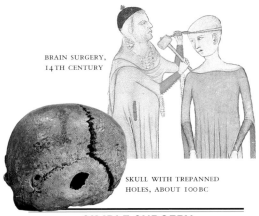

BRAIN SURGERY,
14TH CENTURY

SKULL WITH TREPANNED
HOLES, ABOUT 100 BC

SIMPLE SURGERY
Ancient operations

Using sharpened stones, surgeons of 10000 years ago drilled holes in their patients' skulls, probably to release the spirits thought to be causing mental illness. Ancient skulls from around the world show similar signs of this trepannation operation, which Greek physicians also used to treat head injuries.

Basic operations, including setting fractures and dislocations, removing

HEAD CUT *A healing hole in an ancient skull (below left) is testament to the skills of an early surgeon. Brain surgery was used to treat mental illness in medieval times and beyond.*

thorns and probably stitching wounds, date back to ancient Egypt and Mesopotamia. But because breaching the body's defences frequently led to fatal infections, surgery was not only minimised but confined to the extremities.

From the time Hippocrates practised in the 5th century BC the Greeks knew how to stitch torn muscles, tie off burst blood vessels and remove bladder stones. Techniques were improved, and surgery's prestige enhanced, by the Greek physician Galen around AD 150.

Following the fall of Rome, surgery became the work of pedlars, magicians and rat-catchers. And even in the mid 1700s, barber surgeons were still performing routine operations. An exception was Ambroise Paré, a 16th-century

French surgeon. In Paré's time, the use of gunpowder was increasing. Missiles fired from guns tore into human flesh and pushed what was thought to be 'gunpowder poison' (but was in fact metal and other materials) deep into wounds. Such injuries were routinely sealed or cauterised with hot oil, but in 1536, during the siege of Turin, oil supplies ran out. Instead, Paré used a mixture of egg yolk, rose oil and turpentine, and discovered that with this gentler treatment wounds were less painful and inflamed.

TOOLS AND TECHNIQUES
The art of surgery

Crude flints, or knives made from the volcanic glass obsidian, were the first surgical implements. About 4500 years ago copper blades were used in Egypt for operations such as male circumcision, while wounds were stitched with copper needles. Sumerian surgeons employed similar tools, together with saws for cutting bone.

The only full set of surgical apparatus surviving from these times is a set of tools found in a Minoan tomb on the Greek island of Crete. The copper instruments in this 3500-year-old kit include such familiar items as forceps, drills and scalpels, as well as a dilator for internal examinations.

Roman surgeons performed their operations with cutting blades or *scalpelli* crafted from the best Austrian steel, which remained unmatched until the 18th century. They also favoured catheters—tubes used during the 3rd century BC by the Greek doctor Erasistratus for treating genitourinary blockages.

Ancient surgeons stitched the wounds of patients with strings of animal gut. In ancient India, where both tools and techniques were as advanced as in the Mediterranean

COMPLETE NICKEL-SILVER SURGEON'S FIELD KIT WITH SOME INSTRUMENTS DISPLAYED BELOW, 1875

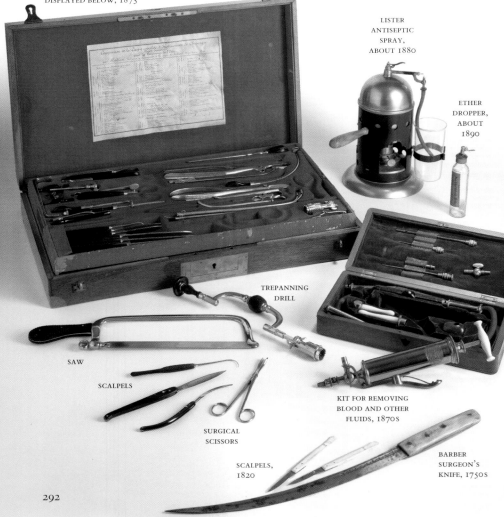

LISTER
ANTISEPTIC
SPRAY,
ABOUT 1880

ETHER
DROPPER,
ABOUT
1890

TREPANNING
DRILL

SAW

SCALPELS

SURGICAL
SCISSORS

KIT FOR REMOVING
BLOOD AND OTHER
FLUIDS, 1870S

SCALPELS,
1820

BARBER
SURGEON'S
KNIFE, 1750S

TOOL KIT *Wielding his curved knife (the sharpened edge is convex) in a single stroke, the skilled barber surgeon was able to amputate a limb in seconds. By the late 19th century a larger range of instruments was being used more safely in antiseptic conditions and on patients who were anaesthetised with ether.*

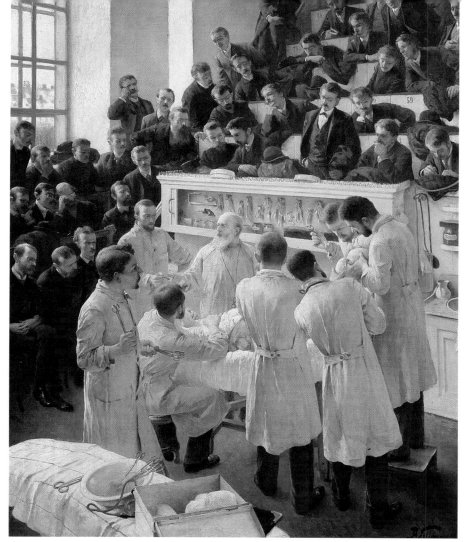

STAR PERFORMER *The German surgeon
Theodor Billroth operates on a patient in
Vienna in 1890, attended by his students.
Billroth pioneered internal surgery; in 1881
he had successfully removed a stomach cancer.*

PREVENTING INFECTION
Killing germs

Following surgery, wounds commonly festered and swelled with pus, now known to be caused by the immune system attacking infective bacteria. For generations this was regarded as an encouraging sign that healing was in progress, and in the Middle Ages pus was commonly hailed as 'laudable'.

The vital link between disease and pus was not realised until the surgeon Joseph Lister carried out the first antiseptic operation, which he did in 1865 on an 11-year-old boy. By spraying the operating theatre with carbolic acid (a chemical he knew as a sewage disinfectant), and dabbing it on the wound to make an 'artificial scab', Lister killed germs—carried from place to place by direct contact and in the air. Suffering no ill effects, the boy healed quickly.

Antisepsis was effective but messy. Asepsis, in which germs are kept away from the wound rather than being killed, began to supersede it after the French microbiologist Louis Pasteur suggested in 1874 that surgical instruments could be sterilised by placing them in boiling water.

civilisations, Hindu surgeons stitched intestines using Bengali ants. Placed side by side along a wound, the creatures clamped it shut with their jaws. The surgeon then severed the ants' bodies (leaving their heads and jaws in place) and stitched up the outer abdominal tissues. As the internal wound healed, the ants' heads dissolved.

FREEDOM FROM PAIN
Giving anaesthetics

To deaden the excruciating pain of surgery the Chinese gave patients a mixture of wine and herbal drugs, probably narcotics derived from the mandrake plant. But it was also thought honourable to ignore pain, and operations were regularly performed without anaesthesia. In the 3rd century AD the Chinese general Guan Yu is said to have carried on playing chess without flinching, even while the surgeon Hua Tuo was scraping away at his arm bone. The

Greeks and Romans also used mandrake extracts. According to the Roman writer Pliny: 'When the mandrake is used as a sleeping draught the quantity administered should be proportional to the strength of the patient'.

Opium was used to quell pain in ancient times and long beyond, as was alcohol, although it often made patients fighting drunk. In 1844 an American dentist named Horace Wells tried using nitrous oxide for pain relief, discussing its problems with a dentist colleague, William Morton. Deciding that ether would be more effective, Morton used it in 1846 to anaesthetise a patient undergoing surgery to remove a neck tumour. Sir James Young Simpson, a British obstetrician, used ether in 1847 before discovering that chloroform better relieved the pain of childbirth.

BLOOD MATCH

Australian Aborigines may have practised blood transfusion for thousands of years, but not until 1667 did Jean-Baptiste Denys, surgeon to Louis XIV, make the first documented transfusion, using lamb's blood. The boy recipient recovered.

In 1825 James Blundell made a successful human-to-human transfusion in London, but the importance of blood compatibility was first realised by Karl Landsteiner, an Austrian pathologist. He identified groups A, O, B and AB in 1900, and from 1908 grouping was routinely ascertained before transfusions.

DONOR CAMPAIGN
POSTER, LATE 1940S

a life in your hands

293

NATURE'S MEDICINE CHEST

*'The Lord hath created medicines out of the earth;
and he that is wise will not abhor them.'*

ECCLESIASTICUS, CH. 38, V. 4

The bark of the Pacific yew tree, *Taxus brevifolia*, was discovered in 1992 to contain taxol, a substance that kills cancer cells. Like this new drug, our first medicines came from plants whose shape or colour often suggested their use. Yellow plants were chosen to treat jaundice; eyebright, named from its resemblance to the eye, was selected to cure optic complaints.

When, about 60000 years ago, a Neanderthal man died in Shanidar (now in Iraq) his body was covered with flowers, many of which are still used in medicines by people of the region. The marsh mallow was valued for soothing sore throats and as a treatment for intestinal upsets, while the grape hyacinth was given to encourage urination.

The Chinese were the first to record their plant remedies, from about 3000 BC. The herbal *Pen Tsao*, probably compiled during the reign of emperor Fo Hi or his son Shen Nung, dates to this period. It describes more than 260 herbal medicines, among them *Ephedra*, whose active ingredient, ephedrine, is still valued for treating asthma.

Ancient Egyptians and Sumerians made use of health-giving plants, and an Egyptian papyrus of 1500 BC lists hundreds of medicinal herbs. Garlic was chewed by the slave workers engaged in pyramid-building to help to ward off infections and fevers.

The Greek physician Hippocrates described some 400 herbal remedies, while much knowledge was spread across Europe by the Romans. As they settled in conquered lands, the Romans planted their favourite medicinal herbs: mint to stimulate the appetite,

POTENT HARVEST Following a long tradition, a woman gathers medicinal plants from the Borneo rain forest. In ancient times 'medicine women' were thought to possess god-given powers.

planted 'physick' gardens with herbs that had been introduced by the Romans. But such practices remained largely unknown until herbals were published from the early 1500s. The herbal published in 1654 by the English apothecary Nicholas Culpeper remains in print today.

By 300 BC the Egyptians were using foxgloves to make heart medicine. The Romans employed the foxglove as a diuretic, but the plant's healing potential was not fully tested until the 18th century when William Withering, an

HERBAL RECORD The Codex *of the Greek physician Dioscorides contained illustrations of hundreds of medicinal plants, including asphodel.*

liquorice to aid digestion and mustard for chest complaints.

Following the collapse of the Roman Empire, Arab physicians became the guardians of herbal knowledge. A treatise written in the early 11th century by Avicenna, a Persian doctor and philosopher who had learnt how to distil essential oils from flowers and herbs, became the standard work of Arab medicine. In the West, medieval monks

English doctor, began searching for a remedy for dropsy, a type of water retention caused by heart disease.

In about 1775 Withering encountered a cure for dropsy, concocted by an old woman, that made patients very sick. Having identified the foxglove as the cause of the vomiting, Withering then went on to investigate its properties. Ten years later, in *An Account of the Foxglove and some of its Medical Uses*, he noted the herb's 'power over the motion of the heart'. Withering did not then connect dropsy with heart failure, but discovered that a dried preparation of

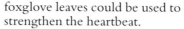

foxglove leaves could be used to strengthen the heartbeat.

To the ancient inhabitants of Peru *Cinchona succirubra* was known as the 'fever tree'. They used its bark, now known to contain quinine, to prepare a concoction to cure malaria, a disease endemic throughout Europe and Asia by the 17th century. A missionary reported on the bark's powers in 1633, but these remained generally unknown in Europe until a Spanish Jesuit missionary took this 'Jesuit's bark' to Rome in the 1630s.

Willow tree bark was probably chewed by country folk to calm fevers long before the English pharmacist Edward Stone used a powdered form to treat the alternating chills and heat typical of ague. More than a century later, in 1876, the Scottish physician Thomas Maclagan gave 100 rheumatic fever patients salicylic acid made from the bark. His patients responded well, but the drug caused gastric problems. After Felix

CRY NO MORE *Medicines for infants, as advertised here in about 1910, contained soothing morphine.*

Hoffman of Bayer in Germany synthesised pure acetylsalicylic acid in 1897 such side effects were eliminated. From 1899 Bayer marketed the drug as aspirin powder.

DANGEROUS PLEASURES

In their religious rituals the Aztecs inhaled the smoke from smouldering tobacco leaves through hollow reeds or canes. And when Christopher Columbus and his men arrived in Cuba in 1492 they were astonished to find local people smoking cigars – probably named from *sik'ar*, a Mayan Indian word meaning 'smoking' – made from rolled corn

WAYSIDE WONDER *Digitalin, the active ingredient of the foxglove, a plant used medicinally by the ancient Egyptians, was not discovered until the early 20th century.*

DELIVERING THE DOSE

- The Egyptians mixed foul-tasting remedies such as castor oil with honey to make them palatable.
- Opium was brought to Europe by the Crusaders from the 11th century.
- The hypodermic was invented in 1853 by the Scotsman Alexander Wood. It may have been based on a syringe invented by the French mathematician Blaise Pascal in the 17th century.

husks filled with shredded tobacco. 'The effect', reported one of the explorers who sampled it, 'is a certain drowsiness of the whole body accompanied by a certain species of intoxication…'.

Tobacco was brought to Europe by the Spanish, who landed in Mexico in 1518. They named the new substance *tabaco* from the Arabic *tabaq*, meaning 'euphoria-inducing herb'. The word was not recorded in English until John Hawkins visited Florida in 1565. After Hawkins brought tobacco home with him the smoking habit, originally described as 'drinking', caught on. Soon tobacco was being recommended as an aphrodisiac and a cure for diseases from 'superfluous phlegm' to lockjaw.

By the 4th millennium BC the potent effects of opium had been widely discovered. The Sumerians wrote enthusiastically of the 'joy plant' and probably introduced this poppy to the Egyptians. Cities such as Thebes were famed for their poppy fields by the 15th century BC, when Egyptians were being entombed with opium supplies for comfort in the afterlife.

The ancient Greeks and Romans were also familiar with opium, whose name comes from *opion*, a word coined by the Greeks for the sap from the poppies' pods. They also recognised opium's sleep-inducing properties. In the 3rd century BC the philosopher Diagoras of Melos obviously realised the risks of addiction when he declared that suffering pain was preferable to dependence on opium.

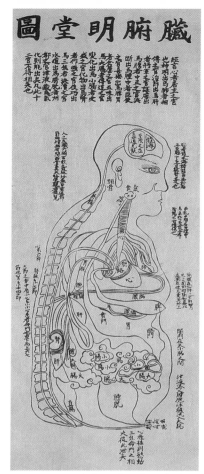

CHINESE CURES *A chart thought to be based on the bronze figures created by Wang Wei-I in the 11th century AD detailing the positions of points and channels shows the internal organs that can be treated by acupuncture.*

about 2600 BC, compiled his *Nei Ching, Su Wen* (*Classic of Internal Medicine*), which included a guide to acupuncture. Around this time the first therapeutic success was recorded after a comatose patient's life was saved.

Bronze needles fashioned during the 8th century BC have been unearthed. But the oldest set undoubtedly used for acupuncture, with five silver needles and four gold, making the standard complement of nine, was discovered in the tomb of Prince Liu Sheng, who died in 113 BC in Hubei Province.

The Illustrated Manual Explaining Acupuncture and Moxibustion with the Aid of the Bronze Figure and its Acu-points, written in AD 1027 by Wang Wei-I, was responsible for refining acupuncture. It was accompanied by a pair of life-size bronze figures on which the acupuncture points were accurately marked. Moxibustion involves placing cones of dried mugwort leaves on the skin and setting them alight.

Wang Wei-I's book was copied onto a pair of huge stone slabs. Copies, taken from it like brass rubbings, helped to ensure the introduction of acupuncture into Europe in 1683 by Willem tem Rhijne, a Dutch doctor who also coined its name.

THE ART OF ACUPUNCTURE
Healing with needles

When, according to ancient Chinese philosophy, the body is in harmony, the contradictory forces of yin and yang are so well balanced that they allow *chi*, the life force, to run through it unhindered. Chi is believed to travel along 12 channels or meridians linked to internal organs. At certain places on the channels an imbalance of chi can be regulated and in acupuncture, which may have been devised to release evil spirits, needles are inserted into these points.

Another version of the origin of acupuncture is that around 5000 years ago Chinese warriors gained relief from disease symptoms after being wounded by arrows penetrating their skin. Whatever its origins acupuncture was probably devised around this time, and performed with stone needles. Techniques were imparted orally until Huang Ti, the 'Yellow Emperor' of

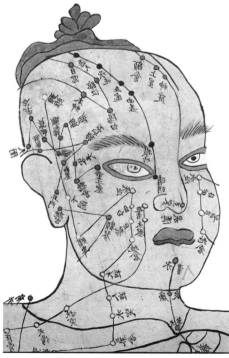

CHART SHOWING ACUPUNCTURE POINTS AND CHANNELS IN THE HEAD

HOMEOPATHIC REMEDIES
Curing like with like

It was his disillusion with orthodox medicine that led Samuel Christian Friedrich Hahnemann, a medical student at Leipzig University in the 1770s, to search for an alternative means of treating the sick. Hahnemann devised his system of homeopathy, named from the Greek words *homos*, 'same', and *pathos*, 'suffering', after observing his reactions when he dosed himself with an extract of Peruvian bark. The bark, which contains quinine, a substance Hahnemann knew was an antidote to

CRITICAL DOSE *Samuel Hahnemann discovered that his homeopathic remedies, many of them highly poisonous, needed to be diluted up to a million times to prevent side effects.*

malaria, produced symptoms similar to those of the disease it was meant to cure. This led directly to Hahnemann's 'law of similars' and to the principle underlying homeopathy that like cures like (*similia similibus curantur*), which he proposed in 1796.

Homeopathy was introduced into Britain, despite vehement opposition, by Dr Frederick Foster Harvey Quin. The fact that Quin was personal physician to Queen Victoria's uncle Prince Leopold and his wife the Duchess of Devonshire, combined with the near-hysterical outcry from the medical profession, helped to publicise his cause. Quin founded the first homeopathic hospital in London's Soho in 1850.

POWERFUL PLANTS *The practice of gathering and crushing plants to extract oils and other ingredients is illustrated in a medieval German version of a work written by the Greek physician Dioscorides around* AD 400.

RESTORATIVE MANIPULATION
Chiropractic and osteopathy

Manipulating the body to cure a wide range of diseases was practised by the Egyptians in the 17th century BC but was not revived until 1895 when a Canadian-born doctor, Daniel David Palmer, cured the deafness of a care-taker named Harvey Lilliard from Iowa by manipulating the vertebrae in his neck. Through this act the system of chiropractic was founded. It was named by a clergyman, who was one of Palmer's patients, from the Greek *kheir*, 'hands', and *praktikos*, 'practical'.

Osteopathy was devised by the American doctor Andrew Taylor Still during the American Civil War. Combining his knowledge of anatomy and his interest in engineering, Still investigated how illness might be caused by misalignments of the body, and worked out effective treatments by manipulating and realigning the spine and other parts of the skeleton. In 1892 he opened the American School of Osteopathy, in Kirksville, Missouri.

PUTTING ON THE PRESSURE

As well as inserting needles into the body at selected points, the ancient Chinese applied pressure at the same places to cure illness. In reflexology, another ancient Chinese therapy, pressure is applied to the feet, where zones on the soles are thought to correspond to different body regions and organs. In 1913 the zones were introduced to the West when the US consultant William H. Fitzgerald devised a system of massage that he called zone therapy. His ideas were further developed in the 1930s by Eunice D. Ingham, who concentrated attention on the feet.

REFLEXOLOGY CHART AND PRACTICE

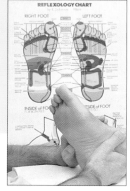

HEALING WITH OILS
Aromatherapy

Early in the 20th century the French chemist René Gattefosse, whose com-pany produced concentrated or essen-tial oils for cosmetics, burnt his hand. He plunged it into some lavender essence and it healed rapidly, leaving no scar. After using essential oils on casual-ties during the First World War, Gattefosse became convinced of their effectiveness and in 1928 coined the word 'aromatherapy' for his treatments.

The medicinal use of plant oils was first recorded in early Chinese writings. In Britain the use of concentrated oils as antiseptics and medicines began in the 13th century. It later became widespread, but essential oils fell out of use when weaker versions were made in the 19th cen-tury. Marguerite Maury, the French biochemist and beautician, was the first to use the oils in therapeutic massage, in the 1950s.

PLANNED FAMILIES
Being in control

POSTER FOR MARIE STOPES' CLINIC AND MONTHLY PUBLICATION, 1930S

Contained in the Kahun papyrus of ancient Egypt and dating to about 2000 BC, the earliest written contraceptive advice advocated inserting gum, a mixture of honey and sodium carbonate, or a paste of sour milk and crocodile dung into the vagina. Another Egyptian prescription involved moistening a lint tampon with honey and ground leaves of the acacia, a plant known to contain lactic acid, which is deadly to sperm.

Aristotle, the ancient Greek philosopher, wrote that women 'anoint[ed] that part of the womb on which the seed falls with oil of cedar, ointment of lead, or frankincense commingled with olive oil' to prevent conception. In modern times Marie Stopes, the pioneer of family planning, found that olive oil did indeed have some spermicidal effects.

In the 2nd century AD the Roman physician Galen listed plants, including juniper, and plant extracts such as the bitter spice asafetida, that women could swallow as oral contraceptives. But most such ancient potions were ineffective, unpleasant and often dangerous.

Reliable oral contraception became possible only after the menstrual cycle was fully understood. Aëtio of Amida, a 6th-century Byzantine scholar, had realised that conception could be prevented if intercourse took place only on 'safe' days of the month. In 1927 the Austrian physiologist Ludwig Haberlandt extolled the virtues of 'hormonal sterilisation based on biologic principles'. But public opinion remained opposed to the idea, despite the work of Marie Stopes in Britain and Margaret Sanger in the USA. Sanger, who coined the phrase birth control, had opened the first birth control advice centre in Brooklyn in 1916.

Impetus for planned parenthood in the 1950s persuaded scientists to reopen their studies. In 1956 the American

THE RIGHT TO CHOOSE *The services of the Marie Stopes birth control clinics, which included caravans, were available free of charge from the 1920s, but aroused public derision.*

PREVENTS NERVOUS STRAIN
DUREX TEAT
The strongest, thinnest and silkiest protectives in the world.

DUREX CONDOMS, 1930S

researchers Gregory Pincus and John Rock published the results of their clinical trials of the contraceptive pill. When it became available in the early 1960s the Pill was believed to fulfil Pincus's prerequisites as 'harmless, entirely reliable, simple, practical, universally applicable and aesthetically satisfactory to both husband and wife.' The yam, used for centuries as an oral contraceptive by Mexican women, played an important part in the development of the Pill. It contains a chemical used to make the female hormone progesterone.

MALE PROTECTION
Cedar gum, recorded as a male contraceptive by the Roman naturalist Pliny the Elder, is one of many ancient substances applied by men. But the first barrier contraceptives used by men were the sheaths applied by the Romans as much to guard against disease as pregnancy. These were probably made from animal gut as were later condoms,

named after the 17th-century Dr Condom, who is thought to have been a physician to Charles II. Such condoms, of which the best came from sheep intestines, were used until 1829 when the American inventor Charles Goodyear made rubber ones practicable. The Durex brand was launched in 1932 by the London Rubber Company.

The cap or diaphragm, originally recorded by a German physician, F.A. Wilde, in 1823, was also improved by rubber technology. But Casanova, the 'Latin lover' of the 18th century, is said to have used halved lemons as caps to protect his conquests from pregnancy.

LIFE BEFORE BIRTH *Leonardo da Vinci's drawing of a foetus in the womb, created in 1511-13, reveals a knowledge of life before birth largely confirmed by modern science.*

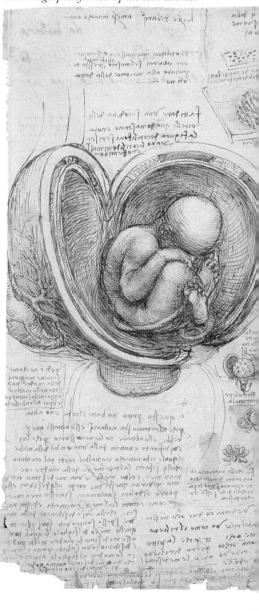

GIVING BIRTH
Into labour

Ancient people tried to lessen the dangers of childbirth for both mother and baby. Greek and Roman doctors could turn in the womb a baby that was presenting feet first. Among North American tribes the mother's belly was massaged to help to expel the placenta.

When women began giving birth in hospital, from the 18th century, many died from puerperal sepsis, a disease recognised by Hippocrates in the 5th century BC. Charles White, the British obstetrician, appreciated the need for cleanliness to prevent puerperal sepsis in the 1730s.

But it took more than a century before any significant advance took place. Ignaz Philipp Semmelweis, who began work in Vienna in 1844, noticed that women whose hospital deliveries were attended by students were at greatest risk. The problem, he realised, was that the students had often come straight from dissecting cadavers of women who had died of puerperal fever.

From 1847 Semmelweis insisted that those examining women during and after labour should wash their hands in a solution of chlorinated lime. Two years later the death rate had plummeted to about one in a hundred. Semmelweis was derided, but

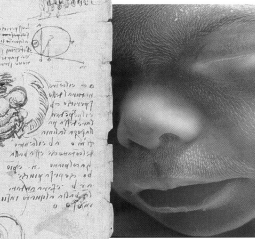

A DELIVERY IN A ROMAN
BIRTHING CHAIR,
2ND CENTURY AD

FOETUS AGED SIX MONTHS

before the century had drawn to a close his theories had been accepted by the British surgeon Joseph Lister, pioneer of antisepsis.

MANAGING LABOUR

When a woman went into labour her mother or another older woman would attend her as a midwife. Propriety excluded men. Women in ancient Egypt gave birth in a crouching or kneeling position or in chairs, and ancient Greek women sat on stools. The Romans had birthing chairs, commonly used in Britain until the 18th century.

From the 7th century BC until at least the 17th century AD women wore eagle stone amulets to protect themselves during pregnancy and childbirth. The

FACTS OF LIFE

- In ancient Greece all mirrors were removed during labour to protect women from the evil eye.
- Roman fathers lifted their newborn children into the air as a sign of accepting responsibility.
- The incubator for premature and sick babies was invented in 1891 by a French doctor, Alexandre Lion.
- Marie Stopes' book *Married Love*, which put forward the idea of sexual equality, was greeted with outrage when it was published in 1918.
- Louise Brown, the first 'test-tube baby' was born in 1978. An egg was removed from her mother's ovary, fertilised outside the body and the embryo implanted into her uterus.

naturally occurring aetites, 'pregnant' stones with sand or a pebble inside them, were used for the same purpose by the ancient Assyrians.

By the late 18th century qualified 'male midwives' had begun to practise. The Chamberlens, a French Huguenot family of male midwives whose forebears had fled to England in 1569, were using forceps in the 17th century. The success of the Chamberlens was built on such instruments, and women were even blindfolded to stop them seeing these powerful, mysterious tools.

Anaesthesia was used to ease the pain of labour from the mid 19th century; Queen Victoria inhaled chloroform while giving birth to Prince Leopold, her eighth child, in 1853. As she recorded in her journal: 'Dr Snow gave that blessed Chloroform & the effect was soothing, quieting & delightful beyond measure.'

One of the oldest surgical procedures is the caesarean section, named after Julius Caesar, the Roman ruler believed to have been cut from his mother's womb. Mentioned in the mythologies of the ancient Egyptians, Indians and Persians, the operation was almost always fatal to the mother—if she was not already dead. The first reports of mothers surviving appeared in the 1500s. Even in the 1850s three mothers in four died during the procedure.

IMPROVING VISION
The first spectacles

An illiterate Italian glazier, who was subsequently bound to secrecy by his employers, was inspired in about 1280 to place a pair of convex glass discs in front of the eyes to make near objects look clearer. Single lenses were already incorporated in magnifying glasses by this time, but these eyeglasses were revolutionary. In the earliest written reference to them, an Italian named Sadro di Popozo commented in 1289: 'I am so debilitated by age that without the glasses known as spectacles, I would no longer be able to read or write.'

Early wearers looped lengths of cord or chain around their head or behind their ears to hold spectacles in place. Otherwise, glasses rested on or gripped the nose. The earliest spectacles found in Britain, made in about 1500, were among the first with pads to help to secure the frames on the bridge of the nose. Glasses with rigid arms or side pieces were originally made in 1727 by Edward Scarlett, a London optician.

Bifocals were invented by Benjamin Franklin, the American statesman. In about 1785 he had the lenses from different pairs of spectacles sawn in half then cemented together to avoid having to swap glasses for close work and seeing at a distance. Before 1864, when the precise means for prescribing glasses were worked out by the Dutch

CLOSE WORK *Most early spectacle wearers were professional men. The Italian Cardinal Hugh Ugone was the first person to be portrayed wearing glasses, by Tomasso de Modena in this likeness painted in the 1350s.*

ophthalmologist Franciscus Cornelius Donders, people picked the pair they thought best from an oculist's selection.

In 1827 the English physicist John Herschel proposed the idea for contact lenses, but they did not become a reality until 1887, when the Swiss physiologist Adolf Eugen Fick had a pair made by a glass-blower to correct astigmatism. These glass discs, 14 mm (more than ½ in) across, were shaped in moulds made of the surface of the eye. It was not until 1933 that a practical version was introduced, by the German ophthalmologist Josef Dallos.

OPERATING ON THE EYES
The ophthalmic surgeon

In attempts to restore failing sight the Babylonians probably performed the first eye operations in about 1800 BC, by pushing lenses clouded by cataracts farther into the eye. The Babylonians may have passed their knowledge to the Indians and to the Romans. Specialist Roman eye doctors regularly removed ingrowing eyelashes. The most skilled among them also used syringe-like

needles to treat cataracts. In his medical writings of the 1st century AD Celsus stressed the great care required: 'the assistant from behind holds the head so that the patient cannot move; for vision can be destroyed permanently by slight movement...'.

The itinerant oculists of the Middle Ages also acted as eye physicians, but only after the German physician Georg Bartisch wrote about eye diseases in the 16th century did ophthalmology start to become a speciality. The first formal courses in ophthalmology were held in 1803 at the University of Göttingen, although these were predated by the first surgery for strabismus or squint, carried out in 1738. Ophthalmology became more precise after 1851, when Hermann von Helmholtz, a German physiologist, invented the ophthalmoscope to create a magnified image of the retina at the back of the eye, where clues to disease can be found.

SIGHT RESTORER *A medieval physician uses a pointed instrument to break up a cataract in the lens of the eye. The Greek physician Rufus of Ephesus had accurately drawn the anatomy of the eye in the 2nd century AD.*

EARLY INSIGHTS

- Concave lenses to aid far vision appeared in a portrait of Pope Leo X painted by Raphael in 1517.
- The Egyptians made artificial clay eyes. Glass was used in Italy in 1578.
- The Inuit put slitted pieces of wood in front of their eyes to protect them from glare. Tinted sunglass lenses were available in the 1700s.
- Italians called early spectacle lenses *lenticchie*, 'lentils', because of their resemblance to lentil seeds.
- In 1921 James Biggs of Bristol painted his stick white to draw attention to his blindness.

THIS WAY *Guide Dogs for the Blind became established in Britain during the 1930s. The Braille alphabet, published in 1829, was extended in 1837 to include codes for words such as 'the' and 'for'.*

AIDS FOR THE BLIND
Guides and alphabets

One day during the First World War a Dr Gorlitz, director of a sanatorium near Stettin (now Szczecin in Poland), was walking with a partially paralysed officer in the garden. Their stroll was interrupted when Gorlitz was called away, but sensing that the officer was in distress the director's dog, an Alsatian named Excelsior, ran indoors to fetch a walking stick. By the time Gorlitz returned, the dog was carefully guiding the soldier home.

Gorlitz was convinced that dogs could be trained to care for the blind. An exploratory programme was set up in 1916 to assist German soldiers who had been blinded in battle. The first guide-dogs were trained by the German Association for Serving Dogs and the Austrian War Dog Institute.

While he was still a teenager the Frenchman Louis Braille, who had been blind since the age of three, devised a system using patterns of up to six raised dots to represent letters of the alphabet. Braille's idea stemmed from the 12-dot military communication system invented for night-time use on battlefields by Captain Charles Barbier, a French army officer, in 1819—the year Braille became a student at the Paris school for blind children.

THE BETTER TO HEAR YOU
Amplifying sound

To boost their hearing, ancient peoples funnelled sounds into their ears with animal horns. The simple ear trumpet was still commonplace in Victorian times—often skilfully disguised. Men would hide one below a beard, while women sported 'acoustic' fans. In 1901 the Acousticon was patented by Miller Reese Hutchinson of New York. It was a large box containing batteries and electric circuitry, including valves to amplify sound. An attached device similar to a telephone receiver was held to the ear.

Queen Alexandra, who had been partially deaf since childhood, used an Acousticon during King Edward VII's coronation in 1902. She was so grateful that she awarded Hutchinson a medal. The 1.1 kg (2½ lb) Amplivox made by A. Edwin Stevens of London in 1935 could be worn, rather than carried, but smaller hearing aids were made practicable by transistors from the 1950s.

EAR TRUMPET WORN ON THE HEAD, 1880

SEE, HEAR *After precise eye testing began in the mid 1860s, patients could be prescribed tailor-made lenses. The deaf had to depend on ear trumpets well into the 20th century, which often made them figures of fun (below).*

SPECTACLES, 1780S DESIGN

EYE TEST CARD, ABOUT 1920

OPHTHALMOSCOPE, ABOUT 1890

SPECTACLES, 1820S

EAR TRUMPET, 1870S

EYE TEST FRAMES AND TRIAL LENS, 1920

'JOHN BULL AT THE ITALIAN OPERA', CARTOON BY THOMAS ROWLANDSON, 1811

TREATING THE TEETH
The dental profession

LOWER SET *These ivory-and-gold dentures are a faithful copy of a set that was made between 1000 and 200 BC and discovered in Sidon, once a Phoenician port.*

'Pain in the teeth', said the Roman encyclopedist Celsus, 'can be counted among the greatest of torments.' Dental treatment in the 1st century AD must have been equally hard to bear. The removal of diseased teeth was common from Egyptian times, when teeth firmly fixed in the jaw were usually knocked out with a stone. Loose ones were pulled free with the fingers.

The Egyptian sage Hesy-Re carried out the first recorded dental work in the 3rd millennium BC, which probably included both rudimentary fillings and extractions. For centuries dentistry was practised by anyone who could acquire the necessary skills, and in medieval times pulling teeth was the job of barbers, surgeons, blacksmiths and horse doctors—or anyone who felt capable of tackling the task.

'Operators for the teeth' extracted the rotten molars of 17th-century Londoners and made dentures for the wealthy, thereby beginning modern dental practice. Britain's first specialist was Peter de la Roche, dentist to the royal household. His patients included the wife of the diarist Samuel Pepys. On March 11, 1661, Pepys recorded what was probably scaling: 'At night home and find my wife come home; and among other things, she hath got her teeth now done by La Roche; and are endeed now pretty handsome…'

The Frenchman Pierre Fauchard, whose definitive reference work, *The Surgeon Dentist*, was published in 1728, effectively made dentistry a science and advocated dental training. By 1760 British practitioners had begun to copy the French and call themselves dentists. Eighty years later in the USA, the world's first dental school was founded in Baltimore, Maryland.

THIS WON'T HURT A BIT

To protect themselves against the agonies of toothache, the ancient Egyptians used burnt mouse dung and burnt angleworms. One ancient Roman cure was to apply olive oil in which earthworms had been boiled.

Until safe anaesthetics arrived, alcohol was used to numb the pain of dental surgery. In 1846 William Thomas Morton of Boston, USA, extracted a tooth from a patient who had been rendered unconscious with ether. Nitrous oxide, also known as laughing gas because of its effects, was preferred from about the turn of the century.

PULL AND FILL
The tools of the trade

The Romans pulled teeth with strong iron forceps and used finer bronze ones for tidying up any fragments. They also employed dental mirrors and probes. Modern versions of these devices, including a range of forceps fashioned to fit different shapes of teeth, date only from the 19th century.

A tooth from a 4500-year-old skull discovered in Denmark bears the marks of a slim flint drill that had once relieved an abscess, but drills were rarely used until the early 1700s, when the French dental pioneer Pierre Fauchard employed a jeweller's bow drill. Strength and speed were added to

the armoury when John Greenwood, dentist to George Washington, adapted a treadle-powered spinning wheel to turn a dental drill in 1790. The hand drill was invented in 1850 by Charles Merry, also in the USA.

The teeth of Egyptian mummies reveal resin fillings, and resin, wax and coral were used to plug cavities up to the Middle Ages. Gold, which is easy to work, resistant to wear and nontoxic, was used in the Middle Ages. Fillings were regarded as symbols of wealth and they remained the preserve of the rich until the 18th century, when tin and lead were pressed into filed or drilled cavities as substitutes for gold.

Mercury was mixed with copper or silver filed from coins to make the first amalgam in the early 1800s. Modern silver amalgam fillings, also containing mercury, were the 19th-century invention of Thomas W. Evans, who was born in the USA but became dentist to the French emperor Napoleon III.

Before the early 18th century, when comfortable wooden armchairs were first provided, patients would sit on the floor. The dentist worked while gripping the patient's head between his knees. Dental chairs with padded headrests, devised by the American Josiah Flagg were first made during the 1790s. Attached to James Snell's reclining chair of 1832 were a mirror and a spirit lamp to shine a light into the mouth.

PULLING IT OUT *A 17th-century French dentist extracts a tooth from his patient with no obvious regard for hygiene. Only in the 19th century did it become clear that the bacteria responsible for tooth decay flourish in food debris left in the mouth.*

BEFORE AND AFTER *An advertisement from 1881 illustrates the advantages of dentures. By the turn of the century more people were taking care of their teeth by using toothpaste.*

A FULL SET
False teeth

The first known false teeth were made by Neferites, who practised in ancient Egypt around 2600 BC, but in the ancient world the Etruscans were the undoubted masters of dentistry. From 700 BC they made partial dentures by mounting extracted teeth, or teeth carved from bone, ivory or ox tooth, on gold bridges supported on each side by healthy teeth. They were unmatched until the 19th century.

A pair of dentures with teeth carved from bone and attached with gut to a hinged side piece are the oldest full set yet discovered. Dug up from a field in Switzerland, they were probably made in the 15th century. Early dentures with wooden plates, especially upper sets, were notoriously hard to keep in place, and in some 18th-century designs they were secured with springs that pressed against the gums. Plaster moulds, used for making accurate casts of the teeth, gums and palate, helped to solve the problem after the 1780s, but it was vulcanised rubber, invented by Charles Goodyear in 1839 and the plates moulded from it from the 1850s onwards, that eventually provided a snug fit.

The first false teeth with the looks and strength of the real thing were the porcelain dentures made by the French apothecary Alexis Duchâteau in about 1770. Many other materials had previously been tried, including ivory which, though durable, made the breath smell. George Washington put his ivory set in port overnight to help to improve both the taste and the odour.

ROUTINE CLEANING
Oral hygiene

The myth that rotten teeth are caused by tooth worms began around 5000 BC in Sumeria and was believed in Egypt, Greece, Rome and China. It also persisted in Europe well beyond the Middle Ages. In fact, a diet of stone-milled flour, which contained grit that wore away tooth enamel, made the ancients prone to dental decay. Many remedies, including the use of tooth-picks, which were recommended by the Sumerians, were intended to drive out tooth worms. The Sumerians included gold toothpicks in toilet sets, but the Greeks discovered the virtues of the resinous wood of the mastic tree, still popular for toothpicks.

Bristled toothbrushes were made in China in the late 11th century, but in Britain they did not go on sale until 1649. Roman toothpowders contained emery to remove stains, but they also abraded the tooth surfaces, leaving blackened stumps. Chalk-based toothpastes were devised in the 19th century. The first tube of toothpaste, called Dr Zierner's Alexandra Dentifrices, went on sale in London in 1891.

EARLY PADDED DENTAL CHAIR, 1840S

TREADLE DRILL, 1870S

OPEN WIDE *The equipment of 19th and early-20th-century dentists reflected their profession's ancient past. On the table, clockwise from the top, are: mirror, 1910; porcelain toothpowder pot, 1890s; tooth mould, about 1920; bridges and dentures of ivory and bone, early 1800s; dental scalers with rosewood handles, about 1860; tooth key, for extractions, about 1860; hand drill, about 1910; dental mouth spray, 1930s. In the centre is an 1810 mouth gag.*

WORDS AND PHRASES

The English language is a complex tapestry. Over the centuries it has been richly interwoven with strands from many tongues, including Greek, Latin, Old Norse, French, Dutch, German, Spanish and, particularly since the advent of the television age, North American English. The language reflects not only the history of English-speaking peoples but also the daily lives of our ancestors of the distant and recent pasts. It speaks of the food they ate, the clothes they wore and the homes they inhabited. It mirrors, too, their customs, festivals and celebrations, the rhythms of their working year and the activities, sports and pastimes that filled and informed their existence.

Because the origins of our language long predate the printed word and mass communications, the sources of many words and phrases remain speculative. Like tracing a family tree, searching for the history of our linguistic inheritance is as frustrating as it is fascinating, and many modern expressions have more than one possible derivation. The entries included here complement and expand on the origins of the words and phrases included in the preceding pages of THE ORIGINS OF EVERYDAY THINGS.

How it All Began

CELTS The name for these ancient Europeans, who included the Britons and Irish, derives via French from the Latin *Celtae*, which comes in turn from the Greek *Keltoi*. The Greek word may imply the Celts were 'hidden people'. The description is apt, because although they could read and write—and inscribed gravestones and pottery—the Celts did not commit any of their history or legends to writing until about the 6th century AD.

DINOSAUR 'Terrible lizard' is the literal meaning of this word, first used in the mid 19th century. It draws on the Greek *deinos*, 'terrible', and *sauros*, 'lizard', to describe the extinct reptiles that existed on Earth from 250 million to 65 million years ago. The word *sauros* was also used in forming the names of such specific types of dinosaur as the brontosaurus, a herbivorous creature named from the Greek *bronte*, 'thunder'.

FOSSIL This word for the preserved remains of a plant or animal came into English in the mid 17th century from the French *fossile*. This term was itself derived from the Latin *fossilis*, 'dug up', from the Latin verb *fodere*, 'to dig'.

GALAXY Our galaxy is the Milky Way, a name reflecting the milky appearance of the star system against a black sky. The Greek word *galaxias* draws on the same image, based on *gala* ('milk'). Through Late Latin the term was borrowed into English as 'galaxy' in the late 1300s. The first recorded use was by Geoffrey Chaucer in his poem *The House of Fame*.

nothing new under the SUN This rather cynical view of the world is Biblical in origin, and appears in Ecclesiastes as 'there is no new thing under the sun'.

TIME and tide wait for no man This proverb, which reinforces the notion that we cannot hold back the relentless march of time, exists in several versions other than its modern-day wording. One that was used in the 16th century was: 'The tide tarrieth no man'. In the 19th century the poet Robert Burns wrote: 'Nae man can tether time or tide'.

brave new WORLD A descriptive phrase that refers to a society of the future. Used by the English writer Aldous Huxley as the title of his novel, published in 1932, it was subsequently applied to negative aspects of modern life such as excessive bureaucracy. The book title owes its origin in turn to Miranda, the heroine of William Shakespeare's *The Tempest*, when she says: 'O brave new world / That has such people in't!'

House and Home

ATTIC In 18th-century England many classical-style buildings had a decorative panel, with flat pillars, above the main façade. The area behind it was called the 'Attic storey', later shortened to the 'attic'. The allusion is to the squarish style of classical Greek pillars—the Attic style that supposedly originated in Attica, the region around Athens.

put on the BACK BURNER This colloquial expression meaning 'to postpone' or 'to demote temporarily' is of 20th-century American origin. The back burner on a stove is a hob or ring that is both relatively cool and positioned to the rear—a doubly apt image of being away from the centre of attention.

a chip off the old BLOCK A person very much like a parent was at first 'a chip *of* the old block'. The block is one of wood or stone; any chip from it consists of the same material. The phrase was in use by the 17th century, but the concept goes back to ancient Greece. The poet Theocritus referred to 'a chip of the old flint' in the 3rd century BC.

CREOSOTE Now a wood preserver, this extract of wood tar was originally used as an antiseptic in medicine. Its name was borrowed from German in about 1835, but derives ultimately from the Greek *kreas*, 'flesh', and *soter*, 'saviour'.

cut the GORDIAN KNOT Cutting the Gordian knot implies taking decisive action to resolve a problem. According to Greek legend Gordius was a peasant who, when he was chosen as King of Phrygia, dedicated his wagon to the god Zeus. He secured the vehicle to a tree with a knot that defied all attempts to undo it. In about 331 BC, during his conquest of the Persian empire, Alexander the Great supposedly came across the knot in Gordium, in modern-day Turkey. He was told that whoever undid it would rule the Asian empire, but he simply sliced through the knot with his sword.

wash one's dirty LINEN in public In a speech to the French Assembly in 1815 Emperor Napoleon I used a version of this expression, based on a French proverb that warns against indiscretion. The concept was soon summarised in this English phrase.

NARCISSUS Greek legend is recalled in this plant, which produces its scented flowers in spring. Narcissus was a handsome youth who fell in love with his own reflection in water. Unable to reach the object of his desire, he pined away and was changed into the flowering plant known by his name. Both his self-love and his name are also remembered in the word 'narcissism'.

NASTURTIUM The Latin name allegedly came from the words *nasus*, meaning 'nose', and *torquere*, 'to twist', apparently in reference to the Romans' reaction to the pungent smell of certain plants. In English the word originally referred to bitter leaves such as those of watercress. Only in the 18th century was it applied to the garden flower.

PANTRY Ultimately derived from the Latin *panis*, 'bread', this word came into English in the early 1300s, both from the Old French *paneterie*, a cupboard where bread was kept, and from the Medieval Latin *panateria*, the room of the person responsible for seeing that bread was supplied to a household.

PAPER over the cracks This expression for disguise reflects the use of wallpaper to hide cracks in walls and ceilings in the 19th century. The original German equivalent is said to have been coined in 1865 by Otto von Bismarck, the Prussian prime minister who was to become the first chancellor of the new German Reich. He apparently used it to describe the outcome of the Convention of Gastein. According to this agreement, which followed the defeat of Denmark, Prussia acquired Lauenburg and administered Schleswig, while Austria was given control of Holstein.

gone to POT This 16th-century phrase for deterioration probably originated in the custom of putting any farm animal for which there was no further use into a pot and cooking it. Another possible source is the smith's melting pot for discarded metal objects.

WALLS have ears This proverb first appeared in print in the early 1600s. It was reinvigorated during the world wars of the 20th century, alongside such slogans as 'careless talk costs lives'. The image may be based on cases of official spying. In the 4th century BC the Greek tyrant Dionysius of Syracuse reputedly eavesdropped on enemy prisoners through a dungeon wall. And the 16th-century French queen Catherine de Medici apparently got wind of plots and state secrets by overhearing conversations on the other side of thin walls in her palace.

Manners and Customs

BAPTISM of fire This expression for a first, usually unpleasant, encounter with a challenging situation was borrowed from the French. It was probably used in the 19th century to describe a soldier's first experience of artillery fire. The phrase has strong Christian overtones. John the Baptist prophesied that the Saviour would baptise people 'with fire', and in later Christian writings the idea was applied to the fate of martyrs burned at the stake.

BONFIRE This contraction of 'bone fire' was used in the 15th century in the form *banefyre* for a blaze fuelled by the

bones left over after meals. The word was later associated with fires marking the Gunpowder Plot of November 5, 1605.

CARNIVAL The 16th-century Italian *carnevale* was a period of merrymaking preceding the fast and self-denial of Lent. The word might have been better applied to the time of abstinence, because it refers literally to the removal of meat—from the Latin *caro*, 'flesh', and *levare*, 'to lift' or 'to remove'. Though the word 'carnival' came into use in English in the mid 16th century, it was only in the 20th century that it came to be used without religious associations, to refer to any celebration.

CATHERINE WHEEL This rotating firework was named in the mid 1900s, after the 4th-century martyr St Catherine of Alexandria, who was tied to a spiked wheel and tortured for publicly defending the Christian faith. According to legend, her bonds were miraculously broken as soon as the wheel began to turn. Traditionally St Catherine is the patron saint of wheelwrights.

CRUSADE Crusades were expeditions or wars that were authorised by the Church for religious ends. In particular the term was applied to the various expeditions made in the 11th, 12th and 13th centuries to recover the Holy Land from the Muslims. The word ultimately derives from the Latin *crux*, meaning 'cross'—Crusaders used the symbol of the Cross to demonstrate their adherence to Christianity.

DARBY AND JOAN A ballad that was published in *Gentleman's Magazine* in 1735 introduced or at least popularised this pair of names for an elderly couple living in long-established harmony. The Darby in question was reputed to be one John Darby of London, the employer of Henry Woodfall, the supposed author of the ballad. However, other sources place the couple in western Yorkshire.

take one's HAT off to someone Until after the Second World War, when men stopped wearing hats as everyday items of dress, a man would remove his hat to someone in a greeting indicating respect or courtesy. The phrase took on its modern use as a figurative expression of admiration in the mid 19th century.

PROTOCOL The Greek *protokollon* was a list of contents glued to the front of a manuscript. The word was formed from *protos*, meaning 'first', and *kolla*, 'glue'. The English word emerged, via Medieval Latin and Middle French, in the mid 1500s and meant an original document. It acquired its more modern meanings—a rule of diplomatic etiquette, an official record and a scientific procedure—in the late 19th century.

pop the QUESTION Making an informal or impromptu proposal has been expressed in this way since the 1700s. An earlier form of the expression appears in *Sir Charles Grandison* (1754), by the English novelist Samuel Richardson: 'Afraid he would now, and now, and now, pop out the question, which he had not the courage to put.'

RED-LETTER day The colour red has been associated with important days since the 15th century or earlier. It was used to highlight saints' days and feast days in ecclesiastical calendars and almanacs. The broader use of the expression, referring to any memorable day, dates from the beginning of the 18th century.

TOUCH WOOD This expression, as well as the gesture itself, invokes good luck. It may hark back to the Druids, a pre-Christian order of priests who lived in Gaul, Britain and Ireland, and regarded certain trees as sacred or as housing benevolent spirits. According to another theory, the phrase comes from an ancient chasing game in which any player who touched wood (the material from which Christ's crucifix was made) was safe from capture.

ZODIAC The Greek word *zoion* meant 'animal' and a *zoidion* was a 'little animal' or the 'carved figure of an animal'. A *zodiakos kuklos* meant a 'circle of carved figures'. It was shortened to *zodiakos* and developed, via Latin and Old French, into the English word in the late 14th century. It denotes the band of 12 signs thought to lie on the celestial sphere, so that the Sun passes through one sign each month. The signs include Aries the ram, Taurus the bull and Cancer the crab.

Food and Drink

AVOCADO In the 16th century the Spanish conquered much of the Americas and brought home foods they discovered there. One of these was the avocado, which they named *aguacate*, adapted from the American Indian word for 'testicle', from the similarity in shape. However, the unfamiliar word was often pronounced *avocado* instead, corresponding to the Spanish word for 'advocate'. 'Avocado' was duly the form that established itself in English in the 18th century.

BISCUIT The original biscuit was a type of unleavened bread, baked and then returned to the oven to dry and crisp. The word's elements suggest 'twice cooked', from the Latin *bis*, meaning 'twice', and *coquere*, 'to cook'. An early form of the word entered the English language from Old French in the 14th century.

sour GRAPES A Greek satire on human nature is the source of this expression, used to describe the attitude of someone affecting disdain for an unattainable object. In 'The Fox and the Grapes', the 6th-century BC fable by Aesop, a fox that fails to reach a bunch of grapes high on the vine exclaims that they are sour, and so not worth eating.

INTOXICATED The 15th-century meaning of this word was not 'drunk' but 'poisoned', as the embedded word 'toxic' suggests. Its origin lies in the ancient Greek practice of spreading poison on arrow tips. *Toxon* was the Greek word for an archer's bow, and *toxicon pharmakon* meant, roughly, 'poison used by archers'. Shortened to *toxicon*, the word was adapted into Latin, French and English.

JERUSALEM ARTICHOKE This plant with edible roots is a member of the sunflower family. The origin of its name, a 17th-century borrowing, is not the city of Jerusalem but the Italian *girasole*, meaning 'sunflower', from *girare*, 'to turn', and *sole*, 'the sun'. The plant tastes similar to, but is no relation of, the globe artichoke. The word *artichoke* itself is Arabic in origin, and was first used in English in about 1530.

the world is your OYSTER The future is bright for those who possess oysters, since they could yield valuable pearls. Shakespeare may have coined this phrase, putting it into the mouth of Pistol, a follower of Sir John Falstaff, in *The Merry Wives of Windsor*: 'Why then, the world's mine oyster / Which I with sword will open.'

PIE in the sky The phrase was popularised in 1911 by a rallying song of the Industrial Workers of the World. Its message was that although religion might promise satisfaction in the afterlife—'pie

---

MAKING NAMES FOR OURSELVES

Many of our ancestors used just one name for themselves, although this was sometimes extended to include a trade— John the Smith and Thomas the Baker, for example. As communities grew larger, surnames were needed to help people to identify each other. This system developed in the south of England in the 13th century, and was well established in most parts of Britain by the 1400s.

The native surnames of the British Isles fall into four broad categories. Names based on the first name of an ancestor include Adam, Gilbert, McArthur, O'Neill, Owens, Peterson and Tomkins. Occupation and status have given rise to names such as Baker, Collier, Glover, Lord, Smith, Thatcher and Waterman.

Names such as Blackwood, Carlisle, Greenwood, Marsh, Salisbury and Woodhouse originate from the locality or type of place where an ancestor lived. Nicknames describing a characteristic of an ancestor's appearance or personality include Black, Doolittle, Fairchild, Longman, Smallbone and Young.

in the sky'—workers deserved a fair deal on Earth. A trade union activist, Joe Hill, is credited with the ironic lyrics of 'The Preacher and the Slave', in which a misguided preacher says: 'You will eat, by and by, in the glorious land above the sky! / Work and pray, live on hay, you'll get pie in the sky when you die.'

buy a PIG in a poke John Heywood, the 16th-century English musician and writer, recorded a version of this phrase in his collection of proverbs of 1546. Its origin is probably the market-day fraud of tying a cat into a bag, or poke, and selling it as a suckling pig. The phrase 'let the cat out of the bag' refers to the revealing of the deception, with luck before purchase.

RECIPE The British have followed 'recipes' since the 16th century, although not in association with food. A recipe then was a prescription for medicine, from the Latin word for 'take'. The word was first used for a set of cooking instructions in the mid 1700s.

TREACLE In Greek *theriake antidotos* meant 'antidote to the venom of a poisonous animal', *ther* being the word for 'wild animal'. It was introduced into English from the Old French *triacle*, 'antidote', and became synonymous with a medicine. The shift of meaning to 'molasses' in the late 17th century was either because the syrup looked like a medicine or because it was used as one, perhaps for its laxative properties.

Fashion and Beauty

have something in the BAG This expression of confidence in a successful outcome comes from the United States of the early 20th century. It probably refers to the hunter's bag used to carry small game after it had been killed, and describes the result of a fruitful hunt.

best BIB and tucker The term for formal attire or best clothes worn on special occasions dates back to the mid 18th century. It probably referred originally to a woman's ornamental bib accompanied by a tucker or frill of lace worn around the neck or shoulders.

a wolf in sheep's CLOTHING In his fables of the 6th century BC, the Greek author Aesop wrote of a wolf who disguised himself as a sheep in order to get closer to his unsuspecting prey. The Bible also refers to this treacherous ploy. In St Matthew's Gospel, Jesus warns: 'Beware of false prophets, which come to you in sheep's clothing, but inwardly they are ravening wolves.'

COMPLEXION This was a medieval medical term that referred to a person's combination of bodily humours—blood, phlegm, yellow bile and black bile—which was thought to determine his or her character or temperament. The word goes back through Old French to the Latin *complecti*, 'to plait' or 'to include'. Facial colouring was considered an important indication of a 'complexion', and by 1450 the word had come to describe the outward appearance of the skin, particularly that of the face.

CRAVAT The Thirty Years' War, which was fought in Europe from 1618, made an impact on fashion. In France, people from Croatia were then known as 'Cravates', and the linen scarves worn by Croatian mercenaries recruited by the French army were apparently given the same name. The fashion for wearing scarves of this type was established in French society around the 1650s, for women as well as for men. Both the name and the fashion soon reached Britain.

MILLINER In 15th-century England, a 'Milaner' was a person who came from Milan. Since the Italian city was then noted for its straw hats and other such finery, the word was probably the source of the 16th-century term 'milliner', which was used for someone who dealt in fancy goods and clothes. The term first came to refer specifically to a maker or seller of women's hats only during the 18th century.

cast PEARLS before swine This phrase, used to suggest there is no point in offering anything of value to people who do not have the capacity to appreciate it, is taken from the Bible. According to St Matthew's Gospel, Jesus taught: 'Give not that which is holy unto the dogs, neither cast ye your pearls before swine, lest they trample them under their feet, and turn again and rend you.'

on TENTERHOOKS This expression for tension or suspense, first recorded in 1748, alludes to a cloth-manufacturing process of the 15th century, in which a piece of damp material was stretched on a wooden frame or 'tenter' and held taut, albeit precariously, by 'tenterhooks'.

Design for Living

AMP or ampere The unit of electric current was named in 1881 in honour of the French physicist and mathematician André-Marie Ampère. He was the first to make the distinction between electric current and voltage.

have an AXE to grind An anecdote told by the 18th-century American writer, scientist and statesman Benjamin Franklin is said to underlie this phrase, which is used of someone acting with an ulterior motive. When he was a boy, Franklin was asked by a man who appeared to be a slow learner how a grindstone worked. Franklin took up the man's axe to demonstrate the process and ended up sharpening it, as the man had intended. So Franklin learnt to beware of people with 'an axe to grind'. The first recorded use of the phrase, however, occurred in 1815—some 25 years after Franklin's death.

have feet of CLAY In the Book of Daniel in the Old Testament, the Babylonian king Nebuchadnezzar dreams of an idol made of gold, silver and brass, standing on feet 'part of iron and part of clay'. The splendid effigy was thus flawed. The poet Lord Byron was the first to use the phrase 'feet of clay', in his *Ode to Napoleon Bonaparte* of 1814.

DERRICK This mechanical crane or hoisting apparatus was given its name in about 1727 from its resemblance to a type of gallows, itself named after a notorious hangman of the 16th and 17th centuries. Thomas Derick is said to have carried out more than 300 executions at London's Tyburn gallows.

a rough DIAMOND People of fine character but lacking social polish have been known as rough diamonds since at least 1700. In that year, John Dryden applied the phrase to his 14th-century fellow-poet Geoffrey Chaucer, author of *The Canterbury Tales*.

pour OIL on troubled waters Mariners of old apparently poured oil onto turbulent seas in an attempt to effect calm. The Venerable Bede, the Anglo-Saxon monk, theologian and historian, alludes to this practice in his *Ecclesiastical History* of 731. St Aidan, he relates, gave a container of holy oil to a priest who was to escort the bride-to-be of King Oswin. A storm arose during the sea-crossing, but it abated when the priest poured the oil onto the waters. As an expression for a soothing of strife, the phrase came into widespread use only in the 19th century.

PAINT the town red This expression, used of wild celebrations, reached Britain from the USA in the early 20th century. It could be based on the alleged habit of North American Indian peoples of setting fire to a town when they were on a spree of destruction, or alternatively to the red nose that can result from drinking.

ROBOT The dramatist Karel Čapek coined the Czech word in 1920, in his play *R.U.R.* (*Rossum's Universal Robots* in English). His robots were artificial beings designed to perform mechanical tasks. They were named from *robota*, meaning 'labour' or 'drudgery'.

TIME flies People have for centuries bemoaned the speed at which time passes. The expression is a translation of the Latin proverb *tempus fugit*, perhaps based on a line written in the 1st century AD by the poet Virgil in his *Georgics*.

VOLT The unit of electromotive force was named in about 1870 in honour of Alessandro Volta, the Italian physicist who studied the theory of electric current and developed the electric battery.

the thin end of the WEDGE The phrase refers to a seemingly unimportant action or decision that could have serious consequences. The allusion is to a wedge

inserted into a block of wood to make it easier to split. The phrase was first used in the 19th century.

WHEELS within wheels Complex, involved situations have been described in this way since Biblical times. The phrase probably derives from the Old Testament Book of Ezekiel, in which the prophet uses the image of one wheel inside another when describing a vision.

tilt at WINDMILLS The phrase means to struggle against imaginary enemies. It comes from the comic adventures of Don Quixote, the hero of the Spanish writer Miguel de Cervantes's 17th-century novel of the same name. In it Don Quixote mistakes some windmills for a gang of evil giants and sets out to 'tilt' at them, that is to attack them with his lance.

Moving About

when the BALLOON goes up A military tactic of the First World War underlies this phrase, referring to the start of dramatic events. The allusion is apparently to the release into the air of the barrage balloons intended as obstacles to enemy aircraft. This served as a clear signal that trouble was expected.

be on one's BEAM ends Beams are the transverse timbers supporting a ship's decks. A vessel on its beam ends is lying on its side and about to capsize. This perilous position reflects the state of those utterly without money, or in a similarly desperate state. This figurative use dates back to the early 19th century.

CANTER The word owes its existence to the English city Canterbury. It refers to the steady and relaxed pace that was adopted by medieval travellers as they rode there on a pilgrimage to the shrine of St Thomas Becket, the 12th-century archbishop who was murdered following a disagreement with Henry II. Geoffrey Chaucer immortalised the pilgrimage in *The Canterbury Tales*, begun in 1387. Variously referred to as Canterbury trot, pace or gallop, or simply the Canterbury, the pace became the shortened 'canter' in the 18th century.

the COAST is clear The risk of getting caught concentrates the mind, for both smugglers and soldiers. A check of the shoreline establishes if 'the coast is clear' and safety assured. The expression was in use by the early 16th century.

DIESEL The diesel engine, in which fuel is ignited by the heat produced by highly compressed air, is named after its inventor. Working in Essen in the 1890s Rudolf Diesel, the French-born German engineer, also developed the petroleum that fuels the engine.

the cut of one's JIB A sailing boat's triangular foresail is its jib. When sailing ships plied the world's oceans, and each country had a particular way of fashioning the jib, sailors could easily identify a ship's 'nationality' at a distance. If a captain did not like the cut of a ship's jib, he avoided it. This figurative description of a person's attitude, manner or appearance was in use by the early 1800s.

JUGGERNAUT The original Hindi and Sanskrit forms of this word mean literally 'Lord of the World', a title given to the Hindu deity Krishna. At religious festivals, an image of the god would be carried on a huge wagon, and the word duly came to refer in English to this massive vehicle. Tales abounded of Hindu devotees sacrificing themselves by diving under the wagon's wheels as it trundled past. This encouraged a new sense of an 'irresistible, crushing force', which developed in the 1860s. The earlier sense was updated in the 1940s, when the word came to be used in Britain to refer to a huge lorry.

shanks's PONY To go by shanks's pony or Shanks's mare is simply to walk—the shank is the lower leg. The expression evokes the image of a snobbish pauper keeping up appearances by boasting of having travelled on a fine horse borrowed from a Mr Shanks. Various forms of the phrase date back to the late 18th century.

take the wind out of someone's SAILS A sailing ship literally takes the wind out of another's if it sails windward of it and deprives it of wind, keeping all the benefits to itself. In its figurative sense, the expression means 'to put someone at a disadvantage' or 'to dent someone's confidence'. An earlier version was used by Sir Walter Scott, the Scottish novelist and poet, in *The Fortunes of Nigel* (1822): 'He would take the wind out of the sail of every gallant.'

TANDEM The word's association with a bicycle comes from an 18th-century pun. A wit deliberately misinterpreted the Latin word *tandem*, which means 'at length' or 'eventually', as 'lengthways', and applied it to a carriage drawn by two horses, one behind the other. The two-person cycle subsequently became a 'tandem', in the 1880s. The word was used in the 20th century to describe two people or forces that act together, especially in the phrase 'in tandem'.

on the WAGON Someone who decides to refrain from drinking any alcohol was formerly described as being 'on the water wagon', a humorous suggestion that the only alternative drink is water. Since the phrase is an American one, the wagon in question was probably one of the familiar horse-drawn carts used to prevent dry dirt roads from becoming too dusty. The modern, shortened phrase dates from the early 20th century.

Living Together

play devil's ADVOCATE The original *advocatus diaboli* was a Catholic priest appointed to argue against the proposed canonisation of a saint in order to ensure his or her worthiness. By extension the phrase came to describe a questioning of the validity of a proposal, typically just for argument's sake. The English phrase dates from the 1700s.

AGNOSTIC This word was coined in 1869 by the English biologist Thomas Huxley to describe someone who holds that knowledge or proof of God is impossible. It is derived from the Greek prefix *a-*, meaning 'not', and *gnostos*, 'known' or 'knowable'.

AMBULANCE Derived ultimately from the Latin *ambulare*, 'to walk', the word was borrowed in 1809 from French.

The word came from the phrase *hôpital ambulant*, meaning 'walking hospital', and was originally used for a mobile military hospital. Only during the Crimean War (1835-56) did it come to refer to a vehicle, and then only to the cart or wagon used for transporting casualties.

upset the APPLECART Evoking the image of market traders' carts being overturned, versions of this phrase for ruining someone's plans or enterprise were in use in English in the late 1700s. The Romans had a similar expression.

throw the BOOK at someone People who are being severely punished for breaking the rules have had 'the book' thrown at them since the early 1920s or 1930s. It was a legal term for the range of charges or penalties applicable to a particular offence or crime.

CURFEW The Old French *covrefeu*, meaning 'cover fire', was the nightly bell-ringing or other signal telling inhabitants of medieval towns—where an unattended blaze could spread rapidly—to extinguish their lights and fires. By the late 18th century the word was being applied to an official order requiring people to be indoors by a certain time, typically to prevent crime or civil unrest.

DRACONIAN So severe were the laws drawn up by the Athenian statesman Draco in 621 BC that his name is associated with disproportionately harsh measures. Even trivial offences could carry the death sentence under Draco's code. The English word is of 19th-century origin, though an earlier form, 'draconic', was used a century before that.

wash one's HANDS of This phrase, which indicates a refusal to accept responsibility for, or have any further association with, someone or something, has been in general use since at least the 16th century. It alludes to the action of the Roman governor of Judaea, Pontius Pilate. He wished to dissociate himself from the decision to crucify Jesus, and St Matthew's Gospel relates that Pilate 'washed his hands before the multitude, saying, I am innocent of the blood of this just person.'

obey the letter of the LAW This expression, which refers to the strict interpretation of a rule according to its wording, is often contrasted with applying the 'spirit of the law', which allows for a more flexible interpretation. The contrast, though not the phrasing, is Biblical, coming from 2 Corinthians.

RAIN cats and dogs Several suggested origins have been proposed for this colloquial expression for heavy rain. One relates to the poor drainage systems of the 17th century and earlier. Flooding was a common occurrence in heavy down-pours, causing the deaths of unwary cats and dogs, which would then float down gutters with other debris. According to another suggestion, the expression relates to the superstition that witches take on the appearance of cats when flying about during storms.

chase RAINBOWS It is probably a traditional legend of the British Isles that lies behind this figurative expression for the pursuit of illusory goals—namely that a crock of gold can be found at the end of a rainbow. The phrase dates from the 19th century or earlier.

save for a RAINY day Putting money aside to provide for future need has been described in this way since the 1500s. In a rural economy, rain could keep agricultural workers off the land and prevent them from earning the day's pay.

read the RIOT ACT The Riot Act lasted for more than 250 years, from the early 18th century to 1973. It decreed that persons engaged in a 'riot' (12 or more people gathered together and considered to be a threat to peace) had to disperse within an hour of being formally warned by an authorised official. By 1850 the phrase was being more widely applied to any stern warning or reprimand.

when in ROME, do as the Romans do This proverbial advice about the wisdom of following local customs is sometimes ascribed to St Ambrose, the 4th-century bishop of Milan. When he was asked by St Monica and her son St Augustine whether they should follow Milanese or Roman fast days, Ambrose is said to have replied: 'When I am here [Milan], I do not fast on Saturday; when I am in Rome, I fast on Saturday.' The proverb had entered the English language by the 16th century.

go to TOWN This expression for great thoroughness or enthusiasm originated in the USA in the 19th or 20th century. It probably stems from the fact that in rural communities travelling to town was a special occasion because of the distances and time involved.

TWELVE GOOD MEN AND TRUE The 'good men and true' of the jury seem to have given rise to this phrase by the 16th century. It was used in a different context by Shakespeare in *Much Ado About Nothing*, in which the constable Dogberry asks the watchmen: 'Are you good men and true?'

The Written and Spoken Word

BLARNEY At Blarney Castle, near Cork in Ireland, visitors make a point of kissing a famous inscribed stone block (or a replica of it), thereby supposedly acquiring skill in the art of persuasion. The custom is first recorded in the 18th century, but its reputed origin goes back to 1602. The local lord, required to surrender the castle to English troops, kept putting them off with eloquent excuses, or 'Blarney talk'. A smooth-talking character called Lady Blarny duly appeared in Oliver Goldsmith's novel *The Vicar of Wakefield* (1766), and Sir Walter Scott used the word as a common noun in a letter of 1796.

GOSSIP The original 'gossip' was the Anglo-Saxon *godsibb*, 'godparent', derived from *sibb*, meaning 'relative' (hence *sibling*, 'little relative'). The word came to refer to a familiar acquaintance or close friend. By the 16th century it had taken on its modern meaning of 'chatterbox' or 'rumour-monger'.

it's GREEK to me In Shakespeare's *Julius Caesar*, Casca, who is one of the conspirators planning Caesar's murder, says of a speech by the statesman and orator Cicero: 'For mine own part, it was Greek to me.' Cicero had actually been speaking in Greek, perhaps to prevent ordinary people from understanding him. In due course the phrase came to be used for unintelligible things in general and those of a specialist or technical nature in particular.

a little KNOWLEDGE is a dangerous thing This warning for the false sense of confidence that incomplete knowledge can confer is in effect a misquotation of Alexander Pope. In *An Essay on Criticism*, the 18th-century English poet wrote: 'A little learning is a dangerous thing.' The idea was not an original one. Some 100 years earlier it had been expressed similarly by both the French essayist Michel Eyquem de Montaigne and the English scientist, writer and politician Francis Bacon.

PATTER As a verb, originally meaning 'to mutter one's prayers quickly', this word dates back about 600 or 700 years. It was adapted rather irreverently from *Paternoster*, the Lord's Prayer (the opening words in Latin are *Pater noster*, meaning 'Our Father'). The modern noun, meaning the 'glib talk' of a salesman, developed in the mid 19th century.

POWWOW When European settlers of North America encountered the Algonquian peoples, they also discovered the medicine man or *powwow*. The word became associated with the ceremony that accompanied his rituals, and perhaps then came to refer to a meeting with him. It was an informal term for a meeting or discussion by the 19th century.

PROPAGANDA Pope Gregory XV set up the *Sacra Congregatio de Propaganda Fide* (Congregation for Propagating the Faith) in 1622. Its purpose was to direct missionary work and also to spread the doctrines of Christianity throughout the world. Some 100 years later 'Propaganda' was being used in English to refer to this committee of cardinals. However, by the late 18th century the word was used to refer to any zealous organisation or pressure group, and during the early part of the 20th century it at last acquired its modern meaning of the dissemination of political dogma.

the WRITING on the wall This colourful warning, which first appeared in print in 1720, is based on a story in the Old Testament Book of Daniel. In it the prophet describes an inscription written on the wall by a ghostly hand during a feast held by Belshazzar, king of the Chaldeans. Daniel warns the king that it foretells his downfall. Later that night Belshazzar was duly killed.

Leisure and Sport

not worth the CANDLE This phrase, which is used of something that is not worth the effort involved, was part of a common English saying by the early 17th century. One version seems to be a translation of the French saying *Le jeu n'en vaut pas la chandelle*, recorded by the 16th-century essayist Montaigne. It referred to a gamblers' card game in which the stake played for was less than the cost of the candle that was needed to light the room.

EASEL The painter's prop is named after the Dutch *ezel*, 'ass' or 'donkey', from the animal used for carrying loads. The word was used in English by the 17th century.

FIDDLING while Rome burns The Roman emperor Nero is the 'fiddler' who gave rise to this expression, although in fact the instrument he is said to have played while watching Rome being destroyed by a fire in AD 64 was a lyre. The expression, used of someone engaged in trivial matters when a crucial one requires attention, was in common use by the 19th century.

NECK AND NECK This is one of many English expressions to be borrowed from horse-racing. It was originally used to describe two mounts running so closely together that it is impossible to predict which one will be the winner. It was adopted in the early 19th century to describe any close competition.

pull a RABBIT out of a hat This conjurer's trick has been a favourite for centuries. The figurative use of the phrase, for last-minute success against the odds, dates from about the 1930s.

back to SQUARE one This vivid way of describing the need to start something again from the beginning owes its wording to an instruction for playing such board games as snakes and ladders. The penalty is also found in the ancient children's game of hopscotch. The phrase is said to have been made so popular by the BBC radio sports commentators of the 1930s that it became virtually a catchphrase. They used a numbered grid representing a football pitch, which was printed in the magazine *Radio Times*, as a reference to help listeners to work out the positions of the players and the ball during matches.

pull out all the STOPS Today's informal way of asserting that no effort has been spared originates in an organist's ancient practice. Pulling out every stop-knob or handle of an organ brings all the ranks of pipe into play to create the loudest and most complex sound. The expression came into common usage only in the 20th century.

WHAT'S IN A NAME?

Britain's ancient invaders and settlers have left their mark in many of the names of villages, towns and cities. King's Lynn and Linlithgow have their origins in the Celtic word 'lin' or 'llyn', a pool or lake, while Dover and Andover derive from 'dubro', water or river. The Celtic word 'aber', a rivermouth, is included in Aberystwyth and Aberdeen.

The Anglo-Saxons settled Britain from the 5th century. Their legacy includes 'burgh', a fortified town or a stronghold, found in Canterbury and Middlesbrough; 'ford', a river crossing, in Oxford; and 'feld', an open space, as in Macclesfield and Petersfield. 'Ham', a homestead or village, is used in Birmingham.

Viking invaders 300 years later left the Norse 'by', farm or town, in Grimsby, and 'thorp', a village, in Scunthorpe. 'Toft', a piece of land or a farm, is found in Lowestoft, and 'gate', a street, in Harrogate.

follow SUIT This expression for imitation comes from card games popular in the late 17th century, such as whist, in which a player has to play cards of the same suit as the player who initiates each trick. The figurative sense dates back to at least the mid 19th century.

steal someone's THUNDER 'They steal my thunder,' was the plaintive cry of the English critic and playwright John Dennis. In 1709 he devised a machine to recreate the sound of thunder in his play *Appius and Virginia*, only to see his idea copied by a rival. The expression eventually came to be applied to anyone claiming the success or effort of another.

throw in the TOWEL This expression for acknowledging defeat comes from the boxing rings, probably in Victorian times. To indicate that he was conceding defeat, a fighter's second or trainer would toss a towel or sponge into the ring.

UMPIRE This word entered the English language in the 14th century as *noumpere*. It was derived from the Old French *nonper*, from *non*, meaning 'not', and *per*, 'equal'. It probably meant 'not even in number'—that is, the third person mediating between two contestants. By the 15th century 'a noumpere' had become 'an oumpere', in the same way that 'an adder' was originally 'a nadder'.

Sickness and Health

BEDLAM This term for a noisy, chaotic scene, first recorded in 1667, had a slightly earlier sense, that of an insane asylum. That derived from the London madhouse known as Bedlam, short for the Hospital of St Mary of Bethlehem.

clean BILL OF HEALTH Dating from the 16th or 17th century, this describes a favourable report on someone's health. Fear of disease prompted the demand for ships or travellers arriving at a port to show 'clean bills of health', proving their last port of call had been disease-free.

the BLIND leading the blind In St Matthew's Gospel Jesus tells his disciples to ignore the Pharisees: 'Let them alone: they be blind leaders of the blind. And if the blind lead the blind, both shall fall into the ditch.' As a proverbial summary of the way ignorance is handed on, the expression has been used for centuries.

turn a BLIND eye Wilfully ignoring another's entreaties or advice has been so described since the mid 15th century. One famous instance popularised the phrase—the reputed action of Admiral Horatio Nelson at the Battle of Copenhagen in 1801. He put a telescope to his blind eye so he could say he had not seen the flagship's signal to withdraw. Nelson went on to trounce the Danes.

bite the BULLET This phrase refers to bravery in the face of the inevitable. According to tradition, soldiers who were undergoing field surgery would bite on a bullet to prevent themselves from crying out. In one version or another, the phrase goes back to the late 19th century or earlier.

DELIRIUM Borrowed from Latin in the late 16th century, this word for a form of madness is derived ultimately from *de*, meaning 'away from', and *lira*, 'furrow'. Like an errant ploughman, a delirious mind fails to maintain a straight line.

EXCRUCIATING The English used 'excruciate' in the late 1500s. The verb was borrowed from the Latin *excruciare*, 'to torture', which derives in turn from *cruciare*, meaning 'to crucify', a method of execution in Roman times. The ultimate origin of both these words is *crux*, 'cross'.

INFLUENZA The English borrowed this word from Italian in 1743 during a Europe-wide outbreak of the illness. In Italian it had earlier referred to any epidemic—the Latin roots, *in*, 'in', and *fluere*, 'to flow', indicate the underlying idea that some flowing force or influence from the stars affected the destiny of people on Earth. The informal 'flu' is a 19th-century contraction.

a fly in the OINTMENT This Biblical metaphor for the flaw in a favourable situation comes from Ecclesiastes: 'Dead flies cause the ointment of the apothecary to send forth a stinking savour.'

INDEX

Page numbers in **bold** indicate a main entry on the subject

A

Academy Awards 249
acrobats 261
acrylic 123
action toys **279**
actors **242–3**
acupuncture **296**
Adams, Thomas 99
additives **107**
adhesives **45**
advertising **195**, **217**
  'lonely hearts' 65
  newspaper placards 229
adzes 146
AEG 251
aerosols 45
Aeschylus 242
Aga 30
'agony columns' 229
agriculture 13, 14, 56,
  82–83, 84–85
air conditioning **31**
aircraft 167, **180–3**
airing cupboards 37
airlines 182
airmail 182, **231**
airports, air safety **183**
airships 181
à la carte 63
alarm clocks **161**
Alcock, John 181
alcohol **112–17**
ale 83, **112–13**
algae 11
algebra **221**
allotments **55**
All Saints' Day 57, **72**
alphabets **214–15**
  Braille **301**
  manual 219
alternative remedies **294–7**
aluminium **149**
  foil **45**
Amati, Andrea 237
ambulances 200
amphibians 11
Amplivox 301
amputation **290**, 292
anaesthesia 292, **293**, **299**,
  300
animals
  domestic 13, 14, 82, 83, 167
  guide-dogs **301**
  performing **261**
  pet **42–43**
  symbolic **216–17**
  toy 276, **277**
anoraks 131
antibiotics **283**
antiseptics 281, 292, **293**,
  299

apartment buildings 189
Appert, Nicolas 103
apples **92**, **113**
apricots 92
April Fools' Day **70**
aqua ardens/vitae **116**
aquaria **261**
Aquascutum 131
aqueducts 208–9
archaeology 14–15
archery **271**
arches 165
Archimedes 144, 145
architecture **165**
Aretaeus 284
Argand, Aimé 26
Aristotle 226, 298
arithmetic **220–1**
Arkwright, Richard 192
armour 123
Army and Navy Co-operative
  Society 195
aromatherapy **297**
art galleries 235, **260**
arthritis 285
artificial limbs **290–1**
Arzt, Walter 69
asbestos 123
Ascot, Royal 269
Ashes, the 266
aspirin **295**
assembly lines 192
Astaire, Fred 241
Astley, Philip 261
Astor, Nancy 190
astrology **78**, 79
astronomy 14, **158–9**, 184,
  185
athletics **262–3**
atlases 184–5
aubergines **93**
Auenbrugger, Leopold 288
Auer, Karl 27
Augustine, St 203
autumn festivals **72–73**
Avicenna 287, 294
axes 12, 142, 145, 146

B

Babbage, Charles 162–3
baby clothes, Babygro **69**
Bacardi, Emilio 117
backgammon 273
bacteria 11, 282
badminton 267
Baedeker, Karl **257**
Baekeland, Leo 157
bags **139**
Bailey, William 37
bains-marie 28
Baird, John Logie 235, **252–3**
baked beans 102, 104
Bakelite 157
Baker, Samuel 171

Ballantine, George 117
ballet **240–1**
balloons, hot-air 180–1
ball-point pens 222, 223
bananas **93**
Band-Aid 289
bank holidays **254**
banknotes, banks 196, **197**
Banks, Joseph 52
banns 66–67
Banting, Frederick **284**
baptism **68**
barbed wire **41**
barber's pole 217
barber surgeons 217, 292
Barbie dolls 277
Barbier, Charles 301
barges 178
barium meal **289**
barley 82
Barnard, Christiaan 291
barographs 207
barometers 158, **159**
barristers 199
Bartisch, Georg 300
baseball 267
basil 101
baskets 142
bathrooms, baths **34–35**
batteries 153
Baudry, Stanislaus 170
bay leaves 101
Bayley, William 25
BBC **233**, 235, 252, 253
beads 138
bears, teddy **277**
beauty care 119, **140–1**
Beaux, Ernest 141
Beck, Harry 185
beds, bedrooms 18, 19,
  32–33
Beecher, Catherine 29
beef 83, **89**
beekeeping **98**
beer 83, **112–13**
beetroot 90
Bell, Alexander Graham 232,
  250
Bell, Patrick 84
Belling, Charles Reginald 31
bell jars 55
bells, church 202
belts 127
Benz, Karl 150, 172
berets 136
Berger, Hans 289
Berliner, Emile **250–1**
Berlioz, Hector 239
Bertin, Rose 132
besoms 38
Bessemer, Henry 149
Best, Charles **284**
betrothal **64–65**
betting **259**
  sweepstakes 269

Bible 202, 203
bicycles **168–9**
bifocals 300
Biggs, James 300
bikinis 135
billhooks 54, 55
billiards **271**
Billroth, Theodor 293
binary code **221**
Bingo **259**
binoculars **158–9**
biological symbols 219
Birdseye, Clarence 103
Biro, Georg *and* Ladislao 223
birth control **298**
birthdays 68
Bissell, Melville 38
bits, horses' 269
black pudding 102
Blackwell, Elizabeth 287
Blanchard, Jean-Pierre 181
blankets 33
blazers 129
bleach 36
Blériot, Louis 180–1
Bligh, Samuel L. 141
blindman's buff **278**
blindness, aids for 300, **301**
blinds 25
blood
  circulation 281
  groups 293
  pressure 281, **288**
  transfusions 292, 293
Bloomer, Amelia Jenks 169
blouses 126–7
Blundell, James 293
board games 234–5, **272–3**
boaters 136
boats 166, 167
Bodley, Thomas 227
Boeing, William 182
boiling 100
bolts **44**
bombers 181
bonbons 99
Bonfire Night 72–73
books 206, 207, **210–11**,
  224–7
  children's **279**
  tokens 226
Boot, Jesse 194
boot cleaners 46–47
Booth, Hubert Cecil 38
boots 137
Boots Co 140
Borden, Gail 96
botanical gardens **260–1**
botany **52–53**
bottle-feeding **68**
Bovril 109
Bowler, Thomas *and*
  William 136
bowling, tenpin 271
bowling greens 51

bows and arrows **271**
boxer shorts 135
boxes 22
box girders 164
boxing **263**
Boxing Day 75
Boyle, Robert 27
braces 129
Bradshaw, George 177
brag 274
Braid, James 285
Braille, Louis **301**
brain surgery **292**
Bramah, Joseph 40
brandy 116
brass 149
brassieres 134, 135
bread 82, 85, **86**
breakfast 60
Brearley, Harry 149
breastfeeding **68**
brewing 82, **112–13**
bricks **20**, 142
bridge (game) 274
bridges **164**
Brightfield, Thomas 35
Brillo steel wool 39
Brindley, James 178
British Library/Museum 227,
  260
broadcasting **233**, **235**,
  252–3
broadsheets 228
brochures, holiday 183
brogues 137
bronze 14, 143, **148**
brooms **38**
Brougham, Lord 171
Brown, Arthur Whitten 181
Brown, 'Capability' 51
Brown, Louise 299
Bruhn, Wilhelm 171
Bruinsz, Pieter 185
Brummell, Beau 59, 129, 132
Brunel, Isambard Kingdom
  179, 192
Brunel, Marc Isambard 164,
  192
brushes **38**
  hair **33**
buckles 127, 137
Budding, Edwin 54–55
buffets 23
building **20–21**, **165**, **174–5**
  blocks 276
  societies 197
Buitoni, Giulia 86
bulbs, flowering **53**
Bulova Accutron 161
Buna rubber 156
Bundy, William 33
bungalows 19
Bunger, G. 291
Burbage, James 243
Burberry, Thomas 130

burial **80**
buses **170**
Butlin, Billy 255
butter **97**
Butterick, Ebenezer 125
buttons 118, **127**, 137

C

cabbages **91**
Cadbury's 99, 189
caddies (golf) 265
caesarean section **299**
cafetières 109
caftans 130
Cailler, François-Louis 99
calculators 162
calendars **206–7**
calico 123
calligraphy **215**
camcorders 253
cameras **246–9**
Campbell, John 185
cams 144, **145**
canal boats 178
canals **165**, 167
canasta 274
cancer surgery 293
candles **26–27**, 75
canes **139**
canned beer 112
canned food 102, **103**
canoes 166
can openers 46, 47
capes 130
caps 136
caravans **171**
carbon dating 14–15
carbon fibre **157**
cardamoms 100, 101
card games **274**, 275
cardigans 133
cards, Christmas 75
Carey, John 185
caricatures **229**
carol singing 74
Carothers, Wallace H. 123, 156
carpet beaters/sweepers **38**
carpets **24–25**
carrots 90
cars 167, **172–3**
  model/toy 276, 277
  police 201
cartoons **229**
carts 167
Cartwright, Edmund 121
cash 113
  dispensers 197
cashmere 121
casinos **258**
caskets 22
castor oil 295
cataract surgery **300**
cat flaps 43
catheters 292
cathode-ray tubes 252
cat's-eyes 175
caviar 95
Caxton, William 195

Cayley, George 181
CBS 251
CD-ROMs 226
CDs **251**
ceilings **21**
cellophane **45**, 157
celluloid 33, 156–7
Celsius, Anders 159
cemeteries **80–81**
central heating **31**
cereals, breakfast 60
chains **41**
chain stores **194**
chairs **22**, 23
  dental **302**, 303
chaises longues 22
chalk, outlines in 217
Chamberlen family 299
champagne 115
chance, games of **258–9**
Chanel, Gabrielle 'Coco' 127, 132, 133, 141
Chancel, Jean 27
chapattis 86
charm bracelets 76
Charnley, John 291
cheese 83, **96**
chefs 63
Chelsea boots 137
cheques 196
  traveller's 256
cherries 92
chess **272**, 273
chests **22–23**
  dower 65
chewing gum 99
chicken **88**
chickpeas 104
childbirth procedures **299**
chillies 100, 101
china **146**
chintz 123
chiropractic **297**
chisels 146
Chivas brothers 117
chocolate 83, **99**, **109**
  Easter eggs 70
christening **68**
Christianity 14, **202–3**
  Cross [symbol] **216**
  dance/drama/music and 235, **236**, 242–3
  festivals 56–57, **70–75**
  marriage 66–67
  symbols **216–17**
Christmas 57, **74–75**
chromium 149
chronometers 185
Chubb, Jeremiah 40, 41
Church, Ellen 183
churches 203
Church of England 202
churns 97
cider **113**
cigars 295
cinema **248–9**
cinnamon 100, 101
circle [symbol] 216
circuits, integrated 163
circuses **261**

cities 14, **188–9**
clairvoyance **78–79**
clarinets **237**, 238
Clark, Edward 195
clay, modelling 276, 277
clerical work **193**
cloaks 130
cloches 55
clocks **160–1**
  clockwork 161
clogs 137
clothes **118–37**, 169
clothespegs 37
cloves 100, 101
clowns 261
coal 30, 149, **150**
coats 128–9, **130–1**, 132
  of arms **218**
Coca-Cola **111**, 117
Cockerell, Christopher 179
Cockran, Josephine 39
cocktails 117
cocoa **109**
coconuts 104
coffee 83, **109**
  grinders/mills 46, 47
cognac 116
coins 148, 196, 197
coke 149
Coke, William 136
colanders 28
collars 127, 129
Columbus, Christopher 93, 101, 178, 184–5, 295
combine harvesters 85
combs **33**
comedy **242**
comic strips 229
commedia dell'arte 243, **244–5**
commercials (TV) 195, 253
communities **14–15**, **186–9**
compasses 184
computers 143, **162–3**
  CD-ROMs 226
  chess 273
  dating 65
  personal 163, 211
concrete **20**, 164
conductors [music] **239**
confetti 66
conjurors **245**
conkers **278**
construction *see* building
construction toys 276
contact lenses **300**
contour lines 185
contraception **298**
Cook, Thomas 183, **256**
cookbooks 226
cookers 29, **30–31**
Cooklin, Len 29
cookware 17, **28**, 29, 82
Cooley, Denton 291
Cooper, Wilson 29
copper 14, 142, 143, **148**
Corby, John 47
coriander 101
corkscrews 114, 115
corn dollies 72
corneal grafts 291

cornets [music] 239
cornflakes 60
corn on the cob **87**
Cornu, Paul 181
coronations 187
corsets 134, 135
cosmetics **140**
costume jewellery 138
cottage industries 192
cotton **122–3**
couches 22, 32
country dances **240**
courtesy **58–59**
courtship **64–65**
crackers 74, 75
cradles **69**
cranks 144–5
Crapper, Thomas 35
cravats 132
creation **10–11**
credit cards 197
cremation **80**
crescent [symbol] 218, 219
cress 91
cricket 235, **266**
crisps 63
croissants 86
crop rotation 82–83
Cross, C.S. 123
Cross [symbol] **216**
  peace cross 219
  Red Cross **219**
crosswords **275**
Crowe, Wilson 29
cruises 179, **256–7**
Crystal Palace 260
Cuba Libre 117
cuffs 127
Cullen, Michael 195
Culpeper, Nicholas 294
cumin 100, 101
Cummings, Alexander 35
Cunard 179
cupboards **22–23**
curling tongs 141
currants, black/red 93
curry 101
curtains **25**
customs **56–81**
cutlery **61**

D

Dacron 123
Daguerre, Louis Jacques
  Mandé **246–7**
Daily Mirror 229
Daimler, Gottlieb 150, 169, 172, 173
Daiquiri 117
Dallos, Josef 300
dams 208
dancing 234, 235, **240–1**
Daquin, Eugène 39
Darby, Abraham 149
d'Arlandes, Marquis 180
Darrow, Charles 273
darts **271**
dating **65**
Davis, Jacob 133

Davy, Humphry 27, 153, 246
'deaf and dumb' language **219**
deafness, aids for **301**
death penalty, abolition of 199
decaffeinated coffee 109
de Chardonnet, Hilaire 123
decimals 220
décolletage 118-19
de Coubertin, Pierre **263**
Deere, John 84
de la Roche, Peter 302
democracy **190**
de Montfort, Simon 191
denim 123, 133
dentistry **302–3**
dentures 302, **303**
Denys, Jean-Baptiste 293
deodorants 141
department stores **194–5**
Derby, the 268, 269
de Rochas, Alphone Beau 172
de Rozier, François Pilâtre 180
desalination 209
Descartes, René 221
de Serres, Olivier 91
designer labels 133
desks 23, 206
detergents **36**
de Thury, César François
  Cassini 185
diabetes, insulin and **284**
dialysis 285
diamonds **151**
dice **258**, 273
Dickens, Charles 226, 229
Dickson, Earle 289
Dickson, James 123
dictionaries **227**
Diderot, Denis 226–7
Diener, Nelly 183
Diesel, Rudolf 176
digitalin **294–5**
digital watches 161
dilators 292
dining rooms 18, 19
Dinky toys 276, 277
dinner 60
  jackets 132
Dior, Christian 127
diplomats 190
discos **241**
dishes **61**
dishwashers **39**
dissection 280–1
distilling **116–17**
DNA 14, 107
doctors **286–7**
dodgems 255
dolls **276–7**
domes 165
Donald, Ian 289
Donders, Franciscus Cornelius 300
doors **20**, 21
dragées 99
drama 234, 235, **242–3**
draughts 272
drawing rooms 19

dreams, interpreting 79
Drebbel, Cornelius 178
dressers, kitchen 29
dresses 119, **126–7**, 133
dressing tables 32
dressmaking 125
dried food 83, **102–3**
drills
  dental **302**, 303
  surgical 292
drinks 83, **108–17**
driving licences/schools/tests
  173
drugs **283**, 293, **294–5**
drums 238
dry cleaning 37
Duchâteau, Alexis 303
Duffle coats 130
dungarees 132
Dunlop, John Boyd 169
Dupain-Triel, Jean Louis 185
Du Pont Co. 123, 156
Durex 298
dusters 38, 39
dustmen 209
dustpans 38
duvets 33
dyes **154**
dynamos 152, 153

E

earrings 138
Earth 10–11
earthenware 146
Easter **70–71**
Eastman, George/Kodak Co
  45, 157, **247**, 249
eating out **62–63**
eau de cologne 141
Ebers papyrus 284, 286
Edison, Thomas Alva 27, 153,
  223, 235, **249**, **250**
Edmondson, Thomas 177
education **204–5**
eggplants 93
eggs **97**
  Easter 70, 71
  whisks 46, 47
Einthoven, Willem 289
elections **190**, 191
electricity **143**, **152–3**
  cooking 31
  gadgets 47
  lighting 26–27
  trains 176, 177
electrocardiograph (ECG) **289**
electroencephelograph (EEG)
  289
electroplating 149
Elsener, Karl 47
emblems **216**
embroidery 125
emergency services **200–1**
Emery, B. 256
employment 192–5
Encyclopaedia Britannica 227
encyclopedias **226–7**
endoscopy **289**
engagement **64–65**

engines
  diesel 176, 178
  electric 176, 177
  internal-combustion 144,
    150, 167, 172, 180, 181
  jet 181
  steam 144, 153, 167, 176,
    177, 178, 179
English 212, **213**
entertainment **233–55**
entrées 63
envelopes 230–1
ephedrine 294
epidemics **282–3**
epilepsy 285
Erasmus, Desiderius 58–59
escalators 177
Escoffier, Georges-Auguste
  62–63
etiquette 57, **58–59**
euchre 274
Euclid 221
Evans, Oliver 192
Evans, Thomas W. 302
evening dress 129, **132–3**
Everitt, Percival 195
exhibitions, industrial 260
eye surgery/tests **300**, 301

F

Faber, Herbert 156
fabrics **120–3**
Factor, Max 140
factories 13, 187, **192**
Fahrenheit, Gabriel 159
fairs **254**
family planning **298**
fans 138
Faraday, Michael 143, 153
farming 13, 56, 82–83,
  84–85
fashion **118–37**
fat substitutes **106**
Fauchard, Pierre 302
fax 233
felt **120**
fences 17
Ferris wheels 254
fertilisers **155**
festivals 56–57, **70–75**
fibre optics 157
fiction 226, **227**, 229
Fielding, Henry and John 201
fighter aircraft 181
figure skating 271
fillings, dental **302**
film **248–9**, **252–3**
  adhesive 45
Financial Times 229
finger-spelling 219
fireplaces, fires **30**
fire services **200–1**
fireworks 73
first aid 289
fish **94–95**
  aquarium **261**
  fried, chips and 95
  smoked **102**
Fisher, Alva J. 37

fishing tackle 13, 94–95, 142
Fitzgerald, William H. 297
Flagg, Josiah 302
flags **218–19**
flamenco **240**
Flanagan, Betsy 117
flats, blocks of 189
Fleming, Alexander **283**
Fliedner, Theodor 200
floor coverings **21**, **24–25**
flour **85**
flowers 48, **52–53**
  valentines 64
  wedding 67
Floyer, John 288
flutes **236–7**, 239
flying **180–3**
folk dance/music **236**, **240**
food **82–107**
  additives **107**
  fast 63
  freeze-dried **103**
  frozen **103**
  genetic engineering **107**
  intensive production **107**
  mixers 47
  preservation 83, **102–3**
  takeaway 63
football 235, **264**
  pools 259
footwear **137**
forceps 292, 299, 302
Ford, Henry 149, 173, 192
foreign travel **256–7**
forks 61
  garden 54–55
Formica 29, 156
fortunetelling **78–79**, 214
fossils 12–13
foxgloves [digitalin] **294–5**
Fox Talbot, William Henry **247**
foxtrot 241
fractions **220–1**
frankfurters 102
Franklin, Benjamin 41, 153,
  300
Fraze, Ermal Cleon 113
Freud, Sigmund **285**
fridges **103**
Frisbees **279**
Froehlich, John 84
fruit **92–93**
  drinks **110–11**
  machines 258
Fry, Elizabeth 200
frying pans 28
Fry's 99
fuel **150**
funerals **80–81**
fungi 82, 91, 103
Funk, Casimir **284**
fur **120**
furniture **22–23**

G

gadgets **46–47**
Gage, William 92
Galen 281, **287**, 292
Galileo 158, 159, 161

galleries, art 235, **260**
galley proofs 225
Galvani, Luigi 289
gambling **258–9**
  sweepstakes 269
games **234–5**
  board **272–3**
  card **274**
  of chance **258–9**
  children's **278–9**
  Olympic **262–3**
  playground **278–9**
  singing **278–9**
  see also sports ; toys
game shows 253
garden cities/suburbs 189
gardens 17, **50–53**
  botanical/zoological **260–1**
garden tools **54–55**
garlic **90**, 294
Garnerin, André Jacques 181
Garrett Anderson, Elizabeth
  287
gas 26–27, 31, **150**
Gattefosse, René 297
gears 144, 145, 169
GEC 252
gems **138**
genetic engineering **107**
geography **184–5**
geometry **221**
Gerard, John 91
germs **282–3**
  control **293**
Gershwin, George and Ira 251
geysers 35
Gibson, Reginald Oswald 157
Giffard, Henri 181
Gilbert, John 178
Gilbert, William 244
Gillette, King Camp 141
gin 117
ginger 100
  ale/beer 111
gin rummy 274
glass **147**
  windows **20**
glasses [eye] 158, **300**, 301
gliders 180, 181
gloves **131**
glue 45
gnomes, garden 51
Godefroy, Alexandre 47
godparents 68
gold **151**
goldfish bowls 26
golf 235, 264, **265**
Good Housekeeping 229
Goodyear, Charles 131, 156
Gordon, John 78
Gorlitz, Dr **301**
grafts (surgical) **291**
Graham, W.G. 169
gramophones **250**
Grand National 269
Grateau, Marcel 141
graves **80–81**
greasepaint 155
greengages 92
greenhouses **55**

Greenwich Meridian 185, 207
greetings 58, **59**
Gregg, John 219
Grégoire, Marc 28
Gregorian chant 236
Greiner, Friedrich 171
Grijns, Gerrit 284
grinders, coffee/spice 46, 47
'grog' 117
grottoes 51
groundnuts 104–5
guidebooks **257**
guide-dogs **301**
guinea fowl 88
Guinness, Arthur 112
guitars 237
guns 271
Gutenberg, Johann 211, 224
Guy Fawkes Day 72–73

H

Haber, Fritz 155
Hadley, John 185
Hahnemann, Samuel Christian
  Frederick **296**
hair 141
  dryers 47
Hall, J. Sparkes 137
Halloween 57, **72**
halls 17, 18, 19
ham **102**
hamburgers 88
hammers 44, 146
hammocks 33
Hammurabi, Code of 280, 286
Hamwi, Ernest A. 97
Hancock, Thomas 156
handbags **139**
handkerchiefs 131
handshaking **59**
handwriting **215**
hang-gliders 180, 181
Hansom, Joseph 171
Harbutt, William 276
Hargreaves, James 121
haricot beans 104
Harington, John 35
Harmsworth, Alfred 229
harps **237**
Harris, Richard 92
Harrison, John 185
Harvest Festival **72**
Harvey, William 281
Hascall, J. 85
hats **136**
  raising 58
hat trick 136
Hauser, Gayelord 97
Hawkins, John 295
he [game] **278**
headscarves 131
health
  and safety laws 193
  care 200, **280–303**
  food and **96–97**, **106–7**
  mental **285**
hearing aids **301**
hearses, motorised 171
heart transplants **291**

Heathrow Airport 183
heating **30–31**
hedges 51
hedge trimmers 54
Hedley, William 176
heels, shoe 137
Heinkel, Ernst 181
Heinz, H.J. 102, 107
helicopters 180, 181
helmets 136
Helmholtz, Hermann von 300
Hennessy, Richard 116
heraldry **218**
herbs **100**, **294–5**
Herodotus 257, 286
herrings, red 102
Hertz, Heinrich 233
Herschel, John 300
Hetherington, John 136
Hewetson, Henry 173
hide-and-seek 278
Hill, Rowland **230**
Hippocrates 280, 285, 286,
  287, 292, 294, 299
hire-car services 171
hire-purchase 195
Hirschowitz, Basil 157
hit parade 251
HMV 250, 251
Hoare, Lawrence 197
hockey 264, **265**
Hockham, George 157
hoes 54, 55
Hoffman, Felix 295
Hogmanay 73
holiday camps 255
holidays **254–7**
  foreign **256–7**
  package **256**, 257
Holland, Henry [architect]19
Holland, Henry [manufacturer]
  139
homburgs 136
homeopathy **296**
Homo sapiens 12–13
honey 82, **98**
honeymoon 67
hoops 279
Hoover, William Henry 38
hopscotch **278**
hormone treatments **284**
Hornby, Frank 276
horns [music] 237, 239
horoscopes **78**
hors-d'oeuvres 63
horse collars 167, 268
horse-racing, riding **268–9**
hoses, garden 55
hospitals **200**, 287
  mental 285
hot dogs 63
hotels 62, **255**
hot-water bottles 33
house numbers 189
house plants **48–49**
houses **16–21**
  doll's **276–7**
housework 17, **38–39**
housing, public 189
hovercraft 179

Howard, Ebenezer 189
Howard, John 199
Hula-Hoops 279
humans **12–13**, 212
Hume, James 38
Hunt, Walter 127
Hutchinson, Miller Reese **301**
Hyatt, John *and* Isaiah 156
hydrofoils 179
hygiene 281, **283**, **293**, 299
  dental 302, **303**
Hyman, A.S. 291
hymns 236
hypnosis **285**
hypodermic syringes 295

I

IBM 163, 211
ice
  cream **97**
  rinks 271
illness **280–7**
illusionists **245**
Imhotep 286
immersion heaters 35
implants **291**
incubators 299
infections **282–3**
  control of **283**, **293**
in-flight services **182–3**
Ingham, Eunice D. 297
ink **222–3**, 224
inns **62**, **255**
inoculation 281, 282, **283**
insecticides 45, **155**
insects 11, 261
instalment system 195
instant cocoa/coffee 109
instruments
  dental **302**, 303
  musical **236–9**
  sterilising 293
  surgical **292–3**
insulin **284**
interest 197
interior decoration **24–25**
interior springing 22, **32–33**
internal-combustion engine
  150, 172, 181
Internet 211
iron 14, 143, **148–9**
ironing boards, irons 29, **37**
irrigation 14, 142, 209
Islam 14, **203**, 215
  crescent [symbol] 218, 219
Issigonis, Alec 173
it [game] **278**
italics 215

J

jackets 126, 128, 129
jacks [game] 278
Jacuzzis 35
Jaeger, Gustav 135
jam **99**
Jarvik, Robert 291
jazz 241
jean(s) 123, 133

Jeffries, John 181
Jenner, Edward 281, **283**
jerseys 133
jets 181
jewellery 14, 118, **138**, 148
Jiffy bags 231
jigsaw puzzles **275**
Johnson, Dennis 168
Johnson, Samuel 227
Johnston, John Lawson 109
jokes 234
Jolly, Jean Baptiste 37
Jolson, Al 249
Jones, Inigo 19
journalists **228**
Judaism **202**
judges 199
judo 262
Judson, Whitcomb L. 127
jugglers 261
jukeboxes 251
Junigl, Georg 22
juries 199

K

Kao, Charles 157
Kapany, Narinder S. 157, 289
karaoke 238
Kato, Satori 109
Kearley, Daphne 183
kebabs 89
Keiller, Janet and John 99
Kellogg, J.H. 60, 105
Kelly, Gene 241
Kent, William 171
Kenwood Chef 47
kettles 28
keys **40**
kidney beans 104
king of the castle 278
kippers 102
kissing **59**
kitchens 18, **28–29**
kites 180, **279**
kiwi fruit 92
knickers 134, 135
knife cleaner 46
knives 61, 82, 142
knitting, knitwear 132, 133
Kodak Co 45, **247**, 249
Koran 203, 215
Korotkoff, Nikolai 288

L

Labour Party 191
lacemaking 125
laces, shoe 137
Ladbrokes 259
Laënnec, René Théophile
  Hyacinthe 288
lager 112
lamb **89**
lamps **26–27**
landscaping 51
Landsteiner, Karl 293
Lane, Allen 227
Langerhans, Paul 284
language **210**, **212–13**

lasers 159
lathes 146
latitudes 184, 185
launderettes, laundries **36–37**
laurels, to rest on one's 101
lavatories 19, **35**, **69**, 209
lavender water 141
Lawler, Richard H. 291
lawn mowers, 54-55
lawns 51
laws 14, 187, **198–9**
lawyers 199
Lea, William 173
lead pencils 222, 223
leap years 65, 206–7
leather **120**
LeBlanc, Nicolas 36
le Brez, Sieur 26
Lee, William 132
leeks **90**
Leeuwenhoek, Anton van 283
Lego 276
Leibniz, Gottfried von 162,
  221
leisure activities **234–79**
Lenoir, Jean Joseph Etienne
  172
lenses 158, **300**
  contact 300
Lent **73**
lentils 104
Leonardo da Vinci 180, 246,
  298–9
Léotard, Jules 261
Lessler, J. 55
lettuce 91
Levasseur, Emile 172–3
levers **144**
Levi's 133
Liberals 191
libraries 227
Liebig, Justus von 155
lifeboats, life jackets **179**
lifts 165
lighthouses **179**
lighting **26–27**, 150, 152,
  153
lightning conductors 41
Lilienthal, Otto 180, 181
Lind, James 284
linen **121**
linen chests 22
Linotype **225**
Lion, Alexandre 299
liqueurs 116
liquorice 294
  All-Sorts 99
Lister, Joseph 281, **293**, 299
lithography **224–5**
Littlewoods **259**
loans **197**
locks **40**
  canal 165
logarithms 162
logos 227
longitudes 184, 185
looms 120–1
Lord, Thomas 266
lotteries **259**
LPs **250–1**

luck, good/bad (signs of)
  76–77
Lucozade 111
ludo 272–3
lullabies **236**
Lumière, Auguste *and* Louis
  246, 248, **249**
lunch(eon) 60
lutes 237, 238
Lycra 123

M

McAdam, John 174
McCormick, Cyrus 84
McDonald, Maurice *and*
  Richard 63
mace 100
machinery 13
McIlhenny, Edmund 101
Macintosh, Charles 131, 156
Macmillan, Kirkpatrick 168
magazines **229**
magicians **245**
magistrates 199
magnets 152–3
make-up 140
mail 211, **230–1**
  order 195
maître d'hôtel 63
maize 83, **87**
mammals 11
mangles 37
manners 57, **58–59**, 61
Manutius, Aldus 227
maps **184–5**
Marconi, Guglielmo 211, **233**
margarine **106**
markets 187, 192, **194**
Markiewicz, Constance 190
Marks and Spencer 194
marmalade **99**
marriage 64–65, **66–67**
  bureaus **65**
Martell, Jean 116
martial arts 262, **263**
Martin, Rémy 116
marzipan 99
mass production 13, 192
matches **27**
mathematics 14, **220–1**
mattresses 32–33
Maundy Thursday 67–68
Maury, Marguerite 297
mausoleums **81**
Maxwell, James Clerk 233
Maxwell, Lily 190
May Day, Maypoles **71**
MCC 266
mealtimes **60**
measures, weights and **206**
meat 82, 83, **88–89**
  curing/smoking **102**
Meccano 276
medicine 14, **280–93**
  alternative/natural **294–7**
  drugs **283**, 293, **294–5**
Meikle, Andrew 84
menageries **260–1**
mental illness **285**

menus 62, 63
Mercator, Gerardus 185
Mercer, John 124
Mergenthaler, Ottmar 225
merry-go-rounds 254
Mesmer, Franz Anton 285
metalworking 13, 14, 142, 143, **148–9**
meteorology **207**
metric system **206**
metronomes 238
Michaux, Ernest *and* Pierre 168, 169
Michelin, Edouard 219
microprocessors 163
microscopes **158**, 282–3
microwave ovens 31
midsummer **71**
midwives **299**
mile 206
milk **96**
  baby **68**
  condensed 96
  pasteurised 96
Miller, Glenn 251
mills
  coffee 46
  paper 222
  water 85, 143, 192
  wind 14, 143
mime 242
mincers 46, 47
mines **150**, 151
mint **101**, 294
mirrors 32, **33**
Mitford, Nancy 59
moccasins 137
models, fashion 133
monarchy 187
money 148, 187, **196–7**
  boxes **41**
Monopoly 273
Montgolfier, Etienne *and* Joseph 180
monuments **81**
Moore, Hiram 85
mopeds 169
morning dress 129
Morris Co. 173
Morris dancing 240
mortar **20**
Morton, William Thomas 293, 302
mosaics 21
mosques 202
Moss Bros 132
motor cars **172–3**
motorcycles 169
motorways 175
mourning **81**
mousetraps 39
Moy, Thomas 179
Muhammad ibn Abdullah 203
Murphy, Gerald *and* Sara 257
Murphy, J.B. 290
museums 235, **260**
mushrooms 91, 103
music 235
  boxes **251**
  halls **244**

instruments **236–9**
  singing 234, **236**
musicals **244**
muslin 123
mussels 95
mustard 294
mutton **89**
Muybridge, Eadweard **248–9**

N

nails **44**
Napier, John 162, 220
National Health Service 200
nativity plays 74
natural remedies **294–7**
navigation **183**, **184–5**
necklaces 138
needles **124**
neoprene 156
Nessler, Karl L. 141
Nestlé 99
Newbery, John **279**
Newcomen, Thomas 176
newspapers 211, 225, **228–9**
Newton, Isaac 43, 159
New Year's Day 73
nickel **149**
Niépce, Joseph Nicéphore **246–7**
Nightingale, Florence 200
999 service 200
noodles 86
notes, musical **239**
noughts and crosses 279
novels 226, **227**, 229
numbers 14, 210, **220–1**
nursery rhymes **236**
nurses **200**
nutmeg 100
nuts **104–5**
nuts, bolts and 44
nylon(s) 123, 157

O

oats 60, **87**
oboes **236–7**
observatories 185
O'Conor, Daniel 156
oculists **300**
offal 88
offices 187, **193**
Ohain, Hans von 181
oil **150**
oils **105**
  essential 294, **297**
olives 101, 105
Olympic Games 234–5, **262–3**
omens **76–77**
omnibuses **170**
one-armed bandits 258
one-way systems 175
onions **90**
opera **244**
ophthalmology **300**, 301
opium 293, **295**
opticians **300**
'Oranges and lemons' 279

orchestras **239**
Ordnance Survey 185
organs (music) **238**
organ transplants **291**
Orlon 123
ornaments 25
  garden 51
'Oscars' **249**
osteopathy **297**
Otis, Elisha 165
Otto, Nikolaus August 172
ovens **30–31**
Owen, Robert 193
Oxford English Dictionary 227
oxygen 11
oysters 95

P Q

pacemakers **291**
pachisi 273
paddle steamers 179
padlocks 40
pain control **293**
paint 12–13, **154–5**
paisley shawls 121
Palladio, Andrea 164
Palmer, Daniel David **297**
palmistry 78, 79
Pan Am 183
Panamas 136
Pancake Day **73**
panelling, wood 24
Panhard, René 172–3
panpipes **237**
pantomime 74, 242, **245**
Papanicolaou, George Nicholas **288**
paper 13, 14, 123, **222**
  clips 45
  mills 222
  money 196, 197
paperbacks 226, **227**
parachutes 181
parasites 282
parasols 138, 139
Parcheesi 273
Paré, Ambroise 281, 290, **292**
parkas 131
Parker, John Joseph 223
Parkes, Alexander 33, 156
parking meters 175
parks 189, **260–1**
parliament **191**, 198
parlours 18, 19
parsley 95, 101
Pascal, Blaise 162, 170, 258, 295
passports 257
pasta **86–87**
Pasteur, Louis 96, 282, 283, 293
pastilles 99
pastry-making 29
patchwork 125
patience [game] 275
patterns, dressmaking 125
paving stones 174
pawnbroking 197, 217

peace cross (CND) 219
peaches 92
  pêche Melba 63
peanut butter 105
peanuts 104–5
pears **92**
peas 104
Peel, Robert 201
pencils 222, 223
pendulums 160, 161
Penguin Books 226, 227
penicillin **283**
penknives 47
penny whistles 239
pens **222–3**
pentathlon 263
pepper **100–1**
peppers 83
Pepsi-Cola 111
percussion 238
perfume **140–1**
periodicals **229**
Pérignon, Dom Pierre 115
Perkins, Jacob 103
permanent waves 141
Persil 36
Perspex 157
pesticides **155**
petrol 150
pets **42–43**, 261
petticoats 119, 134, 135
Peychaud, Antoine-Amadé 117
Pfleumer, Fritz 251
philately **230**
Philips 251
philosophy 14
photocopiers **225**
photography 235, **246–9**
Piaggio Co. 169
pianos **238**
pickled food 102
picnics 63
piers **255**
piggy banks 41
pig in the middle 278
Pill, the **298**
pillar boxes 230, 231
pillows 33
pimiento 101
pincers 146
Pincus, Gregory 298
pineapples **93**
Pinel, Philippe 285
pins **124**
Pitman, Isaac 219
Pitt, William, the Younger 191
pizza 86
placards, newspaper 229
plainsong **236**
planets 10
plants
  garden **52**
  house/pot **48–49**
plaques, commemorative 80
Plasticine 276, 277
plastics 143, **156–7**
plastic surgery 290, **291**
plates **61**
Plato 226

playpens **69**
plays 234, 235, **242–3**
  Nativity 74
pleats 121
Plimsoll, Samuel 136, 179
plimsolls 137
ploughs 84–85
plumbing **208–9**
plums **92**
pockets 139
poker (game) 274
pokers 30
police **201**
  cars 201
  women 200
polish, furniture 39
politeness **58**
political parties **191**
politics 186–7
polo 269
polyester 123
polystyrene 157
polythene 157
pools, football **259**
popcorn 87
porcelain **147**
pork **89**
porridge 60, **87**
port 115
porter 112
'posh' 256
Post, Emily 59
postal services 211, **230–1**
postcards 231
postcodes 231
potatoes 83, 90–91
  crisps 63
pot plants **48–49**
potted fish/meat 102
pottery 14, 17, 142, **146–7**
  wheel 142, 144, 146–7
potties **69**
Poulsen, Valdemar 251
poultry **88**
power boats 178, **179**
power stations 153
prams 171
Pratt, Elijah 68
Pratt, Roger 19
Premium Bonds 258
presents 74
preserves **99**
preserving food **102–3**
Priestley, Joseph 110
print(ed cotton) 123
printing 13, **211**, **224–5**
prisons 199
'problem pages' 229
proofs 225
propellers 179, 181
proposing 65
psychoanalysis **285**
Ptolemy 78, 79, 184
public
  holidays 254
  houses **113**
  transport 170, **176–7**
Pulitzer, Joseph **229**
pulleys 144, **145**
Pullman, George 177

pulse, taking the **288**
pulses 82, **104**
pumps 14
Punch 229
Punch and Judy **244–5**
punched cards 162
punishment, crime and **198–9**
puppets **245**
purses **139**
puzzles **275**
pyjamas, beach 129
Pyrex 28
Pythagoras 221, 239

quadrants, reflecting 185
Quaker Oats 60
quarantine 282
quartz watches 161
quilting, quilts 33, 125
Quin, Frederick Foster Harvey **296**
quinine **295**
Quorn 106

R

rabbit 88
racing **268–9**
radio 211, **233**
  air guidance 183
  broadcasting 233, 235
  transistors 233
radishes 90
rafts 166
railways **176–7**
  underground **177**, 185
raincoats 131
rakes (garden) 54
Ramsay MacDonald, James 191
Ransome, Robert 84
Ransome Co. 54–55
rapeseed oil 105
raspberries **93**
rattles 69
Rawlplugs 44
rayon 123
razors **141**
RCA-Victor 251
real tennis 267
reapers, mechanical 84
recipes 29, 95, 117, 226
recorded sound 235, **249–53**
  digital **251**
record-keeping 14
records, gramophone **250–1**
Red Cross **219**
red crescent **219**
reflexology 297
refrigerators **103**
reins, horses' 269
religion 14, **202–3**
  dance/drama/music in 235, **236**, **240**, 242–3
  festivals **56–57**, **70–75**
  marriage **66–67**
  rulers and **186–7**
Remington, E., and Sons 223
replacement surgery **290–1**
reporters **228**

reptiles 11, 261
restaurants **62–63**
revues **244**
rhymes, children's **278–9**
rice **87**
  weddings, at 66
Richmond, Duke of 185
riding **268–9**
Rimmel, Eugène 140
'ring o'roses' **278–9**
rings 138, 151
  engagement 65
  wedding 67
Ritz, César 62
Riva-Rocci, Scipione **288**
roads 166–7, **174–5**
  signs 175
Rock, John 298
Roentgen, Wilhelm **289**
Roget, Peter Mark 248
Rolex 161
Rollerblades, roller skates **279**
roofs **20–21**
rope 13, **41**
rosaries 202
Roselius, Ludwig 109
rosemary 101
roses **53**
roulette 258
roundabouts 254
rubber **156**
  bands 45
  erasers 222
  gloves 39
Rubik, Erno 275
rugby **265**
rugs **24–25**
rum 117
Rumford, Count (Benjamin Thompson) 30, 109
rummy 274
runner beans 104
Russell, William Howard 228

S

saccharine 106
saddles 268
safes **41**
safety pins **127**
saffron 100
sage 101
sailing ships **178**
St Valentine's Day 57, **64**
salads **91**
salami 102
salaries 187, 192
salmon 95
  smoked 102
Salomons, David 27
salt **100**, **102**
  desalination 209
sandals 136, 137
sandwiches 86
Sanger, Margaret 298
Santa Claus 75
saucepans **28**
Sauerbronn, Karl Drais von 168

sauerkraut 102
Saunders, Clarence 195
sausages **102**
Savery, Thomas 176
saws 146
saxophones 237, 238
scales 207
  musical **239**
scarves **131**
scene, scenery (theatre) 242, 244
scenery, appreciation of 255
scent **140–1**
Schick, Jacob 141
schools **204–5**
Schott, Otto 28
Schueller, Eugene 141
Schweppe, Jacob 110
science 14
scissors **44**
scooters, motor 169
Scotch tape 45
scourers 39
Scrabble **273**
screws **44**, **145**
scripts **214–15**
sea creatures 11
seafood 82, **94–95**
seaplanes 183
seaside holidays **255**
secateurs 54–55
secret ballots 190, 191
securities 197
security systems **40–41**
seed drills 84
Seeley, Henry 37
Selfridge, Harry Gordon 194–5
self-service
  restaurants 63
  shopping **195**
Sellotape 45
semaphore **231**
Semmelweiss, Ignaz Philipp **299**
Senefelder, Aloys 224
sentencing 198, 199
settees, settles 22
sewage systems 208, 209
sewing 120, **124**
  machines **124–5**
sextants 185
Shaftesbury, Lord 193
shampoo 141
shares **197**
shears **44**, 54
sheaths (contraceptive) 298
sheets 33
Shillibeer, George 170
ships **178–9**
shirts **127**, 132
shoe cleaners 46–47
Shoemaker, Robert 289
shoes 119, 137
  ballet 241
  horses' 269
shooting 271
shops **194–5**
  signs **217**
shorthand **219**
shoulder bags 139

shovels 30, 54
showers 35
showjumping 269
Shrove Tuesday 73
shutters 20, 21, **25**
sideboards 23
Siemens, Werner von 176
sieves 28
sightseeing **256–7**
signals **231**
sign language **219**, 301
signs **216–17**
  advertising **217**
  road 175
  shop **217**
  zodiacal **78**, 216, **217**
Sikorsky, Igor 181
silk **122**
  artificial 123
silver **151**
Simms, Frederick 173
Simpson, James 293
Singer, Isaac 124–5, 195
singing 234, **236**
  games **278–9**
sinks 29
skateboards 279
skating **270–1**
  roller skating **279**
skiing **270–1**
skillets 28
skin grafts **291**
skipping 279
skirts **126–7**
skittles **271**
skyscrapers **165**
slalom (skiing) 270
slings, baby 69
Sloane, Hans 260
slot machines 258
smear tests **288**
smelting 14, 143, 148
Smirnoff, House of 117
Smith, Francis Pettit 179
Smith, Hamilton 37
smoked food **102**
smoking **295**
snakes and ladders 272, **273**
Snell, James 302
snooker **271**
soap **34**, **36**
  operas (TV) **253**
Socialists 191
social services 200
soccer 235, **264**
socks 135
sofas 22
soft drinks **110–11**
soldiers, model/toy 276, 277
solicitors 199
solitaire (game) **275**
Sony **25**, 253
Sophocles 242
soup, canned 102, 103
soya beans 104
spades 54
Spangler, James Murray 38
spanners 44
spas 110, **255**
spears 13, 146

special licences 67
spectacles 158, **300**, 301
speech 210, **212–13**
speed limits 175
sphygmomanometers **288**
spices 83, **100–1**
spinning 14, **120–1**, 192
spirits **116–17**
spokes 144
sponges 11
spoons 61
sports 235, **262–71**
  competitive **262–7**
  field and track **262–3**
  holidays 271
  Olympic **262–3**
  wear 135, 137, 169
  winter 257, **270–1**
  see also games
spring festivals **70–71**
springs 22, 32–33
  clockwork 161
  hair 161
sprinklers 54
square roots 220
squash 267
Stair, John 92
stairs 18, 19, **21**
stamps, postage 230
staplers 45
Starley, James 168
Starley, John Kemp 169
Star of David 216
stars **10–11**
stately homes, visiting **260**
stations 177
Staudinger, Hermann 157
steak tartare 88
steam power 153, 167, 170, 172, 176, 179
steel 143, **148–9**
  stainless 149
steeplechases 269
Steiff, Margarete 277
Stephenson, George *and* Robert 176
stethoscopes **288**
Stevene, A. Edwin 301
steward(esses), air 183
sticking plaster 289
sticky tape **45**
stiletto heels 137
Still, Andrew Taylor **297**
stills 116
stirrups 268–9
stitches
  sewing **124–5**
  surgical **292–3**
stockings 134
  Christmas 75
stock markets **197**
stoneware 147
stools 22
Stopes, Marie 298
stores **194–5**
stout 112
stoves 29, **30–31**
Stradivari, Antonio 237
Straub, Ambrose 105
Strauss, Levi 133

strawberries **93**
streets **174–5**
strikes 193
Strite, Charles 47
submarines 178
suburbs 189
sugar 83, **98–99**
  substitutes **106–7**
sugared almonds 99
suites, three-piece 22
suits 119, **128–9**, 139
Sullivan, Arthur 244
sulphonamides 283
summer solstice **71**
Sun 10
sunbathing 257
Sunday Schools 205
Sundback, Gideon 127
sundials 160
sunglasses 300
suntan 257
superglue 45
supermarkets **195**
superstitions 56, **76–77**
surgery **280–1**, **292–3**
Susruta 282, **291**
Swan, Joseph 27, 123
swastika 216
sweaters 133
sweepstakes 269
sweetcorn **87**
sweeteners **106–7**
sweetmeats **99**
swimsuits 135
Swiss Army knives 47
Sylvius, Franciscus 117
symbols **216–17**, **219**
synthetics **123**, **156–7**
syringes 295

tabasco 101
tablecloths 25
table d'hôte 63
table manners 61
tables **23**
tabloids **229**
tag [game] 278
Tagliocozzi, Gaspare **291**
tango **241**
tankards 112, 114
tap dancing 241
tape recorders 250, **251**
tarmac 174–5
tarot cards 78, 79
tartan 121
tattoos 141
taverns **62**
taxes **191**
taxis 171
tea 83, **108**
  afternoon/high 60
teaching **204–5**
teats, rubber 68
technology 14, **142–3**
teddy bears 277
teeth, care of **302–3**
teething rings 69
Teflon 28

telephones 211, **232**
  call boxes 233
  mobile 233
telescopes **158–9**, 185
television 235, **252–3**
  licences 253
Telford, Thomas 174
Tellier, Charles 103
temperatures, measuring 158, **159**
tem Rhijne, Willem 296
tennis 235, **267**
terracotta 146
Terylene 123
Test matches 266
'test-tube' babies 299
textiles 118, 119, **121–3**
Thanksgiving Day 72
thatching **20–21**
theatre 234, 235, **242–3**
thermometers 158, **159**
Thermos flasks 45
thimbles 124
Thompson, Robert 169
thread 124
threshing machines 84–85
thyme 101
tickets [travel] 170, 177, 182, 183
ties 129
tig (game) 278
tiles **20–21**
time, measuring of **206–7**
timekeeping **160–1**
Times, The **229**
time signals 161
timetables 177
timpani **238**
tin 148
tinned food 102, **103**
tips 63
Tizer 111
toast, toasters 47, 86
toasts 115
tobacco **295**
toilets 19, **35**, **69**, 209
tomatoes 83, **93**
  canned/sun-dried 103
tongs, fire 30
tools **12–13**, **44**, 82, **146**
  dental **302**, 303
  surgical **292–3**
toothbrushes 303
  electric 47
toothpaste 303
top hats 136
Tories 191
tortillas 86
totem poles 216–17
tourism **256–7**
towns 14, **188**
toys **276–7**
  action **279**
  soft **277**
trade 187, **192–5**
  guilds/unions 192, **193**
  marks **219**
Tradescant, John 52, 260
traffic lights **175**
tragedy **242**

trains **176–7**
  model/toy 276, 277
trams 171
transfers 132
transformers 153
transfusions 292, 293
transistors 163, **233**
transplants **291**
transport **166–83**
trapeze, flying 261
travel agencies **256**
trees, Christmas 74, 75
trepanation 292
Trésaguet, Pierre 174
Trevithick, Richard 176
trials **198–9**
triangulation points 185
trilbies 136
Trivial Pursuit **273**
Trollope, Anthony 231
trouser presses 47
trousers 129–30, 133
trousseau 65
trowels 54, 55
truffles 91
trumpets **237**
trunks 22
T-shirts 132, 133
tug of war 278
tulips **53**
Tull, Jethro 84–85
tumble driers 37
tunnels **164**
Tupper, Earl Silas 156
turbines
  gas 181
  steam 153, 179
  water 153
Turing, Alan 162
turkey 88
turmeric 100, 101
turnips 90
tutus 240
tuxedos 132
tweed 121
Twelfth Night 74
Tyler, Wat 191
typefaces **224**
typewriters 211, 223
typography **224–5**
tyres 169

U, non-U 59
ultrasound **289**
umbrellas **139**
underwear **134–5**
Union Jack 218–19
universities 205
upholstery 22, 25

vaccination 281, 282, **283**
vacuum cleaners **38**
vacuum flasks 45
valentines 57, **64**
valves 163
van Houten, Conrad J. 109
vanilla 100, 101
vases 48

vaudeville **244**
veal 89
vegetables **90–91**
Velcro 130
vending machines 195
veneer 23
venison 88
video recorders **253**
villages 14, 188, 189
vinyl 157
violas, violins **237**, 239
viruses 282, 283
vitamins **284**, 285
vodka 117
Volta, Alessandro 153
voting 190, 191
V-sign 59
vulcanisation 131, 156

wages 187, 192
wagons 167
waistcoats 128, 129, 132
waiters, waitresses 63
wakes 80
Walker, John 27
Walker, John[nie] 117
walking sticks **139**
Walkman **251**
wall coverings **24**
walls 17, 20
walnuts 104
waltz **241**
Wang Wei-I 296
war correspondents 228
wardrobes 33
Warren, John C. 293
washing **34–35**
  clothes **36–37**
  dishes **39**
  machines **37**
Washington, George 59
watches **161**
water, mineral/soda/tonic **110**
water clocks 160
watercress 91
water gardens 51
water heaters 35
watering cans 54, 55
Waterman, Lewis E. 223
watermarks 197
watermills 143
water pipes 208–9
waterproofing **130**, **156**
waterwheels 142–3
Watt, James 144, 176
weapons 13, 142, **146**
weather forecasts **207**
weaving 14, 118, **120–1**
weddings 57, **66–67**
wedges 144, **145**
Wedgwood, Josiah 147
weeding 55
weedkillers 155
weights and measures **206**, 207
Wellington, Duke of 137
wells 208
Wells, Alice Stebbins 200

Werner, Eugène Michel 169
wheat 82, 85
wheelbarrows 55
wheels **144**
  Ferris ('big') 254
Whinfield, Rex 123
whisk(e)y **116–17**
whist 274
whistles [music] 239
'white horses' 217
white sticks 300
Whitney, Eli 123
Whitsun 71
Whittle, Frank 181
W.H. Smith & Son 194
wigs 141
Wimbledon Tennis Championships 267
winches 144
windmills 14, 143
windows **20**, 21
wine 83, **114–15**
Wingfield, Walter Clopton 267
winter
  festivals **73–75**
  sports 257, **270–1**
Withering, William **295**
Wollstonecraft, Mary 190
women
  actors 243, 244
  doctors **287**
  education 205
  employment 193, 223
  jockeys 269
  midwives **299**
  police 200
  suffrage 190, 231
Wood, Alexander 295
Wood, Ken 47
Woodger, John 102
wool **120–1**
word processors 211
workers' rights 192, **193**
Worlidge, John 113
Worth, Charles Frederick 133
wrestling **263**
Wright, Orville *and* Wilbur 180, 181
wringers 37
writing 14, 206, **210–11**, **214–15**

Xerox **225**
X-rays 281, **289**

yachts 178
Yale, Linus 40
Y-Fronts 135
yoghurt **96–97**
Yo-Yos 279
yule logs 74

zinc **149**
zips **127**
zodiacal signs **78**, 216, **217**
zoos **260–1**
Zworykin, Vladimir Kosma **252**

ACKNOWLEDGMENTS

The publishers wish to thank the following people who helped in the preparation of this book: John Allen ; Fiona Anderson ; Michael Bailey ; David Barber ; John Barnes ; John Berry ; Maggie Black ; Brian Bowers ; Alison Bravington ; John Burnett ; Elinor Clarke ; David Clements ; Arthur Credland ; Malcom Day ; Mary Devine ; Elizabeth Drake ; Dr Brent Elliott ; Dr Jim Fowler ; Stephen Green ; Dr John Gribbin ; Dr Denis Griffiths ; David Hall ; Colin Harding ; James Harpur ; Dan Hayton ; Sue Hayton ; Clare Hill ; Lisa Hirst ; Ken Howells ; Elizabeth Hussey ; Owen Jackson ; John Keyworth ; Rex King ; Nancy Korman ; Gordon Leith ; Hamish McGillivray ; Bob McWilliam ; Richard Onslow ; Erica Plowman ; Lois Reynolds ; Nigel Roche ; Dave Rooney ; Richard Rowley ; Jennifer Salahub ; Libby Sellers ; P.W.B. Semmens ; Denis Smith ; Robert Stewart ; Reena Suleman ; Judith Swaddling ; Dave Thompson ; Pam Thompson ; Dr Larry Trask ; John Trenouth.

The following people and organisations helped in the production of photographs: Angels & Bermans ; Asprey ; BBC costume store ; Beat About the Bush ; Bill & Ben's Greenhouse Ltd ; A Booth Ltd ; British Gas Musem ; BT Museum ; Nigel Cavanagh ; Ken Chaya ; Maxine Clark ; Equinox at the Astrology Shop ; Falkiner Fine Papers Ltd ; Harrods ; Judy Jones ; Larson & Laurens ; Morgans Vintage Wireless & Electrical Goods ; Museum of London ; Robert Opie ; Penfriend ; Red Deer Farm ; Sue Robson ; St Bride Printing Library ; Jill Steed ; Louis Stanton ; STV ; The Chelsea Gardener ; The Geffrye Museum ; The London Toy and Model Museum ; The Museum of Garden History ; Thomas Cook Travel Archive.

Picture credits: The sources of the illustrations in *The Origins of Everyday Things* are listed below. The publishers have made every effort to trace the copyright owners of the illustrations in this book, but the nature of the material has meant that this has not always been possible. Any person or organisation we have failed to reach, despite our efforts, is invited to contact the Picture Editor at Reader's Digest General Books, 11 Westferry Circus, Canary Wharf, London E14 4HE. Names in *italics* indicate work which is Reader's Digest copyright. Abbreviations : T=top ; TL=top left ; TC=top centre ; TR=top right ; C=centre ; CL=centre left ; CR=centre right ; B=bottom ; BL=bottom left ; BC=bottom centre ; BR=bottom right.

6 TL Maringer and Bandi 'Art in the Ice Age', Basel 1953 BL Robert Opie BC Bruce Coleman Ltd/Kim Taylor **7** TL Trebor Bassett Ltd CL Robert Opie C Levi Strauss CR Permission of the Trustees of the British Museum BL Bridgeman Art Library, London/private collection BC Giraudon/Bibliothèque Nationale, Paris **8** TL The National Motor Museum, Beaulieu CL Foto–Georg Goerlipp/Furstenbergischen Museum, Donaueschingen C The Advertising Archives CR Robert Opie BL London Transport Museum BC Bridgeman Art Library, London/private collection BR Museum of London **9** TL The Kobal Collection TR Robert Opie C Permission of the Board of the British Library, London (Ms. Sloane 1975 f.93) CR Science Photo Library BL Hulton Getty Images BR Michael Holford/British Museum **10–11** Science Photo Library/Space Telescope Science Institute/NASA **12** TR Science Photo Library/John Reader **12–13** T Maringer and Bandi 'Art in the Ice Age', Basel 1953 B Permission of the Trustees of the British Museum **13** Science Photo Library/Sinclair Stammers **14** AKG London/Erich Lessing/Heraklion Museum **14–15** Walter Klein/Goethe-Museum, Dusseldorf **15** *Lorraine Harrison* **16** L Edwin Smith CR Royal Horticultural Society, Lindley Library **16–17** Giraudon **17** BL Robert Opie BC Wurttembergisches Landesmuseum, Stuttgart **18** C *David Noonan* BR Edwin Smith **19** CR Hulton Getty Images BL English Heritage/Acton Archives **20** TL Ashmolean Museum, Oxford, brick workers Giraudon CR Bildarchiv Preussischer Kulturbesitz, Berlin/Gemaldegalerie SMPK, Berlin/Photo Jorg P. Anders **21** TL *David Noonan* BL *Patrick Thurston* BR Scala/Museo Nazionale, Naples **22** Lesley & Roy Adkins **22–23** *Jon Bouchier* **23** Bridgeman Art Library, London/Ecole des Beaux-Arts, Paris/Giraudon **24** TL Musée de Breuil de Saint Germain C Old Sturbridge Village/photo Thomas Neill CR Courtesy of the Trustees of the Victoria and Albert Museum, London **25** T Artothek/Allte Pinakothek B Stapleton Collection/Bridgeman Art Library **26** TL Permission of the Trustees of the British Museum TR Rijksmuseum, Amsterdam **26–27** *Jon Bouchier* **27** TL Christie's Colour Library BC Mary Evans Picture Library BR Robert Opie **28** husking tray Ikoma Aldo Durazzi, clay sieve AKG London/Israel Museum, Jerusalem/Erich Lessing, saucepan AKG London/Antikenmuseum SMPK, Berlin, Chinese bronze Asian Art Museum of San Francisco/The Avery Brundage Collection (B60 B4+) C Robert Opie BR Michael Holford **29** CR Peter Newark's Pictures BL Michael Holford BC Bridgeman Art Library, London/private collection **30** TL Giraudon C Trinity College Library, Cambridge, Munby Collection **30–31** *Jon Bouchier* **31** C Mary Evans Picture Library **32** TC Public Record Office C Giraudon/Louvre, Paris CR Retrograph Archive B The Minneapolis Institute of Arts **33** TL Museum of London CL, BC Permission of the Trustees of the British Museum BR ET Archive, London/Edmund Dulac **34** L Permission of the Board of the British Library, London (N.L. 15d. Fig 2 PL.2), recipe Permission of the Board of the British Library, London (Ms. Sloane 1990 f.127) R Bibliothèque Nationale, Paris (Ms. Fr. 6185 F.284) B Mary Evans Picture Library **35** T, L Robert Opie R Arcaid/Lucinda Lambton **36** TL private collection TR Mirror Syndication International B Robert Opie **37** BL Robert Opie BR *Jon Bouchier* **38** TC Stadt Nurnberg C Robert Opie B *Jon Bouchier* **39** TL The National Magazine Company/Good Housekeeping Jan. 1935 BC Marshall Cavendish Ltd BR Ullstein **40** TL Science & Society Picture Library TC *Graham White*, Roman lock and key Permission of the Trustees of the British Museum, padlock and key and combination lock Science & Society Picture Library R Science & Society Picture Library **41** C Courtesy of the Trustees of the Victoria and Albert Museum, London/Mr D.P.P. Naish CR Peter Newark's Pictures BL Courtesy of the Trustees of the Victoria and Albert Museum, London/Sara Hodges BC Worthing Museum & Art Gallery **42** T Rijksmuseum, Amsterdam B Ashmolean Museum, Oxford **42–43** Hirmer Verlag **43** CL Andreas Heumann BL *Sarah Fox-Davies*, budgerigars Trustees of the British Museum (Natural History) **44** TL Permission of the Trustees of the British Museum TC Stadt Nurnberg (Amb. 317.2,f.19r), nail Science & Society Picture Library BR Robert Opie **45** T The Advertising Archives R Robert Opie B Bruce Coleman Ltd/Kim Taylor **46** BR US Patent Office **46–47** *Jon Bouchier* **47** BR John Corby Ltd **48** TR National Gallery of Scotland, Edinburgh BL Werner Forman Archive **48–49** *Jon Bouchier* **50–51** Scala/Museo di Firenze com'era, Florence **51** T Wurttembergisches Landesmuseum, Stuttgart B Courtesy of the Trustees of the Victoria and Albert Museum, London **52** L Permission of the Board of the British Library, London (449.k.4.tp), John Tradescant Junior National Portrait Gallery, London, *Tradescantia virginiana* Permission of the Board of the British Library, London BC ET Archive, London/Victoria and Albert Museum BR Trustees of the British Museum (Natural History) **53** TL Royal Horticultural Society, Lindley Library C Trustees of the British Museum (Natural History) BR Still Life Studies, Amsterdam **54** TL Stadt Nurnberg, spade Permission of the Trustees of the British Museum **54–55** *Jon Bouchier* **55** Scala/Germansches Nationalmuseum, Nuremberg **56** TL Hulton Getty Images **56–57** Courtesy of the Trustees of the Victoria and Albert Museum, London **57** TL AKG London/Bibliothèque Nationale, Paris **58** Giraudon **59** TC The Associated Press/Amy Sancetta Slug TR Giraudon/Louvre, Paris B Express Newspapers **59–60** Courtesy of the Trustees of the Victoria and Albert Museum, London **60** TL Bridgeman Art Library, London/Art Gallery and Museum, Cheltenham TR Hulton Getty Images/Slim Hewitt BC Robert Opie BR private collection **60–61** *Richard Bonson* **61** BL Courtesy of the Trustees of the Victoria and Albert Museum, London BC National Museum of Wales BR Giraudon/Musée Condé, Chantilly **62** T Archives of The Savoy Hotel plc C Bridgeman Art Library, London/Guildhall Library, London BL ET Archive, London/Fondation Auguste Escoffier **63** L Fondation Auguste Escoffier BR Corbis–Bettmann/Tom Brock Corporation **64** CL ET Archive, London/British Library CR Eric Crichton BC ET Archive, London/private collection BR Christie's Colour Library **65** TR Reproduced by permission of the American Museum in Britain, Bath © Eros Robert Harding Syndication/Rolf Richardson, 'Kiss' The Kobal Collection **66** Bridgeman Art Library, London/Christopher Wood Gallery, London **66–67** confetti *Jon Bouchier* **67** TC (St Brides) Hulton Getty Images, photo in frame Hulton Getty Images, *Jon Bouchier* BL Diana Scarisbrick BR Bridgeman Art Library, London /Christopher Wood Gallery, London **68** T MAS, Barcelona/National Library, Madrid CR *Richard Bonson* BL HarperCollins Publishers Ltd From 'Little Grey Rabbit's Birthday' by Alison Uttley, illustration by Margaret Tempest **69** CR Sotheby's, London BL The Image Bank/Joseph van Os **70** T Bridgeman Art Library, London/Cathedral of St Bravo, Ghent/Giraudon CR private collection BC Robert Opie **71** TR Mary Evans Picture Library/Steve Rumney Collection BL, BC Bridgeman Art Library, London/Christie's, London **72** TC (left) Sonia Halliday/Bodrum Museum, Turkey TC (right) Michael Holford CR AKG London/Bibliothèque Nationale, Paris **73** TR Corbis–Bettmann BL Angelo Hornak BR Michael Holford B The Mansell Collection/Time Inc/Katz **74** Bridgeman Art Library, London/Uffizzi, Florence **75** TC Culver Pictures, New York CL Fine Art Photographs CR Bridgeman Art Library, London/Gavin Graham Gallery R *Jon Bouchier*, card Courtesy of the Trustees of the Victoria and Albert Museum, London **76** TC *Jon Bouchier* BL ET Archive, London **77** TR The Mansell Collection/Time Inc/Katz CL, BL *Peter Barrett* BC Images Colour Library **78** T Courtesy of the Trustees of the Victoria and Albert Museum, London CR Mary Evans Picture Library BL ET Archive, London BR ET Archive, London/Civic Museum, Vicenza **79** T *Jon Bouchier* B Bridgeman Art Library, London/Bibliothèque Nationale, Paris **80** CL Arcaid/Martin Jones CR Angelo Hornak **80–81** Hulton Getty Images **81** L *Jon Bouchier* R Corbis–Bettmann **82** TL Royal Horticultural Society, Lindley Library/William Hooker TR Mary Evans Picture Library BR Trebor Bassett Ltd **82–83** Michael Holford **83** TR Giraudon © ADAGP, Paris, and DACS, London, 1998 BL Coca-Cola is a registered trademark **84** BL Sonia Halliday BC Ann Ronan at Image Select **84–85** Michael Holford **85** CL Ann Ronan at Image Select BR Bridgeman Art Library, London/British Library **86** L Michael Holford R Robert Opie **86–87** private collection **87** T Giraudon/Free Library, Philadelphia BC Jean-Loup Charmet/Bibliothèque des Arts Decoratifs, Paris **88** CL ET Archive, London/British Library **88–89** Bridgeman Art Library, London/Guildhall Art Gallery, Corporation of London **89** CL NHPA/Patrick Fagot CR Giraudon/Musée Condé, Chantilly shearer Scala/Biblioteca Marciana, Venice BC ET Archive, London/Museo Civico Sulmona at l'Aquila **90** TL Dave Lewis Nostalgia Collection C Bridgeman Art Library, London/Guildhall Library, Corporation of London **90–91** Jean-Loup Charmet **91** TC Trustees of the British Museum (Natural History) TR The Advertising Archives **92** TR Bridgeman Art Library, London/British Library, London C Royal Horticultural Society, Lindley Library/William Hooker BL Permission of the Board of the British Library, London/Oriental and India Office Collections (Or. 59 a 10. pge IIIa 10) **93** T Robert Opie R Royal Horticultural Society, Lindley Library/Mattiholi Commentaries BL Bridgeman Art Library, London /British Library, London **94** TL Giraudon **94–95** *Jon Bouchier* **95** R Bridgeman Art Library, London/Musée Condé, Chantilly/Lauros-Giraudon **96** TL The National Trust/Derrick Witty CL Permission of the Board of the British Library, London/Oriental and India Office Collections (Add Or 3843) CR Bridgeman Art Library, London/Bibliothèque Nationale, Paris **97** TR Bridgeman Art Library, London/British Library B The Mansell Collection/Time Inc/Katz **98** TR ET Archive, London/Biblioteca Estense, Modena BL Maringer & Bandi 'Art in the Ice Age', Basel, 1953 **99** TC Bridgeman Art Library, London/Bonhams, London CL ET Archive, London/Bibliothèque des Arts Decoratifs, Paris B Trebor Bassett Ltd **100** T, CL *Jon Bouchier* B Bridgeman Art Library, London/Johny van Haeften Gallery, London **101** T *Jon Bouchier* BL Jean-Loup Charmet/Bibliothèque Nationale, Paris **102–3** *Jon Bouchier* **103** L The Advertising Archives R Corbis–Bettmann/George Woodruff **104** TR Corbis–Bettmann/Jonathan Smith CL Trustees of the British Museum (Natural History) C Mary Evans Picture Library **105** CL Robert Opie B Bridgeman Art Library, London/National Gallery of Art, Washington **106** TL Mary Evans Picture Library CR (both) The Advertising Archives **107** TR Science Photo Library/Philippe Plailly/Eurelios BL Ardea, London/Stefan Meyers BR Bridgeman Art Library, London/private collection **108** TL Permission of the Trustees of the British Museum C *Vernon Morgan* CR private collection BL private collection BR private collection **109** CL Museum of London CR Hulton Getty Images BC Permission of the Board of the British Library, London (236 k 44 opp 305) **110** TR Bridgeman Art Library, London/Hermitage, St Petersburg CL Brown Brothers B Mary Evans Picture Library **111** TR Dave Lewis Nostalgia Collection C, CR Robert Opie Collection/*Jon Bouchier* Coca-Cola is a registered trademark **112** TL Michael Holford/British Museum C The National Trust BR ET Archive, London/Biblioteca Estense, Modena **113** TL *John Vigurs* TR Scala/Galleria Sabauda, Turin BR Mary Evans Picture Library **114** *John Chase* **115** T Giraudon/Museo della Civilta Romana CR The National Trust/Mark Fiennes **116** T ET Archive, London/Frederiksborg Castle, Denmark B AKG London **117** L Giraudon © ADAGP, Paris and DACS, London, 1998/Nathalie Gontcharova C ET Archive R private collection/decorations by Gilbert Rumbold/*Jon Bouchier* **118** TR Corbis–Bettmann CR Robert Opie BL Corbis–Bettmann **118–119** Courtesy of the Trustees of the Victoria and Albert Museum, London **119** L The Procter & Gamble Company for permission to reproduce 'Max Factor' © owner of design not traced R Paisley Museum & Art Galleries **120** TL Corbis–Bettmann C Bildarchiv Preussischer Kulturbesitz, Berlin/Antikensammlung SMPK, Berlin BL Bridgeman Art Library, London/Bibliothèque Nationale, Paris **121** T Paisley Museum & Art Galleries CL (both) HarperCollins Publishers Ltd from 'The Clans and Tartans of Scotland' by Robert Bains BL ET Archive, London BR Michael Holford/British Museum **122** TL Jean-Loup Charmet C Sonia Halliday BR Christie's Colour Library **123** TR Courtesy of The Hagley Museum and Library, Wilmington C Science Photo Library/Andrew Syred BL Michael Holford/Science Museum, London **124** TL Bridgeman Art Library, London/Bibliothèque Nationale, Paris TC Corbis–Bettmann B *Patrick Thurston* **125** C C M Dixon/Hermitage, St Petersburg BL Courtesy of the Trustees of the Victoria and Albert Museum, London BR Bridgeman Art Library, London/The Wallace Collection, London **126** TR Courtesy of the Trustees of the Victoria and Albert Museum, London BL Giraudon BC Ashmolean Museum, Oxford **127** TL Hulton Getty Images C Bridgeman Art Library, London/British Museum CR AKG London BR US Patent Office **128** BL Wallace Collection, London BR Réunion des Musées Nationaux/Musée du Louvre **129** TL ET Archive, London/National Gallery, London C Hulton Getty Images BR Kharbine/Tapabor, Paris **130** TC Courtauld Institute of Art C © Burberrys Limited 1998 CR © Burberrys Limited 1998 **131** TL Werner Forman Archive R Scala BL Robert Opie **132** L private collection BR © Mats Gustafson/ A+C Anthology **133** C Levi Strauss BL ET Archive, London BR Corbis–Bettmann **134** C Giraudon/Bridgeman/Wallace Collection, London CR Giraudon/Musée des Beaux- Arts, Mulhouse **135** TL, BL, BR Mary Evans Picture Library BC Robert Opie **136** TR Giraudon **137** T Giraudon BL Metropolitan Museum of Art/Rogers Fund, 1931 (31.6.26) **138** AKG London/SMPK,